P9-DTM-723

*The Papers of*
George Washington

# The Papers of
# George Washington

Dorothy Twohig, *Editor*

Philander D. Chase, *Senior Associate Editor*

Beverly H. Runge, *Associate Editor*

Frank E. Grizzard, Jr., Mark A. Mastromarino,
Elizabeth B. Mercer, and Jack D. Warren, *Assistant Editors*

W. W. Abbott, *Editor Emeritus*

## *Confederation Series*
# 6

*January–September 1788*

W. W. Abbot, *Editor*

.

## UNIVERSITY PRESS OF VIRGINIA

CHARLOTTESVILLE AND LONDON

This edition has been prepared by the staff of
*The Papers of George Washington*
sponsored by
The Mount Vernon Ladies' Association of the Union
and the University of Virginia
with the support of
the National Endowment for the Humanities,
the National Historical Publications and Records Commission,
and the Packard Humanities Institute.

THE UNIVERSITY PRESS OF VIRGINIA
Copyright © 1997 by the Rector and Visitors
of the University of Virginia

*First published 1997*

♾ The paper used in this publication meets the minimum
requirements of the American National Standard for Information
Sciences—Permanence of Paper for Printed Library Materials,
ANSI Z39.48-1984.

Library of Congress Cataloging-in-Publication Data
Washington, George, 1732–1799.
  The papers of George Washington. Confederation
series.
  Includes bibliographical references and indexes.
  Contents: 1. January–July 1784—[etc.]—6. Jan-
uary–September 1788.
  1. Washington, George, 1732–1799—Archives. 2.
Presidents—United States—Archives. 3. United
States—History—Confederation, 1783–1789. I.
Abbot, W. W. (William Wright), 1922–  II.
Twohig, Dorothy. III. Confederation series. IV.
Title.
E312.7    1992         973.4'1'092         91-3171
  ISBN 0-8139-1348-9 (v. 1)
  ISBN 0-8139-1684-4 (v. 6)

Printed in the United States of America

# Contents

NOTE: Volume numbers refer to the *Confederation Series*.

# Editorial Apparatus

Transcription of the documents in the volumes of *The Papers of George Washington* has remained as close to a literal reproduction of the manuscript as possible. Punctuation, capitalization, paragraphing, and spelling of all words are retained as they appear in the original document. Dashes used as punctuation have been retained except when a dash and another mark of punctuation appear together. The appropriate marks of punctuation have always been added at the end of a paragraph. When a tilde is used in the manuscript to indicate a double letter, the letter has been doubled. Washington and some of his correspondents occasionally used a tilde above an incorrectly spelled word to indicate an error in orthography. When this device is used the editors have corrected the word. In cases where a tilde has been inserted above an abbreviation or contraction, usually in letter-book copies, the word has been expanded. Otherwise, contractions and abbreviations have been retained as written except that a period has been inserted after an abbreviation when needed. Superscripts have been lowered. Editorial insertions or corrections in the text appear in square brackets. Angle brackets ⟨ ⟩ are used to indicate illegible or mutilated material. A space left blank in a manuscript by the writer is indicated by a square-bracketed gap in the text [ ]. Deletion of material by the author in a manuscript is ignored unless it contains substantive material, and then it appears in a footnote. If the intended location of marginal notations is clear from the text, they are inserted without comment; otherwise they are recorded in the notes. The ampersand has been retained and the thorn transcribed as "th." The symbol for per (℞) is used when it appears in the manuscript. The dateline has been placed at the head of a document regardless of where it occurs in the manuscript.

Since GW read no language other than English, incoming letters written to him in foreign languages generally were translated for his information. Where this contemporary translation has survived, it has been used as the text of the document and the original version has been included either in the notes or in the CD-ROM edition of the Papers. If there is no contemporary translation, the document in its original language has been used as the text. All of the documents printed in this volume, as well as other ancillary material (usually cited in the notes), may be found in the CD-ROM edition of Washington's Papers (CD-ROM:GW).

Individuals usually are identified only at the first appearance of their names. The index to each volume of the Confederation Series indicates where an identification may be found in earlier volumes of the series.

A number of letters to and from Washington have been printed, in whole or in part, out of their chronological sequence, usually in footnotes. All of these letters are listed in the table of contents with an indication where they may be found in this or another volume.

## Symbols Designating Documents

| | |
|---|---|
| AD | Autograph Document |
| ADS | Autograph Document Signed |
| ADf | Autograph Draft |
| ADfS | Autograph Draft Signed |
| AL | Autograph Letter |
| ALS | Autograph Letter Signed |
| D | Document |
| DS | Document Signed |
| Df | Draft |
| DfS | Draft Signed |
| L | Letter |
| LS | Letter Signed |
| LB | Letter-Book Copy |
| [S] | Signature clipped (used with other symbols: e.g., AL[S], Df[S] |

## Repository Symbols

| | |
|---|---|
| CD-ROM:GW | *See* "Editorial Apparatus" |
| CLjJC | James S. Copley Library, La Jolla, Calif. |
| CSmH | Henry E. Huntington Library, San Marino, Calif. |
| CtY | Yale University, New Haven |
| DeGE | Eleutherian Mills Historical Library, Wilmington, Del. |
| DLC | Library of Congress |
| DLC:GW | George Washington Papers, Library of Congress |
| DNA | National Archives |
| DNA:PCC | Papers of the Continental Congress, National Archives |
| DNDAR | Daughters of the American Revolution, Washington, D.C. |

| | |
|---|---|
| DSoCi | Society of the Cincinnati, Washington, D.C. |
| ICHi | Chicago Historical Society, Chicago |
| ICN | Newberry Library, Chicago |
| MA | Amherst College, Amherst, Mass. |
| MBSC | Society of the Cincinnati of New Hampshire, Boston |
| MdFre | Frederick County Public Libraries, C. Burr Artz Library, Frederick, Md. |
| MdHi | Maryland Historical Society, Baltimore |
| MH | Harvard University, Cambridge, Mass. |
| MHi | Massachusetts Historical Society, Boston |
| MiDbGr | Greenfield Village and the Henry Ford Museum, Dearborn, Mich. |
| Nc-Ar | North Carolina State Department of Archives and History, Raleigh |
| NcD | Duke University, Durham, N.C. |
| NHi | New-York Historical Society, New York |
| NhSB | Strawbery Banke, Inc., Portsmouth, N.H. |
| NIC | Cornell University, Ithaca, N.Y. |
| NjP | Princeton University, Princeton, N.J. |
| NN | New York Public Library, New York |
| NNC | Columbia University, New York |
| NNGL | Gilder-Lehrman Collection, on deposit at The Pierpont Morgan Library, New York |
| NNPM | The Pierpont Morgan Library, New York |
| O | Ohio State Library, Columbus |
| OFH | Rutherford B. Hays Library, Fremont, Ohio |
| PEL | Lafayette College, Easton, Pa. |
| PHi | Historical Society of Pennsylvania, Philadelphia |
| PBMAr | Archives of the Moravian Church, Bethlehem, Pa. |
| PP | Philadelphia Free Library |
| PPAmP | American Philosophical Society, Philadelphia |
| PU | University of Pennsylvania, Philadelphia |
| PWacD | David Library of the American Revolution, Sol Feinstone Collection, on deposit at the American Philosophical Society |
| RG | Record Group (designating the location of documents in the National Archives) |
| ScC | Charleston Library Society, Charleston, S.C. |
| Vi | Library of Virginia, Richmond |
| ViHi | Virginia Historical Society, Richmond |
| ViMtV | Mount Vernon Ladies' Association of the Union |
| ViU | University of Virginia, Charlottesville |

# Short Title List

Bacon-Foster, *Development of Patomac Route.*     Corra Bacon-Foster. *Early Chapters in the Development of the Patomac Route to the West.* Washington, D.C., 1912.

*Biographical Dictionary of the Maryland Legislature.*     Edward C. Papenfuse et al., eds. *A Biographical Dictionary of the Maryland Legislature, 1635–1789.* 2 vols. Baltimore, 1979–85.

Boyd, *Jefferson Papers.*     Julian P. Boyd et al., eds. *The Papers of Thomas Jefferson.* 26 vols. to date. Princeton, N.J., 1950—.

Butterfield, *John Adams Diary.*     L. H. Butterfield, ed. *Diary and Autobiography of John Adams.* 4 vols. Cambridge, Mass., 1961.

Cook, *Washington's Western Lands.*     Roy Bird Cook. *Washington's Western Lands.* Strasburg, Va., 1930.

De Pauw, *Eleventh Pillar.*     Linda Grant De Pauw. *The Eleventh Pillar.* Ithaca, N. Y., 1966.

*Diaries.*     Donald Jackson and Dorothy Twohig, eds. *The Diaries of George Washington.* 6 vols. Charlottesville, Va., 1976–79.

Elliot, *Debates.*     Jonathan Elliot, ed. *The Debates in the Several State Conventions on the Adoption of the Federal Constitution.* 4 vols. Philadelphia, 1836–1901.

Fairchild, *Van der Kemp.*     Helen Lincklaen Fairchild, ed. *Francis Adrian Van der Kemp, 1752–1829: An Autobiography, Together with Extracts from His Correspondence.* New York, 1903.

Fairfax Parish Vestry Minutes.     Manuscript in Christ Church Archives, Alexandria, Va.

Fields, *Papers of Martha Washington.*     Joseph E. Fields, comp. *"Worthy Partner": The Papers of Martha Washington.* Westport, Conn., 1994.

Fitzpatrick, *Writings.*     John C. Fitzpatrick, ed. *The Writings of George Washington from the Original Manuscript Sources, 1745–1799.* 39 vols. Washington, D.C., 1931–44.

Griffin, *Boston Athenæum Collection.*     Appleton P. C. Griffin, comp. *A Catalogue of the Washington Collection in the Boston Athanæum.* Cambridge, Mass., 1897.

Hening.     William Waller Hening, ed. *The Statutes at Large: Being a Collection of All the Laws of Virginia from the First Session of the Legislature, in the Year 1619.* 13 vols. 1819–23. Reprint. Charlottesville, Va., 1969.

*JCC.*     Worthington C. Ford et al., eds. *Journals of the Continental Congress.* 34 vols. Washington, D.C., 1904–37.

Kaminski and Saladino, *Documentary History of the Ratification of the Constitution.*     John P. Kaminski, Gaspare J. Saladino, et al., eds. *The Documentary History of the Ratification of the Constitution.* 16 vols. to date. Madison, Wis., 1976—.

Ledger B.    Manuscript Ledger in George Washington Papers, Library of Congress.

Ledger C.    Manuscript Ledger in Morristown National Historical Park, Morristown, N.J.

Morgan, *Naval Documents.*    William James Morgan, ed. *Naval Documents of the American Revolution.* [vols. 5—]. Washington, D.C., 1970—.

*N.C. State Records.*    Walter Clark, ed. *The State Records of North Carolina.* 26 vols. Raleigh and various places, 1886–1907.

*Papers, Colonial Series.*    W. W. Abbot et al., eds. *The Papers of George Washington. Colonial Series.* Charlottesville, Va., 1983—.

*Papers, Confederation Series.*    W. W. Abbot et al., eds. *The Papers of George Washington. Confederation Series.*    4 vols. to date. Charlottesville, Va., 1992—.

Reardon, *Randolph.*    John J. Randolph. *Edmund Randolph.* New York, 1974.

Rutland and Rachal, *Madison Papers.*    Robert A. Rutland, William M. E. Rachal, et al., eds. *The Papers of James Madison.* [1st series, vol. 9]. Chicago and Charlottesville, Va., 1975.

Rutland and Hobson, *Madison Papers.*    Robert A. Rutland, Charles E. Hobson, et al., eds. *The Papers of James Madison.* [1st series, vols. 10–13]. Chicago and Charlottesville, Va., 1977–81.

Smyth, *Writings of Franklin.*    Albert Henry Smyth. *The Writings of Benjamin Franklin.* 10 vols. New York and London, 1908.

Sparks, *Washington's Writings.*    Jared Sparks, ed. *The Writings of George Washington: Being His Correspondence, Addresses, Messages, and Other Papers, Official and Private, Selected and Published from the Original Manuscripts.* 12 vols. Boston, 1833–37.

*Statutes at Large.*    *The Statutes at Large, from the Twenty-sixth Year of the Reign of King George the Third, to the Twenty-ninth Year of the Reign of King George the Third, Inclusive. . . . Being an Eleventh Volume to Mr. Rummington's Edition, and a Fifteenth to Mr. Ruffhead's.* London, 1789.

Syrett, *Hamilton Papers.*    Harold C. Syrett et al., eds. *The Papers of Alexander Hamilton.* 27 vols. New York, 1961–87.

Turner, *Rumsey.*    Ella May Turner. *James Rumsey:Pioneer in Steam Navigation.* Scottdale, Pa., 1930.

Walker, *New Hampshire Convention.*    Joseph B. Walker. *A History of the New Hampshire Convention.* Boston, 1888.

Warville, *New Travels.*    J. P. Brissot de Warville. *New Travels in the United States of America 1788.* Trans. Mara Soceanu Vamos and Durand Echeverria. Ed. Durand Echeverria. Cambridge, Mass., 1964.

The Papers of George Washington
Confederation Series
Volume 6
January–September 1788

# To William Gordon

Revd Sir,                                   Mount Vernon January 1st 1788

I have recd your letter of the 6th of Septr together with flower-seeds accompanying it for which I beg you will accept of my best thanks.

I am glad to find by your letter that you have begun printing your history of the revolution—you have my best wishes for its success.

Our information from Europe is so various and contradictory as to render it still doubtful whether a rupture will take place between England and France; some accounts have even gone so far as to declare that hostilities have already commenced—others, that vigorous preparations are making on both sides and a war is inevitable—and others again mention pacific dispositions of the Courts. But let their political views and interests be what they may I hope we shall have wisdom enough not to take a part in their quarrels.

I would have forwarded to you a copy of the Constitution proposed by the late Convention for the United States, but as you must undoubtedly have seen it before this through the medium of the news papers or some other publication the necessity of my doing it is superceded. I have pleasure, however, to inform you that there is the greatest prospect of its being adopted by the People, it has its opponents, as any system formed by the wisdom of man would undoubtedly have, but they bear but a small proportion of its friends, and differ among themselves with respect to their objections. Pensylvania, Delawar and Jersey have already decided in its favor, the former by a majority of two to one, and the two latter unanimously. The dispositions in the other States, so far as I have been able to learn, are equally favourable, at least to Pensylvania (unless New York and possibly this State may prove exceptions) and it is expected that their conventions will give it a similar decision. I am &c.

G. Washington

LB, DLC:GW.

# To Thomas Jefferson

Dear Sir,                 Mount Vernon [1 January 1788]

I have received your favor of the 15th of August,[1] and am sorry that it is not in my power to give you any further information relative to the practicability of opening a communication between Lake Erie and the Ohio, than you are already possessed of. I have made frequent enquiries since the time of your writing to me on that subject while Congress were sitting at Annapolis,[2] but could never collect any thing that was decided or satisfactory: I have again renewed them, and flatter myself with better prospect of success.

The accts generally agree as to its being a flat country between the waters of Lake Erie & Big-Beaver; but differ very much with respect to the distance between their sources—their navigation—and the inconveniencies which would attend the cutting a canal between them.

From the best information I have been able to obtain of that Country, the sources of the Muskingham & Cayohoga approach nearer to each other than any water of Lake Erie does to Big-Beaver: But a communication by this River would be more circuitous & difficult; having the Ohio in a greater extent, to ascend; unless the latter could be avoided by opening a communication between James River and the Great Kanhawa—or between the little Kanhawa and the west branch of Monongahela, which is said to be very practicable by a short portage—As testimony thereof, the States of Virginia & Maryland have opened (for I believe it is compleated) a road from the No. branch of Potomack, commencing at, or near the mouth of Savage River, to the Cheat River, from whence the former are continuing it to the Navigable water of the little Kanhawa.[3]

The distance between Lake Erie & the Ohio, through the Big-Beaver, is, however, so much less than the rout through the Muskingham, that it would, in my opinion, operate very strongly in favor of opening a canal between the Source of the nearest water of the Lake & Big-Beaver, altho the distance between them should be much greater and the operation more difficult than to the Muskingham. I shall omit no opportunity of gaining every information relative to this important Subject;

and will, with pleasure, communicate to you whatever may be worthy of your attention.

I did myself the honor to forward to you the plan of Government formed by the Convention, the day after that body rose; but was not a little disappointed, and mortified indeed (as I wished to make the first offering of it to you) to find by a letter from Commod[or]e Jones, dated in New York the 9th of Novr that it was, at that time, in his possession. You have, undoubtedly recd it, or some other 'ere now, and formed an opinion upon it. The public attention is, at present, wholly engrossed by this important subject. The Legislatures of those States (Rhode Island excepted) which have met since the Constitution has been formed, have readily assented to its being submitted to a Convention chosen by the People. Pensylvania, New Jersey, & Delaware are the only States whose Conventions have as yet decided upon it. In the former it was adopted by 46 to 23 and in the two latter unanimously. Connecticut and Massachusetts are to hold their Conventions on the 1st & 2d tuesdays of this Month— Maryland in April, Virginia in June, and upon the whole, it appears, so far as I have had an opportunity of learning the opinions of the people in the several States, that it will be received. There will, undoubtedly, be more or less opposition to its adoption in most of the States; and in none a more formidable one than in this; as many influencial characters here have taken a decided part against it, among whom are Mr Henry, Colo. Mason, Govr Randolph and Colo. R. H. Lee; but from every information which I have been able to obtain, I think there will be a majority in its favor notwithstanding their dissention. In New York a considerable opposition will also be given.

I am much obliged to you, my dear Sir, for the Acct which you gave me of the general state of affairs in Europe. I am glad to hear that the Assemblée des Notables has been productive of good in France. The abuse of the finances being disclosed to the King, & the Nation, must open their eyes, and lead to the adoption of such measures as will prove beneficial to them in future. From the public papers it appears that the Parliaments of the several Provinces, & particularly that of Paris, have acted with great spirit & resolution. Indeed the rights of Mankind, the priviledges of the people, and the true principles of liberty, seem to have been more generally discussed & better understood throughout Europe since the American revolution than they were at any former period.

Altho' the finances of France and England were such as led you to suppose, at the time you wrote to me, would prevent a rupture between those two powers, yet, if we credit the concurrent accts from every quarter, there is little doubt but that they have commenced hostilities before this. Russia & the Porte have formally began the contest, and from appearances (as given to us) it is not improbable but that a pretty general war will be kindled in Europe. should this be the case, we shall feel more than ever the want of an efficient general Government to regulate our Commercial concerns, to give us a National respectability, and to connect the political views and interests of the several States under one head in such a manner as will effectually prevent them from forming seperate, improper, or indeed any connection, with the European powers which can involve them in their political disputes. For our situation is such as makes it not only unnecessary, but extremely imprudent for us to take a part in their quarrels; and whenever a contest happens among them, if we wisely & properly improve the advantages which nature has given us, we may be benefitted by their folly—provided we conduct ourselves with circumspection, & under proper restriction, for I perfectly agree with you, that an extensive speculation, a spirit of gambling, or the introduction of any thing which will divert our attention from Agriculture, must be extremely prejudicial, if not ruinous to us. but I conceive under an energetic general Government such regulations might be made, and such measures taken, as would render this Country the asylum of pacific and industrious characters from all parts of Europe— would encourage the cultivation of the Earth by the high price which its products would command—and would draw the wealth, and wealthy men of other Nations, into our own bosom, by giving security to property, and liberty to its holders. I have the honor to be with great esteem & regard Dear Sir Yr Most Obedt & Most Hble Servt

Go: Washington

ALS, DLC: Jefferson Papers; LB, DLC:GW.

  1. Jefferson's letter is dated 14 Aug. 1787; his postscript is dated 15 August.
  2. See Jefferson to GW, 15 Mar. 1784.

3. For the decision by the Virginia legislature to build the road in conjunction with the state of Maryland, see Enclosure II in James Madison to GW, 9 Jan. 1785.

## From Lafayette

My dear General                    Paris january the 1st 178[8]

I am fortunate in this Opportunity to wish you a Happy New year, and to devote the first Moments of this day to the Heartfelt pleasure to Remind you, My Beloved General, of your Adoptive Son and Most Affectionate, devoted friend. I Beg you will present My Best Respects to Mrs Washington. Madame de Lafayette joins in the Most tender Compliments to you and to Her and I Hope, My dear General, that you will Be so kind as to Mention me Very Affectionately to All the family and friends.

It is Needless for me to tell you that I Read the New proposed Constitution with An unspeackable Eagerness and Attention. I Have Admired it, and find it is a Bold, large, and solid frame for the Confederation. The Electionneering principles with Respect to the two Houses of Congress are Most Happily Calculated. I am only Affraid of two things—1st the want of a declaration of Rights 2dly the Great powers and possible Continuance of the president, who May one day or other Become a State Holder. Should My observations Be well founded, I still am Easy on two Accounts. The first that a Bill of Rights May Be Made if wished for By the people Before they Accept the Constitution—My other Comfort is that you Cannot Refuse Being Elected president—and that if you think the public vessel Can stir without such powers, you will Be able to lessen them, or propose Measures Respecting the permanence, Which Cannot fail to insure a Greater perfection in the Constitution, and a New Crop of Glory to Yourself—But in the Name of America, of Mankind at large, and Your Own fame, I Beseech you, my dear General, Not to deny your Acceptance of the office of president for the first Years—You only Can settle that political Machine, and I foresee it will furnish An Admirable Chapter in your History.

I am Returned from the provincial Assembly of Auvergne, Wherein I Had the Happiness to please the people and the Misfortune to displease Governement to a very Great degree—the

Ministry Asked for an Encrease of Revenue—our province was Among the few who Gave Nothing, and she Expressed Herself in a Manner which Has Been taken Very Much Amiss. the internal Situation of france is Very Extraordinary—the dispositions of the people of which I Gave you a picture are working themselves into a Great degree of fermentation—But Not without a Mixture of levity and love of ease. the parliaments are every day passing the boundaries of their Constitution, But are Sure to be Approued By the Nation, When, Among Many Unrational things, they Have the Good policy to Call for a General Assembly. Governement See that the power of the Crown is declining, and Now want to Retrieve it By an ill timed and dangerous Severity. they Have Monney Enough for this year—so at least they think—for My part, I am Heartily wishing for a Constitution, and a Bill of Rights, and Wish it May Be effected with as much tranquillity and Mutual satisfaction as it is possible.

The Emperor Has Made a foolish Attempt on Belgrade—But Cannot fail to take it an other time—and at the Entrance of the Spring the two imperial Courts will oppen a Vigourous and No doubt successfull Campaign against the turks. these Have Been led into a war by Great Britain, and should france take a decisive part, it is more probable she will side with Russia. But this Governement will avoid Being Committed in the affair, and perhaps will not Be the Better for it. the king of Prussia is Now Courting france, and proposes, I think, to Withdraw His Regiments from Holland. But this is A very insufficient, and probably a very Useless Reparation.

Enclosed, My dear General, are an Arrêt of the Council, and a letter to Mr Jefferson Both of which after long Negotiations we Have Had the Satisfaction to Obtain. I expected it Might Be finished Before My journey to Auvergne, But New difficulties Have Arose and Mr jefferson and Myself Have But lately ended the Business.[1] I am More and More pleased with Mr jefferson. His abilities, His Virtues, His temper, Every thing of Him Commands Respect and Attracts Affection. He Enjoys Universal Regard, and does the Affairs of America to perfection it is the Happiest choice that Could Be Made. Adieu, My dear General, with filial love and Respect I Have the Honour to Be Your devoted and Affectionate friend

Lafayette

ALS, PEL; copy, MH.

1. For the letter of 29 Dec. 1787 from the comptroller general, Claude-Guillaume Lambert, to Thomas Jefferson describing the steps taken to enforce the regulations regarding the farmers-general and the French tobacco trade, enclosing an arrêt of 29 Dec. liberalizing regulations regarding whale oil and other American products, see Boyd, *Jefferson Papers,* 12:466–71.

## From Nicolas Pike

Newbury Port [Mass.]

May it please your Excellency                Jany 1st 1788

Although a Permission to dedicate my Book to your Excellency, the honor of which, however, I had no right to claim, would have afforded me the highest gratification, yet your Excellency's declining to grant it, though in the most obliging and condescending terms, was mortifying to a Breast glowing with Affection and Esteem.[1]

you will undoubtedly observe, Sir, that the date of my Dedication is prior to that of the Letter with which your Excellency was pleased to honor me:[2] The reason of which is, that, although Mr Bowdoin is undoubtedly the first, and one of the best Characters in this State, yet, so unreasonable, cruel & unjust are the popular prejudices, that had I not fixed the date to a time antecedent to the existence of those Prejudices, which are the Offspring of Falshood & Ingnorance, I have great reason to believe it would have ruined the sale of my Book, so far as respects the common People.

Although your Excellency's Library does not admit any useless Books, yet as that, which accompanies this, is the first fruit of my Labors, I hope your Excellency will ⟨*mutilated*⟩ the honor to accept it[3] as a small token of the unfeigned Gratitude and Esteem, of your Excellency's much obliged, and most obedient & hble Servant

Nicolas Pike

Please, Sir, to make my Respects acceptable to Mr Lear.

ALS, PHi: Gratz Collection; Sprague transcript, DLC:GW.

1. See Pike to GW, 25 Mar. 1786, and note 1 of that document.

2. GW wrote Pike on 20 June 1786 declining to give permission for Pike to dedicate his book to him.

3. GW replied from Mount Vernon on 20 June 1788: "Sir, I request you

will accept my best thanks for your polite letter of Jany 1st (which did not get to my hand till yesterday) and also for the copy of your 'System of Arithmetic' which you were pleased to present to me. The handsome manner in which that Work is printed and the elegant manner in which it is bound, are pleasing proofs of the progress which the Arts are making in this Country. But I should do violence to my own feelings, if I suppressed an acknowledgment of the belief that the work itself is calculated to be equally useful and honorable to the United States.

"It is but right, however, to apprise you, that, deffedent of my own decision, the favorable opinion I entertain of your performance is founded rather on the explicit and ample testimonies of gentlemen confessedly possessed of great mathematical knowledge, than on the partial and incompetent attention I have been able to pay to it myself. But I must be permitted to remark that the subject, in my opinion, holds a higher rank in the literary scale than you are disposed to allow. The science of figures, to a certain degree, is not only indispensably requisite in every walk of civilised life; but the investigation of mathematical truths accustoms the mind to method and correctness in reasoning, and is an employment peculiarly worthy of rational beings. In a clouded state of existence, when so many things appear precarious to the bewildered research, it is here that the rational faculties find a firm foundation to rest upon. From the high ground of mathimatical and philosophical demonstration, we are insensibly led to far nobler speculations and subblimer meditations.

"I hope and trust that the Work will ultimately prove not less profitable than reputable to yourself. It seems to have been conceded, on all hands, that such a System was much wanted. Its merits being established by the approbation of competent Judges, I flatter myself that the idea of its being an American production, and the first of the kind which has appeared, will induce every patriotic and liberal character to give it all the countenance and patronage in his power—In all events, you may rest assured, that, as no person takes more i[n]terest in the encouragement of American Genius, so no one will be more highly gratified with the success of your inginious, arduous and useful undertaking than he, who has the unfeigned pleasure to subscribe himself Yrs &c. Go. Washington" (LB, DLC:GW).

# From Lafayette

My dear General                                   Paris january the 2d 1788

I Have writen to You By way of England, and will only inclose a duplicate of the arrêt of the Council and letter to Mr Jefferson which I Hope May Serve the Commerce of the United States[1]— I Am the More wishing for an Encrease of intercourse Betwen the two Nations, as Mr Jefferson and Myself Have pledged ourselves with the Ministry that it would Be the Case. And indeed it is Equally Necessary to Keep up the dispositions of france, and

Change those of Great Britain, who now Have all the profits, while they Grant No favours. You see, my dear General, that a wide field is Now oppened to the Speculations of American Merchants.

The Emperor is determined on a war Against the turks. How far this winter's negotiations May adjust Matters I don't know. But it is probable that the ottomans will Have to fight with the two imperial Courts, and Cannot fail very dearly to pay for the sport. European politics have much changed Since the King of prussia and Grand Signor Gave themselves up to British influence—An alliance with the imperial Courts would Now Better suit france, and She Could not Be a looser in the Bargain. But Her first Aim will Be to Avoid a War. the internal Situation of this Country is Rather Embarassing for Governement, who, alt[h]o they Have insured the Service for the whole year, must still Be a little Busy in Managing a Spirit of opposition Sometimes unrational in the parliaments and A Spirit of freedom in the people which will occupy the Stage untill it is filled By a National Assembly where public affairs will Be Set to Rights. in the Mean while the provincial Assemblies are doing Much good. and I hope that the Constitution of france is improving a Great deal—Adieu, My Beloved General, My Respects to Mrs Washington. Remember me to the family and all friends. Most Affectionately, Most Respectfully, and Gratefully Your devoted and filial friend

lafayette

ALS, PEL.
　　1. See Lafayette to GW, 1 Jan., n.1.

## To Benjamin Fitzhugh Grymes

Dear Sir　　　　　　　　　　Mount Vernon Jany 5th 1788

As you have not yet sent for your Jenny, the presumption is that the many letters which have been written to you requiring of it, have all miscarried; and therefore, you have the trouble of this.[1] She is now in good order, and with foal, which may be lost (as several of my own have been) from the number that are together, struggling for what little I have it in my power from the scantiness of my last years Crop to give them.

I do not mean to charge you for the use of my Jack; nor for the time or expence your Jenny has incurred, but wish she was now taken away;[2] for I again repeat it, that I think she runs a considerable risk by remaining here. I have already lost several Mule Colts, and the Night before last a Jack Colt, from one of my imported Jenny's, for which I would not have taken a large sum of money had he come to maturity. I am Dr Sir Yr Most Obedt Servt

Go: Washington

ALS, MHi: C. E. French Papers.

1. See GW to Grymes, 10 April 1787. No letter of a more recent date has been found.

2. GW records the receipt on 7 Feb. 1787 of £7 from Grymes "for a Jenny sent to R[oyal] Gift" (Ledger B, 262).

## To Peterson & Taylor

Gentlemen,                              Mount Vernon January 5th 1788.

When I wrote to you last upon the subject of furnishing me with scantling, Plank &c. agreeable to the enclosed bill[1] we could not come to any determination with respect to the matter, because the price of herrings, in which I proposed to make payment, could not be fixed. I now make the following proposal, viz.—I will allow you 6/ per Hundred for the scantling, reduced measure, 6/ per Hundred for the inch plank & 7/6 pe[r] do for inch and quarter do—As I understand you will want a large quantity of herrings in the fishing season—you shall give a preference to my landing for a supply provided a price can, at that time, be agreed upon between us; if it cannot, I will pay you for the scantling &c. in Cash after the fishing season is over as I have allotted the fish, or the money arising from the sale of them to supply me with the enclosed bill of scantling. The scantling must be furnished & delivered at my Landing by or before the first of march as I must have the frame &c. prepared before the season for cutting Grass comes on whe[n] my Carpenters will then be obliged to go into the field.

If you accede to the above proposal and will supply the scantling at the time mentioned you will write me a line by the bearer that will put the matter upon a certainty.[2] I am Gentlemen Yr Most Obedt Sert

G. Washington

P.S. If you cannot furnish the scantling so soon as mentioned above you will be so good as to let me know the earliest period in which you can supply it.

LB, DLC:GW.

1. Below the letter the clerk has transcribed: "A Bill of Scantling; and Plank to be provided by Messrs Peterson & Co. for and on acct of the subscriber, to be of the dimensions and exactly agreeable to the following directions.

|  | feet | inches |
|---|---|---|
| 170 Sleepers | 14 long | 10 by 4 |
| 195 Joists | 16 d[itt]o | 8 by 4 |
| 6 Plates | 30 do | 9 by 6 |
| 6 d[itt]o | 15 do | 9 by 6 |
| 2 do | 30 do | 8 by 6 |
| 8 do | 24 do | 8 by 6 |
| 160 Rafters | 20 do | |
| 6 inches at bottom & | | |
| 4½ at top by 3 inches | | |
| 40 Rafters 12½ ft long | | |
| 6 & 4½ by 3 | | |

This Scantling cannot be furnished too soon—at any rate it will be wanted in the month of March—Feby would be preferred—infinitly

|  | feet | inches |
|---|---|---|
| 40 Window beams | 16 long | 4 by 3 |
| 20 do | 11 do | 4 by 3 |
| 31 Studs | 10 do | 6 by 4 |
| 16 do | 11 do | 4 by 3 |
| 8 Rails | 15 do | 6 by 4 |

Note; The whole of the above must be surved⟨,⟩ and good of its kind— Pine—or it will not answer my purpose—10,000 feet of Inch plank (as much of it as possible to be seasoned, and wide as it can conveniently be obtained— 2,000 feet of Inch and quarter &c. seasoned—if to be had and wide also." GW's letter has not been found, but see Peterson & Taylor to GW, 11 Dec. 1787.

2. After the exchanges of these letters during the next few days, GW reached a final agreement on 9 Jan. with the Alexandria firm Peterson & Taylor. Peterson & Taylor replied to GW's letter of 5 Jan. on the same day: "yours

of this day came duly to hand with its Bill of Scantling & plank, therein enclosed. the prices you mention for the Same, and in the manner in Which payment to be made, we therefore, acceed to your, Terms. the Scantling you wish to have delivd by the first of March, but from the presan[t] appearance of the Winter, we cannott Say we can comply with the delivery at that time, however So far there is one of our Vessales that will Leave this town for the Eastern Shore on tuesday next the weather permitting and you may rest assured the Bill Shall be Strictly Attended too and be Sawed as Soon after it reaches our Mr Taylor, now in Maryland, as possible any further Obligation in this matter on account of the Severity of the Weather we would not want to enter into—the Inch & Inch & ¼ plank we belive will be green but they Shall be good, as will the Scantling also, if you Should think favourable of the Above, please to inform by Monday Evening that the Bill may be sent to be complyed with" (DLC:GW).

Two days later GW wrote from Mount Vernon: "Gentln I have recd your letter of the 5th inst. wherein you mention your compliance with the terms proposed so far as to furnish the Scantling, but leave the time for the delivery of it undetermined; this will wholly set aside the object which I had in view in wishing to contract with you to supply me with the bill sent you on Saturday— for I have not the smallest doubt of being able to furnish myself with Scantling upon lower terms than I have proposed to you provided the time which I have allotted to have it framed would permit me to take the chance of procuring it from the Vessels which pass from the Eastern Shore up to Alexandria (or if I could convey a letter seasonably to a Mr Joseph DeShields [Dashiell] of Maryland) who as I have been informed by Gentlemen of veracity that it has been and can generally be bought for 12/ per hundred measured side and edge which makes a difference of near 25 per Cent less than what I have engaged to give you. You therefore see, Sir, that my object in contracting with you is that I may depend upon its being delivered at a particular time and not subject myself to the hazard of not procuring it in time for my people to frame it before the season for cutting grass and Harvest come on—I am very willing to make any reasonable allowance for delays occasioned by weather or the River being blocked up, but still I cannot consent to leave the time of delivering it wholly unfixed. and would thank you to let me know. I am &c. G. Washington" (LB, DLC:GW).

GW received a reply later on that day, 7 Jan: "we receved your Letter of above date, and observe, you are desirous of haveing a time fixed upon for the Lumber being delivd agreable to the Bill Furnished—it is therefore to our Interest to have the Same delivd as soon as possible, and have no doubt but you will make allowances for delays occationed by Weather. we will agree to deliver in All, March Casualities Excepted, if that time should meet your Approbation, we will proceed to the Complyance thereof" (DLC:GW).

On 9 Jan. GW sealed the bargain: "Gentn Your letter of the 7th inst. came duly to hand. I accede to the proposal therein made, for you to have the Scantling and plank delivered at my landing, agreeable to the bill sent you, in all the month of March—as you say it will be for your interest to deliver it sooner if possible—it will be infinitely more pleasing to me to have it done. You will please to have it dilivered at my fishing landing near the ferry, as it will be more convenient for me there than at any other place. I expect the scantling will be of a good quality agreeable to promise, and if any of the plank can be had seasoned, particularly the Inch and quarter, it will be very disireable—I am Gentn Yr Most Obedt Hble Sert G. Washington" (LB, DLC:GW).

Peterson & Taylor wrote on 13 Feb. to say that the company would not be able to make delivery in March. The scantling and planks were delivered in April, but it was not until July that GW made a final settlement. See Peterson and Taylor to GW, 18 April, 14 July, and notes in both documents.

## From Charles Willson Peale

Dr Sir                                    Baltemore Town Jany 6. 1788
Having bussiness in the line of my Profession which will detain me some time in this Place, therefore I take the liberty of intimating, that in case any of your rare Birds should die, that you will oblige me much by sending their remains directed to the care of Captn Elliott of this Town.[1] I am with the greatest regard Dr Sir your much obliged Humble Servant

C.W. Peale

ALS, DLC:GW.
1. Capt. Thomas Elliott (1741–1807), a friend of Peale, was a merchant in Baltimore.

## To William Peacey

Sir,                                    Mount Vernon 7th Jany 1788.
I have received your letter of the 2d of Feby 1787. I am much obliged to you for your attention in sending me the seeds, which arrived agreeable to the bill.

Mrs Bloxham received of Wakelin Welch Esqr. of London £10.1.10, which sum, she informed him, was what she paid you for the seeds on my account.

I am not sorry that Caleb Hall did not come out, for I proposed his coming more to please Bloxham, who was very desireous of having him here, than from a want of his services myself.

I thank you, Sir, for your obliging offer to furnish me with Black-smiths & a Mill-wright; I have two of the former occupation, who, tho' not very neat workmen, answer all my purposes in making farming utensils &c. in a plain way; the latter I shall have no occasion for as I have not work enough to employ him in his own line; and indeed I doubt whether they would find their advantage in coming over at present, because I hardly think they will meet with constant employ: for altho' I should be extreemly glad to see the honest and industrious mechanic come into this Country from any & every part of the Globe, yet I would not wish to encourage them unless they could be benefitted by it. Whenever we have a regular & firm government established, the prospect for those people will be much more pleasing than it is at present.

Bloxham and his family are in good health, and appear to be contented with the country. I am Sir Yr most Obedt Servt

Go: Washington

LS, in the hand of Tobias Lear, ViMtV; LB, DLC:GW.

## To Samuel Athawes

Sir,                                        Mount Vernon Jany 8th 1788.

I have received your letter of the 20th of July last informing me of the death of our much esteemed & worthy friend, George William Fairfax Esqr. I sincerely condole with you and his other friends in England upon the occasion. Altho' the precarious state of his health for several years past must have prepared his friends, in some measure, for his death, yet the event could not take place without being sincerely lamented by all who knew him.

The appointment of Executors & Trustees in each Country for his estates & affairs in each, seperately and without any dependence upon each other, was, in my opinion, a very judicious & necessary step; for the delays and inconveniences which the distance must unavoidably produce, would have been an insuperable objection to their being joined, not to mention the difficulties which must have arisen from the difference of the laws, upon this point, in the two Countries.

The small case which you directed to the care of Colo. Burwell was forwarded by him and came safe to hand. I have sent the watch to Mr Fairfax and the letters to their respective addresses.

Notwithstanding the long & uninterrupted friendship which subsisted between Colo. Fairfax and myself, and however de-

sireous I may be to give every proof of my affection for him &
his amiable relict, yet I must decline acting as an executor for his
estate here. The deranged situation of my own private affairs,
occasioned by my long absence from home during the late war,
and the continual applications which are made to me for information, advice or assistance, in consequence of the publick office
which I sustained, require my constant & unremitting attention,
and would prevent a faithful discharge of the trust, on my part,
if I should accept of it. I am, Sir, Yr most Obedt Hble Servt
Go: Washington

LS, in the hand of Tobias Lear, owned (1977) by Mr. Max G. Lowenherz,
Three Lions, Inc., Publishers, New York; LB, DLC:GW.


## To Bourdon des Planches

Sir,                                    Mount Vernon January 8th 1788
I have recd your letter of the 6th of Decr 1786, wherein you
request me to represent your situation to Congress, and apply
to that body, in your behalf, for a grant of land in some part of
the United States where you may form a settlement.[1]
Altho' no incident in life could afford me more pleasure than
to see all those who have exerted themselves in the cause of this
country amply recompenced for their meritorious services, and
howeve[r] desireous I may be to contribute all in my power towards there obtaining a compensation, yet I cannot, consistant
with the declaration which I made when I quitted my publick
employment, bring forward applications of this nature to Congress. I hope, Sir, you will not think that I act a singular part,
with respect to you by not complying with your request—when
I assure you I have ever declined the repeted applications of
this Kind which have been made to me.
I think it is not improbable but that the Court of France, upon
a reconsideration of the services of the Count de Grass, may be
induced to recompence the merits of him & his friends in the
manner which they deserve. I am Yrs &c.
G. Washington

LB, DLC:GW.
1. Bourdon's letter has not been found, but Bourdon wrote Thomas Jefferson on 10 Aug. 1787 about his letter to GW which he had entrusted to Jefferson "dans le courant du mois de novembre dernier," presumably the letter to

which GW is referring. Bourdon noted that he had enclosed in his letter to GW "un certificat" from de Grasse affirming that Bourdon was his "premier Sécrétaire" during the siege of Yorktown in 1781 (Boyd, *Jefferson Papers*, 12:19).

## To Mauduit du Plessis

Sir,                              Mount Vernon January 8th 1788
    I have to acknowledge the reception of your three letters, viz. of the 12th of Feby the 26th of March and the 20th July.[1] I was exceedingly sorry to hear of the disasters which you met with after you left this place, before you reached Georgia, and was very unhappy to find, when you arrived there, that your expectations, with respect to your property were so much disappointed, and that your misfortunes were aggravated by the death of your family. I sincerely regret the causes which induced you to Return to Europe, not only on account of the loss which America will sustain of a person who would have been a most valuable citizen, but that a worthy man should leave the country with unfavourable impressions and wounded feelings.

    I congratulate you upon your safe arrival in France and hope you will receive that degree of happiness and satisfaction in your return to your family and friends which will compensate for the misfortunes you sustained here.

    Mrs Washington has recd the fans which you were so polite to send to her from Charleston and begs you would accept her best thanks for them. I have likewise received the Ribbon which you did me the honor to send to me and request you to accept my warmest acknowledgements for that as well as for your obliging offer to execute any thing which I might have occasion to do in France, and the very polite expressions with which your letters abounded.

    It would give me a particular pleasure to comply with your request by sending you an engraved copy of my portrait similar to the one which you saw in my dining Room, but as that was a present to me from the Engraver, Mr Brown of London, and the only one of the kind that I ever saw, it is not in my power to gratify your wish.

    When I was in Philadelphia last summer I signed a number

of Deplomas for the foreign officers, members of the Cincinnati, which were sent by the Secretary General to the Counts De Estaing and Rochambeau this, I presume, will supercede the necessity of my sending one to you as you desired. I have the Honor to be with great esteem and regard Yr most Obedt Hble Sert

G. Washington

LB, DLC:GW.

1. Mauduit du Plessis's letters are dated 20 July 1786, 12 Feb. 1787, and 26 Mar. 1787.

## To Edmund Randolph

Dear Sir,                                    Mount Vernon January 8th 1788

The letter which you did me the honor of writing to me on the 27th Ulto, with the enclosure, came duly to hand. I receive them as a fresh instance of your friendship and attention. For both I thank you.

The diversity of Sentiments upon the important matter which has been submitted to the People, was as much expected as it is regretted, by me. The various passions and medium by which men are influenced are concomitants of falibility—engrafted into our nature for the purposes of unerring wisdom; but had I entertained a latent hope (at the time you moved to have the Constitution submitted to a second Convention) that a more perfect form would be agreed to—in a word that any Constitution would be adopted under the impressions and Instructions of the members, the publications which have taken place since would have eradicated every form of it—How do the sentiments of the influencial characters in *this* State who are opposed to the Constitution, and have favoured the public with their opinions, quadrate with each other? Are they not at varience on some of the most important points? If the opponants in the *same* State cannot agree in *their* principles what prospect is there of a coalescence with the advocates of the measure when the different views, and jarring interests of so wide and extended an Empire are to be brought forward and combated.

To my Judgement, it is more clear than ever, that an attempt to amend the Constitution which is submitted, would be productive of more heat, & greater confusion than can well be conceived. There are somethings in the new form, I will readily acknowledge, wch never did, and I am persuaded never will, obtain my *cordial* approbation; but I then did conceive, and now do most firmly believe, that, in the aggregate, it is the best Constitution that can be obtained at this Epocha; and that this, or a dissolution of the Union awaits our choice, & are the only alternatives before us—Thus beliving, I had not, nor have I now any hesitation in deciding on which to lean.

I pray your forgiveness for the expression of these sentiments. In acknowledging the receipt of your Letter on this subject, it was hardly to be avoided, although I am well disposed to let the matter rest entirely on its own merits—and mens minds to their own workings. With very great esteem & regard—I am &c.

G. Washington.

LB, DLC:GW.

## To Rochambeau

My dear Sir,                    Mount Vernon January 8th 1788

I have recd your letters of the 28th of June 1786 & 12th of may 1787. In the former you mentinon your having just returned from Holland and were so obliging as to give me an account of the state of political affairs in that Country. Since the time of your writing their intestine disputes have been brought to a crisis and appear to have terminated rather against the Patriots; What changes may be made in their Government—what revolutions in their political aconomy—and how far their connections with the several powers in Europe may be effected by the termination is yet unknown to us.

I am very glad to here that the Assemblée des Notables has been productive of good in France; the State of your finances was really alarming and required a strict investigation and the sanative hand of the nation to restore them to their proper tone.

I now begin to hope that the period is not very distant when this country will make a more respectable figure in the eyes of Europe than it has hitherto done. The constitution forme[d] by the late Convention appears, as far as my information extends, to be highly acceptable to the people of these States. Jersey, Delawere & Pensylvania having already decided in its favor, the two former unanimously and the latter by a majority of two to one; the Conventions in the other States have not yet determined upon it but their dispositions are very favourable. Whenever this Government is established we shall regain thus confidence and credit among the European powers which a want of energy in the present confideration has deprived us of; and shall likewise feel the benefit of those commercial and political advantage which our situation holds out to us. This event must be extreemly pleasing to every friend of humanity and peculiarly so to you and others, who must feel interested in the happiness and welfare of this country, from the part which you took in establishing her liberty and independence.

I lament with you, my dear Sir, that the distance between us is so great—as to deprive us of the pleasure and satisfaction of a frequent and regular communication by letter, for it often happens either through the inattention of the person to whom letters are committed, or from some other cause, that they do not come to hand till months after their date. You will please to accept the compliments of the season with my sincere wishes for many happy returns of it to you. and believe me to be With the greatest respect My dear Sir, Yr Most Obedt & Most Hble Servant.

G. Washington

LB, DLC:GW.

## To Nicholas Simon van Winter and Lucretia Wilhelmina van Winter

[Mount Vernon 8th Jany 1788]
I have recd your letter of the 26th of Feby accompanied by a Poem entitled Germanicus.[1] I consider your sending the latter to me as a mark of polite attention which merits my warmest acknowledgment, and I beg you to accept my thanks for that, as well as for the many obliging expressions in your letter.

The Muses have always been revered in every age, & in all Countries where letters & civilization have made any progress. As they tend to alleviate the misfortunes, and soften the sorrows of life, they will ever be respected by the humane & virtuous. I am Yr most obedt Hble Servt

Go: Washington

LS, in the hand of Tobias Lear, Amsterdam: Collectie Six; LB, DLC:GW.

1. For the poem, see Nicholas Simon van Winter and Lucretia Wilhelmina van Winter to GW, 26 Feb. 1787, n.1.

## To Wakelin Welch & Son

Gentn                                    [Mount Vernon, 8 January 1788]

I have recd your letter of the 7th of March and 14th of July, the former enclosing my acct current, in which my drafts upon you &c. are justly and properly Stated.[1]

The seeds, Ploughs &c. sent by the Mary Capt. Andrews, arrived safe, but some of the former were injured by being put into the hold of the Vessel; they were in casks, and the Capt. said he did not know the contents of them or they should have been deposited in a more suitable place; however, upon the whole, they arrived in much better order than those things generally do.[2]

I thank you for your attention to Mr Youngs two drafts for £11.12 & £9.12.6 should I have occasion to apply to that Gentn for any thing more I shall advice you thereof, and your further attention to his bills will be very obliging.[3]

Mrs Bloxham's receiving £10.1.10 of you, which she had paid to Mr Peacey for seeds on my acct was perfectly agreeable to me.[4] while I was in Philadelphia last summer I drew upon you for £100 in favor of Robert Morris Esqr. and advised you regularly thereof.[5] I am Gentn yrs &c.

G. Washington

LB, DLC:GW.

1. Letters not found.

2. See GW to Arthur Young, 6 Aug. 1786, and GW to Welch, 5 Aug. 1786 (second letter), printed in note 31 of the Young letter.

3. See note 2. See also GW's accounts with Welch from 1786 to 1788 in Ledger B, 234.

4. See William Peacey to GW, 2 Feb. 1787, and GW to Peacey, 7 Jan. 1788.

5. See Philadelphia Cash Accounts, 9 May–22 Sept. 1787, n.9.

# To John Fitzgerald

Dear Sir, Mount Vernon January 9th 1788

In a card I sent you the other day, at the sametime that I enquired if your express brought any answer from Govr Johnson and Lee I requested to be informed at what precise spot the meeting of the directors was appointed to be held, I should be glad now to know.

I had made my arrangements for setting of on Saturday to proceed on this side of the River; and will do so if I am able but having taken a very severe cold this day Senight in a night ride from Alexandria I have been confined almost ever since getting little rest from a continual cough (which has greatly disordered my breast) and by slow fevers which has constantly attended it.

As I am very desirous that this should be a full meeting, I will make it a point to attend, if the State of my health on Saturday will in any degree enable me to encounter the ride—cold houses and Bad Beds; If it should not I will thank you for assigning the reason (when you get up) for my non attendance—Every paper which we may have occasion for, I hope will be carried. Colo. Humphreys proposed to accompany me. Colo. Gilpin (with Mr Smith) I am informed propose doing some work in their way on the other side of the river. How far it will be convenient to you, to Join our party (If I should be able to go[)], you are best able to decide—of the pleasure we should have in your Company you can have no doubt.[1] I am &c.

G. Washington

LB, DLC:GW.

1. On Saturday, 12 Jan., when "the afternoon became clear, mild & pleasant," GW accompanied by David Humphreys "set off for the meeting of the Directors of the Potomack Co., to be held at the Falls of Shanandoah—but meeting a letter from Colo. Fitzgerald enclosing one from Governer Johnson requesting that the meeting might be postponed till Tuesday," they turned back and the ensuing snowstorm led GW on Monday "to relinquish the journey altogether" (*Diaries*, 5:264, 265). Neither Fitzgerald's nor Thomas Johnson's letter has been found. Mrs. Washington reported to Fanny Bassett Washington, who was at Eltham, on 25 Feb.: "The General did not goe up the river as he intended he got a bad cold and the dismal weather togather prevented—tho he set out satterday with an intention to reach Mr Fairfaxes that night but some disapointment in fixing the day caused him to turn back and the Colo

[Humphreys] seemed to bear his disapointment with tolearable patience—and often said he thought himself quite as well by the fire side at Mt Vernon as he should be at the Shenandoah" (Fields, *Papers of Martha Washington*, 205–7). "Mr Smith" is James Smith.

## From Benjamin Lincoln

Boston Jany 9[–13]th 1788

I have, my dear General, been some time in this town with my son Benjn who has been exceedingly sick for about four weeks. On thursday last we thought his days were fully numbered, and that his last moments were rolling rapidly on and that they would have been terminated before the evening; but in the afternoon he revived, he yet lives, his situation, we trust, is not so critical as it has been, and we cannot help flattering ourselves that there are hopes of his recovery. A bystander might wonder that I should commence a letter to your Excellency on so goolmy a subject, but the part you have always taken in what ever has nearly interested me intitles you to the information and would therefore make an apology as improper as unnecessary.

Our convention meets this morning to take into consideration the proposed plan of government for the United States. Whether it will be adopted or not, in this State, the most prophetic spirit among us cannot certainly determine, I cannot but hope, however, that it will be received here. Whether this hope is well grounded or whether it exists from an ardent wish that it may be, I cannot say, for when we become anxious for the success of any particular proposition we too often weigh with partiality arguments in favor as well as too inattentively those against the measure. I must experience a very great change or I shall give it my most hearty assent.

The constitution has very potent adversaries in this State, it is said that Mr S. Adams, General Warren & Mr Gerry are among them the former only is in convention—All the Gentlemen you know.

I hope and trust that the business will be conducted with moderation candor & fairness, otherwise we may bear down the opposition but we shall never sooth and quiet their minds to do which I consider as a matter of very great importance for it will require all the wisdom aid and attention of all the lovers of order and a good government to bring the system, if adopted into exercise and to avoid that confusion and misery which has too often masked the progress of the various governments now established in the world.

After I had finished my public commission in the western counties I went in June into the eastern one and remained untill about the middle of Novr where I left one son to inspect our saw mills &c. he is very happy in that country and intends to fix there.[1] I think it a valuable part of this State, and as no person has attempted the subject, I have ventured a few observations on the advantages to be enjoyed by settlers in it and have hinted at some measures which should be pursued to bring forward a settlement of it &c. Knowing the great attention your Excellency has paid to obtain a knowledge of the different parts of the United States I have inclosed a copy of my observations (They will also apply pretty generally respecting to the soil produce &c. to New Brunswic only as that is a little farther north)[2] If they shall serve as an hour of amusement, when nothing more interesting shall offer it self, I shall think my self most amply compensated.

13th Since writing the above which I intended for the last post my son has, I think a little recruited tho he yet remains in a very critical situation.

We have been four days in convention organizing the house attending to disputed elections &c. these things being pretty fully over we expect tomorrow morning to have the proposed constitution read & to proceed afterwards upon a discussion of it. I am now as much at a loss to know what will be its fate as I was the first day we met. Should any thing of importance turn up I will have the pleasure of advising you of it by the next post.

Permit me to solicit that my most respectful regards may be presented to Mrs Washington and to assure you My dear General that I am with the highest esteem & warmest affection your Excellencys most obedient servant

B. Lincoln

My regards to Mr Lear tell him, however unwelcome the news may be of the situation of his friend.

N.B. The Docrs are this moment here and they will [not] say that they think my son has gained any for the eight last days I am distressed for his safety.[3]

ALS, DLC:GW.

1. Lincoln wrote GW about his property in Maine and about his younger son, Theodore, in December 1786. See Lincoln to GW, 4 Dec. 1786–4 Mar. 1787, n.1.

2. In reel 8 of the Massachusetts Historical Society's microfilm edition of the Benjamin Lincoln Papers is Lincoln's 22-page essay on the Eastern Provinces, dated 3 Dec. 1787.

3. Benjamin Lincoln, Jr., died on 18 Jan. (Lincoln to GW, 20 January).

# From George Lux

Sir                                   Chatsworth [Md.] 9 Jany [1788]

I beg leave to introduce to your Excy Mr OConnor, who is writing an History of America, & means to make some stay with you—Mrs OConnor, a Niece of Sir Charles Hardy, who commanded the British Fleet last War, means to set up an Academy for the instruction of young Ladies in Alexandria, & I must request your Excellency's patronage & attention—Mr OConnor is warmly recommended to me by my Relations of the Biddle Family in Phila., and as their Friend I beg leave to recommend him to you.[1]

I hope, e'er twelve months are elapsed, that every American may embrace a Citizen of another State more fervently than ever, as a Brother, that we shall be one People, & all local distinctions be obliterated, and am, with Compts to your Excy & Mrs Washington, in which Mrs Lux joins Yr Hume Servt

Geo. Lux

ALS, DLC:GW. Lux dated his letter "9 Jany 1787."

George Lux (1753–1797) inherited Chatsworth at the death of his father, William Lux, in 1778. It was an estate of 956 acres in Baltimore Town, which after visiting it in 1777 John Adams described as "elegant" (*Biographical Dictionary of the Maryland Legislature,* 2:556–57; Butterfield, *John Adams Diary,* 2:257–58). George Lux was married to Catharine Biddle of Philadelphia. During the Revolution he served as the clerk of Baltimore's committee of observation and as an officer in its militia.

1. Eliza Harriot O'Connor at this time opened in Alexandria a short-lived academy for young ladies. Her husband, John O'Connor, an Irishman who came to the United States in 1787 and for two years sought subscriptions to his proposed history of America, visited Mount Vernon in February. Despite the efforts of the O'Connors, GW refused to join the governing board of Mrs. O'Connor's school or to subscribe to Mr. O'Connor's history, which was never

published. For further details of GW's dealings with the O'Connors, see the editors' notes in *Diaries*, 5:272–73, 409.

## From Jonathan Trumbull, Jr.

Dear Sir                                    Hartford [Conn.] 9th Janry 1788

With great satisfaction I have the Honor to inform—that last Evening the Convention of this State, by a great Majority, Voted to ratify & adopt the new proposed Constitution for the United States—Yeas 127—Nays 40.

With additional pleasure I can inform that the Debates on this subject, have been conducted with a spirit of great Candour, Liberality & fairness—and the Decision received with the universal Applause of a numerous Body of the People of the State, who attended the public Deliberations of their Convention—& expressed their cordial Assent, on the moment of Decision, with a general Clap.

The great Unanimity with which this Decision has been made—and the liberality with which its previous Deliberations have been conducted in this State, I hope will have a happy influence on the Minds of our Brethren in the Massachusetts—their Convention is now collecting & will be favored with this Information Tomorrow.

It may not be amiss to mention, that in the List of Affirmants in this State, stand the names of all our principal Characters—with the Men of Liberality, Sentiment & Influence.

Altho not honored with the Appointment of a Delegate (being, in my particular Circle, under the Cloud of Commutation & Cincinnati)[1] I have attended the Debates of this Convention from their beginning to the Close—& have been amply compensated, by the pleasure—the satisfaction & instruction I have participated on the Occasion. With all those sentiments of sincere cordiality & respect with which I have ever had the Honor to address you, my Dear Sir, I now have the pleasure to subscribe myself—Your most obedient & obliged humble Servant

Jona. Trumbull

P.S. While I take the pleasure of congratulating you Sir on this joyous Occasion—I pray you to indulge my Wishes in begging you to present my sincerest respects to Mrs W—— with my tender solicitations for her health & happiness.

ALS, DLC:GW.

1. For Thomas Jefferson's critique of the Society of the Cincinnati and references to GW's attempts to reform it, see Jefferson to GW, 16 April 1784, and note 4 of that document.

## To Richard Butler

Dear Sir,                                    Mount Vernon January 10th 1788

I have received your letter of the 30th of November accompanied by the Indian Vocabulary which you have been so obliging as to forward to me. I am so far from thinking any apology necessary on your part for not having furnished me with the Vocabulary at an earlier period, that I assure you it is a matter of surprise to me to find that you have been able to compleat a work of such difficulty and magnitude, as this appears to be, in so short a time, under the pain which you must have suffered and the delays occasioned by your misfortune in breaking your leg.

The pleasing satisfaction which you must enjoy from a reflection that you have exerted yourself to throw light upon the original history of this Country—to gratify the curiosity of the Philosopher—and to forward the researches into the probable connection and communication between the northern parts of America and those of Asia must make you a more ample compensation for the laborrious task which you have executed than my warmest accknowledgments, which, however I must beg you to accept.

The observations contained in your letter respecting the different tribes of Indians inhabiting the Western Country, The traditions which prevail among them, and the reasoning deduced therefrom, are very valuable and may lead to some useful discoveries. Those works which are found upon the Ohio and other traces of the country's being once inhabitted by a race of people more ingenious, at least, if not more civilized than those who at present dwell there, have excited the attention and enquirries of the curious to learn from whence they came, whither they are gone and something of their history; any clue, therefore, which can lead to a knowledge to these must be gratefully received.

As you have had opportunities of gaining extensive knowledge and information respecting the western territory—its situation—rivers and the face of the Country, I must beg the favor of you, my dear Sir, to resolve the following quæries, either from your own knowledge, or certain information (as well to gratify my own curiosity, as to enable me to satisfy several Gentlemen of distinction in other Countries who have applied to me for information upon the subject.) viz.

1st What is the face of the Country between the sources or Canoe navigation of the Cayahoga (which empties itself into Lake Eire) and the Big-Beaver—and between the Cayahoga and the Muskingum?

2d The distance between the waters of the Cayahoga and each of the two rivers above mentioned?

3d Would it be practicable (and not very expensive) to cut a canal between the Cayahoga and either of the above rivers so as to open a communication between the waters of lake Eire & the Ohio?

4th Whether there is any more direct; practicable, and easy communication between the waters of lake Erie and those of the Ohio (by which The Fur and Peltry of the Upper Country can be transported[)] than these?

Any information you can give me relative to the above quæries, from your own knowledge, will be most agreeable, but if that is not suffiecently accurate for you to decide upon, the best and most authentic accounts of others will be very acceptable.

Your letter to the Marquis de la Fayette shall be particularly attended to and forwarded with mine.[1] I am Dear Sir—With esteem & regard, Yr most Obedt Hble Sert

G. Washington

LB, DLC:GW. GW sent this letter to Clement Biddle on 24 Jan. to be forwarded to Butler.

1. See GW to Lafayette, this date.

## To Henry Knox

My dear Sir,                              Mount Vernon Jany 10th 1788
    I beg you to accept of my thanks for your obliging favor of
the 11th Ult.; which, owing to the dullness of the season, and
want of matter to amuse you, has lain unacknowledged till this
time.
    Three States—to wit—Pensylvania New Jersey, and Delaware
having adopted the New Constitution in so decisive a manner
and those of New Hampshire, Massachusetts & Connecticut
having discovered such favourable sentiments of it, places the
final Success of it, in my judgment, upon unequivocal ground.
Maryland, most unquestionably, will adopt it; from No. Carolina
(so far as accts have been received in this quarter) the disposition
of the People towards it is favourable; from the States South of
it I have no direct intelligence; but in the Situation Georgia is,
nothing but insanity, or a desire of becoming the Allies of the
Spaniards or Savages, can disincline them to a Governmt which
holds out the prospect of relief from its present distresses. The
opposition in this State, tho' headed by very influencial characters, is not, in my opinion (tho' I may be an incompetent judge,
never going from home, & seeing nobody except those who call
upon me) much to be apprehended. My opinion of the matter
is, that the New form on the final decision in our Convention,
will be acceded to by a large majority. The determination of New
York, of all others, seems most problematical; and yet, I can
hardly entertain an idea that She will be disposed to stand alone,
or with one or two others, if the States bordering on her should
Confederate.
    Whether War or Peace will be the issue of the dispute between
France and England, seems as yet undecided. If the former, we
shall certainly get involved, unless there is energy enough in
Government to restrain our People within proper bounds; and
that the power of the present Government is inadequate to accomplish this, I believe none will deny.
    Mrs Washington joins me in offering compliments of congrat-
ulation to Mrs Knox and yourself on the increase of yr family by
the birth of a son, and I pray you to accept the acknowledgment
of my sense of the honor you have conferred on me by giving
him my name. I hope he will live to enjoy it long after I have

taken my departure for the world of Spirits and that he may prove a blessing and comfort to you both in your declining years. With sentiments of the greatest esteem & regard I am— My dear Sir Yr Most Obedt & Affecte friend

Go: Washington

P.S. Colo. Humphreys has lost no flesh since he came to Virginia. He undertakes a journey to morrow with me to the upper falls of this River whither I am called on business of the Potomack Company. How far this ride—The cold weather &ca may effect a change can best be determined after our return in about ten days.[1]

ALS, NNGL: Knox Papers; LB, DLC:GW.
   1. According to Mrs. Washington, David Humphreys was not displeased when the expedition fell through. See GW to John Fitzgerald, 9 Jan., n.1.

## To Lafayette

My dear Marqs                    Mount Vernon January 10th 1788
   I fear my dear marqs, you will believe me to have been remiss in attentions to you. my last letters, I find, have been unaccountably concentered in the same hands and unreasonably delayed; entirely contrary to my expectation. when you shall have received them by the Chevalier Paul Jones, you will acquit me of any intended or real neglect. one of these letters containing the form of Government which has been submitted by the fœderal Convention to the People of these States I wished to have got to your hands by the first conveyance as it was my intention that you should have been among the first to be informed of the proceedings of that body.[1]
   It is with great pleasure I transmit to you, by this conveyance, a Vocabulary of the Shawanese & Delaware languages. your perfect acquaintance with Genl Richard Butler, the same worthy officer who served under your orders, and who has taken the trouble to compile them, supersedes the necessity of my saying any thing in support of their veracity [and] correctness. I likewise send a shorter specimen of the language of the Southern Indians. It was procured by that ingenious gentleman, the Hble Mr Hawkins, a member of Congress from North Carolina, &

lately a Commissioner from the United States to Indians of the South.[2] I heartily wish the attempt of that singular great character, the Empress of Russia, to form a universal Dictionary, may be attended with the merited success. To know the affinity of tongues, seems to be one step towards promoting the affinity of nations. Would to god, the harmony of nations was an object that lay nearest to the hearts of Sovereigns; and that the incentives to peace (of which commerce and facility of understanding each other are not the most inconsiderable) might be daily encreased! Should the present or any other efforts of mine to procure information respecting the different dialects of the Aborigines in America, serve to reflect a ray of light on the obscure subject of language in general, I shall be highly gratified. For I love to indulge the contemplation of human nature in a progressive state of improvement and melioration: and if the idea would not be considered as visionary and chimerical, I could fondly hope that the present plan of the great Potentate of the North, might, in some measure, lay the foundation for that assimilation of language, which, producing assimilation of manners and interests, should one day remove many of the causes of hostility from amongst mankind.

At this moment, however, it appears by the current of intelligence from your side of the Atlantic, that but too many motives & occasions exist for interrupting the public tranquillity. A war between the Russians and Turks, we learn, has broken out. How far, or in what manner this may involve other nations seems to us, at this distance, uncertain. Extraordinary speculations and expectations arise from the conduct of the King of Prussia in the Dutch and the Emperor of Germany in the Austrian Netherlands. Nothing as yet, has come to our knowledge, which indicates with certainty, whether hostilities will take place between France & England, or, in that event, how extensively the flames of war will spread. we are apprehensive we have but too much reason to bewail the fate of the Dutch Patriots.

To guard against the similar calamities of domestic discord or foreign interposition, and effectually to secure our liberties, with all the benefits of an efficient Goverment, is now the important subject that engroses the attention of all our part [of] America. you will doubtless have seen, in the public papers, in what manner the new Constitution has been attacked and defended.

There have been some compositions published in its defence, which I think will, at least, do credit to American genius. I dare say its principles and tendencies have, also, before this time been amply discussed in Europe. Here, that is in United America, it is strongly advocated by a very great and decided majority. The Conventions, in the States of Jersey and Delaware, have *unanimously* adopted it: and that of Pennsylvania by a majority of two to one. no other State has yet had an opportunity of deciding. New England (with the exception of Rhode Island, which seems itself, politically speaking, to be an exception from all that is good) it is believed will chearfully and fully accept it: and there is little doubt but that the three Southern States will do the same. In Virginia and new york its fate is somewhat more questionable: though, in my private opinion, I have no hisitation to believe there will be a Clear majority in its favor, in the former: of the latter, I can say nothing from my own knowledge, its advocates, there, generally conclude that they shall carry it.

Upon this summary view, you will perceive, my dear Marquis, the highest probability exists that the proposed Constitution will be adopted by more than nine States, by some period early in the coming summer.

To morrow, I shall set out on a Journey to vew the progress which has been made in clearing the upper falls of the Potomack, This business, in general, has been attended with as much success as could possibly have been expected.

I have nothing more to add, but that Mrs Washington & those under this roof desire to be affectionately presented to yourself and those under yours. for myself, my dear Marquis, I am &c.

G. Washington

P.S. Under cover with this letter, is one from Genl Butler which I forward to you at his request.[3] as this Gentlemans knowledge of the Indian languages is more extensive and accurate in the Shawane than it is in Delaware and the vocabulary less copius in the latter than in the former—I send you the Delaware Indian & English spelling Book by Mr Zeis berger, as it may throw light on the Subject.[4] Go. W.

LB, DLC:GW.

1. GW's letter to Lafayette enclosing a copy of the new Constitution is dated 18 September. See John Paul Jones to GW, 9 Nov. 1787.

2. See Richard Butler to GW, 30 Nov. 1787, and notes.
3. See GW to Richard Butler, this date.
4. David Zeisberger published in Philadelphia in 1775 and 1776 his *Essay of a Delaware-Indian and English Spelling-Book, for the Use of the Schools of the Christian Indians on the Muskingum River.*

# To James Madison

My dear Sir,                    Mount Vernon Jany 10th 1788.
I stand indebted to you for your favors of the 20th & 26th Ult.; and I believe for that of the 14th also, & their enclosures.

It does not appear to me that there is any *certain* criterian in this State, by which a decided judgment can be formed of the opinion which is entertained by the mass of its Citizens with respect to the New Constitution. My belief on this occasion is, that whenever the matter is brought to a final decision, that not only a majority, but a large one, will be found in its favor.

That the opposition should have gained strength, among the members of the Assembly in Richmond, admitting the fact, is not to be wondered at when it is considered that the powerful adversaries to the Constitution are all assembled at that place, acting conjunctly; with the promulgated sentiments of Col. R.H.L. as auxiliary. It is said however, and I believe it may be depended upon, that the latter (tho' he may retain his sentiments) has with-drawn, or means to withdraw his opposition; because, as he has expressed himself, or as others have done it for him, he finds himself in bad Company; such as with M——r Sm—th's &ca &ca.[1] His brother, Francis L. Lee on whose judgment the family place much reliance, is decidedly in favor of the new form, under a conviction that it is the best that can be obtained, and because it promises energy—stability—and that security which is, or ought to be, the wish of every good Citizen of the Union.

How far the determination of the question before the debating club (of which I made mention in a former letter) may be considered as auspicious of the final decision in Convention, I shall not prognosticate; but in this Club, this question it seems, was determined by a very large majority in favor of the Constitution;[2] but of all the arguments which may be used at this time, none will be so forcible, I expect, as that nine States have acceded to it. and if the unanimity, or majorities in those which are to follow, are as great as in those which have acted, the power of these arguments will be irrisistable.

The Governor has given his reasons to the Publick for with holding his signature to the Constitution. A copy of them I send you.[3]

Our Assembly has been long in Session—employed chiefly (according to my information) in rectifying the mistakes of the last, and committing others for emendations at the next. Yet, "who so wise as we are"—We are held in painful suspence with respect to European Intelligence—Peace or War, by the last accts are equally balanced a grain added to either scale will give it the preponderancy.

I have no regular corrispondt in Massachusetts; otherwise, as the occasional subject of a letter I should have had no objection to the communication of my sentiments on the proposed Government as they are unequivocal & decided.[4] With the greatest esteem & regd I am My dear Sir Yr Most Obedt & Affe. Ser⟨vt⟩

Go: Washington

P.S. I have this momt been informed, that the Assembly of No. Carolina have postponed the meeting of the Convention of that State until July—This seems evidently calculated to take the Tone from Virginia.

ALS, MA; LB, DLC:GW.

1. The opposition of Meriwether Smith of Essex County in the house of delegates in 1785 to the bill for the payment of British debts had met with GW's disapproval. See David Stuart to GW, 18 Dec. 1785. "Col. R. H. L." is Richard Henry Lee.

2. See the postscript in GW's letter to Madison of 7 Dec. 1787.

3. See Edmund Randolph to GW, 27 Dec. 1787, n.1.

4. See Madison to GW, 20 Dec. 1787, n.5.

## To Frederick Weissenfels

Sir,                              Mount Vernon January 10th 1788

I have received your letter of the 10th of December in answer to that, as well as those which you wrote to me in June last,[1] I am sorry to inform you that I cannot, with any propriety, make application to Congress had [I] the offices to bestow or any other publick body in your behalf for an appointment; because it would be acting directly contrary to a resolution which I made, when I quitted the publick service, not to make application for, or interfere with appointments of any kind.[2]

It is a matter of regret as well as surprize that you should apply to me in an affair of this nature in preferrence to those persons among whom you live and have been more immediately employ'd and who must, from their long acquaintance with you, have a much better knowledge of your merits and sufferings than I can be supposed to have. If you expect relief from the Cincinnati, it is to the State Society you must look for it, or apply to the General-meeting, when convened, for I cannot, as an individual, transact any business of this kind relating to the Society. I am Sir Yr Most Obed. Sert

G. Washington

LB, DLC:GW.
  1. Letters not found.
  2. For Weissenfels's earlier and subsequent applications to GW, see Weissenfels to GW, 21 Feb. 1785, source note.

# To William Irvine

Dear Sir,                    Mount Vernon January 11th 1788
   When I had the pleasure to see you in Philadelphia last summer, I think (if my memory serves me) that you mentioned, in the course of conversation, your having lately been in that part of the Western Country which lies between the sources of the Cayahoga, the muskingum and Big-[Beaver] River. As I am desireous of learning some particulars relative to that part of the Country (as well to gratify my own curiosity as to enable me to satisfy several Gentlemen of distinction in other countries who have applied to me for information upon the subject), I shall take it as a particular favor if you will resolve the following quæries—viz.[1]

   1st What is the face of the Country between the sources, or Canoe navigation of the Cayahoga (which discharges itself into Lake Eire) and the Big-Beaver—and between the Cayahoga and the Muskingum?

2d The distance between the waters of the Cayahoga and each of the two rivers above mentioned?

3d Would it be practicable (and not expensive) to cut a canal between the Cayahoga and either of the above rivers so as to open a communication between the waters of Lake Eire and the Ohio?

4th Whether there is any more direct; practicable, and easy communication between the waters of Lake Eire and those of the Ohio (by which the Fur and Peltry of the upper Country can be transported) than these?

Any information you can give me relative to the above quæries, from your own knowledge, will be most agreeable; but if that is not sufficiently accurate for you to decide upon, the best and most authentic accounts of others will be very acceptable.[2]

As a determination of the points here referred to, may tend to promote the commerce, population and welfare of the Country, I know it will, to you my dear Sir, be a Suffi[ci]ent apology for any trouble which this letter may give. I am Sir, Yr most Obedt Hble Sert

G. Washington.

LB, DLC:GW.

William Irvine (1741–1804) came from Ireland in 1763 and settled in Carlisle, Pennsylvania. He served as a brigadier general in the Revolution and at this time was a member of Congress.

1. GW on 10 Jan. posed the same questions to Richard Butler. See also GW to Thomas Jefferson, 1 January.

2. Irvine responded on 27 January.

## To John Francis Mercer

Sir,                                Mount Vernon January 11th 1788

The People on board Mr Spriggs Vessel have been already supplied with Provisions, and shall receive every other aid they may require, and I can give. The conduct either of the Skipper, or your Overseer, has been egregiously wrong. The Vessel, it seems, came up in the night of thursday; but not till near dusk on friday had I any information of it, and then by [way] of enquiry from your People after their Overseer, whom they said was put on shore at my point, opposite to Mr Digges and had[1] not at that time Joined them. In strong terms I then urged them to go immediately on board and get the Vessel as near as possible to my warf *that night* as there was every appearance of a severe frost. Instead of doing this the Vessel kept her position (more than a mile of,) and, as I expected, was frozen up next morning and unable to deliver a grain of the Corn until the afternoon of Saturday Then but 16 Barriels whereas had they stopped on thursday the whole might have been landed before friday evening & the Vessel discharged, as I had a large Boat of my own and had collected my Plantation Carts (as soon as I was advised of the Vessels being here) to expedite the work.[2]

Mr Whites, letter is returned to you and I should be glad to know precisely whether I am to expect any and what part of the £200 on[3] which you assured me in Philadelphia I might absolutely rely and the half of which you informed me in november should be sent to me by your Servant in ten days if you could not get the residue? I have put the Sheriff of this County off 3 times—if he comes again—I must if I have no further expectn from you suffer him to make distress, as I raised nothing last year for sale, and allotted this money for the payment of my taxes.[4]

Mrs Washington and myself would have been glad to have seen you and Mrs Mercer here—This she would do still—In the morning I shall leave home for a meeting of the Directors of the Potomack Co. at the Falls of Shanandoah from whence I do not expect to be returned in less than ten days. I am Sir Yr most obedt Sert

G. Washington

LB, DLC:GW.

1. The manuscript reads "hand."

2. GW wrote in his diary on 4 Jan.: "A Vessel with 130 Barls. of Corn, sent by Colo. Mercer arrived here but from mismanagement of the Overseer on board no notice thereof was given till Sundown. Consequently no endeavor used to land it tho' the Weather indicated a severe frost" (*Diaries*, 5:261). A photocopy of GW's receipt to Mercer for the corn and other items, dated 23 Mar. 1788, is in Kenneth W. Rendell's catalog, 1991, p.33. Richard Sprigg of Annapolis was Mercer's father-in-law. William Digges's Warburton Manor was opposite Mount Vernon on the Potomac. GW credited Mercer's account for £102.18.4 for the corn (Ledger B, 221).

3. The manuscript reads "or."

4. Mr. White may have been the lawyer Alexander White with whom GW had frequent dealings. GW on 5 Nov. had reminded Mercer of his promise. See GW to Mercer, 5 Nov. 1787, n.1.

## To Charles Carter

Dear Sir,             Mount Vernon January 12th 1788

I find that an extract of my letter to you, is running through all the news papers; and published in that of Baltimore with the addition of my name.

Altho' I have no dis-inclination to the promulgation of my Sentiments on the proposed Constitution (not having concealed them on any occasion) yet I must nevertheless confess, that it gives me pain to see the hasty, and indigested production of a private letter, handed to the public, to be animadverted upon by the adversaries of the new Government. Could I have supposed that the contents of a private letter (marked with evident haste) would have composed a news paper paragraph, I certainly should have taken some pains to dress the Sentiments (to whom know is indifferent to me) in less exceptionable language, and would have assigned some reasons in support of my opinion, and the charges against others.[1]

I am persuaded your intentions were good, but I am not less persuaded, that you have provided food for strictures and criticisms. be this however as it may, it shall pass of unnoticed by me, as I have no inclination, and still less abilities for scribling. With very great esteem and regard I am Sir yr most Obed. and Affe. Sert

G. Washington

LB, DLC:GW.

1. GW's letter to Charles Carter of Ludlow in which he expressed support for the new Constitution is dated 14 Dec. 1787. Carter had written GW on 21 Dec. 1787 about the publication of the excerpt, but GW had not yet received Carter's letter, which has not been found. See GW to Carter, 20, 22 January. Apparently the excerpt of GW's letter was first printed in the *Virginia Herald* (Fredericksburg) in the missing issue of 27 Dec. 1787. Before the end of March it had been printed in at least forty-nine newpapers (Kaminski and Saladino, *Documentary History of the Ratifaction of the Constitution*, 8:276–81). Kaminski and Saladino compare the extract printed in the *Maryland Journal* (Baltimore), 1 Jan. 1788, with the passage in GW's letter-book copy.

# To William Thompson

Sir,　　　　　　　　　　　　Mount Vernon January 12th 1788

I have recd your letter of the 7th inst.[1] When I requested my nephew to apply to you for a craft, I expected that he would have engaged your largest, which he had last winter, upon the same terms that he then employed her viz.—at £20 for the trip and allow her to be detained below for four days on his account if she exceeded that time by his desire, he was to give 20/ per day for every day she might be so detained over the four Stipulated.

My corn will be received about the place where your Vessel was last year. I shall have enough to employ your largest two trips,[2] which I had rather do than engage two Crafts. If you are willing to let me have the same Vessel which Majr Washington had last winter, and upon the same terms above mentioned, I would thank you to drop me a line by the post.[3] I am going from home to day and shall not return in less than 10 days. I should wish, if you agree to let me have the Vessel, that she might be ready to go down as soon as the frost and weather will permit. I am Sir, yr most Obedt Hble Sert

Go. Washington

LB, DLC:GW.

1. William Thompson, a friend of GW's who was a merchant in Colchester, wrote GW on 7 Jan.: "Major Washington Called here Yesterday when I happened to be from home, & left a ⟨Verble⟩ Message; Informing me you Wanted Craft to goe round to Pomonkey River for about 2500 Bushells Corn, I have one Craft that will Carry 1600 & Another 900 which I coud send for it Whenever the Weather Permits, at the rate of four pence ₱ Bushell, which is as Low a freight as I cou'd possibly take" (DLC:GW).

2. In writing "your largest two trips," instead of "ships," the copyist evidently was in error. See note 3.

3. Thompson replied on 17 Jan.: "I shoud have Answered your favor of the 12th Inst. ere this, but Expected you ware from home. I am Willing my Craft shoud goe to York River for your Corn, on the same Termes she was Chartered Last Winter to Majr Washington, which is Exactly those you have Mentioned, she is now at Norfolk, & I expect her up as soone as the Weather Permits, when she shall Imediately proceed on your Business, After having her put in Proper Order" (DLC:GW). For GW's purchases of the corn from the John Parke Custis estate, see GW to David Stuart, 5 Nov. 1787, and note 4 of that document.

# From Henry Knox

My dear Sir                              New York 14 January 1788

Some time has elapsed since my writing to you as I had nothing to offer but what you were acquainted with through the medium of the public papers.

The new constitution has hitherto been as well received as could have been expected, considering the various existing opinions prejudices, and parties in the respective states.

In addition to Delaware Pensylvania, and New Jersey, Connecticut has adopted the Constitution by a noble majority of 127 to 40. This event took place on the 9th instant. I call the majority a noble one because it included every character in the convention of any real importance excepting Genl James Wadsworth, whom you may remember commandant of a brigade of Connecticut militia in the year 1776. Colonel Wadsworth writes me that the present Governor and Lieutenant Governor The late Governor, The judges of the supreme Court and the Council were of the convention and all for the constitution excepting Jas Wadsworth.[1]

The Massachusetts Convention were to meet on the 9th. The decision of Connecticut will influence in a degree their determination and I have no doubt that the Constitution will be adopted in Massachusetts—But it is at this moment questionable whether it will be by a large majority.

There are three parties existing in that state at present, differing in their numbers and greatly differing in their wea[l]th and talents.

The 1st is the Commercial part, of the state to which are added, all the men of considerable property, The clergy—the Lawyers—including all the judges of all the courts, and all the officers of the late army, and also the neighbourhood of all the great Towns—its numbers may include ⅗th of the State. This party are for the most vigorous government perhaps many of them would have been still more pleased with the new Constitution had it been more analagous to the british Constitution.

The 2d party, are the eastern part of the state lying beyond New Hampsher formerly the Province of Main—This party are cheifly looking towards the erection of a new state, and the Majority of them will adopt or reject the New Constitution as it may facilitate or retard their designs, without regarding the merits of the great question—This party ⅔ths.[2]

The 3d party are the Insurgents, or their favorers, the great majority of whom are for an annihilation of debts public & private, and therefore they will not approve the new constitution— This party ⅔ths.

If the 1st and 2d party agree as will be most probable, and also some of the party stated as in the insurgent interest, the Constitution will be adopted by a great majority notwithstanding all the exertions to the Contrary.

Mr Samuel Adams has declared he will oppose it in the Convention, to the very great disgust of the people of Boston his constituents It is said Boston were about to take some spirited measures to prevent the effect of this opposition.

You will see by the enclosed paper that the affairs between france & England are accomadated.[3] I am my dear Sir Your affectionate

H. Knox

Mrs Knox unites in presenting our affectionate compliments of the season to you & Mrs Washington and Also to Colo. Humphreys.

ALS, DLC:GW; ADfS, NNGL: Knox Papers.

1. Colo. Jeremiah Wadsworth of Hartford, a member of the Connecticut Ratifying Convention who voted for ratification, wrote to Henry Knox on 9 January. James Wadsworth (1730–1817) of East Haven, Conn., was major general of the Connecticut militia during the Revolution and at this time was state comptroller of finances. He was the leading Antifederalist in Connecticut.

2. In the draft of his letter, Knox wrote: "This party may not be less than ⅔ of the State," and at the end of the next paragraph he wrote: "This party may be more than ⅔ths."

3. Knox did not include in his letter the last sentence in his draft: "I have been confined to my chamber for a fortnight with the Rheumatism but am gettin[g] better."

# From James Madison

Dear Sir　　　　　　　　　　　　　　　　N. York Jany 14. 1788

The Daily Advertizer of this date contains several important articles of information, which need only be referred to.[1] I enclose it with a few other late papers. Neither French nor English packet is yet arrived; and the present weather would prevent their getting in if they should be on the Coast. I have heard nothing of Consequence from Massachusetts since my last. The accounts from New Hampshire continue to be as favorable as could be wished. From South Carolina we get no material information. A letter from Georgia, of the 25. of Decr says that the Convention was getting together at Augusta and that every thing wore a fœderal complexion. N. Carolina it seems, has been so complaisant to Virginia as to postpone her Convention till July. We are still without a Congress. With perfect esteem & attachment I remain Dear Sir Your Obedt humble servt

Js Madison Jr

ALS, DLC:GW; copy, DLC: Madison Papers.
1. The *New York Daily Advertiser* on 14 Jan. included a statement by Robert Yates and John Lansing giving their objections to the Constitution and a report on the ratification of the Constitution by Connecticut.

## To David Stuart

Dear Sir,                          Mount Vernon January 15th 1788
In answer to your enquiries in behalf of Mr Custis and which you requested I would commit to writing, you will please to receive and convey, the following information.[1]

Namely. That the lands which I have to dispose of beyond the Alligany mountains, are contained in the following tracts.

2314—Acres in Botteteurt County on the Ohio—beginning about 4 miles below the mouth of the little Kankawa and bounded by the Ohio 1720 poles. being the first large bottom on the East side of that River, below the mouth of the little Kankawa.

2448—Acres in the same rout and on the said river about 16 miles below the above tract being the 4th large bottom on the east side, below the little Kankawa. this tract is bounded by the Ohio 1012 poles—has a fine Creek running through it which (as I am informed) Mill seats.

4395—Acres, in the same County, and on the Ohio also about 3 Miles below the past mentioned Tract and on the same that is the East side & above the great bend which is about 25 Miles from the mouth of the Great Kankawa bounded by the River 1670 poles.

In all 9,157 Acres on the Ohio; betwn the great and little Kankawa.

10,990—Acres, on the great Kankawa, West side of it in Montgamery County—Beginning about 2 or 3 Miles from its Conflux with the Ohio. Bounded by the former, that is the Kankawa, 5491 poles or 17 Miles and 51 poles. Having many valuable streams passing through it.

7276—Acres, about 2 Miles above the latter on the other or East side of the said river in Green brier County and bounded thereby. 3947 poles or 12½ Miles.

2000—Acres about 6 Miles above the last mentioned tract on the west side of River laying in the fork of the Kankawa and Coal River—binding on the first 1400 and on the latter 588 poles.

2950—Acres on the east side of the Kankawa in Green brier County part whereof is opposite to the last mentioned tract. this is bounded by the River 1939 poles.

In all 23,216 Acres on the Great Kankawa—and on the Ohio 9.157

Total 32.373 on both Rivers.

That these several tracts, *some* from my own observation, and *all* from good information, are of the richest low grounds; being the first choice of the Country, by a competent Judge and are well watered, and superabounding in fine meadow.

That the whole are to be let, on the Conditions hereafter mentioned.

That the two first mentioned on the Ohio—and the two last named on the Kankawa may be purchased—as indeed all of them may if any one person for himself or in behalf of a number, will strike for the whole. without this and not because they are of inferior quality, but because what remains will be more concentered I incline to sell those that are farthest apart first.

That if I sell these, I shall expect (considering the quality of the Soil there situations on navigable waters; and the advantages they possess on account of Fish wild fowl &c.) Twenty Shillings pr Acre—part of the monies to be paid down, and such credit as can be agreed upon, given for the residue. I have been·in treaty with some foreigners (thro' there agent Mr Charson)[2] who have large tracts of land back of or in the vicinity of some of these Lands of mine and who know them perfectly well for the *whole* of them at the price of 30,000 guineas—but as they are not yet returned from Europe and the time is elapsed in which they ware to have given me a difinitive answer, I do not consider myself bound any longer to them—tho' it has been the cause (in a great measure) of the lands remaning unsold.

That the enclosed Gazette will explain *my* ideas of what I conceive the Rents *ought* to be.[3] but as this, it seems, is not the mode which is practiced by, and most agreeable to, the people in that Country possible from the scarcity of money or want hitherto must conform to the custome of it and of established markets. I have accordingly within the course of the last month authorized Colo. Thomas Lewis who lives (at Point Pleasent, a town at the mouth of the Great Kankawa in which I am told 30 or 40 families are settled and which) in the center between my several tracts to let them on the following terms[4]—that is to say.

First—With an exemption from the payment of rent 3 years. provided in that time a reasonable quantity of land is cleared and cultivated; a comfortable House, or houses for the accomodation of a family is built and a reasonable number of frute trees planted. And provided also (if it be customary) that the Land tax of whatever the tenant may be inclined to hold is paid by them.

Second—That after the expiration of the third year Rents shall commence and as the custom of the Country is to be received in the specific articles that are raised on the tenement and in the proportion of one third, by my Collector, or agent beaing near the premises.

Third—That under this tenure the tenant may have a certainty of holding their places (if they incline to remain and will continue to improve them) for a certain number of years (but not for lives) which may be agreed on.

Fourth—That all mines and minerals; with free egress and regress, shall be reserved. and an extra allowance made for Mill-Seats, or a reservation of them if there is not.

Altho', in the hands of Industrious tenants, and a good & faithful Collector, Rents paid in this manner and proportion, would far exceed what I have required in my printed proposals, yet I must confess that it is not a pleasing thing to me to let them on these terms because there is no certainty in the revenue which will arise from it. Idle tenants will pay little—dishonest ones will cheat me—and indolent, or speculating Collecter, will make poor returns. Otherwise as I have already observed no money rents that can be fixed would be so productive—for Instance—Suppose a farm of 100 acres (which of such land is enough for any man who has only a wife and their children to assist him) and ten only of these for the land is most easely cleared, is in cultivation, Corn we will say at the expiration of the 3d year—this it is agreed *on all hands*, will yield from 60 to 100 Bushels to the acre—but call it 50 only, it makes 500 Bushels the ⅓ of which is 166 bushels—the demand for which in a Country whose population is encreasing every year by thousands of emegrants will hardly ever let this article be under a Shilling; but was it not more than *half*, which is scarcely within the bounds of possibility, it would amount to £4.3 ℔ Hundred Acres.

If Mr Custis, or his neighbours of whom you made mention to me has any inclination [to] buy or rent any of my Lands here discribed—It would not be improper to suggest to them that the sooner something is resolved on the better; for as well formerly as lately, it has been told me, that I may soon fill my lands, with tenants agreeably to the terms on which Colo. Lewis has been empower'd to grant them; and on which if nothing more pleasing to *both* parties can be agreed, Mr Custis's neighbours may have them.

Should these circumstances, & conditions on which I have offered to sell part or Rent the whole of these lands induce Mr Custis to take a trip by water, or land, to this place, I will shew him the plats of the several tracts, the manner in which the land lays—give him a more ample description of the advantages which attends it and if any terms can be agreed upon between us will endeavour in time to prevent the seating of them by Colo. Lewis, by whose agreements I must be bound, if he makes any, as I have given him full powers to let the Land. I am &c.

G. Washington

LB, DLC:GW. GW enclosed this letter to be given to Custis in his letter to Stuart of 18 January.

1. It has not been determined when Stuart made this request. Mr. Custis probably was Edmund Custis who at this time was in Richmond with Stuart as a delegate from Accomac County on Virginia's Eastern Shore.

2. This is Henry L. Charton. See GW to Charton, 20 May 1786.

3. For GW's advertisement of his western lands, see GW to Charles Simms, 22 Sept. 1786, n.7.

4. See GW to Thomas Lewis, 25 Dec. 1787.

*Letter not found*: from Charles Carter, of Ludlow, 17 Jan. 1788. GW wrote Carter on 22 Jan. about letters he was "so obliging to forward to me under cover of the 17th."

## To Samuel Powel

Dear Sir,                                    Mount Vernon Jany 18th 1788.

Having nothing, either interesting or entertaining in these parts to communicate—our faces being turned to the Eastward for news—I felt no inclination to give you the trouble of perusing a dull scrawl, merely to acknowledge the receipt of your obliging favor of the 12th Ult., & to thank you for the information it conveyed, being in hopes that a little time might be productive of occurrences more worthy of attention; of this however I am disappointed.

It is with pleasure, I find that the States of Pensylvania, New Jersey & Delaware, have adopted the proposed Constitution, for a Fœderal Government; the two latter unanimously, and the former by a majority of two to one. Connecticut, Massachusetts and New Hampshire are to appear next on the theatre, in the order they are mentioned; and will, I hope, with a decision equal to those which have preceeded them, give their voices in favor of it. Of the unanimity of Maryland there can be little question; and tho' the Constitution in this State has powerful adversaries, little doubt of the adoption of it, has a place in my mind; but in this I may be mistaken; for as I seldom go from home, & see few besides travellers, my conjectures on this subject may be founded in error. North Carolina, has it seems, postponed the meeting of the Convention of that State to a later period than that of Virginia; which is indicative, in my opinion, of a disposition to take her tone from hence. From the States more Southerly, I have received no information that can be relied on; except that Georgia has accompanied her act of appointment, with powers to alter, amend & what not; But if a weak state, with powerful tribes of Indians in its rear, & the Spaniards on its flank, do not incline to embrace a strong *general* Government there must, I should think, be either wickedness, or insanity in their conduct.

The unanimity, & generosity with which the County of Philadelphia has been proposed for the Seat of the Fœderal Government, by the Landholders thereof, gives much weight and merit to the Invitation; and will, probably, induce others to follow the example.

I offer my best wishes, and affectionate regards to Mrs Powell; and assurances to you, of the esteem & regard with wch I am, Dear Sir Yr Most Obedt & Very Hble Servt

Go: Washington

ALS, ViMtV; LB, DLC:GW.

# From Rochambeau

My Dear General          Paris on the 18th of January [1788]

I have received by M. Shippen's hands the letter which you have honoured me with, and I made him the reception that he deserves by himself, and Especially, being honoured of your recommandation. I formerly received another one of you by the way of M. Rutlege bearing also your recommandation for that gentleman, but as I was in the Country when he Came to Paris, that has deprived me of the pleasure of Seeing him, but they assure me I Shall be incessantly indemnified of that privation on his return from England.[1]

Poor Count de Grasse, our Colleague in the expedition against Cornwallis, is dead the day before yesterday of an apoplexy. he had an unhappy End—the pains he had after his unlucky fighting of the 12th of april, and having being latly marry'd again with a woman of bad a character, all that occasioned him a great sorrow—I made all it has been in my power to soften his pains, but by the vivacity of his head he did take always violent parts which spoiled all what his friends could make in his favour.[2]

We have been, as you know, at the moment to have a violent war with our neighbours—the finances of france and those of England Should have been set on the same Barrel of gunpowder on the occasion of the troubles of holland, that has been appeased, but the war which breaks out in turky that was excited by the ministers of England and of Prussia against the Empress of Russia and the Emperor of Germany, will Set incessantly all Europe in fire, and I do not know how all the ocean of the politics Could put out that Combustion.

I long, my Dear General, to see your convention passed upon the plurality of the states and to see you President of a confederation strongly settled. I have the honour to be with the most respectful attachment my Dear General your most obedient and Very humble servant

le comte de rochambeau

ALS, DLC:GW.

1. GW's letter to Rochambeau of 30 June 1787, introducing young Thomas Lee Shippen, is printed in note 1 of GW's letter to Lafayette of that date; GW's letter introducing John Rutledge, Jr., dated 6 June 1787, is printed in note 3 of his letter to Chastellux of that date.

2. For the "unlucky fighting of the 12th of april" 1782, see de Grasse to GW, 15 Mar. 1784, n.1.

## To David Stuart

Dear Sir,                        Mount Vernon Jan: 18th 1788

As the enclosed will be transmitted to Mr Custis, I will blend nothing else ⟨w⟩ith it; but beg, for the reason therein as⟨si⟩gned that you would contrive it by the first ⟨sa⟩fe conveyance.[1]

The Certificates which I thought had ⟨b⟩een sent to you, are found—I suppose, after ⟨th⟩e list was taken, it was found unnecessa⟨ry to⟩ send them, & they were, consequently, with⟨h⟩eld.[2]

When Mrs Stuart was here, I inform⟨e⟩d her that Peters year, according to his own ⟨a⟩cct, which is all the acct I have; was up at ⟨C⟩hristmas, and she would direct what ⟨w⟩as to be done with him—She answered, he ⟨m⟩ight stay here till you returned—when th⟨is hap⟩pened, the hurry we were both in occasi⟨one⟩d my forgetting to mention it to you—he ⟨n⟩ow waits your orders.[3]

Patcy has been a little unwell bu⟨t *mutilated*⟩ better. all join in love & best wishes ⟨to⟩ Mrs Stuart & the family with Dear Sir Yr affecte Hble Servt

Go: Washington

ALS, ViU. The left margin is torn. The portions of the letter in angle brackets were taken from Fitzpatrick, *Writings*, 29:387.

1. The enclosed was his letter to Stuart, 15 January.

2. For the public certificates that GW sent to Stuart, see GW to Anthony Singleton, 1 Mar. 1788, nn.1 and 2. See also GW to Charles Lee, 4 April.

3. For earlier correspondence about the slave Peter who handled race-horses, see GW to Stuart, 12 Feb. 1787. See also GW to Stuart, 22 Jan. 1788.

# To Charles Carter

Dear Sir,                    Mount Vernon January 20th 1788

Your favor of the 21st of last month, came to my hands last neight *only*.[1] where it has been resting, or through whose hands it has passed, I know not. I wish it had reached me in time for the prevention of the hasty and indegested sentiments of my former letter, going to the press. not, as I observed in my last, because I had the least repugnance to the communication of them in a proper dress accompanied with reasons for there support if any person whatever was desireous of knowing them.[2]

You give me some reason to hope for the result of your *thoughts*, or *experiments*, on a more eligable system of agriculture. To receive it would afford me pleasure. That the one which is now in general practice (if it can be called a system) is beyond description ruinous to our lands, need no other proof of the fact than the gullied, and exhausted State of them, which is every where to be met with—but what chanse[3] is most likely to restore the land with such means as is in our power to apply which will at the same time be productive to the Proprietor, is the ques-tion—and an important one. a question too which admits of no other satisfactory solution than such as is derived from a *course* of experiments by intelligent and observant farmers; who will combine things and circumstances together—Theoratical opin-ions should have no share in the determination and what is good, and profitable husbandry in one Country, may not be so in another—Articles which are very saleable in Europe might find no market in america and if produced abundently would answer no other end than to encumber our Barns, or Graneries. Consequently two things must be engrafted into our plan 1st Crops which are useful on our farms, or saleable in our mar-kets—& 2d the intermixing these c[r]ops by such ralations[4] and with such dressings as will improve, instead of exhausting of our lands. To effect these is the great desederata of Farming, and ought to be the pursuit of every farmer. on this ground every experiment is a treasure—and the authors of them valuable members of Society. Hence also the Societies which are formed for the encouragement, and promulgation, of these experiments in other Country's have rendered such assential services to the imp[r]oved and improving States of agriculture in the old world and are so worthy of imitation in the vew.[5] My best respects, in which Mrs Washington Joins, is offered to Mrs Carter and your family. I am Dr Sir &c.

G. Washington.

LB, DLC:GW.

    1. Letter not found.

    2. GW's "hasty" letter was that of 14 Dec. 1787; his "former letter" is that of 12 Jan. 1788.

    3. The copyist should have written "change."

    4. The copyist should have written "rotations."

    5. The copyist should have written "new."

# To John Jay

Dear Sir,                  Mount Vernon Jan. 20 1788.

    Your goodness upon a former occasion, accompanied with assurances of forwarding any dispatches I might have for Europe in future, is the cause of my troubling you with the letters herewith sent.

    The one for the Marquis de la Fayette contains a vocabulary of the Delaware and Shawanese languages for the Empress of Russia. I beg leave therefore to recommend it to your particular care. To send it by Post from Havre I am informed would be expensive. To trust it to chance might be still worse. I leave it therefore to your own judgement to convey it, and my other letters in such a manner as you shall think best and least expensive.[1]

    We are locked fast in Ice—expecting as soon as the weather breaks, to hear what the Conventions of Connecticut and Massachusetts have resolved on with respect to the proposed Government. The decisions of New York and Virginia on this important subject are more problimatical than any others; yet, with respect to the latter, little doubt remains in my mind of the adoption of it.[2] In this however I may be mistaken, for going seldom from home and seeing few, except travellers, my conjectures may be erroneous. North Carolina it seems has fixed a late period for the meeting of its Convention; hence, it is not unfair to infer, they mean to take the tone from this State.

With much concern I have heard that Mrs Jay and you have been indisposed. I hope both of you are perfectly restored. The best wishes and affectionate regards of Mrs Washington and myself are presented and I am with much truth and sincerity Dr Sr Yr Most Obedt & Most Hble Servant

Go: Washington

Transcript of ALS, owned (1971) by Mr. Randolph Chetwynd, Carmarthenshire, Wales; LB, DLC:GW.

1. GW's letter to Lafayette is dated 10 January. For the Indian vocabularies, see Richard Butler to GW, 30 Nov. 1787, and notes.

2. The letter-book copyist, Howell Lewis, had this incomprehensible version: "The determination of your States and of this important subject seem more problematical than any other, yet, little doubt remains in my mind of the adoption of it."

## From Benjamin Lincoln

My dear General                              Boston Jany 20, 1788

In my last,[1] I mentioned to your Excellency the critical situation in which I consdeered my son though I entertained hopes that appearances were in his favor; my hopes were alive untill friday morning last; a manifest change then took place in him— He died at four in the afternoon.

In him I have lost a beloved son, an agreeable companion, and a sincere and confidential friend—With him expired the fond and pleasing hope that he would have lived a support to me in the evening of life.

My feelings which are alive on this occasion are rendered, if possible, more poignant when I see the distressed situation of my daughter, the widow, with two babes in her arms and observe the silent grief of a tender and most affectionate mother—our loss is great our wound is deep—I must not proceed I must not cause a momentary uneasiness in your mind—We have a source from which we may draw the most substantial consolation if we reflect justly.

Having been detained from convention for a number of day[s] I requested one of my friends to give me a general state of matters which statement I do my self the pleasure to inclose with the last papers from them[2]—your Excellency will learn in what stage the business of convention is in—I hope the constitution will be adopted I think matters wear a better face than they did.

My dutiful respects to Mrs Washington & regards to my young friend—I will write again next week. With sincere esteem & affection I have the honour of being My Dear General Your obedient servant

B. Lincoln

ALS, DLC:GW; ADf, MHi: Benjamin Lincoln Papers, dated 21 January.

1. Lincoln wrote in the postscript dated 13 Jan. in his letter of 9 Jan. about the grave condition of his son.

2. The statement, a typescript of which is in CD-ROM:GW, is devoted largely to an account of the controversy that arose when Elbridge Gerry was denied an opportunity to speak to the ratifying convention on Saturday, 19 January. Gerry, who had attended the convention in Philadelphia and had declined to sign the Constitution, had not been elected to the Massachusetts Ratifying Convention but had been invited to attend and answer questions.

# From James Madison

Dear Sir　　　　　　　　　　　N. York Jany 20. 1788.

The Count de Moustier arrived here a few days ago as successor to the Chevr de la Luzerne. His passage has been so tedious that I am not sure that the despatches from Mr Jefferson make any considerable addition to former intelligence. I have not yet seen them, but am told that this is the case. In general it appears that the affairs of Holland are put into pacific train. The Prussian troops are to be withdrawn, and the event settled by negociations. But it is still possible that the war between the Russians & Turks may spread a general flame throughout Europe.

The intelligence from Massachusetts begins to be very ominous to the Constitution. The antifederal party is reinforced by the insurgents, and by the province of Mayne which apprehends greater obstacles to her scheme of a separate Government, from the new system than may be otherwise experienced. And according to the prospect at the date of the latest letters, there was very great reason to fear that the voice of that State would be in the negative. The operation of such an event on this State may easily be foreseen. Its Legislature is now sitting and is much divided. A majority of the Assembly are said to be friendly to the merits of the Constitution. A majority of the Senators actually convened are opposed to a submission of it to the Convention. The arrival of the absent members will render the voice of that branch uncertain on the point of a Convention. The decision of Massachusetts either way will involve the result in this State. The minority in Penna is very restless under their defeat. If they can get an Assembly to their wish they will endeavor to undermine what has been done there. If backed by Massts they will probably be emboldened to make some more rash experiment. The information from Georgia continues to be favorable. The little we get from S. Carolina is of the same complexion.

If I am not misinformed as to the arrival of some members for Congress, a quorum is at length made up. With the most perfect esteem & attachment I remain Dear Sir Your obedt humble servant

Js Madison Jr

ALS, DLC:GW; copy, DLC: Madison Papers.

*Letter not found*: from Alexander Spotswood, 20 Jan. 1788. On 13 Feb. GW wrote Spotswood about "Your favor of the 20th Ult."

# From George Mason, Jr.

Dr Sir                  Lexington 21st Jany 1788

Some time ago Mr Massey sent me his Subscription papers (as sent herewith) I never untill very lately showed them to any Person as I wished to decline the Office of Collector & Solicitor but finding I cou'd not do it without giving offence I have been obliged to submit—Mr Massey wrote me yesterday to know if I had received any Money for him as he had engaged some Corn to be delivered the middle of this Week—in consequence of this I send the Bearer into your Neighbourhood & have desired him to call on you if convenient you will please send by him the amount of your last years Subscription[1]—With much respect I am Yr Most Hbe St

G. Mason Jr

ALS, DLC:GW.

1. GW's entry in his cash accounts for 22 Jan. reads: "By Mr [Lee] Massey pd him my subscriptn for the year 1787 by the hands of Geo. Mason Junr Esqr. [£]8.00" (Ledger B, 262). Massey was rector for Truro Parish.

## To Charles Carter

Dear Sir,                    Mount Vernon January 22d 1788

I return the letters which you were so obliging as to forward to me under cover of the 17th[1]—I am satisfied you had no agency in publishing the extract of my letter to you which is now to be traced through all the news Papers, and am sorry that I signifyed any concern on this occasion, as it has given you so much trouble.[2] With very great esteem and regard I am—Dear Sir, Yrs &c.

G. Washington

LB, DLC:GW.

1. Letter not found.
2. See GW to Carter, 12, 20 January.

## From John Rumney, Jr.

Sir                         Alexandria 22d Jany 1788

I now inclose you all the Papers that I have recd from Mr Swan of Baltimore respecting the Estate of Mr Colville deceas'd, for your Perusal, also a Letter from Mr Scorer of Whitehaven to myself on the same Business.[1] If there is any Thing remaining after the Discharge of the Debts, I believe it would be of great Use to the Claimants. You have inclosed the Opinion of Council, respecting their Claim, which I wish may prove satisfactory.[2] With the greatest Respect I am Sir Yr most obt Servt

John Rumney

ALS, DLC:GW.

1. GW wrote to Rumney on 6 April 1787 about Thomas Colvill's estate.

See also GW to John Swan, 23 May 1785, and notes. "Mr Scorer" has not been identified.

2. None of the enclosures has been found.

## To David Stuart

DEAR SIR:                        MOUNT VERNON, *Jan'y* 22d, 1788.

As you have no immediate occasion for Peter in the *only* line in which he will be useful to you, I shall be very glad to keep him, as well on acct of my Jacks, Stud Horses, Mares, etc., as because he seems unwilling to part with his wife and Children.

When you are in this way (and if it is not more profitable to you, than it is to me, you had better keep out of it) he may be serviceable, but hardly in any other, as he will do nothing but peddle about the stables, and conceives it to be a kind of degradation to bestow his attention on horses of plebean birth.[1] With great esteem and regard, I am, Dear Sir, Yr Obedt and affect. Serv.,

G. WASHINGTON.

*Historical Magazine*, 3(1859), 243.
1. See GW to Stuart, 18 January.

## To Clement Biddle

Dear Sir,                        Mount Vernon January 24th 1788.

I wrote to you on the 3d Ulto and as I have not received any answer to my letter of that date, I am led to suspect that it never reached your hands; I therefore enclose you a duplicate of it.

My reason for requesting you to pay Mr Pettit £18.5s.1d. (as mentioned in the enclosed duplicate) when I was not certain of your having money of mine in your hands to that amount, was in consequence of his informing me, in his letter, that you had offered to discharge it at the time the Backs & Jambs were shipped, but he then declined accepting it, not knowing how far it might comport with my arrangements to do so; and I likewise expected that a sum of money would, very shortly after my writing to you, have been lodged in your hands, on my account, by Thomas Smith Esqr.—If you have not paid the money to Mr

Pettit & should find the smallest inconvenience in so doing I wish you to inform me of it that I may convey it to him through some other channel.

I will thank you to forward the enclosed letter to General Butler by the first safe & direct conveyancce,[1] & am, Dear Sir, Yr most Obedt Hble Servt

Go: Washington

LS, in the hand of Tobias Lear, PHi: Washington-Biddle Correspondence; LB, DLC:GW.

1. GW's letter to Richard Butler is dated 10 January.

## To James Keith

Sir,                                      Mount Vernon January 24th 1788

The friends of Miss Anderson; and the residuary legatees named, or described in the will of the deceased Colo. Thomas Colvill are frequently applying to me; the first for the legacy which is bequeathed to that Lady—the others (but more particularly one who claims under the name of Shott) to know what the residue of that Estate is.[1]

No man can be more anxious to have all these matters finally settled upon equitable and legal ground than I am. and so far as my agency in the Administration of that Estate has gone there can be no difficulty in closing the Accts—and at any moment to satisfy the claims of every one, if there is no interference by the laws which passed during the Revolution and may be in force— In a word to do every thing which I can do with safety.

Let me entreat therefore, Sir, that you would inform me.

1st—What progress you have made in the statement of these Accts.

2d—Whether any more papers for the better illustration of them have been handed to you by Mr Thomas West (Son of Mr Jno. West)? By the Revd Mr William West? or by any others who have been applied to by me for this purpose?

3d—Whether you have yourself obtained any lights with respect to the Bills of Exchange which are unaccounted for, and which I have reason to beleive were applied by Mr John West in discharge of a protested bill due to Mr Thomas Kirkpartrick?

4th—What, if any, are the impediments which oppose a final settlement with the Court?[2]

5th—Wheather there is any prospect of overcoming them *satisfactorily?*

6th—What steps, if there is no further expectation of aid from the papers of Mr John West, ought to be taken to close them? and—

7th—What measures are necessary for me to adopt for my safety and Justification under such circumstances?

It will never, I fear, be more in my power to make Mr West's Estate answerable for neglects, or misapplications (if any there be) in his administration than at present; this then is among other important reasons which makes me extreemly anxious to bring this business to a close. I therefore pray that you will favor me with answers, as soon as it is convenient, to the foregoing questions—and if there is no further hope (which I am fully persuaded is the case) of aid from the heirs and Executors of Mr John West that the Accts may be made up in the clearest & best manner the nature of the case will admit; and that you will be so good as to accompany them with your advice in writing in what manner I shall proceed.

1st—I[n] submitting them to the Court.

2d—In case it should appear, as has already been mentioned, that the transactions of Mr West cannot be satisfactory accounted for, and a consequent delinquency, what in that case is incumbent on me to do?

3d—Whether the legacy due to Miss Anderson may safely be paid? whether it ought to bear interest? and in that case, from what period?

4th—In case a surplus should be found after all the debts and legacies are paid—what mode will be best for me to adopt— and safest—in the disposal of it; so as not to defeet the Testators intentions, nor to draw myself into a scrape from the variety of claims which have been presented—some of which are now in the hands of Mr Remney of Alexandria.[3]

And lastly, I wish to know what debts—by the papers in your hands, appear to be due *to* & *from* the Estate—and what measures I had best take to obtain the former—especially in the case of the Bond from Mr Montgomerie & others.[4] In the close investigation of this business, other matters, not herein enumerated, may occur on which your advice may be equally necessary and for which I shall be not less obliged. I am &c.

G. Washington.

LB, DLC:GW.

James Keith (1734–1824) practiced law in Alexandria.

1. For GW's correspondence since 1785 regarding Harriot Rebecca Anderson's legacy from the Colvill estate, see Henry Hollyday to GW, 30 April 1785, and note 2 of that document. For some claims on the Colvill estate by members of the Stott (not Shott) family, see Advertisement, 10 Mar. 1768, and note 1 of that document, GW to William Peareth, 20 Sept. 1770, and James Balfour to GW, 10 May 1772.

2. The copyist wrote "count."

3. See GW to John Rumney, Jr., this date, and notes.

4. See Thomas Montgomerie to GW, 24 Oct. 1788, and notes.

# From Moustier

Sir,                                            New York 24th January 1788

In order to have rendered the satisfaction which I felt upon my arrival in the United States compleat, I should have landed near enough to the place where you reside, to have immediately gratified the desire, which I have long since had, of seeing the man, to whose virtues & talents these States are so much indebted. My departure from Paris was hasty in consequence of the anxiety which I felt to reach the place of my destination. From this cause I am not charged with those marks of acknowledgments & remembrances which I should otherwise have been loaded with from my Countrymen, who have been sensibly struck with your goodness from the time that they have had an opportunity of admiring you & profiting by the Example which you have given to your Cotemporaries & to posterity. The Marquis de la Fayette, more provident than others, has just been able to seize a moment to favor me with the two letters which accompany this—The Chever de la Luzerne has likewise charged me with a letter.[1] If I had been so happy as to have handed these letters to you myself—I should have been at the same time the interpreter of those two persons who were formed to be precious & dear to you.

I earnestly wish that some favourable circumstance may hasten the moment of fulfiling the desire which I have so long formed of having the satisfaction to ask your friendship which I wish I might deserve. I shall never be able, but in a very imperfect manner, to express the sentiments of esteem, admiration, & I ought to say veneration, with which I have the Honor to be Sir, Yr very Hbe & Obedt Servt

Le Cte de Moustier

Translation, in the hand of Tobias Lear, DLC:GW; LS, in French, NN: Washington Collection. The French version of the letter is in CD-ROM:GW.

  1. The letters from Lafayette are dated 9 and 15 Oct. 1787; La Luzerne's letter is dated 12 Nov. 1787.

## To John Rumney, Jr.

Sir,                                      Mount Vernon January 24th 1788

  In answer to your letter of the 22d I can only, in addition to what I have formerly written to you on the subject of the claims on the surplus (if any) of the estate of the deceased Colo. Thomas Colvill, say, that *I*, who in fact had very little to do in the administration of that Estate *previous* to the dispute with Great Britain, and nothing during the continuation of it for the nine or ten years that I was absent, have done every thing in my power, since my return home, to bring the accts to a close in some manner or another. To this end I have called upon the Son and Heir of Mr John West (deceased) who was the principal acting Executor of Colo. Colvill—upon the Revd Mr West & Colo. George West his Brothers, the former of whom is, and the latter was (before his death) the Executors of John West—and upon Major Little, the Agent of Lord Tankerville, for all the papers and information that can throw lights on these accts.[1] and such as I have been able to obtain—imperfect indeed they are!—are placed in the hands of a Gentleman of the Law, well acquainted with this kind of business to make a proper digest and arrangement of them, which, when accomplished, will be exhibited in the Court.[2] and then—as I mentioned in a former letter, whatever is right and proper for me to do under the will, agreeable to Law, I shall do with out delay, or hesitation.[3]

  It must seem strange to persons not acquainted with the Circumstances, that a matter of this sort should lye in an unfinished state so long. The truth of the case is—that Colo. Thomas Colvell's affairs were so blended with his brother John Colvell (to whom he was sole Executor and a Legatee)—and these again so entangled with debts, to the Tankerville family—also with an important sale of land made by Thomas Colvell, as Executor of John Colvell, to John Semple which involved disputes, references &c. and moreover with Law-suits in other cases—all of which together, with more exertion than I believe fell to the lott of Mr West, could not have brought matters to a close before hostilities commenced; and the Courts of Justice were shut;[4] after this, the death of Mr West, and my absence (Mrs Colvell the Executrix of the will being also dead) put an entire stop to this business; and since, the disordered state in which that Gentleman has left his papers—or rather no papers—has occasioned more trouble and vexation to me engrossed as my time is with a multitude of other matters than any private circumstance of my life has ever done to renew and bring this business if possible to a satisfactory issue. However, I am determined that the accounts and disputes shall be liquidated—and the best, or worst known without much more delay; for this purpose I have this day written to the Gentleman who is vested with all the Papers to have them adjusted upon the best ground he can take for the accomplishment of this work. I am &c.

G. Washington

LB, DLC:GW.

1. Thomas West was the son and heir of John West, Jr., who died in 1777. The Rev. Mr. West was William West (d. 1791) of Baltimore. George West died in 1786. Charles Little (d. 1813) bought the Colvill plantation Cleesh. Lord Tankerville was the main beneficiary under John Colvill's will. For GW's dealing with Thomas West regarding papers relating to Thomas Colvill's estate and for references to GW's continuing efforts to settle the estate, see GW to Thomas West, 27 June 1786, n.1.

2. The "Gentleman of the Law" was James Keith. See GW to Keith, this date.

3. The "former letter" has not been found.

4. For summaries of GW's vain efforts before the war and in the 1780s to settle the Colvill estate, see the notes in GW to John West, Jr., December 1767, and Thomas Montgomerie to GW, 24 Oct. 1788.

## From James Keith

Sir                                                    [25 January 1788]

Your man has just delivered me your Favor, desiring to be informed, in what State the papers respecting Colo. Colvills Estate, delivered me to arrange, now stand.¹ I have delayed closing that Buseness to this distant period, hoping to discover some Traces of a Claim, which by Mr Riddles accts Mr West appears to have satisfyed, but for which no account is lodged, among the papers, and to procure a Receipt from Mr Adams for his Claim, which I am inclined to think has been satisfyed by Mr West;² I have several times applyed to him to satisfy me in that particular, which he has repeatedly promised but without performing as yet. The first I doubt will never be cleared up, the other I will proceed upon as it now appears, and whenever Mr Adams's Receipt can be procured it will then become a Credit for Mr West: Neither Capt. West nor the Parson have furnished me with any papers or Information[.] In the course of next week I will wait upon you with the papers—I have them stated from those Lights with which I have been furnished and Information upon the several Points contained in your Letter. I am Sir your most obedt Servt

Jas Keith

ALS, DLC:GW.
    1. See GW to Keith, 24 Jan. 1788.
    2. Mr. Riddle may be Joseph Riddle, a merchant in Alexandria; Mr. Adams was Robert Adam, also a merchant in Alexandria (Ledger C, 14).

## From James Madison

Dear Sir                                         N. York Jany 25. 1788.

I have been favoured since my last with yours of the 10th inst: with a copy of the Governours letter to the Assembly. I do not know what impression the latter may make in Virginia. It is generally understood here that the arguments contained in it in favor of the Constitution are much stronger than the objections which prevented his assent. His arguments are forceable in all places, and with all persons. His objections are connected with his particular way of thinking on the subject, in which many of the Adversaries to the Constitution do not concur.

The information from Boston by the mail on the evening before last, has not removed our suspence. The following is an extract of a letter from Mr King dated on the 16th inst.

"We may have 360 members in our Convention. Not more than 330 have yet taken their Seats. Immediately after the settlement of Elections, the Convention resolved that they would consider and freely deliberate on each paragraph without taking a question on any of them individually, & that on the question whether they would ratify, each member should be at liberty to discuss the plan at large. This Resolution seems to preclude the idea of amendments⟨;⟩ and hitherto the measure has not been suggested. I however do not from this circumstance conclude that it may not hereafter occur. The opponents of the Constitution moved that Mr Gerry should be requested to take a seat in the Convention to answer such enquiries as the Convention should make concerning facts which happened in the *passing of the* Constitution. Although this seems to be a very irregular proposal, yet considering the jealousies which prevail with those who made it (who are certainly not the most enlightened part of the Convention) and the doubt of the issue had it been made a trial of strength, several friends of the Constitution united with the opponents and the Resolution was agreed to and Mr Gerry has taken his Seat. Tomorrow we are told certain enquiries are to be moved for by the opposition, and that Mr Gerry under the idea of stating facts is to state his reasons &c.—this will be opposed and we shall on the division be able to form some idea of our relative strength—From the men who are in favour of the Constitution every reasonable explanation will be given, and arguments really new and in my judgment most excellent have been and will be produced in its support. But what will be its fate, I confess I am unable to discern. No question ever classed the people of this State in a more extraordinary manner, or with more apparent firmness."[1]

A Congress of seven States was made up on Monday. Mr C. Griffin has been placed in the chair.[2] This is the only step yet taken. I remain with the highest respect & attachmt Yrs affety

Js Madison Jr

ALS, DLC:GW; copy, DLC: Madison Papers.

1. This is the complete text of the letter from Rufus King, as printed in Rutland and Hobson, *Madison Papers*, 10:376.

2. Cyrus Griffin (1748–1810) of Virginia served as president of Congress until the dissolution of the Continental Congress.

*Letter not found*: GW to John Fitzgerald and George Gilpin, 27 Jan. 1788. Advertised in Goodspeed's catalog no. 150, item 3140, March–April 1923.

## From William Irvine

Sir                                        New York January 27th 1788

I have been honored with your letter of the 11th instant. I need not tell you how much pleasure it would give me to be able to answer your queries, to your satisfaction, but I am persuaded that no observations short of an actual Survey will enable you to gratify your correspondents abroad—(particularly relative to your 3d querie) with such accuracy as to hazard any thing positively; I will however relate to you such facts, and observations as actually came within my own knowledge, as well as accounts of persons who I think may be confided in.

From a place called Mahoning on the big Beaver to the falls of Cayahoga[1] is about thirty miles; the Country is hilley, tho not Mountainous, the chief is called the Beech ridge in this rout, which is not high, but pretty extensive, being several miles over a flat moist Country on the summit; in some places it inclines to be marshey and the difficulty of travelling is encreased much by the roots of Beech trees with which it is heavily loaded. The Cayahago above the great falls is rapid, rocky, and interrupted by sundry lesser falls, on the branch that heads towards that part of the big Beaver called Mahoning—This account I had from an intelligent person, then at Mahoning who was loading a Sloop with flour at the mouth of Cayahoga for Detroit; he added that an old Indian assured him it was not more than 15 miles from Mahoning to a navigable Creek, a few miles East of Cayahoga—that he had employed the Indian to blaise a road, and intended when that was done to explore the Country himself —I presume however this service was not performed, as this gentlemans Men & Horses were soon after killed and his store house burned by the Savages.

Captain Brady,[2] a Partizan officer, says that the sources of the big Beaver, Muskingum, and a large deep Creek which empties into Lake Erie, 15 or 20 miles above Cayahoga, are within a very few miles of each other, (perhaps four or five) and that the Country is level. Several other persons of considerable credibility and information, have assured me the portage between Muskingum, and the Waters falling into the Lake, in wet seasons—do not exceed 15 miles—some say two miles, but I believe the first is the safest to credit.

At Mahoning, and for many miles above and below, I found the general course of the Beaver to be East & West, from which I concluded this place to be the nearest to the main branch of Cayahoga—and on comparing the sundry accounts I am led to think, that, the shortest communication between the Waters of Beaver, Muskingum, and Lake Erie, will be found to lie East and west of Cayahoga. I have also been informed by a young gentleman of veracity, that the sources of the grand River (laid down in Hutchins's map) and a branch of Beaver which falls into Big Beaver, called Shinango, are not more than twelve miles apart—the Country hilley—I know this to be a fine Boatable str[e]am its confluence with the Big Beaver about 20 miles from the Ohio. I droped down the Beaver from Mohoning to the great fall about seven miles from the Ohio, in a Canoe on the first of July without any difficulty—it is true that at this season when all the western waters are remarkably low, some small riffles appear—but nothing to cause any material obstruction—The great falls appear at first view impracticable, at low water; indeed too tremendous, at any season, notwithstanding it has been passed at all seasons—I met two Men in a flat Boat a few miles above, who had carried their Cargo half a mile on shore and then warped up the empty Boat—they set with poles the rest of the way to Mahoning—This Boat carried about a ton and a half—but at some seasons there will undoubtedly be water sufficient for Boats with five tons in—Canoe's tis said have ascended 25 miles higher than Mahoning, which must certainly be very near one branch of Muskingum—as it continues a westerly course—and this most Easterly branch of that River, it is agreed by all who have been in that quarter approaches very near to waters falling into Lake Erie—all agree likewise that the Rivers north of the dividing ridge are deep and smooth the Country being flat, particularly those, west of the Cayahoga—Following the Indian path, which generally keeps in the low ground, along the River, the distance from the mouth of Big Beaver to Mahoning is 50 miles, which with the 30 computed from thence to Cayahog makes 80. but I am certain a much better road will be found by keeping along the high grounds which divide the waters of the big, and little Beaver, and the distance shortened at least 20 miles—but this digression I must beg your pardon for—to your 4th querie I flatter myself I shall be able to afford you more satisfaction, as I think I can point out a more practicable and easy Communication by which the articles of trade you mention, can be transported from Lake Erie, to the Ohio, than any other hitherto mentioned—at least untill Canals are cut—This is by a branch of the Alegheny, which is navigable, by Boats of considerable burden to within 8 miles of Lake Erie—I examined the greatest part of this communication myself, and such as I did not, was before and subsequent to my being there, by persons whose account can scarce be doubted. From Fort Pitt to Venango by land on the Indian, & French, path is computed to be 90 miles—by water it is said to be at least a third more; but as you know the Country so far, I will forbear giving any account of it—but proceed to inform you that I set out from Vinango and traveled, by land, tho frequently, on the ⟨beach⟩ or within high water mark—(the Country in many places being almost impracticable for a Horse) to the Confluence of a branch or Creek called Caniwagoo,[3] about 65 miles from French Creek—the general course of the River between these two Creeks is North East—the course of Caniwagoo is very near due north—it is upwards of 100 yards wide 30 miles up from the mouth to a fork—deep and not very rapid—to this fork the navigation is rather better from Vinango, than from thence to Fort Pitt.

I traveled about 25 miles a day, two Indians pushed a large Canoe loaded, and encamped with me every night, as the River is crooked I think it must have been near 40 miles by water[.] One fork of the Caniwago continues a north direction about 7 miles to a beautifull Lake, this Lake is noticed in Hutchins map by the name Lake Jadaque,[4] but is badly executed—it extends by the best information I could obtain, to within 9 miles of Lake Erie—is from one quarter to two miles broad, and deep enough—I was taken sick which prevented my intended Journey to Lake Erie; The following account I had from an Indian Chief of the Seneca tribe—as well as from a white Man named

Mathews, of Virginia, who says he was taken by the Indians at the Canhawa in the year 1777, he has lived with the Indians since that time; as far as I could Judge he appeared to be well acquainted with this part of the Country—I employed him on this tour as interpreter—That from the upper end of Jadaque Lake, to Lake Erie, is not more than 9 miles along the path, or road, for they with great confidence assured me that there was formerly a Carriage road between the two Lakes—The Indian related this, that he was about fourteen years old when the French first went to establish a post at Fort Pitt—That he accompanied an Uncle of his a Chief warior, who attended the French on that occasion, that the head of Lake Jadaque was the spot the Detachment embarked at; that they fell down all the way to Fort Pitt without obstruction—in large Canoes, with Artillery, Stores, provision &ca—he added that French Creek was made the communication afterward—for what reason he could not tell—but always wondered at it as he expressed himself, knowing this other to be so much better—This Seneca also related a number of circumstances to corroberate, and convince me of the truth of his account—among which the most remarkable are—That he was constan[t]ly employed by the British last war in this quarter had the rank of Captain—that he Commanded the party who were defeated up the Aligheny by Col. Broadhead[5]—That in the year 1782 a Detachment composed of 300 British and 500 Indians were formed, and actually embarked in Canoes on Lake Jadaque—with 12 pieces of Artillery, with an avowed intention to attack Fort Pitt—this Expedition he says was laid aside occasioned by reports of the repair & strength of the place, carried by a person from the neighborhood of the Fort—They then contented themselves with, the usual mode of sending small partys on the frontiers, one of whom burned Hannas town. I recollect very well that in august 1782 we picked up a number of Canoes which drifted down the River—and I received repeated accounts in June & July—as well from friendly Indians, who I employed as from a Canadian who Deserted to me, of this armament, but I never knew with precision, before this account, of the spot of formation—Both the Seneca and Mathews wanted to conduct me as farther proof of their veracity—to where an Iron four pounder lies on the bank of Jadaque Lake—which the Indian says was left there by the French—Major Finley,[6] who has been in that Country since I was, informs me he saw the Gun—Mathews wished me much to explore the East fork of Caniwagoo—but the reason already mentioned prevented me—his Account is—that it is navigable about 40 miles up from the Junction with the north or west branch, it suddenly terminates in a Swamp—which is half a mile wide—that on the north side of this swamp a very large Creek has its source, called Cateraque,[7] which falls into Lake Erie about 40 miles from the head, that he has three several times been of a party—who went up the one & down the other, carrying the Canoe over the swamp only—he added that Cateraque waters much the finest Country between Niagara and Presque Isle.

A letter has been lately published in a Philadelphia News paper, written by one of the Gentlemen who was employed last summer in running a boundary line between New York and Pennsylvania, which I think supports the foregoing accounts very much—his words are as near as I can recollect "We pushed up a large branch of the Alegheny called Caniwango, to a beautifull Lake called Chataghque—(so he spells the names) which is from one half mile to three or four broad, and upwards of twenty long; the Country is level and land good to a great extent on both sides. we ascended the dividing ridge between this and Lake Erie, from this place a most delightfull prospect was open to us["]—here he dwells on the scene and future prospects of grandeure &ca not to the present purpose; but concludes by saying that in his opinion "the waters of Lake Erie can not be brought to the Ohio as the summit of the dividing ridge is 70 feet higher than that Lake but we continued along the common path to Lake Erie which is only nine miles though the path is crooked—a good waggon road may be made which will not exceed seven miles as the hill is not steep.["] This gentleman has overlooked the Eastern branch, which is extraordinary if his view was to find out a communication as there is very little difference in the size of the two at the Junction—I suppose the Commissioners have reported to the Executives of New york & Pennsylvania—which I doubt not I can have access to. If I find any thing more particular than what is herein mentioned, I will inform you.[8]

I am sorry this detail has been spun out to such length, as I doubt will rather weary than afford you real satisfaction, but being obliged to blend other persons information with what came within my own knowledge, rendered it in some degree unavoidable—I have the honor to be with the greatest respect, Sir Your Excellencys Most obedient Humble Servant

Wm Irvine

ALS, DLC:GW.

1. Cuyahoga.

2. Captain Brady was probably Samuel Brady (1756–1795) who served in the Pennsylvania regiments during the Revolution. Famous as an Indian scout and fighter, he was chosen by Anthony Wayne in 1792 to command his scouts. It also is possible, however, that he was William Brady who along with Irvine testified in April and May 1779 in Gen. Lachlan McIntosh's investigations of Col. George Morgan and the Indian interpreter Daniel Sullivan (DNA:PCC, item 152). On 18 Feb. 1786 this William Brady was one of the signers of the "Memorial in behalf of the Inhabitants of Pittsburgh and others living on or near the waters of the Rivers Monongahela, Allegany and Ohio" in support of a company being formed by Irvine, Stephen Bayard, and others "residing at or near Pittsburgh . . . for the purpose of trading with the Friendly Indians, and at the same time of extracting Salt, from the water of certain Springs, situated near great Beaver Creek between the Ohio and Lake Erie" (DNA:PCC, item 42). Whether either of these is the Capt. William Brady who is referred to in Armand to GW, 25 April 1784, Enclosure II, n.4., or in note 1, John Sedwick to GW, 8 Aug. 1785, has not been determined.

3. Conewango.

4. Chauktaugua.

5. Gen. Daniel Brodhead (1731–1809) was colonel of the 8th Pennsylvania regiment and commandant at Pittsburgh in September 1779 when he led an expedition of 600 men up the Allegheny "against the Senecas and Muncy nations" (Brodhead to GW, 16 Sept. 1779; see also *JCC*, 15:1212–13). The leader of the small Seneca scouting party which was defeated by a contingent of Brodhead's troops has been identified in various sources as either Cornplanter or Guyashuta (Kiasuta). "Mathews" has not been identified.

6. Major Finley was probably either Joseph L. Finley (1748–1839) or John Finley (1748–1838), both of whom served in Pennsylvania regiments throughout the Revolution and had long service on the frontier. Both men were promoted to captain. Joseph Finley, who served at one time as a brigade major, after the war was appointed U.S. surveyor for Westmoreland County in Pennsylvania. John Finley seems to have been referred to as "major" during the mid-1780s.

7. Cattaraugus.

8. The Pennsylvania–New York boundary dispute was partially settled before the Revolution. In 1786 Pennsylvania appointed David Rittenhouse and Andrew Ellicott commissioners to complete the running of the line. James Clinton and Simeon De Witt were the New York commissioners. The work was not completed until August and September of 1787, by which time Andrew Ellicott and Col. Andrew Porter were acting for Pennsylvania and Abra-

ham Hardenberg and William Walton Morris for New York. See William Bar-
ton, *Memoirs of the Life of David Rittenhouse* (Philadelphia, 1813), 239–46, and
Catharine Van Cortlandt Mathews, *Andrew Ellicott: His Life and Letters* (New
York, 1908), 61–66.

Portions of two letters written by Andrew Ellicott and Andrew Porter in
August and September 1787 appear in slightly different form in two Philadelphia newspapers (*Pennsylvania Packet, and Daily Advertiser*, 3 Oct. and 3 Nov.
1787; *Pennsylvania Herald, and General Advertiser*, 2 and 31 Oct. 1787). Each
newspaper account agrees with a portion of the information in Irvine's letter.
It appears that Irvine read the accounts in both papers.

## From Benjamin Lincoln

My dear General                          Boston Jany 27th 1788
I have the pleasure of enclosend two news papers in which
are the debates of the convention to saturday the 19th[1]—they
are not forward enough to give your Excellency a just state of
the business I therefore am inclined to observe that yesterday
we were on the 9th sect.—The oposition seem now inclined to
hurry over the business and bring on as soon as possible the
main question—however this they are not permitted to do it is
pretty well known what objections are on the minds of the
people—it becomes therefore necessary to obviate them if possible—we have hither to done this with success the oposition see
it and are alarmed for there are a vast many people attending
in the galleries (we now assemble in one of our meeting houses)
and most of the arguments are published in the papers both are
of use.

Your Excellency will see in the paper propositions for adopting the constitution on conditions, this will not be attended to—
It is possible if we adopt it absolutely that the convention may
recommend certain amendments—It will never I presume be
adopted on any conditions, It will pass absolutely or be rejected.
I have now higher expectations that it will pass than when I last
wrote I think the friends to it increase daily, however I would
not raise your Excellencys expectations to high—it is yet impossible to determine absolutely its fate.

Mr Gerry as mentioned in my last left the convention in du-
geons he has not since returned to it I presume he will not re-

turn. With the highest esteem I have the honor of being my Dear Genl your most obedient servant

B. Lincoln

ALS, DLC:GW.

1. Among the Boston newspapers that reported the debate of the state's ratifying convention, which began its meetings on 9 Jan., were *Massachusetts Gazette*, 11 Jan., and *American Herald*, 14 January.

## From Chartier de Lotbinière

Sir,                                                         New York 27 Jany 1788

Immediately upon my return from Philadelphia I was seized with the tertian ague which was so violent in its first attacks that I still feel the effects of it—This has hitherto prevented me from giving you, by letter, some proof of my acknowledgements for the kind attention with which your Excellency honored me for the short time I was with you—But I should first have offered you the compliments of the season by wishing that you may have all the success & happiness which you deserve.[1]

You have already learnt, Sir, & with the same satisfaction that I have, that his Britanic Majesty has been obliged to restrain (I judge for near a year & perhaps more) the resentment which he has felt against his most Christian Majesty ever since your independence, by the firm & manly answer which the Archbishop of Toulouse ordered to be given to his minister by the Ct de Mountmorin to the artful & impudent requisition made on the part of his master.

You see at the same time, into the conduct of our good King whom the safety of the United Provences had equally engaged, & how happy they were, amidst all the furious & violent measures which were taken against them, to have an ally so exact & generous as he is. & what flatters me more than anything else in the event of this business is, that it has given time to your States to unite themselves firmly under the wise Constitution which you have presented to them: And by speaking you would find him ready to disengage you very quickly by some severe examples of those troops of Spies scattered about here by half dozens upon the arrival of every British Packet, whose sole occupation is to foment divisions & spread confusion—and give an account of the success to their chief in their Country—who are, in my opinion the only enemies whom you have to fear, & whom you may no longer dread when you have arranged yourselves under a constitution sufficiently energetic.

I have with me here at present, a young man of 13 years & two months old of the same name & family as myself but of the Branch of *Allainville* seperated from our's about three centuries ago who is deficient neither in information nor abilities suitable to his birth. I will not hide it from your Excellency, that seeing my only son without Children & without a prospect of having any by his present wife, my views are to perpetuate my branch (which is the oldest in France) by his means, in case my only son of our branch dies without issue; and my design is, in the first place, to fix this young shoot in your States. I placed him, soon after my arrival here at an Acadamy at Flat Bush on Long Island, chiefly with a view for him to learn English & to be instructed in writing—He has begun his studies & speaks English well enough to enter into common conversation. When I find him properly formed, I shall have the honor to offer him to you (that you may, if you have occasion, make him one of your aid de Camps, as his ruling passion is military) and I will venture to foretell that he will not be long with you before he will merit the honor of your protection, and under a master such as you, sir, he will soon display a sufficiency of genius to render him remarkable.[2]

Altho I have not yet had the honor to be known to Madam Washington, I dare flatter myself that you will not object to presenting my himble respects to her & with this sentiment joined to that of the most lively attachment, I have the honor to be Yr Excellency's Most Hbe & Obedt Servt

le Mis de Chartier de Lottiniere

Translation, in the hand of Tobias Lear, DLC:GW; LS, DLC:GW.

1. See Chartier de Lotbinière to GW, 8 July 1787, and notes.

2. GW replied on 22 Feb. from Mount Vernon: "Sir, I have been honored by the receipt of your letter of the 27th Ulto and am sorry to find, by it, that you have been so violently attacked by the tertian ague. I hope the bad effects of it are removed before this, and that you will not be afflicted by any returns of it.

"I am very happy to find that matters have been adjusted between the Courts of Versailles & London without coming to an open rupture; for notwithstanding the exploits that may be performed, or the eclat which may be acquired by military operations, yet the effects of war must be sincerely regreted by every humane & feeling mind.

"I thank you, Sir, for your politness in offering me the services of the young Gentleman, your relation, who is at present with you, as my Aid de Camp; I have not the smallest doubt but his abilities & dispositions are such as would do him credit in any post, but, sir, I must decline the honor which you would do me, for, at the close of the war, I resigned my military employments & quitted publick life, I have, therefore, no occasion for the services of an Aid de Camp, and I hope that a continuance of peace in this Country will render them unnecessary at any future period. I have the Honor to be, sir, Yr most Obedt Hble Servt Go: Washington" (LS, in the hand of Tobias Lear, MHi: Jeremiah Colburn Papers; LB, DLC:GW).

*Letter not found*: from Embree & Shotwell, 28 Jan. 1788. On 22 Feb. 1788 GW wrote to Embree & Shotwell: "I have received your letter of the 28th Ulto."

# From John Lathrop

Sir,                                        Boston 28 Jany 1788

Our worthy an amiable friend General Linclon asked me the other day, whether I had sent one of my Discourses ⟨de⟩livered before the Humane Society to General Washington, I told him I had not, and indeed the reason I had not was, that I had not confidence enough in its merit, to think it worth sending so far. But as Genral Linclon assurd me Your excellency wished to see every thing of the kind publishd in America, and that he would take the trouble of sending it, I will ask your acceptance of one of those Discourses for your self, and one for any friend to whom you may please to give it.[1]

I also take the liberty to Send a Discourse deliverd on the Peace.[2] ⟨I⟩ felt myself greatly interested in the events of the w⟨ar I⟩ never enjoyed a more happy Day than that which ⟨brough⟩t peace, with innumerable Blessings.[3] With ev⟨ery s⟩entiment of respect ⟨I⟩ beg leave to Subscribe myself Your Excellency's most obedient & humbe Servt

John Lathrop

ALS, DLC:GW.

1. John Lathrop (c.1739–1816) published many of the sermons that he delivered during his long tenure as minister of the Second Church in Boston. *A*

*Discourse, before the Humane Society, in Boston: Delivered on the Second Tuesday of June, 1787* was printed by E. Russell in Boston in 1787.

2. Lathrop's *A Discourse on the Peace; Preached on the Day of Public Thanksgiving, November 25, 1784* was printed by Peter Edes in Boston in 1784.

3. GW replied from Mount Vernon on 22 Feb.: "Sir, I have received your letter of the 28th Ulto—accompanied by the three pamphlets which you did me the honor to send me. You will do me the favor, Sir, to accept of my best thanks for the mark of polite attention in forwarding your discourses to me.

"The one delivered before the Humane Society is upon a subject highly interesting to the feelings of every benevolent mind. The laudable view of Institutions of this nature do honor to humanity. The benefices resulting from them is not confined to any particular class or nation—it extends its influence to the whole race of mankind and cannot be too much applauded. I am, Sir, Yr most Obedt Hble Servt Go: Washington" (LS [photocopy], PU: Armstrong Photostats; LB, DLC:GW).

# From James Madison

Dear Sir                                    New York Jany 28. 1788

The information which I have by the Eastern mail rather increases than removes the anxiety produced by the last. I give it to you as I have recd it in the words of Mr King.

Boston 20 Jany 88

"Our Convention proceeds slowly. An apprehension that the liberties of the people are in danger, and a distrust of men of property or education have a more powerful effect upon the minds of our opponents than any specific objections against the Constitution. If the opposition was grounded on any precise points, I am persuaded that it might be weakened, if not entirely overcome. But every attempt to remove their fixed and violent jealousy seems hitherto to operate as a confirmation of that baneful passion. The opponents affirm to each other that they have an unalterable majority on their side. The friends doubt the strength of their adversaries but are not entirely confident of their own. An event has taken place relative to Mr Gerry, which without great caution may throw us into confusion. I informed you by the last post on what terms Mr Gerry took a Seat in the Convention. Yesterday in the course of debate on the Construction of the Senate, Mr G. *unasked*, informed the Convention that he had some information to give the Convention on the subject then under discussion. Mr Dana and a number of the most respectable members, remarked upon the impropriety of Mr G——s conduct. Mr G. rose with a view to justify himself. He was immediately prevented by a number of objectors. This brought on an irregular conversation whether Mr G. should be heard. The Hour of adjournment arrived and the President adjourned the House. Mr Gerry immediately charged Mr Dana with a design of injuring his reputation by partial information, and preventing his having an opportunity to communicate important truths to the Convention. This charge drew a warm reply from Mr Dana. The members collected about them, took sides as they were for or against the Constitution, and we were in danger of the utmost confusion—However the gentlemen separated, and I suppose tomorrow morning will renew the discussion before the Convention. I shall be better able to conjecture the final issue by next post."[1]

There are other letters of the same date from other gentlemen on the spot which exhibit rather a more favorable prospect.[2] Some of them I am told are even flattering. Accounts will always vary in such cases, because they must be founded on different opportunities of remarking the general complexion; where they take no tincture from the opinions or temper of the writer. I remain Dear Sir with the Most perfect esteem & attachment Your Obedt servt

Js Madison Jr

ALS, DLC:GW; copy, DLC: Madison Papers.
1. The letter is printed in Rutland and Hobson, *Madison Papers*, 10:400–401.
2. The editors of the *Madison Papers* have found no other letters to Madison of this date.

## To Benjamin Lincoln

My dear Sir,                           Mount Vernon Jany 31st 1788
Your favor of the 9th instt came to hand last evening. As you know what ever concerns your happiness & welfare cannot be indifferent to me, you will very readily believe me when I assure you, that I take a feeling part in your anxiety and distress on account of your Son, and most sincerely wish for his recovery.

I thank you, my dear Sir, for your observations upon the advantages which might accrue from a Settlement of the Eastern parts of your State—&ca. And also for the information contained in your letter. I am very sorry to find that there is like to be so powerful an opposition to the adoption of the proposed plan of Government with you; and I am entirely of your opinion that the business of the Convention should be conducted with moderation, candor & fairness (which are not incompatible with firmness) for altho' as you justly observe, the friends of the New system may bear down the opposition, yet they would never be able, by precipitate or violent measures, to sooth and reconcile their minds to the exercise of the Government; which is a matter that ought as much as possible to be kept in view, & temper their proceedings.

What will be the fate of the Constitution in this State is impossible to tell at a period so far distant from the meeting of the Convention; my private opinion of the matter however is, that it will certainly be adopted; There is no question however but the decision of other States will have great influence here; particularly of one so respectable as Massachusetts.

You have undoubtedly seen my sentiments upon the Constitution in an extract of a letter written by me to a Gentleman in Fredericksburgh, which I find has circulated pretty generally through the Papers. I had not the most distant idea of its ever appearing before the public, for altho' I have not the least wish or desire to conceal my sentiments upon the subject from any person living, yet, as the letter containing the paragraph alluded to was written upon several other matters quite foreign to this, & intended only for that Gentleman's own inspection, I did not attend to the manner of expressing my ideas, or dress them in the language I should have done, if I had had the smallest suspicion of their ever coming to the public eye—through that Channel.[1]

I feel myself much obliged by your promise to inform me of whatever transpires in your Convention worthy of attention, and assure you that it will be gratefully received. With the sincerest regard and the most ardent desire in which Mrs Washington joins me—that your distresses may be removed by the recovery of your Son I am My dear Sir, with great regard Yr Most Obedt Hble Servt

Go. Washington

ALS, MH; LB, DLC:GW.
  1. See GW to Charles Carter, 12 January.

## From Benjamin Tasker Dulany

Dear General                              Springhill Feby 1st 1788
  Nothing but the inclemency of the Weather has prevented my
going to Maryland for your Rent, and can assure you I have no
other apology to make.
  As soon as I can cross the potomac you may rely on my going
to Maryland, and immediately waiting on you on my return with
your Rent, in the mean time Mrs French will rest satisfied[1]—
With respectful Compliments to Mrs Washington I am Dear
Genl with true esteem Your Obedt servt
                                              Benjn Dulany

ALS, DLC:GW.
  1. In March Dulany paid GW £120 which he owed for rent of GW's Dow
property where Dulany and his wife, Elizabeth French Dulany, lived (Ledger
B, 132). The Dow tract was to become the property of the Dulanys at the death
of Mrs. Dulany's mother, Penelope Manley French, to whose property on
Dogue Run GW held reversionary rights. For a description of GW's arrangements with the Dulanys and Mrs. French with regard to these landholdings,
see GW to Charles Lee, 20 Feb. 1785, n.1.

## To Andrew Lewis, Jr.

Sir,                          Mount Vernon February 1st 1788
  The white Doe with which you have been pleased to present
me, and which is indeed, a very great curiosity, came safe to
hand, this day; for which and so obliging a mark of your attention and politeness I beg you to accept my best acknowledgments and thanks.[1]
  Doctr Stuart informed me by letter from Richmond, that you
had it in contemplation of offer me a Buffaloe calf, of which you
were possessed; & desired to know if it would be acceptable. In
answer, I assured him it would be very much so, as I had been
endeavouring for sometime to get a pair (male and female with
a view of propagating the Breed for the drought) and requested
him to inform you thereof; but it seems you had left Richmond

before my letter which was enclosed in it for your Brother Colo. Thomas Lewis who I requested, and had accordingly empowered, to rent my Lands on the G. Kankawa—and Ohio above it. This last was, I believe, sent by a Mr Clendenia, and I should be glad to know whether it got safe to hand, and whether the Colo. will act as my agent in that Country or not. with the letter was enclosed draughts of all these Lands.[2]

Is it with you, or your Brother I hold the Burning spring⟨s⟩ and a small quantity of surrounding Land, in Partnership? What is, or can be done with it?[3] Mr Porter tells me you are expected at Alexa. this spring should you fulfil your intention of coming thither I can, with out a compliment assure you that I shall have great pleasure in seeing you at this place for though I have not the honor of an intimate acquaintance with you I had such with your deceased Father for whom I had a very sincere friendship and regard. I am Sir—Yr Most Obedt Sert

                                            Go. Washington

LB, DLC:GW.

Andrew Lewis, Jr. (1759–1844), a son of Gen. Andrew Lewis, was living at his place on the south bank of the Roanoke River in Botetourt County.

1. See GW to David Stuart, 29 Dec. 1787. The doe was brought to Mount Vernon by a "Waggoner" (Ledger B, 262).

2. See GW to Thomas Lewis, 25 Dec. 1787. George Clendinin had been Greenbrier County's delegate in the Virginia Assembly since 1781.

3. GW and Gen. Andrew Lewis together in 1775 claimed the 250-acre Burning Springs tract near present-day Charleston, W.Va., and on 14 July 1780 they received the grant from Gov. Thomas Jefferson (GW to Samuel Lewis, 1 Feb. 1784, n.3). Thomas Lewis in 1795 sold 125 acres of the tract. For the litigation after GW's death over title to the property, see Cook, *Western Lands*, 66–68.

# From James Madison

Dear Sir                                    N. York Feby 1. 1788

The Eastern Mail which arrived yesterday brought me a letter from Mr King, of which a copy follows. "Our prospects are gloomy, but hope is not entirely extinguished. Gerry has not returned to the Convention, and I think will not again be invited. We are now thinking of Amendments to be submitted not as a condition of our assent & ratification, but as the Opinion of the Convention subjoined to their ratification. This scheme may gain a few members but the issue is doubtful."[1]

In this case as in the last Mr King's information is accompanied with letters from other persons on the spot which dwell more on the favorable side of the prospect. His anxiety on the subject may give a greater activity to his fears than to his hopes; and he would naturally lean to the cautious side. These circumstances encourage me to put as favorable a construction on his letter as it will bear.

A vessel is arrived here from Charlestown which brings letters that speak with confidence of an adoption of the fœdl Government in that State; and make it very probable that Georgia had actually adopted it. Some letters on the subject from N. Carolina speak a very equivocal language as to the prospect there.

The French Packet arrived yesterday. As she has been out since early in November little news can be expected by her. I have not yet got my letters if there be any for me and I have heard the contents of no others. I remain Dr Sir with the utmost respect & attachment Yr Affte servt

Js Madison Jr

ALS, DLC:GW; copy, DLC: Madison Papers.
    1. Rufus King's letter to Madison is dated 23 January.

*Letter not found*: from John Fowler, 2 Feb. 1788. GW wrote Fowler on 2 Feb.: "I have received your letter of to day."

# To John Fowler

Sir,          Mount Vernon February 2d 1788

I have received your letter of to day,[1] and in answer to it must inform you that I have no inclination to purchace the Negro fellow which you mention as I have already as many Slaves as I wish, and I cannot engage to give another, or others in exchange for him, because I do not think, it would be agreeable to their inclinations to leave their Connexions here, and it is inconsistent with my feelings to compel them. I did agree to take him from Mr Robt Alexander but it was in part payment of a debt which he owed me & upon any other consideration I would not receive him.[2] I am &c.

G. Washington

LB, DLC:GW.
John and George Fowler were merchants in Alexandria with whom GW had dealings as early as 1772.
1. Letter not found.
2. For Robert Alexander's debt to GW, see GW to Alexander, 14 Nov. 1786, and note 1 of that document.

## To Burwell Bassett, Jr.

Dear Sir,                    Mount Vernon February 3d 1788
Mr Dandridge for reasons which he can better explain to you than I, have requested that the enclosed Bonds may be put in Suit. I beg it may be done accordingly.[1]

Upon so great a change as has lately taken place in your career of life I ought, possibly to have begun this letter with compliments of congratulation but as they are not less sincere on account of there being made the second Paragraph of the epistle you will please to accept and present them to your lady the manner which will be most pleasing to you both In doing which includ your Aunts.[2]

It is unnecessary, I hope, for me to add that whenever, and at all times, that you & Mrs Bassett can find inclination and leizure to visit your friends at Mount Vernon we shall be happy to see you at it. I am &c.

Go. Washington

P.S. Inform me by the first Post after this letter is received of its safe arrival that I m[a]y be relieved from any apprehension of its miscarriage.

LB, DLC:GW.
John Dandridge (d. 1799), a lawyer in New Kent County and the eldest son of Bartholomew Dandridge, wrote his aunt Martha Washington on 18 Jan. asking her if she did not "see any impropriety in it" to intervene with GW on his behalf to promote "the welfare of my Mother & her younger children." Bartholomew Dandridge at his death in 1785 left his slaves to his children to be held by his wife and mother for their lifetime. As his father's executor John Dandridge was instructed to sell Dandridge lands, and not slaves, to settle his

father's debts. Dandridge reported to his aunt that the returns on the land that he had been able to sell had proved insufficient to repay outstanding debts, with the result that the creditors "have sued, & will issue executions against the Negroes as soon as they get judgt." When he earlier had asked Martha Washington about the debt owed by Bartholomew Dandridge's estate to GW, she had told him, her nephew said, that GW "wished me not to sell anything on his acct. immediately; but as the negroes will be sold by somebody, before I can raise money from the land, he is better intitled to them than almost any other creditors. If however he can wait longer with us for the money, & does not see any impropriety in the measure, I would request him to send the bonds immediately to B. Bassett as his attorney, & let me give him a judgt. at March court next: Directing it to be levied on the Negroes, including such as (among which I can have included such as my Mother is particularly attached to) & have them purchased for him. They may then remain his & subject to his claim till I can raise money enough from the lands to sell & Debts due the Estate, to satisfy him.... I intend not thus by any means to defraud any creditor of his just Debt; for if there shall not be enough after paying the Genl, to satisfy the balance I will sell the negroes secured under his Judgt. & all my own individual property, to do it—But this will not be the case—" (Fields, *Papers of Martha Washington*, 202–5). Bartholomew Dandridge borrowed £600 sterling from his sister Martha Custis before her marriage to GW. At the death of Mrs. Washington's daughter in 1773, most of the bonds that Bartholomew Dandridge had given her in the place of interest payments were assigned to GW (see Settlement of Daniel Parke Custis Estate, 20 April 1759–5 Nov. 1761, printed above). In the March 1788 court in New Kent County, the attorney secured judgments for GW against Bartholomew Dandridge of £143.11.9 sterling, "with Interest from the Twenty third Day of April" 1771, and against John Dandridge and William Armistead, "executors of Bartholomew Dandridge decd," of £207.4.1 sterling (ViHi: Custis Papers).

1. GW again wrote Bassett on 9 Mar. to explain why the bonds were to be put in suit.

2. Bassett and Elizabeth McCarty were married on 10 January.

*Letter not found*: from Clement Biddle, 3 Feb. 1788. On 5 Mar. GW wrote Biddle: "In your letter of the 3d of February. . . . "

# From John Jay

Dear Sir                    New York 3d Feby 1788

an English Gentleman having been so obliging as to procure for me some Rhubard Seed which, from his account of it, there is Reason to believe is of the best kind, I take the Liberty of sending you a little Parcel of it—If the seed prove good you will soon be able to determine whether it will flourish in your climate, & in what Soil & Situation best.

It is a prevailing and I believe a just opinion that our Country would do well to encourage the breeding of mules; but the Difficulty of obtaining good male Asses, as yet much retards it. as you have one of the best kind, would it not be useful to put him to some of the best females now in the Country; and by that means obtain at least a tolerable Breed of asses? The few that I have seen are indeed very small, and it is to be wished that two or three Females of the largest Size could be imported; for we might then have from Yours, as good a Race of those animals as any in the world.[1]

our Legislature has agreed to call a Convention—the opponents to the proposed Constitution are nevertheless numerous & indefatigable; but as the Ballance of abilities and Property is against them, it is reasonable to expect that they will lose ground as the People become better informed: I am therefore inclined to think that the Constitution will be adopted in this State; especially if our Eastern neighbours should generally come into the Measure—our accounts, or rather Calculations from Massachusetts are favorable, but not decisive.

Your favor of the 20th Ult. was delivered to me this morning. The Letters which accompanied it, shall be conveyed by the most early & proper opportunities that may offer. are you apprized that all American Letters, and indeed most others, which pass thro' the french Post office are opened! so is the fact—while in that Country I never recd a single one from the office that did not bear marks of Inspection.

The influence of Massachusetts on the one Hand, and of Virginia on the other, renders their Conduct on the present occasion, very interesting—I am happy that we have as yet no Reason to despair of either. Connecticut has acceded, and the Gazettes tell us that Georgia has done the same. A few months more will decide all Questions respecting the adoption of the proposed Constitution. I sincerely wish it may take Place, tho' less from an Idea that it will fully realize the sanguine Expectations of many of its Friends, than because it establishes some great Points, and smooths the Way for a System more adequate to our national objects. Its Reputation & Success will I think greatly depend on the manner in which it may at first be organized and administred—but on this head we have no Reason to despond.

Mrs Jay's Health which was a little deranged by her too kind attendance on me while sick, is again pretty well established— For my own Part I have much Reason to be thankful, for altho a constant pain in my left Side continues to give me some, but no great Trouble, yet I am happy that my long and severe Illness has left me nothing more to complain of—we are both obliged by your kind attention, & assure you & Mrs Washington of our best wishes—I am with the greatest Respect & Esteem Dear Sir Your affectionate & hble Servt

John Jay

ALS, DLC:GW; ADf, NNC.

1. See GW to Jay, 3 March.

## From Benjamin Lincoln

My dear General,                                    Boston Feby 3 1788

Your Excellency will find by the papers of yesterday, which I do myself the pleasure to inclose, that the Governour has taken his seat as President of the Convention and that he came forward with a motion for the adoption of the constitution and sub joined a recommendation that some alterations may take place in it;[1] The motion has taken up a considerable time; those in the opposition want the constitution to be accepted *upon condition* that the alterations be made; this they will not be able to carry— Yesterday noon, a motion was made that the motion under consideration should be committed. This was agreed to, and a large Committee was raised, consisting of two members from each of the large Counties, and of one for two small ones. It was also agreed that each County should nominate their own members & that they should take one who had given his opinion for, and one who had given his opinion against the constitution, in each County wherein two were chosen; I expect they will report to-morrow afternoon to which time convention stands adjourned. I hope Good will arise from the measure & that the main question will be taken by wednesday next. The Gentlemen in the opposition urge that the Governour's motion ought to be divided, and that the first question be taken simply "whether they will or will not accept the constitution"; They are opposed in this, and I hope the large Committee will adjust the matter and put an end to any further dispute upon the question.

We find ourselves exceedingly embarrass'd by the temper which raged the last winter in some of the Counties. Many of the insurgents are in Convention, (even some of Shay's Officers.) a great proportion of those men are high in the opposition. We could hardly expect any thing else, nor could we I think, justly suppose that those men who were so lately intoxicated with large draughts of liberty, and who were thirsting for more would in so short a time submit to a constitution, which would further take up the reins of government, which in their opinion were too strait before; I hope people abroad will consider this matter and make proper allowances for a clog of this kind—I think the constitution will pass. I have the honor of being my dear General with perfect Esteem yr Excellency's most obedt Servt

B. Lincoln

LS, DLC:GW; ADfS, MHi: Benjamin Lincoln Papers.
    1. Gov. John Hancock was also presiding officer at the convention.

# From James Madison

Dear Sir                                    N. York Feby 3d 1788.

Another mail has arrived from Boston without terminating the conflict between our hopes and fears. I have a letter from Mr King of the 27 which after dilating somewhat on the ideas in his former letters, concludes with the following paragraph— "We have avoided every question which would have shewn the division of the House. Of consequence we are not positive of the numbers on each side. By the last calculation we made on our side, we were doubtful whether we exceeded them or they us in numbers—They however say that they have a majority of eight or twelve against us. We by no means despair." Another letter of the same date from another member gives the following picture.[1] "Never was there an assembly in this State in possession of greater ability & information than the present Convention— Yet I am in doubt whether they will approve the Constitution. There are unhappily three parties opposed to it—1. all men who are in favour of paper money & tender laws; those are more or less in every part of the State. 2. all the late insurgents & their abettors. In the three great western Counties they are very numerous. We have in the Convention 18 or 20 who were actually in Shay's army. 3. A great majority of the members from the province of Main. Many of them & their Constituents are only squatters upon other people's land, and they are afraid of being brought to account. They also think though erroneously that their favorite plan, of being a separate State will be defeated. Add to these the honest doubting people, and they make a powerful host. The leaders of this party are a Mr Wedgery Mr Thomson, & Mr Nason from the province of Main—A Docr Taylor from the County of Worster & Mr Bishop from the neighbourhood of R. Island.[2] To manage the cause agst them are the present and late Govr 3 Judges of the supreme Court—15 members of the Senate—20 from among the most respectable of the Clergy, 10 or 12 of the first characters at the bar, Judges of probate, High Sheriffs of Counties & many other respectable people Merchants &c.—Genls Heath, Lincoln, Brooks & others of the late army. With all this ability in support of the cause, I am pretty well satisfied we shall lose the question, unless we can take off some of the opposition by amendments—I do not mean such as are to be made conditions of the ratification, but recommendatory only. Upon this plan I flatter myself we may possibly get a majority of 12 or 15, if not more."

The Legislature of this State has voted a Convention on June 17. I remain Yrs most respectfully & Affecly

Js Madison Jr

ALS, DLC:GW; copy, DLC: Madison Papers.

1. The letter to Madison is from Nathaniel Gorham.

2. These Antifederalists were William Widgery (c.1753–1822) of New Gloucester, Maine, Samuel Thompson (1735–1797) of Topsham, Mass., Samuel Nasson of Sandford, Maine, John Taylor (1734–1794) of Douglas, Worcester County, Mass., and Capt. Phanuel Bishop of Rehoboth, Massachusetts.

## From Samuel Griffin

Sir—                                        WilliamsBurg 4th February 1788

As Rector of the Visitors, & Governors, of William and Mary College, for the present year—I do myself the Honor to inclose you a Copy of a Resolution which passed at the last Convocation, And I am directed by the Convocation, to assure you, that your acceptance of the appointment, will be esteemed of the highest honor confered on them.[1] should you wish to be possessd of one of the Books which contains the Charter, & Statutes, and which Authorises the appointment of a Chancellor, I will with the greatest pleasure forward one by the first safe conveyance.[2] I have the Honor to be with the greatest respect & esteem Sir Your Friend & most Obedt Servt

Saml Griffin

ALS, DLC:GW.

Samuel Griffin (1746–1810) at this time represented Williamsburg in the house of delegates, and in 1789 he was elected to the U.S. House of Representatives.

1. The resolution reads: "At a Convocation of the Visitors & Governors of the William and Mary College held the 16th day of January 1788 Resolved unanimously that George Washington esquire be appointed Chancellor of the College of William and Mary and that the Rector be requested to Notify to him the said appointment. A Copy. Will. Russel Ck" (DLC:GW).

2. GW consulted David Stuart about the duties of the chancellor of the college, either when Dr. Stuart was at Mount Vernon on 10–11 Feb. or by a written message, for on 17 Feb. Stuart wrote from Abingdon that he thought the college's board of visitors met twice a year and that the chancellor would be expected to attend. In a "private communication" on 20 Feb., GW informed Griffin that as much as he would like to accept the honor, he could not do so were he expected to attend the visitors' meetings. Griffin on 15 April assured GW that no duties whatsoever were attached to the office, and on 30 April GW wrote accepting the appointment.

# From Lafayette

My dear General                                        Paris February the 4th 1788

Your letters Become More and More distant, and I Anxiously Wish for your Speedy Appointement to the Presidency, in order that You May Have a More Exact Notice of the Opportunities to Write to Me. This Will not tell you Much of politics. The two Imperial Courts are preparing for a Vigorous Campaign Against the turks. Russia intends Sending a Squadron into the Mediterranean, and altho' it does not Much Suit either England or france, None, I think, Will Earnestly Expostulate Against it. The turks would fight, as lord Cornwallis once wrote about me, if they knew How. They shall be Beaten without doubt, and Cannot fail to pay dearly for their New Connection With Great Britain. I am told that the king of prussia also Repents for What He Has done, but He is too Wild to Be trusted. He is Strenghtening the Germanic Confederacy Set on foot By the late King, and England Has taken into Her Pay a Good Number of German princes. it seems affairs are slowly working towards an Alliance Betwen the Imperial Courts, france and Spain. it Goes on as Gently as it is possible for politics to Move. france is Afraid for Her levant trade. She wants to Mend Her deranged finances. Governement is not a little Embarassed By a Spirit of Opposition that Has of late introduced itself. So that Every Means to pacify, to Mediate, and to lay still will Be Emploied By France. Yet is she so powerfull By Her Ressources, Her fertility, Her position, and all the Advantages She is Endowed with, that She Must Be Calculated Much Above the Mark Where Her Rivals Now place Her—and the Moment She Gets a National Assembly, She Will leave far Behind Every Thing in Europe. England Has Gone a little too far for Her own abilities and intentions. I am told there is a deficiency in the last Quarter. She is Uneasy at the fermentation kept up in Holland By the Horrid Conduct of the State Holderians—and at the Prospect of the Quadruple Alliance. Yet as our Ministry are known to Seek Peace with Great Perseverance, the British Cabinet think themselves Enabled to take a Higher tone than what they seriously intend.

We are Anxiously waiting for the Result of the State Conventions. The New Constitution Has Been Much Examined and Admired By European philosophers. it Seems the want of a declaration of Rights, of An insurance for the trial by juries, of a Necessary Rotation of the President, are, with the Extensive powers of the Executive, the principal points objected to. Mr Jefferson and Myself Have Agreed that those objections Appear'd to Us Both well Grounded, But that None Should Be Started Untill Nine States Had Accepted the Confederation— then Amendments, if thought Convenient, Might be Made to take in the dissidents.[1] as to What Respects the powers and possible permanency of the president I am Easy, Nay I am pleased with it, as the Reducing of it to what is Necessary for Energy, and taking from it Every dangerous Seed will Be a glorious Sheet in the History of My Beloved General.

You Have Received an Arrêt du Conseil and letter to Mr Jefferson Which I Hope will prove Advantageous to the trade.[2] The former Has Excited a pretty Considerable fermentation Among Some Commercial and financeering people who think we Have Been too partial to the United States. I Have Requested the Ministers to Call the Opponents in a Committee, and Hope to Support Every Article to their Satisfaction. it is Better Not to Mention this Circumstance for fear of Giving Some Unnecessary Uneasiness to the Merchants in America.

The Edi[c]t Giving to the *Non Catholic Subjects of the king* a Civil Estate Has Been Registered. You Remember, My dear General, What I wrote to You Three Years Ago.[3] You Easely Guess that I was well pleased last Sunday in introducing to a Ministerial table the first protestant Clergyman Who Could Appear at Versailles Since the Revolution of 1685.

Mde de Lafayette, Anastasia, George Your Son, and Virginia are all Well and Beg to Be Most Respectfully presented to You and to Mrs Washington to whom I Beg You to offer My affectionate Respects. Remember me, My dear General, to the family and all friends. inclosed is a letter from M[arqu]is de Bouillé who Has Been Much flattered with the one He Received from You.[4] Adieu, My Beloved General, for God's Sake don't Miss any opportunity to write to Your Most Respectfull loving, and filial friend

lafayette

ALS, PEL.

1. For Thomas Jefferson's familiar objections to the new Constitution, see Jefferson to James Madison, 20 Dec. 1787, in Boyd, *Jefferson Papers*, 12: 438–42.

2. See Lafayette to GW, 1 Jan., n.1.

3. Lafayette wrote to GW on 11 May 1785 about the mistreatment of Protestants in France and his determination to take a lead in securing rights for them. He is referring here to the revocation in 1685 of Henry IV's Edict of Nantes granting civil rights to Protestants.

4. The letter of François-Claude-Amour de Bouillé, marquis de Bouillé, has not been found. See GW to Bouillé, 1 June 1787 and 1 Oct. 1788.

# To Charles Carter

Dear Sir,                                Mount Vernon Feby 5th 1788

At length I have got *some* answer to my application for Wolf Dogs—I wish it was more satisfactory—but such as it is, I give it; as suspence, of all situations, is the most disagreeable.[1]

The information comes from Sir Edward Newenham, a Gentleman of family & fortune in Ireland; and is in these words. "I have just received a letter from your noble & virtuous friend the Marquis de la Fayette, in which he communicates your wish to obtain a breed of the *true* Irish Wolf dog; and desires me to procure it; I have been these several years endeavouring to get that breed without success; It is nearly annihilated; I have heard of a dog in the South, and a bitch in the North of Ireland, but not of a couple any where; I am also told that the Earl of Altamont has a breed that is *nearly* genuine, if he has, I will procure two from him; The Marquis also wants some at his domain, where he is troubled by the Wolves; If Mastiffs would be of any Service I could send you some valuable *large* ones; which are our guard dogs; you will honor me with your commands about them. They are very fierce—faithful—& longlived."[2]

If under this information, you think I can be further useful, I shall be happy to render any services in my power. Mastiffs, I conceive, will not answer the purposes for which the wolf dog is wanted—They will guard a pen, which pen may be secured by its situation, by Cur dogs, & various other ways—but your object, if I have a right conception of it, is to hunt and destroy wolves by pursuit for wch end the Mastiff is altogether unfit. If the proper kind can be had I have no doubt of their being sent by Sir Edward who has sought all occasion to be obliging to me.[3]
I am—Dear Sir Yr Most Obedt & Affecte Servt

Go: Washington

ALS, ViMtV.

1. Carter may have inquired about wolf dogs in his missing letter to GW of 21 Oct. 1787. See GW to Carter, 14 Dec. 1787.

2. Sir Edward Newenham's letter of 10 Aug. 1787 has not been found.

3. See GW to Newenham, 24 February.

# To Henry Knox

My dear Sir,                                        Mount Vernon 5th Feby 1788.

Soon after my last was dispatched to you, I was favoured with the receipt of your letter of the 14th Ult.; by which, and other accts of more recent date, I am sorry to find that the important question under deliberation in Massachusetts, stands on such precarious ground. The decision of that State will, unquestionably, have considerable influence on those which are to follow; especially on the one in which you now are; at the sametime that an unfavourable issue, will strengthen the cords of dissention in others, which have already decided.

What may be the final determination on this Subject in Virginia, is more, I believe, than any man can say with precision. Every one, with whom you converse, delivers his own sentiment as the sentiments of the State; whilst there is *no* just criterian that *I* know of, to form a decided judgment. My own opinion of the matter is, as I observed to you in my last, that it will certainly be received; but, for the reasons then assigned, I may be mistaken; not having been from home ten miles (my journey up the river being prevented by bad weather & a slight indisposition) since I returned from Philadelphia, and from not having seen many beyond that circle, except travellers & strangers, whose means of information is too often defective to be relied on.

The poor Patriots of Holland, must either have been greatly decieved, or they have acted from weakness & precipitency. The first, I conceive to be the case—& the peculiar situation of the affairs of France—perhaps too, divisions among themselves, will acct for it. Be this as it may, their case is pitiable.

The Navigation of this river has been stopped for near five weeks—at this moment we are locked fast by Ice—and the air of this day is amongst the keenest I ever recollect to have felt.[1] Mrs Washington joins me in every good wish for you & Mrs Knox—and I am My dear Sir, Yr Sincere frd & Affece Servt

                                                            Go: Washington

P.S. Pray, if it is not a secret, who is the author, or authors of Publius?[2]

ALS, NNGL: Knox Papers; LB, DLC:GW.

1. GW's entries in his diary for January, February, and early March are filled with descriptions of the frigid weather.

2. Knox wrote on 10 Mar. that the "publication signed *Publius*" was "attributed" to John Jay, James Madison, and Alexander Hamilton. Hamilton on 13 Aug. affirmed that he and Madison wrote the papers "with some aid from Mr Jay."

## To James Madison

My dear Sir,                    Mount Vernon Feby 5th 1788.

I am indebted to you for several of your favors, and thank you for their enclosures. The rumours of War between France and England have subsided; and the poor Patriots of Holland, it seems, are left to fight their own Battles or negotiate—in neither case with any great prospect of advantage—They must have been deceived, or their conduct has been divided, precip-[it]ant, & weak—the former, with some blunders, have, I conceive, been the causes of their misfortunes.

I am sorry to find by yours, and other accts from Massachusetts, that the decision of its Convention (at the time of their dates) remained problematical. A rejection of the New form by that State will envigorate the opposition, not only in New York, but in all those which are to follow; at the sametime that it will afford materials for the Minority in such as have adopted it, to blow the Trumpet of discord more loudly. The acceptance by a *bare* majority, tho' preferable to rejection, is also to be depricated.

It is scarcely possible to form any decided opinion of the *general* sentiment of the people of this State, on this important subject. Many have asked me with anxious sollicitude, if you did not mean to get into the Convention; conceiving it of indispensable necessity. Colo. Mason, who returned here only yesterday, has offered himself, I am told, for the County of Stafford; and his friends add, he can be elected not only there, but for Prince William & Fauquier also.[1] The truth of this I know not. I rarely go from home and my visitors who for the most part are travellers and strangers, have not the least information.

At the time you suggested for my consideration, the expediency of a communication of my sentiments on the proposed Constitution, to any corrispondent I might have in Massachusetts, it did not occur to me that Genl Lincoln & myself frequently interchanged letters—much less did I expect that a hasty, and indigested extract of one which I had written—intermixed with a variety of other matter to Colo. Chas Carter, in answer to a letter I had received from him respecting Wolf dogs—Wolves—Sheep—experiments in Farming &ca &ca &ca—was then in the press, and would bring these sentiments to public view by means of the extensive circulation I find that extract has had.[2] Altho' I never have concealed, and am perfectly regardless who becomes acquainted with my sentiments on the proposed Constitution, yet nevertheless, as no care had been taken to dress the ideas, nor any reasons assigned in support of my opinion, I felt myself hurt by the publication; and informed my friend the Colonel of it. In answer, he has fully exculpated himself from the *intention*, but his zeal in the cause prompted him to distribute copies, under a prohibition (which was disregarded) that they should not go to the press. As you have seen the rude, or crude extract (as you may please to term it) I will add no more on the subject.

Perceiving that the Fœderalist, under the signature of Publius, is about to be republished, I would thank you for forwarding to me three or four Copies; one of which to be neatly bound, and inform me of the cost.[3]

Altho' we have not had many, or deep Snows since the commencement of them, yet we have had a very severe Winter; and if the cold of this day is proportionably keen with you, a warm room, & a good fire will be found no bad, or uncomfortable antidote to it. With sentiments of perfect esteem and friendship I am—Dear Sir Yr Affecte & Obedt Servt

Go: Washington

ALS, MA; LB, DLC:GW.

1. On 17 Feb. David Stuart reported new rumors about George Mason's intentions regarding the state ratifying convention, but in the end he represented Stafford County where he outpolled GW's friends Charles Carter of Ludlow and William Fitzhugh of Chatham.

2. It was in his letter to GW of 20 Dec. 1787 that Madison suggested that a good word about the new Constitution from GW to one of his friends in Massachusetts "would be attended with valuable effects." See note 5 of that document. See also GW to Charles Carter, 12 Jan. 1788, and note 1 of that document.

3. There were two two-volume sets of the *Federalist* in GW's library at his death (Griffin, *Boston Athenæum Collection*, 518–19). On 24 Mar. 1788 John Jay wrote GW: "Mr Jay presents his Compliments to his Excellency General

Washington, & sends him herewith enclosed the 1 vol. of the Fœderalist"
(DLC:GW). GW responded from Mount Vernon on 15 April: "Dear Sir, Your
Card of the 24th Ult., and first Vol. of the Fœderalist came safe, for which I
pray you to accept my thanks, and assurances of the sincere esteem & regard
with which I am Dear Sir Yr Most Obedt & Affecte Hble Servt Go: Washington" (ALS, ICN: Ruggles Collection). See also Alexander Hamilton to GW, 13
Aug. 1788.

# From Thomas Smith

Sir,                                        Carlisle [Pa.] 5th February 1788
   On my return from the Western Courts, two weeks ago I was
honored with your letter of the 3d of December last inclosing a
duplicate of another letter dated the 16th Septr. Since my return
I have had no opportunity of writing to Philadelphia till now. I
did not receive the letter of the 16th Septr till the middle of
november & having by my letter of the 26th October anticipated
an answer to it excepting as to one point,[1] I did not think it
proper to take the liberty of writing again to you at a time when
affairs of such infinite importance to your county must greatly
engage your attention. My business requiring me to go to Philadelphia in November I did not think myself at liberty to express
myself on the excepted point untill I should take the opinion of
some of my law friends there nor untill I should see Mr Ross I
mean on your proposition respecting the trial fees in the
ejectments in Washington County—According spending an afternoon with Mr Wilson I asked his opinion informing him that
it was not my wish; & I was satisfyed that it ⟨was⟩ not Mr Ross's
to receive any extraordinary fee, but that as you had put the
matter on so delicate a point as leaving the quantum to me, I
wished to be guided by My friends advice—Mr Wilson replied
he was not at liberty to give his opinion intimating as I concieved
you had spoke to him on the same subject & that he had declined forming an opinion I then requested Mr Yeates to favor
me with his opinion—he replied that he thought £100 to each
would be a reasonable & liberal fee—Permit me to assure you
that I shall be perfectly satisfyd with less & so will Mr Ross I am
convinced, although he would not name any sum when I asked
him at the last circuit, but he leaves the whole to me. However
in order that you may guess with what sum I will be satisfyed, I

have retained only £50 for myself, & paid Mr Ross the like sum including a sum which he was to recive from one Jackson on your account by my order[2]—Besides these sums I have received £200 in part of the bonds which Mr Freeman put into my hands payable to you. These debtors were all ready to pay & others offered to pay the money into the Prothonotary's office at the day it became due; therefore no suits were brought against them nor could I charg them Interest which was but a trifle 'till the time I recd the money—I have brought actions against those that did not pay & expect the greatest part if not the whole of the money which I will send down according to your direction together with the account by the first safe conveyance after I shall receive the money I will send the £200 to Mr Biddle by the first good conveyance[3]—I would send it by the bearer but he is only a lad & going without company, I think it is too great a risque—The executions for the Court charges in the ejectments have been put into the hands of Mr Scott the Prothonotary of Washington County.[4] I have the honor to be with profound respect, Sir your most obt & Hbl. St

Thomas Smith

ALS, copy, in Smith's hand, PWacD. The letter, labeled "copy," is written on the reverse of the letter cover of GW's letter to Smith of 3 Dec. 1787.

1. Letter not found. On 3 Dec. 1787 GW acknowledged its receipt.

2. GW agreed that the fee for Smith and James Ross would be £50 each (GW to Smith, 5 Mar. 1788). Jasper Yeates was a leading member of the Pennsylvania bar. "One Jackson" is Samuel Jackson of Red Stone Fort.

3. Clement Biddle wrote GW on 5 Mar. that he had received from Smith the day before a payment of £200 (actually £192.13.4 specie) and that he was now forwarding to GW "Bank Notes for four Hundred Dollars." GW may have consulted James Wilson while attending the Constitutional Convention.

4. Thomas Scott had been prothonotary and clerk of the court for Washington County since its formation in 1781.

# To Jonathan Trumbull, Jr.

My dear Sir,                    Mount Vernon February 5th 1788
    I thank you for your obliging favor of the 9th Ulto which came duly to hand, & congratulate with you on the adoption of the new Constitution in your State by so decided a Majority and so

many respectable Characters. I wish for the same good tidings from Massachusetts but the accts from thence are not so favourable—The decision, it is even said, is problematical; arising, as I believe ⁹⁄₁₀th of the opposition does, from local circumstances and sinister views, The result of the deliberations in that State will have considerable inf[l]uence on those which are to follow—especially in that of New York where I fancy the opposition to the form will be greatest.

Altho' an inhabitant of this State, I cannot speak with decision on the publick sentiment of it with respect to the proposed Constitution—my private opinion however of the matter is, that it will certainly be received but in this opinion I may be mistaken. I have not been ten miles from home since my return to it from Philadelphia—I see few who do not live within that circle, except Travellers and strangers and these form[1] opinions upon too slight ground to be relied on—The opponants of the Constitution are indefatigable in frabricating and circulating papers, reports &c. to its prejudice whilst the friends *generally* content themselves with the goodness of the cause and the necessity for its adoption suppose it wants no other support.

Mrs Washington, and others of this family with whom you are acquainted (among which is Colo. Humphrees) Join me in every good wish for you Mrs Trumbull and family and with sentiments of the sincerest regard and friendship I am Dear Sir—Yr Affect. & very Hble Sert

Go. Washington

LB, DLC:GW.
   1. The copyist wrote "from."

# From Rufus King

Sir                                           Boston 6 Feb. 1788

Our convention this day ratified the constitution 187 affirmatives 168 negatives the majority although small are very respectable, and the minority in addition to great Temper & moderation, publickly declare that the Discussion has been fair & candid, and that the majority having decided in favor of the constitution, they will devote their Lives & Fortunes to support the

Government—with perfect respect I have the Honor to be Sir
your obt Hble Servt

Rufus King

ALS, DLC:GW.

## From Benjamin Lincoln

My dear General                          Boston Feby 6th 1788

The convention this evening ratified the constitution. present
three hundred and fifty five members One hundred & Eighty
seven Yeas & one hundred & sixty eight Nays 19 majority in
favor of the adoption.

As I mentioned to you in my last the spirit which operated the
last winter had its influence in the appointment of members for
the convention and was a clog upon us through the whole business, to this source may be ascrib⟨ed⟩ the great opposition we
have experienced through the long debates, and the smallness
of the majority. I hope the neighbouring States will consider this
and not suffer it to weigh in their decisions.

Yesterday there was a motion for an adjournment which cost
us the whole day[.] Upon the question at evening there were
about 100 Majority against it this was a damper upon the opposition and they had little hope after. When this evening the question went against them some of the leaders arose and assured
the convention that they were convinced that the debates had
been conducted with fairness and candor and that they should
return with dispositions to satisfy the minds of their constituents
and to preserve the peace & order of the people at large I hope
and trust they will and that ⟨we⟩ shall soon enjoy the blessings
of ⟨a⟩ good government.

I shall continue to write to your Excellency whilst any thing
relative to this great subject shall turn up here worthy your
notice—forgive the haste ⟨or⟩ the post office will be shut and
believe me with the sincerest esteem & regards I am my Dr
General your affectionate Servant

B. Lincoln

Upon the issue of the question every demonstration of joy was
discoverd among the people.

ALS, DLC:GW.

# To Lafayette

My dear Marqs,                    Mount Vernon February 7th 1788
You know it always gives me the sincerest pleasure to hear from you, my dear Marquis, and therefore I need only say that your two kind letters of the 9th & 15th of Octr so replete with personal affection and confidential intelligence, afforded me inexpressible satisfaction. I shall myself be happy in forming an acquaintance and culivating a friendship with the new Minister Plenipotentiary of France, whom you have commended as "a sensible & honest man"—these are qualities too rare & too precious not to merit on[e]'s particular esteem—you may be persuaded he will be well received by the Congress of the United States, because they will not only be influenced in their conduct by his individual merits, but also by their affection for the nation of whose Sovereign he is the Representative. For it is an undoubted fact, that the People of America entertain a greateful remembrance of past services as well as a favourable disposition for commercial and friendly connections with your Nation.

You appear to be, as might be expected from a real friend to this Country, anxiously concerned about its present political situation. So far as I am able I shall be happy in gratifying that friendly solicitude. As to my sentiments with respect to the merits of the new Constitution, I will disclose them without reserve (although by passing through the Post offices they should become known to all the world) for, in truth, I have nothing to conceal on that subject. It appears to me, then, little short of a miracle, that the Delegates from so many different States (which States you know are also different from each other in their manners, circumstances and prejudieces) should unite in forming a system of national Government, so little liable to well founded objections. Nor am I yet such an enthusiastic, partial or undiscriminating admirer of it, as not to prerceive it is tinctured with some real (though not radical) defects. The limits of a letter would not suffer me to go fully into an examination of them; nor would the discussion be entertaining or profitable, I therefore forbear to touch upon it. With regard to the two great points (the pivots on which the whole machine must move) my Creed is simply:

1st That the general Government is not invested with more Powers than are indispensably necessary to perform [the] functions of a good Government; and, consequently, that no objection ought to be made against the quantity of Power delegated to it.

2ly That these Powers (as the appointment of all Rulers will forever arise from, and, at short stated intervals, recur to the free suffrage of the People) are so distributed among the Legislative, Executive, and Judicial Branches, into which the general Government is arranged, that it can never be in danger of degenerating into a monarcchy, an Oligarchy, an Aristocracy, or any other despotic or oppressive form; so long as there shall remain any virtue in the body of the People.

I would not be understood my dear Marquis to speak of consequences which may be produced, in the revolution of ages, by corruption of morals, profligacy of manners, and listlessness for the preservation of the natural and unalienable rights of mankind; nor of the successful usurpations that may be established at such an unpropitious Juncture, upon the ruins of liberty, however providently guarded and secured, as these are contingencies against which no human prudence can iffectually provide. It will at least be a recommendation to the proposed Constitution that it is provided with more checks and barriers against the introduction of Tyranny, & those of a nature less liable to be surmounted, than any Government hitherto instituted among mortals, hath possessed. we are not to expect perfection in this world: but mankind, in modern times, have apparently made some progress in the science of Government. Should that which is now offered to the People of America, be found an experiment less perfect than it can be made—a Constitutional door is left open for its amelioration. Some respectable characters have wished that the States, after having pointed out whatever alterations and amendments may be judged necessary, would appoint another federal Co[n]vention to modify it upon these documents. For myself I have wondered that sensible men should not see the impracticability of the scheme. The members would go fortified with such Instructions that nothing but discordant ideas could prevail. Had I but slightly suspected (at the time when the late Convention was in session) that another Convention would not be likely to agree upon a better form of Government, I should now be confirmed in the fixed belief that they would not be able to agree upon any System whatever: So many,

I may add, such contradictory, and, in my opinion, unfounded objections have been urged against the System in contemplation; many of which would operate equally against every efficient Government that might be proposed. I will only add, as a farther opinion founded on the maturest deliberation, that there is no alternative—no hope of alteration—no intermediate resting place—between the adoption of this and a recurrence to an unqualified state of Anarchy, with all its deplorable consequences.

Since I had the pleasure of writing to you last, no material alteration in the political State of affairs has taken place to change the prospect of the Constitution's being adopted by nine States or more. Pennsylvania, Delaware, Jersey and Connecticut have already done it. It is also said Georgia has aceeded. Massachusetts, which is perhaps thought to be rather more doubtful than when I last addressed you, is now in Convention.

A spirit of emigration to the western Country is very predominant. Congress have sold, in the year past, a pretty large quantity of lands on the Ohio, for public Securities, and thereby diminished the domestic debt considerably. Many of your military acquaintances such as the Generals Parsons, Varnum and Putnam, the Colos. Tupper[,] Sprout and Sherman, with many more, propose settling there. From such beginnings much may be expected.[1]

The storm of war between England and your Nation, it seems, is dissipated. I hope and trust the political affairs in France are taking a favorable turn. If the Ottomans wod suffer themselves to be precipitated into a war, they must abide the consequences. Some Politicians speculate on a triple Alliance between the two Imperial Corts & Versailles.

I think it was rather fortunate, than otherwise, that the incaution of an Ambassador and the rascality of a Rhinegrave prevented you from attempting to prop a falling fabric.

It gives me great pleasure to learn the present ministry of France are friendly to America; and that Mr Jefferson & yourself have a prospect of accomplishing measures which will mutually benefit and improve the commercial intercourse between the two Nations. Every good wish attend you & yrs & I am &c.

Go. Washington

LB, DLC:GW.

1. GW is referring to the settlement at Marietta, Ohio. The men he names are Samuel Holden Parsons, James Mitchell Varnum, Rufus Putnam, Benjamin Tupper, Ebenezer Sprout, and Isaac Sherman.

## To La Luzerne

Sir,                                    Mount Vernon February 7th 1788

The Compte de Moustier your successor in office hath forwarded from New York, the letter in which you did me the honour to bring me acquainted with the merits of that Nobleman.[1] Since it is the misfortune of America not to be favored any longer with your residence, it was necessary, to diminish our regrets, that so worthy and respectable a character should be appointed your successor. I shall certainly be happy in cultivating his acquaintance and friendship. The citizens, from gratitude as well as from personal considerations, will, I am persuaded, treat him with the greatest respect. Congress, I doubt not, will by every means in there power desire to make his sojourn in the United States as agreeable as it possible can be.

But, Sir, you may rest assured your abilities and dispositions to serve this Country were so well understood; and your services so properly appreciated, that the residence of no public Minister will ever be longer remembered or his absence more sincerely regretted. It will not be forgotten that you was a witness to the dangers, the sufferings, the exertions and the successes of the United States from the most perilous crises to the hour of triumph. The influence of your agency on the Cabinet to produce a co-operation and the prowess of your Countrymen co-operating with our's in the field to secure the liberties of America have made such an indelible impression on the public mind as will never be efaced. Wherever you may be, our best wishes will follow you. And such is our confidence in your disinterested friendship, that we are certain you will wish to be useful to us, in whatever Mission you may be honored by your King: it has been surmised, on I know not what authority, that there was a probability of your being employed in the Diplomatique Corps at the Court of London; shod this particularly be the case, your zeal m[a]y still find occasions of being servicable to America and profetable to your own Country at the same time—for I conceive the commercial interests of the two nations are in many instances blended and in opposition to those of great Britain.

By intelligence of a more recent date than that brought by the Compte de Maustier, we learn that the political clouds which threatened to burst in a storm on France and England are blown over. The poor Dutch Patriots, however, seem to have had the objects for which [      ] off (if I m[a]y use the same metaphor) by a cornes of the hurrican, The Dutch Patriots, I fear have been disunited imprudent, impetuous: and that the King of Prussia has not acted worthily or wisely—should his measures drive the Corts of Versailles & Vienna into an union of plans—should the embers of war be but imperfectly quenched, he may yet repent the temerity of intermeddling with the internal affairs of a foreign Power. In the mean time the new scene that is opened in the north, by the rupture between the Russians and Turks must call men's attention to that quarter; as it can hardly avoid producing e[ve]nts, which will be attended with serious, extensive, and durable consequences.

I feel, sir, not only for myself but in behalf of my Country, under great obligations for the affectionate wishes you have the goodness to make with respect to the tranquility and happiness of America. Seperated as we are by a world of water from other Nations, if we are wise we shall surely avoid being drawn into the labarynth of their politics and involved in their distructive wars.

You will doubtless have seen long before this time the Constitution which was proposed by the Fœderal Convention for the United States. Only four States as yet (to my knowledge) have [had] an opportunity of acting upon it. The Pensylvania State Convention adopted it by a Majority of two to one, those of Jersey and Delaware Unanimously, and that of Connecticut by more than three to one; In Massachusetts the Convention is now in session. The Merits of this Constitution have been discussed in a great variety of news paper and other Publications. A periodical Essay in the New York Gazetts, under Title of the Federalist, has advocated it with great ability. In short it seems (so far as I have been able to learn) to be a prevalent opinion that it will be accepted by nine States or more by some period early in the ensuing summer. with Sentiments of great respect and Considn I have the honor to be &c.

                                                    Go. Washington

LB, DLC:GW. Sparks made several corrections in the letter-book copy. See GW to Moustier, this date, source line.

1. La Luzerne's letter is dated 12 Nov. 1787.

# To Moustier

Sir,                                        Mount Vernon February 7th 1788

I have received the letter which your Excellency did me the honor to address to me on the 24th of January, and take the earliest occasion of expressing my warmest acknowledgments for your favourable opinion as well as offering my sincerest congratulations on your safe arrival in this country. I am at the same time to return you my thanks for the trouble you had the goodness to take in conveying to me the letters of my noble friends the Marquis de la Fayette and the Chevr de la Luzerne, indeed nothing was wanting to the pleasure afforded by their communications, but that of having received them at your hands and thereby having had an opportunity of demonstrating the promptitude of my attention to their recommendations. In the mean time I have taken the liberty (which I beg your Excellency to excuse) of remitting my answers for them to your care.

The fidelity, honour & bravery of the troops of your nation, to which I have been a witness; the enlightened sentiments of patriotism and the delicate feelings of friendship which have actuated great numbers of your compatriots, with whom I may bost the happiness of being intimately connected; and above all that lively interest which your illustrious Monarch and his faithful subjects took in the success of the American Arms and the confirmation of our Independence have endeared the National Character to me, formed attachments and left impressions which no distance in time or contingency in event can possibly remove. Though but a private citizen myself and in a measure secluded from the world, I am conscious the assertion will be founded, while I venture to affirm such are the feelings & such the affections of the American People.

Deprived of the felicity of having been able to form a personal acquaintance with your Excellency, by your arrival at a distance: it is mine peculiarly to regret that misfortune and earnestly to wish some favorable circumstance may hasten the moment so desirable to me. And I pray you will be persuaded that I should be truly happy to receive you, in the plain unceremonious American style, on the banks of the Potowmack.

The partial knowledge of your merits which had preceded your advent and the very honorable testimonials of our friends in France, added to the advantage you possess in being the Representative of a Sovereign, (the earliest, most faithful & most powerful Ally of these infant States) cannot fail to make your presents extremely agreeable to Congress and the American People.

Permit me to add the assurance, Sir, that your Mission cannot be more acceptable, to, or your friendship more flattering to any American, than to him who hath the honour to subscribe himself Sir Yr Excellency's &c.

Go. Washington

LB, DLC:GW. The manuscript is sprinkled with corrections made by Jared Sparks in the nineteenth century, which in fact may bring the text closer to what GW himself wrote. They have been disregarded here as elsewhere, however, except in rare cases when they are retained in square brackets.

## From James Madison

Dear Sir                                    New York Feby 8 [17]88

The prospect in Massts seems to brighten, if I view in the true light the following representation of it. "This day, (Jany 30) for the first our President Mr Handcock took his seat in Convention, and we shall probably terminate our business on Saturday or tuesday next. I can not predict the issue, but our hopes are increasing. If Mr Hancock does not disappoint our present expectations, our wishes will be gratified."[1] Several reflections are suggested by this paragraph which countenance a favorable inference from it. I hope from the rapid advance towards a conclusion of the business, that even the project of recommendatory alterations has been dispensed with.

The form of the ratification of Georgia is contained in one of the papers herewith inclosed.[2] Every information from S. Carolina continues to be favorable. I have seen a letter from N. Carolina of pretty late date which admits that a very formidable opposition exists, but leans towards a fœderal result in that State. As far as I can discover, the state of the question in N. Carolina is pretty analogous to that in Virginia. The body of the people are better disposed than some of a superior order. The Resolutions of New York for calling a Convention, appear by the paper to have passed by a majority of two only in the House of Assembly. I am told this proceeded in some degree from an injudicious form in which the business was conducted; and which threw some of the fœderalists into the opposition.

I am just informed by a gentleman who has seen another letter from Boston of the same date with mine, that the plan of recommendatory alterations has not been abandoned, but that they will be put into a harmless form, and will be the means of saving the Constitution from all risk in Massts. With the highest respect & attachment I remain Dear Sir, your affe. hble servt

Js Madison Jr

ALS, DLC:GW; copy, DLC: Madison Papers.

1. This is taken from Rufus King's letter to Madison of 30 January.

2. On 5 Feb. the *New York Journal* printed the text of the ratification of the Constitution by the Georgia convention.

## From Caleb Gibbs

Dear General                                    Boston Feby 9th 1788.

It is with infinite satisfaction that I take the earliest oppertunity of Informing your Excellency that on the 6th Inst. at evening the Convention of this Commonwealth, assented to & Ratified the proposed Constitution for the United States.

It gives all ranks of people great pleasure, thus to see a glimmer of a hope that this Country is in a fair way of appearing respectable both at home and abroad by the Establishment of a government wherein Justice & Energy preside; I have done myself the honor of transmitting your Excellency the best news papers in this Capitol which contains allmost all the debates of the Convention but it was impossible to obtain the whole. There is a subscription on foot to have the Whole in a pamphlet if it is accomplished I will endeavour to forward one to your Excellency. The Minority your Excellency will please to observe by the last paper seem to be easy & Concilatory. it was said by many of them on the day of Ratification at the Senate Chamber, that

If the vote was to be reconsidered & Call again there would be but few against the adoption of the Constitution.

It would take more time than the post would allow me to give you an account of the whole of the characters of the Minority, but thus much I will say that a large proportion of them of the Eastern Counties of Lincoln, Cumberland & York (or Province of Main) who have for these several years been Endeavouring to bring about a separation from this Commonwealth, Others of the Western & Southern Counties of whom more than *twenty* have this moment a *State Warrant* against them for being some of the foremost in the last winters Rebellion, & Principal part of the remainder are Insurgents & some of the most attrocious Characters in existence. This is real fact, that very few of them are men of very little property & very much In debt & wish only to oppose the Constitution because if not adopted they may have it in their power to pass tender Acts, & emit paper money to pay a just debt they owe in Specie. Genl Warren who was Pay Mr Genl in 76 is one of the greatest *Antifederalists* we have among us.[1] but he could not obtain to get his Election for Convention. *he acts like the snake in the grass.* N. Hampshire Convention meets on Tuesday next. I had the pleasure to See the Honbl. Mr Langdon who attended several days of our Convention & he told me that If Massachutts adopted the Constitution, N. Hampshire would not be one week in Session.[2] Some of the principal Gentlemen of Newport & Providence have been attending the debates here, & they said the same a[s] Mr Langdon did, *that is*, A Convention they were Certain would be called immediately & no doubt but the Constitution would be adopted. I cannot write your Excellency as full as what the papers will communicate & by Compareing those in the opposition specially those who debated on the Constitution—You will see the Characters I have alluded to. those are the feeble Speakers of the Rabble. I shall be happy to hear from your Excellency after receipt of this & any thing in my power to Communicate worth notice I shall endeavour to forward.

Mrs Gibbs (altho a stranger to your Mrs Washington) desires her most respectfull Compliments may be offered.[3] & pray Sir make mine to Mrs Washington & all freinds—Mr Hancock's Indisposition was such as prevented his attendance in the early part of the Convention, but fortunately he recovered so much as to be in the house a week or more previous to the great question, & many of our ableest politicians say if he had not been well enough to have come out & appeared in Convention, it was more than probable the *important* question would have been lost. I have the honor to be With the greatest respect and Esteem Dear General Your most Obedient & very humble Servant

C. Gibbs

ALS, DLC:GW.

1. James Warren (1726–1808) was elected to the Massachusetts house of representatives in 1787 after Shays' Rebellion, and the house elected him speaker.

2. John Langdon at this time was president of New Hampshire.

3. Gibbs married Catherine Hall in 1787.

## From Benjamin Lincoln

My dear General                                   Boston Feby 9th 1788

In my last I had the pleasure of announcing to your Excellency that we had adopted the reported constitution. Nothing very material has taken place since saving what is mentioned in the enclosed paper by that you will learn what was the temper of many of those who had been in the oposition I think they discovered a candour which does them honor and promises quiet in the State. Some however will I fear sow the seeds of discontent and attempt to inflame the minds of the people in the country—They have no really object as they cannot be certain it will ever pass nine State I hope and trust this consideration will quiet them at present when it shall have passed nine State it will be too late for any one State to think of opposing it.

Considering the great disorders which took place in this State the last winter, and considering the great influence the spirit which then reigned has had since upon all our operations it must be supposed that we have got through this business pretty well and considering also that when we came together a very decided majority of the convention were against adopting the constitution—Every exertion will be made to inform the people & to quiet their minds. It is very fortunate for us that the Clergy are pretty generally with us they have in this State a very great influence over the people and they will contribute much to the general peace and happiness.

Subscription papers are out for printing all the debates in the convention they will probably be printed if they are I will forward to your Excelly one of the books—Should they not I will forward the remaining news papers as they come out.

By the paper your Excellency will observe some account of the parade of the Eighth[1] the printer had by no means time enough to do justice to the subject⟨.⟩ to give you some idea how far he has been deficient I will mention an observation I heard made by a Lady the last evening who saw the whole that the description in the paper would no more compare with the original than the light of the faintest star would with that of the Sun fortunately for us the whole ended without the least disorder and the town during the whole evening was, so far as I could observe perfectly quiet. I have the honour of being my dear General your Excellencys most obedient servant

B. Lincoln

P.S. Upon a review of the last paragraph I think it of little importance have therefore X it out.[2]

ALS, DLC:GW.

1. An account of the parade, of its march and order of procession, appeared in the *American Herald* (Boston) on 11 Feb. and in the *Massachusetts Gazette* (Boston) on 12 February. Some 5,000 tradesmen and mechanics assembled at Faneuil Hall at 11:00 on 8 Feb. and marched to the houses of the members of the ratifying convention to give each "three huzzas," before returning to the hall at 4:00 for refreshments.

2. The crossed-out paragraph reads: "The Gentlemen provided at Fanuel Hall some biscuit & cheese four qrs Casks of wine three barrels & two hog-[head]s of punch the moment they found that the people had drank sufficiently means were taken to over set the two hog[head]s punch this being done the company dispirsed and the day ended most agreeably."

# From Henry Knox

New York 10 February 1788

I thank you my dear Sir for your favor of the 10th of last month which I duly received.

The constitution has labored in Massachusetts exceedingly more than was expected. The opposition has not arisen from a consideration of the merits or demerits of the thing itself as a political machine, but from a deadly principle levelled at the existence of all government whatever; The principles of insurgency expanded, and deriving fresh strength and life from the impunity with which the rebellion of last year was suffered to escape.

It is a singular circumstance that in Massachusetts, the property, the ability and the virtue of the state are almost solely in favor of the constitution—Opposed to it are the late insurgents and all those who abetted their designs constituting ⅘ths of the opposition—a few very few indeed well meaning people are joined to them.

The friends of the constitution in that state without overrating their own importance conceived that the decision of Massachusetts would most probably seal the fate of the proposition—They therefore proceeded most cautiously and wisely—debated every objection with the most guarded good nature and candour but took no questions on the several paragraphs and thereby prevented the establishment of parties—This conduct has been attended with the most beneficial consequences—It is now no secret that on the opening of the conventions a majority were prejudiced against it—But the federalists are now well assured that the scale is turned in their favor—The question to approve and ratify in the form contained in the enclosed papers was most probably taken somewhere between the 5th & 8th instant—Although the federalists presume on a majority they do not flatter themselves with a large one—The recommendatory alterations are to be considered as conciliatory propositions, and in no degree militating with an unconditional adoption[.] As the form of ratification, and the propositions for alterations were the mature productions of the federalists, it is probable that they will pass without any material alterations.

Mrs Knox desires me to associate her in the most affectionate respects to you and Mrs Washington. I am my dear Sir Your most obedient humble Servant

H. Knox

Mr Saml Adams seconded Mr Hancocks motion.

ALS, DLC:GW.

*Letter not found*: to Henry Knox, 11 Feb. 1788. On 10 Mar. Knox wrote GW: "Your favor of the 11th ultimo was duly received."[1]

1. Knox may have been referring to GW's letter of 5 February. See Knox to GW, 10 Mar., n.1.

## To Benjamin Lincoln

My dear Sir,                              Mount Vernon. Feb. 11th 1788.

As you must be convinced that whatever effects your happiness or welfare cannot be indifferent to me, I need not tell you that I was most sensibly affected by your letter of the 20th of January. Yes, my dear Sir, I sincerely condole with you the loss of a worthy, amiable & valuable Son! Altho' I had not the happiness of a personal acquaintance with him, yet the character which he sustained, and his near connection with you, are, to me, sufficient reasons to lament his death.

It is unnecessary for me to offer any consolation on the present occasion; for to a mind like yours, it can only be drawn from that source which never fails to give a bountiful supply to those who reflect justly. Time *alone*, can blunt the keen edge of afflictions. Philosophy & Religion holds out to us such hopes as will, upon proper reflection, enable us to bear with fortitude the most calamitous incidents of life, and these are all that can be expected from the feelings of humanity; & all which they will yield.

I thank you, my dear Sir, for the information you forwarded me of the proceedings of your Convention. It is unhappy that a matter of such high importance cannot be discussed with that candour & moderation which would through light on the subject, and place its merits in a proper point of view: but in an Assembly so large as your Convention must be, & composed of such various & opposite characters, it is almost impossible but that some things will occur which would rouse the passions of the most moderate man on earth. It is, however, to be hoped that your final decision will be agreeable to the wishes of good men, and favorable to the Constitution.

Mrs Washington thanks you for your kind remembrance of

her & joins me in the sincerest condolence for your loss. With sentiments of the highest estm & regard—I am—My dear Sir Yr Most Affecte & Obedt Ser⟨vt⟩

Go: Washington

ALS, MH; LB, DLC:GW.

# From James Madison

Dear Sir                                             N. York Feby 11. 88.
    The Newspaper inclosed with the letter which follows, comprises the information brought me by the mail of yesterday.[1]

Boston Feby 3d
    "I inclose a Newspaper containing the propositions communicated by Mr Hancock to the Convention, on thursday last. Mr [Samuel] Adams who contrary to his own sentiments has been hitherto silent in Convention, has given his public and explicit approbation of Mr Hancocks propositions—We flatter ourselves that the weight of these two characters will ensure our success; but the event is not absolutely certain. Yesterday a Committee was appointed on the motion of a doubtful character to consider the propositions submitted by Mr Hancock and to report tomorrow afternoon—We have a majority of fœderalists on this Committee and flatter ourselves the result will be favorable: P.S. We shall probably decide on thursday or friday next when our numbers will amount to about 363."

    With greatest esteem & attachment I am Dear Sir Yr Obedt & affee Servt

Js Madison Jr

ALS, DLC:GW; copy, DLC: Madison Papers.
    1. This letter from Rufus King, 3 Feb., quoted here, is in Rutland and Hobson, *Madison Papers*, 10:465–66. On 31 Jan. John Hancock found himself sufficiently recovered from the gout to appear at the convention in which he had been elected to preside. He declared himself in favor of the Constitution and offered a series of amendments to be sought after ratification. See Benjamin Lincoln to GW, 3 February. It was on this basis that the convention moved to a final vote on 6 Feb. when the Constitution was adopted by a vote of 187 to 168 along with the recommended amendments. The enclosed newspaper was the *Massachusetts Centinel* (Boston) of 2 Feb. 1788.

*Letter not found*: from Thomas Cushing, 12 Feb. 1788. On 10 Mar. GW wrote Cushing acknowledging the receipt of "Your letter of the 12th Ulto . . . last Saturday."

## From William Hartshorne

General Washington                 Alexandria February 13th 1788
   Enclosed is your Accot with W.H. & Co. Amot £34.19.5 also an accot of what will be due to the Potowmack Co. the 15th next Mo. say £33.14.8 Virga Currency[1]—If agreeable to you I will take your draft on London payable at 30 days sight for either, or both these accounts, at the Excha. of 40 ⅌ct.[2] I am very Respectfully Yours

                                             Wm Hartshorne

ALS, DLC:GW.
   1. The enclosed accounts show charges by Hartshorne on 27 Nov. 1787 of £23.17 for red clover seed and, on 4 Jan. 1788, £5.16.2 for seventeen bars of iron, and £5.6.3 for one barrel of sugar, making a total of £34.19.5 in Virginia currency. The Potomac River Company charges were £6.10 sterling for each of the five shares that GW held, but deducting £9.12 Virginia currency for the expenses GW had incurred on company business in 1787 leaves a total of £33.14.8 Virginia currency owed by GW to the company.
   2. On 17 Mar. GW wrote from Mount Vernon to Wakelin Welch & Son: "Gentn Of this date, and at thirty days sight I have drawn upon you in favor of Wm Hartshorn Esqr. for Sixty Seven pounds Sterling which please to pay, and place to the Acct of Your Most Obedt Hble Servant Go. Washington" (LB, DLC:GW). The payment of £67 sterling comes to £93.16.2 in Virginia currency, and Hartshorne's account (note 1) shows only £68.14.1 due from GW, but in March, after sending the account, Hartshorne had supplied GW with iron valued at £25.6.1 (Ledger B, 258).

## From Peterson & Taylor

Sir                                    Alexandria February 13. 88
   on account of the Severity of the Winter, it never has been in our power to convey your Bill of planke & Scantling to the Eastern Shore which will render it out of our power to furnish Said Bill, at the time mentioned, and will likely delay, when delivered untill Early the Month of May. however there now appears a

prospect of the Navigation being open very Soon—at which time we will Send the Bill, and exert every means to have it delivered, as much Sooner as possible. the plank likely will be delivered Soon, as that we suppose is Sawed. Save the Inch & ¼.[1] We are Sir your Obt Sevts

                                        Peterson & Taylor

P.S. a few lines will be expected in Answer.[2]

LS, DLC:GW.

    1. See GW to Peterson & Taylor, 5 Jan., and notes.

    2. GW wrote in answer from Mount Vernon on 15 Feb.: "Gentn I have received your letter of the 13 inst. and am sorry to find that my bill of Scantling has not yet been forwarded to the Eastern Shore. I should have thought, notwithstanding the communication by water was stopped, that it might have been conveyed by land—I am now, in a manner, reduced to the necessity of depending upon you for the Scantling, because I have, in expectation of being supplied by you, imployed my own Carpenters in other matters when they would have been preparing it.

"As the River is now open I should imagin that it might be delivered much sooner then you mention in your letter; if it should not, I shall sustain a great injury, to say nothing of the disappointment. I am &c. Go. Washington" (LB, DLC:GW).

## To Alexander Spotswood

Dear Sir,                    Mount Vernon February 13th 1788

Your favor of the 20th Ult., accompanied by a bag of Seeds, did not get to my hands untill the middle of last week or it should have received an earlier acknowledgment; as you now do my thanks for the latter.[1]

I feel myself obliged by the measures you have pursued to stock me with Turnip seed; but if I am *tolerably* lucky, I shall raise a sufficiency from seed sent me by Arthur Young Esqr.; many hundreds of the Turnips being set out for that purpose: injudiciously tho' I fear, as they will be exposed to Poultry, especially Turkies—a circumstance that did not ocur to me when I made choice of the spot (in other respects favourable) for the transplantation of them. I am not less obliged to you for the offer of sp[r]ing Wheat; but a little of this also I got from England, from the same Gentleman—Mr Young—to gether with the winter Vetch, Sainfoin and other seeds. But from a neglect too common among Master's of Vessels (of stowing them in the hold) I fear

vegitation in most of them is injured, if not entirely destroyed—
This was the case *nearly* with a little wheat, the Sainfoin and some
other seeds which were imported and sown last Autumn. With
care and attention however I may, possibly raise a little from
each in which case I shall [be] very ready to oblige you in my
turn. Exchanges, and Services of this kind, are what Farmers
owe to one another; and in the practice of which I should feel
much pleasure.[2]

I think with you that the life of a Husbandman of all others,
is the most delectable. It is honorable—It is amusing—and with
Judicious management, it is profitable. To see plants rise from
the Earth and flourish by the superior skill, and bounty of the
labouror fills a contemplative mind with ideas which are more
easy to be conceived than expressed.

I am glad to find that your first essay to raise Indian Corn in
drills has succeeded so much to your satisfaction; but I am inclined to think—unless restoratives were more abundant than
they are to be found on Common farms, that 6 feet by 2 will be
too oppressive to your land. Experiance has proved that every
soil will sink under the growth of this plant; whether from the
luxuriancy and exhausting quality of it, or the manner of tillage
or from both, is not *very* certain, because instead of 2420 plants
which stand on an Acre at six feet square, with 2 stalks in a hill
(as is usual in land of midling quality) you have 3630 at 6 feet
by 2, single stalks. How far the exposing of land to the rays of
the Sun in Summer is injurious, is a question yet more difficult
to solve than the other. my own opinion of the matter is, that it
does; but this controverts the practice of Summer fallows, which
(especially in heavy land) some of the best practical Farmers in
England contend for as indispensibly necessary notwithstanding the doctrine of Mr Young, & many others who are opposed
to them.

The reason, however, which induced me to give my Corn rows
the wide distance of ten feet, was not because I thought it assential to the growth of that *plant*, but because I introduced
other plants between them. And this practice, from the experience of two years—one the wettest and the other the driest that
ever was felt on my Estate, I am resolved to continue untill the
inutility of it, or something more advantageous, shall point out
the expediency of a change: but I mean to practice it with varia-

tions, fixing on 8 by 2 feet as the medium, or standing distance which will give more plants by 300 to the acre than six feet each way with two stalks in a hill will do.

As all my Corn will be thus drilled, so between all, I mean to put, in drills also, Potatoes, Carrots (as far as my seed will go) and Turnips alternately; that not one sort, more than another, may have the advantage of Soil; thereby to ascertain the comparitive quantity, and value of each of these plants as food for horses and stock of every kind. From the trials I have made (under the disadvantages already mentioned) I am well satisfied that my crop of Corn in this way, will equal the yield of the same fields in the usual mode of cultivation—and that the quantity of Potatoes (proportionate to the number of Rows) will quadruple the Corn. I entertain the same opinion with respect to Carrots, but being more unlucky in the latter, I cannot speak with so much confidence, & still less can I do it with respect to Turnips.

From this husbandry, and statement then of what I conceive to be facts, any given number of acres will yield as much Corn in the *new* as they will in the *old* way—and will, moreover, with *little* or *no* extra labour, produce four times as many Potatoes or Carrots, which adds considerably to the profit from the field but here it may be asked if the land will sustain these Crops—or rather the Potatoes in addition to the Corn. This is a question my own experience does not enable me to answer. The received opinion however of many practical Farmers in England is, that Potatoes and Carrots are amelioraters, not exhausters of the Soil—preparing it well for other Crops; But I do not scruple to confess, that notwithstanding the profit which appears to result from the growth of Corn and Potatoes, or Corn and Carrots, or both, thus blended, my wish is to exclude Indian Corn altogether from my system of Cropping, but we [a]re so habituated to the use of this grain, and it is so much better for negros than any other that [it] is not to be discarded; consequently, to introduce it in the most profitable, or least injurious manner ought to be the next consideration with the Farmer.

To do this, some are of opinion that a small spot, set apart *solely* for the purpose, and kept highly manured is the best method; and an instance in proof, is adduced of a Gentleman near Baltimore, who for many years past from the same ground has not made less than ten Barrels to the Acre in Drills, 6 feet a part, and (if I recollect rightly) 18 Inches in the rows. But quæry, where the Farmer has no other resource than the manure of his own Farm, will not his other crops be starved by this extra allowance to the Indian Corn? I am inclined to think it will. and for that reason shall try the intermixture of Potatoes, Carrots and Turnips, or either (as from practice shall be found most profitable) with my Corn, which shall be[c]ome a componant part of some regular, and systematic plan best adapted to the nature of my soil.

To Societies which have been formed for the encouragement of agriculture, is the perfection to which husbandry is now arrived in England, indebted. why then does not this Country (Virginia I mean) follow so laudable and beneficial an example? and particularly, why do not the Gentlemen in the vicinity of Fredericksburg begin this Work? Your lands are peculiarly well adapted for it. There are more of you, in a small circle than I believe is to be found in the same compass almost any where.[3] And you are well able to afforde experiments; from which and not from theory are individuals to derive useful knowledge, and the Public a benefit. My love, to which Mrs Washingtons is Joined, is presented to Mrs Spotswood and I am &c.

Go. Washington

LB, DLC:GW.

  1. Letter not found.

  2. See Arthur Young to GW, 1 Feb. 1787, and GW to Young, 1 Nov. 1787.

  3. See GW's correspondence since the war with Spotswood, William Fitzhugh of Chatham, and Charles Carter of Ludlow.

# From Henry Knox

My dear Sir                            New York 14th February 1788

It is with great satisfaction that I inform you that last evening the news arrived here of the adoption of the new constitution in Massachusetts on the 6th instant. The members present in the convention on the decision of the question 355—187 affirmatives, 168 negatives—majority 19.

It may be asserted with great truth, that the subject was most candidly examined and debated. Many of the minority declared their determination of inculcating the principles of acquiesence, and union, among their constituents.

The opposition arose from local causes, which existed previously to the general convention of Philadelphia in May and is to be classed under the following heads.

1st The part of the insurgent interest who oppose every species of government, that may prevent their return to great Britain. The persons who influence the insurgents, have been fixed on this point, and consider the constitution, as the greatest obstacle to the accomplishment of their wishes.

2. Desperate debtors who are warmly attached to paper-money and tender Laws.

3. Honest men, without information, whose minds are apprehensive of danger to their liberties, but like people groping in the dark, they possess, no principle whereby to ascertain the quality, degree or nearness of the danger—Their suspicions render them incapable of conviction.

The 1st and 2d classes constitute probably ⁸/₁₀ths of the opposition in the convention of Massachusetts. 45 members were present from the Province of main 25 of whom voted for the constitution.

I enclose a news paper containing a description of the demonstrations of Joy by the people of Boston on the occasion.[1]

There is not a doubt but that the Majority will be perfectly efficient within the State of Massachusetts, But the example to the other States particularly to this, will not be so influential as if the majority had been larger.

The Convention of New Hampshire assembled yesterday. About 20 days hence I hope to have the pleasure of informing You of the adoption of the constitution in that State. I am my dear Sir with the sincerest affection Your most obedient humble Servant

H. Knox

ALS, DLC:GW; ADfS, NNGL: Knox Papers.
1. See Benjamin Lincoln to GW, 9 Feb., nn.1 and 2.

# From James Madison

Dear Sir                                    N. York Feby 15. [1788]

I have at length the pleasure to inclose you the favorable result of the Convention at Boston. The amendments are a blemish, but are in the least offensive form. The minority also is very disagreeably large, but the temper of it is some atonement. I am assured by Mr King that the leaders of it as well as the members of it in general are in good humour; and will countenance no irregular opposition there or elsewhere. The Convention of N. Hampshire is now sitting. There seems to be no question that the issue there will add a *seventh* pillar, as the phrase now is, to the fœderal Temple. With the greatest respect & attachmt I am Dr Sir Yrs

Js Madison Jr

ALS, Universiteitsbibliotheek, Amsterdam; copy, DLC: Madison Papers.

# From David Stuart

Dear Sir,                                    Abingdon 17th Feby 88

As well as I can recollect the College Charter, the Governor for the time, is expressly declared Chancellor—None of them I belive, ever took upon them the duties of the office, before Lord Botetourt—Visitations are I think appointed to be held twice in the year. The only business of these meetings formerly used to be, to enquire into the conduct of the Professors, and to prescribe rules for them—Tho' it is not absolutely necessary that the Chancellor should be present at these meetings, (the Rector being the active office) it will no doubt be expected.[1]

I have just returned from a tour round part of the County— I mean about the middle of the week to set out again—I find that Pope, and Chichester in particular, have been very active in alarming the people. The latter Gentleman and myself were near meeting at several houses—He had his pockets full of Mason's objections; which he leaves wherever he calls—He is trying to persuade some one opposed to the Constitution, to offer for the Convention—Mr Pollard informed me that he applied to him, but that he declined it. I am happy to find, that he has met with no success except with old Broadwater—Mr Little informs me, that he appears to be changed, and to be disposed to offer himself in opposition to those who approve of the Constitution[2]—I almost think that Mason, doubtful of his election in Stafford will offer for this County, notwithstanding his declarations—I think he might have been satisfied with the publication of his objections, without taking the pains to lodge them at every house[3]—I find it commonly believed in this County, that you consider amendments necessary. It therefore appears to me, that it would be of advantage to the Constitution, to undecieve the people in this respect; by some communication or other. Would not Mr Blair your fellow labourer in the business, be a proper person, through whom to introduce it to the Publick? If you should think proper to take any step of this sort, it would be particularly useful, to take some short notice of the difference between the Objections—I find this argument to have the most weight with the common class. I am Dr Sir, with the greatest respect Your affecte Servant

David Stuart

ALS, DLC:GW.

1. See Samuel Griffin to GW, 4 Feb., and GW to Griffin, 20 February.

2. Mr. Pope was probably John Pope of Prince William County who in 1787 was elected to the state senate for Fairfax and Prince William counties. Mr. Chichester was probably Richard Chichester, a large landholder in the Accotink area of Fairfax County and a justice of the peace. His wife was Sarah McCarty Chichester, daughter of Daniel McCarty. "Old Broadwater" was Charles Broadwater (d. 1806), who, with GW, was elected in 1775 to represent Fairfax County in the House of Burgesses and was replaced in 1784 as a delegate to the house by Thomas West. Mr. Pollard may be Thomas Pollard who was a member of the Truro Parish vestry, Fairfax County, from 1774 until he moved out of the parish in 1784.

3. See GW to James Madison, 5 Feb., n.1.

# To William Irvine

Sir,                              Mount Vernon February 18th 1788

I have to acknowledge the receipt of your favor of the 27th Ulto and to thank you for the information contained in it.

As a Communication between the waters of lake Eire and those of the Ohio is a matter which promises great public utility, and as every step towards the investigation of it may be considered as promoting the general interest of our Country I need [not] make an apology to *you* for any trouble that I have given upon this subject.

I am fully sensible that no account can be sufficiently accurate to hazard any operations upon without an actual survey. My object in[1] wishing a solution of the Quæries proposed to you, was that I might be enabled to return Answers, in some degree satisfactory, to several Gentlemen of distinction in foreign Countries who have applied to me for information on the subject in behalf of others who to engage in the fur trade,[2] and at the same time to gratify my own curiosity and assist me in forming a Judgement of the practicability of opening a communication should it ever be seriously in contemplation.

1st—Could a channel once be opened to convey the Fur, Peltry &c. from the lakes into the Eastern Country,[3] its advantages would be so obvious as to induce an opinion that it would, in a short time, become the channel of conveyance for much the greatest part of the commodities brot from thence.

2d—The trade, which has been carried on between New York and that quarter is subject to great inconveniences from the length of the Commun[ication]—number of Portages—and at seasons from Ice—yet it has, notwithstanding, been prosecuted with success.

I Shall feel myself much obliged by any further information that you may find time and inclination to communicate to me on this head—& am sir with great esteem Yr Most Obedt Hble Sert

Go. Washington

LB, DLC:GW. The same letter, dated 20 Feb. and probably taken from the ALS, appeared in the *Daily National Intelligencer* (Washington, D.C.), 2 May 1823. One significant difference in wording has been noted.

1. The copyist wrote "is."

2. GW posed his "Quæries" on 11 January. For one example of such an inquiry, see GW to Henry L. Charton, 20 May 1786, and note 2 of that document.

3. Instead of "Eastern Country," the printed letter reads: "waters of the Ohio, and from thence into the Atlantic States."

# From John Armstrong

Dear General                        Carlisle [Pa.] 20th Feby 1788

As a Citizen of the united States, I always consider my Self your debtor, and the annual tribute of a Short letter, the smallest remittance we can well conceive. It is perhaps more than a year past since I took the liberty of telling you, that however attatched to retirement & rural life, you must suffer a little more interruption to domestick enjoyments & give some more attention to the suffrages of yr countrymen in publick employ.[1] this you see Sir, has proved true, and the same Object & same motives induce me to think, that one other tour of this kind of duty will fall to your Lot.

Old as I am, I rejoice at the high probability and therefore, near prospect of a general adoption of the Federal Constitution; this hope leads us on to the use of that System, in which the Federal voice of Pennsylvania stands ready to announce your Excellency the first President of the union. of this there need be little hesitation amongst the Citizens, but not so with you; persuaded as I am, it will cost you much anxious thought—nevertheless if the call of God, is manifested to you in a plenary or unanimous call of the people, I hope that will obviate every objection; if not for the whole term of four years, at least for half that time if health admit: considering as you will, that we were not made for our Selves, therefore must not live to our Selves. my sole reason for these early hints, is that by a divine blessing you may be made instrumental of giving a wise & useful *Example to successors* in more things than what may be merely essential to the office; I had like to be so imprudent as to mention a few, but am checked, not by modesty alone, but by former demonstration that you will have in full view, all I mean and much more— the more dissipated customs of the age, prompted by elevation of rank, National dignity & other inflated ideas, will but too probably contrast themselves, to National Economy, real dignity, & private virtue too; this battle you will have in your own breast, it must principally be fought with yourself, an opponent harder to be overcome & more ready to give the foil, than any in all creation except One—but resistance on behalf of the publick & of the Church of God, is worthy of double praise: nor is any man who has this as his motive, likely to fight this battle alone—the wise medi⟨um⟩ an indulgent providence will direct, tho' no precise & invariable rule is admissable in the case.

The proposed Federal Constitution is well approved of this way by the more candid & better informed part of the people, some of whom are even Surprized at the propriety of the first draught, all things considered, but look up for some amendments or alterations in the way prescribed in the Constitution itself, when experience & time shall point out the expedience of the measure—these perhaps will be of two kinds, some truly salutary, others in the way of explanation, merely to please. We have in this State had the most sanguine & unreasonable Opposition of any I have yet heard of, and hope that none other of the Union will follow the insiduous example, and had it not been assiduously contrasted might have proved very injurious to the union and peace of this country; nor has this evil & demented Spirit yet subsided—you cannot have read the Centinel in his numerous & baneful productions, the Old Whig—and the reasons of dissent exhibited by the minority of our Convention— without discovering the treasonable & delusive views of the junto from whom our Confusions proceed,[2] a Sordid & contemptible junto too, but they have their emissaries & interpreters over a great part of the State, whereby they have allarmed the fears & deranged the commonsense of the otherwise Sober & orderly Citizens, beyond any thing you can well conceive. this wild & destructive Spirit appears to abate, but we are Sorry that yr State has postponed their decision to so late a day—the Susspence of that large State, keeps our Opposition in countenance—some of whom, (men of some note too) have lately declared that if Virginia do not adopt, they entertain no doubt but that the Maelcontents of the two States, will prevent the Execution of the proposed Federal plan! this is very rediculouse, yet very disagreeable, nor much to be doubted, but that some of the Western people talk together in this Stile. The Struggle we hear of in the Convention of Massachusetts, must principally be owing to the redundancy of their numbers, of whom like our Selves, too many must be unacquainted with the Science & principles of Government—Old Sam: Adams amazes me more than any other individuel, because I cannot conceive what can induce one of his years to overlook the immediate necessity of at least begining to make a reform—Mr R. Lees letter too, tho' wrote with decency, contains more of the air, than the Substance of the Statesman; and in which he has fallen below himself.[3] The Federalist *Publius*, in my Opinion deserves much of his Country—at first from his Sage manner, I took the Author to have been Mr Jay, but it's now said he is not—that these Nos. are wrote by a small junto, of whos names none are gone out, but that of Coll Hamilton. be the Author who may, he has great merit & his papers may be of farther use, than a present inducement to embrace the new System.

I hope Dr Nisbets discourse on litterature & address to the Students of this College has met your approbation[4]—he is a good man, a great Scholar, a kind of moving library, with as little vanity or parrade on the whole, as any man I ever Saw—yet I am afraid thro' the weakness of our funds, that we must Lose him, as unable to pay his Salary with the various other expences. this College was precipitately undertaken, and the present scarcity of money not sufficiently foreseen, deters many from sending their children abroad tho' the College & boarding which includes Washing makes but 32£ a year. If our New Congress should think of a Federal University, Dr Nisbet would be the man to lay the foundation of it, but this appears to be at some distance.

Coll Blain informed me of yr request that he should give you a Call before he left the City in order to carry a line to me,[5] this he forgot, and knowing your embarrassed situation & the impediments of the City, I charge him only in the account—this letter please to accept in the ruff, as I cannot well copy—therefore cannot correct, tho' sensible of the need. I am dear General with great truth Affectionately Yours.

John Armstrong

ALS, DLC:GW.

1. As far as can be determined, GW's letter of 25 April 1788 in response to this was the first that he made to one of Armstrong's postwar "annual" letters, although GW did say in his April letter that he had written a note to Armstrong before leaving Philadelphia in September 1787. Armstrong's most recent letter was dated 2 Mar. 1787.

2. Between 5 Oct. 1787 and 9 April 1788, the Philadelphia newspapers printed a total of eighteen essays signed "Centinel," written in opposition to the new Constitution. Samuel Bryan (1759–1821), eldest son of George Bryan, is now thought to have written the essays (Kaminski and Saladino, *Documentary History of the Ratification of the Constitution*, 13:326–57).

3. Richard Henry Lee's letter of 16 Oct. 1787 to Edmund Randolph spelling out his objections to the proposed federal Constitution was printed in December. See GW to Madison, 7 Dec. 1787, n.8.

4. In March 1787 Armstrong sent GW two pamphlets by Charles Nisbet, principal of Dickinson College. See Armstrong to GW, 2 Mar. 1787, n.4.

5. Ephraim Blaine (1741–1804), former commissary general in the Continental army, lived in Carlisle.

## To Samuel Griffin

Dear Sir,                         Mount Vernon Feby 20th 1788

I have been duly honored & gratefully affected with the receipt of the Resolution of the Visitors & Governors of William & Mary College, appointing me Chancellor of the same; and have to thank you for your polite attention in the transmission.[1]

Not knowing particularly what duties, or whether any active Services are immediately expected from the person holding the Office of Chancellor; I have been greatly embarrassed in deciding upon the public answer proper to be given. It is for that reason I have chosen to explain in this private communication my situation & feelings; and to defer an ultimate decision until I shall have been favored with farther information on this subject.

My difficulties are briefly these. On the one hand, nothing in this world could be farther from my heart than a want of respect for the worthy Gentlemen in question; or a refusal of the appointment with which they have honored me—provided its duties are not incompatible with the mode of life to which I have entirely addicted myself. And on the other hand, I would not for any consideration disappoint the just expectations of the Convocation, by accepting an Office, whose functions I previously know (from my pre-engagements & occupations) I should be absolutely unable to perform.

Although, as I observed before, I know not specifically what these functions are, yet, Sir, I have conceived that a principal duty required of the Chancellor might be a regular & indispensable Visitation once or perhaps twice a year[2]—Should this be expected, I must decline accepting the Office. For, notwithstanding I most sincerely & ardently wish to afford whatever little influence I may possess, in patronising the cause of Science,

I cannot, at my time of life & in my actual state of retirement, persuade myself to engage in new and extensive avocations.

Such being the *sentiment* of a heart unaccustomed to disguise; I flatter myself the candid manner in which I have explained it, could not be displeasing to the Convocation; and that the intervening delay, between the *present* and the *moment* in which I shall have the pleasure of receiving such ulterior explanations as may enable me to give a *definitive answer* will not prove very detrimental to the Collegiate interests.[3] With great esteem and regard I am—Dear Sir Yr Obedt Hble Servt

Go: Washington

ALS, owned (1989) by the Gallery of History, Las Vegas; LB, DLC:GW.
1. See Griffin to GW, 4 Feb., n.1.
2. See David Stuart to GW, 17 February.
3. See Griffin to GW, 4 Feb., n.2.

## From Benjamin Lincoln

My dear General                    Boston Feby 20th 1788
New hampshire convention is setting the accounts are vague and uncertain things do not look as well as we wish they did we however flatter ourselves that the constitution will go down among them—Governour Sullivan & Mr Langdon, who have been in oposite boxes, are in this matter united and they are uniting their whole interest in favor of the constitution.

Our supream judicial Court opened here yesterday the Chief justice in his charge to the grand jury stated the imperfections of the old and the wisdom & necessety of the new constitution and answered many objections which have been thrown out against it—People here are quiet and are daily more and more attracted to the new—a proposed government.

I have the pleasure of inclosing the three last papers if none of my letters misscarry your Excellency will have the debates regularly in the several papers I have & shall forward. I have the honour of being my dear General with the highest esteem & affection your Excellencys most Obedient servant.

AL, DLC:GW.

# From James Madison

Dear Sir                         New York Feby 20. 1788

I am just favored with yours of the 7th inst:[1] and will attend to your wishes as to the political essays in the press.

I have given notice to my friends in Orange that the County may command my services in the Convention, if it pleases. I can say with great truth however that in this overture I sacrifice every private inclination to considerations not of a selfish nature. I foresee that the undertaking will involve me in very laborious and irksome discussions; that public opposition to several very respectable characters whose esteem and friendship I greatly prize may unintentionally endanger the subsisting connection; and that disagreeable misconstructions, of which samples have been already given, may be the fruit of those exertions which fidelity will impose. But I have made up my determination on the subject; and if I am informed that my presence at the election in the County be indispensable, shall submit to that condition also; though it is my particular wish to decline it, as well to avoid apparent solicitude on the occasion; as a journey of such length at a very unpleasant Season.

I had seen the extract of your letter to Col. Carter, and had supposed from the place where it first made its appearance that its publication was the effect of the zeal of a correspondent. I cannot but think on the whole that it may have been of service, notwithstanding the scandalous misinterpretations of it which have been attempted. As it has ev[i]dently the air of a paragraph to a familiar friend, the omission of an argumentative support of the opinion given will appear to no candid reader unnatural or improper.

We have no late information from Europe, except through the English papers, which represent the affairs of France as in the most ticklish state. The facts have every appearance of authenticity, and we wait with great impatience for the packet which is daily expected. It can be little doubted that the patriots have been abandoned; whether from impotency in France, misconduct in them, or from what other cause is not altogether clear. The french apologists are visibly embarrassed by the dilemma of submitting to the appearance of either weakness or the want of faith. They seem generally to alledge that their engagements being with the Republic, the Nation could not oppose the regular Authority of the Country by supporting a single province, or perhaps a party in it only. The validity of this excuse will depend much on the real connection between France and the patriots, and the assurances given as an encouragement to the latter. From the British King's speech it would seem that France had avowed her purpose of supporting her Dutch friends; though it is *possible*, her menaces to England might be carried farther than her real promises to the patriots. All these circumstances however must have galled the pride of France, and I have little doubt that a war will prove it as soon as her condition will admit of it; perhaps she may be the sooner forced into it on account of her being in a contrary situation.

I hear nothing yet from the Convention of N. Hampshire. I remain yours most respectfully & Affectly

Js Madison Jr

ALS, DLC:GW; copy, DLC: Madison Papers.
1. Madison is referring to GW's letter of 5 February.

## To James Wilkinson

Mount Vernon Feby 20th 1788

I have received your letter of the 30th of December, written at George-Town.[1] I am very sorry that your business was so pressing as to deprive me of the pleasure of seeing you at this place, while you was in the neighbourhood of it.

Doctor Stuart handed me the Indian fabricks which you did me the honor to send by him, and for which I beg you to accept of my warmest thanks. Altho' they are not novel to me, yet the sight of them will undoubtedly be highly pleasing to those who have never before had an opportunity of seeing work of this kind; and peculiarly gratifying to the curiosity of an European. I regret the loss of the Seeds, having long been endeavouring to possess myself of the curious shrubs of the Western Country, but sincerely congratulate you on your own fortunate escape.

I feel myself much obliged, Sir by the offer of your Services which you are so polite as to make me, and shall always retain a grateful remembrance of them. My compliments if you please

[to] Mrs Wilkinson.[2] With much esteem I am—Dear Sir Yr Most Obedt Servt

Go: Washington

ALS, ICHi; LB, DLC:GW. The letter was addressed to "General Wilkinson Kentucke," and GW wrote on the cover: "recomd to the care of Colo. Biddle Philada."

1. Letter not found. For Wilkinson's trip through Virginia, see GW to James Madison, 7 Dec. 1787, n.7.

2. During the Revolution Wilkinson married Ann Biddle, sister of Clement Biddle.

## To Clement Biddle

Dear Sir,                                    Mount Vernon 22d Feby 1788

If this letter should get to your hand in time, I beg you would send me five bushels of clean and fresh red-clover seed, and the like quantity of Timothy by the Vessel which you say would sail for Alexandria, soon after the Delaware should be freed from Ice.

By a letter which I have just received from Mr Smith of Carlisle dated the 5th Instt I am informed that he had at that time £200 of my money in his possession which he would send to you by the first safe conveyance—out of this please to pay yourself.

I will write more fully to you in a few days. In the meanwhile I am—Dear Sir Yr Most Obedt Servt

Go: Washington

ALS, Bodleian Library, Oxford; LB, DLC:GW.

## From J. Huiberts

Sir!                                         Baltimore feby 22d 1788

Being on the eve of going to Europe, I should undoubtedly do myself the honour of waiting on your Excellency, but unavoidable buseness attending a voyage of this kind rendering it quite impossible to acquit myself of this duty personally, I take the liberty to do it by this letter, and to thank You and your friendly family most Cordially for all the unmerited attentions and civilities shewn me while in America, and to tender my Services to your Excellency and your friends, where ever you think they can be usefull either to you or to them; worthless as they are, I must beg you'll receive them, with the addition of my Sincere wishes, for your health and prosperity in every respect.[1]

My Stay in Holland shall not be long, as the trip is only intended to fetch my only child and property over to America, where I hope to bring it up, and Spend the remainder of my life, in that true freedom and under the protection of Such Laws, as by a Fœderal Gouvernment, duly administered, can make its peaceful Citizens the happyest people on the globe.[2]

Allow me Sir! to recommand me in Your & Mrs Washingtons friendly and much esteemed remembrance; to request my Sincere compliments to Major Washington and his Lady, also to Master George, and be pleased to believe, that no time nor distance can alter the real Sentiments of gratitude and due reguard, with which I have the honour to be Your Excellency's Most obedient & most humb. ser.

J. Huiberts.

ALS, DLC:GW.

1. GW replied from Mount Vernon on 3 Mar.: "Sir, I have received your polite letter of the 22d Ulto—and am much obliged to you for the kind tender of your services to execute any commissions for me in Holland; but as I have no business, at present in that quarter I cannot avail myself of your obliging offer, I have however, a no less grateful sense of it on that acct. You will please, Sir, to accept of my best wishes for a safe voyage, a prosperous completion of your business in Europe, and a happy return to this Country. Mrs Washington and the rest of the family Join in this wish. I am Sir Yr Most Obedt Hble Sert Go. Washington" (LB, DLC:GW).

2. Huiberts wrote GW on 23 July 1790 to explain why he had not returned to America.

## To Thomas Smith

Sir                          Mount Vernon February 22d 1788

I have, at this late period, to acknowledge the rect of your letter of the 22d of may last.[1] The reason of my not doing it in course, was not owing to any neglect or inattention on my part, but to the want of knowing that it was in my hands, for I received the Title papers of my land in Washington County which you sent to me in Philadelphia, and not expecting that any thing was contain'd in the enclosure more than those, I delay'd opening it till a few days since.[2]

I have forwarded the letter to Mr Bushrod Washington which was under the same cover with my papers, but I expect the contents of it have been anticipated by a letter from you since that time.[3]

You have undoubtedly recd a letter from me before this, requesting you to retain whatever you consider as a compensation for the trouble of yourself and Mr Ross in prosecuting my land suit, out of the money which you may recover on my acct from the bonds in your hands and transmit the residue to Clement Biddle Esqr. in Philadelphia.[4] I am yrs &c.

Go. Washington

LB, DLC:GW.

1. Letter not found.

2. See GW to Smith, 16 Sept. 1787. "A few days since" was in fact 29 Dec. 1787, or earlier (see note 3).

3. GW sent Bushrod Washington the letter on 29 Dec. 1787, with an explanation for the delay in its being forwarded.

4. GW asked Smith to name his fee in his letters of 16 Sept. and 3 Dec. 1787. For the decision reached, see Smith to GW, 5 Feb. 1788, and GW to Smith, 5 Mar. 1788.


# From Charles Lee

Dear Sir                               Alexandria 23 Feby 1788

A bill drawn on you by the Treasurer of the James River Company for sixty five pounds balance of the requisitions accompanied with the account has been transmitted to me which I have the honour to enclose. Please to inform me when and to whom application is to be made for payment.[1] With every consideration of respect and esteem I remain your most obed. sert

Charles Lee

ALS, DLC:GW.

1. In August 1785 GW authorized Edmund Randolph to purchase for him five shares in the James River Company, which were priced at £60 a share. GW paid £15 in 1786, £50 in 1787, and £65 on 21 June 1788. The remaining £170 he paid in 1791 (Ledger B, 354). See also John Hopkins to GW, 1 May 1786.

# From Caleb Gibbs

Dear Sir. Boston Feby 24th 1788.

On the 8th Instant[1] I did myself the honor of addressing your Excellency and Communicating the agreable Information that this Commonwealth had assented to and Ratified the proposed Constitution for the United States of America. I also transmitted several news papers of this Metropolis containing Part of the Debates of the Convention. In the same Letter I gave your Excellency some hope that as New Hampshire was soon to meet in Convention, they would (by the best Information) adopt the Constitution, They Convened on the 13th at Exeter, and Continued doing business till the 22d when I am sorry to inform your Excellency they adjourned till June next, This was owing to a very large proportion of the Delegates, having received positive Instructions from their Constituents, to vote against the adoption of the Constitution. The Gentlemen in favour found if they went on doing business ⟨till⟩ the final question was called, that a decided Majority would be against the Constitution, and finding that several who came so Instructed were in some measure converted, but having their hands tied dare not vote for the adoption, It was therefore thought advisable by the Gentlemen in favour, and those Converted, that they had best adjourn and Return to their Constituents, and give up their Instructions, and if they would not Consent for them to act according to the dictates of their own reason, they would resign & they may choose new Delegates to meet in June at Exeter. It is thought this measure will have its desired effect, for before June the Illiberal and Ignorant will be brought in to do what is right and Just.[2]

Nothing more worth notice can I find to Communicate, but refer your Excellency to the Inclosed news papers which I do myself the honor to transmit by this Conveyance.

Mrs Gibbs Joins with me in most respectful regards to your Excellency and Mrs Washington, pray offer me in terms of esteem to Inquireing freinds. With the greatest respect regard and esteem I have the honor to be your Excellency's most Obedient and most humble servant

C. Gibbs

ALS, DLC:GW.

1. Gibbs's letter is dated 9 February.

2. John Langdon on 28 Feb. reported from Portsmouth more fully on the adjournment of the New Hampshire Ratifying Convention.

## From Benjamin Lincoln

My dear General                    Boston Feby 24th 1788

I was the last evening honoured by the receipt of your favor of the 31st Ulto.

Your feelings and wishes which have been called up by the distresses of my family are such as fully evince your concern for our happiness and welfare are additional proofs of your affection and demand our most grateful acknowledgments.

A Gentleman of this town who attended the New Hampshire convention the last week has returned and informs us that many of the members came instructed that tho convinced, some of them, of the propriety and importance of adopting the proposed constitution yet felt themselves so bound by their instructions that they must vote against it from this view of the matter it was thought best to adjourn, & as it was not probable that a majority were in favor of the adoption an adjournment accordingly on friday last took place to the third wednesday in June— They could not well have it at an earlier day as the General Court, or their assembly meets and a Governour is to be elected between this and that time. Those who are best acquainted with the temper of that State say that there is no reason to doubt but the constitution will be finally adopted there.

Federalism I am confident daily gains ground in this State. I think to have federal ideas will soon be the fashion if not the rage of the day. With the highest esteem I am My dear General your most obedient humble servant

B. Lincoln

ALS, DLC:GW.

## To Edward Newenham

Dear Sir,                                    Mount Vernon Feby 24th 1788.

I have been favoured with your letter of the 10th of Augt[1] and am very sorry to find by it, that your intended voyage to this Country was prevented, and especially after you had made your arrangements and was upon the point of Sailing. The cause of your detention must have made it still more displeasing to you, for, of all the vexations in life, that of a tedious & perplexing Law-suit is the most disagreeable. I am, however, in hopes that your visit is not wholly given up, but only postponed.

You will be so good, my dear Sir, as to inform your friend Colo. Persse that I have a grateful sense of the favourable sentiments which he entertains of me, and present my best thanks to him for the Hay seed & Gooseberry bushes wch he is so polite as to propose sending me.[2]

I must beg that you would not put yourself to any trouble or inconvenience in obtaining the wolf dogs for me, for however desirous I may be to procure a breed of them, I should think they were too dearly purchased if you met with any difficulty in getting them.[3]

At the time you complain of having been deluged by incessant rains, we were, in this part of the Continent, distressed by the opposite extreme. The drought in this neighbourhood, was as severe last Summer & fall as was ever known in the memory of man. The grass & small grain were greatly injured by it, and the Indian corn (maize) in some places, almost entirely cut off. My farms were among the number of those which felt it in its greatest severity—but happily, it was not general. The middle & Eastern States had favourable Seasons & good Crops. A very severe winter has added to the inconvenience of short Crops. We have, since Christmas, experienced a series of cold weather which is very seldom felt in this climate. The navigation of our rivers has been stopped by the frost since the first of January.

I thank you, my dear Sir, for your information upon the general state of Politics in Europe; and would, in return, give you some acct of our public affairs here had any thing of importance transpired since I had the honor of writing to you last. I can only say that we are still in a state of expectation, waiting the result of the State Conventions, relative to the proposed plan of

Government. Six States only have as yet decided upon it; they are favourable. The Convention of New Hampshire is now in Session. The most formidable to it, is expected to come from New York and Virginia. But as nine States will have determined upon it (and in all probability adopt it) before their Conventions take place it is expected that its opponents in those States will not have sufficient influence to prevent its adoption there when it is found to be the general voice of the Union. Rhode Island has discovered some symptoms of recovering from the delirium into which she had fallen. The papers mention the Votes of several Towns instructing their delegates in the Legislature to have a Convention of the People for the purpose of considering the New Constitution.

Mrs Washington joins me in Compliments to Lady Newenham and yourself—with great esteem & regard I am—Dear Sir Yr Most Obedt Hble Servt

Go: Washington

ALS, DeGE; LB, DLC:GW.

1. The letter has not been found, but GW quotes part of it in his letter to Charles Carter of 5 February.

2. For GW's earlier contact with William Persse of county Galway, Ireland, see Alexander McCabe to GW, 26 June 1786. See also Persse to GW, 11 Oct. 1788, and GW to Persse, 2 Mar. 1789.

3. See GW to Charles Carter, 5 February.

## To Caleb Gibbs

Sir,       Mount Vernon February 28th 1788

I have received your letter of the 9th inst. accompanied by the papers which you was so polite as to send me. I must beg you to accept my thanks for your attention in forwarding to me the pleasing decision of your convention upon the proposed Government. The candid and concileating behaviour of the minority places them in a more favourable point of view than the debates of the Convention gave room to expect, and sufficiently shews the good effects of the full and fair discussion which the subject met with.

The adoption of the Constitution in Massachusetts will, I presume, be greatly influential in obtaining a favourable determination upon it in those States where the question is yet to be agitated.

No person can, at this moment pretend to say what *will* be its fate here, and I am perhaps less qualified to give an opinion upon it, from my own observation, than almost any one, as I very seldom ride off my farms, and am indebted to Gentlemen who call upon me for any information which I have of the disposition of the people towards it, but from what I can collect, I have no doubt of its being accepted here. I am &c.

Go. Washington

LB, DLC:GW.

# From John Langdon

Sir                          Portsmouth [N.H.] Feby 28. 1788

The Convention of this State met the 13 Ins⟨t⟩. to take into Consideration the fœderal plan of Government; contrary to the expectation of almost ev'ry thinking man, a small majority of (say four persons) appeared against the system. this was the most astonishing to ev'ry man of any information, as Massachusets had accepted it, and that this State in particular had ev'ry thing to gain and nothing to loose, by the adoption of the Government and almost ev'ry man of property and abilities for it; however, this can be accounted for. just at the moment of choice for members for our convention (in one of our principal counties) took place, a report was circulated by a few designing men who wished for confusion that Massachusets Convention who had just met, were against the plan & would certainly refuse it. the liberties of the people were in danger, and that the great men (as they call them) were forming a plan for themselves together with a thousand other absurdities, which frightened the people almost out of what *little* senses they had. This induced them to choose not only such men as were against the plan but to instruct them positively against receiving it. the absurdity of such conduct is too plain to observe upon, however notwithstanding the exertion of the opponents, (both without doors and within) after spending ten days in debating on the plan, a number of those Gentlemen who came from home with different sentiments, were convinced of their Mistake and only wished an opportunity to lay the matter before their Constituents. this they mentioned to those in favor of the plan who seeing the difficulty which those men laboured under & the unceartainty of the Vote if the general question was then call'd for, agreed that I should move for an adjournment to some future day to take the final question this was done and carried. the Convention adjourned to meet the third day of June next tho' greatly opposed by those against the plan.

That this State must and will receive it, I have but very little doubt, notwithstanding their late Conduct, which to be sure is very mortifying, as we have ev'ry thing to expect from its adoption. I have the Honour to be Your Excellency's Mo' Ob'dt St

John Langdon

LS, DLC:GW.

## To Rufus King

Sir,                          Mount Vernon 29th Feby 1788

I have received the letter with which you were pleased to honor me from Boston,[1] and pray you to accept my thanks for, & congratulations on, the important information it contains.

Happy, am I, to see the favorable decision of your Convention upon the proposed Government; not only on acct of its adding an important State to the number of those which have already accepted it, but because it must be productive of good effects in other States, whose determination may have been problematical. The candid, and open behaviour of the minority, is noble and commendable. It will have its weight.

From my own knowledge, I cannot undertake to say what will be the fate of the Constitution in this State. I am altogether indebted to Gentlemen who visit me for information respecting the disposition of the people towards it, not having gone Six miles beyond the limits of my own farms since my return from Philadelphia. From these accounts, no doubt, from the first, has been entertained in my mind, of the acceptance of it here; notwithstanding the *indefatigable* pains which some very influencial characters take to oppose it.

I beg you to present me in respectful terms to Mrs King[2]— and to receive assurances of the esteem & regard with which I have the honor to be, Sir, Yr Most Obedt Hble Ser⟨vt⟩

　　　　　　　　　　　　　　　　　　Go: Washington

ALS, NHi: King Papers; LB, DLC:GW. The letter-book copy, dated 28 Feb., differs somewhat from the ALS and seems to have been copied from a different version of the letter.

　1. King's letter is dated 6 February.

　2. In 1786 King married Mary Alsop of New York City.

## To Benjamin Lincoln

My dear Sir,　　　　　　　　Mount Vernon Feby 29th 1788

　I have to acknowledge the receipt of your three letters of the 3d 6th & 9th int. The information conveyed by the last was extremely pleasing to me, tho' I cannot say it was altogether unexpected, as the tenor of your former letters had in some measure, prepared me for the event, but the conduct of the minority was more pleasing and satisfactory than could have been looked for from the debates. The full & fair discussion which you gave the subject in your Convention was attended with the happiest consequences; it afforded compleat information to all those whose minds were open to conviction and at the sametime gave an opportunity to confute, and point out the fallacy of those specious arguments which were offered in opposition to the proposed Government. Nor is this all, the concitiating behaviour of the minority will strike a damp on the hopes which opponents in other States might otherwise have formed from the smallness of the majority: and must be greatly influencial in obtaining a favourable determination in those States which have not yet decided upon it.

　There is not perhaps a man in Virginia less qualified than I am, to say from his own knowledge & observation, what will be the fate of the Constitution here for I very seldom ride beyond the limits of my own farms, and am wholly indebted to those Gentlemen who visit me for any information of the disposition of the people towards it, but from all I can collect I have not the smallest doubt of its being accepted.

　I thank you, my dear Sir, for the accts which you have, from time to time, transmitted me since the meeting of your Convention, nothing could have been more grateful or acceptable to me, I am also obliged by your promise to inform me of any important matters that may transpire, and you know I shall, at all times to hear of your welfare. Mrs Washington joins me in every good wish for you and your family—and with sentiments of the greatest esteem & regard—I am, My dear Sir Yr Obedt & Affecte Servt

Go: Washington

ALS, MH; LB, DLC:GW. The letter-book copy is dated 28 February.

## To John Pendleton

Sir,                                        Mount Vernon March 1st 1788

When Doctor Stuart was in Richmond I sent a number of public securities to him that he might receive the interest due upon them; among them was a Certificate for a Negro executed in the year with Interest due from the date, which he informs me he left in your hands to have the Interest paid thereon and transmitted to me as it could not be done while he was there. As I find, by the Revenue act, that the Interest drawn upon Certificates of this kind will be received in taxes for the year 1787, I shall be much obliged to you Sir, if you will take the trouble to have every thing which is necessary to be transacted respecting the matter done, and transmitted to me as I expect a visit from the Sherrif very soon.[1] I am Sir, Yr Most Obedt Hble Sert

Go. Washington

LB, DLC:GW.

John Pendleton, Virginia state auditor, was the son of Edmund Pendleton's brother John (1719–1799).

1. Pendleton sent the warrant on 6 March. For GW's successful efforts to collect payment for his executed slave, see GW to David Stuart, 11 Dec. 1787, n.2.

## To Anthony Singleton

Sir,                                        Mount Vernon March 1st 1788

Two of the enclosed Certificates dated Jany 4th 1788 were received at the Auditors office on my acct by Doctor Stuart when he was in Richmond, but as he was, by some means or other, prevented from having the necessary business respecting them transacted at the Treasurer's Office before he left that place, and has informed me that you will be so good as to do whatever is proper to be done respecting them, I have taken the liberty of sending them to you, requesting that you will be so kind as to return them to me compleated, as soon as possible, because I depend upon them for discharging a part of my taxes of the Year 1787.[1]

I have likewise enclosed to you five others recd in the year 1786.[2] as I see they are of the same tenor And I suppose require the same to be done with them as the above two. These last mentioned warrants have laid by me since their dates—I am so little acquainted with matters of this kind that I hardly know the use of them, much less the necessary forms they must pass before they are receivable in taxes.[3] I am &c.

Go. Washington

LB, DLC:GW. Immediately following GW's letter in the letter book is a list of the auditor's warrants sent to Singleton.

Upon the passage by the Virginia legislature of "An act providing a sinking fund for the gradual redemption of the public debt" in December 1787 (12 Hening 452–54), Anthony Singleton of Richmond was made the state's agent for the sinking fund. Singleton, who served as a captain in the 1st Continental infantry from 1777 to 1783, married in 1788 Lucy Harrison Randolph, daughter of Benjamin Harrison (d. 1791) of Berkeley and widow of Peyton Randolph of Wilton. In 1792 he was named a director of the new bank of Richmond (13 Hening 599–607).

1. The warrants dated 4 Jan. 1788 were for £43.4.10 on loan certificate no. 252, dated 26 Mar. 1779, and £6.9 on certificate no. 237, dated 24 June 1780 (see source note).

2. One of these five warrants, dated 18 April 1786, was for £17.16.4 on loan certificate 237 (see note 1). The other four, all dated 29 Nov. 1786 and totaling £87.16.6, were "for sundry articles furnished for the use of the Mil[iti]a in the year 1774 allowed by the Court of claims in Fairfax County" (see source note).

3. On 12 Jan. 1786 GW received £171.6.10 from the state treasurer in payment "on Certificates whc. had been Recd for Loans, to this State." See GW to David Stuart, 18 Dec. 1785, n.2.

# To James Madison

My dear Sir,                          Mount Vernon March 2d 1788.

The decision of Massachusetts, notwithstanding its concomitants, is a severe stroke to the opponents of the proposed Constitution in this State; and with the favorable determinations of the States which have gone before, and such as are likely to follow after, will have a powerful operation on the minds of Men who are not actuated more by disappointment, passion and resentment, than they are by moderation, prudence & candor. Of the first description however, it is to be lamented that there are too many—and—among them, *some* who would hazard *every* thing rather than their opposition should fail, or the sagacity of their prognostications should be impeached by an issue contrary to their predictions.

The determination you have come to, will give pleasure to your friends. From those in your own County you will learn with more certainty than from me the expediency of your attending the Election in it. With *some*, to have differed in Sentiment, is to have passed the rubicon of their friendship, altho' you should go no further—with others (for the honor of humanity) I hope there is more liberallity; but the consciousness of having discharged that duty which we owe to our Country, is superior to all other considerations, and will place smaller matters in a secondary point of view.

His Most Ch——n M——y speaks, & acts in a style not very pleasing to republican ears, or to republican forms; nor do I think this language is altogether so to the temper of his own Subjects at *this* day. Liberty, when it begins to take root, is a plant of rapid growth. The checks he endeavors to give it, however warrantable by ancient usage, will, more than probably, kindle a flame which may not easily be extinguished; tho' for a while it may be smothered by the Armies at his command, & the Nobility in his interest. When the people are oppressed with Taxes, & have cause to suspect that there has been a misapplication of their money, the language of despotism is but illy brooked. This, & the mortification which the pride of the Nation has sustained in the affairs of Holland (if one may judge from appearances) may be productive of events which prudence will not mention.

To-morrow, the Elections for delegates to the Convention of this State commences—and as they will tread close on the heels of each other this month becomes interesting and important. With the most friendly sentiments, and affectionate regards, I am, My dear Sir Your Obedient

Go: Washington

ALS, NN: Lee Kohns Memorial Collection; LB, DLC:GW.

## To Clement Biddle

Dear Sir                    Mount Vernon March 3d 1788.

If this should reach you before the sailing of the vessel which you informed me in your last was bound to Alexandria, I must request you to put on board her, on my acct two good Linnen Wheels, one dozn good strong wool-Cards with strong[1] teeth, and one hundred pounds of Clover seed in addition to the quantity which I have before desired you to get.[2] I am, Dear Sir, Yr most obedt Hbe Servt

G. Washington

P.S. Pray send me as soon as you conveniently can 40 yards of Lace, of the width & colour of the enclosed—that, or any other figure will do.

LS, in the hand of Tobias Lear, PHi: Washington-Biddle Correspondence; LB, DLC:GW. The postscript of the signed letter, which is in GW's hand, does not appear in the letter-book copy.

   1. Tobias Lear as clerk wrote "long," which GW changed to "strong." The letter-book copy has "long."
   2. See GW's letter to Biddle of 22 February.

## To John Jay

Dear Sir,                    Mount Vernon March 3d 1788

In acknowledging the receipt of your obliging favor of the 3d Ult., permit me to thank you for the Rhubarb seed which accompanied it. To the growth of which, if good, a fair trial shall be given.

I have two imported female asses from the Island of Malta; which, tho' not quite equal to the best Spanish Jennies, will serve to establish a valuable breed of these animals in this Country. Besides, I have disseminated the breed of my Spanish Jack to *many* of the smaller kind of this Country. And if you have one of these, or a better sort, and should think the trouble of sending her here not too great, she shall have the free use of the Jack— every necessary attendance—and I shall have great pleasure in obliging you.

I was not unapprised of the treatment of letters in the Post Offices of France; but am not less obliged by the friendly hint you have given me respecting this matter. mine contain nothing which will be injurious to the receiver, if the contents of them are inspected.

The decision of Massachusetts would have been more influencial had the Majority been greater, and the ratification unaccompanied by the recommendatory act. As it stands however, the blow is severely felt by the antifederalists in the equivocal States. This adoption added to the five States whh have gone before it, and to the favorable decision of the three which is likely [to] follow next, will (as there can be little doubt of Rhode Island following the example of her Eastern brethren) be too powerful, I conceive, for locallity and sophistry to combat.

On this day our Elections of Delegates to the Convention of this State, commences. They will progress as our Court days in this Month shall arrive, and form an interesting epoch in our annals. After the choice is made, the probable decision on the proposed Constitution (from the characters of the members) can with more ease be conjectured: for myself I have never entertained much doubt of its adoption, tho' I am incompetent to judge, never having been six miles beyond the limits of my own Farms since my return from Philadelphia; and receive information of the sentiments of the people from Visitors only.

It gives me much pleasure to hear that Mrs Jay's health is restored, and that you have the slight remains only of your long & painful indisposition. A little time and more moderate weather (if it should ever arrive, for at present there is no appearance of it) will, it is to be hoped, set you quite right again— In wishes for this purpose, and in offering compliments to Mrs Jay, I am joined by Mrs Washington. With sentiments of the highest esteem & regard I am—Dear Sir Yr most obedt & Affecte Servt

Go: Washington

ALS, NNC; LB, DLC:GW.

## To Henry Knox

My dear Sir,                    Mount Vernon March 3d 1788
    I pray you to accept my acknowledgements of your favors of the 10th and 14th Ulto and congratulation on the acceptance of

the new Constitution by the State of Massachusetts—Had this
been done without its concomitants, and by a larger Majority the
stroke would have been more severaly felt by the antifederalists
in other States. As it is, it operates as a damper to their hopes,
and is a matter of disappointment and chagreen to them all.
Under the circumstances enumerated in your letters, the favourable decision which has taken place in that State, could
hardly have been expected; nothing less than the good sense,
sound reasoning, moderation and temper of the Supporters of
the measure, could have carried the question. It will be very
influencial on the equivocal States—Of the two which are next
to Convene, (New Hampshire and Maryland) there can be no
doubt of its adoption and So. Carolina but little, which will make
nine States without a dissentient—the force of this argument
is hardly to be resisted by locallity sophistry—candor and prudence therefore, it is to be hoped will prevail, and yet I believe
there are some characters among us who would hazard, *every*
thing rather than cease their opposition or leave to the operation of the government the chance of proving the fallacy of their
predictions of it, by which their sagacity and foresight might be
impeached.

This day introduces the Elections for the Convention of this
State, and they will progress regularly thro' the month as the
Court days shall arrive—After which a more accurate opinion
may be formed of the probable decision of the State.

From the last European intelligence, the Political state of affairs in France seem to be in a delicate Situation—what will be
the issue is not easy to determine—but the spirit which is diffus-
ing itself may produce changes in that Government which a few
years ago could hardly have been dreamt of. all these things,
together with the importance assumed by G.B. on the occasion
of her dispute with this power and the State of other powers on
the Continent are strong additional motives for us to establish a
well toned Government.

Mrs Washington Joins me in every good wish for you, Mrs
Knox and the family—and with sentiments of the most friendly
and affect. regard. I am dear Sir Yr Obedt & Obliged

Go. Washington

LB, DLC:GW. ALS offered for sale by Sotheby Parke-Bernet, no. 4114 of Sang
Collection, item 293.

# From James Madison

Dear Sir N. York. March 3d 1788

The Convention of N. Hampshire has afforded a very disagreeable subject of communication. It has not rejected the Constitution, but it has failed to adopt it. Contrary to all the calculations that had been made it appeared on the meeting of the members that a majority of 3 or four was adverse to the object before them, and that on a final question on the merits, the decision would be in the negative. In this critical state of things, the fœderalists thought it best to attempt an adjournment, and having proselyted some of the members who were positively instructed agst the Constitution, the attempt succeeded by a majority of 57 agst 47, if my information as to the numbers be correct. It seems to be fully expected that some of the instructed members will prevail on their towns to unfetter them and that in the event N. Hampshire will [be] among the adopting States. The mischief elsewhere will in the mean time be of a serious nature. The second meeting is to be in June. This circumstance will probably be construed in Virga as making cotemporary arrangements with her. It is explained to me however as having reference merely to the conveniency of the members whose attendance at their annual elections & Courts would not consist with an earlier period. The opposition I understand is composed precisely of the same description of characters with that of Massts and stands contrasted to all the wealth, abilities, and respectability of the State.

I am preparing to set out for Orange, and promise myself the pleasure of taking Mount Vernon in the way.[1] Meantime I remain Yours most respectfully & Affetly

Js Madison Jr

ALS, DLC:GW; copy, DLC: Madison Papers.

1. GW wrote in his diary on 18 Mar.: "Mr. Madison on his way from New York to Orange came in before dinner and stayed all Night," and on 20 Mar.: "Mr. Madison (in my Carriage) went after breakfast to Colchester to ⟨fall⟩ in with ⟨the Stage⟩" (*Diaries*, 5:287).

# From Chavannes de La Giraudière

*4 March 1788.* This letter is almost illegible. From what can be read it appears to be a reprise of his letter to GW of 10 July 1787.

ALS, DLC:GW.

# To Richard Peters

Sir,                                        Mount Vernon March 4th 1788
    When I had the pleasure to be at your house last Summer you shewed me a triangular harrow with trowel tines for the purpose of cultivating your dell Crops. The appearance was preposs[ess]ing. But I forgot whether you spoke of its merits from theoritical, or practical knowledge. If the latter, will you permit me [to] request the favor of you to direct your workmen to furnish me with one compleat in all its parts accompanied with lines[1] or trowells sufficient for 4 more. Colo. Biddle will pay the cost, upon demand.
    That you may be enabled to Judge of the proper sizes—I will inform you for what particular uses they are intended.
    From the experience of two years, one the wettest, the other the driest that evey was felt in *this* neighbourhood I am persuaded that as much (Inidian) Corn can be raised in rows as in any manner which has yet been tried in such (midling) land and with such management as is usually allowed for this Grain and that by drilling Potatoes between, the quantity of the latter will at least quadruple that of the former. whether Potatoes in addition to the Corn will bear too hard upon the soil is a question that has received an affirmative and negative answer. and both (it is said) from the experience of Husbandry I mean therefore to learn that which seems most profitable & in the practice of which I am already engaged. These Harrows then are to work the intervals between the Corn and Potatoes; which being 4 feet *only*, the dementions of them must be proportioned to the space they are to operate in. But, notwithstanding the levelness of my land—the straitness and equi-distance of my rows, it would seem nevertheless dangerous to depend upon a *single* bout of this implement because if perchance the width between the Rows should exceed 4 feet the ground will not be broken—and

if it falls short the plants will be cut up—twice therefore in each Row—seems necessary for safe and proper tillage. I mention it for your consideration only—my own opinion of the matter I must confess is (but it yields to experiance) that two feet from center to center of the hindmost lines would be a proper Medium—this, with the outer lins[2] of the trowel, will stir near, or quite 2½ feet of earth; and under certain circumstances may be sufficient without going twice in the same row for cultivation of the plants; at all events, two bouts will give part of it a double stirring.

I will not trouble you with an apology for this request as it affords an opportunity to Mrs Washington and myself to present our best wishes to Mrs Peters and yourself and an occasion for me to assure you of the esteem with which—I am Sir Yr Most Obedt & very Hbl. Sert

Go. Washington

LB, DLC:GW.

Richard Peters (1744–1828) was secretary of the Board of War throughout most of the Revolution and served in the Continental Congress in 1782 and 1783. He was at this time a member of the Pennsylvania assembly and carried on extensive agricultural experiments at Belmont, his country estate on the Schuylkill River near Philadelphia. Peters married Sarah Robinson in 1776.

1. GW either wrote or intended to write "tines."

2. See note 1.


## To Clement Biddle

Dear Sir,                               Mount Vernon 5th March 1788.

In your letter of the 3d of February[1] you mentioned Messrs Dunlap & Claypole having put into your hands one Vol. of their News Papers for the years 1785 & 86, which they desired might be forwarded to me and my acceptance thereof requested. I must now beg the favor of you to return them my best thanks for their politness, and, at the same time, to inform them that I beleive they misunderstood me in my application for their paper when I was in Philadelphia, for it was my intention to have taken it after my return home as well as in Philadelphia; they will, therefore, be so good as to forward them to me by every post, and at the end of each year I shall be glad to have a Vol. of them bound. I have, hitherto taken the Pensylvania Herald, but, from some cause or other, it has been discontinued for a number of weeks past; I will thank you to discharge whatever may be due on my account for that paper, and inform the printers, in decent terms, that it need not be sent on to me in future, as I conceive one will be sufficient to give all the information that is necessary.[2]

I have recd a Letter from Thomas Smith Esqr. of the 5th ultimo, wherein he informs me that he has £200 in his hands for me, which he should forward to you by the first safe conveyance. Whenever you receive it you will please to discharge the balance which may be due to you for articles purchased on my acct since our last settlement, and forward the remainder to me in the manner mentioned in a former letter, reserving in your hands about £20 to pay for any articles I may have occasion to procure in Philadelphia.[3]

I must beg the favor of you [to] forward the enclosed letters to their respective addresses by the first conveyance that may offer after you receive them. I have, in the one to Mr Peters, desired him to have a harrow made for me similar to one which I saw when I was at his house[4] with some spare teeth; I will thank you to pay his bill for the same, and have them sent to me by the first vessel bound to Alexandria, after the one which I suppose is now about sailing for that place, provided they cannot be compleated in time to be sent by her. I am, Dear Sir, Yr most Obedt Hble Servt

Go: Washington

LS, in Tobias Lear's hand, PHi: Washington-Biddle Correspondence; LB, DLC:GW.

1. Letter not found.

2. Biddle wrote GW about the volume of Dunlap & Claypoole's *Pennsylvania Packet, and Daily Advertiser* (Philadelphia) and about the *Pennsylvania Herald* (Philadelphia) on 5 and 16 March.

3. See Biddle to GW, 5 March.

4. GW inserted "at his house" in place of "in Philadelphia," which his secretary, Tobias Lear, had written. GW's letter to Richard Peters is dated 4 March.

# From Clement Biddle

March 5 1788

I shipd the Grass seed and volume of Newspapers on bd the Sloop Charming Polly Capn Ellwood for Alexandria who was on the point of Sailing but a severe frost again closed our River and the Navigation is stopped, probably for some Days [to] Come but the Vessel will sail on the first opening—the Bill for the Seed is inclosed.[1]

Yesterday I recd from Thomas Smith Eq. one hundred ninety two pounds thirteen shillings & 4d. specie for your Account. He sent £200 but some of the Gold being Bad I returned it to the Gentleman by whom he sent it & only receipted for the above Sum, & I have now inclosed you our Bank Notes for four Hundred Dollars, which for security against Loss I have had made payable to you on Order in Ten days therefore when you part with them you will please to endorse as they Cannot be paid without it.[2] I am &c.

C. Biddle

ADfS, ViMtV; Clement Biddle Letter Book.

1. The *Charming Polly* sailed for Philadelphia on 16 Mar. (Biddle to GW, 16 March).

2. See Thomas Smith to GW, 5 Feb. 1788.

# To Thomas Smith

Sir, Mount Vernon March 5th 1788

Your letter of the 5th Ulto came duly to hand—The sum of £50 which you and Mr Ross have received for bringing and prosecuting my Ejectments is perfectly satisfactory to me, I only wish it may be so to you—if it is not I must repeat my request that you will satisfy yourself.

I find that the greatest part of the money which you have received on my acct has been paid without suits being brought as in this case you have all the trouble of a collector, without the benefit of a Lawyer, it is my wish that you would retain whatever is the customary commission for collecting, or receive a compensation for your trouble in some other way.

Major Freeman, in a letter to me before he left Fayette

County, mentioned his having deposited in the hands of a Mr Richd Noble at Red-Stone about £30 for me and sundry papers which he was to forward to me—I have written to him twice upon the subject but have recd no answer, I will, therefore, be much obliged to you, Sir, if you will get them from Mr Noble whenever you are again in that part of the Country, and convey them to me.[1] I am Sir Yr Most Obedt Hble Sert

Go. Washington

LB, DLC:GW.

1. Thomas Freeman's letter has not been found, but GW quotes it with regard to Richard Noble in his letter to Smith of 16 Sept. 1787. See also GW's letter to Smith, 3 April 1788.

## From John Pendleton

Sir            Richmond Audrs Office March 6th 1788

I enclosed lately the Warrants on your claim for a negroe exe-cuted to Mr Henderson of Dumfries requesting he would for-ward them by the first safe conveyance; I am sorry Sir, the delay in transmitting them occasioned yo. the trouble of an Applica-tion but begg you'll be assured it did not proceed from inatten-tion to the business.

The Appropriation Law passed October Session '84 (the first which has taken any notice of those claims since the Revolution) charged the interest on a particular branch of the Revenue with-out fixing a period for the Commencement and the Auditors being in doubt whether they could admit the allowance of inter-est prior to the Passage of the Law refered the matter to the then Attorney General (the present Governor) who advised that it could only be allowed from the time of passing the Law; and the Board have uniformly followed that opinion, so that on your claim, Sir, only three years interest were allowed.[1] I am, with the highest respect & esteem, Sir Your mo. obt hble servt

J. Pendleton

ALS, CSmH; Sprague transcript, DLC:GW.

1. See GW to Pendleton, 1 March.

# From Gouverneur Morris

Dear Sir                                    Williamsburgh 7 March 1788

Enclosed with this you will receive two Books which I recd some considerable Time since at Richmond; but being then about to depart for this Place, brought them hither in the Hope of an Opportunity to send them direct to Mount Vernon. Failing in that Expectation, I now put them in the Office; as I recollect you will not have to pay the Postage which otherwise would be worth at least as much as the Books.[1]

I should not forgive myself if I omitted this Occasion of congratulating with you on the Accession of Massachusetts to the new Constitution. This Event is in all Probability conclusive and gives to our Country the Chance for national Felicity. Should the new Government be set agoing speedily and well I verily beleive the political Situation of american Citizens, under the Presidency of the Man of their unanimous Choice will be the most happy in the World. Permit me to express the ardent Wish that Events so desirable may speedily take Place, and to assure you of my sincere and respectful Affection; in which, and in the proper Remembrances to Mrs Washington, Mr Morris[2] begs Leave to join with Dr Sir your obedt & humble Servt

Gouv. Morris

ALS, DLC:GW.

1. These volumes have not been identified.

2. Gouverneur Morris and Robert Morris were both in Virginia for several months on business pertaining to Robert Morris's contract for a monopoly on the sale of tobacco to the French farmers-general.

# To William Deakins, Jr.

Sir,                                    Mount Vernon March 8th 1788

This will be handed to you by my overseer who goes to George Town to procure a quantity of twine suitable for making a Sein, as there is none in Alexandria fit for that purpose. Should you have any such as he may chuse, I will thank you to let him have 150 lb.; and if the Balance of the Bond assigned to me by Mrs Kirk has not yet been paid into the hands of Colo. Simms, you will please to retain that as part payment of the amount of the twine, and charge me with the surplus. Should you not have any yourself, you will oblige me by assisting Mr Fairfax in getting it, if to be sold in George Town, and, if the above mentioned Balance has been paid to Colo. Simms, I will discharge the amount of the twine at the end of the fishing season.[1] I am Sir—Yr Most Obedt Hble Sert

Go. Washington

LB, DLC:GW.

1. For an earlier reference to Mrs. Kirk's indebtedness to GW, see GW to Bridget Kirk, 20 Feb. 1787. Charles Simms, a lawyer in Alexandria, on 29 Oct. paid GW the balance of £7.18.5 due on James Kirk's bond (Ledger B, 275). The overseer that GW sent to Georgetown is probably John Fairfax, overseer at the Home farm, rather than Hezekiah Fairfax, overseer at the Ferry farm.

## From William McWhir

Sir                                        Alex[andri]a March 8th [1788]
     In consequence of an unexpected addition to my family and the smallness of my house it will be inconvenient for me to accommodate Master George and Laurence any longer than their quarter is out. I should have changed my house in order to accommodate them but find it neither suits them nor me—I'm under the necessity of being often out: Then they like other boys will do as they please. Again my Servants do not pay as much attention to their Clothes as I could wish, and they are very inattentive themselves: Only think Sir of their being totally without shirts for four or five weeks after they came to live with me I think they must have disposed of them in some improper manner or they could not have been totally without—I apprehend it will not be very difficult to get Lodgings for them now. I shall at all times be happy to do every thing in my power for them And am Sorry it is not convenient for me to keep them longer.[1] I have the Honor to be Your Excellencies Much Obliged and Very Hble Servt

W. McWhir

ALS, DLC:GW.

1. GW's nephews Lawrence Augustine and George Steptoe Washington had been boarding at the house of their schoolmaster, William McWhir, only for a short time. See Samuel Hanson to GW, 18 Nov. 1787, n.2.

## To Burwell Bassett, Jr.

Dear Sir,                              Mount Vernon March 9th 1788
   If my last letter to you, containing the Bond of the deceased
Mr Dandridge on which you were requested to bring suit, was
not sufficiently explanatory of the intention,[1] I now beg leave to
inform you that my meaning is after Judgement shall have been
obtained and execution levied on the Slaves belonging to the
estate of the decd Gentn that you, or Mr John Dandridge, in
behalf of his Mother, wd purchase for her use such as she may
want, on my acct. In a word, as it is at the request of Mr John
Dandridge that suits are instituted, my wish is to accomodate
the family as far as I can consistently. the mode of doing it I
leave to you.[2] being with very great esteem and regard Dr Sir,
Yr Obedt & Affect. Sert
                                                    Go. Washington

LB, DLC:GW.
   1. See GW to Bassett, 3 February.
   2. John Dandridge wrote Martha Washington on 29 Feb.: "The Genl's Letter inclosing the Bonds I have not delivered to B Bassett yet: He has not been
in New Kent since his marriage, but is expected now daily—. I suppose the
Genl has informed him that when judgment is obtained & an execution levied
on the negroes of my Fathers Estate, he or myself may purchase on the Genl's
acct—" (Fields, *Papers of Martha Washington*, 207–8).

*Letter not found*: from Samuel Chamberline, 10 Mar. 1788. On 3 April
GW wrote Chamberline: "I have been favored with your letter of the
10 Ulto."

## To Thomas Cushing

Dear Sir,                              Mount Vernon March 10th 1788
   Your letter of the 12th Ulto inclosing the recommendatory
Amendments to the proposed plan of Government by your Convention, did not come to hand till last Saturday, or it should have
had an earlier acknowledgement.[1]
   The adoption of the Constitution by the State of Massachusetts will undoubtedly have a very happy influence upon the
decision of those States which have yet to determine upon the
important question. The respectability of your Majority, added

to the canded and manly behaviour of the minority, will obviate any improper impressions which might have been made by its smallness. The full and fair discussion which the subject met with in your Convention evidently shew the advantage of it by its effects, for, from every information which we could obtain here, it appears that there would have been a decided majority against the Constitution, had the matter been determined early in the session; nor will this be the only benefit derived from it, the publication of the debates will serve to remove objections in the minds of unprejudiced persons in other States who seek for information.

It is not in the power of the best informed among us to say, at present, how it will terminate in this State; at the end of this month some Judgement may be formed, as we shall then have a return of the delegates from the several Counties who are to compose the convention. There is perhaps no person less qualified than I am to give an opinion upon the matter from his own observation, as I am wholly indebted to those Gentlemen who visit me for any knowledge that I have of the dispositions of the people, not having been ten miles from home since my return from Philadelphia, but from every information, I have not a doubt of its being adopted here. Mrs Washington Joins me in Compliments to Mrs Cushing and yourself. I am Dear Sir, Yr Most Obedt Hble Servant

Go. Washington

LB, DLC:GW.
    1. Letter not found.


# From Henry Knox

My dear Sir                         New York 10 of March 1788
    Your favor of the 11th ultimo was duly received.[1]

The publication signed *Publius* is attributed to the joint efforts of Mr Jay, Mr Maddison and Colo. Hamilton It is highly probable that the general conjecture on this case is well founded.

I have not written to you since the untoward event of New Hampshire⟨.⟩ The conduct of the convention was so contrary to expectations of every person who conceived themselves informed of the dispositions of that State, that I knew not what to write.

I have received a letter from President Sullivan in which he says that the adjournment will be attended with the hapiest consequences, and that the convention in their next session will adopt the constitution by a majority of three to one.

The business in this state is critically circumstanced, and the parties nearly balanced—The issue will depend greatly on the industry of the different sides—I am apprehensive that the anti-federalists will be the most indefatigable. The federalists say they shall have a small majority certainly—but it is to be apprehended that their confidence will prove highly injurious to the cause—Nothing has been received from Rhode Island that can give any immediate hopes that that state will endevor to establish a different character.

I beg the favor that you would present Mrs Knox and myself to Mrs Washington—and my Compliments to Colo. Humphreys—I am my dear Sir with great sincerity Your most affectionate humble Servant

H. Knox

ALS, DLC:GW.

1. No letter from GW of 11 Feb. has been found, but Knox may have mistaken the date of GW's letter and be referring instead to GW's letter of 5 Feb. in which he asks Knox about the identity of Publius.


## To Benjamin Lincoln

My dear Sir,                          Mount Vernon March 10th 1788

Your favor of the 20th Ult., and the papers accompanying it came duly to hand; I believe none of your letters to me have miscarried as I have received the Gazettes containing the debates of your Convention very regularly.

I am sorry to hear that the issue of the proposed Government in New-Hampshire is, in any measure, dubious: Our accounts from that quarter have been favorable in the highest degree, they would have justified the expectation of an unanimous vote in their Convention.

The growing attachment of the People in your State to the

proposed Constitution is certainly a strong proof of its general excellence; It shews that a due & impartial consideration of the subject will decide in its favor.

At the end of the present Month we shall be able to form a tolerable judgmt of what may be its fate here, as our returns for the delegates to the Convention will be known at that time, and the characters chosen will be pretty generally decided in their opinions upon the matter before their delegation, as that will determine the people in their choice. The general tenor of the information, which I derive from those Gentlemen who call upon me, seems to agree in the oppositions loosing ground here; and that nothing is wanting to render the people so favourably disposed towards it as to put the decision beyond a doubt but a proper representation of, and information upon the subject. The opponents are indefatigable in their exertions, while the friends to the New form seem to rest the issue upon the goodness of their Cause. There will undoubtedly be a greater weight of abilities against the adoption in this Convention than in any other; It was to be expected from the characters who first declared against it here, but notwithstanding this, my opinion is (as it ever has been) that it will be received—With the highest esteem & regard I am My dear Sir, Yr most Affecte Ser⟨vt⟩

Go: Washington

ALS, MH; LB, DLC:GW.

# From Auguste, Comte de Grasse

My General                                    Paris [March] 11th 1788.

The real grief, which the death of my Father occasioned me, prevented me from having the honour of imparting to your Excellency the news, in the first moments of the melancholy event.[1] The friendship which he professed for you was founded upon esteem, & I fondly flatter myself that the friendship you accorded him was established upon a basis equally solid. It was by your means my Father obtained the flattering compensations for the services which he was so happy as to render America in conjunction with your Excellency. It is to you, my General, that I owe the four peices of Cannon taken at York Town. This glori-

ous testimony of your Suffrage & of that of the U. States is a
precious triumph for me. It adorns my arms at this day & will
perpetuate eternally in my family the acknowledgment which
my father hath always entertained for you. It would be very flattering for his memory & extremely agreeable to me, to be able
to preserve in his name, one other proof of the satisfaction of
Congress. The Eagle of Cincinnatus was originally instituted to
perpetuate from age to age the remembrance of the American
Independence. Deign, my General, to obtain for me permission
from the States to wear that Insignia with which they had decor-
ated my father. It is a favour which I entreat with earnestness of
your Excellency, & I pray you to be fully persuaded beforehand
of my gratitude.[2] I am, My General, with great respect Your Excellency's most humble & most obedt Servant

                    The Count Augustus de Grasse

Translation, in David Humphreys' hand, DLC:GW; ALS, DLC:GW. Bourdon
des Planches sent de Grasse's letter to Thomas Jefferson on 29 Mar. 1788 for
him to forward to GW (Boyd, *Jefferson Papers*, 12:694). Humphreys misdated
the translation 11 May instead of 11 March.

   Alexandre-François-Auguste de Grasse-Rouville, comte de Grasse, marquis
de Tilly (1765–1845), became a captain in the Royal Guienne regiment of cavalry and in 1789 wrote to GW from Santo Domingo where the regiment was
then stationed. De Grasse came to the United States in 1793 and was admitted
to the Georgia Society of the Cincinnati in 1796. He returned to France in
1800.

   1. For Admiral de Grasse's court martial and references to his death, see his
letter to GW, 15 Mar. 1784, n.1, and Rochambeau to GW, 18 Jan. 1788. De
Grasse's grief did not prevent him from writing to Thomas Jefferson on 19
Jan. 1788, five days after his father's death, to ask that he be allowed to become
a member of the Cincinnati (Boyd, *Jefferson Papers*, 12:521).

   2. See GW to Auguste, comte de Grasse, 18 Aug. 1788.

*Letter not found*: from Thomas Smith, 11 Mar. 1788. On 3 April GW
wrote Smith of "the reception of your letter of the 11th Inst." GW
should have written "ulto."

*Letter not found*: from James Wilson, 11 Mar. 1788. On 4 April GW
thanked Wilson for his "favr of the 11 Ulto."

# From Richard Peters

Sir                                      Belmont [Pa.] March 12. 1788

It is with the greatest Pleasure that I recieve your Commands respecting the Harrows.[1] I have in Consequence spoke to the Smith & pointed out some Improvements, where I think mine has Defects. I never had seen one in the Construction of mine & therefore the Idea was theoretical but it has answered in Practice to my utmost Expectations. I have never however applied it on so large a Scale as to meet your Views having only intended it for drilled Crops of Carrots, Cabbage, Pease, Roots of Scarcity & other Vegetables of this Tribe. In these it has done every Thing I wished. I have one in Contemplation for Corn of a stronger Construction & with fewer Tines. I believe they will not exceed three & I am told you have such in your Country but I know not their Success. I shall have one Harrow made similar to mine with Tines for another that you may judge from your own Experience of your Inclination to multiply them. I shall take the Liberty of sending you one for Corn but cannot vouch for its Utility. I shall venture to throw on you the same Risque I shall hazard myself.

I have tried on a small Scale your Plan of raizing Indian Corn. It answered well one Year but did not in a second Experiment. I shall however repeat it as at any Rate it will be an excellent Fallow Crop & it has been from a Prosecution of this System that I have rendered a miserably worn Farm surprizingly productive considering its Quality.

I find my Roots of Scarcity so perfectly answerable to everything I had heard of them that I shall either send you some Roots from which to raize Seed or save you a Quantity from a Number I shall plant out this Spring & this will forward your Cultivation of them equally with your having Roots now, which are subject to Accidents in Transportation. I did not forget my Promise to send you the Cones of the White Pine. But on Examination of a vast Number of them I found them barren—A Circumstance I never met with before & cannot account for unless the long Drought of the last Year occasioned it.

Be assured Sir that it will always be highly gratifying to me to have any oppertunity of proving how much I wish to shew my

Esteem & Respect for you—Do not therefore hesitate to command my Services when ever you think proper.

I have sent you a few of the Seeds of the Roots of Scarcity & have extracted from a German Book an Account of them to which I have added some Observations of my own lest you should not have met with the Information necessary to cultivate this excellent root.[2] If you think of going into its Culture trench plough in the Fall. I should concieve Trench ploughing advantageous to your Land if I have a proper Idea of its Quality. I have found most surprizing Benefit from it. Mine is a Loam inclining to Sand on a red brick Earth. Have you ever seen any Effects yet of your Plaister?[3] I had some that did not appear for four Years & now it is in great Heart. I never knew it so generally fail as it has with you. Altho' I am a little *hobby horsical* as to this Matter I would wish to know how it succeeds with others. I have made much Enquiry about it & tho' it is constant with me I frequently find it whimsical & capricious with others.

Mrs peters begs her sincere & respectful Compliments may be presented to you & Mrs Washington. Be pleased to accept the unfeigned Assurances of the Truth & Regard with which I am your very obed. Servt

Richard Peters

P.S. I send to Mr Biddle's Care two small Roots proportioned to the Size of my Box more than to my Inclinations; & they will produce as good Seed as the largest.

ALS, DLC:GW.

1. GW wrote Peters on 4 March.

2. In the enclosure Peters begins by quoting about two pages on the root of scarcity printed in "the Leipzig Magazine of Arts, Natural Knowledge & Agriculture" in 1781. Then he describes at length his own "Experience of the Ease & Cheapness" in the cultivation of this vegetable which he believes "would be an incomparable Acquisition to the Agriculture of this Country." GW wrote in his diary on 29 Oct. 1788 of harvesting the plants grown from the root of scarcity seed sent him by Peters (*Diaries*, 5:413–14). A copy of Peters's enclosure running to more than seven typescript pages appears in CD-ROM:GW. GW had been given some roots of scarcity by Elizabeth French Dulany in 1785 (GW to Dulany, c.23 Nov. 1785).

3. The "Plaister" Peters refers to is probably plaster of paris. GW several years before began experimenting with plaster of paris (gypsum) as a fertilizer. He recorded in his diary on 9 May 1785 that he saw no benefits from it on the

grass in his courtyard, but he continued to use it on grass and other crops. The plaster was pounded into a powder before being spread over the ground.

*Letter not found*: Richard Butler to GW, 13 Mar. 1788. On 3 April GW wrote Butler: "I have received your letter of the 13th ulto."

# From Clement Biddle

March 16. 1788

My last of 5 covered four hundred Dollars in Bank Post Notes which I hope Came safe to your Hands since whch I am favd with yo[ur]s of 3 & 5d—I have accordingly put on bd the sloop Polly Ellwd in addition to the Volume of Newspapers & 2 Casks Grass seed, 2 Spinning wheels & 1 Box of 12 Wool Cards—this Vessel has staid much longer than expectd but as she has at last sail'd this Day I hope she will be with you in time for the Grass seed—As I had put 25 Bushels of Clover seed more than first ordered it answers to your Additional Order of one hundred pounds weight of that article I have made diligent search for Livery Lace but not being able to find any in the shops or Stores that would answer, a man has engaged to make 40 yards but not in time for the Conveyance—Capt. Stewart is hourly expected and will be another good Conveyance for Powtomack I forwarded the Letters for Thomas Smith Esq. by a Mr Semple who was going to Carlisle just as I recd it—That for General Wilkinson shall go by first safe Conveyance—I delivered the Letters to Mr Peters[1] & desired him to send the harrow when finished to me & I wod pay for & forward it—The Pennsa Herald being discontinued I paid up your Subscription £1.14.2 & to Mr Carey for the museum 9/[2]—Mr Dunlap to whom I delivered your thanks for the volume of Papers says that those from his Office not reaching you since your Return has been owing to some new regulation in the Post office but he has put up a Bundle of the past which I have sent by Capt. Ellwood & he has promised to Cover your Papers by each Post & Mr Bryson Dep. Post Master Genl has Promised to forward them in the Mail.[3] I have inclosed the Bill of Lading of the Goods by Cap. Ellwood which must be sent to Alexandria to enter & receive them[4]—the whole being of the manufacture of this State the Cap. has the necessary Certificates to save duties.

The Certife to save the Duties I thought proper to keep from the Captain & inclose it to you herein.

C. Biddle

ADfS, ViMtV: Clement Biddle Letter Book.

1. GW's letter to Wilkinson is dated 20 Feb.; that to Thomas Smith, 5 Mar.; to Richard Peters, 4 March. Mr. Semple may be David Semple (Sample), a prominent Pennsylvania attorney who practiced in Westmoreland, Washington, and Fayette counties.

2. Mathew Carey (1760–1839) had come to America from Ireland in 1784 after being involved in several newspapers critical of English rule. He had spent a short time in France during the American Revolution where he had become known to Benjam Franklin and Lafayette. In Philadelphia where he became a printer and bookseller, he in 1785 began publishing the *Pennsylvania Herald* and in 1786 was briefly concerned in publication of the *Columbian Magazine* before in 1787 becoming editor of the *American Museum, or Repository of Ancient and Modern Fugitive Pieces, Prose and Poetical*. The *American Museum* continued publication until 1792. At his death GW had in his library volumes 1 through 10, dated 1787–91. See GW's letter to Mathew Carey of 25 June showing his enthusiastic support of the *American Museum*.

3. James Bryson had been assistant postmaster under Ebenezer Hazard since 1782. See GW to Biddle, 5 Mar., and Biddle to GW, 3 April. For the "new regulation in the Post office," see GW to John Jay, 18 July 1788.

4. The copy of the bill of lading shows total charges of £26.1.3. This was for two casks of grass seed—£22.7.6, two spinning wheels—£2, and one dozen wool cards—£1.13.9. It also included: "A Volume of Papers present from Mr [John] Dunlap," no charge.

## From Samuel Hanson

Sir                                    Alexandria 16th March 1788

I have just been informed by Mr McWhir that it will be utterly inconvenient to him to accommodate your Nephews any longer.[1] After your late indulgence of me upon this Subject, it will appear extraordinary that I should so soon apply to you to let me have them again.[2] The fact is the Gentlemen whom I had engaged, have quitted me; one, on acct of his marriage; the other, to make an unexpected voyage to the West Indies. I now therefore purpose, to take 6 or 8 young Gentlemen, Students at the Academy.

I will not conceal from you that there have been many disagreements between your Nephews & myself & family. The principal Subjects of those are the following: An obstinate habit they have contracted of Keeping Company with Servants; So that I could never Keep them out of the Kitchen—Going out, without my permission, to dine with their School-mates, who had invited them, perhaps, without the Consent or Knowledge of their Parents—Wearing their best Cloathes upon common Occasions and staying out late of Evenings, and sometimes the whole Night. I pass over the disrespect and insults with which they have frequently treated Mrs H. and myself, because that kind of Offence may have possibly originated in unreasonable Expectations on our part.[3] Upon those Occasions I have frequently, by Letter complained to Mr McWhir; but from an aversion to have them chastized, merely upon my own representation, I have always (except in one Instance) Subjoined a request that, instead of proceeding to actual punishment, he would only admonish & reprove them. This tenderness & forebearance, had, as you will readily conceive the effect of making them disregard my Authority & set me & my family at defiance. *Lawrence* had dressed himself one Morning to go to the Dancing School. In the meantime I had sent to Know if the Dancing-Master were in Town, & found he was not. I therefore told Lawrence to put on his common Cloathes and go immediately to the Academy. But he would do nothing. He was out the whole day, and returned at Night with his Cloathes very much torn. I therefore wrote Mr McWhir and declared that unless Laurence should be punished for this transgression, my authority over him would be merely nominal & by no means correspondent to that degree of Confidence with which *you* had been pleased to honour me. But, unfortunately for me, & I think, for the youth himself, His Teacher is an Enemy to corporal Punishments. Lawrence, therefore, was only kept in School during Dinner-time; a species of punishment to which he had been too much accustomed to derive any benefit from it. I am, I confess, no Advocate for corporal punishments; but it was plain that, in the present Case, those which Mr McWhir wished to substitute in their place were defective. For Laurence was after this more perverse than before. So far was he from discovering any Symptoms of penitence, that I was convinced, from his subsequent behaviour, it would be needless to trouble Mr McWhir again on the Subject.

George is of an obliging Disposition. His Offences have been

much less frequent than those of his Brother. They have proceeded perhaps from the circumstance of his being of an Age
& Stature verging to Manhood. On this Acct he is impatient of
Such a Controul as must still Keep him in the rank of Smaller Boys.

Sir, the Intention of these remarks is by no means, to injure
your Kinsmen in your Opinion, but to suggest the propriety of
investing me not only with a nominal, but an actual, authority,
over them. It will be impossible for me to restrain, without the
power to punish, them. I say *them*; without any Idea of proceeding against George, who is at a time of Life when rough treatment would be improper. In *his* Case, therefore⟨,⟩ I would, when
necessary, only complain to his Teacher, or, if that should be insufficient, finally to yourself. But I have hopes that if they should
be impressed with an Idea that my Authority is not confined to
the making of Complaints, the encrease of it would be unnecessary.

I should, Sir, be extremely hurt could I suppose you would
suspect me of a desire to encrease my former Authority, with the
resentful & malignant view of revenging their former Conduct.
On the Contrary, it would be extremely painful to me to adopt
harsh Measures, & nothing could urge me to it but the regard I
have for their Wellfare, as well as for the peace of my own family.
I can conscientiously declare that, in subjecting them to some
restraints, which they thought rigid, I have been determined by
the reflection that they were the same I should impose on Sons
of my own.

If you think proper to invest me with the proposed Authority,
I shall continue to discharge my duty to them. As to the Price, I
hope you will not think 30£, (to be advanced quarterly), too
much. I received from the Gentlemen 20 Guineas for Dinner
alone. Scarce as money now is, we cannot at this moment, buy in
market Beef under 4½ pr lb. Should the price Keep up (which is
hardly possible) it must be only from having a considerable
number that I can expect to reap any profits. The advance of
the money at the beginning of Each Quarter, tho unusual, I
hope will not be objected to, as it enables me to provide at a
Smaller Expence than I could otherwise do.[4]

I should have done myself the honour of waiting on you to

propose this Subject, & thus have spared you the trouble of reading a long and tedious Letter, but that the Situation of Mrs H. prevents my leaving Home.

I beg Mrs H. and my Compliments may be presented to your Lady, and remain, with perfect respect & Esteem, Sir Your much-obliged and obedient humble Servt

S. Hanson of Saml

ALS, DLC:GW.
   1. See William McWhir to GW, 8 March.
   2. See Hanson to GW, 18 Nov. 1787.
   3. Mrs. Hanson was the former Mary Key (Kay) of New Jersey.
   4. See GW's reply, 18 Mar. 1788.

*Letter not found*: from Thomas Smith, 17 Mar. 1788. GW wrote Smith on 3 April: "your letter of the 17th ulto has come to hand."

## To Samuel Hanson

Sir,                                      Mount Vernon March 18. 1788

Your letter of the 16th Inst. was handed to me yesterday in Alexandria as I was going to dinner: previous to that I had seen my Nephew George Washington, and asked him if he had heard of any suitable place for himself and Lawrence to board at after their quarter with Mr McWhir expired; he told me that it was probable a place might be obtained at a Mrs Sandford's;[1] I desired him to inform himself of the terms &c. and let me know them; as I had not an opportunity of seeing him again before I left town to know the result of his enquiries, it is not, at this moment, in my power to give a decided answer to your offer of taking them again into your family.

Your candid and free communications respecting the conduct of my Nephews, while with you, meets with my warmest approbation and deserves my best thanks, and I should think myself inexcusable, if, upon this occasion, I did not act a part equally open and candid, by informing you of several allegations which they have, from time to time, offered on their part, viz., There having been frequently detained from school in the morning beyond their proper hour, in consequence of not having their breakfast seasonably provided, and sometimes obliged to go to school without any. They have likewise complained of their not being permitted to dine with company at the House; & served indifferently in a nother place afterwards: and, after being a short time with Mr McWhir, they made application for shirts, and upon being asked what they had done with those which were made for them not long before, they replied that the manner of washing at Mr Hansons (in Lye with out soop) had entirely distroyed them.[2] This communication, Sir, cannot, I think, be displeasing to a person of your candar. I do not state the above a[s] *facts* but merely as the reports of the boys, and if they should live with you again it will undoubtedly have a good effect by shewing them that their reports will always be made known to you, and the truth or falsehood of them discovered.

The motive which first induced me to put the Boys with you explained upon a former occasion to gether with the advantage of throwing them into company will still operate, and incline me to give a preferrence to your House upon terms nearly equal in other respects but I cannot decide upon the matter till I know the result of Georges enquiries,[3] and so soon as I do, you may depend upon hereing further from Sir Yr Most Obedt Hble Sert

Go. Washington

LB, DLC:GW.

1. A number of Sanfords lived in and about Alexandria at this time. GW may have been referring to the widow of Richard Sanford, Sr., a resident of the town who died in 1786.

2. See Hanson to GW, 23 March. See also William McWhir to GW, 8 March.

3. The boys soon were back at Hanson's, probably by 15 April. See Ledger B, 251, 256, and Hanson to GW, 4 May 1788.

## From Lafayette

My dear General              Paris March the 18th 1788

I wish I Could Begin this letter With the Aknowledgement of a late favour from You, But None Having Come to Hand I Have No other Comfort But to Attribute it to ill fortune and Not to Any fault of Yours. I am so Happy to Hear from You, My Beloved General, and so Uneasy When I do not, that I Hope You Will Never Willingly deprive me of a Satisfaction so dear to me, Yet so short of the Happy Habits I Had taken in America.

The Politics of Europe Begin to Unfold themselves, in the Eastward at least. Russia is preparing for a Vigourous Campaign, and Will soon Besiege Oksarkow, While an other Army is Combining itself With an Austrian Body of troops. The Grand Army of the Emperor, Commanded By Himself Assembles about Belgrade, Which He Endeavoured to surprise But did not succeed. The Russians are sending a fleet With five thousand Men into the Mediterranean—and the Venitians are also Arming a fleet. The turks Have Raised Numerous Flocks of Armed men. Their Cavalry, Which in the first shock, is not despicable, Has, it is Said, Surrounded Three Thousand of the Austrians and Cut of their Heads, as is Usual Among Them. They also Had a Successfull Skirmish Against the Russians. But There is No doubt of the Advantage Which Such disciplined Armies as those of the Allied Empires will Have over a Banditti of Men Who are totally strangers to discipline, Military Knowledge, and Rational Calculations. They May Succeed with detached Corps, and Must disperse Before the Main Body of their Ennemies. The only difficulties Will be the Want of provisions, the Bareness of the Country, And the dangers of the plague—and Should the imperial Courts, Not wistanding those Embarrassements, Go So far as Constantinople, there they Will find a Bone of Contention to Know who Will possess that Metropolis.

The King of Prussia Has taken No Part as yet. Poland is Uneasy, and fears to loose Something in the General Arrangement. Holland is Making a treaty With Prussia and one with England. Nothing in Great Britain Has the Appearance of a War. france Wants Peace at Any Rate. Spain is Arming and objects to the Entrance of the Russians in the Mediterranean, But will probably Yeld to the demands of france. it is not improbable that the two Imperial Courts Will, after one Campaign, Content themselves for the Present With a Considerable Encrease of their Possessions. But it Could also Be foreseen that a War May Be kindled through all Europe, and End with the total destruction of the Ottoman Empire in Europe. So that it is Not Easy to determine Which of the two Events Will take place.

The internal Affairs of france are not yet Settled. Many Considerable Reforms Have taken place in the Expense. But a Great deficiency Still Subsists, and as the Parliaments Have declared themselves Unfit to Assent to taxes, as the provincial Assemblies are not Yet the Representatives of the people, I think the king will be obliged to Assemble the Nation sooner than is Expected by His Ministers. The printed Account of the finances is to Come out in a few days. I know that Governement intend to postpone the States Generals to the latest period Consistent With their Engagement Which is Before 1792. But I Believe this desireable Event Will take place Next Summer twelve Month. it is the only Way to put things to Rights, and to fix Unalterable principles in the Administration of this Country.

I have Some Reasons to think that Governement is preparing an Attack on the Parliaments, who altho' they are only a judicial Court Have Shown a Spirit of Resistence, and Refused to Register any New tax untill the States Generals Have Met.

The Troops Have Been divided into Armies, and grand divisions. the four Generals will Be Marshals of france—The Grand divisions under lieutenant Generals—I Have Asked to Be Emploied with the duke d'ayen My father in law in the Southern provinces and am the Eldest general[1] officer Under Him.[2] the divisions are About ten thousand Men. the Commands of us Major Generals are called Brigades. two Corps of light infantry Will Be added to My Regiments—We Will serve two Months.

Adieu, My Beloved General, My Best Respects Wait on Mrs Washington and family. With Most tender Respect and filial love I Have the Honour to be Your Affectionate and devoted friend

lafayette

ALS, PEL; copy, NNGL.

1. Lafayette wrote "gal" with an expand mark over it.
2. Jean-Paul-François de Noailles, duc d'Ayen (1739–1824), Adrienne de Lafayette's father, was lieutenant general in the French army.

## From Carl von Leuchsenring

Sr                              Durlach the 18th March 1788

The known fame throughout the World of your Excellencies humanity, emboldens me to Address myself to you; and altho unknown to recommend me to your particular favors. from various papers I have remark'd that the United States intending to establish a Chore of Six thousand regular Infantry Troops, I have therefore determind within my self, that should I receive a favorable account from the Hands of your Excellency, of a reasonable Advancement in the American Service, I should then devote my self to the Art Military in America.

My intentions last Warr were, to go to America as an Officer in the Hessian Service, but sickness prevented it, after which I enterd into the Hereditary Prince of Prussia's regiment Garrisond at *Pottsdam*, my Parents & relations however wishing me near them, did not rest until I took my discharge and entered the present Service, where Officers may expect more Honor then in the Service of great Potentates—but in this Service I am inactive & Dissatisfied. Therefore wishing to be employed in the American Service, and that so much the more, because I hear that Troops are to be Established where Officers may shew there activity and where a Man of Talents may sooner make his fortune then in old regiments where a Person is only a slave to rank. I now am Thirty two Years old, five feet—10 Inches in length prussian Measure, my Studies in my younger Years were that of Oconnomy and Merchandize, but this ten years past had devoted my self to the Art Military, in which Charractar notwithstanding all my endeavers, I yet remain what I first was, Say a Leiutenant, But convinced of the goodness of my Prince, I doubt not but he will be graciously pleased to dismiss me under the Title of Captain, for my farther Advancement—Therefore should I have the good fortune of being made a Field Officer in the American Service, I should not hessitate one Moment to take my discharge, and by your ordar to undertake the Journey. The bearar of these Lines Mr Myer, with whom I have oftimes been in Company during his stay in these parts had an oppertunity of becoming acquainted with me, and therefore the better enabled (if required) to give your Excellency a farther account of me.[1] And altho I am not acquainted with the English Language, yet I flatter myself in a short time to make some progress therein, ⟨and⟩ I have equal knowledge of the French and German Languages. The Charractor your Excellency bears in Germany is a Sufficient Security to me that you will Honor me with your notice, at least so far as to favor me with your Answer. In this Confidential expectation, I have the Honor to be with the utmost Respect, Your Excellencys most Obediant and Very Humle Servt

Charles de Leuchsenring
Leiut. & Adjudant of the
Battalion of the Hereditary
Prince of Baden

Translation, DLC:GW; ALS, DLC:GW. The translator Philip Marsteller, a merchant in Alexandria, wrote at the top of his translation: "N.B. the Title in the Orriginal is in a very high & decent Stile, but not Customary in the English Language."

1. "Mr Myer" has not been identified.

## From Benjamin Lincoln

My dear General                     Boston March 19th 1788

I was this morning honoured with the receipt of your Excellencys favor of the 29th Ulto.

Nothing very material has taken place since the convention was dissolved, saving the meeting of our General court. An attempt was made by some in the house of representatives, in a proposed answer to the Governours speach, to reprobate the doings of the convention held at Philadelphia and of the one in this State. In order to avoid a greater evil an answer will be omitted.

Your Excellency will recollect that our last house of assembly was chosen under the influence of the insurgents most of whom are against the proposed constitution at the least—Had it been submitted to our house of representatives it would have been negatived—We had different men in our convention they were chosen at a time when the spirit of insurgency had in a degree subsided.

We have much to apprehend yet from the remains of the same temper and are anxious what may be its effects on the choice of our next General Court.

I have the pleasure to forward for your Excellencys inspection the debates in our late convention they would have been forwarded sooner could they have been obtained from the printer.[1]

I hope my young friend is well I feel my self much interested in his happiness I wish my particular regards may be tendered to him.[2]

I am much obliged by yours and Mrs Washingtons kind wishes I wish my most dutiful respects to her and that the children might know that I remember them with affection—With the highest esteem I have the honour of being my dear General your most obedient & most humble servant

B. Lincoln

ALS, DLC:GW.

1. *Debates, Resolutions and Other Proceedings of the Convention of the Commonwealth of Massachusetts . . .* (Boston, 1788) was in the library at Mount Vernon.

2. Lincoln is referring to GW's secretary, Tobias Lear.

## From Battaile Muse

Honorable Sir,                                March 19th 1788

I stand Indebted in acct Current with you at this Time about Seventy pounds on acct of my Collection of rents—I wish it was in my Power To Convey the money as it's on hand—I shall be down the First of may and Expect with the above Sum I shall be able To Pay £130 altho what is not in hand is Very [un]Certain—if you have not Paid in your Propotion To the Potomack Company—Mr Hartshorne Drawing on me In Favour of Colo. W. Darke To whome the Company is Indebted, the money by direction Shall be Paid at my House the Seventh day of april—it will be uncertain To Find me at Home before that day.[1]

Should you stand in need of money before the first week in may I will be down by the 21st day of april with what Ever sum I may have in my hands—it would be more Convenient for me To Pay the 1st Week in may as I shall then draw money below without the risk of Conveyance.

I have wrote To Messrs Danl & Isaac McPherson To Pay To your order £25 in 15 days after they receive my Letter which will be delivered about the 22d day of this month—also wrote to Mr William Hunter Junr To Pay To your order on demand Ten or Fifteen pounds—Mr Lear Can Call on those Gentlemen with your order when in Town.[2]

I have Visited all your Tenants once many Twice Since Christmas—on wenesday next I Set out again If they do not make

Payment I beleave I shall Execute the Law the First week in april.

I shall be oblige to you To write To me by Post after Mr Lear has seen Messrs McPherson & Hunter with your advice.

I am Very Sorry To see, & hear, that their is So Many People of this state against the Proposed Govourment—still in hopes their will be a Magority In Favour of it. I have the Honor To be Sir your Obedient Humble Servant

Battaile Muse

ALS, DLC:GW.

1. See William Hartshorne to GW, 13 Feb., and notes. William Darke (1736–1801), who during the Revolution rose from captain to lieutenant colonel in the Virginia regiments, lived in Berkeley County.

2. GW's cash accounts show that he received in payment of rents on 15 Mar. Muse's bill of credit for £15 drawn on William Hunter, on 15 April Muse's bill for £25 drawn on "D. & I. McPherson," and on 21 April £46.15.5 from Muse (Ledger B, 264, 265). See also GW to Muse, 31 March.

## From Edward Pemberton

London, at Mr Priddens, No. 100 Fleet Street[1]

May it please Your Excellency                    21st March 1788

The Distinguishd Rank which You will hold in the Annals of Mankind, might rather descourage me from an address of this kind to Yr Excellency, was it not, that Your Merit as a Man, is not inferior to that of a Statesman or Soldier.

I know that Your Excellency is above Flattery which You stand not in need of, as I am above Flattering. What I have said in the few Verses, which I have herewith subjoin'd, was dictated by voluntary Inclination alone.[2] should therefore Your Excellency read them with some small degree of Approbation, my purpose will be answer'd, and I must say that then I shall be flatter'd, who give my Praises not so much to the Splendor and Titles of Men as to their Actions and Virtues.

Timoleon proclaiming Liberty to the States of Greece ⟨is⟩ a more Exalted Character in my Eye, than Cæsar or Alexander. Not that Alexander, as Some have Supposed went upon a mere Project of Conquest, or Glory, but to avenge the Grecian States of the Attempts, which the Persians had made to bring them under Subjection. In the same manner the Arming the Christian

States to drive the Moors and the Særacens from the Holy Land, was to retaliate in part the Injuries they had attempted to bring upon Christendom by the repeated Invasions of Various parts, and the Conquest of Several.

What Your Excellencys Actions have been a later Period may testify better than the present, when their Effects will be more fully known. As to the Policy of Great Britain respecting Your Country, I ever Condemn'd it as harsh, and unjust, and ever shall do so.

Had Britain been truly wise, She wd have been Satisfied with even less than the Act of Navigation gave at all events nothing should have provoked Hostilities: rather than have come to such, I would have made amicable concessions, a conduct since observed respecting Ireland.

What was the intent of Greece, in founding Colonies? It seems not to have been with a View of drawing Taxes, or Commercial Benefits from them—but to Extend their Fame and their power amongst the Barbarians: and to assure them as Allies to themselves against the Common Enemy—This seems to have been the Policy of the Grecians and also of the Roman People—Two of the most enlightened Nations that ever Existed. Had this Idea been more nearly adopted by Britain than it was, She wd still have had an ample Share of the Riches of America, without restraint or Compulsion—was She to found Colonies, in every part of the Globe no doubt but from Affection they wd in the first Instance seek their Mother Country, tho able to Support themselves. A Wide extended Empire Seperated in its diverse parts—cannot long be held together—therefore is it wise to relinquish the superfluous or useless parts, or those that are too Luxuriant in their Growth, that the Trunk or the Centre, may ever be strong and Vigorous. I had written the above to Your Excellency long ago, but from a diffidence relative to such an address, I put off the sending it from time to time since which some great Occurrences have arose in Your States which are worthy of abler Pen than mine to celebrate. This may now probably reach Your Excellency at a Season when all the Beauties of Nature will universally concur to render delightful great designs founded upon the Love of Liberty, and the happiness of Mankind.

You have a Vast World to work in, favour'd with every diversity of Climate and Soil Capable of every improvement which Ingenuity and art can Suggest.

I believe there may already be a Junction form'd between the Rivers Ohio and Missisippi—but whether it may have been Suggested that a Junction with the Atlantic and Pacific Ocean may be a work hereafter practicable by means of Rivers and Canals I do not know—but in some Latitude from South to North, it may be possible—was the interior Continent peopled throughout. that Your Excellency may long continue in health to consult for the welfare of the rising and flourishing States is the sincere wish of Your most humble and Obedient Servant

Edwd Pemberton

P.S. As I am not much used to approach Great Men, I hope Your Excellency will excuse the ⟨*mutilated*⟩tions and Inaccuracies ⟨*mutilated*⟩ Sentiments, and Stile.[3]

ALS, DLC:GW.

1. "Mr Pridden" is probably John Pridden (1758–1825), curate of St. Bride's, Fleet Street, from 1783 to 1803. He was a renowned antiquarian and philanthropist.

2. The enclosed poem of 41 lines, which appears in its entirety in CD-ROM:GW, begins:

> Accept Great Chief the Tribute of my Lay:
> Foremost in Arms Thoust clos'd a glorious Day:
> And the thick Laurels shade thy Evening Ray.

And it ends:

> A Cato Thou to bring the Tyrants down:
> And wear with Modest Worth the Civic Crown—
> The People Sav'd a Monument shall raise
> With Songs of Triumph, and thy Endless Praise
> Shall live in Verse; that Spurns the dreary Grave
> To Die the tuneful Muse forbids the Brave

No published work by Pemberton has been identified.

3. GW wrote Pemberton from Mount Vernon on 20 June: "Sir, I have Just received the letter and peice of poetry which you did me the favour to address to me, on 21st of March last: and take an early opportunity of acknowledging the receipt of them and of expressing my sense of the sentiments you are pleased to entertain for me. It cannot fail of being agreeable to me, that my conduct (th[r]ough the difficult scenes in which I have been called to act) should be approved, where my person is unknown.

"Not arrogating to myself any particular skill in deciding critically on the merits of poetical compositions, you will excuse me for being silent on a subject

In which I pretend not to Judge and for adverting rather to the friendly wishes you make for myself and Country; than to the style and numbers in wh[ic]h they are communicated. You may be assured, Sir, that the good opinion of honest men, friends to freedom and well-wishers to mankind, where ever they may happen to be born or reside, is the only kind of reputation a wise man would ever desire.

"Although your observations on antient Colonization and the recent Contest between Great Britain and America seem to be founded: yet it only remains now to profit of our actual situation by a liberal commercial intercourse. In the mean time, your disinterested friendship for this Country will probably be gratified, on the adoption of measures now in contemplation, in finding that it will arrive at a degree of respectability and happiness, to which it hath hitherto been a stranger. I am with all due regard Sir Your most huble Servant Go. Washington" (LB, DLC:GW; the ALS was listed in the Alvin Schener catalog no. 4, item 1903-A, 1928).

## To Nathaniel Ingraham

Dear Sir,                              Mount Vernon March 22d 1788

When I requested you to procure a Gardener for me in Holland, which you was so obliging as to promise to do, I fear I was not explicit enough with respect to the terms &c. upon which I would wish to have him.[1]

If one properly qualified for the business, could be obtained to come over in the nature of a redemptioner or which will be more certain, who will indent himself for a certain term years it would be most agreeable to me, because he would be much cheaper; but if one of a proper description cannot be procured in this way, I should be willing to give a good Gardener £15 Sterling per annum. more than this I do not incline to offer, because I presume they might be obtained for that sum in this Country. I should prefer a single man, but have no objection to one who is married provided his wife understands spinning &c. and will indent as her husband does. and provided they have not a number of Children. middle aged man will suit me best, as the necessary services cannot be expected from, or performed by, one advanced in years.

I should likewise be glad to procure a good coarse Weaver, and will be much obliged to you if you will endeavour to get one for me to come over on the terms mentioned above—I should give the preference to one who understands weaving both woollen and linen, but would be satisfied with one who could do either well.

If it is necessary (or would be more convenient for you) for me to make any advance for defraying the charges &c. which may arise from this business, I will thank you to let me know it and will provide accordingly. As I also shall be for your telling me with the *utmost* candor if the request here made will be attended with the smallest inconvenience to you—It not being by any means, my intention to lay you under the most trifling difficulty by the request. Wishing you a prosperous voyage and a speedy return—I am Dear Sir Yr Most Obedt Hble Sert

Go. Washington

LB, DLC:GW.

1. Ingraham, who as recently as 28 Feb. had been at Mount Vernon with his business partner Thomas Porter, was at the point of sailing for Amsterdam. He returned to Alexandria in November, without either a Dutch gardener or a weaver for GW (*Diaries*, 5:280).

*Letter not found*: from Edward Newenham, 22 Mar. 1788. On 29 Aug. GW wrote Newenham: "your obliging letters of the 22th and 25th of March afforded me particular satisfaction."

## From Samuel Hanson

Sir                        Alexandria 23d March 1788

Your favour of the 18th Inst. did not come to hand 'till last Night; an account that has given me some concern, lest you should have concluded that my Silence has been owing to any difficulty in replying to the charges made by the Boys.

with respect to the 1st "their being obliged to go sometimes to School without breakfast" I will not deny that it has been sometimes the Case. that it has not happened *often* Mr McWhir acknowledges. I declare that they never complained to me on this score, to the best of my recollection, more than once. But had it happened oftener, you would excuse me, when informed that it was their constant custom to sleep till eight or nine O'clock in the morning; So that very often our breakfast was over before they got up. One of our most frequent Subjects of difference was their sitting up late and their consequent late risings. The most violent offence that George ever received here was the omitting to awake him when it was, by my own watch, past 9 O'Clock. Had they got up at the proper hour for Students, the Servants would have had some warning of the approaching hour of Breakfast; a matter which they might easily mistake, from my having no Clock, and sometimes neglecting to leave my watch at home, or from it's not being right.

As to the 2d charge "Their not being permitted to dine with company" I admit it in part. But they have done it oftener than the contrary. I do not remember that they were ever prevented when there were not more than one or two guests; and we much oftener entertain that number than a greater. But, Sir, the mention of one Circumstance would excuse me tho I had excluded Lawrence all together. (*George's* behaviour at Table was unexceptionable) His unmannerly Conduct at Dinner was such as has been taken notice of by the Company. If there was any Dish considered as a rarity or delicacy, of that *Alone* he would be sure to make his dinner. As to their fare on such days as they did not dine with Company, every Person who has lived in Towns must be immediately convinced that this part of the Charge must be a misrepresentation; Since the Dinners on Such occasions are much superior in quality to those provided for the family. Upon this head I would only remark in general, that they fared precisely as I did myself, except in the article of *brown* Sugar with their Tea instead of *white*.

The 3d Charge is the Injury done to their Shirts "by washing them with Lye instead of Soap." Admitting this to be true, and that it was done by our orders, knowledge, or consent, it places the exactness of our Œconomy on such a pitiful point of view that I confess I should be ashamed to acknowledge it. However, not knowing but the Servants might have done it inadvertently, I applied to them, before it was mentioned to their mistress, to know how they had washed the Boys Shirts. I did it in such a manner as to make them think it was a mere cursory question, and that it was of no consequence to them to conceal the Truth. They, both, answered, "they had always washed them with *Soap*" upon being asked if they never made use of *Lye*? they answered "never." Mrs H. declares she never gave them such Orders. I, therefore, chearfully submit to you whether it is probable that

Servants should be capable of such an uncommon degree of par-
simony, of their own Accord? As for the Destruction of their
Linen I can suggest a much more obvious cause viz. their wearing it sometimes a week without a Change—This has been a
frequent cause of altercation; though, if I had been actuated by
the views that they impute to me, I should certainly have been
silent on that head; since it is less trouble to furnish them with
clean shirts once a week than twice—Sir, I can not help suspecting that your Nephews have been prompted to prefer those
Complaints agt me by an apprehension of my being beforehand with them. They have frequently threatened to inform you
agt me, in the hearing of my family. Upon hearing of George's
threats on acct of his not being awaked to Breakfast after 9
*O'Clock*, I sent him a message that, in my turn, would inform
also. I am really ashamed to employ so much of your time upon
a subject that, so far as it relates to myself, must appear frivolous.
But I cannot sit down contented under the imputation of
Charges for which there is no foundation but their own Misbe-
haviour. If you have any doubts of their Misconduct, I could, if
it were worth the trouble, at once refer you for proof to Mrs
Dade, with whom they lived.[1] I have no view in wishing to make
such an impression besides guarding you agt any future complaints; which, I trust, you will listen to with some Grains of Allowance. To effect this purpose, & to prove the difficulty of
managing those Boys, I will mention two Cases, which they will
not deny. In less than 1 month after their living here, Lawrence
whipped (rather severely) one of my Children, a Girl of 5 years
old. I do not know what was the provocation or that she was not
in fault. But I well know that it was her *first* offence against him,
because they had never 'till then had any Quarrels.[2] George was
in a short time exceedingly affronted by setting for his Breakfast
Milk, and Bread made of Indian-Meal. Offence was taken at this
kind of Bread, (tho it is so much esteemed in our family that we
are never willingly without it) merely, as I suspect, from it's being the common food of Negroes. Many times have they refused
Supper, because coming in late, Tea was over, and they could
not eat meat; although when I was at School, meat twice a day,
instead of a grievance, was considered as a rare Instance of
good-fortune.

But, Sir, I will no longer trespass upon your time & patience. The Proofs to which I have already put your politeness and indulgence are, I fear, scarcely compatible with that degree of respect with which I have the honour to subscribe myself Sir Your most obedt & most humble Servant

S. Hanson of Saml

P.S. after the description I have given of your Nephews, it may be very naturally asked "Why I would wish to engage with them?" To this I answer: Being desirous to pursue this business upon a large Scale, & the conditions respecting Controul (& perhaps the *price* also) being unusual, I conceive, Sir, that others may be influenced by your Example & Encouragement. I am &c. S. H. of Saml.

ALS, DLC:GW. The letter was marked "Favd by master G: Washington."
1. The boys lived with Mrs. Parthenia Alexander Massey Dade in 1785 when they first enrolled at the Alexandria Academy.
2. The child Lawrence Augustine Washington whipped was probably Maria Hanson (b. 1781).

## To Clement Biddle

Dear Sir,                                   Mount Vernon March 24th 1788
    Your letter of the 16th Inst. enclosing the Bill of Lading & Certificate of the Articles shipped on my Acct came duly to hand. The Packet has not yet arrived unless she passed by here yesterday.
    I thank you for your attention to the letters which I committed to your care. As I do not know whither you may have received the Interest due upon my Certificate in your hands, and some charges will arise from the harrow furnished by Mr Peters, and the livery lace, I enclose you a Bank Bill for forty Dollars which you will please to pass to my credit. I am, Dear Sir, Yr most Obedt Hble Servt

Go: Washington

LS, PHi: Washington-Biddle Correspondence; LB, DLC:GW.

# From James Rumsey

Dr General                    Shepherds town March 24th 1788

With this you will Receive five pamphlets Respecting My Boat and other plans, the Subject is not handled Quite to my wish as I was Obliged to get a person to Correct my Coppys In Doing which my Ideas in Several places ware new modled but not So much as to Injure the truths I wished to Introduce, But has made Sum things Rather Obscure.[1]

I hope Sir that the nessisaty there was of Such an Explanation being made to the public, will plead my Excuse for Taking the Liberty of Introduceing your name into my Concerns, and Shall Do my best Endeavours to Conduct my Self In Such a manner as in Sum Degree to Deserve the Honor it Does me, you may Rest ashored that all that I have proposed is within my power to perform, I have proven them all Experimentally, and have modles by me Sufisiantly Large to Convince any Compitant Judge (that may Exammon them) of the truth thereof.

Tomorrow morning I throw myself upon the wide world In persuit of my plans, being no longer Able to proceed Upon my Own foundation, I Shall bend My Course for philidelphia where I hope to have it in my power to Convince a Franklin and a Rittenhouse of their Utility, by actual Experiments, as Mr Barnes is to Set out in about ten days after Me with all the Machinery in a waggon and halt at Baltimore untill I write him from philidelphia what Encouragement we may Expect there, if none we will push Immediately for South Carolina.[2]

There is no period in life that Could give me more Satisfaction than to have it in my power to Stop the mouths of the Envious few (I might add Ignorant) that has taken the Liberty to Cast Reflections on the gentlemen that was kind anough To give me Certificates; one of this Discription would have got Roughly handled by the Gentlemen of this place if he had not made a Very timely Escape. I must Say that I am under great Obligations to the gentlemen of this County, on hearing my Intentions to travel, a number of them Vollentarily furnished me with Letters to gentlemen of their acquantances in Different States, and ten of the magistrates has given me a Recommendation that would do Honor to a much worthyer person,[3] I mention this Sir because I Conceive I am Indebted to you for a great part of the Zeal they have Shewn Upon this Occasion, and Should be ungratefull If I Did not feel the weight of the great obligations I am under To you—you Shall hear from me if I meet with any Occurance that I Conceive is worthy of your Attention—I am Sir with Every Sentiment of Esteem & Regard your much Obliged and Very Hbl. Servt

James Rumsey

P.S. Just as I was Sealing this Letter I Receivd a notice from the Director of the potomack Company that a motion would be made to Recover £20 Sterling of me alreadey Called for. I have Mr Hartshorns Receipt for five Dollars and the Boats the Valuation of which when Passed to be applyed to pay two ten pound Devidends for Winecoop⁴ One for me and the Ballance to my Credit with Hartshorn and Co. as I furnished the Boats their Valuation was then £57.12.0 Virginia money as I owed Mr hartshorn & Co. but about £5. there is nearly as much Comeing to me As will Discharge the third & fourth Devidends It is out of my power to pay the 5th Devidend In time must therefore abide by the Cansequences, I have Mr Stuarts Receipt for the Boats which Mr Hartshorn has Seen I Shall have a Statement of the hole forwarded to the Directors as Soon as posable I am &c.

J. Rumsey

ALS, DLC:GW.

1. Rumsey's pamphlet, *A Plan, Wherein the Power of Steam Is Fully Shewn, by a New Constructed Machine, for Propelling Boats or Vessels, of Any Burthen, against the Most Rapid Streams or Rivers with Great Velocity. Also, a Machine, Constructed on Similar Philosophical Principles, by Which Water May Be Raised for Grist or Saw-Mills, Watering of Meadows, &c. &c.* (1788), which he printed in Shepherdstown, Va., was in GW's library at his death.

2. Rumsey went to Philadelphia where he remained until May when he sailed for England to raise money for his experiments, with the blessings of Benjamin Franklin and others. See Rumsey to GW, 15 May, and notes. Rumsey's brother-in-law Joseph Barnes served as his mechanic.

3. For the names of some of the men in Berkeley County who were following Rumsey's experiments, see Rumsey to GW, 17 Dec. 1787.

4. Richardson Stewart was Rumsey's successor as manager of the Potomac River Company's work. "Winecoop" is probably Cornelius Wynkoop who held shares in the Potomac River Company. Wynkoop was one of the witnesses to Rumsey's steamboat experiment on the Potomac of 11 Dec. 1787 (Turner, *Rumsey*, 93).

# From Richard Bland Lee

Very honored Sir,                    Alexandria March 25th 1788
    After what passed between your Excellency and Col. Lee, and
our subsequent conversation touching my undertaking to write
a memoir of the events of the late revolution, for some time past
you may have expected my determination:[1] and undoubtedly I
should have written to you long ago, if I could have removed
those struggles in my mind, which were excited by the grandeur
of the subject, and the consciousness of my want of information,
and of talents, equal to the description of actions and virtues,
which merit and would have ennobled the pen of a Sallust or
a Tacitus. I considered that so great an undertaking, so full of
glory, so flattering to my ambition, ought not lightly to be attempted by a young man, who in point of literary attainments,
feels himself deficient in what is necessary to fulfil the duties of
Society even in the mediocrity of station in which fortune has
placed him. I considered too that such a subject merited a mind
totally devoted to *itself*, free from the avocations of the world;
and that in my case, the necessary attention to provide the easy
competence so grateful to the feelings of a freeman, and for the
discharge of the sacred obligations due to the memory of a much
honored Father, precluded the quiet and leisure indispensable
to the proper execution of the design.[2] Notwithstanding these
insuperable difficulties pressed upon my mind, the desire of
fame still led me to deliberate; Fancy painted to my view the
flattering distinction of being honored with the confidence of
the most illustrious Character and the glory of transmitting to
Posterity that series of events, full of danger, replete with Mag-
nanimity by which their country was delivered from oppression
and obtained the dear privilege (if we use it with wisdom) of
founding a government on the immutable rights of nature. But
it becomes me to correct the illusions of Fancy, and to yield however reluctantly this rich harvest of glory to some one, to whom
fortune has been more indulgent, and on whom Nature has bestowed the qualities requisite for the undertaking. So fruitful
and so grand a subject cannot fail to employ the attention of the
ablest pens. If ever I should think myself capable of engaging
in it; and find the necessary leisure, beleive me, Sir, there is

nothing in this world to which I should so fondly devote my attention.[3]

Permit me now to make my most thankful acknowledgements to your Excellency for the friendliness with which you offerred me every accomodation and assistance in the execution of the design: a friendliness which I shall ever remember with gratitude and affection. I will trouble your Excellency to make my most respectful devoirs to Mrs Washington and beleive me, Sir, to be with every sentiment of gratitude and esteem both as a citizen, and a man your Excellency's much honored and very hume Sert

Richard Bland Lee

ALS, DLC:GW. The letter was sent "By favr of Mr Lear."

1. Richard Bland Lee was most recently at Mount Vernon on 24–25 Oct. 1787. "Col. Lee" was Richard Bland Lee's brother Henry (Light-Horse Harry) Lee.

2. Richard Bland Lee's father, Henry Lee of Leesylvania, had died the previous year.

3. GW replied from Mount Vernon on 10 April: "Dear Sir, The letter which you did me the favor of writing to me the 25th Ult. came safe, & receives this acknowledgment of it. I can only repeat, that if it had accorded with your Inclination & business, to have devoted your time in writing a history of the late revolution, any aid that could have been derived from my papers, or information, would have been afforded with pleasure, being Dear Sir Yr Most Obedt Hble Servt Go: Washington" (ALS, University Library, King's College, Aberdeen, Scotland).

*Letter not found*: from Edward Newenham, 25 Mar. 1788. On 29 Aug. GW wrote Newenham: "your obliging letters of the 22th and 25th of March afforded me particular satisfaction."

## To Moustier

Mount Vernon Mar: 26th 1788

I have received the letter wch your Excellency did me the honor of addressing to me by the hand of Mr Madison.[1]

While I am highly gratified with the justice you do me in appreciating the friendly sentiments I entertain for the French Nation; I cannot avoid being equally astonished & mortifyed in learning that you had met with any subject of discontent or inquietude since your arrival in America. Be assured, Sir, as nothing could have been more unexpected: so nothing can now give me greater pleasure than to be instrumental in removing (as far as might be in the power of a private citizen as I am) every occasion of uneasiness that may have occurred. I have even hoped, from the short time of your residence here, and the partial acquaintance you may have had with the characters of the persons, that a natural distance in behaviour, & reserve in address, may have appeared as intentional coldness & neglect. I am sensible that the apology itself, though it should be well founded, would be but an indifferent one—yet it would be better than none: while it served to prove that it is our misfortune not to have the same chearfulness in appearance, & facility in deportment, which some nations possess. And this I believe, in a certain degree, to be a real fact; and that such a reception is sometimes given by individuals as may affect a foreigner with very disagreeable Sensations, when not the least shadow of an affront is intended.

As I know the predilections of most of our leading characters for your Nation; as I had seen the clearest proofs of affection for your King given by the people of this country, on the birth of the Dauphin; as I had heard before the receipt of your letter that you had been received at your public audience by Congress, with all the marks of attention which had ever been bestowed upon a Representative of any Sovereign Power; And as I found that your personal character stood in the fairest point of light; I must confess, I. could not have conceived that there was one person in public office in the United States capable of having treated with indifference, much less with indignity the representative from a Court with which we have ever been upon the most friendly terms. And confident I am that it is only necessary for such conduct to be known to be detested.

But in the mean, so ardently do I wish to efface any ill impressions that may have been made upon Your Excellency's mind to the prejudice of the Public, by individuals; that I must again repeat, that I am egregiously deceived if the people of this Country are not in general extremely well affected to France. The prejudices against that Kingdom had been so rivetted by our English connection & English policy that it was sometime before our people could entirely get the better of them. This, however, was thoroughly accomplished in the course of the

War—and I may venture to say that a greater revolution never took place in the sentiments of one people respecting another— Now as none of their former attachments have been revived for Britain, and as no subject of uneasiness has turned up with respect to France, any disgust or enmity to the latter would involve a mystery beyond my comprehension. For, I had always believed that some apparent cause, powerful in its nature & progressive in its operation, must be employed to produce a change in National Sentiments. But no prejudice has been revived, no jealousy excited, no interest adduced, and, in short, no cause has existed (to my knowledge) which could have wrought a revolution unfriendly to your Nation. If one or a few persons in New York have given a different specimen of thinking & acting; I rely too much upon your candor to apprehend that you will impute it to the American people at large.[2]

I am happy to learn that your Excellency is meditating to strengthen the commercial ties that connect the two Nations: and that your ideas of effecting it by placing the arrangements upon the basis of mutual advantage coincide exactly with my own. Treaties which are not built upon reciprocal benefits are not likely to be of long duration. Warmly as I wish to second your views, it is a subject of regret that my little acquaintance with commercial affairs & my seclusion from public life, have not put me in a state of preparation to answer your several questions with accuracy. I will endeavor to inform myself of the most interesting particulars & shall take a pleasure in communicating the result.[3]

At present I can only remark that I think the taste for many articles of French Merchandize is rather encreasing. Still there are three circumstances, which are thought to give the British Merchants an advantage over all others. 1st their extensive credit: (which, I confess; I wish to see abolished[)]. 2dly their having in one place Magazines containing all kinds of Articles that can be required: and 3dly their knowledge of the precise kind of Merchandize & fabric which are wanted.

For my own part I could wish as I have just observed to see the time when no credit should be given. Attention and experience in the American trade would enable the French Merchants, I apprehend, to accomodate our Markets in other respects. Between this Country & England many causes of irritation exist: and it is not impossible but that the ill-policy of the British Court may accelerate the removal of our trade into other channels. With sentiments of the greatest respect and consideration I have the honor to be Your Excellency's Most Obedt Hble Servt

Go: Washington

ALS, Ministre des Affaires Etrangères, Paris: Mémoires et Documents, Etats-Unis, vol. 5–6; LB, DLC:GW.

1. Letter not found, but see note 3. Madison undoubtedly delivered Moustier's letter on 18 Mar. when he spent the night at Mount Vernon en route from New York to his home in Orange County.

2. For another reference to Moustier's dissatisfaction, see Lafayette to GW, 25 May. After GW wrote Moustier on 17 Aug. 1788, Moustier wrote of his wish to visit GW at Mount Vernon, and GW promptly extended a cordial invitation (Moustier to GW, 5 Oct.; GW to Moustier, 18 October). After Moustier and his party visited Mount Vernon in early November, GW wrote Lafayette: "I can with pleasure inform you that the Count de Moustier seems at present to be perfectly well satisfied with the country and to be persuaded that some little uneasinesses about etiquette, originated from misunderstanding alone, and not from intention" (GW to Lafayette, 27 Nov. 1788). When writing to Jefferson, on 25 Nov., John Jay said that Moustier had "expected more particular and flattering Marks of minute Respect than our People in general entertain Ideas of, or are either accustomed or inclined to pay to anybody" (Boyd, *Jefferson Papers*, 14:290–92).

3. On 2 Mar. Moustier addressed to Madison a series of eight questions about matters relating to the possible development of trade between Virginia and France, including a query about Virginia's opinion of the tobacco contract that Robert Morris had with the farmers-general. It may be that Moustier wrote his letter to GW on the same day, and it is certain that the queries about trade that he asked GW were very similar, if not identical, to those that he asked Madison. For Moustier's letter to Madison, see Rutland and Hobson, *Madison Papers*, 10:551–52. On 25 July Thomas Pleasants, Jr., sent to GW, for his perusal before forwarding them to Madison, his suggested answers to Moustier's queries which he had drafted at Madison's request. GW wrote to Moustier on 17 Aug. 1788 giving his response to Moustier's questions. He also reported on this exchange to Thomas Jefferson, on 31 August.

# From John Ettwein

Bethlehem [Pa.] March 28th 1788

May it please your Excellency to spend a few moments in kind remembrance of Bethlehem in Pensilvania and to accept as a Small Token of my continuing thankfulness for your Excellencys kindness during the War, a copy of some remarks or annotations concerning the customs, Language &c. of the Indians, which I took from the memoirs of our Missionaries, to gratify an enquiring Gentleman; As also a printed Copy of the stated Rules of a Society for propagating the Gospel among the Heathen, lately incorporated by an Act of Assembly in this State.[1] That health and all hapiness may long attend your Excellency's person and Lady Washington is the sincere prayer of Your Excellencys Humble Servant

John Ettwein[2]

ALS, PHi: Gratz Collection; ADfS, PBMAr: Ettwein Papers; Sprague transcript, DLC:GW.

John Ettwein (1721–1802) was born in Germany and came to America in 1754. He promoted and himself undertook missions to the Indians, first in the South and, after 1766, in Pennsylvania and the Ohio country. In 1784 he became bishop of the Moravian Church in America.

1. Ettwein's enclosures included: (1) "Extract from the Instruction, or Rules, for ⟨*illegible*⟩ of the United Brethren, as are used as missionaries, or Assistants, in propogating the Gospel among the Indians"; and (2) "Some Remarks and Annotations concerning the Traditions, Customs, Languages &c. of the Indians in North America, from the Memoirs of the Reverend David Zeisberger, and other Missionaries of the United Brethren." The second of these included 5½ pages headed "1. Of their old Traditions"; 2½ pages headed "2. Of the political Constitution of the Indians"; and 5 pages headed "3. Of their Customs &c." Finally Ettwein enclosed "A Collection of Words," a 6-page vocabulary of several Indian tribes.

2. GW replied from Mount Vernon on 2 May: "Revd Sir, I have received your obliging letter of the 28th of March enclosing a copy of some rema[r]ks on the Customs, Language &c. of the Indians, and a printed pamphlet containing the stated rules of a Society for propagating the Gospel among the Heathen, for which tokens of polite attention and kind remembrance I must beg you to accept of my best thanks.

"So far as I am capable of Judging, the principles upon which the society is founded and the rules laid down for its government appear to be well calculated to promote so laudable and arduous an undertaking, and you will permit me to add that if an event so long and so earnestly desired as that of converting the Indians to Christianity and consequently to civilization, can be effected, the Society of Bethlehm bids fair to bear a very considerable part in it. I am Revd Sir, With sentiments of esteem Yr most Obedt Hble Servant Go. Washington" (LB, DLC:GW).

# To Henry Knox

My dear Sir,                    Mount Vernon 30th March 1788

Your favor of the 10th came duly to hand, and by Mr Madison I had the pleasure to hear that you had recovered from a severe indisposition, on which event I sincerely congratulate you.

The conduct of the State of New Hampshire has baffled all calculation, and happened extremely mal-apropos for the election of delegates to the Convention of this State; For be the *real* cause of the adjournment to so late a day, what it may, the anti-federal party with us do not scruple to declare, that, it was done to await the issue of this Convention before it would decide— and add, that if this State should reject it, all those which are to follow will do the same; & consequently, the Constitution cannot obtain, as there will be only eight States in favor of the measure.

Had it not been for this untoward event, the opposition in this State would have proved entirely unavailing, notwithstanding the unfair conduct (I might have bestowed a harsher epithet without doing injustice) which has been practiced to rouse the fears, and to inflame the passions of the people. What will be the result *now*, is difficult for me to say with any degree of certainty, as I have seen but a partial return of the delegates, and not well acquainted with the political sentiments even of those few. In the Northern part of the State the tide of Sentiment— I know—is *generally* in favor of the proposed system. In the Southern part—*I am told*—it is the reverse. While the middle, it is said, is pretty much divided. The Kentucke district will have great weight in deciding this question; and the idea of its becoming an impediment to its seperation, has got hold of them; while no pains is spared to inculcate a belief that the Government proposed will—without scruple or delay—barter away the right of Navigation to the River Mississipi.

The postponement in New-Hampshire will also, unquestionably, give strength and vigor to the opposition in New York; and possibly will render Rhode Island more backward than she otherwise would have been, if all the New England States had *finally* decided in favor of the measure. Mrs Washington joins in every good wish for Mrs Knox, yourself & family, with Dear Sir Yr Affecte friend & obedt Sert

Go: Washington

ALS, NNGL: Knox Papers; LB, DLC:GW.

# To John O'Connor

Sir,                                          Mount Vernon March 30 1788
I was favored with your polite letter, and ticket of admittence
to Mr OConners lecture on Elequence, at a time yesterday when
it was not in my power to give it an acknowledgment.[1]
Business (and indeed disinclination to leave my own bed
when I am within a few miles of it) would not permit my atten-
dence at the lecture last evening for the invitation to which you
will please to accept the thanks of Sir Yr Most Obedt Hble Sert
                                                            Go. Washington

LB, DLC:GW.
John O'Connor, an Irishman who advertised himself as a barrister-at-law,
dined at Mount Vernon on 3 Feb. 1788. For his attempt to promote his history
of the Americas, which, if written, was never published. See *Diaries*, 5:272–73.
GW had further dealings with Eliza Harriot O'Connor as the headmistress of
the academy for young ladies in Alexandria (see Eliza Harriot O'Connor to
GW, 17 June).
   1. O'Connor's letter has not been found.

# To Francis Speake

Sir,                                        Mount Vernon March 30th 1788
Mr Lee requested that the enclosed letter and bag accompanying it, might be sent to your care which is the cause of the
trouble you now receive from me.[1]
I cannot omit the occasion of communicating a piece of information I have received—to wit—that your Boat is engaged
to meet passengers on this side to take them to the other by
which I am deprived of the Ferriages—I hope the practice will
not be continued except for yourself—I find the Ferry inconvenient, and unprofitable enough without this, to wish the discontinuance of it. A little matter more wid induce me to put it down
and stop up the Road leading thereto. I am Sir Yr Very Hble
Servant
                                                            Go. Washington

LB, DLC:GW.
Francis Speake was a planter in Charles County, Md., and a tobacco inspec-
tor at Chicamuxen warehouse.
   1. "Mr Lee" has not been identified.

# From Clement Biddle

Ph[iladelphi]a March 31 1788

Your esteemed favour of 24 Inst. with 40 Ds. in Bank Notes Came to hand by last post. No other vessel has yet offered for Alexandria. Mr Peters having sent me two Letters & a small Box to forward and the Letters containing some Garden seed I have covered them by post & shall not fail to send the Box which Contains some Roots by first Conveyance[1] I am &c.

C. Biddle

ADfS, ViMtV: Clement Biddle Letter Book.

1. Richard Peters wrote GW on 12 Mar. and enclosed seed of the root of scarcity, or mangel-wurtzel. The box contained roots of the plant. The second letter to which Biddle refers may be Peters's extract of a work on the root of scarcity (see note 2 in Peters to GW, 12 March).

# From David Griffith

Dear Sir, March 31st 1788

The enclosed paper contains a Statement of your Subscription to the first of August last, when, by a resolution of the vestry, at their last meeting, the Pew rent was to commence in lieu of it. If it be convenient, should be greatly obliged to you for the balance.[1] With respectful Compliments to Mrs Washington, I am, Dr Sir Your most humble & obedt Servt

D. Griffith

ALS, DLC:GW.

1. GW wrote in his diary on 31 Mar. that "a Son of Revd. Mr. Griffiths came here on business of his fathers & stayed to dinner" (*Diaries*, 5:293). The "Subscription" had been the annual payment the parishioners made for the minister's support.

A new vestry was elected for Fairfax Parish on 28 Mar. 1785 after the incorporating of the Protestant Episcopal Church by the Virginia legislature in 1784. The church no longer received tithes, and on 25 April 1785 GW and seven other pewholders at the Alexandria church signed an agreement to pay an annual pew rent of £5 for the support of the minister and the church. The next year, on 21 Mar. 1786, the members were asked to sign a subscription "to pay to the Minister and Vestry of Fairfax Parish yearly to commence the first day of May next . . . the sums affixed to our respective names" for the support of the ministry and church. At the "last meeting," on 22 Aug. 1787, however, the resolution was made "that a subscription be offered to such Members of the Church as do not pay pew rent in aid of the Salary to be raised for the Minister exclusive of the Glebe And that the money arising from such subscription together with that arising from the Pew-rents be applied to wards furnishing such salary not exceeding One Hundred and fifty pounds ℔ annum Which shall be paid to The Revd Doctr David Griffith for his support" (Fairfax Parish Vestry Minutes). For GW's earlier affiliation with the Alexandria church, see GW to John Dalton, 15 Feb. 1773, n.1. Griffith sent his son again to GW in November to collect the pew rent for 1787–88 (Griffith to GW, 3 Nov. 1788). See also Griffith to GW, 26 April 1787, n.1.

## To Battaile Muse

Sir,                                        Mount Vernon March 31st 1788
I have received your letter of the 19th Inst. and Mr Lear has, agreeable to your request therein, called upon Messrs D. & I. McPherson & Wm Hunter Junr Esqr. who have informed him that the money shall be paid conformable to your advice.[1]
It would have suited me exceedingly well to have discharged my proportion of the assessment on the Potomack Company in the manner mentioned in your letter, could I have received it previous to the 15th Inst. as I paid Mr Hartshorne on that day.[2]
As you say it will be more convenient for you to pay me the money which you have, or may receive on acct of my Rents, in the first week in May than ⟨so⟩oner, I have no objection to its being delayed 'till that ⟨time⟩. I am, Sir, Yr Most Obedt Hble Servt

                                        Go: Washington

LS (photocopy), in the hand of Tobias Lear, owned (1991) by Gallery of Art, Las Vegas, Nev.; LB, DLC:GW.
    1. See Muse to GW, 19 Mar., n.2.
    2. See William Hartshorne to GW, 13 February.

## To John Langdon

Sir,                                        Mount Vernon April 2d 1788
Your letter of the 28th of February came regularly to hand. The conduct of New Hampshire respecting the proposed Government was a matter of general surprize in this, and I believe in every other part of the United States; for her local situation, unconnected with other circumstances, was supposed to be a

sufficent inducement to the people of that State to adopt a general Government which promises more energy & security than the one under which we have hitherto lived, and especially as it holds out advantages to the smaller States equal, at least, to their most sanguine expectations. Circumstanced as your Convention was, an adjournement was certainly prudent, but it happened very mal-apropos for this State, because the concurrent information from that quarter would have Justified the expectation of an unanimity in the convention, whereas an account so opposit to every former one having arrived at the very time when the elections were carrying on here, gave an opportunity to the opponents of the proposed Constitution to hold up to the people an idea of its not having been so generally approved of in other States as they had been taught to believe, and of consequence prepared them to receive other impressions unfriendly to the Government and tending to influence their votes in favor of antifederal charaters—However I am still strong in the expectation of its being adopted here notwithstanding the unjust and uncanded representations which have been made by the opponents to inflame the minds of the people and prejudice them against it. I am Sir Yr Most Obedt Hble Sert

Go. Washington

LB, DLC:GW.

## To Benjamin Lincoln

My dear Sir,                                    Mount Vernon April 2d 1788.
    I have to acknowledge the reception of your favor of the 24th of Feby; which I have delayed answering till this time in expectation of being able to give you some information of what will probably be the determination of this State, upon the Constitution; but the proceedings of New Hampshir, so directly opposite to what we had reason to hope for, from every account, has entirely baffled all calculation upon the subject; and will strengthen the opposition here; the members of which are not scrupulous in declaring, that, the adjournment was with design to know the result of this Convention.
    The only ground upon which an opinion can be formed of what will be the decision here, is, the return of the members for

the Convention; of these I have as yet seen but a partial list, and of this list there are many who are unknown to me; so that I am not able to give you any more satisfactory information upon the Subject than when I wrote last to you. This, however, I may say, that the Northern, or upper Counties are *generally* friendly to the adoption of the Government, the lower *are said* to be generally unfriendly, the Sentiments of the Western parts of the State are not fully known, but no means have been left untried to prejudice them against the system. Every art that could inflame the passions or touch the interests of men has been essayed. The ignorant have been told, that should the proposed Government obtain, their lands would be taken from them and their property disposed of. and all ranks are informed that the prohibition of the Navigation of the Mississipi (their favourite object) will be a certain consequence of the adoption of the Constitution. But notwithstanding these unfair and unjust representations, I do not despair of its adoption in this State. With the sincerest regard & esteem, I am, my dear Sir, Your Affecte & Obedt Servt

Go: Washington

ALS, MH; LB, DLC:GW.

## From Clement Biddle

Phil[adelphia] April 3d 1788

I expected from what Mr Dunlap had informed me that your papers had been forwarded you regularly since I wrote on that subject[1] but on enquiry at the post office & finding they had not been sent (owing to some misunderstanding between the office & Printers) I have directed the papers to be brought to my Office & now put up in a Bundle with those of last month & shall inclose them in future by the Different Mails as Mr Bryson & Capt. Patton who direct the Post Office here[2] have shewn an anxiety to forward them to you with Care—No vessels yet offers by which to send the small Box from Mr Peters.

C. Biddle

ADfS, ViMtV: Clement Biddle Letter Book.

1. See Biddle to GW, 16 March.
2. Robert Patton was the postmaster at Philadelphia. James Bryson was Postmaster General Ebenezer Hazard's assistant.

# To Richard Butler

Dear Sir,                           Mount Vernon 3d April 1788.

I have received your letter of the 13th ulto[1]—My not acknowledging the reception of the printed Vocabulary must have been an omission, for it came safely to hand with the manuscript one.[2]

Your observation respecting the instability & inefficacy of our general Government is very just; they are not only apparent in the instances which you mention, but have, for a long time, strongly marked all our national transactions. This, in my opinion, is a powerful argument for adopting the proposed Constitution, even if it was less perfect than it is, and while a constitutional door is left open for amendments whenever they may be found necessary.

I thank you, my dear Sir, for your information respecting the opposition to the proposed Government in the Country west of the Susquehanna. Notwithstanding the rancour & activity of the opponents in Pensylvania, I trust that they are, generally speaking, persons of too little importance & of too contemptable characters to endanger the general welfare of the Union by extending their influence to other States, or even any further in their own than to a few Counties, or over persons whose characters, dispositions & situations are conformable to their's.

How the important question will be decided in this State is yet uncertain. Opinions are various, & I can say nothing upon the subject from my own knowledge, as I but very rarely ride off my farms, and am wholly indebted to the publick papers & those Gentlemen who visit me for any information which I have; however, from everything that I can collect, I am still confident of its adoption here. I am, Dear Sir, Yr most Obedt Hbe Servt

Go: Washington

LS, in the hand of Tobias Lear, MiDbGr; LB, DLC:GW.

1. Letter not found.

2. For the Indian vocabulary compiled by Butler and sent to GW, see Butler to GW, 30 Nov. 1787, and enclosure and note.

# To Samuel Chamberline

Sir,                                 Mount Vernon April 3d 1788

I have been favored with your letter of the 10 Ulto and feel myself much obliged by the communication of your mode of cropping, which you have been pleased to make to me.[1]

Every improvement in husbandry should be gratefully received and peculiarly fostered in this Country, not only as promoting the interest and lessening the labour of the farmer, but as advancing our respectability in a national point of view; for, in the present State of America, our welfare and prosperity depend upon the cultivation of our lands and turning the produce of them to the best advantage.

The method of treading out wheat with horses is certainly a very execrable one, and nothing but the necessity of getting it out by some me[a]ns or other can justify the practice. Your mode of cropping (with the assistance of the Winlaw Thrasher) claims the preference to every other if only considered as getting the wheat out so expeditiously as to preserve it from the ravages of the fly.[2]

I wrote sometime in January last, to Arthur Young Esquire (Editor of the Annals of Agriculture) requesting him to send over to me one of Winlaw's thrashing machines, if it was found, from the experience which it must have had in England, to possess that merit is ascribed to it in his Annals; I hope to receive it in time to prove it after the next ha[r]vest, and should its operation be as favourable as is represented, I shall conceive the cultivation of wheat to be infinitely more worthy of the farmer's attention in this country than it is at present.[3]

If, in the course of your farming, you should meet with any thing further that is interesting and worthy of attention I shall be much obliged to you for a communication of it. I am Sir Yr Most Obedt Hble Sert

Go. Washington

LB, DLC:GW.

This may be Samuel Chamberlaine (1742–1811) who had large landholdings in Talbot County, Md., and, in 1783, 66 slaves.

1. Letter not found.

2. GW is referring to the Hessian fly.

3. No letter from GW to Arthur Young in January 1788 has been found,

but GW did write to Young on 1 Nov. 1787 asking him to send a Winlaw mill, or thresher, provided that Young was certain of its utility. See also Young to GW, 1 July 1788, and note 4 of that document.

## To Caleb Gibbs

Dear Sir, Mount Vernon April 3d 1788

Your letter of the 24th of Feby and the enclosed news papers came duly to hand. The conduct of New Hampshire has I believe, been a matter of surprize in eve[r]y part of the Country, and from what I can learn, wholly unexpected by a considerable part of the Convention themselves; The adjournment was, however, (circumstanced as they were) a very prudent step, for it appears that the great question would have been lost if the sense of the convention had been taken upon it at that time.

It is still uncertain what the determination of this State will be; the Northern Counties are generally favourable to the adoption of the Constitution, The Southern are said to be unfavourable: and the Sentiments of the western parts of the State are not fully known; no pains, however, has been spared, and no art untried to inflame the minds of the people & prejudice them against the proposed system of Gove[r]nment. I am, Dear Sir, Yr Most Obedt Hble Sert

Go. Washington

LB, DLC:GW.

## From William Gordon

My Dear Sir London Apr. 3. 1788

I had proposed writing by the present opportunity, before I received your letter of Jany the 1st on tuesday last. Return you my most sincere thanks for your good wishes. The second volume will be printed off I expect by the end of the week after next. The first begins with the settlement of the several colonies, & comes down to & takes in the Lexington engagement. The second finishes with the Saratoga convention.[1] The storm is blown over for the present, & the continuance of peace is expected. But whenever war breaks out among the European powers, I hope & pray with you that the United States may have no interference therein, other than as carriers between the belligerent powers. And yet this may lead on to a war, should Britain assume the exercise of the powers which they had long practiced before the armed neutrality. It is a very desirable thing for the Americans to obtain an insertion in all their treaties of this principle that neutral bottoms make neutral goods. Would the different kingdoms of Europe make it a part of the law of nations, though Britain should dissent; that might most probably prevent the latter's being so insolent because of her marine.

I conjecture from what has taken place, that the New Constitution will be established, & most sincerely hope it will promote the general interests of the United States. Strength of government is certainly wanting: but as to the plea that the court of London makes for not entering on a commercial alliance from a deficiency of power in Congress I consider it as deceitful. A disinclination to the business is the main reason; & was I in the councils of America I should advise to send no more an ambassador to London, till this court was disposed to do the like. A consul at Westminster may suffice for a consul at New York.

We are not yet settled, but am going tomorrow to a place in the neighbourhood of where I was first fixed for thirteen years; should all parties suit upon a trial, may probably set down there before summer is over for the remainder of my days.[2]

Mrs Gordon the beginning of last November was seized in the night with a throbbing in her right thumb, which continued, spread, inflamed her hand & near to her shoulder. It was attended with a violent fever. When it pleased God to restore her health, her hand & fingers were crippled by the inflammation so as to be useless. They are come to in measure, so that within this month she has been able to dress & undress herself. We are in hopes that the summer weather will nearly perfect the cure: but are very thankful that she is so much better.

Reports represented the duke of York as a most deserving & temperate person. Since then we are told, that he has lost by gaming most or all of his Yorkshire estate, & that he is frequently intoxicated. His brother the sea captain it is said, made an entertainment at Plymouth & invited the ladies to whom he introduced his black mistress, but they considered it as so coarse a compliment that they withdrew. After that he made another &

invited all the neighbouring negro men & women, who were well pleased with the company of the prince's favorite. We have a hopeful generation of princes. The Americans will not regret their separation from them.[3]

Government are sending troops to the East Indies to take possession of the East India company's territories. In a course of years these will be lost to Great Britain, for they are as far again from the seat of power as America. The means taken to prevent may, as in the other instance, hasten the catastrophe.

Expect the pleasure of having to congratulate your Excellency before the year is out upon being chosen President to the American parliament. I know of no one whom I could wish so heartily to fill that place as yourself. But I do not wish you to have Mr Hancock for your vice-president; there are many I think much better qualified, on one of whom I hope the choice will fall.[4] I feel myself interested in the prosperity of the American States. May they be ever a virtuous free & happy people. I remain my Dear Sir Your Excellency's most obedient & very humble servant

William Gordon

Mrs Gordon unites with me in best wishes for your lady & family. Suffer me to drop a hint in favor of the Post Master General, whose attention to business, when I was in America, made me desirous that whatever revolutions in state government might exist, he might continue in office.[5] Should Cornwallis be the watch word agreed upon, of which I wish to be absolutely certain, be pleased to introduce it in your next.[6]

ALS, DLC:GW.

1. Gordon was overly optimistic: he wrote to GW on 24 Sept. and again on 28 Oct. to explain the delay in the publication of his *History*. It was not until February 1789 that he could report its publication and send a set of the work to GW. See Gordon to GW, 16, 23 Feb. 1789.

2. The Gordons did not at this time go to Ipswich in Suffolk, "where we settled in the early part of life & have many friends" (Gordon to GW, 16 Feb. 1789), but instead they first went for a few months to Ringwood in Hampshire, where one of Mrs. Gordon's brothers lived, and then shortly thereafter to St. Neots, Huntingdonshire, where Gordon became rector of the parish. It was not until 1802 that the two returned to Ipswich. Gordon died there in 1807.

3. Frederick Augustus, duke of York (1763–1827), was the second of George III's nine sons. "His brother the sea captain" was the third son, William Henry, duke of Clarence (1765–1837), who later became King William IV.

4. John Hancock (1737–1793) at this time was governor of Massachusetts

and had just served as president of the state's ratifying convention, though absent for most of it.

5. Postmaster General Ebenezer Hazard (1728–1807), Gordon's friend and himself a historian of parts, did not secure a reappointment from GW after GW became president. See GW's criticism of Hazard in his letter to John Jay, 18 July 1788.

6. Gordon is referring here to the cipher which he had sent GW in 1786 to use in corresponding with him. See Gordon to GW, 16 Feb., 28 Sept. 1786, 24 Sept. 1788, and GW to Gordon, 20 April 1786, 23 Dec. 1788.

## From Thomas Mahony

Honourd Sir                                    Alexandria Aprill 3d 1788

I woud esteem it as a great Favour if you have considered that Affair of my working with your (Honour) I am willing to Engage for the Year at Twenty Six pounds with all other Articles wch was made mention'd of your Honour's Answer I Humbleley waite for.[1]

Thos Mahoney

Copy, DLC:GW.

1. On 1 Aug. 1786 Mahony (Mahoney) first signed Articles of Agreement (printed above) to serve GW at Mount Vernon as a house carpenter and joiner for one year for £30 and keep. Tobias Lear responded to Mahony's letter for GW on 4 April: "The General has received your letter of yesterday and desires me to inform you that he [will] not give you any more than twenty four pounds per year and the making of Clothes Shoes &c. as he mentioned to you here. He thinks this sum is fully equal if not better than the wages which he gave you when you worked for him last year, as every article of produce &c. by which wages should be regulated is much cheaper now then at that time. If you incline to come upon those terms you will inform me by the bearer or come down your self tomorrow or next day" (DLC:GW). Mahony signed articles of agreement on 15 April 1788 (DLC:GW) accepting GW's terms. He continued in GW's employ until 1792 (see Ledger B, 236, 271, and 331).

## To Thomas Smith

Sir,                                    Mount Vernon April 3d 1788

Previous to the reception of your letter of the 11th Inst.[1] Colo. Biddle advised me of his having received from you £192.13.4 on my acct he mentioned £200 having been brought to him by the Gentleman into whose charge you had given it but £7.6.8.

being in bad gold, he did not incline to receive it, and had therefore returned it to the Gentleman by whom it was sent[2]—
I am &c.

Go. Washington

P.S. Since writing the above your letter of the 17th Ulto has come
to hand.[3] Mr Smith of Baltimore transmitted to me the sum of
£75.15.10. which you lodged in his hands, for me in October
last.[4]

LB, DLC:GW.
   1. GW may have meant 11 Mar., but no letter from Smith more recent than
5 Feb., which GW answered on 22 Feb., has been found.
   2. Clement Biddle's letter is dated 5 March.
   3. Letter not found.
   4. This is probably the William Smith, who moved from Pennsylvania to
Baltimore in 1761 to establish a mercantile business. He had served briefly in
the Continental Congress and was a member of the First Congress.

## To Barbé-Marbois

Sir,                                   Mount Vernon April 4th 1788.
   I have regularly received the letter you did me the honor to
write to me on the 30th of November last, accompanied by one
from the Count de la Luzerne,[1] respecting the claim of the M.
de Saqui des Tourets to be admitted a member of the Society of
the Cincinnati.
   I should certainly find myself extremely happy in an opportunity of gratifying the wishes of so meritorious an officer as M.
des Tourets; if I thought myself at liberty to take any part whatever in the premises. Recommended strongly as he is by the
Count de la Luzerne & yourself I cannot have a doubt that he
would be an acquisition & a credit to the institution: nor can I
have a hesitation in believing that his pretensions are as good as
those of some who have found admission into the society. Yet as
I have (amidst the almost innumerable applications that have
been made to me) scrupulously avoided giving any decision and
only referred the documents I had received to the General
Meeting; I flatter myself I shall be considered as having done
every thing that was properly within my sphere, by making a
similar reference in the present instance.

You are sensible, I perceive Sir, that, from the constitution of our Society, it would not have been right in me to have given a positive determination on the question. It would now be less proper than ever for me to take that upon myself. For, having by a circular letter to the several State Societies requested that I might not be re-elected President, on account of my numerous avocations: the last General Meeting was pleased so far to indulge me, as to make it a condition to induce my acceptance, that I should be absolutely excused from all trouble & application incident to the office; and that the whole business should devolve on the Vice-President, General Mifflin. As I shall not be present at the next General Meeting, I will transmit the application of Monsieur des Tourets to General Knox, the Secretary of the General Meeting.[2]

The appointment of the Count de la Luzerne to the office of Minister of Marine & his *consequent removal to Europe*, will, I presume, supersede the necessity or expediency of my addressing him on this subject. Had that not been the case, I should have seized with eagerness the occasion of paying the tribute of my homage to his acknowledged talents & virtues.

I am truly rejoiced to hear of the felicity of Madame de Marbois & yourself: and hope you will still be made more happy *in the growing cement* of the two nations to which you allude. With great regard & esteem, I have the Honor to be, Sir, Yr most Obedt & very Hble Servt

Go: Washington

LS, in the hand of Tobias Lear, Mitchell Library of New South Wales, Sydney, Australia; LB, DLC:GW.

1. La Luzerne's letter was dated 12 Nov. 1787.

2. GW wrote Henry Knox from Mount Vernon on 4 April: "Dear Sir, The enclosed, Mr de Marbois has been informed, will be submitted to the General Meeting of the Society of the Cincinnati—and for that purpose would be transmitted to the Secretary General. With great esteem & regard I am—Dear Sir Yr Obedt Hble Servt Go: Washington" (ALS, DSoCi). The docket on the letter includes the information, signed by George Turner, "Produced in Extra-Gl Meetg May 1788."

## To Clement Biddle

Dear Sir,                                   Mount Vernon April 4th 1788.

The articles which you shipped on my Acct on board of the Charming Polly have arrived safe & in good order.[1]

As I am under the necessity of purchasing, every year, a quantity of coarse Linen, Blanketings &ca for the clothing of my negroes, and sundry other articles for various purposes, and Goods of every kind being sold in Alexandria at a high advance, I am desireous of knowing if I could not supply myself from Philadelphia, or some other place, upon lower terms. I will therefore be much obliged to you if you would inform me of the price of the following articles, as soon as is convenient after you have received this, viz. German & British Oznaburgs of the best quality, suitable for making Negroes shirts & shifts—a kind of Rolls proper for summer Petticoats & Trousers—Dutch Blanketings—Nails from 6d. to 20d.—and good ditching Spades by the dozen or single one.[2]

I will thank you to be so good as to forward the enclosed letters to their respective addresses by the first safe conveyances[3] & am, with great esteem & regard, Dear Sir, Yr most Obedt Hble Servt

                                   Go: Washington

LS, in the hand of Tobias Lear, PHi: Washington-Biddle Correspondence; LB, DLC:GW.

1. See Biddle to GW, 5, 16 March.
2. See Biddle to GW, 21 April, and GW to Biddle, 12 May, and notes.
3. See Biddle to GW, 21 April.

## To Charles Lee

Dear Sir,                                   Mount Vernon April 4th 1788

I am very sorry that I have not yet been able to discharge my acct with the James River Company for the amount of which you presented me with an order.[1]

The almost total loss of my crop last year by the drought which has obliged me to purchace upwards of eight hundred Barrels of Corn, and my other numerous and necessary demands for cash, when I find it impossible to obtain what is due to me, by any means, has caused more perplexity & given me more uneasiness than I ever experienced before from the want of money. In addition to the disappointments which I have met with from those who are indebted to me, I have in my hands a number of indents and other public securities which I have received from time to time as the interest of some Continental loan office certificates &c. which are in my possession; as I am so little conversant in publick securities of every kind as not to know the use or value of them, and hardly the difference of one species from another, I have kept them by me from year to year without having an idea that they would depreciate as they were drawn for interest, and never doubting but they would be received in payment of taxes at any time, till I have found by the Revenue Law of the last Session, that only a particular description of them will pay the taxes of the year 1787[2]—the others pay all arrearages of taxes and I am informed are not worth more than 2/6 in the pound, the injustice of this measure is too obvious and too glaring to pass unobserved; it is taxing the honest man for his punctuality, and rewarding the tardy or dishonest with the sum of 17/6 in every pound which is due from him for taxes.

As you are now in Richmond I take the liberty of enclosing to you (in a letter from Mr Pendleton) a Certificate for a negro executed in the year 1781 Amounting to £69. which I will thank you to negociate for me there upon the best terms you can, and pay the proceeds thereof in behalf of what is due from me to the James River Company—The principal for the negro, and three years interest thereon (which is all that was allowed) amounted to £138. which was divided into two Cirtificates, one receivable in the taxes now due, which I retain, to discharge part of my taxes for the year 1787 and the other you have with this[3] upon what principle of Justice interest is allowed on the above certificates from the 1st of Jany 1785 *only* my ideas are not sufficiently comprehensive to understand and if it should fall in your way to enquire should be glad to know; As also what will or is likely to be the final result of my holding the Certificates which have been given to me for interest of the money I lent to the Public in the day of its distress. I am well apprised that these are negotiable *things* and when a person is *obliged* to part with them, he must, as with other commodities at market, take what they will fetch, but the object of my enquiry, is to know, as above, what the final end of them will be if retained in my chest. Strange indeed it seems—that the Public Offices should take in the original Certificates—Issue new, by a scale of their own—reducing the money as *they* say, to specia value—give warrents for interest accordingly—and then behold! these specia warrents are worth 2/6 in the pound. To commit them to the flames, or suffer this is a matter of indifference to me. there can be no Justice where there is such practices. You will pardon me for dwelling so long upon this subject—It is a matter which does not concern me *alone* but must affect many others—with great esteem and regard—I am &c.

Go. Washington

LB, DLC:GW.

1. See Lee to GW, 23 February.

2. For a description of GW's public certificates and for the amount of the interest due on them, see GW to Anthony Singleton, 1 Mar. 1788, nn.1 and 2. "An act to amend the laws of revenue, to provide for the support of civil government, and the gradual redemption of all debts due by this commonwealth" was passed on 1 Jan. 1788 (12 Hening 412–32).

3. GW's letter to John Pendleton is dated 1 March. For the certificate that GW received in recompense for an executed slave, see GW to David Stuart, 11 Dec. 1787, n.2. For the certificates GW retained, see Charles Lee to GW, 11 April 1788. For GW's payment to the James River Company, see Lee to GW, 17 April, n.2.

## To James Wilson

Dear Sir,                                    Mount Vernon April 4th 1788

You will please to accept of my best thanks for the copy of the debates of your late convention which you have been so polite as to send me—That, together with your favor of the 11 Ulto was handed to me by Mr Madison.[1]

The violent proceedings of the ememies of the proposed constitution in your State are to be regreted as disturbing the peace of society; but in any other point of view they are not to be regarded; for their unimportance effectually precludes any fear of their having an extensive or lasting influence, and their activity holds up to view the general cast & character of them, which need only be seen to be disregarded.

It is impossible to say, with any degree of certainty, what will be the determination of the Convention in this State upon the proposed plan of Government. I have no opportunity of gaining information respecting the matter but what come through the medium of the news papers or from those Gentln who visit me, as I have hardly been ten miles from any farms since my return from Philadelphia. Some Judgement may be formed when the members chosen by the several Counties to serve in Convention, are known, as their sentiments will be decided, and their choice determined, by their Attachments or opposition to the proposed System. A majority of those names I have yet seen are said to be friendly to the Constitution but these are from the Northern parts of the State from whence least opposition was to be expected. It is however certain that there will be a greater weight of abilities opposed to it here than in any other State. I am, Dear Sir—Yr Most Obedt Hbl. Sert

Go. Washington

LB, DLC:GW.

1. Letter not found. *Debates of the Convention of the State of Pennsylvania on the Constitution* was printed in Philadelphia by Thomas Lloyd in February.

*Letter not found*: to Richard Peters, 6 April 1788. On 27 April Peters wrote GW: "I was honoured yesterday with yours of the 6th instant."

# From John Porter

New York

April 9h 1788

May it please your Excellency.

With the advice of many of my military frinds of rank & respectability I am induced to address this on a subject of which I but too sinsibly feel the misfortune—'Tis that of my discharge from the Army, by a Court Martial for going beyond sea without proper leave for that purpose, &c. which will no doubt immediately occur to your mind; I have been mostly in Europe & the West Indies since the conclusion of the war, but on my return to America some time since, I presented a memorial to Congress praying a restoration to my rank, & the Emoluments to which I might have been intitled had my better fortune prevailed, To this I was recommended & assisted by my military friends, both in & out of Congress, The memorial has been attended to, refered, & is now before a very rispectable Committee, As I have not heard any thing particularly discouraging I hope it will meet with a favorable Issue[1]—But to put the matter beyond a doubt, I presume to request of your Excellency, (If consistent with your own feelings and Idea of the matter) some kind of recommendation to the indulgence of Congress on this head. If 'tis only to say there is no objection in your mind to any act Congress in their wisdom & goodness may be induced to pass in my favor therein.

Were it possible for this to be done it would give my memorial every success I could wish, & in some measure relieve me from a misfortune, causing the most embittering circumstance of my life. As the army has been long since disbanded I flatter myself there cannot remain an objection in the mind of any Officer to my succeeding in my wishes—Relying on your well known goodness & benevolence I beg leave to submit my case to your consideration—If any assistance can be given me in my present situation with propriety, it will be laying me under a never to be forgotten Obligation.[2] Wishing every prosperety & happiness to your illustrious House permit me to Subscribe myself with sentiments of the most profound respect & veneration Your Excellency's most Obedient & Very humble Servant

John Porter late Major 6 Massts Battln
Address Coffee House New York.

ALS, DLC:GW.

1. Porter's memorial to Congress is dated 26 Mar. 1787 (DNA:PCC, item 41). The committee of Congress to whom Porter's memorial was referred reported on 10 April: "*Resolved* that Major Porter be Considered as meriting the Approbation of Congress for his long and faithful Services in the Army untill the time of his Absence which Occasioned his dismission, but that the privileges and emoluments granted to those who continued in the Service to the end of the war cannot be Allowed to him" (*JCC*, 32:170). Porter, who came from Bridgewater, Mass., died in Port-au-Prince in 1791.

2. GW replied from Mount Vernon on 30 April: "Sir, I have received your letter of the 9th instant by the Post, and have found myself not a little at a loss to know how to answer it.

"While rivetted to the toils and perplexities inseperable from the Commission of Commander in Chief; I sought not to avoid trouble, I shunned not to enter into the minutest investigation of innumerable disagreeable subjects— for, unfortunately, in our army, they were but to[o] numerous and too troublesome to my repose. But to rip open again the disagreeable subjects that seemed to be forever closed with the war and my retirement, would be an irksome and an endless employment. I could not think of doing it, unless I would first consent to give up all the prospects of tranquility, which, I flattered myself, awaited the last years of a life, that had been devoted almost invariably to the services of others. The sacrifice would be too great—and the expectation unreasonable. All that I can be expected to do in your case is to observe upon the state of it (not from a recurrence to papers which are packed away but according to the best of my recollection) that your absence from the Army apppeared to be rather the effect of an unaccountable indisection [indiscretion] than of a premeditated criminality; and that, altho' precedent and the good of service made your dismission indispensable on account of your having gone beyond Sea without a regular permission, your character in other respects stood unexceptionable: insomuch that considerable interest was made in your behalf by Officers of good reputation.

"Upon this State of facts; although it would be highly improper for me to give any opinion to Congress, yet so far am I from wishing to prejudice an impartial examination into the Justice of your applications, that I cannot have the least objection to their investigating and determining the matter, in whatsoever manner may seem most proper to them. In whatsoever manner the business may result, I cannot ever with propriety say any thing more on the subject. I am, Sir, Your most obedient & Hble Servant Go. Washington" (LB, DLC:GW).

# From James Madison

Dear Sir                                                Orange April 10. 1788

Having seen a part only of the names returned for the Convention, and being unacquainted with the political characters of many of them, I am a very incompetent prophet of the fate of the Constitution. My hopes however are much encouraged by my present conjectures. Those who have more data for their calculations than I have, augur a flattering issue to the deliberations of June. I find that Col: Nicholas, who is among the best judges, thinks on the whole, that a majority in the Convention will be on the list of fœderalists; but very properly takes into view the turn that may be given to the event by the weight of Kentucky if thrown into the wrong scale, and by the proceedings of Maryland and South Carolina, if they should terminate in either a rejection or postponement of the question.[1] The impression on Kentucky, like that on the rest of the State was at first answerable to our wishes: but, as elsewhere, the torch of discord has been thrown in and has found the materials but too inflammable. I have written several letters since my arrival, to correspondents in that district, with a view to counteract anti-federal machinations. I have little expectation however that they will have much effect, unless the communications that may go from Mr Brown in Congress, should happen to breathe the same spirit: and I am not without apprehensions that his mind may have taken an unlucky tincture from the difficulties thrown in the way of the separation of the district, as well as from some antecedent proceedings of Congress.[2] I have taken the liberty of writing also to a friend in South Carolina on the critical importance of a right decision there to a favorable one here.[3] The inclosed letter which I leave unsealed will shew you that I am doing the same with respect to Maryland. Will you be so good as to put a wafer in it and to send it to the post office for George Town, or to change the address to Annapolis, if you should have reason to conclude that Mr Carrol will be there? I have written a similar letter to Docr McHenry.[4] The difference between even a postponement and adoption in Maryland, may in the nice balance of parties here, possibly give a fatal advantage to that which opposes the Constitution.

I have done nothing yet in preparing answers to the queries. As facts are to be ascertained as well as opinions formed, delay will be of course, counted upon.[5] With every sentiment of respect and attachment I remain Dear Sir, your Obedient & humble servt

Js Madison Jr

ALS, DLC:GW; copy, DLC: Madison Papers.

1. See George Nicholas to Madison, 5 April, in Rutland and Hobson, *Madison Papers*, 11:8–10.

2. John Brown (1757–1837) of Augusta County studied at both the College of New Jersey and the College of William and Mary and served as an officer in the Revolution. A lawyer, he moved to Kentucky in 1786 or 1787 and became a leader in the movement to separate the Kentucky district from Virginia. He at this time was a member of Congress from Virginia and a supporter of the Constitution. Brown was elected to the first Congress under the new Constitution, and he was elected to the U.S. Senate when Kentucky was admitted to the Union in 1792.

3. The editors of the *Madison Papers* tentatively identify this as a missing letter to Charles Pinckney (ibid., 21).

4. The editors of the *Madison Papers* were unable to find the letters to Daniel Carroll and James McHenry.

5. See GW to Moustier, 26 Mar., n.2.

# From Richard Ratcliff

Most Renown'd sir                    Aprill 10th 1788

I am Sorry that after Serving in the Capacity of a Publick Servant for Eight years Succesfully, and haveing (I flatter myself) Discharged my Duty therein faithfully, that I Shou'd now at this Period be loaded with Injustice threats &c.—& that for no Other Cause, than haveing Innocently given you, or Some friend an Affront, for Sir with Respect to the Tax Recd for yr Slaves in Fairfax Parish for 1785 As Conceale'd Property I have Accounted for in the most Lawfull & Just manner, by Stateing An Acct giveing Creditt for them Taxes & Double as much more in Simaler Cases Recd for that year, against which I Chargd for the Insolvence's, which I allways was taught to believe was Honest Dealing. & never untill now, Know'd that a Collector was to make good all Insolvence's, & pay for Conceal's, which Acct by me Stated, Remains Among the Clerks Papers free for to be Seen by Any Person, which Fairfax County Court have Inspecte'd, Sir I am Senciable your Anger hath been Rais'd against me, not for any wrong offered or done to you or the Publick, but from false Acusations & misrepresentation &c. I Shou'd be Sorry you or Any other Gentleman Shou'd think, that The Small Tax rec'd from Mr Lund Washington for that Propy which was only £12.0.0 in the Revenue & £13.10 in the Certificate Tax would Induce me to Act Dishonestly for Perhaps I as Little Regard Such a Sum, as most men do who Possess one hundred Times as much as I have, which is but Little—for I dispise proffitt Dishonestly Acquired—Pray Sir Consider the matter in your Own mind (and if I have Stated It Truly to you), I Doubt not you will think as I do—I am Ever Ready & willing to Submit all my Disputes to two Worthy Carectors, (Truth & Justice) Consiouss that I Deserve not those Malishious Reproaches[1]—Sir I have a family among which are Six Children whoe's welfares are Deare to me, on Acct of whoom with myself & wife, you must expect my feelings to be much hurt[2]—I appeale to the County in Generall for my Carector both in a Private & publick Life, and I Defy the man, or Sett of men, to Say with Truth that ever I Indeavour'd in the most distant Degre, to Extortion, rob, or Injure Either individuals or the Publick, Except I did so, in Executig the Lawfull Dutys of my Office—which Perhaps hath been

done with as much Tenderness ⟨*mutilated*⟩ntage to my County
men, as Ever they found Practised ⟨*mutilated*⟩ Previous to myself.
I am far from desireing to ⟨*mutilated*⟩ to you or to mankind.
The Reverse, being always my Choice & Desire, I hope these
things (altho faintly Represented) will Appeare to you in a True
Light, and that they will have Such weight with you as they Deserve, that I am & always was Ready & willing to goe into a full
Investigation of All my Actings & Doings as a Publick Servant
or Otherways, is a Determin'd & fixed Principle in my Breast,
Regardless of Any Injury that Can Arise from my Conduct
(Where Truth & Justice Determine) But if Power Shou'd Rob
me of Justice & Right, I must Submissively Submitt & beare the
great & Grevious Load with as much fortitude as is Posses'd by
your Much Injure'd Obt Humbe Servt

Rd Ratcliff

ALS, DLC:GW.
   Richard Ratcliff (Ratcliffe; d. 1825) was associated with and succeeded his
father-in-law Gerrard Bowling in a mercantile business in Alexandria. In 1799
he donated four acres of his land in Fairfax County to be used for the site of
the courthouse that was completed in 1800 and is still in use. Ratcliff at this
time was a commissioner of the tax in Fairfax County.
   1. It was the legal duty of the tax commissioner to maintain a list of the
property in the county upon which taxes were by law to be levied and collected
by the county sheriff. The act defining the duties of the commissioner also
specified the penalties for taxpayers who concealed from the commissioner
taxable property (12 Hening 243–54). GW wrote David Stuart the year before,
on 12 Feb. 1787, about the sheriff and Ratcliff's attempt to collect his county
taxes.
   2. Ratcliff and his wife Louisiana (Lucian) Bowling Ratcliff eventually had
nine children.

## To Clement Biddle

Dear Sir,                          Mount Vernon 11th Apl 1788
   I have recd your favor of the 31st Ulto enclosing a letter &
some seeds from Mr Peters, and will thank you to send me,
by the first Vessel bound this way, a good Wheat-fan (if there
have been any late improvements on the common sort, which
have been found useful, I shall prefer one with such improvements)—and a steel-plated Whip-saw of the best kind, seven &
an half feet long; if you are not a competent judge yourself of

the quality of the saw, I will thank you to get somebody to chuse one who is, as I wish it to be free from flaws & good in every respect.[1]

You will oblige me by conveying the enclosed letter to Mr Peters by the first good opportunity.[2] I am, Dear Sir, Yr most Obedt Hble Servt

Go: Washington

LS, in the hand of Tobias Lear, PHi: Washington-Biddle Correspondence; LB, DLC:GW.

1. See GW to Biddle, 14 April, and Biddle to GW, 21 April.

2. On 27 April Richard Peters acknowledged GW's letter of 6 April, which has not been found.

# From Charles Lee

Dear Sir                                     Richmond 11th april 1788

I had the honor to receive by post your letter inclosing a certificate for sixty nine pounds a moity of what was due for a slave executed in 1781 and I have endeavoured to negotiate it but I find the terms so disadvantageous to you that I have retained it for your further directions. The value of all the state certificates depends upon the laws of taxation & revenue and as tobacco is receivable in all taxes at a price above the real market price so in the like proportion the securities which may pay taxes are reduced in their value. The offer made for your certificate is in the ratio as 20/ is to 28/ these being supposed as the average cash price and tax price of tobacco, respectively. I do not think that by keeping this certificate another year, more will be got for it because I believe the same system of revenue will be continued, but I have declined parting with it until you were informed of the loss that would follow from so doing. I have examined the law respecting claims for slaves executed: the commencement of interest is not expressly fixed and it seems to be a prevailing principle among the officers of goverment here, to construe all laws most strongly against the claims of individuals and to allow only such as are literally within the laws—Before the act of 1784 there was no interest allowed on claims for slaves executed &c. I suppose it is understood to operate in future only—Though

this be a mistake in the construction of the act, I apprehend it
will not be altered, the practice of the auditor having been so
long fixed; but the justice of demanding interest from the year
1781 when the slave was executed is so strong, that I will state
the case to the Attorney General.[1]

Our Legislature has pursued a system, it may be said ever
since the beginning of the commonwealth, tending to efface
every principle of virtue and honesty from the minds of the
citizens and this is particularly obvious in the laws respecting
delinquent officers and delinquent individuals as to taxes. There
has scarcely been a session of the General Assembly but some
law has been made to favor and relieve (as it is expressed) those
who might have failed to pay what was rightly due to the commonwealth. By this sort of conduct an opinion now generally
prevails among the delinquents that they will never be compelled to pay and though the act of the last assembly has most
unjustly enabled such persons to pay up the arrearages in de-
pretiated securities yet it is not expected that any considerable
part of the arrearages will even yet be paid.[2]

What the result will be, of retaining your public securities, is
a thing of great uncertainty upon which opinions are very different: Unless there be a quiet and peaceable transition from the
present american government, into another more powerful and
independent of the people, the public debts and even private
debts will in my opinion be extinguished by acts of the several
Legislatures of the several states. The temper of the people in
general, their habits, their interests all combine in producing
such an event, and against these, natural justice will make but a
feint opposition. If the proposed constitution be agreed to, and
the administration be mild, just and wise, if it be so conducted
as to engage the affections of the people, the public securities
will appretiate and in a few years perhaps, be of considerable
value.

Upon the accession of this commonwealth to the constitution,
the happiness of America seems to me to depend & it is distressing to find upon the best information yet had respecting
the sentiments of the conventioners that this remains very uncertain. Exclusive of Kentucky, I beleive there is a majority of
ten or twelve in favor of taking it as it is; except a few characters,

the members of most knowledge and abilities and personal influence are also in favor of the constitution: It seems too to be gaining ground among the people in this part of the country from which last circumstances I have strong hopes that it will be agreed to by our convention. Kentucky is said to be divided but their representatives are as yet unknown here. Governor Randolph is Very busy with those who declare themselves undetermined, and as his mind does not seem to be yet fixed, I cannot tell how his influence will operate. I am told he has declared if nine states accept it, that he will vote for its adoption. With every sentiment of esteem and respect I have the honor to remain sir your most obedient humble servant.

Charles Lee

ALS, DLC:GW.
    1. See GW to Lee, 4 April, and note 3 of that document.
    2. For "the act of the last assembly," see GW to Charles Lee, 4 April, n.2.

## To Clement Biddle

Dear Sir,                       Mount Vernon April 14th 1788
    Your favor of the 3d inst. and the news-papers accompanying it came to hand by the last mail.

    In my letter to you of the 11th inst. I requested you to procure a wheat fan for me, but since that time I have found one more than I then knew of[,] which compleated the number of my several farms and supersedes the necessity of your sending the one which I wrote for, provided this letter reaches you in time to prevent your procuring it.

    I will thank you to inform me of the price of good Shad and Herring per Barrel and if a quantity of them would meet with a ready sale in Philadelphia. With great esteem and regard I am dear Sir, Yr Most Obedt Hble Sert

Go. Washington

LB, DLC:GW.

# From Benjamin Rush

Philadelphia April 14th 1788.

Dr Rush presents his most respectful compliments to General Washington, and has the pleasure of sending him herewith a print of the celebrated Mr Napier, which was committed to the Doctors care, for the General, from the Right Honble the Earl of Buchan of Scotland.[1]

AL, DLC:GW.

1. The response from Mount Vernon, dated 28 April, was: "General Washington presents his best compliments and thanks to Doctor Rush, for the polite attention manifested in forwarding the elegant engraving from the Right Hble the Earl of Buchan. The General takes the liberty of requesting that the Doctor (whenever an occasion may happen) will have the goodness to make his most grateful acknowledgments to that patriotic Nobleman, for so flattering a token of his esteem and friendship" (LB, DLC:GW). The eccentric and very wealthy David Steuart Erskine, eleventh earl of Buchan (1742–1829), of Dryburgh in Scotland, was a political and agricultural reformer, a zealous antiquarian and historian, a prolific writer, and an avid courter of men of distinction. In 1787 he and Walter Minto published their study of Francis Scott, fifth Lord Napier of Merchiston (d. 1773), the engraving of whom he sent to GW.

# From Samuel Griffin

Dr Sir                                    WmsBurg 15th of April 1788

I had the Honor of recieveing your polite favor of the 20th of February, in regular time by the Mail. and on the 26th of March had the pleasure of laying it before a Convocation of the Vissitors, they thought themselves much honord, by the freindly Manner in which you were pleased to Mention that Body, and desired me to make their sincere Acknowledgements to you in behalf of the Convocation, and as the difficulties which you are apprehensive of, can never exist, they earnestly hope that you will do them the favor to accept of the Chancellorship.

I have inclosed Sir a part of the Statute, that points out the duties of the Chancellor[1]—the Bishop of London was the last Chancellor, neither an Oath, or Personal attendance is Necessary. the Chancellor is Considered as the Mecænas or Patron, of the University, to promote its Interests when he may have it in his power, either by his Influence in the Legislator, or with any public Bodies who may have it in their power to lend their aid to the College, the Bishop of London, formerly engaged and sent over the Professors, and all applications, either to King, or parliment, were made through him, but that part of the duty is of course done away.

I hope Sir, that a severe illness which has confined me from the last day of the seting of the Convocation will plead my excuse for not writeing you sooner. permit me Sir to present you with most sincere thanks, for your freindly expressions towards me, and to assure you that I am with the greatest respect esteem & regard Dr Sir Your sincere friend & Humble Sert

Saml Griffin

ALS, DLC:GW.

1. The enclosure reads: "Duties of the Chancellor. The Chancellor is to be the Mecænas [Maecenas] or Patron of the College, such a one as by his favor with the King, and by his Interest with all other persons in E[n]gland, may be enabled to help on all the College affairs. his advice is to be taken, especially in all such arduous and Momentous affairs, as the College shall have to do in England. if the College has any petitions at any time to the King, let them be presented by their Chancellor. If the College wants a new President, or Professor, or Master, let the College Senate rely chiefly on his assistance, advice, and Recommendation. very little of this will be necessary" (DLC:GW).

# From Daniel of St. Thomas Jenifer

My dear Sir                               Annapolis Apl 15. 1788

It affords me great pleasure to have it in my power to inform you that our Elections are now over, & in general in favor of the New Constitution. But three Counties in the State have chosen Members Antifederal to wit Ann Arundel Baltimore & Harford & the Elections of these three will be controverted as to these Members to wit Mr Saml Chase for Ann Arundel on Account of being a Non resident. the same objection to Mr Paca & Luther Martin in Harford. Baltimore a Double return 4 for & 4 against the Constitution—Tho' I am opinion when the ultimate decision happens that Mr Paca will vote for the proposed plan as it stands—& recommend amendments—rather than risque a new Convention.[1] With my respectful Compliments to your

Lady and Family I am as much as I can be Dear Sir Your most
Affectionate & obedt Servt

Dan. of St Thos Jenifer

ALS, DLC:GW.

1. At the Maryland Ratifying Convention, William Paca pressed for amendments to the proposed constitution, but when faced with the vote to accept or reject it, he voted to ratify. GW responded to Jenifer from Mount Vernon on 27 April: "Dear Sir, Accept my thanks for the obliging information contained in your letter of the 15th inst. The great, the important question must ere this, have received its first features in, if not the fi[n]al of your Convention. If they are decisive and favourable, it will most assuredly raise the edifice. Seven affermatives without a negative carries weight with them, that would almost convert the unerring Sister and yet, but in place of what I was going to add, I will say that, I am Dear Sir &c. Go. Washington" (LB, DLC:GW). The copyist clearly botched the job of copying this letter worse than usual.

# From L'Enfant

Sir                                      new york april the 15 1788
   Having already taken the liberty of troubling your Excellency
with the particular of my circumstances owing to the Cincinnati
affaire[1]—and finding that thier resolutions of the last general
meeting in consequences of my application on this subject has
been of no relief to me it is become incumbent on me that I
should once more sollicite your Excellency patronage on the occasion therefore I take the liberty to inclose here in an adresse
to the Honable the general assembly of the society which I am
inform is to be held in philadelphie in may next & I beg you will
Sir do me the favour of laying it before them. your Excellency
will see by its content that I have only received 229 dollrs as part
of the money which they have voted in my favor in may 1787.
also that I have not been reimbursed of any part of the tow other
sums the payment of which had been recommanded to the Road
Island and So. carolina societies and consequently that I have
been forced to go from my words which I had engaged under
the assurances, that had been given me, of reciving some money
in September last. which circumstances deprived me of the facility which I hoped I should otherwaise have obtained and more
over so much roused those people whom had trusted my words

that they are now determine to procsecut me without mercy.

on an other part Marquis de lafayette to whom I sent at the time a copy of the last resolutions of the Cincinnati respecting to this affaire and on whose support I much depended to make those people easy—appear to have himself misunderstood the matter and belive that the money voted for has been paid to me at the time appointed which mistake as I am informe by some of my frind in paris has made him Exclaim much against me for not having sent that money to the people to whom it belong —and your Excellency will doubtless be sorry to ear that the marquis himself positively opposed my interest in france on that account, a circumstance which made me fel in an attempt I had lately made to obtain from the Court some favour that had been promised me long befor and on which I now depended consid-iring the good disposition of severals of the present ministry to-ward me. not only this Sir but I am at this instant summoned to discharge the whole of the capital own on my former engage-ments and also the interest there on for three year a circum-stance most chagrining considering that the sum of the interest was not considered at the last general meeting of the society and that it is to be feared will not be easely obtained at present When Every thing demonstrate the backwardness with which the sev-eral society complay with the last requisition for the money voted in may 1787. indeed should they refuse to Exerte them-selves on this new occasion and on the other saide should the people persist in demanding both the principal with the interest of thier money I must be utterly ruined.

your Excellency well known how little Sparfull I have been of my personal means trought all the transaction of the Cincinnati affaire and what has been my wish to conceal the causes of my Embarassment—but for ietherto I could depend upon the gen-erous assistance of a parant whose frindship for me supply'd all my want but unfortunatly and in this juncture of affairs I am deprived of the best of father and With him I may say of all most all my fortune because the largest portion of his incom he derived it from the King favor and consequently I can have no raite to it after his death.[2]

from this your Excellency may easely conceive what my Em-barasment must be, and you will no doubt also perceive the ne-cessity there is that the cincinnati endeavour at this next meeting to paid me the 3014 dollor which they had voted in may last and also that they will take charge of the 886 dollor more own by the Road Island and So. carolina society which will bring the principal they shall have to pay to 3671 dollors deduction being made of the 229 doll. already paid as is said above.

as with what relate to the interest money should the society, be out of power to facilitat on the payement thereof I should wish they would then enter into some resolution such as may serve me to obtain from the people concerned the termes which I may propose them.[3] I beg your Excellency will excuse the liberty I take and I am With great respect Sir your Excellency Most obeident and humble Servant

P. ch. L'Enfant

ALS, DSoCi.

1. L'Enfant wrote GW on 6 Dec. 1786 enclosing a long memorial regarding the Cincinnati medals that he had secured in France and for which he had not been paid. See Thomas Jefferson to GW, 7 Jan. 1786, n.1.

2. L'Enfant's father, Pierre L'Enfant, was an artist, a painter who had been in the employ of the king of France.

3. GW wrote L'Enfant from Mount Vernon on 28 April: "Sir, I have been duly favoured with your letter of the 15 Instt, enclosing a Memorial to the General Meeting of the Cincinnati; and, agreeably to your request, shall transmit the Enclosure to the Secretary, to be laid before the meeting.

"As your embarrassments have been a source of long & severe inquietude, I should be truly happy in knowing that they were removed. But, as it was the express condition of my accepting the Presidency of the Society, 'that I should be exempted from all applications & cares respecting it': I trust when this stipulation shall be generally known that all addresses will be made to the Vice-President or Secretary.

"While I sincerely condole with you on the loss of your good father; you will permit me to remind you, as an inexhaustible subject of consolation, that there is a good Providence which will not fail to take care of his Children: and be assured, Sir, it will always give me real satisfaction to find that prosperity & felicity have been attendant on all your steps. With sentiments of great esteem and regard I am—Sir Yr Most Obedt Hble Servt Go: Washington" (ALS, OFH). On the same day GW wrote Henry Knox: "My dear Sir Enclosed is a letter and Memorial from Major L'Enfent which he is informed shall be transmitted to you, to be laid before the General Meeting of the Society of the Cincinnati, about to be held in Philadelphia. With sentiments of great esteem and friendship I am Yr Affecte Servt G: Washington" (ALS, DSoCi; LB, DLC:GW).

# From Hector St. John Crèvecoeur

Sir                                    New York 17 April 1788

I have this moment receiv'd a Letter by the French Packet just come into this Port—inclosed in one of our Ministers dispatches addressed to you, which he has most particularly requested I shou'd forward to you, not knowing when the Post sets out, I thought it most prudent to inclose it in this, & put the whole into the hands of the Presidt of Congress, I hope it will reach your Excellency's hands speedily & safely.[1]

I embrace with great pleasure this opportunity of offering your Excellency the unfeign'd testimonies of the Veneration & Respect with which I have the Honor to be Your Excellency's Most obedient & most humble Servant

St John

LS, DLC:GW.
1. Cyrus Griffin of Lancaster County in Virginia was president of Congress. The letter has not been identified.

# From Charles Lee

Dear Sir                          Richmond 17th april 1788

Since writing my last I have exchanged your warrant for £69 payable in the aggregate fund for warrants payable in the present taxes as well as the arrears and this being done upon equal terms is an advantage to you.[1] If you choose to apply these to the payment of your taxes for the year 1787, in case there remain any such taxes to be paid by you, I will retain them till an opportunity shall offer of returning them.[2]

I take the liberty of mentioning to you, that a few days ago Mr Robert Renick sheriff of Green Brier was in the Clerks office and in his conversation to Mr Brown observed that your lands in that county were to be advertised for sale in june for the arrears of taxes for 1785, 1786 and 1787. Mr Brown referred him to Mr John Hopkins who has requested me to make the matter known to you and has furnished me with the inclosed state of the taxes demanded. The sheriff has said that he should decline advertising, till he had an opportunity of knowing from Mr

Hopkins what steps you intend to take respecting payment and that he should be here at the June court. The easiest mode of paying this years taxes is in tobacco at the state-price and Mr Hopkins desires me to mention him to you as at all times ready to execute your commands in this or any other matter.[3] With every sentiment of respect and esteem I have the honor to remain your most obed. sert

Charles Lee

ALS, DLC:GW.

1. See Lee to GW, 11 April.

2. GW wrote Lee on 27 April and at first suggested that the £69 in warrants be applied to what he owed the James River Company. On 14 May Lee wrote that the warrants were not "receivable in discharge of the claims of the James River Company." In his account with the company GW records paying £65 on 21 June 1788 (Ledger B, 354).

3. John Brown was the clerk of the Virginia General Court, and John Hopkins was commissioner of the Continental Loan for Virginia. For GW's taxes, see GW to Lee, GW to Hopkins, both 27 April, and notes.

*Letter not found*: from John Vaughan, 17 April 1788. On 27 April GW wrote Vaughan: "I have received your two letters of the 17th and 21st Inst."

## From Peterson & Taylor

Honoured Sir                           Alexandria Apl 18th 1788

We have the pleasure to inform you that by Capt. Levingston you will receive the Bill of Scantlin compleat together with 2300 feet of 1¼ In. Plank as well 1300 feet of 1 In. D[itt]o all of which we flatter ourselves will meet your approbation as theire hath been nothing lacking on our part to have it procured in the best mannor theire will be still wanting some 2 In. Plank which shall be forwarded immediately the Vesel not being large enoug to bring the Quantity at once the 1¼ is well seasoned but Quartered, broader could not be had seasoned.[1] Theirefore we hope this will answer your purpose as well you will please to direct the Scipper whare to discharge that he may not be detaind longer than necessary.[2] permit us to Subscribe Your very Hume St

Peterson & Taylor

LS, DLC:GW.

1. For GW's purchase of scantling and plank for his new barn from the Alexandria firm Peterson & Taylor, see GW to Peterson & Taylor, 5 Jan., and notes. GW's diary for 30 April includes the entry: "Drawing, with the Plantation Carts, & Waggon, the Scantling from the landing to the New barn" (*Diaries*, 5:313).

2. GW complained to Peterson & Taylor when writing from Mount Vernon on 10 May: "Gentn Enclosed is a Bill of the Scantling which you sent me according to the measurement of it. There is a deficiency of 21 pieces, as you will see by the bill annexed which is a copy of the one sent to you last winter; you will see the dimensions of the deficient pieces by comparing the two bills— There are 15 pieces among those sent which are not conformable to any mentioned in the original bill, and of course are useless to me, unless 7 of them, which are 12 ft long—6 by 4, should be included with the studs 10 ft long 6 by 4, of which you will observe there is a deficiency of 19—I would wish to be informed whether you could supply those pieces which are wanting immediately because if you cannot I must get them myself.

"Should you have any doubts respecting the proper measurment of the Scantling they can easily be removed (and it is my wish that th[e]y may) by being measured by yourselves or by a person of your own appointing as the pieces are now stocked and can be run over in a few hours. I am Gentlemen &c. Go. Washington" (LB, DLC:GW).

Peterson & Taylor responded on 2 June: "your Letter of the 10th May mentiones a deficiency of 21 peices of Scantling not delivd agreable to your Bill, we are at a Loss to Know by whome the Neglect, or deficiency may be with wheather the Skipper or those that got the Scantling, as we was very particular in our Instructions to have it got in a particular manner, and have, accounted for the same agreable to the Bill sent. however, as yours of 10th May have not been parused by us untill the 30 following, we expect you have supplyed said 21 peices else where, and most Likely the peices you mention received and not sent for may answer some part of the Building, and yours, Inclosed, respecting the measurement we have not the Least doubt of, and Submitt thereto, you will therefore in complyance to the agrement Receive by the Bearer Capt. Fountan 10 M. feet of good, Inch plank and seasoned we might have sent the plank Sooner but, your former, advised that you was not in haste, p[r]ovided they ware good & seasoned which we have no doubt, but thay will meet your approbation. . . .

"P.S. if you should want any more than 10 M. the Bearer will supply them" (DLC:GW).

George Augustine Washington acknowledged from Mount Vernon on 5 June the letter of Peterson & Taylor of 2 June: "Gentlemen I am unable to reply to Your Letter of the 2d Inst. as the General is absent and have not the agreement respecting the plank and scantling—the ten thousand feet has been recd. ⟨W⟩hen the General returns the plank will be ⟨exam⟩ined and You shall recieve an ans⟨wer⟩ to your Letter" (DLC:GW). See also Peterson & Taylor to GW, 14 July.

# From John Jay

Dear Sir                                          New York 20 Ap. 1788

Your favor of the 3d Ult. gave me great Pleasure, and I thank you for the friendly offers contained in it.[1] Some Gentlemen here and in Jersey have it in Contemplation to form a Society to promote the Breeding of good Horses and mules—in that Case we will endeavour to introduce some Jennies, of which we have none at present, and send them to your Jack.

The Constitution still continues to cause great party Zeal and Ferment, and the opposition is yet so formidable that the Issue appears problematical. I inclose the latest publication of any Consequence that we have on the Subject.[2] Adieu my dear Sir— I am with the greatest Respect and Esteem your affectionate & hble Servt

John Jay

ALS, DLC:GW; ADfS, NNC; ADf, NNC. The drafts are dated 12 April 1788.

1. Jay's draft contains at this point the following lines which he deleted from the final letter: "As yet we have no four footed Asses in this State, and I sincerely wish we could exchange some of the other Sort for them—we might then obtain a much more valuable Race of Mules than those we now have."

2. The pamphlet, *An Address to the People of the State of New York*, signed A Citizen of New York and written by John Jay, was published in New York in April.

# To Thomas Johnson

Dear Sir,                                   Mount Vernon April 20th 1788.

As well from report, as from the ideas expressed in your letter to me in December last, I am led to conclude that you are disposed (circumstanced as our public affairs are at present) to ratify the Constitution which has been submitted by the general Convention to the People;[1] and under this impression, I take the liberty of expressing a *single* sentiment on the occasion.

It is, that an adjournment, (if attempted), of your Convention, to a later period than the decision of the question in this State, will be tantamount to the rejection of the Constitution. I have good ground for this opinion—and am told it is *the blow* which the leading characters of the opposition in the two States have ⟨meditated⟩[2] if it shall be found that a direct attack is not likely

to succeed in yours. If this be true, it cannot be too much depre-
cated, & guarded against.[3]

The postponement in New-Hampshire, altho' made without
any reference to the Convention of this State, & altogether from
the local circumstances of its own; is ascribed by the opposition
*here* to complaisance towards Virginia; and great use is made of
it. An event similar to this in Maryland, would have the worst
tendency imaginable, for indecision there, wd have considerable
influence upon South Carolina, the only other State which is
to precede Virginia, and submits the question almost wholly to
the determination of the latter. The *pride* of the State is already
touched upon this string, & it will be strained much higher if
there is an opening for it.

The sentiments of Kentucky are not yet known here. Independent of these, the parties with us, from the known, or presumed opinions of the members, are pretty equally balanced.
The one in favor of the Constitution preponderates at present—
but a small matter cast into the opposite scale may make it the
heaviest.

If in suggesting this matter, I have exceeded the proper limit,
my motive must excuse me. I have but one public wish remaining—It is, that in *peace* and *retirement*, I may see this Country rescued from the danger which is pending, & rise into respectability maugre the Intrigues of its public & private enemies.
With very great esteem & regard I am, Dear Sir Yr Most Obedt
Hble Servt

Go: Washington

ALS, MdFre; LB, DLC:GW.

1. Johnson's letter is dated 11 Dec. 1787.

2. The manuscript is mutilated; "meditated" is taken from the letter-book
copy.

3. GW may have been taking his cue from James Madison. See Madison to
GW, 10 April; see also James McHenry to GW, this date, and GW to McHenry,
27 April. For the false accusation that Johnson took this letter to be an unwelcome intrusion in Maryland's deliberations, see GW to Johnson, 31 Aug. 1788,
and note 2 of that document.

## From James McHenry

My dear General.                    Baltimore 20 April 1788

Your election for members of convention being over must have furnished data by which to form an opinion of the probable fate of the constitution in your State. I wish you to favor me with a line on this subject, and whether you think an adjournment of our convention would operate with yours against its adoption. Our opposition intend to push for an adjournment under the pretext of a conference with yours respecting amendments. As I look upon such a step to amount to a rejection in both States I shall do every thing in my power to prevent it. Your sentiments may be useful. You will be kind enough therefore if you have leisure, to write to me at Annapolis whither I shall go in the morning.[1] Present appearances are flattering; but we should be provided with the means of guarding against any change. Yours truly and sincerely

James McHenry

ALS, DLC:GW.
1. See GW's letter to Thomas Johnson of this date. See also GW's response to McHenry, 27 April.

## From Clement Biddle

Philade[lphia] April 21st 1788

I have your favours of 4th & 11th Inst. before me unanswered—The Letter for Mr Smith I forwarded by a safe Conveyance to Carlisle—Genl Butler having just arrived in Town from New York I delivered that for him myself—the one for Mr Peters under Cover of the 11th I sent to him in the Country —No vessel having yet sailed for Port au Prince I have the Letter for Mr De Marbois but it will go some Day this Week by a Schooner Bound directly there.

About a Week ago Mr Peters sent me Word that he could not get a Workman to make the Harrow (which I was in hopes had been ready) and desired me to send him a Workman to make it—I wrote to him that if he would be so obliging to inform me when he next came to Town (which he frequently does) that I would Wait on him with a Workman to take his directions for making it. A Sloop Capt. Reed had set up for Alexandria & was to have sailed last Week but freight Offering slowly & Capt. Ellwood arriving he has delivered what freight he had over to Capt. Ellwood who is near full & will sail about Wednesday by whom shall send the small Box of Roots the livery Lace wheat fan and Whip saw.

German & British Oznabrigs Rolls & Blankets are scarcer than when you were here owing to our spring Vessels not having arrived (except one on Saturday Eveng from London) but as severral Vessels are expected I will examine for those kinds of Goods & give you the prices of them in a short time.[1] The Importation of Nails is nearly at an End, that Article being manufactured here of Better quality than the English in very large quantities & Can be shipped to Virginia without paying Duty there the prices are set down at book—Ditching spades are also made here which are reckoned better than the Imported but I have not time to get the prices for this post

C. Biddle

ADfS, ViMtV: Clement Biddle Letter Book.

1. Biddle made these notes on 4 May for the letter to GW that GW acknowledged on 12 May:

"A ⟨*illegible*⟩ of Goods ℔ Ellwood & sending bills loading & Certificate &c. &c.

"Price of Herring 18/9—Shad 30/ to 32/6 & plenty.

"Oznabrigs & coarse Linens scarce as when he was here—none cheaper—no blankets—Dry Goods not plenty.

"The Acct of Goods ℔ Ellwood is Entered" (ViMtV: Clement Biddle Letter Book).

## From Samuel Holden Parsons

Sir                                    Carlisle [Pa.] 21st Apl 1788.

I am now on my Road to the Settlements forming on the River Ohio; and take this only Method in my power to take leave of your Excellency & to assure you of my most cordial Wishes for your Happiness; should any Occurrances render my Services in that Country of Use to you, I shall never be more happy than in devoting myself to the execution of your Wishes—The State of our Country must give very sensible trouble to every good

Citizen & to none more than to your Excellency who has acted so conspicuous a part in effecting our Independance—in the eastern States I think Opposition to the fœderal Government is nearly ended; we have our Eyes now turnd to Virginia, if there is Wisdom to adopt the propos'd plan in that State; I think we may hope to restore to our nation the Honor their folly has lost them; I view the Adoption of the present plan with all its Imperfections as the only Means of preserving the Union of the States & securing the Happiness of all the parts of this extensive Country; I feel myself deeply interested in this Subject as it will affect the Country of which I am now commencing an Inhabitant. I am sure it must ever be our Interest to continue connected with the Atlantic States, to them we must look up for protection, and from them we can receive such Supplies as we want with more facility than from our other Neighbours; but without an efficient Government we can expect no Benefits of a Connection and I fear it will lead Us to improper Measures— the Navigation of the Potomac is very interesting to our Settlement, if it is perfected according to the proposd Scheme, we Shall Save a land transportation of five Hundred Miles, the Rout we at present Pursue, our new Settlement progresses rapidly⟨;⟩ Two Hundred Families will be within our City by July & I think we are sure of a thousand families from New England within One Year if we remain in peace.[1] I am with every Sentiment of Esteem & Respect Your Excellencys Obedt Servt

Saml H. Parsons

ALS, DLC:GW. GW docketed the letter: "recd the 30th June."

Samuel Holden Parsons (1737–1789), a graduate of Harvard and trained as a lawyer, was a major general in the Continental army during the Revolutionary War. In 1787 he became one of the three directors of the Ohio Company and the first judge of the Northwest Territory.

1. Parsons is referring to the settlement at Marietta, Ohio. See Benjamin Tupper to GW, 26 Oct. 1785, n.1.

*Letter not found*: from John Vaughan, 21 April 1788. On 27 April Vaughan wrote GW: "I have received your two letters of the 17th and 21st Inst."

# From Victor Marie Du Pont

Sir                                    New York April's 22, 1788.
    I have the honor of forwarding your Excellency a letter which I received at Paris from the Marquis de la Fayette few days before I left that city, and which I had intended to have delivered myself. But fearing least it might contain some matters of importance, I have applied to Général Knox who has promised to inclose it in his own.[1]
    I am very sorry that circumstances should have prevented me to be presently Bearer of it and from embracing at the same time that opportunity of offering your Excellency that testimony of vénération and respect which your elevated character and justly deserved fame has filled me with,[2] and where with I have the honor of suscribing myself Your Excellency's Most obedient and very humble servant

                                                  V. du Pont

ALS, DLC:GW; copy, in Du Pont's hand, DeGE. The copy is dated 20 April.
    Victor Marie Du Pont (1767–1827) had come to the United States to become an attaché of the French legation in New York. He was the older brother of Eleuthère Irénée Du Pont (1771–1834).
    1. Du Pont visited Mount Vernon from 2 to 6 Nov. with Moustier, Madame Bréhan, and her son (*Diaries*, 5:417). In his response to Du Pont (see note 2), GW indicates that Lafayette's letter introduced Du Pont, but no such letter has been found.
    2. GW responded from Mount Vernon on 12 May: "Sir, I have lately had the honor of receiving your polite letter of the 22d of April, enclosing one from the Marquis de la Fayette, which would have given me double pleasure to have received from your own hands by informing me of the welfare of that much esteemed character, and giving me an opportunity of paying a proper attention to a person recommended by him; this pleasure, however, I flatter myself I shall yet receive by your visiting Mount Vernon.
    "You will please, Sir, to accept of my best wishes that your tour to this Country may be perfectly pleasing, & conformable to your expectations, and that you may return to your native land with impressions favourable to America and its Citizens. I have the honor to be, Sir, Yr most Obedt Hbe Servt Go: Washington" (LS, in Tobias Lear's hand, DeGE; LB, DLC:GW).

# From Charles Pettit

Sir                                    Philadelphia 22d April 1788

An Accident happening to one of the Boats prevented part of the Iron Castings ordered by your Excellency from coming round before the Winter set in, and the long continuance of the Frost with other Circumstances have delayed them since till within a few Days.[1] Col. Biddle having been so obliging as to undertake the forwarding of them, they were delivered yesterday & put on board a Vessel bound to Alexandria.[2] One of the Plates being somewhat thicker & heavier than I expected, owing to a Misconception of the Workman in construing the Orders given him, the whole are charged 2/6 ₱Ct less than they otherwise would have been. I should have directed another to be made in lieu of this large one if I had discovered it in Time, but the Furnace is now out of blast, & I hope this extra Thickness will be no Disadvantage. I have the Honor to be very respectfully Sir, your most obedient Servant

                                                       Chas Pettit

ALS, DLC:GW.

1. For GW's order of firebacks for his fireplaces at Mount Vernon and reference to his correspondence with Pettit about these, see GW to Pettit, 7 Sept. 1787, and note 1 of that document.

2. See Clement Biddle to GW, 21 April, n.1.

*Letter not found*: from Jeremiah Wadsworth, 22 April 1788. On 18 May GW wrote Wadsworth: "Your favor of the 22d Ulto . . . arrived safe."

# From John Jay

Dear Sir                                New York 24 April 1788

It occurs to me that you would probably be glad to know when and in what manner the Letters you sent to me to be forwarded were sent on.

The large Packet for the Marqs de la Fayette was committed to the Care of the french minister, who was so obliging as to take Charge of it.

Those for Count de Rochambeau, Countess d'Essarts, Gen: Duplessis, Mesdames Van Winter Van Merken &c: Monsr de Bourden, Mr James McIntosh, and Monsr Roussilles were sent under Cover to Mr Jefferson, by the french Packet No. 1 commanded by Monsr de Sionville—she sailed 21 Feby.

Those for Mrs Macauly Graham, Revd Dr Gordon, Wakelin Welsh Esqr. and Saml athawes Esqr. were sent by the Grantham Packet Capt. Richard George, who also sailed the 21 Feby.[1]

The Letter for Sr Edw. Newenham[2] was sent by Mr Thomas Randall of this City to his Correspondent in Newry,[3] by the Brig Brownlow Capt. McMacken—she sailed the same Time. I am Dr Sir with the greatest Respect and Esteem your affte & hble Servt

John Jay

ALS, DLC:GW.

1. Letters to all of these people, dated in January, have been printed above, except that to Catharine Macaulay Graham, which has not been found.

2. GW wrote to Edward Newenham on 24 February.

3. Thomas Randall (died c.1797) was a prominent New York merchant and a former privateer. He later was coxswain of the ceremonial barge that carried GW to New York for his inauguration as president. Newry is in county Down, Northern Ireland.

## To John Armstrong

Dear Sir,                                    Mount Vernon April 25. 1788

From some cause or other which I do not know your favor of the 20th of February did not reach me till very lately. This must apologize for its not being sooner acknowledged. Altho Colo. Blain forgot to call upon me for a letter before he left Philadelphia, yet I wrote a few lines to you previous to my departu[r]e from that place; whether they ever got to your hands or not you best know.[1]

I well remember the observation you made in your letter to me of last year, "that my domestic retirement must suffer an interruption."[2] This took place, notwithstanding it was utterly repugnant to my feelings, my interest and my wishes; I sacrificed every private consideration and personal enjoyment to the earnest and pressing solicitations of those who saw and knew the alarming situation of our public concerns, and had no other end in view but to promote the interest of their Country; and conceiving that under those circumstances, and at so critical a moment, an absolute refusal to act, might, on my part, be construed

as a total dereliction of my Country, if imputed to no worse motives. Altho' you say the same motives induce you to think that
another tour of duty of this kind will fall to my lot, I cannot but
hope that you will be disappointed, for I am so wedded to a
state of retirement; and find the occupations of a rural life so
congenial; with my feelings, that to be drawn unto public at the
advanced age, would be a sacrifice that could admit of no compensation.

Your remarks on the impressions which will be made on the
manners and sentiments of the people by the example of those
who are first called to act under the proposed Government are
very Just; and I have no doubt but (if the proposed Constitution
obtains) those persons who are chosen to administer it will have
wisdom enough to discern the influence which their examples
as rulers and legislators may have on the body of the people,
and will have virtue enough to pursue that line of conduct which
will most conduce to the happiness of their Country; and as the
first transactions of a nation, like those of an individual upon his
enterance into life, make the deepest impression and are to form
the leading traits in its character, they will undoubtedly pursue
those measures which will best tend to the restoration of public
and private faith and of consequence promote our national respectibility and individual welfare.

That the proposed Constitution will admit of amendments
is acknowledged by its warmest advocates but to make such
amendments as may be proposed by the several States the condition of its adoption would, in my opinion amount to a compleat
rejection of it; for upon examination of the objections which are
made by the opponents in different States and the amendments
which have been proposed, it will be found that what would be
a favourite object with one State is the very thing which is stren-
ously opposed by another; the truth is, men are too apt to be
swayed by local prejudices, and those who are so fond of amendments which have the particular interest of their own State in
view cannot extend their ideas to the general welfare of the
Union—they do not consider that for every sacrifice which they
make they receive an ample compensation by the sacrifices
which are made by other States for their benefit—and that those
very things which they give up will operate to their advantage
through the medium of the general interest. In addition to these

considerations it should be remembered that a constitutional door is open for such amendments as shall be thought necessary by nine States. When I reflect upon these circumstances I am surprized to find that any person who is acquainted with the critical state of our public affairs, and knows the variety of views, interests, feelings and prejudices which must be consulted and conciliated in framing a general Government for these States, and how little propositions in themselves so opposite to each other, will tend to promote that desireable an end, can wish to make amendments the ultimatum for adopting the offered system.

I am very glad to find that the opposition in your State, however formidable it has been represented, is, generally speaking, composed of such characters as cannot have an extensive influence; their fort, as well as that of those of the same class in other States seems to lie in misrepresentation, and a desire to inflame the passions and to alarm the fears by noisy declamation rather than to convince the understanding by some arguments or fair and impartial statements—Baffled in their attacks upon the constitution they have attempted to vilify and debase the Characters who formed it, but even here I trust they will not succeed. Upon the whole I doubt whether the opposition to the Constitution will not ultimately be productive of more good than evil; it has called forth, in its defence, abilities (which would not perhaps have been otherwise exerted) that have thrown new lights upon the science of Government, they have given the rights of man a full and fair discussion, and have explained them in so clear and forcible a manner as cannot fail to make a lasting impression upon those who read the best publications on the subject, and particularly the pieces under the signiture of Publius.[3] There will be a greater weight of abilities opposed to the system in the convention of this State than there has been in any other, but notwithstanding the unwearied pains which have been taken, and the vigorous efforts which will be made in the Convention to prevent its adoption, I have not the smallest doubt but it will obtain here.

I am sorry to hear that the College in your neighbourhood is in so declining a state as you represent it, and that it is likely to suffer a farther injury by the loss of Dr Nisbet whom you are afraid you shall not be able to support in a proper manner on account of the scarcity of Cash which prevents parents from sending their Children hither. This is one of the numerous evils which arise from the want of a general regulating power, for in a Country like this where equal liberty is enjoyed, where every man may reap his own harvest, which by proper attention will afford him much more that what is necessary for his own consumption, and where there is so ample a field for every mercantile and mechanical exertion, if there cannot be money found to answer the common purposes of education, not to mention the necessary commercial circulation, it is evident that there is something amiss in the ruling political power which requires a steady, regulating and energetic hand to connect and control. That money is not to be had, every mans experience tells him, and the great fall in the price of property is an unequivocal, and melancholy proof of it; when, if that property was well secured—faith and Justice well preserved—a stable government well administered—and confidence restored, the tide of population and wealth would flow to us, from every part of the Globe; and, with a due sense of the blessing, make us the happiest people upon earth. with sentiments of very great esteem and regard I am Dr Sir &c.

Go. Washington

LB, DLC:GW. The letter is out of place in GW's letter book. At the end of his copy of the letter, the copyist, Howell Lewis, wrote: "Note This preceding letter dated in April was not given to be recorded until after those for the year 1788 had been entered—which is the reason of it being in this place." The *New York Times*, 11 Mar. 1968, announced the ALS was to be sold by Sotheby's on 9 April.

1. No letter from GW to Armstrong written in 1787 has been found.

2. In his letters of both 2 Mar. 1787 and 20 Feb. 1788 Armstrong refers to having warned GW earlier of the likelihood of his having to give up his retirement to Mount Vernon, but no such letter has been found.

3. I.e., the *Federalist Papers*.

# To Chastellux

Mount Vernon<br>April 25th[–1 May] 1788

My dear Marquis,

In reading your very friendly and acceptable letter of the 21st of December 1787, which came to hand by the last mail, I was, as you may well suppose, not less delighted than surprised to come across that plain American word—"my wife."[1] A wife! well my dear Marquis, I can hardly refrain from smiling to find you are caught at last. I saw, by the eulogium you often made on the happiness of domestic life in America, that you had swallowed the bate and that you would as surely be taken (one day or another) as you was a Philosopher and a Soldier. So your day has, at length, come. I am glad of it with all my heart and soul. It is quite good enough for you. Now you are well served for coming to fight[2] in favour of the American Rebels, all the way across the Atlantic Ocean, by catching that terrible Contagion—domestic felicity—which time like the small pox or the plague, a man can have only once in his life: because it commonly lasts him—(at least with us in America—I dont know how you manage these matters in France) for his whole life time. And yet after all the maledictions you so richly merit on the subject, the worst wish which I can find in my heart to make against Madame de Chastelux and yourself is, that you may neither of you ever get the better of this same—domestic felicity—during the entire course of your mortal exestence.

If so wonderful an event should have occasioned me, my dear Marquis, to have written in a stra[n]ge style—you will understand me as clearly as if I had said (what, in plain English, is the simple truth) do me the Justice to believe that I take a heartfelt interest in whatsoever concerns your happiness. And in this view, I sincerely congratulate you on your auspicious Matrimonial connection. I am happy to find that Madame de Chastellux is so intimately connected with the Dutchess of Orleans, as I have always understood that this noble lady was an illustrious pattern of connubial love, as well as an excellent model of virtue in general.

While you have been making love, under the banner of Hymen—the great Personages in the North have been making war, under the inspiration, or rather under the infatuation of Mars. Now, for my part, I humble conceive, you have had much the best and wisest of the bargain. For certainly it is more consonant to all the principles of reason and religion (natural and revealed) to replenish the earth with inhabitants, rather than[3] to depopulate it by killing those already in existence, besides it is time for the age of Knight-Errantry and Mad-heroism to be at an end.

Your young military men, who want to reap the ha[r]vest of laurels, dont care (I suppose) how many seeds of war are sown: but for the sake of humanity it is devoutly to be wished that the manly employment of agriculture and the humanizing benefits of commerce would supersede the waste of war and the rage of conquest—that the swords might be turned into plough-shares, the spears into pruning hooks—and, as the Scripture expresses it, the nations learn war no more.

Now I will give you a little news from this side of the water, and then finish. As for us, we are plodding on in the dull road of peace and politics.[4] We, who live in these ends of the earth, only hear of the rumours of war, like the roar of distant thunder. It is to be hoped, our remote local situation will prevent us from being swept into its vortex.

The Constitution, which was proposed by the fœderal Convention, has been adopted by the States of Massachusetts, Connecticut, Jersey, Pennsylvania, Delaware and Georgia. No State has rejected it. The Convention of Maryland is now setting and will probably adopt it: as that of South Carolina is expected to do in May. The other Conventions will assemble early in the summer. Hitherto there has been much greater unanimety in favour of the proposed government than could have been reasonably expected. Should it be adopted (and I think it will be) America will lift up her head again and in a few years become respectable among the nations. It is a flattering and consolatory reflection, that our rising Republics have the good wishes and[5] of all the Philosophers, Patriots and virtuous men in all nations: and that they look upon us [as] a kind of Asylum for mankind. God grant that we may not disappoint their honest expectations, by our folly or perverseness![6] With sentiments of the purest attachment and esteem I have the honor to be My dear Marquis Yr most obedient and Most humble Servant

Go. Washington

P.S. If the Duke de Lauzun is still with you, I beg you will thank him, in my name, for his kind remembrance of me, and make my Compliments to him.

May 1st. Since writing the above I have been favoured with a duplicate of your letter in the hand-writing of a lady, and cannot close this without acknowledging my obligations for the flattering Postcript of the fair Transcriber. In effect, my dear Marquis, the Characters of this interpreter of your sentiments are so much fairer than those through which I have been accustomed to decypher them, that I already consider myself as no small gainer by your Matrimonial connection. Especially, as I hope, your amiable amanuensis will not forget, at sometimes, to add a few annotations of her own to your original text—I have just received information that the Convention of Maryland has ratified the proposed Constitution, by a Majority of 63. to 11.

LB, DLC:GW; copy, ScC. From some slight differences in wording of this and other letters in the collection, it is possible that the copies of letters to Chastellux at ScC were taken from the ALS's.

1. Letter not found. Chastellux married in October 1787 Marie-Josephine-Brigitte-Charlotte de Plunkett (1759–1815), daughter of Thomas, baron de Plunkett, an Irish-born officer in the Austrian service. She was lady-in-waiting to Louise-Marie-Adélaïde de Bourbon-Penthièvre, duchesse d'Orléans (1753–1821), who married in 1769 Louis-Philippe-Joseph de Bourbon, duc d' Orléans (1747–1793), and gave birth to Louis-Philippe who became king of France in 1830. Chastellux died in October 1788.

2. The letter-book copyist wrote "light."

3. The letter-book copyist wrote "that."

4. In the South Carolina copy it is "side the Atlantic" instead of "side of the water" and "*dark* road" instead of "dull road."

5. "And" is omitted in the South Carolina copy.

6. The South Carolina copy reads: "God grant that we may not be disappointed in our honest expectations by our folly or perverseness."

*Letter not found*: from Richard Dobbs Spaight, 25 April 1788. On 25 May GW wrote Spaight that he had received the "letter with which you honored me the 25th of last month."

# From Benjamin Rush

Sir/                        Philadelphia 26th April 1788.

I received a small quantity of the mangel wurzel or Scarcity root Seeds a few days ago from Dr Lettsom of London. In distributing these Seeds among the friends of Agriculture in this country, I should have been deficient in duty, and patriotism, to have neglected to send a small portion of them to your Excellency.

The pamphflet which accompanies the Seeds will furnish your

Excellency with a particular account of the method of cultivating—as also—of the great encrease, & useful qualities of this extraordinary Vegetable.

From an acurate examination of the plant, the botanists have agreed in its being a mongrel Species of the Beet. Dr Lettsom has called it the "Beta hebrida."[1] with respectful Compliments to Mrs Washington in which Mrs Rush joins, & sincere wishes for your Excellency's health & happiness, I have the honor to be your most Obedient Servant

Benjn Rush

ALS, PHi: Gratz Collection.

1. Rush corresponded regularly with the Quaker physician John Coakley Lettsom (1744–1815) of London. Lettsom published treatises on a wide variety of subjects. GW wrote in his diary for 29 Oct. 1788: "Took up the Mangel Wurzel, or Roots of Scarcity in the Inclosure below the Stable. Had those raised from the seeds sent me from Doctr. Rust (coming immediately from Doctr. Letsum) 48 in number—put by themselves; being of the grey or marble coloured sort" (*Diaries*, 5:413–14). Lettsom had recently published in London under the title *An Account of the Culture and Use of the Mangel Wurzel, or Root of Scarcity* a translation of a work by the abbé de Commerell. On 12 Mar. Richard Peters sent GW mangel-wurzel seed and an extract of a disquisition on the plant printed in Germany.

# To John Hopkins

Sir, Mount Vernon April 27. 1788.

I received the enclosed Tax bill by the last post in a letter from Mr Charles Lee who informed me that you had furnished him with it, and was so obliging as to offer to settle it with the Sheriff.[1] I must beg you to accept of my best thanks for your kind offer, and shall take the liberty to trouble you upon the occasion.

The specie Tax for the years 1785 & 6 amounts to £107.11.9 which I find, by the Revenue act passed the last Session, may be discharged in Certificates of a particular description, and for the payment of which I have enclosed you 8 Warrants amounting to £107.12.2.[2]

To discharge the Certificate tax for the above mentioned years, amounting to £91.12.8 I have enclosed 305⁵³⁄₉₀ Dollars in Indents, which, if I am rightly informed, will pay all arrears of the Certificate tax.[3]

I shall endeavour to procure Tobacco notes to pay £71.14.6 due for the year 1787, and will forward them to you as soon as I can obtain them.[4]

I observe that the Sheriff, of Green Briar has, in the enclosed bill, given in a tract containing 10,990 acres which lies on the west side of the Great Kanawa, and has omitted one of 7276 Acres patanted in my name and that of George Muse but now my sole property laying on the East side of said River. If the Great Kanawa seperates the County from Green Briar from any other (as I conceive it does) this statement is erroneous; however I am not sufficiently acquainted with the bounds and divisions of those Counties to decide upon it; the Sheriff ought to know whether it is right or not, and I will thank you to mention the matter to him. The tract of 2000 Acres is also on the West side of the Great Kanawa, tho' by the tax bill it is placed in the County of Green Briar[5]—Independently of the tracts here mentioned, I have 3 other lying on the Ohio, between the mouths of the Great and little Kanhawa, but in what Counties they be or under what predicament they are, I know not *possibly sold*; tho no application has ever been made to me, or any person in my behalf, to my knowledge, for the taxes—these contain 2314 and 2448 Acres and 4395 Acres making together 9157 Acres—I have also, higher up the Ohio a small tract of 587 Acres called the round bottom but how it is taxed, or what steps have been taken to collect it I know not.[6]

Upon the reception of this you will be so obliging as to inform me if the warrants & Indents are such as will answer the purpose. I am yours &c.

Go. Washington

LB, DLC:GW.

1. See Charles Lee to GW, 17 April. The letter-book copy of GW's tax bill for Greenbrier County shows tracts of 2,000, 10,990, and 2,950 acres to be taxed, valued at 6 shillings an acre, for a total value of £4,782. The specie tax on the three tracts was £35.17.3 in 1785 and £71.14.6 in 1786 and 1787; the certificate tax was £45.16.4 in 1785 and 1786; there was no certificate tax for 1787. GW listed the payments he made in his account with John Hopkins and his account of "Taxes and Parish Levies" (Ledger B, 267, 268).

2. The correct total is actually £107.13.2, which is what GW has correctly recorded in the enclosed list of warrants. The eight warrants listed in the letter book include the four warrants issued on 29 Nov. 1786 for articles supplied to the Fairfax County militia in 1774, totaling £87.16.6 (see GW to Anthony

Singleton, 1 Mar. 1788, n.2), one warrant of £4.16 issued 8 Dec. 1783 payable to Thomas Swain for services in the Fairfax County militia, one of £2.14.8 issued on 5 Aug. 1782 to Joshua Smolley for his services in the Loudoun County militia, one for £9 issued by the Prince William County court of claims on 2 Nov. 1783 to Mathew Whiting "for Corn furnished the Continent," and one for £3.6 issued on 4 Oct. 1783 in Loudoun County to William Smith "for waggon hire" (27 April 1788, LB, DLC:GW). For the ultimate disposition of these warrants, see Hopkins to GW, 14 May.

3. The indents are not listed in the letter book.

4. For the payment of this, see the postscript in GW to Charles Lee, this date.

5. On 20 June Hopkins confirmed that the Great Kanawha was the county line and attempted to explain why GW was to pay tax to Greenbrier County on land not in Greenbrier County and was not to pay tax on some of the land in that county. The sheriff of Greenbrier was Robert Renick.

6. For GW's land on the Great Kanawha and Ohio rivers, see the references in the source note, GW to Thomas Lewis, 1 Feb. 1784, and GW's advertisement printed above as an enclosure in GW to John Witherspoon, 10 Mar. 1784.

## To Charles Lee

Dear Sir,                              Mount Vernon April 27th 1788

Your two favors of the 11th & 17th Inst. have been duly received—I am much obliged to you for the trouble which the negotiating the Certificate that I forwarded to you has given, and must further intrude upon you by requesting that you will dispose of the certificates which are in your hands to the best advantage and have the proceeds of them passed to my Credit with the James River Company—As I have already discharged my taxes here for the last year, I shall have no occasion for them on that score.[1]

I thank you, my dear Sir, for your kind attention in forwarding the Acct of my taxes due upon my lands in Green Briar, and as you inform me that Mr Hopkins is so obliging as to offer to settle with the Sheriff for them, I shall write to him upon the subject, and enclose him Certificates to discharge all that is due previous to the year 1787, for the payment of which I shall endeavour to procure Tobacco notes, which shall be forwarded to him as soon as I can obtain them. With great regard and esteem I am, Dear Sir, Yr Most Obedt Hble Sert

Go. Washington

P.S. Enclosed is a letter to Mr Hopkins under a flying seal, which you will be so good as to close and deliver to him;[2] you will see by the contents what steps I have taken to discharge the tax bill which you forwarded to me, and as it is probable that others of a similar nature will be rendered in (if the lands are not already sold) I think it would be best to lodge the Certificates which you have in the hands of Mr Hopkins to pay that part of the tax which is due for 1787, and I will devise some other method to answer the demands of the James River Company.[3]

LB, DLC:GW.

1. GW is referring to the certificate for £69 that he received from the state in partial payment for the slave executed in 1781, which he had forwarded to Lee on 4 April. Lee wrote GW on 17 April that he had exchanged the certificate for warrants payable for taxes. Before finishing this letter of 27 April, GW changed his mind about the disposal of the warrants. See the postscript and note 3.

2. On 17 April Lee sent GW information about the taxes due on his land on the Great Kanawha in Greenbrier County, and GW's letter to John Hopkins attempting to arrange the payment of these taxes is dated 27 April.

3. On 14 May Lee informed GW that he had followed instructions and turned the warrants over to John Hopkins. See note 1.

# To James McHenry

Dear Sir                 Mount Vernon 27th April 1788

Not having sent to the Post office for several days your favor of the 20th inst. did not get to my hand till last night. I mention this circumstance as an apology for my not giving it an earlier acknowledgment.

As you are pleased to ask my opinion of the consequences of an adjournment of your Convention until the meeting of ours, I shall [(]tho' I have meddled very little in this political dispute less perhaps than a man so thoroughly persuaded as I am of the evils and confusions which will result from the rejection of the proposed Constitution, ought to have done) give it as my sincere and decided opinion that the postponement of the question would be tantamount to the final rejection of it—that the adversaries of the new Constitution [in] Virginia and Maryland view it in this light—and the[y] will pass for the accomplishment of this measure as the denier resort. I have very good reason to

believe to adduce arguments in support of this opinion is as unnecessary as they would be prolex—They are obvious, and will
occur to you on a moments reflection.

Tho' the period to which the adjournment in new Hampshire
was fixed, no respect to the meeting of the Convention in this
State, but was the effect, *solely* of local circumstances within itself.
yet, the opposition *here* ascribe it wholy to complaisance towards
Virginia—Make great use of it and undertake to pronounce that
all the States thereafter whose Convention were to precede hers
will pursue the same line of Conduct, and of course that those
which are to follow will receive the ton[e] from it—Should Maryland fulfil this p[r]ognostic South Carolina may indeed be stag-
gered and the prediction of the foes to the Constitution will
thereby be realized—for the assertion so far as it respects North
Carolina may with some truth I believe be applied while the opposition in New York it is well know[n] will avail itself of every
pretext for rejection.

The sentiments of the Western district of this State, are not
yet brought to my view—Independently thereof the Majority,
so far as the opinions of the Delegates are know[n] or presumed
is in favor of the adoption and is encreasing but as the parties
from report are pretty equally poized a small matter cast into
either scale would give it the preponderancy—Decisions, or
indecisions then with you, will in my opinion, determine the fate
of the Constitution. and with it, whether peace and happiness—
or discord and confusion is to be our lot. The fœderalests here
see and depricate the idea of the latter, and there opponents
doing all they can to encouraging it as thier last hope. Thus
stands the matter in my eyes at present. with very great esteem
and regard I am Dear Sir Your Most Obedt and very Hble
Servant

Go. Washington

LB, DLC:GW.

# From Richard Peters

Dear Sir                                    Belmont [Pa.] April 27th 1788
    I was honoured yesterday with yours of the 6th instant.[1] I am
glad the Scarcity Seeds came to Hand. It will not be too late

to plant the Roots as they will be preserved sufficiently by the Sand I had them packed in. When you come to make the Comparison of this to any other Forage dont forget to take into your Account the Summer ⟨str⟩ippings which come in when Clover is burnt up. This with the Advantages over Vegetables subject to Worms & Flies has with me fixed this as a *peerless Root* to which I shall lay myself out to pay much Attention. Whether it will do as well in your Ground or whether it will thrive in your Manner of Culture among Corn which will undoubtedly shade it much, is yet to be tried. I believe it requires Exposure as the Leaves grow rapidly after stripped & that in the driest Season. Mine were the worst near any Shade. *Potatoes* I shall never abandon as they are very productive & valuable. *Carrots* when raized I have a high Opinion of, but the weeding & Hand hoeing I find expensive to me who have to hire all Sorts of Labourers. Your Situation is different as you may employ those who would otherwise be nearly idle. *Cabbages* have scarcely ever succeeded well with me. Vermin have forever destroyed them—I have too been cheated in my Seed nor do I believe my Ground suits them as they require a strong & good Soil—They do not like *Shade. Turnips* are watery & not very nutritious. A fatting Bullock will eat between 2 & 300 Weight of them in 24 Hours nor can they be used here as in Europe as Winter Fodder for Sheep as our Snows forbid it. With you they may do better as your Climate is milder.

Except Lime (which you may have I should concieve from Oyster Shells tho' the Shells unburnt are I believe as good If not better) I have no other resource than my Barn Yard for Manure. I made a Sort of Bargain with myself in the Beginning of the War that if I could get off with the Loss of half my Property & gain the Point I would be contented. The D——l has so contrived it as to oblige me to keep my Contract except as to that Part of being perfectly contented—Among the Portion I have lost went most of my Money. What Degree of *Freedom* I have gained by having thus got rid of *my Bonds* is yet to be known. The Necessity consequent upon it however has compelled me to a thousand Shifts to save Expence on my Farm, which have gained me more Experience hitherto than Money. I have been careful in collecting Manure & have tried many Sorts of Green Manures & they have my decided Approbation. I prefer them

in some Respects to Dung because they destroy instead of producing Weeds. I have not however gone on your Plan of distributing to all Crops their Proportion of Dung. I have rather les-
sened Crops as to Number & Extent to do well what I did. I
have *thought* this ⟨*illegible*⟩y & I do not know that I have been
decieved. I have not yet been able ⟨to g⟩et a Years Stock of Barn
Yard Manure a Head, but I am aiming at it as the most advantageous. I have Water in my Yard by Means of a Pump which I
prefer to running or stagnant Water which are subject to be dirt-
ied & frozen in Winter. This is a great Assistance to my Dung
Heap as the Cattle never leave the Yard.

You ask me if Carrots & Potatoes are Exhausters? In my Opinion they are not. Tuberose & tap-roots I have never considered
exhausting. But fibrous rooted Vegetables except of the Le-
gumineres Tribe I have ever deemed Exhausters, because they
live only in the Vegetable Mould their Roots running horizon-
tally & shallow nor do their Tops shade, or collect Support in so
great a Degree from the Atmosphere. Whatever be the Cause or
Reason I know they (the roots of the tuberose & tap Kind) leave
the Ground better than they find it; & if this be the Case, it
matters not whether it is owing to any inherent Qualities or the
Effects of the clean & good Culture they require. Is not Corn
an Exhauster?

In your Rotation or Fallow System I percieve Corn the principal Object & what I have made sole fallow Crops only follow in
its Train. Your large Stile of Farming I presume requires it. With
so excellent a Preparation the first Year & the Buckwheat the 2d
I should think a Wheat Crop would do well the 3d Year. I have
constantly followed the Buckwheat with Winter Grain the same
Season. A naked Fallow I much disapprove of. A Neighbour of
mine never had a superior Crop 'till he ploughed in the Teazel
(a most villainous Weed) when in a sappy State. This tho' not
shading shews the Benefit of green Manures & how to make
the best of a bad Thing—Your 4th Year in Pease will be a great
Preparation for the next Years Crop especially if the shed Pease
sprout & are ploughed in towards Winter—The ⟨Callavanse⟩ or
native Pea I find the best.[2] The others as well as Beans being
much subject to Blights Mildews & Vermin. 5. Barley & Clover
are well—but Oats I hold exhausting & little valuable when obtained. They foul Ground & in short I have an Antipathy to

them on every Account—6 & 7—I presume you will plough in your Clover of the last rotatory Year, in the Fall & its roots will be as good as a dunging. I am happy to find you, who will do it so much Justice, are beginning the best System of Agriculture possible—What do you think of Wheat on the Clover Ley[3] harrowed in? I had a great Crop in this Mode—This might succeed the Clover & then your Corn &c.

If I am successful in raizing Scarcity Seeds I will with Pleasure supply you with what I can spare.

The Harrow I have had made on my new Plan I have tried & yours would have been ready but I could not get a Workman I could depend upon. I have now one making them here as I chose he should be near me. It answers every Expectation I had formed of it & I have a Thought of improving it still farther. If I do I will inform you. I have too an Idea that by adding a small Box or Hopper I can by Means of the Wheel drill in many Sorts of Crops. The first Tooth or Hoe behind which the Seed should fall opens & the two latter completely cover the little Trench leaving the Ground in small ridges all completely stirred. If you wish to level it where not seeded the other Harrow will do it. My Intention was to do more than Chatevieux's Cultivator which only (somewhat better but in the Manner of the Hoes you describe) mines under the Surface & leaves the Ground superficially nearly the same.[4] But by Means of the Upper Wing to my Hoes I can stir & turn the whole. They will penetrate as deep as you would wish. Some Slight is required in giving them when foul a sudden Motion sideways to get off the Weeds &c. This your Workmen will soon learn.

In trench ploughing I have a light Plough & two Horses to pare off the Sod, & I care not how shallow, to precede the larger Plough which runs in the same Furrow directly after it. The 2d plough is little different from the common Plough. It has only its Coulter a little more perpendicular to go the deeper. It is large & strong & its Mould Board calculated to cast off more Earth. It must be narrower in the Share about an Inch & an half than the first Plough it will otherwise eat in to the unploughed Ground *latterally*. Two Oxen & two Horses go in this Plough. I find some Inconvenience in their going a Breast but their working in a Line has also its Disadvantages especially in turning. I plough 10 Inches deep in general & often 14—One Driver to the first Plough—A Man to hold & a Boy to drive the 2d. I never kept any exact Account of Days Work. I value this Preparation so much that I am content with half an Acre a Day but believe they can & frequently do an Acre. But I generally perform this Operation towards Winter when Days are short & Weather uncertain—A *Winter Fallow* I think much of tho' I think with you as to naked *Summer Fallows*.

Had I known the Nature of your Ground I should not have expected anything from the Plaister of Paris which with few Exceptions has not succeeded in Clays. On your Coast where Sands, if they are not blowing, prevail it would I think do well— Vegetation is also with us backward but my Plaister even strewed in the Beginning of March begins to shew. I do not recollect that it ever failed me & I have now tried it 16 Years in smaller or more extended Experiments as my Oppertunities of procuring it occurred.

If I have not fully answered the Points you were pleased to enquire about I will endeavour to do it should you require it as it is with the most sincere Pleasure I comply with any Request you may think proper to make & it is but in small Matters I can evince the Esteem & Respect with which I am your very obed. Servt

Richard Peters

Mrs Peters begs her Compliments to you & Mrs Washington to whom be pleased to add mine.

A large Hoe on the Construction of the Harrow Tooth is excellent for Horse hoeing. I could wish the Angle of the Upper Wing was more acute but the Smith did not quite please me in it. I have a Mind to add to the Shank a shifting Plate & something in the Manner of that to the Hand Hoe of Cooke's Drill Plough.[5]

Most of the Cape Wheat I have heard of in this Country Mr Morris's excepted is killed by the Winter. I fear we are too far North for it—I heartily congratulate you on my Paper being out, lest your Patience tho' known to be of the most excellent. Bottom might have been ⟨*illegible*⟩ not *distanced*.

Before closing my letter a Man I employed to make me a simple Machine for separating the larger from the smaller Potatoes has been with me. I made one from a sudden Thought (which I have improved on) that has saved me Twenty Times its Value in Wages. I dont expect it will cost half a Joe & if you choose to have one made at the same Time with mine I will have it done & I think you will approve of it as it both separates the Potatoes & cleans the Dirt from them at one Operation. It is a riddle fixed in a Box moving in a lower Frame to receive the small ones as the Riddle retains the larger & the Dirt drops thro the lower Frame which holds the smaller after passing thro the large riddle.[6]

ALS, DLC:GW.

    1. Letter not found, but see Peters to GW, 12 March.

    2. The calavance, or garvance, is the chickpea.

    3. Ley, or lay, was land that remained untilled for some time, or arable land under grass. It was also land "laid down" for pasture or in grass or clover.

    4. Michel Lullin de Chateauvieux (1695–1781), a native of Geneva, constructed and improved many agricultural instruments. His *Expériences et réflexions sur la culture des terres, faites aux environs des Genève, dans les années 1754, 1755 et 1756* is frequently quoted in Duhamel's *A Practical Treatise of Husbandry,* the 1762 edition of which GW had in his library at his death.

    5. James Cooke, an English clergyman, in 1782 patented a widely used drill plow. In 1784 he published *Drill Husbandry Perfected* and, in 1789, *Improved Patent Drill and Horse-Hoe.*

    6. There follows here in the manuscript a "rough Sketch of a Corn Brake with a proposed Addition for drilling in Seed." The legend for the sketch is in CD-ROM:GW.

# From Jonathan Trumbull, Jr.

Dear Sir                          New York 27th April 1788

    I Yesterday in this City, happened to fall in the Way of a Leiut. How, an officer of the New Hampshire Line, who Your Excelly will doubtless recollect was, in the latter part of our being at NewBurgh, acting with Mr Colfax as a Leiut. of the Guards— enquiring his wellfare, he informed me, that since the War he had been residing in this City & doing Business here—& that he was now engaging in an Enterprize to some part of the Spanish settlements in America—& expressed an anxious wish to obtain from your Excelly a Certificate of his services as an officer in the American Army, & particularly of his being attached to your Guards. such Credentials, together with what he expected to procure from Gov. Clinton he conceived would be of eminent Service to him in his Adventure. On this Ground he has prevailed on me to solicit the favor he wishes from your Exy—I have made some Enquiry—& so far as I have been able to possess myself of his Character in the Course of his Business since the War, I do not find any thing unfavorable to his reputation as a Gentleman—a man of probity & Honour and could therefore wish, if your Exclly sees no impropriety in the matter, that he may be gratified in his Desire.

should you be pleased to grant his request, he will be particularly obliged in receivg the Certificate by the 20th May, addressed to him in this City, where he expects to remain till that time.[1] With perfect Respect & Regard I am Dr Sir Your Excellencys Most Obet & Obliged hume Servant

Jona. Trumbull

ALS, DLC:GW; ADfS, ViMtV.
1. For the text of GW's statement dated 12 May 1788 recounting Bezaleel Howe's wartime service in the commander in chief's guard and attesting to his good character, see the note in Howe to David Humphreys, 30 Mar. 1790, printed below.

## To John Vaughan

Sir,                                          Mount Vernon April 27th 1788
I have received your two letters of the 17th and 21st Inst. and the papers containing the four numbers of Fabius whih accompany'd them.[1]

I must beg you to accept of my best thanks for your polite attention in forwarding those papers to me. The writer of the pieces signed Fabius, whoever he is appears to be master of his[2] subject; he treats it with dignity, and at the same time expresses himself in such a manner as to render it intelligible to every capacity. I have no doubt but an extensive republication of them would be of utility in removing those impressions which have been made upon the minds of many by an unfair or partial representation of the proposed Constitution, and would afford desireable information upon the subject to those who seek for it.[3]

I am happy to hear of your farthers safe arrival in Jamaica; you will please to tender my regards to him whenever you write.[4] I am &c.

Go. Washington

LB, DLC:GW; copy, PHi: Robert R. Logan Collection; copy, PPAmP: Madeira-Vaughan Collection.

John Vaughan (1756–1841), the son of GW's friend Samuel Vaughan, was a merchant in Philadelphia who helped arrange the publication of Dickinson's "Fabius" essays.

1. Letters not found.

2. John Dickinson's copy, undoubtedly made from the receiver's copy, has "this" instead of "his." The other differences between it and the letter-book copy are inconsequential.

3. John Dickinson's "Fabius" pieces began appearing in the *Pennsylvania Mercury and Universal Advertiser* (Philadelphia) on 12 April.

4. In late 1787 Samuel Vaughan went from Philadelphia to Jamaica where he had extensive property and remained there for a year or more. He again sailed from Philadelphia in 1790 at which time he returned permanently to London. See Vaughan to GW, 4 Nov. 1788, written from Jamaica.

# To Lafayette

Mount Vernon April 28th[–1 May] 1788

I have now before me, my dear Marqs your favor of the 3d of August in the last year; together with those of the 1st of January, the 2d of January and the 4th of February in the present— Though the first is of so antient a date, they all came to hand lately, and nearly at the same moment. The frequency of your kind remembrance of me, and the endearing expressions of attachment, are by so much the more satisfactory, as I recognise them to be a counterpart of my own feelings for you. In truth, you know I speak the language of sincerity and not of flattery, when I tell you, that your letters are ever most wellcome and dear to me.

This I lay out to be a letter of Politics. We are looking anxiously a cross the atlantic for news and you are looking anxiously back again for the same purpose. It is an interesting subject, to contemplate how far the war, kindled in the north of Europe, may extend it[s] conflagrations, and what m[a]y be the result before its extinction. The Turke appears to have lost his old and acquired a new connection. Whether England has not, in the hour of her pride, overacted her part and pushed matters too far [for] her own interest, time will discover: but, in my opinion (though from my distance and want of minute information I should form it with diffidence) the affairs of that nation cannot long go on in the same prosperous train: in spite of expedients and in spite of resources, the Paper bubble will one day burst. And it will whelm many in the ruins. I hope the affairs of France are gradually sliding into a better state. Good effects may, and I trust will ensue, without any public convulsion. France, were he[r] resources properly managed and her administrations wisely conducted, is (as you justly observe) much more potent in the scale of empire, than her rivals at present seem inclined to believe.

I notice with pleasure the additional immunities and facilities in trade, which France has granted by the late Royal Arret to the United States. I flatter myself it will have the desired effect, in some measure, of augmenting the commercial intercourse.[1] From the productions and wants of the two countries, their trade with each other is certainly capable of great amelioration, to be actuated by a spirit of unwise policy. For so surely as ever we shall have an efficient government established; so surely will that government impose retaliating restrictions, to a certain degree, upon the trade of Britain, at present, or under our existing form of Confederations, it would be idle to think of making comercial regulations on our part. One State passes a prohibitory law respecting some article—another State opens wide the avenue for its admission. One Assembly makes a system—another Assembly unmakes it. Virginia, in the very last session of her Legislature, was about to have passed some of the most extravigant and preposterous Edicts on the subject of trade, that ever Stained the leaves of a Legislative Code. It is in vain to hope for a remedy of these and innumerable other evils, untill a general Government shall be adopted.

The Convention of Six States only have as yet accepted the new Constitution. No one has rejected it. It is believed that the Convention of Maryland, which is now in session; and that of South Carolina, which is to assemble on the 12th of May, will certainly adopt it. It is, also, since the elections of Members for the Convention have taken place in this State, more general believed that it will be adopted here than it was before those elections were made. There will, however, be powerful and elequent speeches on both sides of the question in the Virginia Convention. but as Pendelton, Wythe, Blair, Madison, Jones,[2] Nicholas, Innis[3] and many other of our first characters will be advocates for its adoption, you may suppose the weight of abilities will rest on that side. Henry and Masson are its great adversaries—The Governor, if he opposes it at all will do it feebly.

On the general Merits of this proposed Constitution, I wrote to you, some time ago my sentiments pretty freely.[4] That letter had not been received by you, when you addressed to me the last of yours which has come to my hands. I had never supposed that perfection could be the result of accomodation and mutual concession. The opinion of Mr Jefferson & yourself is certainly a wise one, that the Constitution ought by all means to be accepted by nine States before any attempt should be made to procure amendments. For, if that acceptance shall not previously take place, men's minds will be so much agitated and soured, that the danger will be greater than ever of our becoming a disunited People. Whereas, on the other hand, with prudence in temper and a spirit of moderation, every essential alteration, may in the process of time, be expected.

You will doubtless, have seen, that it was owing to this conciliatory and patriotic principle that the Convention of Massachusetts adopted the Constitution in toto; but recommended a number of specific alterations and quieting explanations, as an early, serious and unremitting subject of attention. Now, although it is not to [be] expected that every individual, in Society, will or can ever be brought to agree upon what is, exactly, the best form of govenment; yet, there are many things in the Constitution which only need to be explained, in order to prove equally satisfactory to all parties. For example: there was not a member of the convention, I believe, who had the least objection to what is contended for by the Advocates for a *Bill of Rights* and *Tryal by Jury*. The first, where the people evidently retained every thing which they did not in express terms give up, was considered nugatory as you will find to have been more fully explained by Mr Wilson and others:[5] And as to the second, it was only the difficulty of establishing a mode which should not interfere with the fixed modes of any of the States, that induced the Convention to leave it, as a matter of future adjustment.

There are other points on which opinions would be more likely to vary. As for instance, on the ineligibility of the same person for President, after he should have served a certain course of years. Guarded so effectually as the proposed Constitution is, in respect to the prevention of bribery and undue influence in the choice of President: I confess, I differ widely myself from Mr Jefferson and you, as to the necessity or expediency of rotation in that appointment. The matter was fairly discussed in the Convention, & to my full convictions; though I cannot have time or room to sum up the arguments in this letter. There cannot, in my Judgment, be the least danger that the President will by any practicable intrigue ever be able to continue himself one moment in office, much less perpetuate himself in it—but in the last stage of corrupted morals and political depravity: and even then there is as much danger that any other species of domination would prevail. Though, when a people shall have become incapable of governing themselves and fit for a master, it is of little consequence from what quarter he comes.

Under an extended view of this part of the subject, I can see no propriety in precluding ourselves from the services of any man, who on some great emergency, shall be deemed, universally, most capable of serving the Public. In answer to the observations you make on the probability of my election to the Presidency (knowing me as you do) I need only say, that it has no enticing charms, and no fascinating allurements for me. However, it might not be decent for me to say I would refuse to accept or even to speak much about an appointment, which may never take place: for in so doing, one might possibly incur the application of the moral resulting from that Fable, in which the Fox is represented as inveighing against the sourness of the grapes, because he could not reach them. All that it will be necessary to add, my dear Marquis, in order to shew my decided predelection, is, that, (at my time of life and under my circumstances) [t]he encreasing infirmities of nature and the growing love of retirement do not permit me to entertain a wish, beyond that of living and dying an honest man on my own farm. Let those follow the pursuits of ambition and fame, who have a keener relish for them, or who may have more years, in store, for the enjoyment!

Mrs Washington, while she requests that her best Compliments may be presented to you, Joins with me in soliciting that the same friendly and affectionate memorial of our constant remembrance and good wishes may be made acceptable to Madam de la Fayette and the little ones—I am &c.

Go. Washington

P.S. May 1st.

Since writing the foregoing letter, I have received Authentic Accounts that the Convention of Maryland have ratified the new Constitution by a Majority of 63 to 11.

LB, DLC:GW. The copyist, Howell Lewis, who was perhaps more careless than usual when entering this long letter in the letter book, often wrote *or* for *on* and *he* for *the*; they have been transcribed here as *on* and *the* respectively.

    1. See Lafayette to GW, 1 Jan. 1788, and note 1 of that document.
    2. This is Gabriel Jones.
    3. This is Col. James Innes.
    4. See GW to Lafayette, 7 February.
    5. GW probably is referring to James Wilson's speech of 6 Oct. 1787 which was widely printed.

## To Rochambeau

My dear Count,           Mount Vernon April 28th 1788

I have Just received the letter which you did me the honor to write to me on the 18th of January; and am sorry to learn that the Count de Grasse, our gallant coadjutor in the capture of Cornwallis, is no more. yet his death is not, perhaps, so much to be deplored as his latter days were to be pitied. It seemed as if an unfortunate and unrelenting destiny pursued him, to distroy the enjoyment of all earthly comfort. For the disastrous battle of the 19th of April, the loss of the favor of his king and the subsequent connection in marriage with an unworthy woman, were sufficient to have made him weary of the burden of life, your goodness, indeavouring to sweeten its passage, was truly commendable; however it might have been Marred by his own impetuosity. But his frailties should now be buried in his grave with him, while his name will be long deservedly dear to this Country, on account of his, successful co-operation in the gloreious campaign of 1781. the Cincinati in some of the States have gone into mourning for him.[1]

Altho' your nation and England have avoided, from prudential motives, going into a war, yet, I fancy, their affections have not been much encreased by the affair in Holland. The feeling occasioned to France by the interference of Prussia and Britain, may not pass away altogether without consequences. I wish, indeed, the affairs of France to be on a footing which would enable her to be the arbiter of peace to the neighbouring nations. The poor Dutch Patriots seem, by some means or another, to have been left sadly in the lurch and to be reduced to a most humiliating condition. And as if the two Powers, who reinstat'd the Stadt-Holder, had not done enough to set the middle nations together by the ears; they have embroiled, forsooth, all the north of Europe by bringing the Turks into hostility with the two Imperial Courts. Should France Join with the latter, or even should she continue neuter, I can scarcely conceive that the Ottomans will be permitted to hold any of their possessions in Europe. The torch of hostility, being once kindled, commonly spreads apace; but it is beyond my prescience to fortell how far this flame will extend itself, before it shall be entirely extinguished.

Here, in America, we have not much news worth the trouble of communicating to you, my dear Count, Though I know what is to ourselves often [a] matter of indifference, is to our friends at a distance a subject of curiosity. For that reason, I will subjoin, in one word, a State of affairs on this side of the water. All the public attention has been, for many months past, engrossed by [the] new Constitution. It has met with some opposition from men of abilities, but it has been much more ably advocated. Six States, that is to say, those of Massachusetts, Connecticut, Jersey, Pennsylvania, Delaware and Georgia have accepted it. The opinion is that Maryland and South Carolina will soon do the same. One more State, only, will be wanting to put Government into execution. And as the other Convention[s] are to meet early in the summer, we hope for the best.

As t[o] the intimation which your partiality for me has prompted you to make on my behalf: I need only say that every body knows that private life is my decided choice in preferrence to any thing the world can bestow. I am &c.

Go. Washington

LB, DLC:GW.

1. For the problems faced by the French commander after the victory at Yorktown in 1781, see de Grasse to GW, 15 Mar. 1784, n.1. See also Auguste, comte de Grasse, to GW, 11 Mar. 1788.

## From Gouverneur Morris

Dear Genl                              Richmond 29 April 1788

I cannot prevail on myself to omit the present Occasion of offering my Respects, altho I have Nothing to say which is worth your Perusal. It may not however be quite unsatisfactory to receive even Conjecture on a Subject whose Importance is great and whose Situation precludes Evidence. As far as one who avoids much Enquiry can judge I am led to decide that the Opposers to the new Constitution are fewer and more feeble than they were in this Quarter And would almost venture to predict that if Carolina and Maryland shall be tolerably unanimous in the Adoption particularly the latter the Convention of this State will not long hesitate. I am mistaken if some Leaders of Opposition are not more solicitous in the present Moment how to make a good Retreat than how to fight the Battle. It is you know a sad Thing for a great and deep Politician to make a great Blunder and fall in a deep Ditch and yet this may easily happen when Men walk on *bad Ground*. Adieu. As this was intended meerly to convey my Respects to You and your Lady and to my worthy friend Humphreys if still with you will detain you no longer than to repeat the Assurances of that sincere Esteem with which I am yours

Gouv. Morris

ALS, DLC:GW.

## From Robert Morris

Dear Sir                              Richmond April 29th 1788

My detention here having been so much longer than expected, the Season in which Mrs Morris promised a Visit to Mount Vernon being come, and my Sons being arrived at Philada these circumstances induced me to propose the journey to which she very readily consents. I am therefore sending up my Servants & Horses to bring down Mrs & Miss Morris attended by my Sons Robert & Thomas, all of them being ambitious to pay their respects to that character which they so much admire.[1] You see my Dear Sir the Liberty I take & the trouble I am about to bring on your Household by such a Host of Strangers but I shall shew my confidence that it will give you pleasure to receive them by declining to make any appology. Mrs Morris in her last letter mentioned that you had desired her to lay by for Mrs Washington, some Cambrick Book Muslins & she believes some large Book Muslin Handkerchiefs, out of Capt. Bells Cargo from the East Indies, will you be good enough to give John a note of the particulars Mrs Washington wishes to have & Mrs Morris will bring them with her[2]—I pray my best respects to Mrs Washington & to assure her that the same Considerations determine me not to make an appology to her for the trouble She is likely to have with so large a part of my Family, especially as I hope they will render their Company very agreable & pleasing to that of Mount Vernon. With the most sincere esteem I am Dear Sir Your most obedient & humble Servant

Robt Morris

ALS, DLC:GW. Morris wrote on the cover of the letter "by John Adam," who may have been the John Adam who was the son of the Alexandria merchant Robert Adam.

1. See GW to Mary White Morris, 1 May.

2. Captain Bell is probably Thomas Bell (d. 1805), who in 1784 sailed from Philadelphia to trade in Sumatra and India. He returned to the United States the following year.

## To Samuel Griffin

Dear Sir,                                    Mount Vernon April 30th 1788

I am now to acknowledge to receipt of your letter of the 15th of April, in which you did me the favor to enclose an extract from the original Statute, designating the duties of the Office to which I had been appointed.

Inf[l]uenced by a heart-felt desire to promote the cause of Science in general and the prosperity of the College of William and Mary in particular, I accept the office of Chancellor in the same; and request you will be pleased to give official notice thereof to the learned Body, who have thought proper to honor me with the appointment. I consider fully in their strenuous endeavour's for placing the system of Education on such a basis as will render it most beneficial to the State, and the Republic of letters, as well as to the more extensive interests of humanity and religion. In return, they will do me the Justice to believe that I shall not be tardy, in giving my chearful concurrence to such measures as may be best calculated for the attainment of those desirable and important objects.

For the expressions of politeness and friendship blended with your communications, you are desired to receive my best acknowledgments. I am Dear Sir Yrs &c.

Go. Washington

LB, DLC:GW.

## To Mary White Morris

Madam,                            Mount Vernon May 1st 1788.

With infinite pleasure Mrs Washington & myself received from Mr Morris the News of your intended visit to Mount Vernon—and that you will be accompanied by Miss Morris and the young Gentlemen who are lately returned to you (on which happy event we sincerely congratulate you). We have only to wish, further, that you could make it convenient to bring the other Children; for with much truth we can assure you of the pleasure it would give us to see them all under this roof with you and Mr Morris.[1]

Being engaged in my Mornings ride when John came, and he anxious to proceed, I detain him no longer than I can unite Mrs Washingtons best wishes and compliments to mine, for you, and the family—in a particular manner I beg you to assure the young Gentlemen of the cordial reception they will meet from⟨,⟩ Madam, Yr Most Obedt & Obliged Hble Servant

Go: Washington

P.S. Mr Morris in his letter to me says, you will be so obliging as to bring (sending it to Colo. Biddle if it is the least inconvenient will do equally well) Muslins agreeably to the inclosed Memorandum.

G.W.

ALS (photocopy), DLC:GW.

1. See Robert Morris to GW, 29 April. On 14 May, three days before the arrival at Mount Vernon of Mrs. Morris with sons, Robert (b. 1769) and Thomas (1771–1849), and daughter, Esther (1774–1816), George Augustine Washington wrote the Alexandria storekeeper Thomas Porter: "The General

will beg the favor of You to procure for him a Box of Lemons if they are not to be had 6 or 8 doz. Limes as he is daily expectg company and those who I doubt not from use are attached to the good things of this world—we are much in want of Butter and will thank You to have the pot left at Your store filled the first Opporty as the Boat will probably be in Town in a few days" (PHi: Gratz Collection). The two Morris boys had just returned from Europe where they had been sent in 1781 for their schooling.

## To William Stephens Smith

Dear Sir,                                     Mount Vernon May 1st 1788
 I consider myself the more indebted to your obliging care in transmitting the letter of the Marquis de la Fayette, as by that means you have given me the double advantage of hearing from two of my distant, military friends at once.[1]
 It is so long since I have had the satisfaction of holding any immediate intercourse with you, that I may be allowed to touch on a subject rather obsotute[2] indeed, but not (I presume) the less pleasant on that account: I mean your entrance upon the road of connubial life. Permit me, then, to wish that it may be strewed with flowers, and that every possible happiness may attend you and the partner of your Journey, who, (if I am not egregiously misinformed by those who are well acquainted with her) is worthy of that distinguished lot of felicity. Mrs Washington wishes that her compliments may be presented with mine to yourself and Lady. You may ever count upon my sincere regard, and believe me to be, Dear Sir yours &c.

                                        Go. Washington

LB, DLC:GW.
 1. In his letter to Lafayette of 28 April, GW acknowledges having received of late a number of letters from Lafayette. Smith had recently returned to the United States from London with his bride Abigail, daughter of John and Abigail Adams. No letter from Smith at this time has been found.
 2. Perhaps GW wrote "obsolete."

## From Thomas Jefferson

Sir                                          Paris May 2. 1788.
 I am honoured with your Excellency's letter by the last packet & thank you for the information it contained on the com-

munication between the Cayahoga & Big beaver.¹ I have ever considered the opening a canal between those two watercourses as the most important work in that line which the state of Virginia could undertake. it will infallibly turn thro the Patowmack all the commerce of Lake Erie & the country West of that, except what may pass down the Missisipi. and it is important that it be soon done, lest that commerce should in the mean time get established in another channel. having in the spring of the last year taken a journey through the Southern parts of France, & particularly examined the canal of Languedoc through it's whole course, I take the liberty of sending you the notes I made on the spot, as you may find in them something perhaps which may be turned to account some time or other in the prosecution of the Patowmac canal. being merely a copy from my travelling notes, they are indigested & imperfect, but may still perhaps give hints capable of improvement in your mind.²

The affairs of Europe are in such a state still that it is impossible to say what form they will take ultimately. France & Prussia, viewing the Emperor as their most dangerous & common enemy had heretofore seen their common safety as depending on a strict connection with one another. this had naturally inclined the Emperor to the scale of England, and the Empress also, as having views in common with the Emperor against the Turks. but these two powers would at any time have gladly quitted England to coalesce with France, as being the power which they met every where opposed as a barrier to all their schemes of aggrandizement. when therefore the present king of Prussia took the eccentric measure of bidding defiance to France by placing his brother in law on the throne of Holland, the two empires immediately seised the occasion of solliciting an alliance with France. the motives for this appeared so plausible that it was believed the latter would have entered into this alliance, and that thus the whole political system of Europe would have taken a new form. what has prevented this court from coming into it, we know not. the unmeasurable ambition of the Emperor & his total want of moral principle & honour are suspected. a great share of Turkey, the recovery of Silesia, the consolidation of his dominions by the Bavarian exchange, the liberties of the Germanic body, all occupy his mind together, and his head is not well enough organised to pursue so much only of all this as is practicable. still it was thought that France might safely have co-alesced with these powers, because Russia & her, holding close together, as their interests would naturally dictate, the emperor could never stir but with their permission. France seems how-ever to have taken the worst of all parties, that is, none at all. she folds her arms, lets the two empires go to work to cut up Turkey as they can, and holds Prussia aloof neither as a friend nor foe. this is withdrawing her opposition from the two empires without the benefit of any condition whatever. in the mean time England has clearly overreached herself. she excited the war between the Russians & Turks, in hopes that France, still sup-porting the Turks, would be embarrassed with the two empires. she did not foresee the event which has taken place of France abandoning the Turks, and that which may take place of her union with the two empires. she has allied herself with Holland, but cannot obtain the alliance of Prussia. this latter power would be very glad to close again the breach with France, and there-fore, while their remains an opening for this, holds off from England, whose fleets could not enter into Silesia to protect that from the Emperor. thus you see that the old system is unhinged, and no new one hung in it's place. probabilities are rather in favour of a connection between the two empires, France & Spain. several symptoms shew themselves of friendly disposi-tions between Russia & France, unfriendly ones between Rus-sia & England, and such as are barely short of hostility between England & France.[3] but to real hostilities this country would with difficulty be driven. her finances are too deranged, her internal union too much dissolved, to hazard a war. the nation is pressing on fast to a fixed constitution. such a revolution in the public opinion has taken place that the crown already feels it's powers bounded, and is obliged by it's measures to acknowlege limits. a states general will be called at some epoch not distant. they will probably establish a civil list, and leave the government to tem-porary provisions of money, so as to render frequent assemblies of the national representative necessary. how that representative will be organised is yet incertain. among a thousand projects, the best seems to me that of dividing them into two houses of commons & nobles, the commons to be chosen by the provincial assemblies who are chosen themselves by the people, & the no-bles by the body of noblesse as in Scotland. but there is no reason to conjecture that this is the particular scheme which will be preferred. the war between the Russians & Turks has made an opening for our Commodore Paul Jones. the Empress has invited him into her service. she ensures to him the rank of rear-admiral, will give him a separate command and it is understood that he is never to be commanded. I think she means to oppose him to the Captain Pacha on the black sea. he is by this time probably at St Petersburg.[4] the circumstances did not permit his awaiting the permission of Congress, because the season was close at hand for opening the campaign. but he has made it a condition that he shall be free at all times to return to the orders of Congress whenever they shall please to call for him, and also that he shall not in any case be expected to bear arms against France. I believe Congress had it in contemplation to give him the grade of Admiral from the date of his taking the Serapis. such a measure now would greatly gratify him, second the efforts of fortune in his favor, and better the opportunities of improving him for our service whenever the moment shall come in which we may want him.

The danger of our incurring something like a bankruptcy in Holland, which might have been long, and even fatally felt in a moment of crisis, induced me to take advantage of mr Adams's journey to take leave at the Hague, to meet him there, get him to go on to Amsterdam, and try to avert the impending danger. the moment of paying a great sum of annual interest was approaching. there was no money on hand; the board of treasury had notified that they could not remit any, and the progress of the loan which had been opened there, had absolutely stopped. our bankers there gave me notice of all this, and that a single day's failure in the paiment of interest would have the most fatal effect on our credit. I am happy to inform you that we were able to set the loan a going again, and that the evil is at least postponed. indeed I am tolerably satisfied that if the measures we proposed are ratified by Congress, all European calls for money (except the French debt) are secure enough till the end of the year 1790[5] by which time we calculated that the new government might be able to get money into their treasury. much conversation with the bankers, brokers, & money holders gave me insight into the state of national credit there which I had never before been able satisfactorily to get. the English credit is the first, because they never open a loan without laying & appropriating taxes for the paiment of the interest, and there has never been an instance of their failing one day in that paiment. the Emperor & Empress have good credit, because they use it little, and have hitherto been very punctual. this country is among the lowest in point of credit. ours stands in hope only. they consider us as the surest nation on earth for the repaiment of the capital. but as the punctual paiment of interest is of absolute necessity in their arrangements, we cannot borrow but with difficulty and disadvantage. the monied men however look towards our new government with a great degree of partiality & even anxiety. if they see that set out on the English plan, the first degree of credit will be transferred to us. a favourable occasion will arise to our new government of asserting this ground to themselves. the transfer of the French debt, public & private, to Amsterdam is certainly desireable. an act of the new government therefore for opening a loan in Holland for this purpose, laying taxes at the same time for paying annually the interest & a part of the principal will answer the two valuable purposes of ascertaining the degree of our credit, and of removing those causes of bickering & irritation which should not be permitted to subsist with a nation with which it is so much our interest to be on cordial terms as with France. a very small portion of this debt, I mean that part due to the French officers, has done us an injury of which those in office in America cannot have an idea. the interest is unpaid for the last three years; and these creditors, highly connected, & at the same time needy, have felt & communicated hard thoughts of us. borrowing as we have done 300 thousand florins a year to pay our interest in Holland, it would have been worth while to have added 20 thousand more to suppress those clamours.[6] I am anxious about every thing which may affect our credit. my wish would be to possess it in the highest degree, but to use it little. were we without credit we might be crushed by a nation of much inferior resources but possessing higher credit. the present system of war renders it necessary to make exertions far beyond the annual resources of the state, and to consume in one year the efforts of many. and this system we cannot change. it remains then that we cultivate our credit with the utmost attention. I had intended to have written a word to your Excellency on the subject of the new constitution, but I have already spun out my letter to an immoderate length. I will just observe therefore that according to my ideas there is a great deal of good in it. there are two things however which I dislike strongly. 1. the want of a declaration of rights. I am in hopes the opposition of Virginia will remedy this, & produce such a declaration. 2. the perpetual re-eligibility of the President. this I fear will make that an office for life first, & then hereditary. I was much an enemy to monarchy before I came to Europe. I am ten thousand times more so since I have seen what they are. there is scarcely an evil known in these countries which may not be traced to their king as it's source, nor a good which is not derived from the small fibres of republicanism existing among them. I can further say with safety there is not a crowned head in Europe whose talents or merit would entitle him to be elected a vestryman by the people of any parish in America. however I shall hope that before there is danger of this change taking place in the office of President, the good sense & free spirit of our countrymen will make the changes necessary to prevent it. under this hope I look forward to the general adoption of the new constitution with anxiety, as necessary for us under our present circumstances.

I have so much trespassed on your patience already by the length of this letter that I will add nothing further than those assurances of sincere esteem & attachment with which I have the honor to be Your Excellency's most obedient & most humble servant

Th: Jefferson

ALS, DLC:GW.

1. See GW to Jefferson, 1 Jan. 1788.

2. Jefferson headed the enclosure: "Extract from notes made on a journey through the south of France 1787" (DLC:GW). For Jefferson's travel notes and the portions that he extracted, see Boyd, *Jefferson Papers*, 11:446–54; see also p. 463. Jefferson also sent GW an engraved map of the canal in Languedoc.

3. Although GW received frequent reports on the developments in European politics and diplomacy, most often from Lafayette, this from Jefferson is probably the most comprehensive review of the European situation that he had received since the war.

4. John Paul Jones went from St. Petersburg to the Black Sea where he took command of a Russian squadron as a volunteer in the fleet of the Prince of Nassau (Karl Heinrich Nicholas Otto, Prince of Nassau-Siegen). Captain Pacha was Ghazi Hassan, commander of the Turkish Black Sea fleet.

5. For Jefferson's role in the recent negotiations with Holland, see the editor's note to this letter, ibid., 13:128–29.

6. See GW's forceful response to Jefferson's sympathetic report of the "clamours" of the French officers, in his letter to Jefferson of 31 August.

## To Benjamin Lincoln

My dear Sir,                Mount Vernon 2d May 1788.

I have now to acknowledge the receipt of your favor of the 19th of March, which should have been done at an earlier period had any thing transpired in these parts which was worth communicating. I can now, with pleasure, inform you that the State of Maryland adopted the proposed Constitution last monday by a very large majority; this you will undoubtedly have announced by the publick papers before this letter reaches you, but that State will not receive the sole benefit of its adoption, it will have a very considerable influence upon the decision in Virginia, for it has been strongly insisted upon by the opponents in the lower & back Counties in this State that Maryland would reject it by a large majority; the result being found so directly opposite to this assertion will operate very powerfully upon the sentiments of many who were before undecided and will tend to fix them in favor of the Constitution; it will, if I am not misinformed, have this effect upon many who are chosen to the Convention and who have depended, in a great measure, upon the determination of Maryland to confirm their opinion. But, exclusive of this influence, the most accurate returns of the members of the Convention, with their sentiments, so far as they were known, annexed, gave a decided majority in favor of the Constitution, and the prevailing opinion is, that it gains advocates daily. I have never, for my own part, once doubted of its adoption here, and if I had at any time been wavering in my opinion the present appearances & concurrent information would have compleatly fixed it.

I am sorry to find by your letter that there is so much of the spirit of insurrection yet remaining in your State, and that it discovered itself so strongly in your last Assembly, but I hope the influence of those Gentlemen who are friendly to the proposed Constitution, and the conciliatory disposition which was shewn by many of the minority in your Convention will so far pervade the State as to prevent that factious spirit from gaining ground.

Mrs Washington & the Children thank you for your kind remembrance of them & unite with me in the best wishes for your happiness. With sentiments of the highest esteem & regard, I am, my dear Sir, Yr most Obedt & Hble Servt

Go: Washington

P.S. Enclosed is a letter from your young friend.[1]

LS, in the hand of Tobias Lear, MH; LB, DLC:GW.

1. In his letter, dated 2 May, Tobias Lear apologizes for not having written for nearly a year and informs Lincoln of his intended visit to New England within a month's time.

## To James Madison

My dear Sir,                              Mount Vernon May 2d 1788

Your favor of the 10th Ult. came duly to hand, and the enclosure for Mr D. Carroll was forwarded the next day by a direct & safe conveyance.[1] That Gentleman, however, was not of the Convention. But the body of which you supposed him to be a member, by a large and decided Majority (of Sixty odd to twelve) have ratified the New Constitution. A thorn this in the sides of the leaders of opposition in this State. Should South Carolina give as unequivocal approbation of the system, the opposition here will become feeble; for eight affirmatives without a negative carries *weight* of argument, if not of eloquence along with it, which might cause even the unerring sister to hesitate.

Mr Chace, it is said, made a display of all his eloquence. Mr Mercer discharged his whole Artillery of inflamable matter— and Mr Martin did something—I know not what—but presume with vehemence—yet no converts were made—no, not one.[2] so the business, after a very short Session, ended; and will if I mistake not, render yours less tiresome. With Sentiments of sincere regard & Affect. I am—Yours

Go: Washington

ALS, MA; LB, DLC:GW.

1. Daniel Carroll on 28 April acknowledged receipt of Madison's letter of 10 April, which has not been found (Rutland and Hobson, *Madison Papers*, 11:21, 30–31).

2. The ratifying convention met in Annapolis on 21 April and began debate

on the Constitution itself on 23 April. Vote on ratification was taken on 24 April, sixty-three delegates voting for and eleven voting against. After agreeing to recommend a number of amendments, the convention adjourned on 29 April. John Francis Mercer and Luther Martin had both left the Federal Convention, and neither had signed the new Constitution.

## To Gouverneur Morris

Dear Sir,            Mount Vernon [2 May 1788]

Your letter of the 29th Ult. reminds me of an omission which I should be ashamed of, did I not conceive that my apology will be as satisfactory as it is just. The omission alluded to, is not acknowledging the receipt of your former favor which accompanied the Books, and thanking you for your care of them.[1] The apology is, the hourly expectation of seeing you at this place on your return to Philada—Of the adequacy of the one to the other, you are to judge. Be this as it may, it is the best I can offer.

I have not at any moment dispaired of this State's acceptance of the New Constitution, and entertain more confidence since the ratification of it in Maryland by so large & decided a Majority. The *fury* of the opposition I believe is spent. The grand push was made at the Elections. failing of success here, the hopes of the leaders begin to flag, & many of them (or I am mistaken) wish the business was to commence de nova—in which a different line of March would be taken up by some of them.

It was with very singular pleasure I received information of the intended visit of Mrs Morris &ca[2]—I take it for granted, though Mr Morris has not said as much, that he will add to our happiness by becoming one of the party—to repeat the same to you is, I hope unnecessary, as you cannot doubt of the pleasure it would give me. Mrs Washington offers her Compliments to you, and with sentiments of sincere esteem & regard I am—Dear Sir Your friend & Servt

                   Go: Washington

P.S. Colo. Humphreys who is here, thanks you for your kind remembrance of him, and prays you to accept of his best wishes[3]—G.W.

ALS, NjP: deCoppet Collection; LB, DLC:GW. The ALS is addressed to Morris "at Richmond."

1. Morris's letter is dated 7 March.

2. See Robert Morris to GW, 29 April, and GW to Mary White Morris, 1 May.

3. David Humphreys had been at Mount Vernon since 18 November.

## To Robert Morris

Dear Sir,                                        Mount Vernon May 2d 1788

Permit me to assure you in unequivocal terms, that the proposed visit of Mrs Morris, and such parts of your family as are mentioned in your letter of the 29th Ulto will give sincere pleasure at Mount Vernon—Mrs Washington and myself only wish that you had not confined it to Miss, and the two Mr Morris— of this I have taken the liberty to inform Mrs Morris in a letter; hoping that she may find it convenient to bring the other parts of your family along with her—I hope you will not (tho' you are silent on the head) let us not want the pleasure of your Company to make the party perfectly happy.

On the safe arrival of your Sons I heartily congratulate you as I hope I may do on the recovery of your finger from the severe blow we are told it received in your tour to Norfolk—Mrs Washington Joins me in every good wish for you—& with Sentiments of very great esteem and regard I am Dear Sir &c.

Go. Washington

LB, DLC:GW.

## From Samuel Hanson

Sir                                        Alexandria, 4th May 1788.

It is extremely painful to me to be so soon under the necessity of troubling you again with a Complaint against one of your Nephews. Master George has slept from Home the 3 last Nights. The first night he went away, and desired his Brother to inform me where he intended to lodge. This message did not, from accident, come to my ears till after he had slept out the next night. Last night he went away again, contrary to my express prohibition. I have told him I should acquaint you with his conduct; but he does not seem unwilling to submit the propriety of it to your determination. You will be told that he lodged with a Mr Keith, a young Gentleman of sober manners, and good reputation. That cannot be denied. But, perhaps it may occur to you, Sir, that, under the pretence of sleeping with a Companion, great irregularities may be committed.

I should be unjust to the Boys if I did not take this method to inform you that, except George in the present instance, & one other, they have behaved extremely well. Lawrence's Conduct is unexceptionable. From a perverse, insolent, unmannerly Boy, He is transformed into an obliging, civil, & respectful one; a change which may, I trust, without being uncharitable be imputed in some measure, to the increased sphere of my Authority over him: Since it is very certain that there have been no greater pains taken to please lately, than before.[1] I remain with the utmost respect, Sir Your most obedt hble Sert

S. Hanson of Saml

ALS, DLC:GW.

1. GW's nephews had returned in April to live again with Samuel Hanson after boarding for several months at the house of their schoolmaster, William McWhir. See GW to Hanson, 18 Mar., and Hanson to GW, 23 March.

## From Lafayette

My dear General                              Paris May the 4th 1788

I Have Been Requested to Present to You M. de Saint fris a Captain in the french Regiment of dragoons who is Going as a traveller through the United States, and of Course wishes to Pay His Respects to General Washington.[1] He Has Been Particularly Recommended to me, and as I don't know When this introductory letter will Reach you and I am sure it will not Arrive Before My dispatches of a later date I shall only Present You with the Affectionate Respects of Your filial friend

lafayette

ALS, PEL.

1. On 15 Nov. 1788 the chevalier de St. Trys (St. Tries, St. Trise, St. Fris) visited Mount Vernon with Brissot de Warville. See the editors' note, *Diaries*, 5:424–25.

## To Hector St. John Crèvecoeur

Sir,                                    Mount Vernon May 5th 1788.
   The letter with which you were pleased to honor me, dated the 17th ult., & the enclosure, came safe. For your attention & care of the latter I pray you to accept of my best thanks, at the sametime that I entreat you to pardon the liberty I now take in requesting the favor of you to forward the letters herewith sent by the Packet, or any other safe Conveyance.[1] With sentiments of great esteem I am Sir Yr Most Obedient & Most Hble Servant
                                    Go: Washington

ALS, DLC: Crèvecoeur Papers; LB, DLC:GW.
   1. The letters enclosed may have been those of 25 April to Chastellux and of 28 April to Lafayette and to Rochambeau.

## To Samuel Hanson

Sir,                                    Mount Vernon May 5th 1788
   Your letter of yesterday was handed to me last evening. I am sorry that the conduct of one of my Nephews has been such as to render a complaint to me necessary, but I am extreemly obliged to you for the communication. George has now advanced to that time of life when it is absolutely necessary that his conduct should be regulated by some means or other. Coertion would be extreemly painful to me, but if advice, remonstrance and gentle methods will not answer the purpose others must be taken. Enclosed is a letter to him which I have left open for your perusal.
   I am glad to find that Lawrence has behaved so well, I rather suspected that trespasses would have commenced on his part than on that of George. I am, Sir, Yr most Obedt Hble Sert
                                    Go. Washington

LB, DLC:GW.

## To George Steptoe Washington

Dear George,                           Mount Vernon May 5th 1788
   I yesterday received a letter from Mr Hanson informing me that you slept from home three nights successively and one con-

trary to his express prohibition. Complaints of this nature are extreamly painful to me, as it discovers a degree of impropriety in your conduct, which, at your time of life your good sense & discretion ought to pount out to you and lead you to avoid. Altho' there is nothing criminal in your having slept with a companion of good manners and reputation as you say you have, yet your absenting yourself from your own lodgings under that pretence may be productive of irregularities and disagreeable consequences—and I now insist upon it, in the most pointed terms, that you do not repeat it without the consent and approbation of Mr Hanson.

One strong motive for my placing you in your present lodgings was that you might, in your conduct out of school, be guided by Mr Hanson's advice and directions, as I confide very much in his discretion & think that he would requ[i]re nothing of you but what will conduce to your advantage; and at the age to which you have now arrived you must be capable of distinguishing between a proper and improper line of conduct and be sensible of the advantages or disadvantages which will result to you through life from the one or the other.

Your future character and reputation will depend very much, if not entirely, upon the habits and manners which you contract in the present period of your life; they will make an impression upon you which can never be effaced. You should therefore be extreemly cautious how you put yourself into the way of imbibing those customs which may tend to corrupt your manners or vitiate your heart. I do not write to you in this style from knowing or suspecting that you are addicted to any vice, but only to guard you against pursuing a line of conduct which may imperceptably lead on to Vicious cources.

Mr Hanson has done you and Lawrence Justice in saying that your behaviour since you have been last with him has been unexceptionable except in this instance and one more which he has not mentioned, and I hope this is the last complaint I shall ever hear while you remain in your present situation at least, as it will prevent me from using means to regulate your behaviour which will be disagreeable to us both. I am—Yr sincer[e] friend & affectionate Uncle

Go. Washington

LB, DLC:GW.

*Letter not found*: from Bouillé, 6 May 1788. On 1 Oct. 1788 GW wrote Bouillé about the letter, "which you did me the honor to write to me on the 6th of May."

## To John Fitzgerald and George Gilpin

Gentln                                                  Mount Vernon May 6th 1788

If you have fixed upon Monday next for the meeting of the Directors of the Potk Company at the Falls of the Shanandoah— Have given Messrs Johnson and Lee notice of it—and informed Mr Stuart and his accusers thereof you will please to let me know it—(having heard nothing yet of the determination)[1] In these cases, and that I may have nothing to retard my speedy return after the business of the meeting is finished I shall set off on thursday—take the great and Seneca Falls in my way up—make a visit or two in Berkiley—and be at the place of meeting by ten oclock on monday. I am &ca

Go. Washington

LB, DLC:GW.

1. The meeting of the directors of the Potomac River Company was not held, and GW remained at Mount Vernon. But see GW to George Gilpin, 29 May. On Saturday, 10 May, the treasurer of the company, William Hartshorne of Alexandria, "came in before Dinner to get notices (to the Subscribers to the Potomack Co. that motions would be made for judgments upon their Arrearages at the next Genl. Court) signed" (*Diaries*, 5:319–20). These suits were to be instituted under the terms of the acts of the Virginia and Maryland legislatures recently passed at the behest of the Potomac River Company (see GW to George Mason and David Stuart, 4 Nov. 1787, and note 1 of that document). For the meeting which took place on 1–2 June, see GW to George Gilpin, 29 May 1788, notes 1 and 3.

## From Battaile Muse

Sir,                                                    Alexandria May 7th 1788

The bad state of Health and Business Since I have been down Prevented my Caling at Mount vernon untill this day—I was Sorry not To Find you at Home—My Engagements at this Place Prevented my staying for your return—If you desire To See me I will Endeavour To waite on you on Friday otherwise I wish

To Push towards Home[1]—If Mr Lear Should be at this place Tomorrow I will Pay the Ballance To Close my acct £21.1.1 altho I have a Quantity of Flour at this place I received of Sundrie Pooer Tenants at 26/ ℔ Barrel and now will not sell @ 22s/ Cash, as it's my Conduct I must Submit To it.[2] For your Sattisfaction I here Inclose a List of Ballances that may be Collected—as the Chief of them will be recovered by Law[3] you'll Please To Consider the opperation in this state and not Expect more than half the sum this Summer, suppose £60. I shall be down in Less than three Month & will then give my Self Time To attend on you with all the money I can raise. Henry Shover and Mrs Lemart has made Tolerable Payment this year they Pray Indulgence To another year, in which you will Please To advise me.[4] I will For Your Sattisfaction make out a General rental by next Fall with all the Debts & Credits as Fully as Circumstances will admit of—with all the notes I can make respecting Each Tenament.

Mr Smith Slaughter Sheriff in Berkeley County has Entered a warrant with the Surveyor of sd County To be Levied on 1100 & odd acres Land of Colo. G. W. Fairfaxes under Lease to Mr Giles Cooke with a Pretence that the said Land is not Entered in the Proprietors office. Mr Cooke the Tenant is Very unneasy about the matter Requested of me To ask the Favour of you To Inform Him by me whether their is a deed For the Land as you Surveyed the Land & the Papers are with you the Best information will be From you.[5]

If I Should not hear From you Tomorrow I Shall Leave £21.1.1 with Mr A. Wales—If you can make it Convenient I wish Mr Lear to ride up. I am Sir your Obedient Humble Servant

Battaile Muse

ALS, DLC:GW. Muse wrote on the cover: "By negroe Dennis."

1. On Wednesday, 7 May, GW "Visited all the Plantations—Mill, & Brick Yard" (*Diaries*, 5:317). GW does not indicate that Muse returned to Mount Vernon.

2. GW records the payment from Muse on 8 May (Ledger B, 265).

3. The list of balances has not been found.

4. Muse writes frequently about the chronic difficulties that the impoverished tenants Henry Shover and Ann Lemart had in paying their rent. See Lists of Tenants, 18 Sept. 1785, nn.12, 19.

5. GW lists a survey, 6–8 Nov. 1750, for George William Fairfax, of vacant land between the fork of Bullskin Run and the Shenandoah River, for which

no grant has been found or any indication in GW's field book that the plat was drawn. He lists a second survey, 1 April 1751, of 217 acres on a branch of Long Marsh Run, for which no grant has been found, but the field book indicates the plat was drawn and copied (*Papers, Colonial Series*, 1:26, 28, 36 n.39, 37 n.43). Both tracts in 1788 were in Berkeley County.

## To James McHenry

Dear Sir,                                       Mount Vernon May 8th 1788.

To a letter which I wrote to you somedays ago, I beg leave to refer you.[1] I congratulate with you on the happy decision of your Convention; having no doubt of its weight on those States which are to follow.

In a letter (just received) from Colo. Spaight of North Carolina he informs me of his having sent a small bag of Pease to your care, for me. Have you received them? If so, be so good as to forward them by the Stage (the Cost of which I will pay; without dispatch they will come too late) to Alexandria.[2]

A Monsr Campion who brought over my Asses, says he is in distress, and has written to me for money. Pray what is his character in Baltimore, and what has he been employed about this year and half, in that place? Though he had no demand upon me for the service he performed, yet, I gave him a sum of money as an acknowledgment of my sense of the proper discharge of the trust reposed in him. He told me at that time (fall was twelve months) that he should spend the Winter in Baltimore & Sail for France in the Spring. In the spring (as I was going to Phila.) he told me he should sail in the Fall. In the fall, as I returned from thence, he assured me he should sail in a fortnight—Since which I have heard nothing from, or of him till now, his application to me for money.[3] Your answer (soon) to this part of my letter will be very acceptable to Dear Sir Yr Most Obedt & Affecte Servt

Go: Washington

ALS (photocopy), PU: Armstrong Photostats; LB, DLC:GW. The ALS was listed for sale in Robert F. Batchelder Autographs catalog no. 5, item 119, September 1973.

1. GW's letter is dated 27 April.

2. The letter from Richard Dobbs Spaight of 25 April has not been found, but see McHenry to GW, 18 May, and GW to Spaight, 25 May.

3. For GW's earlier dealings with Jaques Campion, see particularly GW to McHenry, 11 Nov. 1786, n.1. See also McHenry's response of 18 May 1788.

## From Thomas Mifflin

Sir,                    Philadelphia May 8th 1788.
I have the honor to transmit to your Excellency the copy of a circular letter to the State-Societies of the Cincinnati from the Gentlemen who have attended here in consequence of the recommendation of the General-Meeting in May last.[1]
The Members present not making a Quorum no other business could be entered on. I am with the greatest Respect Your Excellencys Obedient & humble Serva⟨nt⟩
Thomas Mifflin
V.P.G.C.

ALS, DSoCi; LS, in the hand of William Jackson, DLC:GW; ALS (retained copy), DSoCi.

1. On 11 May George Turner, secretary of the Society of the Cincinnati, wrote GW from Philadelphia: "I must apologize for not forwarding to your Excellency with General Mifflin's Letter of the 8th Instant (which was committed to my Care) the Copy of the Circular Letter it was intended to enclose. It was an Omission occasioned through Hurry, and which I did not recollect 'till this Moment. I have now the honour to send it herewith" (DLC:GW). The circular letter of 8 May signed for the Society of the Cincinnati by Turner and the other ten members of the Society in attendance at the "Extra-Meeting" of the Society in Philadelphia reported their inability to take any actions due to a lack of a quorum but included this statement regarding L'Enfant's predicament: "The Considerations which induced the last General-Meeting to admit the Claims exhibited by Major L'Enfant against the Society, still existing in full Force, and the Honour of the Society being pledged for the payment of the Money, we cannot avoid expressing our earnest Wish, that the final Settlement of this Business may sustain no farther Delay; and that the several State-Societies, who have not yet complied with the Requisition, would immediately take Measures for remitting their Quotas, as directed in the Resolution of the General-Meeting" (DLC:GW). See L'Enfant to GW, 15 April.

## To Benjamin Rush

Sir,                    Mount Vernon May 10th 1788
Your favour of the 26th ulto together with the seeds of the manget[1] werzel and the Pamphlet respecting the cultivation and

use of this valuable plant, came safe and claims my particular acknowledgments. I thank you for both, and shall endeavor to propogate the former with care and attention. Mrs Washington Joins me in compliments to Mrs Rush. I am Sir &c.

Go. Washington

LB, DLC:GW.
    1. The copyist should have written "mangel."

# From Oliver Pollock

Sir                                 Philad[elphi]a 11th May 1788.
    The late Conflagration of the Town of New Orleans (which was the place of my residence during the Grand Contest with Great Britain) I hope will in some measure appoligize for troubling your Excellency's repose on this Occasion.
    I have bussiness of importance to settle in that Country and have now to request from you a letter of introduction to His Excellency Governor Stephen Miro Commander in Chief of Louissiana to wch place I purpose to set out by the first favourable Opportunity.[1] I have the honor to be with the most profound respect Your Excellency's Most Obedient & Most Humble Servant

Or Pollock

ALS, DLC:GW. The letter was forwarded to GW from Richmond by Robert Morris on 26 May.
    Oliver Pollock (1737–1823) left Ireland and settled in New Orleans before the American Revolution. During the war he served as a commercial agent in Louisiana for both the United States and Virginia. For the continuing disputes over Pollock's accounts, see Beauregard & Bourgeois to GW, 14 Oct. 1789, and the notes of that document.
    1. Esteban Rodríguez Miró y Sabater (1744–1795) was made acting governor of Spanish Louisiana in 1782, governor in 1785, and intendant as well on 10 May 1788. He pushed forward on the reconstruction of New Orleans after the devastating fire of 1788, until he left office at the end of 1791. GW responded to Pollock from Mount Vernon on 8 June: "Sir, I received your letter of the 11th of May at the moment when I was setting out for a pre-concerted journey to meet the Directors of the Potomack Company on business of importance at the Shenandoah falls—that circumstance has necessitated me to defer giving an acknowledgment until this time.
    "It would be with particular pleasure that I should write to his Excellency the Governor of Louisiana on your behalf if I did not think that there would

be a glaring impropriety in my assuming that liberty with that representative of the Spanish King—especially as I have never had the honor of a personal acquaintance or any corrispondence with the Governor—I do not feel myself authorised to take a greater latitude of freedom in this respect than any other unknown private citizen these motives of delicacy on my part I hope will be considered in the same point ⟨of light, and of the same weight by you as they have appeared to me. With sentiments of consideration & respect I am Sir Your Most Obed. & Most Hble Servant Go. Washington⟩" (ALS, in private hands; LB, DLC:GW). The portion in angle brackets is taken from the letter-book copy.

## To Clement Biddle

Dear Sir,                                    Mount Vernon 12th May 1788

I have received your two letters of the 29 of April & 4th of May.[1] Since my application to you for the prices of Linen & Blankets I have had an opportunity of supplying myself with both, upon pretty reasonable terms, but am no less obliged to you for the trouble of your inquiries respecting them.

The Philadelphia Packet has not yet arrived, but if she sailed at the time you mention she may be expected very soon.

I will thank you to inform me whether you have received the Interest due upon my Certificate in your hands, as there is a balance due to you in consequence of those articles last purchased on my Acct which shall be remitted if it is not adjusted by the above Interest.[2]

Will you be so obliging as to let me know in your next what the price of double & single refined Sugar is with you?

Nails from 8d. to 20d. can be purchased cheaper in Alexandria than in Philadelphia. 20d. can be had in the former place @ 10/2 per M—allowing 20 lb. to the M—whereas 20 lb. at 9d. would amount to 15/ Pensylvania Currency; but I beleive all under 8d. would come cheaper @ 9d. per pound. With great esteem, I am, Dear Sir, Your most Obedt Hble Servt

Go: Washington

P.S. Pray forward the Letter to Genl Armstrong when a good conveyance offers. G.W.[3]

LS, in the hand of Tobias Lear, PHi: Washington-Biddle Correspondence; LB, DLC:GW.

1. No letter from Biddle dated 29 April has been found. The contents of

GW's letter make it certain that he is referring to the letter from Biddle dated 21 April, a copy of which is in Biddle's letter book. Biddle's notes for his letter of 4 May are printed in note 1 of Biddle's letter of 21 April.

2. At the dissolution of their partnership at Washington's Bottom, Pa., in 1785, GW secured from Gilbert Simpson a U.S. certificate, which GW sent to Biddle to dispose of. Biddle converted it to a Pennsylvania certificate and sent the interest to GW. See GW to Biddle, 1 Feb. 1785, n.8.

3. The postscript is in GW's hand. GW's letter to John Armstrong is dated 25 April.

*Letter not found*: From John Cowper, 12 May 1788. On 25 May GW wrote Cowper: "I have been duly favored with your letter of the 12th Inst."

# From John Hopkins

Sir                                        Richmond May 14 1788
    I was favor'd with your Letter of the 27th Ulto by Mr Charles Lee, covering sundry Warrants for articles furnished the Army during the late War, to the Amount of £107.12.2 & 305 Dollars 53ths in Indents of Interest[1]—And Mr Lee has placed in my hands the sum of £69 in Warrants for Interest on Loan Office Certificates of this State, to be applied to the payment of your Taxes;[2] but you will be pleased to observe, by the Statement of these Taxes, which I have the honor of transmitting for your information, that I am obliged to make a different arrangment, of them, than what you have supposed. Indents are not admissable in discharge of the Certificate Tax, nor are Certificates or Warrants for Articles furnished the Army received in payment of the revenue, or Specie Taxes, as you will observe by the Statement above mentioned. So many therefore of the Warrants as are necessary to pay the Certificate Tax, as well as the proper proportion of Indents, admissable in discharge of the Specie Tax, I have taken from the sums sent me, and the balance, I return by Mr Lee.[3]
    The Sherif of Green Briar will be down during the Sitting of the Genl Court in June next, when I will make the enquiry respecting your Lands and inform you.[4]
    I beg leave to assure you Sir, that I will with very great pleasure execute this Commission, and on all occasions shall be happy in the opportunity of shewing you with how much re-

spect and Esteem, I have the honor to be Sir Your Mo. obt hble servant

Jno. Hopkins

ALS, DLC:GW.

    1. See GW to Hopkins, 27 April, nn.1, 2.

    2. See GW to Charles Lee, 27 April, and note 1 of that document.

    3. Hopkins enclosed this statement of the action he had taken:

Genl Washingtons Taxes may be paid in the followg form. Viz.

| | |
|---|---:|
| Half Tax for the Year 1785—⅔ds in Indents | £23.18.2 |
| ⅓d in Specie, or Warrants on Certain funds | 11.19.1 |
| | £35.17.3 |
| Tax for the Year 1786. ⅓d in Indents | 23.18.2 |
| ⅔ds Specie, or warrants as above, or Tobo | 47.16.4 |
| | £71.14.6 |
| Tax for the Year 1787—no part payable in Indents | |
|    but in Warrants of the foregoing description, or Tobo | £71.14.6 |
| Certificate Tax's for 1785, and 1786, payable in any | |
|    Auditors Certificates or Warrants | £91.12.8 |

Below this are Hopkins's notes giving the information about the taxes owed in Greenbrier County which GW sent him on April 27 (see note 1 of GW's letter) and Hopkin's copy of two receipts. The first reads: "Received June 16. 1788 of John Hopkins the above sum of One hundred and Seventy nine pounds 6/3, for the above Taxes, on account of Genl Washington. Robert Rennik Do." This is followed by a copy of Rennick's receipt of the same date of £95.12.8 for "Certificate Taxes."

    4. See GW to Hopkins, 27 April, and note 5 of that document, and Hopkins to GW, 20 June.

## From Charles Lee

Richmond 14th april [May] 1788

Dear Sir,
    I have received your Letter covering one to Mr John Hopkins to whom I have delivered it.[1] The warrants in my hands not being receivable in discharge of the claims of the James River Company have been deposited in Mr Hopkin's hands as you directed.[2] He informs me (and he is right in my opinion) that the securities you enclosed to him will not answer in the payment of your taxes for 1785 & 1786 exactly as stated in your letter and I have desired him to retain such as can be applied to those taxes and to return to me the residue with a Sketch of his account enclosed to you.[3] As to your other lands not contained in the account of the Green Brier Sheriff, I suppose they cannot have

been sold because a previous advertisement in some newspaper has been necessary.

The Court of Appeals after much consideration have determined that the District Law of the last session is contrary to the constitution and therefore ought not to be executed. This they have represented to the Executive who are this day to decide whether the Genl Assembly ought not immediately to be called which I think probable. However the Governor does not seem to like the idea and this aversion is attributed to the circumstance, that the district bill was drawn by him. I apprehend the public opinion will be much divided respecting the conduct of the Judiciary and that it will be a source of uneasiness and distraction among the people at large.

With regard to the proposed constitution, it seems that the newspapers have mispublished the delegates from Kentucky and the governor informs me that they are to a man opposed to it—He seems to be fixing in favor of it, and this stroke of the Judiciary will have some effect upon his mind and perhaps on the minds of others shewing the incompetency of our present government to maintain us in society. I have the honor to remain Dear Sir with great regard and esteem your most obed. hble Sert

Charles Lee

P.S. The Assembly are to meet on the 23d June by order of Council.[4] C. Lee

ALS, DLC:GW. Lee dates this letter 14 April, but it is written in response to GW's letter of 27 April, in which he enclosed a letter to John Hopkins of the same date dealing with the same matter. Hopkins's reply is dated 14 May, and it has been assumed that Lee mistook only the month and not the day of the month as well. The date, 14 May, fits the contents of the letter.

1. See GW to Lee and to John Hopkins, both 27 April.

2. See GW to Lee, 27 April, nn.1, 3.

3. See GW to Hopkins, 27 April, and notes 1 and 2 of that document, and Hopkins to GW, 14 May, and notes.

4. The Virginia assembly on 3 Jan. 1788 passed a bill establishing district courts in Virginia to be presided over by the judges of the general court, whose number were to be increased by four (12 Hening 532–58). On 12 May the judges of the court of appeals drew up a remonstrance objecting to the act on the grounds that it infringed on the independence of the judiciary, and they presented it to Gov. Edmund Randolph to be forwarded to the assembly. On 14 May after Randolph informed the executive council of the remonstrance, it was decided that the legislature should be called into special session on 23

June. In the special session, 24–30 June, the legislature voted to suspend the operation of the district court act (Reardon, *Randolph*, 161–62). A new district court bill was passed in the next session, on 22 Dec. 1788 (12 Hening 730–63).

## From Osborn Parson

May 14th 1788

May it Please your Excellency for an unfortuneate unhappy friendless stranger to adress you with a few lines to claim your Excellency's Bounty being distitute of the necessary's of life and in a strange land no friends nor relations to commiserate my misfortunes nor relieve my distress. Five years of my time was spent in defence of my country with many hardships and the loos of Blood having been wounded at the Battle of the Green Spring Virginia[1] But when the happy tidings of Peace arriv'd I then thought myself happy having made some speculation and my own income amounted to a sum I thought would put me above the frowns of this world five years have I spent in the enjoyment of my friends since the war but hearing of that flourishing Country of Kantucky I converted all my property into Ready money and took my journey By the way of Philadelphia having Business at Baltimore but on my journey Betwen Philadelphia and Baltimore near Bush Town I was attacked by some Ruffins and Robed of all my money except one Guinea Thus being depriv'd of all my flattering Prospects of settleing myself in that flourishing Country I am redused to necessity and want and am now a wandering about this wretched world like a wave tosed upon the Otion with Grief sorrow and bitter anguish companions of my way if I return to my native soil I have no prospect before me if I Go on I have no means to procure any subsistance O that Heaven (or some friendly hand) would assist or direct me what cource to take and indue me with fortitude to bare up against the frowns of Divine Providence. When I look round this world and behold my fellow mortals in the heights of happiness Possesed of Riches and Grandure and spend their Days in peace and plenty it fills my heart with inexpressable Grief to think while they injoy their happyness I am doomed to spend my Days in moloncoly reflection upon my past Misfortune But why do I reflect upon the will of Divine Providence as it is my unhappy lot I submit to my fate, but knowing the goodness of your Excellency's Heart I make thus bold to unbosom my misfortunes hoping and praying your Excellency will consider my unhappy Circumstances and not impute it to forwardness but real necessity Perhaps your Excellen[c]y may ask why I did not deliver this in an extemporary manner to which I answer your Excellencys dread presence would so abash me that I should not have the power of utterence.

So submitting my unhappy circumstances to your Excellency's perusal I subscribe praying for the choicest of Heavens Blessing to desend and light on you and your noble consort and may your live happy all the days of your appointed time and at last receive that immortal Crown of Glory which is your just Reward.

Osborn Parson

May it please your Excellency to excuse the inaccuracy of my writing.

ALS, DLC:GW.

1. The battle at Green Spring, near Jamestown, took place on 6 July 1781 when false information induced Anthony Wayne to attack the British army under Cornwallis. Lafayette came to Wayne's support and ordered a retreat, leaving 139 Americans killed, wounded, or captured. Most of the troops involved were Pennsylvanians with a large contingent of Virginia troops from Augusta County. Parson's name has not been found in listings of soldiers in either the Pennsylvania or the Virginia forces.

## From Thomas Green

Dear Sr                                                    May th[e] 15. 1788

I Humbley beg your parden for my Neglet of Duty to you and I hope you will take it in Consideration and over look it this time and I will take Care for the time to Come that you never shall have any thing of the like happen any more when my farther and I left work a monday Night a took a little Grog and I found it hurt me the next day so that I was not fit to do any thing the next day and for Mohonys part he was wors then my self so we took a wark as far as Colo. ⟨stiff⟩[1] house and there was fool a nough to be perswaded by Mohony to go up to town which he promesed me that he hould not stop half a hour and when we got to town I never Could git site of him any more untill about Nine or ten OClock yesterday when I beged of him to Come home with me which he promesed me that he hould if I hould stop for him aboute ½ a hour which I did to git him home with me which we both set oute to Come home togather and Mohony Come on all most to the turnpike and then turned back a gain and I have not seen him since so I Came home by my self Dear Sr I hope you will take it in Consideration and over look it this time and you never shall have any a thing to find fort with me again for I will not ever be perswaded by any person like him again.[2] Sr I am Yours

Thos Green

ALS, DLC:GW.

1. "Colo. ⟨stiff⟩" is probably Buckner Stith who owned about 300 acres on the north and south branches of Little Hunting Creek (deeds of mortgage, Buckner and Ann Stith to William Herbert, 9 Mar. and 9 July 1787, Fairfax County Deed Book Q [1785–88], 495–500). This may be the man of that name who was a son of Drury Stith (c.1718–1770) of Brunswick County, or the Buckner Stith (d. 1800) who was the son of GW's old boyhood friend Buckner Stith (see Stith to GW, 22 Mar. 1787). Both men had wives named Ann.

2. Thomas Green was the overseer of the carpenters at Mount Vernon for a decade beginning in 1783. For earlier references to his misbehavior, see GW to George Augustine Washington, 1 July and 2 Sept. 1787. Thomas Mahony was a carpenter whom GW had recently rehired (see Mahony to GW, 3 April 1788).

# To John Jay

Dear Sir,                                       Mount Vernon May 15th 1788

I am indebted to you for your favors of the 20th & 24th Ult. and thank you for your care of my foreign letters. I do the same for the Pamphlet you were so obliging as to send me.[1] The good sense, forceable observations, temper and moderation with which it is written cannot fail, I should think, of making a serious impression even upon the antifœderal mind where it is not under the influence of such local views as will yield to no arguments—no proofs.

Could you, conveniently, furnish me with another of these pamphlets I would thank you, having sent the last to a friend of mine.

Since the Elections in this State little doubt is entertained of the adoption of the proposed Constitution with us (if no mistake has been made with respect to the Sentiments of the Kentucke members). The opponents to it I am informed are *now* also of this opinion. Their grand manœuvres were exhibited at the Elections, and some of them, if report be true, were not much to their credit. Failing in their attempt to exclude the friends to the New Government, from the Convention, and baffled in their exertions to effect an adjournment in Maryland, they have become more passive *of late.* Should South Carolina (now in Session) decide favourably, and the government thereby (nine States having acceded) get in motion, I can scarcely conceive that any one of the remainder, or all of them together, were they to convene for the purpose of deliberation would (seperated from each other as they then would be in a geographical point of view) incline to withdraw from the Union with the other nine—Mrs Washington unites with me in Compliments and good wishes for you and Mrs Jay—and with sentiments of very great esteem & regard—I am Dear Sir Yr Most Obedt & Affecte Sert

Go: Washington

ALS, NNC; LB, DLC:GW.
 1. See Jay to GW, 20 April, n.2.

*Letter not found*: from Henry Emanuel Lutterloh, 15 May 1788. On 3 June 1791 Lutterloh wrote to GW: "I took the Liberty to state My Reasons in My Answer of the 15th of May following [1788]."

# From James Rumsey

Dr General,                                   philedelphia May 15th 1788.

    When I Last had the honor of writeing to you I was about Seting out on a Very uncertain Expedition.[1] I Came to this place with an Intention of astablishing my prior Right to The Invention of the Steam boat and have met with great Oppozetion from Mr Fitches Company who Seem to Stop at nothing to Carry their point[.] by advice of Several freinds we attempted an N[e]-gotiation of the matter and I was met Several Times by Deputyes from his Company in The Course of which I offered to make an Eaqual Join of the matter with them which They Refused, &

they offered me one Eighth which I Refused, when all negotiation Ceased.

I Laid the Drafts of Several Mechines before the philosophical Society Expecting thereby to Secure Such Inventions to myself[.] among these Drafts was my new Invented Boiler for Genereateing Steam my papers was In possesion of his Excellencey Docter Franklin Several Days before the Day of Meeting But on that Day three other Drafts was handed in of Boilers on the Same princeples as mine but Varyed a Little in form two of these was a Mr Voights a partners of Mr Fitches, the other by a person of Influance a teacher in the Collage I found who it was by axedent. Inclosed you have the Report of a Committee of the philosophical Society on the above mentioned Mecheines,[2] also the proposials of a plann I published to form a Company and the names of the persons that has subscribed to it,[3] when this was known Mr Fitches party Immediately Sent a Draft of the boiler to Urope, with Letters and Instructions to apply for a pattent for it. the Gentlemen That formed my Company was Roused at Such Treatment and at the next meeting after the first formation of it, they Subscribed 1000 Dollars more for the Express purpos of Sending me to Urope and I am to Set of in the morning, Docter Franklin and a number of other Gentl. write Letters by me to their freinds in Europe.[4] If you think Sir that you Could with propriaty mention me in a Line the first opertunity to the Marquis La Fayette Mr Jefferson or any other Gentlemen that you may think proper the favor Should always be most Greatfully Remembered.[5] Benjamin Vaughn Esqr. Jeffreys Square and Mr Robert Barclay[,] Thralers Brewery[,] Southwark London are to be two of my Confitent⟨ial⟩ freinds—Doctr Franklin is to name one or two more In his Letters which I have not got yet but am to Call on him in the Evening for them. I am Sir with Every Sentiment of Esteem your much obliged hble Servt

James Rumsey

P.S. If Mr hartshorn would give me Credit for the Boats and Sum Other Small accounts that Lye with him It would nearly pay what was Called for by the Company before I Came from home

ALS, DLC:GW.

1. See Rumsey to GW, 24 March.

2. The enclosed printed extracts of the meetings of the American Philosophical Society on 18 April and 2 May show that on 18 April the society had received a letter from James Rumsey "accompanied with a drawing and description of an improved boiler for a steam engine, as also drawings and descriptions" of improvements on "Dr. Barker's Grist-Mill" and "the Saw-Mill" and the mode of "raising water, by means of a Steam-engine." Henry Voight, John Fitch's assistant, also submitted a letter with drawings and descriptions of boilers for generating steam. A committee of three, including David Rittenhouse, was appointed to examine and make a report on "the several papers on the production and use of Steam," which also included one by John Stevens. The committee's report made on 2 May reads: "The principle which Mr. Rumsey, and Mr. Voight seem to have adopted, in the construction of their proposed boilers for Steam-Engines, viz. to increase the surface, and diminish the quantity of water exposed to the action of the fire, appears to your committee, in general to be just. But what may be the best application of this principle, must, no doubt, in some measure be determined by actual experiments.

"The improvement which Mr. Rumsey proposes in Dr. Barker's Grist-Mill; that in the Saw-Mill; and that in raising of water, by means of a Steam-Engine, are certainly ingenious, in theory, and will deserve a full trial."

3. The enclosed broadside is headed in various sized types: "Proposals for forming a Company, to enable James Rumsey To carry into Execution on a Large and Extensive Plan, his Steam-Boat And sundry other Machines herein after mentioned." Rumsey's list of names of the nineteen men who bought at least one share in the Rumseyan Society is headed by Benjamin Franklin and includes such men as Arthur St. Clair, William Bingham, William Barton, Levi Hollingsworth, and Charles Vancouver. Rumsey also at this time published *A Short Treatise on the Application of Steam* to bolster his case for having "fixed on a method of applying steam to propel a boat before Mr. Fitch" (quoted in Turner, *Rumsey*, 113).

4. Rumsey boarded the ship bound for England on 14 May and among the letters he took with him were one from Benjamin Rush to the famed Dr. John Coakley Lettsom and one from Franklin to GW's friend Benjamin Vaughan.

5. GW does not seem to have written letters for Rumsey, who was still in London when he became ill and died in December 1792.

# From Francis Adrian Van der Kemp

Sir!                                        New-york 15 May 1788

Being honoured with a recommendatory letter of the Marquis de La Fayette to your Excellency, in view to adsist my endeavours to Settle my in this commonwealth with my wife and two children, who followed their husband and father from the Unhappy Nethelands I thougth it my duty to Sent that letter to your Excellency, as soon Possible. Althoug I lost the greatest part of my fortune in the defence of the Rigths of the enhabitants of a country—before my fellow-citisens—now Subdued by an unlawful power, with the adsistance of two mighty forein allies I flatter my Selv with the hope, that it wil be Sufficient to procure me and my family a henest Susestance in one of the other Part of America if my unrelented endeavour are blessed by Providence. as i have no larger views formed than to Subsisst, and enjoy of that indepence with belongs to a member of a free State I think it wil be So.

I am personally acquainted—Since Several years by Mr John Adams. This man can inform your Excellency of my character of what I have done. If I am happy enough to be honoured by length of time—with your Excellency's adprobation and may enjoy—for the present—of your advie—this wil give a new ⟨Surcroit⟩ to my Contentment. It is my design to make a tour to Philadelphia to deliver my recommandatory letters, as I did in this town; and if I am happy enough to know before me departur that the paying a vsit to your Excellency wil not be Ungrateful I wil make that digression of Some days. my duty of making no expences, without necessity is the reason of this question—and my departur to Philadelphia wil not have place before the arrival of the French Packet. It sh⟨all be⟩ always for me a blessing to tell to my children—that I Saw and Spoke that Man, who was the principal foundator of all those blessings, which Surely wil be their property—if they chuse to live in a virtuous manner.

Be Sure Sir! that no born American, who was an eye-witness of your uncommon deeds, wil pay, with more Sincerity, the respect and admiration, due to your Person, than He, who is Sir Your most obedient Servant

Fr. Adr. van der Kemp

ALS, DLC:GW.

1. Lafayette wrote GW from Paris on 6 Mar.: "My dear General Give me Leave to Present to you Mr Van der Kemp a Gentleman Whose Conduct in the Patriotic Cause of Holland Entitles Him to Your Attention and Patronage—He is Recommended to Me Most Particularly By the first Characters Among the Patriots. I Have Many Opportunities to See the Refugees from Holland, Many of Whom Had Wished to Entrust their Military Affairs to one Who Had Been Educated at General Washington's Head Quarters. they Have Spoken to me of Mr Van der Kemp their fellow Sufferer in Such terms as Make me Happy

to introduce Him to You. With filial love and Respect I Have the Honour to Be My dear General Yours Lafayette" (PEL). Thomas Jefferson wrote James Madison on 8 Mar. to introduce Francis Adrian Van der Kemp (1752–1829), who had been recommended to him "for his extraordinary zeal in the cause of liberty, his talents, & his sufferings" (Rutland and Hobson, *Madison Papers*, 11:1–2). Van der Kemp settled in the state of New York. See GW's response to Van der Kemp, 28 May.

# From John Lathrop

Much Hond Sir,                              Boston May 16. 1788

Please to accept of my best thanks for your letter of Feby 22, and the very obliging manner in which you are pleased to accept mine of Jany 28, together with the pamphlets, which I took the liberty to send you—Your approbation of the institution which I had the honour of introducing to you, encourages me to send the inclosed, which have been published by order of the Society.[1]

The President & Trustees, thought it might be acceptable to the Friends of Humanity to have the method of Treatment to be used with persons apparently dead from drowning and other accidents, expressed in a very plain & concise manner, so that those who may have it in their power to give assistance on such occasions may know at once what is proper to be done; at the same time they were glad of an opportunity to advertise several successful cases, which have happened since the last year: several have been recoverd from apparent Death, & several have been saved from pereshing by cold, in one of the Shelters erected by the Society—I know Sir, every information of this kind, will afford you real pleasure; and since you are pleased to allow me the honour, I will communicate to you all such cases as shall be authenticated by the Society.

This Sir, is an age of astonishing improvement: Americans I hope will not be wanting in their exertions to come up with Europeans in whatever tends to the dignity of human Nature, and the increase of human felicity. Nothing seems wanting but a good general Government, to make the Inhabitants of this part of the World as respectable and happy as the Inhabitants of any quarter of the Globe.[2]

We are looking with vast expectation and hope to your ancient and venerable state. Massachusetts, in the most difficult and trying times prided herself in acting in strict concert with Virginia: we hope to be unitd with her and all the Sister States, in that form of Government which was drawn up by the Philadelphia convention, and with all its imperfections, has more to recommend it, than any Constitution formed heretofore, by the wisdom of man.

That this Constitution may be adopted, that America may rise to glory and influence among the Nations of the Earth, and that you Sir, may reap the just fruit of your toils and dangers, is the prayer of Hond Sir Your most obedt & most humbe Servt

John Lathrop

ALS, DLC:GW.

1. Lathrop's pamphlet (see Lathrop to GW, 28 Jan., n.1) included in its appendix a description of "the method of treatment to be used with persons apparently dead from drowning &c." The copy in GW's library was inscribed: "His Excellency General Washington from his humbl. Servt the Author" (Griffin, *Boston Athenæum Collection*, 119).

2. See GW's endorsement of these sentiments in his response to Lathrop of 22 June.

## From Robert Morris

Dear Sir                    Richmond May 16th 1788

Having been honoured with the receipt of your very obliging letter of the 2d Inst. I waited to hear of Mrs Morris's setting out on her journey before I gave you the trouble of my thanks for its Contents; Before you receive this Mrs Morris & three of her children will feel them selves happy under Your Hospitable roof, I am not ready, but shall make every exertion to finish my tedious & troublesome business here, so that I may personally make those acknowledgements which will be due to Mrs Washington & yourself for the kind reception I know my Family will meet at Mount Vernon. the Mail is just making up & I have only time to assure you of my respect & Esteem being ever my Dr sir Your most obedient humble Servant

Robt Morris

ALS, DLC:GW.

*Letter not found*: from William West, 17 May 1788. GW wrote West on 28 June: "I was favoured with your letter of the 17th Ult."

# From James McHenry

Dear General.                                    Baltimore 18 May 1788.

It has not been in my power to acknowlege the receipt of your letters of the 27 Ulto and the 8 inst. before to-day.

Immediately on my return from Annapolis I sent the peas by Capn Mann with orders, if the wind would admit, to drop them at Mount Vernon, otherwise, to leave them with Col. Hoe; so that I expect they will have reached you long before this comes to hand.[1]

Campion for some time taught fencing—he then tried the billiard table, and within these few days past has decamped (I am told) to New York. I understand he has cheated as many as would trust him.

You will have concluded from the address of our minority that the convention were a little embarassed on the subject of amendments. A very good friend of yours for whom I have the greatest respect brought us into the difficulty, and we were obliged to leave him to get out of it. The amendments were intended to injure the cause of federalism in your State, and had we agreed to them they were well calculated to effect it.[2] With the greatest regard and affection I am Dr General your

James McHenry

ALS, DLC:GW.

1. McHenry is referring to peas sent by Richard Dobbs Spaight to GW from North Carolina by way of Baltimore. See GW to McHenry, 8 May, and note 2 of that document. GW records in his diary planting on 1 and 2 July the seed sent by Spaight; and on 22 Oct. he writes in his diary: "Those Pease which were sent me by Colo. Spaight and planted at this place [Muddy Hole] at the same time were quite ripe and had been pulled great part of them many days ago—qty. of these latter about 9 bushels from about [    ] Acres of grd. These are a very forward kind, and must be reserved for Seed" (*Diaries*, 5:353, 354, 410).

2. Daniel Carroll wrote James Madison on 28 May: "The truth is Mr [Thomas] Johnsons accomodating disposition and a respect to his charac[ter] lead the Majority into a Situation, out of which they found some dificulty to extricate themselves" (Rutland and Hobson, *Madison Papers*, 11:66–68). This was with reference to the report of the committee appointed by the Maryland Ratifying Convention to make recommendations regarding William Paca's twenty-eight proposed amendments to the Constitution.

# From Robert Morris

Dear Sir                                    Richmond May 18th 1788

The enclosed letter will probably deprive you of the Company of your guests sooner than you expected, & my partiality for them leads me to believe you will feel a disapointment in that event.

But by way of attonement we must pass a few days with you on our return. The business which has detained me so long being now in such train that I cannot leave it, and my presence for a Couple of Weeks longer likely either to finish it entirely, or so near as to render further attention unnecessary I determine to ⟨sort⟩ it out at all events. My anxiety to see my Family after so (unexpectedly) long absence, is surely excusable & I have desired Mrs Morris to come on,[1] the journey is not long and they may make it easy by coming Thursday to Mr Fitzhughs, on Friday to the Bowling Green (where if I can I will meet them that Evening) & the next day here.[2] They will have an opportunity of seeing more of this Country & of making some valuable acquaintances and can pass their time very agreably untill I am ready to return. Mr G. Morris joins in my request to be remembered most respectfully to Mrs Washington as also in the assurance of the esteem & regard with which I have the honor to profess myself Dr Sir Your most obedient & humble Servant

Robt Morris

ALS, DLC:GW.

1. Mary White Morris, two of her sons, and a daughter arrived at Mount Vernon on 17 May and left for Richmond on 22 May after she received the letter that her husband had enclosed for her. On 12 July Robert Morris, his wife and children, and Gouverneur Morris came up to Mount Vernon from Richmond and remained there until 15 July, before continuing their journey to Philadelphia (*Diaries*, 5:326, 329, 360, 361).

2. This is William Fitzhugh who lived at Chatham across the river from Fredericksburg. Bowling Green is between Fredericksburg and Richmond, about forty miles from the latter.

## To Sarah and Thomas Porter

[18 May 1788]

*General* and Mrs *Washington presents* their *Compliments* to Mr and Mrs Porter *and requests* the favor of their *Company at* dinner tomorrow Monday 19th May 1788. An answer is requested.

AD, ViMtV. The italicized words of the invitation are printed; the remainder are in the hand of GW. GW struck out the final "s" in "presents."

Sarah (Sally) Ramsay, daughter of William Ramsay, and the Alexandria merchant Thomas Porter were married on 5 Feb. 1788.

## To Jeremiah Wadsworth

Dear Sir,                                        Mount Vernon May 18th 1788

Your favor of the 22d Ulto and a Barrel of Barley have arrived safe, & I pray you to accept my thanks for the latter. I lost no time in committing it to the Ground; & shall, (as it was good) look for a prolific return. My People, however, tell me it is a grain that is called Bare, and considered more as a Winter than Summer grain, tho' it is, *sometimes* sown in the Spring they say.[1]

Mrs Washington joins me in Compliments, & good wishes for you and Mrs Wadsworth[2]—and with sentiments of great esteem & regard I am Dear Sir Yr most Obedt Hble Ser⟨vt⟩

Go: Washington

Colo. Humphreys is here, & begs to be remembered to you.

ALS, O.

1. Wadsworth's letter of 22 April has not been found. Wadsworth was a businessman in Connecticut who also took an active interest in experimental agriculture and cattle breeding.

2. Wadsworth married Mehitabel Russell in 1767.

## To Thomas Lewis

Sir,                                        Mount Vernon May 19th 1788

Enclosed is the duplicate of a letter I wrote to you agreeably to the date, but having heard nothing from you since, I am apprehensive it may have met with a miscarriage and therefore send this copy by your Brother who will endeavor to contrive it safe to you.[1]

I have been called upon for Taxes, and threatned at the same-time with a Sale of the Land after June, if the money is not paid before, by the Sheriff of Green brier County—As I have been suffering loss after loss for near ten years while I was in the public Service and have scarcely had time to breath sence. to this proceedure seems to me to be a little hasty, no regular application bee'n made to me—nor I might add any application at all but by these threats indirectly sent. to be threatned with a Sale when I cannot upon enquiry find that others who have lands in the same County has been treated in that rigorous manner seems to carry with it singular appearince. I am however, endeavouring to provide for the payment but wish to meet that measure and indulgence which is shewn to others.[2]

I have heard also, that People, under some other authority than mine, are settling in the point of a Fork between Cole River an[d] the great Kankawa; as I have a tract of two thousand Acres which encludes this spot these persons should be informed thereof to prevent deception to themselves, or trouble to me. The authority (if you encline to act under it) with which you are invested will enable you to settle this matter with them and to continue them thereon if you can agree on terms.[3] I am &ca

Go. Washington

LB, DLC:GW.

1. See GW to Thomas Lewis, 25 Dec. 1787. The brother referred to was Andrew Lewis, Jr. (see GW to Andrew Lewis, Jr., 1 Feb. 1788).

2. See GW to Henry Banks, 22 Nov. 1787, GW to Bushrod Washington, 3 Dec. 1787, and, especially, Charles Lee to GW, 17 April 1788, and the references in note 2 of that document.

3. For this tract of land, see GW to Thomas Lewis, 1 Feb. 1784, n.6. This letter of 1 Feb. 1784 was to Thomas Lewis, the brother of Gen. Andrew Lewis, whereas the letter printed here was written to Gen. Andrew Lewis's son Thomas. GW's letter to Lewis of 25 Dec. 1787 had given Lewis authority to act for him, but Lewis wrote on 27 Aug. 1788 refusing the commission.

# From Lafayette

My dear General                                   Paris May the 20th 1788

I Have Been Requested to introduce to You Mr de Chastel de la Vallée a french Gentleman Who intends to Visit the United States, and Will probably Settle in one of them. He is Particularly Recommended to Me By the Marquis de Boüillé to Whose lady He is Related, and I Beg, My dear General, you Will Honour Him with Your Advices in His intended plan.[1]

Not knowing When this Can Reach You, and Having a Speedy Opportunity to write I shall only Present You, My Beloved General, with the filial Respect and Affection of Your Most devoted friend

lafayette

ALS, PEL.

1. For the identity of the marquis de Bouillé, see GW to Bouillé, 1 June 1787. There is no mention in GW's diaries of a visit from Chastel de La Vallée to Mount Vernon. For Thomas Lee Shippen's letter introducing Chastel de La Vallée to his father in Philadelphia, see Boyd, *Jefferson Papers*, 13:120. See also the reference to a letter to Jefferson from Chastel, 27 Sept. 1788, ibid., 640.

## To Lachlan McIntosh

Dear Sir,                                            [Mount Vernon, 20 May 1788]

This letter will be presented to you by Mr Stevens, and is introductory of him; He has been an Officer in the Virginia line of the Army during the War, and as far as hath come to my knowledge behaved with zeal and propriety in the Service of his Country.[1] Business carrying him to the State of Georgia, I could not refuse him this recommendation, & myself the pleasure of assuring you that I am Yr Most Obedt and very Hble Servt

Go: Washington

ALS, NjP: deCoppet Collection.

1. Mr. Stevens may be Edward Stevens (1745–1820) of Culpeper County, former colonel of the 10th Virginia Regiment and at this time a state senator, or he may be Richard Stevens of Caroline County who served as captain in the 18th (and 16th) Virginia Regiment from 1777 to 1781. It is less likely that he was William Stevens (Stephens; d. 1825), a lieutenant in the 3rd and 5th Virginia regiments from 1777 until his capture in May 1780.

## From Jean Gibo

My Lord,                                            Alexandria 22d May 1788

Pardon me for presuming to take the Liberty of troubling your Excellency, to whom every moment is so precious—your name so much respected among us was the Cause I did not in the smallest degree hesitate to Comply with every request that your dear Nephew Mr Ferdinand Washington ever made to me;[1] when at the Warm Springs I supplied him with every thing he asked me for, and when I was returning home I presented him my accot against him, which he recd and promised to leave the amount of it with Mrs Hannah, at the Coffee house, in this Town, with whom I left the Note he was good enough to give me for the Same[2]—Indeed had he asked me for twice the amot he should have had it most chearfully, considering he was so nearly connected with a personage So illustrious as yourself. Had not a premature Death prevented him, I am thoroughly convinced I should have been paid long ago. From a very considerable Robbery that has been committed in my absence by my Servant, and from the many Instances of bad faith I have met with from allmost every person I have had any dealings with, I find my self most unhappily circumstanced in my affairs. I shall hold myself exceedingly obliged to your Excellency for this Small Sum (the amot of which your Excellency can See by the inclosed Note)[3] and the payment of it will most certainly greatly add to your well known honor as you can have no other motive for paying it than that of generosity altogether disinterested, and for which your Excellency has always been most justly praised. I hope your Excellency will graciously consider what a Loss I should Sustain in not receiving this Small Sum, which would be So inconsiderable to your Excellency & which would be a very principall means of retreiving my affairs which I am Sorry to Say are truly distressing—I cannot expect to receive it from any other person but your Excellency, as the Guardians of your dear Nephew have no right to pay it, as the Transaction happened before he was of age. I will not murmur should your Excellency decline settling this small matter, but when I consider the character of your Excellency with respect to the unfortunate I have not the smallest doubt but your Excellency will do every thing in your power to serve me.[4] In expectation of your gracious Answer, I have the honor to be My Lord, Your most obedeint and very Hble Servt

jean gibo

LS, DLC:GW.

Jean (John) Gibo's name appears on several occasions in the Fairfax County court records in 1789 and 1792.

1. Samuel Washington's son Ferdinand died in February 1788.

2. Nicholas Hannah (died c.1794) owned a coffeehouse in Alexandria. See his advertisement in the *Virginia Journal, and Alexandria Advertiser,* 4 Jan. 1787.

3. The enclosed note has not been found.

4. No reply to Gibo's letter has been found.


## From William Heth

Sir                                        Alexandria 24th May 1788

My extreme impatience to get home after so long an absence, prevents my doing myself the honor of calling on you. Inclos'd you have a Philadelphia paper, containing a piece, which may probably have some influence on our approaching convention—I mean to have it reprinted at Richmond, immediately after my arrival.[1]

I have completed the important business respecting the North Western territory ceded to Congress, in a way, which I flatter myself will give entire Satisfaction to every Man of sense in the State, acquainted with the circumstances attending that business, and must deprive Many of the opposers of the new constitution of a weapon, which might have been used, with too much success—*The disposition of the eastern States, to oppress and take every advantage of the southern.*[2] My compliments of respect, and esteem attend the Ladies & Gentlemen at Mount Vernon—I have the honor to be, sir, Your Most obedient servt

Will. Heth

ALS, DLC:GW.

1. The "piece" in the Philadelphia newspaper has not been identified.

2. William Heth (1750–1807), formerly colonel of the 3d Virginia Regiment, had been in Philadelphia acting as the commissioner for Virginia to settle the state's accounts with Congress for its cession of western lands.


## From Charles Cotesworth Pinckney

Dear General,                      Charleston [S.C.] May 24th 1788

South Carolina has ratified the fœderal Constitution. Our Convention assembled the 12th Instant, & yesterday the vote of ratification was taken—149 Ayes—& 73 Noes—I enclose you a list of the Members who voted on each side. You will be pleased to find that the names you are best acquainted with, were in favour of the Constitution, and that those who were against it, have declared they would do all in their power to reconcile their Constituents to its adoption, and would exert themselves in its support.

Mrs Pinckney joins me in tendering our best respects to Mrs Washington & yourself, & to Major Washington & his Lady, & I remain with sincere gratitude for all your favours, Your devoted & affectionate humble Sert

Charles Cotesworth Pinckney

Major Butler out of a principle of delicacy too refined, declined serving in the State Convention, you will not therefore see his Name among the Yeas or Nays.[1]

ALS, DLC:GW.

1. Pierce Butler (1744–1822), a member of the Federal Convention in Philadelphia in 1787 from South Carolina, at this time was a member of Congress, though not attending, which may be why he declined serving in the South Carolina Ratifying Convention.

## To John Cowper

Sir,                                          Mount Vernon May 25th 1788

I have been duly favored with your letter of the 12th Inst.[1] In answer thereto I beg leave to inform you that I am not disinclined to part with my moiety of the land purchased (by the deceased Colo. Fielding Lewis and myself) in North Carolina, provided a reasonable and adequate price can be obtained for it.

For this land, that Gentleman and myself paid (to the best of my recollection) a pistole an Acre 20 odd years ago, and expended considerable Sums in ditching to reclaim the low parts thereof. If under this information you should feel disposed To give a sum that would in some measure make us whole, I would in order to accomodate the Execters of Colo. Lewis who are desirous of selling his moiety, part with mine also; and will as soon as Mr John Lewis can be consulted, communicate the terms to you.[2] Without such disposition on your part, it would be useless to fix on any price or the credits because I am not inclined to sell my part at any considerable loss being fully convinced that if a good government is established and property thereby secured that Land *generally*, will again be in demand and consequently rise, and those which are situated as *this* is will command almost any price, if the Cut between Elizabeth River and Pasquetank (to make which nothing in my opinion is easier) should be effected. I am Sir Yr Most Obedt Hble Sert

G. Washington

LB, DLC:GW.

John Cowper was a merchant in Portsmouth, Virginia. He was made the manager at Portsmouth "for receiving and entering subscriptions" to a new Dismal Swamp Company, created in December 1787 by an act of the Virginia assembly, "for cutting a navigable Canal from the waters of Elizabeth river, in this state, to the waters of Pasquotank river, in the state of North Carolina" (12 Hening 478–94).

1. Letter not found.

2. John Lewis wrote GW on 15 Dec. 1787 about selling the land in North Carolina acquired jointly by GW and his father, Fielding Lewis, before the Revolution. For the location of the land in North Carolina and for references to further correspondence between GW and John Lewis regarding its sale to Cowper on 18 May 1791 for £950, see Lewis to GW, 15 Dec. 1787, n.4, and Lewis to GW, 7 Dec. 1788, n.1. See also GW to Cowper, 26 Oct. 1793, 27 Jan., 9 Mar., 30 July, and 4 Sept. 1794.

# From Henry Knox

New York 25th May 1788.

I have to acknowledge my dear Sir the receipt of your several favors in March and yours of the 28th of april enclosing the application of Major LEnfant.[1]

I intended to have written You from Philadelphia while attending on the Cincinnati but being only three days there, and being much hurried by public business I could not obey my wishes in that respect.

I have this day been putting on board the french packet the eldest son of our highly esteemed friend the late General Greene. He goes to the Marquis de la Fayette in order to receive some years of education in France. It is proposed he should return in about six years. Indeed this will be long enough lest he should receive habits inconsistent with those necessary to be pra[c]ticed in his own country—He is a lively boy and with a good education will probably be An honor to the memory of his father and the pride of his friends.[2]

We have received no explicit information from South Carolina, the convention of which has been in session nearly a fortnight—Nobody doubts that it will be adopted, although it is well ascertained there will be a considerable party against it—Much will depend on Virginia—Her conduct will have a powerful influence on this state and North Carolina.

In this state it appears to be conceded on the part of the federalists that numbers will be against them in the convention, but they hope so many states will previously have adopted the constitution that they shall prevail—It is however doubtful—the party against it in this state are united under the auspices of the Governor and he is supposed to be immoveable—And yet one would think they could not persist in an opposition fraught with the most deadly consequences—The elections will be known in a few days, when a better judgement will be formed than at present.

Colonel Smith has lately arrived from England and informs that Doctor Price and all the friends of liberty in great Britain highly approve the Constitution and ardently wish its adoption—Mr John Adams who probably has arrived in Massachusetts is exceedingly pleased with it, and thinks it the first production ever offered to the human race—It is spoken of by the English Ministers as an admirable form of government and which if adopted will place the American character in a new point of view highly deserving respect.[3]

The turks are oppressed by the plague and what is worse and perhaps more cruel War. If they extricate themselves out of such complicated calamities, it will probably be owing to some work of chance The calculations being greatly against them.

Mrs Knox and her little family are well and unite with me in presenting our respectful compliments to Mrs Washington and I am my dear Sir Your sincere and affectionate humble Servant

H. Knox

If Colo. Humphreys is still with you I will thank you to present my love to him.

ALS, DLC:GW.

1. GW wrote Knox on 3 and 30 March.
2. For an account of young George Washington Greene's sojourn in France

and his tragic death after his return, see GW to Jeremiah Wadsworth, 22 Oct. 1786, n.1.

3. John and Abigail Adams's son-in-law, William Stephens Smith, communicated with GW upon his return from England. See GW to Smith, 1 May.

## From Lafayette

My dear General                                    Paris May the 25th 1788
    In the Midst of our internal troubles, it is a Comfort to me that I May Rejoice in the Happy Prospects that oppen Before My adoptive Country. Accounts from America Give me Every Reason to Hope the New Constitution will Be Adopted. Permit me once More, My Beloved General, to insist on Your Acceptance of the Presidency. The Constitution as it is Proposed Answers Most of the Purposes, But, Unless I am Much Mistaken, there are Some Parts Which Would not Be Quite Free of some danger Had Not the United States the Good fortune to Possess their Guardian Angel, Who May feel the Advantages and inconveniences of Every Article, and Will Be able, Before He Retires Again, to ascertain to What degree Government Must Necessarily be Energic, What powers Might Be diverted into a Bad Use, and to Point out the Means to Attain that Perfection, to which the New Constitution is Already Nearer than Any past or present Governement.
    The affairs of france are Come to a Crisis, the More difficult to Manage as the people in General Have no inclination to Go to Extremities—liberty or death is Not the Motto on this Side of the Atlantic—and as all classes are More or less dependant, as the Rich love their Ease, and the poor are depressed By Want and ignorance, the only Way is to Reason or persuade the Nation into a Kind of Passive discontent or Non obedience which May tire out the Levity and Undo the Plans of Governement. The Parliaments, Notwistanding the inconveniences Attending them, Have Been Necessary Champions to Stand forth. You will See By the Publications, for We Have Sent over Every thing, that the King Has Assumed Pretentions, and the Courts of justice Have Stated principles Which so widely differ that one Could Hardly Believe those Assertions are Made in the Same Country and Century. Matters Could not Rest there. Governement Have

Employed the force of Arms Against Unarmed Magistrates, and Expelled them—and the people will you say? The people, my dear General, Have Been so dull that it Has Made me sick, and phisicians Have Been obliged to Cool My inflammed Blood. What Has the More wounded Up My Anger, is a Bed of justice wherein the King Has Established a *Court pleniere* Composed of judges, peers, and Courtiers, Without one Single Representative, and their Ministers Had the imprudence to Say that all taxes and loans Should Be Registered. thank God, we Have Got the Better, and I Begin to Hope for a Constitution. the Magistrates Have Refused Sitting in the *Cour pleniere*—the Peers, who are Thirty Eight, a few of whom Have Sense and Courage, Will not However Obey—some, like my friend La Rochefoucauld Behaved Nobly. the others follow at a distance. The parliaments Have Unanimously protested and Made an Appeal to the Nation. Most of the inferior Courts Reject the New Regimen—discontents Breack out Every Where, and in Some Provinces are Not despicable. The clergy who Happen to Have an Assembly are Remonstrating. The lawyers Refuse to plead. Governement are Embarrassed and Begin to Apoligise. Their Commandants Have Been in some Parts Pursued with dirt and stones—and the Midst of these troubles and Anarchy the friends of liberty are daily Reinforced, shut up their Ears Against Negociations, and Say they Must Have a National Assembly or Nothing. Such is, my dear General, our Bettering Situation, and I am for My Part Very Easy when I think that I shall Before long Be in an Assembly of the Representatives of the french Nation, or at Mount Vernon.

I am so taken up with those Affairs, that I can tell you But little of European politics. My disapprobation of Ministerial plans, and what little Exertions I Could Make Against them Have induced me to Cease My visits at the Arch Bishop's House, and the More I Have Been Connected with Him and the keeper of the Seals, the Greater indignation I Have professed Against their infernal plan.[1] I am Glad our American Arrêt du Conseil Has taken place Before the full tide of these troubles, and Am Now, through other Ministers, Endeavouring to Bring about a plan for the total Enfranchisement of duties on the Whale oil, Which Would put the American Merchants on the same footing with the french, Even With Respect to Bounties, and that Without obliging the fishermen to leave their Native Shore. Should we succeed in that, our Next object Must Be the trade With the west indias. I am Happy in the Ambassador we Have in this Country, and Nothing Can Excell M. jefferson's abilities, virtues, pleasing temper, and Every thing in Him that Constitutes the Great States man, zealous Citizen, and Amiable friend. He Has a Young Gentleman with Him, Mr Short, a Virginian, who is a very able, Engaging, and Honest Man;[2] This letter Will Be delivered By Mr de Warville, a Man of letters, Who Has writen a pamphlet Against Chattelux's journal, But is However very clever, and wishes very Much to Be presented to You. He intends to write the History of America, and is of Course very desirous to Have a Peep at Your papers Which Appears to me a deserved Condescension as He is Very fond of America, writes pretty Well, and Will set Matters in a proper light. He Has an officer with Him whom I also Beg leave to Recommend—M. de la terriere is His Name.[3]

But to Come to politics, I Must tell you that the War Betwen the Imperial Powers and the turks is Going on—the Emperor Has Made several attempts, But there is a fatality in that Man which Makes Him Ever Begin and Never finish Any Thing. The Skirmishes Have Generally Been doubtfull. He Has taken a town, But was Severely Brushed in an other Assault, and the Same day met with a second defeat. Those Matters, However trifling, show that the turks are either very ill attaked, or More lucky than We did Expect. The siege of Belgrade will Be the Grand Expedition that Way and is Not Begun. There Has Been a jonction Made By the Austrians and Russians in an other Quarter, But they Have Not Much the Means to Operate. The Grand Army of the Russians are Moving toward Ozakow which Prince Potemkin, a former lover, and the Bosom friend of the Empress is Going to Besiege.[4] Paul jones Has Entered the Russian Service and Will Command a Squadron on the Black Sea. all the powers are Negociating for a peace, But at the Same time Spain, Sweden, danemark are Arming. Those will Be observation fleets, and it is Expected that a Peace will take place this Winter. We Must of Course Wish for decisive Actions. Should they be Unfavourable to the Christians it May disgust them. and you Never Can Get a Concession from the turks, Untill the

Prophet Has shown His displeasure By suffering them to Be flogged. in Case Both Parties Maintain their Ground, a General war is Aprehended for the Next Year.

I Beg, My dear General, You will present My Most affectionate Respects to Mrs Washington, And to Your Respected Mother. Remember me to the family, the young ones, your Relations, to all friends. Mde de lafayette and Children join in the Best Respects to You and Mrs Washington. My younger daughter Virginia is Now Under inoculation. Adieu, My Beloved General, I don't live one day without Grieving for this Hard Separation which deprives me of the Blessed Sight of What is dearest to me, and leaves me so few opportunities to tell you, My dear General, With all the love of a devoted Heart that I am forever With the Most affectionate Respect Your filial, gratefull friend

lafayette

I Had a letter from M. de Moustier who (Betwen us) appears to me not well pleased. We Must Humour Him a little, that His Representations Be favourable.[5] it is Said that the Russian fleet destined to the Mediterranean is Counter Manded altho Spain Had Consented. How far this is Certain I don't know. I Have just Received an official Communication of a Resolve Signed By more than three Hundred Gentlemen of the order of Noblesse in Britanny *declaring it infamous* to Accept a place in the New Administration—to which I very plainly Have Given My Assent—Adieu, my dear General.

ALS, PEL.

1. Etienne-Charles de Loménie de Brienne, archbishop of Toulouse, was comptroller general of finance for Louis XVI.

2. William Short (1759–1848), a native of Surry County who graduated from the College of William and Mary in 1779, went to France with Thomas Jefferson in 1784 as his secretary.

3. Jacques-Pierre Brissot de Warville (1754–1793) in 1786 published *Examen critique des voyages dans l'Amérique septentrionale de m. le marquis de Chatellux*. He arrived in the United States in July 1788 as an agent for European financiers interested in making American investments. A journalist, he was an admirer of the United States and was thinking of writing its history. While traveling through different states until the end of the year, he visited Mount Vernon for two days in November (*Diaries*, 5:423–25). Brissot de Warville does not mention La Terrière in his *Nouveau voyage dans les Etats-Unis de l'Amérique septentrionale, fait en 1788* (1791).

4. Ochakov was besieged for six months and fell on 17 Dec. 1788.

5. See GW to Moustier, 26 Mar., and note 2 of that document.

## To Richard Dobbs Spaight

Sir,                                      Mount Vernon May 25th 1788.

The letter with which you honored me the 25th of last Month,[1] and the Pease (by way of Baltimore) are safe at hand. I pray you to accept my thanks for them. I shall cultivate the Pease with care—this year in hills, to accumulate Seed—next year in broadcast, for a crop.[2]

I am sorry to find by your letter that the State of North Carolina is so much opposed to the proposed Government. If a better could be agreed on, it might be well to reject this; but without such a prospect (& I confess none appears to me) policy I think, must recommend the one that is submitted.

The sentiments of this State will soon be known—The second day of June the Convention is to meet. Since the election of delegates to it, the prevailing opinion is that a majority of the members are in favor of the Constitution, but as they are soon to speak their own sentiments it would be imprudent to anticipate them, even, if they were reduced to certainty. Maryland has ratified by a very large Majority, Sixty three to Eleven. With great esteem & regard I have the honor to be—Sir Yr Most Obedt Hble Servt

                                              Go: Washington

ALS, Nc-Ar: George Washington Papers; LB, DLC:GW.

Richard Dobbs Spaight (1758–1802) was a member of the Federal Convention of North Carolina in 1787.

1. Letter not found.
2. See GW to McHenry, 18 May, n.1.

*Letter not found*: Clement Biddle to GW, 26 May 1788. On 20 July GW wrote Biddle: "Your favors of the 26th of May, 13th of June and 7th instt are before me."

## From Robert Morris

Dear Sir,                                  Richmond May 26th 1788

I had the pleasure to meet Mrs Morris & my Children at the Bowling Green about two oClock on Friday & have since Conducted them safe to this place. We reserve our Acknowledgements for Mrs Washington & your kind Attentions untill they can be made in person as I hope it will not be long before we shall have the pleasure of waiting on you again at Mount Vernon—The letters Enclosed herewith were brought by Mrs Morris under a Sealed Cover directed to me on the supposition of my being with you. The French letter is from a meer *aventurier* who took me in for 100 Dollrs & has now put me to an expense of 50/ for Postage from Charles Town. these Circumstances will guard you against his importunities.[1]

Mr Pollock's request you will be best able to judge of. He wishes me to solicit for him what I would not ask for myself.[2] With perfect esteem & regard I remain Dear Sir Your obliged & obedient humble Servant

Robt Morris

ALS, DLC:GW.
1. The "French letter" has not been identified.
2. See Oliver Pollock to GW, 11 May.

## To Lafayette

My dear Marquis,                    Mount Vernon May 28th 1788

I have lately had the pleasure to receive two letters by which you introduced to my acquaintance M. Du Pont and M. Vanderkemp and (altho' those gentlemen have not as yet been to visit me[)], you may be persuaded that whensoever I shall have the satisfaction of receiving them, it will be with all that attention to which their merits and your recommendations entitle them.[1]

Notwithstanding you are acquainted with Mr Barlow in person, and with his works by reputation, I thought I would Just write you a line by him, in order to recommend him the more particularly to your civilities.[2] Mr Barlow is considered by those who are good Judges to be a genius of the first magnitude; and to be one of those Bards who hold the keys of the gate by which Patriots, Sages and Heroes are admitted to immortality. Such are your Antient Bards who are both the preist and doorkeepers to the temple of fame. and these, my dear Marquis, are no vulgar functions. Men of real talents in arms have commonly approved themselves patriots of the liberal arts and friends to the poets of their own as well as former times. In some instances by acting reciprocally, heroes have made poets, and poets heroes. Alexander the great is said to have been enraptured with the Poems of Homer and to have lamented that he had not a rival muse to celebrate his actions. Julias Ceesar is well know[n] to have been a man of a highly cultivated understanding and taste. Augustus was the professed and munificent rewarder of poetical merit—nor did he lose the return of having his atcheivments immortalised in song. The Augustan age is proverbial for intellectual refinement and elegance in composition; in it the harvest of laurels and bays was wonderfully mingled together. The age of your Louis the fourteenth, which produced a multitude of great Poets and great Captains, will never be forgotten: nor will that of Queen Ann in England, for the same cause, ever cease to reflect a lustre upon the Kingdom. Although we are yet in our cradle, as a nation, I think the efforts of the human mind with us are sufficient to refute (by incontestable facts) the doctrines of those who have asserted that every thing degenerates in America. Perhaps we shall be found, at this moment, not inferior to the rest of the world in the performances of our poets and painters; notwithstanding many of the incitements are wanting which operate powerfully among older nations. For it is generally understood, that excellence in those sister arts has been the result of easy circumstances, public encouragements and an advanced stage of society. I observe that the Critics in England, who speak highly of the American poetical geniuses (and their praises may be the more relied upon as they seem to be reluctantly exhorted) are not pleased with the tribute of applause which is paid to your nation. It is a reason why they should be the more caressed by your nation. I hardly know how it is that I am drawn thus far in observations on a subject so foreign from those in which we are mostly engaged, farming and politics, unless because I had little news to tell you.

Sence I had the pleasure of writing to you by the last Packet,[3] the Convention of Maryland has ratified the federal Constitution by a majority of 63 to 11 voices. That makes the seventh State which has adopted it, nex[t] monday the Convention in Virginia will assemble—we have still good hopes of its adoption here: though by no great plurality of votes. South Carolina has probably decided favourably before this time. The plot thickens fast. A few short weeks will detirmine the political fate of America for the present generation and probably produce no small influence on the happiness of society through a long succession of ages to come. Should every thing proceed with harmony and consent according to our actual wishes and expectations; I will confess to you sincerely, my dear Marquis; it will be so much beyond any thing we had a right to imagine or expect eighteen months ago, that it will demonstrate as visibly the finger of Providence, as any possible event in the course of human affairs can ever designate it. It is impracticable for you or any one who has not been on the spot, to realise the change in men's minds and the progress towards rectitude in thinking and acting which will then have been made.

Adieu, my dear Marquis, I hope your affairs in France will subside into a prosperous train without coming to any violent crisis. Continue to cherish your affectionate feelings for this country and the same portion of friendship for me, which you are ever sure of holding in the heart of your most sincer[e] Friend &c.

Go. Washington

LB, DLC:GW.

1. Victor Marie Du Pont de Nemours enclosed in his letter to GW of 22 April Lafayette's letter of introduction, which has not been found. Lafayette's letter introducing Francis Adrian Van der Kemp, dated 6 Mar., is printed in a note of Van der Kemp's letter to GW of 15 May. See also GW to Van der Kemp, 28 May.

2. GW on this day wrote both La Luzerne and Rochambeau about Joel Barlow. Barlow sailed for Europe on 25 May as European agent for the Scioto Company. He remained abroad until 1805.

3. GW wrote to Lafayette on 28 April.

## To La Luzerne

Sir,                                    Mount Vernon May 28th 1788

As not any thing which is interesting to your happiness and glory can be indifferent to me, I have a sincere pleasure in congratulating you on your appointment as Ambassador from the most Christien King to the Court of London.

Altho your Excellency may possibly have had some knowledge of Mr Barlow (the gentleman who will put this letter into your hands and of whom it is recommendatory) during your residence in America; yet his celebrity as a writer was not then so great as to have attracted the same admiration and applause, which he hath since merited and obtained by the publication of his celebrated Poem entitled the Viseon of Columbus.[1] That Work is dedicated by permission to the King of France, and is intended as an honorable testimony of America['s] gratitude and affection for the Frence nation. I observe that it has been republished in London, and that the Critical Reviewers have treated the Author, in their Strictures upon it, as a person possessed of a very distingueshed and sublime Genius. I will only trespass on your time to add that Mr Barlow's character and talents are such as authorize me to commend him to your particular notice: and to assure you, my dear Marquis, with how great personal consideration and esteem[2]—I have the honor to be Your most Obedt and Most humble Servant

Go. Washington

LB, DLC:GW.

1. GW purchased ten copies of Joel Barlow's *Vision of Columbus* upon its publication in 1787. See GW to Elizabeth Powel, 6 June 1787, n.1.

2. On the same day GW wrote a similar letter of introduction to Rochambeau: "My dear Count. I take the liberty of introducing to your acquaintance Mr Barlow, the person who will have the honor of handing this letter to you. He is a Gentleman of liberal education, respectable character, great abilities, & high reputation for literary accomplishmts. He is peculiarly & honorably known in the republic of Letters both here and in Europe, for being the Author of an admirable Poem, in which he has worthily celebrated the glory of your Nation in general & of yourself in particular—Attended, as he is, with so many interesting circumstances & under so many unusual advantages, I need add no more than just a recommendation to your attention & civilities.

"Since I had the pleasure of writing to you by the last Packet, nothing worthy of notice has happened in America, except the adoption of the Constitution in Maryland by a very great majority. I embrace you, my dear Count, with all my heart; and have the honor to be—with the highest sentiments of friendship and esteem Your most Obedt and Most Hble Servant Go: Washington" (ALS, DLC: Rochambeau Papers; LB, DLC:GW).

## To Francis Van der Kemp

Sir,                                      Mount Vernon May 28th 1788.

The letter which you did me the favor to address to me on the 15th of this instt from New York has been duly received, and I take the speediest occasion to well-come your arrival on the American shore.[1]

I had always hoped that this land might become a safe & agreeable Asylum to the virtuous & persecuted part of mankind, to whatever nation they might belong; but I shall be the more particularly happy, if this Country can be, by any means, useful to the Patriots of Holland, with whose situation I am peculiarly touched, and of whose public virtue I entertain a great opinion.

You may rest assured, Sir, of my best & most friendly sentiments of your suffering compatriots, and that, while I deplore the calamities to which many of the most worthy members of your Community have been reduced by the late foreign interposition in the interior affairs of the United Netherlands; I shall flatter myself that many of them will be able with the wrecks of their fortunes which may have escaped the extensive devastation, to settle themselves in comfort, freedom and ease in some corner of the vast regions of America. The spirit of the Religions and the genius of the political Institutions of this Country must be an inducement. Under a good government (which I have no doubt we shall establish) this Country certainly promises greater advantages, than almost any other, to persons of moderate property, who are determined to be sober, industrious & virtuous members of Society. And it must not be concealed, that a knowledge that these are the general characteristics of your compatriots would be a principal reason to consider their advent as a valuable acquisition to our infant settlements. If you should meet with as favorable circumstances, as I hope will attend your first operations; I think it probable that your coming will be the harbinger for many more to adventure across the Atlantic.

In the meantime give me leave to request that I may have the pleasure to see you at my house whensoever it can be convenient to you, and to offer whatsoever services it may ever be in my power to afford yourself, as well as to the other Patriots & friends to the rights of Mankind of the Dutch Nation.[2] I am —With sentiments of great esteem & respect—Sir Your Most Obedt & Very Hble Servant

Go: Washington

ALS, PHi: Autograph Letters of the Presidents of the United States, 1788–1864; LB, DLC:GW; copy, PHi: Letters of John Adams, 1781–1825.

1. See also GW to Lafayette, 28 May.

2. See Van der Kemp to GW, 16 July, n.2.

# To Clement Biddle

Dear Sir,                              Mount Vernon May 29th 1788
    Enclosed is a bill of lading for Ten Barrls of Shad, and Forty
Barrls of Herrings which you will please to dispose of on Com-
mission to the best advantage[1] for the benefit of—Your Most
Obedt Hble Servant

                                            Go. Washington

LB, DLC:GW.
    1. The shad remained unsold at summer's end; see Biddle to GW, 24 Aug.,
and GW to Biddle, 16 September.

# To George Gilpin

                                [Mount Vernon, 29 May 1788]
    My Nephew informs me that you propose to set off for Shen-
andoah tomorrow. Particular matters which I have on hand will
prevent my doing of it till Saturday—possibly in the afternoon
of that day, time enough to reach Mr. Fairfax's. Early on Sunday
I will call at the Great, & proceed to the Seneca Falls and if business should not require Mr. Smith to proceed before that time, I
should be glad to meet him at the first place, but not otherwise.[1]
    It is my earnest wish that the meeting should be full—busi-
ness requires it—& for that reason I hope Colo Fitzgerald will
attend, and that the Maryland Members could be carried[2] on.
Barring accidents I will be at the place of Rendezvous by 10
o'clock on Monday.—Such papers as will be wanting be so good
as to take with you, particularly the charges &c. against Stuart.[3]

L (incomplete), printed in Goodspeed's catalog no. 106, item 5787, 1914.
    1. GW begins his full account in his diary of his attendance at the meeting
of the directors of the Potomac River Company with this entry of Saturday, 31
May: "After an early dinner, in company with Colo. Humphreys, I set out for
a meeting of the Directors of the Potomack Company to be held at the Falls of
Shenandoah on Monday next. Reached Mr. Fairfax's about an hour by Sun,
who with his lady were at Alexandria; but a cloud which threatend rain induced us notwithstanding to remain there all night" (*Diaries*, 5:334). James
Smith was the assistant manager of the company.
    2. Perhaps GW wrote "counted."
    3. Before adjourning on Tuesday, 2 June, GW and the directors on Monday
wrote the following letter to Richardson Stewart (Stuart): "We met today by
appointment to hear the charges against you but could not with propriety go

into an examination of witnesses in your absence, which however to be regretted we believe is involuntary. On a general view of the situation of the Company's affairs being of the opinion that the present funds or prospects will not warrant our continuing two managers we have come to the inclosed resolution. It is with reluctance we found ourselves under the necessity to make an arrangement which at this point of time may possibly be thought by your enemies to be occasioned by the charges against you, but it has proceeded solely from our duty and inclination to promote the Company's interest without being influenced in any degree by facts alleged and not examined into. The preference given to Mr. Smith is on different principles and we expect cannot surprise you or hurt your feelings. We request on the expiration of your present year you will deliver up the property of the Company under your care to his hands. . . . G. WASHINGTON, P[,] THOS. JOHNSON[,] T.S. LEE[,] GEO. GILPIN" (Bacon-Foster, *Development of Patomac Route*, 82). For the recommendation of the directors to James Smith, see ibid., 83, and *Records of the Columbia Historical Society*, 15 (1912), 173–74.

## From John Jay

Dear Sir                          New York 29 May 1788—

I was two Days ago favored with yours of the 15th Instant. it gives me pleasure to find that the Probability of Virginias adopting the proposed Constitution rather encreases—such an Event would undoubtedly disarm the opposition. It appears by recent advices from Charleston that we may count on South Carolina, and the New Hampshire Delegates assure me that their State will come into the Measure.

There is much Reason to believe that the Majority of the Convention of this State will be composed of antifœderal Characters;[1] but it is doubtful whether the Leaders will be able to govern the Party. Many in the opposition are Friends to Union and mean well, but their principal Leaders are very far from being sollicitous about the Fate of the Union. They wish and mean (if possible) to reject the Constitution with as little Debate and as much Speed as may be. It is not however certain that the greater part of their Party will be equally decided, or rather equally desperate—an Idea has taken air, that the Southern part of the State will at all Events adhere to the union, and if necessary to that End seek a Separation from the northern. this Idea has Influence on the ⟨Fears⟩ of the Party. I cannot find that they have as yet so looked forward to contingent Events, or even to those the most probable, as to have united in or formed any System adapted to them[2]—with perfect Respect & Esteem I am Dear Sir your affectte & hble Servt

John Jay

ALS, DLC:GW; ADf, NNC.

1. Jay's draft has several lines here that he deleted from the final letter: "It is to be wished that ⟨their⟩ Election had been a little longer delayed; for the constitution continues gain ground daily. very improper Means hav⟨e⟩ been used to decieve and alarm the People, and with very considerable Success, but Truth is constantly extendg & will prevail, of Men who express much Indignation at the misrepresentations by which they were led into opposition."

2. On the reverse of the draft is the following notation which may or may not have been intended to go with the letter: "In addition to the pamphlets you mention I enclose one on the other Side of the Questio⟨n⟩."

## From John Moss

Sir.                                                30th May 1788.

Not attending to your list of Titheables when I receaved it, did not discover you had not made the necessary distingtion between Blacks above Sixteen, and over Twelve and under Sixteen. I inclose the list that you may make the alteration.[1] Should also be glad to receave Major Washingtons list. Colo. Wren also desired me to ask you for your list in Truro Parish. The whole you may send me to Mrs Peakes if convenient. Or lodge them for me at Mr Hepburns Store in Alexandria.[2] I am Sir with due Esteem your Hble Servt

John Moss

ALS, DLC:GW. Moss wrote on the cover of the letter: "The Lists may be left at Mr [William] Hepburns Store, as I dont Stay at Mrs Peakes."

John Moss became a justice of the Fairfax County Court in 1785 and tax commissioner for Fairfax parish in 1786. During the Revolutionary War he served first as a captain in the 1st Virginia Regiment and later as Virginia's agent for stores.

1. After receiving Moss's letter, GW made additions in his own hand to the lists of his taxable property in Truro and Fairfax parishes in April 1788, indicating which of his slaves were "undr 16." The list of *Blacks above 12 years of age*" in Truro Parish included: Will, Frank, Auston, Hercules, Nathan, Giles, Joe, Paris, Gunner, Boatswain, Sam, Anthony, Tom, Will, Isaac, James, Sambo, Tom Nokes, Nat, George, Simms, Joe, Jack, Bristol, Peter, Peter, Scumburg "(past labor)," Frank, Jack, Betty "(past service)," Doll, Jenney, Charlotte, Sall, Caroline, Sall Rass, Dorchia, Alice, Myrtilla, Kitty, Moll, Billy "undr 16," Joe "D[itt]o," Christopher "Do," Cyrus "Do," Uriah "Do," Godferry "Do," Sinah

"Do," Mima "Do," Lylla "Do," Oney "Do," Anna "Do," Beck "Do," Virgin "Do,"
Patt "Do," Will, Will, Charles, Gabriel, Jupiter, Nanney, Kate, Sarah, Alice,
Nanny, Peg, Sackey, Darcus, Amy, Nancy, Molly "undr 16," Morris, Robin,
Adam, Jack, Jack, Dick, Ben, Matt, Morris, Brunswick "(past service)," Han-
nah, Lucy, Moll, Jenny, Silla, Charity, Betty, Peg, Sall, Grace, Sue, Agga "Undr
16," Will, Paul, Abraham, Paschal, Rose, Sabeen, Lucy, Delia, Daphne, Grace,
Tom "undr 16," Moses "Do," Isaac "Do," Sam Kit, London, Cæsar, Cupid,
Paul, Betty, Doll, Lucy, Lucy, Flora, Fanny, Rachael, Jenney, Edy, and Daphne,
a total of 121. Also reported were 98 Horses, 4 Mules, "1 Covering Horse @
2 Guineas," and 1 Chariot.

The *"Blacks above 12 Years of age"* in Fairfax Parish included Davy, Breeche,
Nat, Ned, Essex, Bath, Johnny, Will, Robin, Ben, Molly, Ruth, Dolly, Peg,
Daphne, Mwnia, Agnus, Jack, Sucky, Judy, Judy, Hannah, Cornelia, Lidya,
Esther, Cloe, Fanny, and "Alice under 16[,] Rose under 16, Ben Do Do," a total
of thirty. There were twenty-six horses (DLC:GW).

2. James Wren (c.1728–1815), a justice of the Fairfax County Court and a
member of vestry of Fairfax Parish, took his oath as tax commissioner for the
Truro district of Fairfax County on 19 May 1788 (*Diaries*, 5:351). Mrs. Peake
was probably Mary Stonestreet Peake (c.1738–1805), widow of Humphrey
Peake (1733–1785), who lived in Fairfax Parish next to Thomson Mason.

## From James McHenry

Dear Sir.                                        Baltimore 1st June 1788.

Captn Barney being the bearer of the present from the merchants of Baltimore would, I am persuaded, be a sufficient introduction, and insure to him without any thing further a favorable
reception. I cannot however omit the occasion this offers me
of placing it more upon his own merit. Permit me therefore to
mention, that the federal cause in this Town is not only greatly
indebted to his exertions, but that he has rendered his country
valuable services as a brave sea officer in the late revolution.[1]

I congratulate you upon the adoption of the constitution by
South Carolina and am, Dear Sir, with the most sincere regard
and affection your obt & hble servt

James McHenry

ALS, NIC.

1. Captain Joshua Barney (1759–1818) was the hero of the naval action in
April 1782 in which the *Hyder-Ally* captured the much larger *General Monk*. On
9 June GW wrote in his diary: "Captn. Barney, in the Miniature Ship Federalist—as a present from the Merchants of Baltimore to me arrived here" (*Diaries*,
5:339). The 15-foot *Federalist* had been featured in the parade through the
streets of Baltimore on 1 May in celebration of Maryland's ratification of the

new Constitution (*Maryland Journal* [Baltimore], 6 May and 3 June 1788). See also GW to William Smith, 8 June.

# From Francis Peyton

Sir                                                          June 1st 1788

I have the Honor to inclose you an Acct which I am Satisfied you have forgot or thought it must have been paid by Mr Washington in your Absence which I suppose would have been the case had I have been in possession of Dawsons Order but as I had delivered it to you I had nothing to Support the Charge. I once Wrote to Mr Washington on the Subject requesting him to inquire of you as to it's legality but never received any answer from him—if you remember the Matter and find no mistake in the Acct you will please Order me payment when Convenient[1] I have the Honor to be with great respect Your Mo. Obt Servt

                                                          Francis Peyton

ALS, DLC:GW.

1. In November 1774 when GW conducted the sale of George Mercer's Bull Run land in Loudoun and Fauquier counties, he stayed at Col. Francis Peyton's house for three nights. Peyton at the time was a justice in Loudoun County and represented it in the House of Burgesses. The sale of Mercer's land in Frederick County immediately followed, and it was held at the house of William Dawson, who was George Mercer's overseer. "Mr Washington" is Lund Washington. The enclosed account shows Peyton's charges of £19 against GW in November 1774 for William Dawson's delivery to GW of a wagon of George Mercer's wheat. Peyton credits GW with £5.10 for "Surveyors Compass & Chain" in 1775 and with £1.0.7½ for "Sundry Surveyors Instruments sent me from Philadelphia" on 1 June 1775 (DLC:GW). Peyton wrote GW about this account a second time on 12 Feb. 1789.

# From Tobias Lear

My dear Sir,                          Portsmouth N.H. 2d June 1788.

As I know you feel deeply interested in the fate of the proposed Constitution, considering its adoption or rejection as deciding upon the happiness & prosperity of your fellow-citizens, I shall take the liberty to give you an account of its present situation in this State so far as I have been able to learn it from the best information which I can obtain; beging, at the same time, that you will not answer this, or any other letter which I may write to you before my return, unless something more particular (which I do not at present know of) should require it, because I am so well acquainted with your numerous avocations as to be sensible that you have not (especially at this busy season) an hour that could be conveniently spared.[1]

I was surprised to find, in conversing with some of the first Characters here, that so little information respecting the Constitution has been diffused among the people of this State; there have been few, or no original publications in the papers & scarcely any republications; the valuable numbers of Publius are not known,[2] the debates of the Pensylvania & Massachusetts conventions have been read but by few persons, and many other pieces which contained useful information have never been heard of. Fabius is now republishing in the papers of this town,[3] and as the papers under this Signiture are written with perspicuity & candour I presume they will have a good effect. The enemies of the Constitution have been indefatigable in disseminating their opinions personally among the interior inhabitants of this State, and had they acted like good politicians would effectually have prevented its adoption here, but instead of alarming the fears of the people by telling them that their immediate & individual interest would be effected by the adoption of the Constitution they acknowledged that this State would be more benefited thereby than any other in the Union, but declared that if the Constitution obtained[,] the rights & liberties of all American citizens would be destroyed, and that the people of this State, as a part of the Community, wo⟨*mutilated*⟩ for in the general wreck; this apparent disinterestedness & patriotism was relished for some time and was the means of producing so large & unexpected an opposition in the last convention, but since that period the friends to the proposed System have been at some pains to counteract their opponents by personal information, and their success (they say) is as great as they could wish; for the people, upon reflecting, & duly considering those Characters who had stood forth as the Champions of the general rights of America, were convinced that they had been imposed upon by a specious parade of patriotism, thought it highly absurd to pretend that the inhabitants of other States were not as competent to the judging of what was injurious to their liberties as they were, and as they have more to hope & less to fear from its obtaining than almost any other State it would be doing injustice to themselves not to accept it. This is taken to be now the general sentiment which prevails, and I think the friends to the Constitution would not feel so secure of its adoption as they do, (after the unexpected opposition which they met with ⟨la⟩st winter) unless they were possessed of some certain information to ground their faith upon; they now only appear to be mortified that New Hampshire will not make the ninth State, as it is probable South Carolina & Virginia will adopt it before them, and coming in at the tenth hour will rather have the appearance of submitting to, than accepting of it; the only method which can be devised to save appearances is to adopt it before the ratification can reach them from Virginia; this they expect to do, as it is thought the Convention will not be many days in session.

You will be so obliging as to tender my best respects to Mrs Washington, & beleive me to be, With sentiments of the highest respect & warmest attachment, My dear Sir, Yr most Obedt & Hble Servt

Tobias Lear

ALS, DLC:GW.

1. Lear returned home to New Hampshire for a visit and remained until September (*Diaries*, 5:393). See also Lear to GW, 22 June and 31 July.

2. These are the *Federalist Papers*.

3. GW refers to John Dickinson's "Fabius" papers in his letter to John Vaughan, 27 April.

## From Thomas Pleasants, Jr.

Sir                                        Raleigh 2d June 1788.

I have just recieved a Letter from Mr John Dydsbury, formerly a noted shoe & Boot Maker Pall-Mall London,[1] but now residing at south Multon in Devonshire, requesting of me to procure him information of an allotment of Land made to Capt. Jacob Van Braam. and as your Exellencys name is mentioned, as having procured the land for Capt. Braam so I have taken the liberty of enclosing an extract of Mr Dydsbury Letter, as the most likely person to whom I could apply, to give me the information wanted, or to put me into the best way of obtaining it[2]—

Which Will greatly oblige one, who is With great regard, and respect, Yr Most ob. Hble St

Thomas Pleasants jr

ALS, DLC:GW.

Thomas Pleasants, Jr. (c.1737–1804), lived at Raleigh in Goochland County where he was both a planter and a merchant. Pleasants served as a commissary agent for Virginia during the Revolutionary War.

1. For more than a decade beginning in 1758, GW had John Didsbury of London make his shoes.

2. Pleasant's extract of Didsbury's letter reads: "I beg the *favour* of you, if in your power to procure me an acct of a particular Lot of land on the Ohio, that you may know exactly what I mean, I must acquaint you that in 1774 Genl Washington, then procured for my friend Capt. Jacob Van Braam his quota of Land on the Ohio, amounting to *9000* acres, and in December 1775, I purchased *6000* of these Acres from the Captain who retains the *3000*, and depends on my doing with his whatever I may do with my own. You may perhaps recollect this Gentleman who afterwards acquired the rank of major, sold out of the Army and at present resides in France. What I think is in favor of the quota of land, is that a Governeur, secretary, and Judges are appointed on the Ohio, from this it is Certain that some part of the Country there must be well peopled—and each of us will be particularly obliged to you, if you Can get this lot exactly described separate from any other, and learn if my part of it is occupied, and what may be the Value of it.

"By the acct I have here it is lot 15, survey the 2d Containing *28,400* acres to be divided thus—Robert Stobo—*9000* Jacob Van Braam 9000 James Towers *6000* and *4400* to 11 privates at 400 each." Jacob Van Braam, who was taken as a hostage by the French after the capitulation of Fort Necessity in 1754, was entitled to land under the terms of Governor Dinwiddie's Proclamation of 1754. Born in 1725, Van Braam was reported to have died in 1784. For the allocation of the land to Van Braam in 1771 and GW's attempt to purchase it from him, see GW to Robert Adam, 22 Nov. 1771, n.1.

# From Benjamin Lincoln

My dear General                           Boston June 3d 1788

I have had the pleasure of receiving the several letters answers to those which I have had the honour of writing to your Excellency.

In one of my last I suggested to your Excellency what appeared to me to be the temper of our last house of representatives relative to the new constitution and my apprehensions lest the same spirit which they possessed would be by them difused through the different parts of the State. Their professed design was to shift the Governour and to appoint one, and a Leiutenant Governour of their own sentiments, hence federalism & antifederalism were pitted one against the other—The antifederalists were in hopes of throwing such an influence into the Government, by a change of its officers, as to prevent an organisation of the general Government by this State should it be adopted by nine.

Mr Hancock was put up by the federalists and Mr Gerry by the oposite party for Governour Mr Adams and Mr Lincoln were put up by the federalists as Lieutenant Governour and General Warren by the other party. The division of votes beetween Adams & Lincoln prevented a choice of Lieutenant Governour by the people, they had about two thirds of the votes General Warren had the greatest part of the remainder. As no person was chosen the four Gentlemen who had the most votes were by our constitution candidates, from whom the house must chuse two and send their Names to the Senate one of whom must be chosen by them Lieutenant Governour. Adams, Warren, Gerry & Lincoln were the candidates. The votes for them by the people stood as followeth Warren 6,157 Adams 3495 Gerry 669 Lincoln 10,204—Warren & Lincoln were returned to the Senate—they elected Lincoln who had 20 votes out of 28. He accepted the trust I hope he will discharge the duties of his office with fidelity.

I have been thus particular in returning the numbers as the contest as I said before seemed to be between the federalists & those of a different character that you might judge of the temper of the people & of the state of the parties. Federalism is manifestly fast gaining ground.

In our last house of representatives the antifederalists could carry any vote they pleased and there cannot be a doubt but if it had been with them to determine the question they would instantly have rejected the constitution with triumph—In the present house it has I am confident a great majority in its favor, much greater than it had in the convention.

In this State the people are manifestly returning to that train of thinking and line of duty necessary and indeed indispensible to their well being.

Though the majority have much to do yet they must take care

that they do not do too much, the utmost good temper and moderation must be used and we must make haste slo⟨w⟩ly.

On the whole if we act with judgment temper and moderation we shall, I have no doubt, in a short time have a government established the influence of which will not only promote and preserve the happiness and interest of the United States but that the beneficial effects of it will be enjoyed by all the different nations of the world.

I wish my most dutiful respects to Mrs Washington and that the children may be assured and early taught that General Lincoln loves them and that he wishes they may live long happily and be the most honored & useful among their brethren. With the sincerest esteem I have the honour of being My Dr General Your Obt Servant

B. Lincoln

ALS, DLC:GW; ADf, MHi: Benjamin Lincoln Papers. The draft is dated 31 May.

## From Samuel Hanson

Sir                                          Alexandria, 4th June, 1788

To whom but the powerful and the benevolent should the unfortunate apply?

The partiality of my Friends has suggested the expediency of soliciting your influence in procuring for me an appointment under the new Government. I mention that the idea originated entirely with them, in order to acquit myself, as far as I can, of the blame of preferring a Suit which may, perhaps, be considered as premature, if not improper—They possibly hoped that the Consideration of my misfortunes, might, in your opinion, confer a kind of merit upon one who cannot justly boast of any other. What those misfortunes are I beg leave to relate. You may probably have heard of the depredations committed on my Father's fortune by the severe operation of the Tender-Law, which deprived him of ⅞ths of his debts.[1] This event necessarily occasioned him to lessen the provision he intended for me. To recover what in this manner I had lost, I was induced to become one of those numerous adventurers, who, on the establishment of peace, were seized with a rage for mercantile engagements. What was the issue of my attempt you have, probably, understood. My ill Success Sir, was not owing, as I conceive, to inattention, Mismanagement, or extravagance, but to causes which no human prudence could controul.

Thus, Sir, I find myself, with a large family, reduced, from flattering prospects, to a situation the most uncomfortable. Upon this ground, chiefly, I must rest my pretensions to your favour. In *misfortunes* I may, I conceive, claim a melancholoy pre-eminence.

I know it is usual with Suitors to employ the advocation of others. But I also know that these commendations are generally obtained either through the solicitous importunity of the Candidate, or the partiality of his Friends. It cannot, therefore, be the effect of conceit in me to believe that I could procure the advocation of Gentlemen of great respectability both in this, and my native, State. But, not to mention the irksomeness of this business to one unhackneyed, as I am, in the ways of Solicitation, I wish to owe to your own goodness any Service you may render me. Indeed, abstracted from that wish, I do not perceive how I can be benefited by the representations of my Friends. I was, and am still, Sir, in hopes that, if during my residence for the last 4 Years in your own neighbourhood, there has been no impeachment of my Character or integrity, you will generously conclude that none can be exhibited of an earlier date.

Thus, Sir, I do not hope for success through the partial recommendation of my Friends, or the efficacy of illustrious advocation. It is in the form of a *poor but honest man*, that I prefer my Suit. In this character I am not ashamed to solicit you. Sir, let me not be the *first* who, in this character, ever solicited you in vain.

It has, doubtless, occurred to you that, the new government not being yet established, my application is premature. I take it for granted, Sir, that the proposed Government, or some other efficient one, must be adopted; and the reason of my early application is that, if it should meet your approbation, I may have as much time as possible for qualifying myself for any office of which you may think me capable. This it will be my earnest desire to do, in order by a faithful execution of my duty, to justify your friendly Patronage.

I must beg, Sir, that if, in pursuing this Subject, I have been imperceptibly carried beyond the true line of Decorum, you will ascribe it, not to any deficiency of respect, but to the anxious, yet natural, feelings of a Husband and a Father.[2] With every sentiment of the most exalted respect, I have the honour to remain, Sir, Your most obedient and most humble Servant

S. Hanson of Saml

P.S. I have the pleasure to inform you, for your satisfaction, that the behaviour of the boys ⟨is une⟩xceptionable.

ALS, DLC:GW.

    1. The elder Samuel Hanson (1716–1794) of Charles County, Md., before the Revolution held more than 5,000 acres in Charles and Frederick counties and, in 1783, twenty-five slaves; at his death he had twenty-six slaves and about 2,000 acres in Charles County.

    2. On 8 June GW made clear, not for the last time before his election to the presidency, that an inquiry such as Hanson's did indeed go beyond "the true line of Decorum."

## From James Madison

Dear Sir                          Richmond June 4. 1788

    Your favor of the 2d Ulto was not recd till my arrival here on monday evening. I found, contrary to my expectation that not only a very full house had been made on the first day, but that it had proceeded to the appointment of the President & other officers. Mr Pendleton was put into the chair without opposition. Yesterday little more was done than settling some forms and Resolving that no question general or particular should be propounded till the whole plan should be considered & debated clause by clause. This was moved by Col. Mason, and contrary to his expectations, concurred in by the other side. To day the discussions commenced in the Committee of the whole. The Governor has declared the day of previous amendments past, and thrown himself fully into the federal scale. Henry & Mason made a lame figure & appeared to take different and awkward ground. The federalists are a good deal elated by the existing prospect.[1] I dare not however speak with certainty as to the decision. Kentucke has been extremely tainted, is supposed to be generally adverse, and every piece of address is going on privately to work on the local interests & prejudices of that & other quarters. In haste I am Dr Sir Yrs Affecly

Js Madison Jr

ALS, DLC:GW; copy, DLC: Madison Papers.

1. During the Virginia Ratifying Convention, 2–27 June, Madison communicated with any regularity only with GW, Alexander Hamilton, and Rufus King. The editors of the *Madison Papers* fully document Madison's role in the ratifying convention in 11:72ff. Edmund Pendleton was elected president of the convention on Monday, 2 June.

*Letter not found*: from Christopher Gadsden, 5 June 1788. On 18 Aug. GW wrote Gadsden of the letter that Gadsden wrote him "on the 5th of June last."

*Letter not found*: from David Stuart, 4 June 1788. On 8 June GW wrote Stuart: "I have received your favour of the 4th."

# From Richard Henderson

Sir                              Bladensburgh [Md.] June 5th 1788

The impression made upon me by the inclosed letter, has surmounted the hesitation I felt, at the thought of troubling you with it; for the *Queries* are beyond my capacity of answering, as I was desired to do, and seem worthy of attention from the greatest.

I know not the writer. He lives in the north of Scotland, where the body of the people are useless to society, by the neglect of their rulers; and miserable, by the engrossed state of land, and the expensiveness of landlords, which leaves not a subsistence to their tenants.

It is a pity that a vigorous people, who are easily ruled by humane usage, should remain in misery, as recruits some day to pester us, when they might be improving the soil or navigation of this country, to their own felicity.

The letter has been some time in this country, & deserved no attention, untill the prospect of a good government opened. But now I think it proper to submit it to your observations, hoping that you will bestow a little time, in giving information, that may be transmitted either as coming from you, or not, as you please, to a man who may become an usefull fellow citizen.[1]

The love you have shewn to our country, produced that sincere respect and regard which have led me to trouble you on this occasion—And this is the only apology which can with truth be made by Sir Your most Obedt Servt

Rd Henderson

ALS, DLC:GW.

Before the Revolution Richard Henderson of Bladensburg, Md., in partnership with his fellow townsman Dr. David Ross and others, owned the Frederick ironworks on the Potomac River at the mouth of Antietam Creek. When on his way to the Federal Convention in Philadelphia in May 1787, GW dined at Henderson's house after crossing over the river from Mount Vernon on 9 May (*Diaries*, 5:153).

1. In his response of 19 June GW indicates that the enclosed letter, which has not been found, was from someone named St. Clair. It probably was from John Sinclair (1754–1835) of Caithness in Scotland, the first president of Britain's board of agriculture and author of the influential *The Statistical Account of Scotland*, the first volume of which appeared in 1791. On 18 May 1792 Sir John sent GW agricultural "Pamphlets & Papers" which GW acknowledged on 20 Oct., beginning a correspondence in which the two men exchanged dozens of letters before GW's death in 1799. For a listing of pamphlets and other works that Sinclair sent to GW during these years, see Griffin, *Boston Athenæum Collection*, 89–95.

*Letter not found*: from James Swan, 5 June 1788. On 18 Aug. GW wrote Swan: "I have received your favor of the 5th of June from Havre de Grace."

## From Bushrod Washington

[7 June 1788]

The convention has hitherto made a very slow progress towards finishing the business before them, and leads me to apprehend, that we shall be detained here much longer than I at first expected. We have determined to go through the constitution clause by clause, before any question shall be put. This regulation, if attended to, would expedite the business, by confining us to the particular parts objected to. But the debates have hitherto been general and desultory, although we have proceeded no farther than the third section of the first clause. The defects of the old confederation, and the necessity of framing an entirely new one, seem to have claimed the principal share of our attention.

Mr. Henry on Thursday called upon the friends to the proposed plan to point out the objections to the present federal constitution. This challenge, which was given with an appearance of great confidence, drew from the governor yesterday a very able and elegant harangue for two hours and a half; for I suppose you have been informed of Mr. Randolph's determination to vote for the proposed government without previous amendments. He pointed out those defects, and painted in a masterly and affecting manner the necessity of a more solid union of the States. Mr. Henry's confidence in the power and greatness of Virginia, which he said she might rest upon though dismembered from her sister States, was very well exposed by the above speaker. Mr. Madison followed, and with such force of reasoning, and a display of such irresistible truths, that opposition seemed to have quitted the field. However, I am not so sanguine as to trust appearances, or even to flatter myself that he made many converts. A few I have been confidently informed he did influence, who were decidedly in the opposition. Mr. Nicholas concluded the day with a very powerful speech, inferior to none that had been made before as to close and connected argument. Were I to attempt to predict the fate of the constitution, it must be founded on conjecture.

Sparks, *Washington's Writings*, 9:378n. Sparks dates the letter 6 June, but Bushrod refers to Edmund Randolph's "harangue for two hours and a half" of "yesterday," which was 6 June. See the editors' notes in Kaminski and Saladino, *Documentary History of the Ratification of the Constitution*, 10:1580–81. Bushrod Washington represented Westmoreland County in the house of delegates and in the ratifying convention.

## To Joseph Barrell

Mount Vernon June 8th 1788.

General Washington, having lately received with great satisfaction the medal which the Owners of the adventure to the Pacific Ocean have been pleased to transmit to him, begs leave to return his best acknowledgments to those Gentlemen for the very acceptable Compliment, and to assure them that his hearty wishes for success attend their enterprise, he hopes and even flatters himself that the day will arrive (at no very distant period) when the sources of commerce shall be enlarged and replenished; and when the new Constellation of this Hemisphere shall be hailed and respected in every quarter of the terraqueous globe![1]

LB, DLC:GW.

Joseph Barrell (1739–1804), one of the merchants whose economic position in Boston was greatly enhanced during the Revolution by his privateering activities and the removal of Loyalist competitors, was one of the partners in the joint-stock plan founded in Boston in 1787 to establish a China-northwest coast trade. See Barrell to GW, 20 Mar. 1790, and notes.

1. Copyist Howell Lewis wrote "globle."

## To Samuel Hanson

Sir, Mount Vernon June 8th 1788

Your letter of the 4th instant, which was delivered to me on my return from my late Journey, is now before me; and requires that I should say something in reply on a subject, in which I feel myself more embarrassed and more awkwardly situated than ever I have been before.

It is but Justice to my own feelings to observe, that I am conscious I have never been indisposed to do whatever might be in power in favor of those whose misfortunes had been unavoidably brought upon them, without any fault of their own. In this predicament, I doubt not, I was not a little concerned at an application for employment under a Government which does not yet exist, and with the Administration of which (in case it should be adopted and carried into execution,) it is *much more* than possible I may never be concerned. The chaos of uncertainty in which we are involved, and the impropriety of my anticipating events or hazarding opinions, would scarcely permit me to touch, however slightly, on these delicate topics.

These circumstances, I observe, had not entirely escaped your attention—you will not, therefore, think hard that I should mention the subject as peculiarly distressing and perplexing to me. Delicacy forbids that I should enlarge as to myself—as to yourself, I will only add that I know nothing but that your character stands in the fairest possible point of light, and consequently cannot be actuated by any prejudice against your pretentions.

I beg, Sir, that the candour and freedom which I have used on this occasion may not be misinterpreted to give you any unintended and unnecessary anxiety; or to induce you to believe that I have taken in ill part the application, although I thought it to be altogether untimely and improper.

On the contrary you may rely upon my protestation, that I am in every personal consideration, with real esteem and Friendship. Sir, Your most Obedt and Most Hble Servant

Go. Washington

LB, DLC:GW.

## To John Jay

Dear Sir,                                    Mount Vernon June 8th 1788.

By the last Mail, I had the pleasure to receive your letter of the 29th of May—and have now the satisfaction to congratulate you on the adoption of the Constitution by the Convention of South Carolina.

I am sorry to learn there is a probability that the majority of members in the New York Convention will be Antifederalists. Still I hope that some event will turn up before they assemble, which may give a new complexion to the business. If this State should, in the intermediate time, make the ninth that shall have ratified the proposed Government, it will, I flatter my self, have its due weight. To shew that this event is now more to be expected than heretofore, I will give you a few particulars which I have from good authority & which you might not, perhaps, immediately obtain through any public channel of conveyance.[1]

On the day appointed for the meeting of the Convention, a large proportion of the members assembled & unanimously placed Mr Pendleton in the Chair. Having on that & the subsequent day chosen the rest of their Officers & fixed upon the mode of conducting the business, it was moved by some one of

those opposed to the Constitution to debate the whole by paragraphs, without taking any question until the investigation
should be completed. This was as unexpected as acceptable to
the Federalists; and their ready acquiescence seems to have
somewhat startled the opposition for fear they had committed
themselves.

Mr Nicholas opened the business by very ably advocating the
system of Representation.[2] Mr Henry in answer went more
vaguely into the discussion of the Constitution, intimating that
the Fœderal Convention had exceeded their powers & that we
had been, and might be happy under the old Confederation—
with a few alterations. This called up Governor Randolph, who
is reported to have spoken with great pathos in reply: and who
declared, that, since so many of the States had adopted the proposed Constitution, he considered the sense of America to be
already taken & that he should give his vote in favor of it without
insisting previously upon amendments. Mr Mason rose in opposition & Mr Madison reserved himself to obviate the objections
of Mr Henry and Colo. Mason the next day. Thus the matter
rested when the last accounts came away.

Upon the whole, the following inferences seem to have been
drawn—that Mr Randolphs declaration will have considerable
effect with those who had hitherto been wavering. That Mr
Henry & Colonel Mason took different & awkward ground—&
by no means equalled the public expectation in their Speeches—
That the former has, probably, receded somewhat from his violent measures to coalesce with the latter—and that the leaders
of the opposition appear rather chagreened & hardly to be decided as to their mode of opposition.

The *sanguine* friends to the Constitution counted upon a majority of twenty at their first meeting, which number they imagine will be greatly encreased: while those equally strong in their
wishes, but more temperate in their habits of thinking speak less
confidently of the greatness of the majority and express apprehensions of the arts that may yet be practised to excite alarms
particularly with the members from the Western District (Kentucke). All, however, agree that the beginning has been as auspicious as could possibly have been expected. A few days will now
ascertain us of the result. With sentiments of the highest esteem

and regard—I am—Dear Sir Your Most Obedt & Affecte Hble
Servt

Go: Washington

ALS, NNC; LB, DLC:GW.

1. GW's account of these developments at the ratifying convention are almost certainly based on a missing letter from David Stuart of 4 June. In the past, Stuart had reported to GW regularly on developments in the Virginia house of delegates when it was in session, and he wrote to GW a number of times during the ratifying convention which he attended as a delegate for Fairfax County. None of these letters from Stuart to which GW refers have been found. See GW to Stuart, 8 June. James Madison and Bushrod Washington also wrote to GW from the convention.

2. This is George Nicholas of Albemarle County.

## To James Madison

My dear Sir,                                Mount Vernon June 8th 1788.

I am much obliged by the few lines you wrote to me on the 4th and though it is yet too soon to rejoice one cannot avoid being pleased at the auspicious opening of the business of your Convention. Though an ulterior opinion of the decision of this state on the Constitution would at any time previous to the discussion of it in the Convention have been premature yet I have never dispaired of its adoption here. What I have mostly apprehended is that the insiduous arts of its opposers to alarm the fears and to inflame the passions of the Multitude may have produced instructions to the Delegates that would shut the door against argument and be a bar to the exercise of the judgment— If this is not the case I have no doubt but that the good sense of this Country will prevail against the local views of designing characters and the arragent opinions of chagreened and disappointed men—The decision of Maryland & South Carolina by such large majorities and the moral certainty of the adoption by New-Hampshire will make *all* except desperate men look before they leap into the dark consequences of rejection.

The ratification by eight States without a negative—By three of them unanimously—By Six against one in another—By three to one in another—By two for one in two more—and by *all* the weight of *abilities* & *property* in the other is enough one would think to produce a cessation of opposition—I do not mean that number alone is sufficient to produce conviction in the Mind, but I think it is enough to produce some change in the conduct of any man who entertains a doubt of his infalibility.

Altho' I have little doubt of your having received a copy of the enclosed pamphlet, yet I send it. It is written with much good sense & moderation—I conjecture, but upon no certain ground, that Mr Jay is the author of it. He sent it to me sometime ago, since which I have received two or three more copies.[1] With the sincerest esteem & most affecte regard I am ever Yours

Go: Washington

ALS, NjP: Straus Autograph Collection; LB, DLC:GW.

1. Jay sent to GW one copy of his pamphlet *An Address to the People of the State of New York* on 20 April and, apparently, a second copy in his letter of 29 May (Kaminski and Saladino, *Documentary History of the Ratification of the Constitution*, 9:804).

*Letter not found*: to Richard Peters, 8 June 1788. On 27 June Peters wrote GW: "I have the Honour of your Letter of the 8th inst."

## To Thomas Pleasants, Jr.

Sir;                                    Mount Vernon June 8th 1788

I have been duly favored with your letter of the 2d instt containing an extract from Mr Disbury⟨'s⟩ letter to you. In addition to what he has there recited, I can only inform you that the tract in which Major Vanbraam holds or held a share, lays on the *little* Kankawa. but in what County (whether Greenbrier, Ohio—or Harrison) I am not sufficiently acquainted with the boundaries of them to decide. nor can I say whether or in what manner the tract of 28,400 has been divided or give the least information with respect to the *quality* of the land; consequently can say nothing as to the value of it. The natural situation of it is exceedingly advantageous for it is not only a part of the highest survey on the Ohio (that was made under the Proclamation of 1754) but it lays on the Communication which is opened, or opening under the authority, and at the expence of the State from Morgan Town (Harrison Court House) to the Ohio.[1] From Judge Mercer you may, possibly, get a more particular acct of this matter for if my memory does not deceive me, his brother Colo. George Mercer (for whom he was acting Attorney) either by purchase, or by the advanc[e] of his (Vanbraams) quotas of the expence of Surveyg Patentg &c. is involved in this business.² I am Sir Yrs &c.

Go. Washington

LB, DLC:GW.

1. The Virginia general assembly in its session of October 1786 passed "An act appropriating certain public taxes to the opening a waggon road from the State road to the mouth of the Little Kanawha . . . ," which provided for the building of a road through Harrison County from the mouth of the Little Kanawha River to the state road as well as one from Morgantown, seat of Monongahela County, to the mouth of Fishing Creek on the Ohio River (12 Hening 295–97).

2. In 1774 George Mercer paid the fees due on Van Braam's share of the Ohio lands. See GW to James Mercer, 12 Dec. 1774. GW himself at one point made some attempt to purchase Van Braam's claims. See GW to Robert Adam, 22 Nov. 1771, n.1.

## To William Smith

Gentlemen,                                 Mount Vernon June 8th 1788.

Captn Barney has just arrived here in the miniature Ship called the Federalist; and has done me the honour to offer that beautiful *curiosity* as a Present to me, on your part. I pray you, Gentlemen, to accept the warmest expressions of my sensibility for this *specimen of American ingenuity*: in which the exactitude of the proportions, the neatness of the workmanship, and the elegance of the decorations (which make your Present fit to be preserved in a Cabinet of Curiosities) at the sametime that they exhibit the skill & taste of the Artists, demonstrate that Americans are not inferior to any people whatever in the use of mechanical instruments & the art of Ship-building.¹

The unanimity of the Agricultural State of Maryland in general, as well as of the commercial Town of Baltimore in particular, expressed in their recent decision on the subject of a general Government, will not (I persuade myself) be without its due efficacy on the Minds of their Neighbours, who, in many instances, are intimately connected not only by the nature of their produce, but by the ties of blood and the habits of life. Under these circumstances, I cannot entertain an idea that the voice of the Convention of this State, which is now in Session, will be dissonant from that of her nearly-allied Sister, who is only seper-ated by the Potomack.

You will permit me, Gentlemen, to indulge my feelings in re-iterating the heart-felt wish, that the happiness of this Country may equal the desires of its sincerests friends; and that the patri-otic Town of which you are Inhabitants (in the prosperity of which I have always found myself strongly interested) may not only continue to encrease in the same wonderful manner it has formerly done—but that its trade, manufactures and other re-sources of wealth may be placed, permanently, in a more flour-ishing situation than they have hitherto been. I am with senti-ments of respect Gentlemen, Your Most Obedt & Most Hble Ser⟨v⟩t

Go: Washington

ALS, from an anonymous donor; LB, DLC:GW. Addressed to "William Smith Esqr. and the other Gentlemen Proprietors of the Ship Federalist." GW's letter was "Honoured by Captn Barney." It was printed in the *Pennsylvania Gazette* (Philadelphia) on 2 July.

William Smith (1728–1814), a member of the Continental Congress in 1777–78, was a Baltimore merchant.

1. See James McHenry to GW, 1 June, n.1.

## To David Stuart

Dear Sir,                                    Mount Vernon June 8th 1788
I have received your favour of the 4th, and am happy to find that matters so far as you had proceeded, had assumed an auspi-cious aspect.[1] I hope the good sense of the Country will be supe-rior to, and overcome the local views of some, and the arrogant and malignant pride of others. The decided majority by which the proposed Constitution was ratified in South Carolina, and the almost absolute certainty of its adoption in New Hampshire, will contribute, more than a little to dispel the mist which may, have blinded the eyes of the wavering (if they have minds open to conviction and capable of foreseeing the consequences of re-jection & seperation) & must one would think, turn them into the right road. I am just returned from meeting of the directors of the Potomack Co. at the Mouth of Shanendoah—veiwing the

Works at the Great falls, Seneca falls, and one between them, on my way up[2]—The constant rains, and consequent high waters have retarded the progress of them, but exhibit nothing discouraging; on the contrary it was observed with pleasure that our operations hitherto have bid defiance to both freshes and Ice. Stand firm & look well—I am, Dear Sir Your obed. & affect. Servt

Geo. Washington.

Copy, MH: Sparks transcripts. The addressee is not named, but the concluding sentence and closing indicate it was to David Stuart who helped keep GW informed about developments in the ratifying convention and all of whose letters from the convention are missing. See GW to Stuart, 23 and 27 June. See also GW's reference to Stuart's letter of 4 June in his letter to John Jay of this date.

1. Letter not found.
2. See GW to George Gilpin, 29 May, and notes.

## To Jonathan Trumbull, Jr.

My dear Sir                    Mount Vernon June 8th 1788

Although a multitude of avocations joined to a recent journey which I have been obliged to make in order to visit the works on the Potomack, have occasioned me to postpone giving an answer to your letter in favor of Lieutt How, yet I delayed not to forward the necessary certificate for that Gentleman, so that it might come to him before the time fixed for his departure.[1] I have at length found a moments leizure to take up my pen & to tell you in few words the state of politics in this part of the Union.

Our Convention has been assembled about a week, & so far as I am advised of their proceedings seem to have made as auspicious a beginning as could have been expected. Mr Mason & Mr Henry are at the head of the opposition. In favor of the Constitution are many very able men—among these we count Messrs Pendleton, Madison, Wythe, Blair, Nicholas, Innis, Marshall & a long train of other worthies—Governor Randolph (in answer to a speech in which Mr Henry insinuated that the Fœderal Convention had exceeded their powers, and that nothing forbade us to live happy under the old Confederation with some alterations) described pathetically our perilous situation as a full Justification of the proceedings of the Fœderal Convention; and declared, since so many of the States had adopted the Constitution without alterations that he should vote for it in its present form; Upon the whole (tho' great and unwearied artifices have been practiced to prejudice the people in many parts of the State against the New Government) I cannot avoid hoping, and believing, to use the fashionable phraze that Virginia will make the ninth column in the fœderal Temple. May all things turn out for the best in respect to this highly favoured Continent, is the constant & unfeigned prayer of My dear Trumbell Your most Affecte friend

Go: Washington

ALS, PP; LB, DLC:GW.

1. For reference to GW's certificate for Bezaleel Howe, see Trumbull to GW, 27 April, n.1.

## From Samuel Hanson

Sir                                    Alexandria, 12th June, 1788

Your favour of the 8th instant was left here when I was out of Town; whither I did not return till this moment.

It is with extreme Concern I find you have been involved, through my means, in a considerable embarrassment. Believe me, Sir, nothing could have been farther from my intention than a procedure that should reduce you to a Situation productive of the smallest perplexity. I beg your indulgence whilst I defend, by explaining, myself.

I solemnly assure you that the expedient of obtaining a provision for my family by an appointment under the new Government, did not originate with me, but in the partiality of my Friends. It was mentioned to me, for the first time, not more than 4 Weeks ago. It was objected that any application, before the establishment of the new Government, would be unseasonable. To this it was replied that, as there must be a new Government, of some kind, there would be no impropriety in soliciting the influence of your *private* Capacity. It was this Interest, Sir, which I wished to procure; without any intention of applying to you, *at that time*, as a future Magistrate of the new Government. No, Sir—It would have been indeed, highly presumptuous in me to wish to anticipate the disclosure of a determination which has for some months engaged the anxiety of all fœderal America. Though, in the course of my Letter, Some expressions escaped me that might seem to have reference to you in a future official Station; yet, my only view was to solicit the patronage of your private one. The efficacy of this interest I conceived to be sufficient; and an unavoidable conviction upon this point, leading me to consider your advocation as tantamount to an appointment, occasioned the ambiguity of my Letter, & your consequent misconception of it's true design.

I beg you, Sir, to accept my most grateful acknowledgements for the condescending, indulgent, & obliging Sentiments contained in your Reply. Be assured, it is with the utmost ⟨*mutilated*⟩ I declare that, whatever may be ⟨*mutilated*⟩ fate of my application to the new Government, your good-Opinion confers in my estimation, an honour upon me greater than any I could receive from a public appointment, however splendid or illustrious. With unfeigned Sentiments of respect, Esteem, & Gratitude, I remain, Sir, your much-obliged, and most obedt Servt

S. Hanson of Saml

ALS, DLC:GW.

## From William MacIntosh

Avignon 12th June 1788

The Letter, Sir, which you did me the honor to write, at Mount-Vernon, the 8th January, saluted me, here, the 28th May.[1]

It appears, that the same Patriotic Zeal, & unaffected Equanimity, which have suffused your fame, both as a General, & as a Politician, accompany & guide your ideas into the recesses of a Citizen, & intercourse with Individuals. It is to such elevated Sentiments, Sir, that I feel myself indebted, for the ingenuous condescension of gratifying me with a Copy of the New Constitution composed by a Convention of the States of America, in September last. The memorable retreat, from a high military Command which terminated successfully, and from the dignities inseperable from Great achievements, to the Private Station of a Citizen, on your hereditary domain, without Show or Emolument, (which your Country, the unanimous Voice of all Europe, and even the Enemies to Your Cause, have admired with Veneration) originated the institution of a Military Order, the Lustre whereof has been, in some degree, obscured by its universality; but, Sir, the late measure, was the well-timed ordeal, which promises to Crown with Permanency, the vigilant, perillous, & unremitted toils & dispositions of a Six Years Supreme Military Station in constant action. That *conclusive* measure, called you forth again, from a Private Station, to uphold the New Superstructure, not yet consolidated; and to rescue your Jarring Country from impending danger, by the powers of reasoning, & the irresistible confidence due to recent illustrious Services as a General. The result claims another honorary institution, which may properly be denominated the *Civick* Order, or the Order of *Solon*—a decoration, qualified to incite future emulation in the bosoms of Legislators, Magistrates, Cultivators, & merchants, & to inspire them with ideas worthy of those Characters; the true Springs of public Wealth & Grandeur; which are the natural qualities, & birth-right inheritances, of the People of North America.

It is flattering to me, Sir, on comparing the paper which you were pleased to transmit, & that which I took the liberty of submitting to your Consideration, (although the one was crossing the Atlantic, while the other was under decision in Philadelphia) to perceive so striking a resemblance in their Outlines & features. By the latest accounts from Great Britain (our most frequent vehicle of intelligence concerning the affairs of America) I see with pleasure, that the number of Provinces required to establish the new Constitution, by adopting the act of the Convention, were nearly completed. Without offending delicacy, may I presume, Sir, on this occasion also, to intrude an humble opinion, as a Salutary maxim in Legislation; It is—To be tender of *amending acts*, hastily—to avoid a multiplicity of articles—and to admit no terms or phrases in any Code of Jurisdiction, or Jurisprudence, that can be construed ambiguously. Some improvements may be found indispensable, at the beginning, but, perhaps, it may be productive of good, that *Explanations, amendments*, and *abrogations* be stored up, *as in petto*, for discussion & determination at the termination of a certain period of years. The reasonings & Votes on the several objects, during the term of *one presidentship*, being minuted & preserved apart, after such an experience, every obscurity, ambiguity, & necessity, will become evident to the plainest demonstration. The Example of Britain, and of many other States in Europe, should open the Eyes & Senses of New Legislators. The original Constitution, and the rights of a free-people, should be so sacred & inviolable, that strong, emphatical, unequivocal words, should be selected from an entire language, as an infallible barrier, to preserve both, by a clause, solemnly and incontestably declaring the Congress of the United States, *ipso facto*, & *in toto*, suspended from all Legislative functions, (without discomposing the wheels of the Executive government,) and the people authorised, & obliged, to proceed to new Elections, on any rash assumption of power, derogatory to the original Constitution, or to the rights of the people, or innovations on either; unless accompanied with clauses suspending their Execution, untill the consent of the Provincial States are legally, and deliberately obtained.

Constitutionally frank, even to the borders of Enthusiasm, my mind disdains to flatter. Admiring virtue, Truth, & Generosity, in others, by inclination, I have always wished to practice them. These are not Spiritual, but they may be temporal Crimes, in the present Political age, to which I plead guilty. Therefore, the man who means well, and does not utter absurdities, or follies, cannot offend; far less will it receive so haughty an interpretation, when it comes addressed under the language of respect to General Washington. On this foundation I build my faith—and without apprehension of offending, I take my leave with sentiments of profound Esteem Sir Your most obedient, & most Humble Servant

W. MacIntosh

ALS, DLC:GW.

1. GW's letter of 8 Jan. is an acknowledgment of the receipt of MacIntosh's letter of 20 Aug. 1787; it is printed in a note of MacIntosh's letter.

*Letter not found*: Clement Biddle to GW, 13 June 1788. On 20 July GW wrote Biddle: "Your favors of the 26th of May, 13th of June and 7th instt are before me."

# From James Madison

Dear Sir                              Richmond June 13th 1788.

Your favour of [        ] came to hand by the mail of Wednesday. I did not write by several late returns for two reasons; one the improbability of [your] having got back to Mount Vernon; the other a bilious indisposition which confined me for some days.[1] I am again tolerably well recovered.

Appearances at present are less favorable than at the date of my last. Our progress is slow and every advantage is taken of the delay, to work on the local prejudices of particular setts of members. British debts, the Indiana claim,[2] and the Mississippi are the principal topics of private discussion & intrigue, as well as of public declamation. The members who have served in Congress have been dragged into communications on the first which would not be justifiable on any other occasion if on the present. There is reason to believe that the event may depend on the Kentucky members; who seem to lean more agst than in favor of the Constitution. The business is in the most ticklish state that can be imagined. The majority will certainly be very small on whatever side it may finally lie; and I dare not encourage much expectation that it will be on the favorable side.

Oswald of Philada has been here with letters for the antifederal leaders from N. York and probably Philada. He staid a very short time here during which he was occasionally closeted with H——y Ma—s—n &c.[3] I learn from N. York that the elections have proved adverse to the Constitution. Yours Affectly

Js Madison Jr

ALS, DLC:GW; copy, DLC: Madison Papers.

1. GW wrote Madison on 8 June, but he does not mention in that letter his intention to go to Fredericksburg on Wednesday, 10 June, to visit his mother. GW got back to Mount Vernon on 16 June (*Diaries*, 5:343). The "your" in square brackets is taken from the copy at DLC.

2. The Indiana Company, formed of traders and others who had suffered losses in Pontiac's War, was granted a tract of land between the southern boundary of Pennsylvania and the Little Kanawha River by the Six Nations at the Treaty of Stanwix in 1786. Their claim, however, was swallowed up by the Grand Ohio Company. After the Revolution broke out, the Indiana Company was reorganized and began selling land. The Virginia legislature claimed the land lay in Virginia and refused to approve the Indian grant. In 1789 after the Constitution was in effect, the company brought suit against the state of Virginia, which the U.S. Supreme Court finally dismissed.

3. Eleazer Oswald, printer of the Philadelphia *Independent Gazette*, arrived in Richmond on 7 June with letters from New York Antifederalist leaders addressed to members of the Virginia Ratifying Convention, Patrick Henry, George Mason, and William Grayson, each of whom sent letters back to New York when Oswald left Richmond two or three days later. For a full account of Oswald's mission, see Kaminski and Saladino, *Documentary History of the Ratification of the Constitution*, 9:811–13.

## From Charles Morrow

Honoured Sir,                                    Shepherds Town June 13th 1788

Having the greatest veneration possible for your Character & high Station I should never have thought of calling your attention for a Moment to any thing that might affect myself as an Individual and almost a Stranger to your Person, (tho, not to your Character) But where the Character of my friend who is of a growing Genius & has made some discoveries that are likely to be of Public Utility is traduced, and apprehending it will be fully in your power to relieve him from the Imputation, I have ventured upon the expedient.

Mr James Rumsey who has now sailed for England under favour & with Testimonials from a Respectable Company of Citizens of Philadelphia of whom Govr Franklin was one, has had sundrie attacks made on his Character by a Mr Fitch & Co. and the more effectually to rival & traduce him in his absence have confidently Reported in the City of Philada that Mr Rumsey left the Service of the President & Directors of the Potomack River Company in *Disgrace*. This is the single point that sundrie Gentlemen of this place, with myself, would pray Your Excellency to determine either in a Letter to Govr Franklin or in any other way that you may think proper.[1] I am with every possible Sentiment of Unfeigned Respect Yr Excellencys Mo. Devoted Sert

Charles Morrow

ALS, DLC:GW.

Charles Morrow of Berkeley County, Rumsey's brother-in-law, had followed closely James Rumsey's experiments with steam power and river navigation at Shepherdstown since 1785 and had witnessed the progress of Rumsey's boat upstream on the Potomac on 3 Dec. 1787. He provided Rumsey with affidavits about these experiments which Rumsey included in his treatise on steam that he published in January 1788. See Rumsey to GW, 15 May, n.3.

1. GW responded from Mount Vernon on 25 June: "Sir, Your letter of the

13th instand from Shepherds town came duly to hand[.] In answer to the question you have propounded to me, consequent you add of a report, 'that Mr Rumsey left the Service of the President and Directors of the Potomack Company in *disgrace*'—I answer the fact is—otherwise; and that his quitting superintendency of the Companies concerns was an act of his own acquiesced in, at his desire by the P[resident] & Directors. I am Sir, Yr Very Humble Servant Go. Washington" (LB, DLC:GW). For Rumsey's trip to England, see James Rumsey to GW, 15 May.

*Letter not found*: from David Stuart, 13 June 1788. On 23 June GW wrote Stuart of "the receipt of your favor of the 13th instt."

## From Rochambeau

Rochambeau near Vendôme

My dear General June the 15th 1788.

I have received, but Since a few days, the letter of the 8th January the last, which you have honoured me with—I See in it with the greatest Satisfaction that your confederation is to take a solid and respectable form, and that you are going to play at its head a part where your Virtues and your merit naturally place you. our constitution, tho' monarchical, is in a moment of crisis that has Some ressemblance with that in which your has been till now. our twelve parliaments which arrogated the title intermediate between the Sovereign and the people, have had always principles of administration entirely dissonant, and grounded upon privileges of place. the King will reduce all that different wills to, an only King, an only law and an only court for registering, that they Shall call, according to an old Set form of the monarchy, *cour-pleniere*, plenary court; it has been recorded by the Strength of the Sovereign authority, many Edicts very good and very useful, which the last is the complement that establish a plenary court wherein all the laws will be recorded, and Shall have alone the right of remontrance. all depend on the Composition of that plenary court, if it remains as it is made Known, Composed of the delegates of the parliaments which refuse to Seat in, it Should remain only the Princes and peers and Courtiers that one could get easily, and our King Should become, against his intention, a despotic sovereign. but if, as it is assured, he calls members of the three orders lawfully elected by each province then we could acquire a very legal Constitution that will make respect our credit and render to us the consideration that We have lost by the bad administration of M. de Calonne—that plenary court is to be assembled the first of next december, and it is, its good or bad composition, that will decide of our constitution.

We are going to make this year two Camps of peace one under the orders of the marschal de Broglie at ⟨Metz⟩ and t'other in the provinces where I command, under the orders of the Prince de Condé. The King Since the death of the Mareschal de Levis has re-united the Province d'artois to my Command of Picardie.[1] The Camp Shall be probably at St omer or at Lens in the artois. I am to go at the end of this month to give orders for the preparation of it—I Shall begin my turn by the artois and I Shall fix myself at Calais till the Epoch of the camp, which Shall be about the 15th of September, after the plain will be discovered of its harvests.

my Respect to Madam Washington, my Dear général and be very persuaded that my heart draw near again continually the immense distance Which Separates our persons. I am with respect my Dear General Your most obedient and Very humble servant

le comte de Rochambeau

LS, DLC:GW.

1. François-Gaston, duc de Lévis (1719–1787), who fought for France in Canada during the war with Britain in the 1750s, was made maréchal de France in 1783 and duc de Lévis in 1784. He died at Arras in Artois where he was in command.


# To Henry Knox

My dear Sir,                              Mount Vernon June 17th 1788.

I received your letter of the 25th of May, just when I was on the eve of departure for Fredericksburgh to pay a visit to my mother from whence I returned only last evening.[1]

The information of the accession of South Carolina to the New Government, since your letter, gives us a new subject for mutual felicitations. It was to be hoped this auspicious event would have had considerable influence upon the proceedings of the Convention of Virginia; but I do not find that to have been the case. Affairs in the Convention, for some time past, have not worn so good an aspect as we could have wished: and, indeed, the acceptance of the Constitution has become more doubtful than it was thought to be at their first meeting.

The purport of the intelligence, I Received from my private letters by the last nights mail, is, that every species of address & artifice has been put in practice by the Antifederalists to create Jealousies & excite alarms.[2] Much appears to depend upon the final part which the Kentucke members will take; into many of whose minds apprehensions of unreal dange[r]s, respecting the navigation of the Mississipi & their organization into a seperate State, have been industriously infused. Each side seems to think, at present, that it has a small majority, from whence it may be augured that the majority, however it shall turn, will be very inconsiderable. Though, for my own part, I cannot but imagine, if any decision is had, it will be in favor of the adoption. My apprehension is rather that a strenuous—possibly—successful effort may be made for an adjournment; under an idea of opening a corrispondence with those who are opposed to the Constitution in other States. Colo. Oswald has been at Richmond, it is said with letters from Antifœderalists in New-York & Pensylvania to their Co-adjutors in this State.[3]

The Resolution, which came from the antefederalists (much to the astonishment of the other party) that no question should be taken until the whole Plan should have been discussed paragraph by paragraph; and the remarkable tardiness in their proceedings (for the Convention have been able as yet only to get through the 2d or 3d Section) are thought by some to have been designed to protract the business until the time when the Assembly is to convene, that is the 23d instant, in order to have a more colorable pretext for an adjournment. But notwithstanding the resolution, there has been much desultory debating & the opposers of the Constitution are reported to have gone generally into the merits of the question. I know not how the matter may be, but a few days will now determine.

I am sorry to find not only from your intimations, but also from many of the returns in the late Papers, that there should be so great a majority against the Constitution in the Convention of New York. And yet I can hardly conceive, from motives of

policy & prudence, they will reject it absolutely, if either this
State or New-Hampshire should make the 9th in adopting it—
as that measure which gives efficacy to the system, must place
any State that shall actually have refused its assent to the New-
Union in a very awkward & disagreeable predicament.

By a letter which I have just recd from a young Gentleman
who lives with me, but who is now at home in New-Hampshire,[4]
I am advised that there is every prospect that the Convention of
that State will adopt the Constitution almost immediately upon
the meeting of it. I cannot but hope then, that the States which
may be disposed to make a secession will think often and seriously on the consequence.

Colo. Humphreys who is still here, occupied with literary pursuits, desires to be remembered in terms of the sincerest friendship to you & yours.[5] Mrs Washington & the family offer, with
me, their best Compliments to Mrs Knox & the little ones—You
will ever believe me to be, with great esteem & regard My dear
Sir Yr affecte & Obedt Servt

Go: Washington

ALS, NNGL: Knox Papers; LB, DLC:GW.

1. GW left Mount Vernon with Mrs. Washington for Fredericksburg on 10
June.

2. The "private letters" that GW is referring to are undoubtedly those of
James Madison and David Stuart of 13 June. For Stuart's missing letter of 13
June, see GW to Stuart, 23 June.

3. See James Madison to GW, 13 June, n.3.

4. Tobias Lear's letter is dated 2 June.

5. Humphreys may well have been working on the biography of GW which
he never completed. See Comments on David Humphreys' Biography of
George Washington printed at the end of volume 5 of the *Papers, Confederation Series*.

## From Eliza Harriot O'Connor

Sir                                    Alexandria June 17th 1788
When Mr O'Connor had the honor of dining with you before
I opened the Academy for young Ladies in Alexandria you was
kind enough not only to express your approbation of the Institution but likewise your wish for its permanancy and support,

and intimated likewise that you would have no objection to be one of the visitors at the Examinations.

Impressed with an Idea of the goodness and benevolence of your heart, and its wishes for the promotion and encouragement of seminaries of Learning in the United States, I most earnestly request your attendance on Tuesday the 24th Instant to the first Examination, when I trust I shall prove myself not unworthy yours or Mrs Washingtons patronage.[1]

If Mr O'Connors attention to the history of America permitted him to be in Alexandria he would do himself the honor to request this favor in person—but his engagement to the public respecting that work which he looks upon to be indispensible prevents his attendance here.

Your presence Sir will be a sanction to this arduous undertaking, and will be conferring a very essential obligation, on Sir your obliged and most Obedient Hum. Sert

Eliza Harriot O'Connor

ALS, DLC:GW.

1. George Lux of Chatsworth at Baltimore wrote GW on 9 Jan. recommending to him Eliza O'Connor and her husband Robert. See note 1 of that document. John O'Connor dined with GW on 3 Feb., and shortly thereafter Mrs. O'Connor opened her school in Alexandria. GW wrote Mrs. O'Connor on 20 June declining to serve on the board of visitors for her school. For a summary of GW's subsequent dealings with Mrs. O'Connor, see the editors' note in *Diaries*, 5:409.

## To Lafayette

Mount Vernon June 18th 1788

I cannot account for your not having received some of my letters, my dear Marquis, before you wrote yours of the 18th of March; as I have been writing to you, at short intervals, constantly since last autumn. To demonstrate the satisfaction I enjoy on the receipt of your favours; I always answer them almost as soon as they arrive—Although, on account of my retirement from the busy scenes of life and the want of diversity in the tenour of our affairs, I can promise to give you little novelty or entertainment in proportion to what I expect in return. Were you to acknowledge the receipt of my letters, and give the dates

of them when you write to me, I should be able to ascertain
which of them had reached you—and which of them had miscarried. I am left in doubt whether the Indian Vocabularies &c.
&c. have got to you or not.[1]

There seems to be a great deal of bloody work cut out for this
summer in the North of Europe. If war, want and plague are
to desolate those huge armies that are assembled, who that has
the feelings of a man can refrain from shedding a tear over the
miserable victims of Regal Ambition? It is really a strange thing
that there should not be room enough in the world for men to
live, without cutting one anothers throats. As France, Spa[i]n
and England have hardly recovered from the wounds of the late
war, I would fain hope they will hardly be dragged into this.
However, if the war should be protracted (and not end in a cam-
pain as you intimate it possibly may) there seems to be a probability of other powers being engaged on one side or the other.
by the British papers (which are our principal source of intelle-
gence, though not always to be relied upon, as you know) it appears that the Spaniards are fitting out a considerable fleet and
that the English Ministry have prohibited the subjects of their
Kingdom from furnishing transports for the Empress of Russia.
France must be too intent on its own domestic affairs to wish to
interfere; and all have not heard that the King of Prussia, since
his exports[2] in Holland, has taken it into his head [to] meddle
with other people's business. I cannot say that I am sorry to hear
that the Algerines and other piratical powers are about to assist
the Porte, because I think Russia will not forget and that she will
take some leisure moment, Just to keep her fleets in exercise,
for exterminating those nests of Miscreants.

I like not much the situation of affairs in France. The bold
demands of the Parliaments and the decisive tone of the King,
shew that but little more irritation would be necessary to blow
up the spark of discontent into a flame that might not easily be
quenched. If I were to advise, I would say that great moderation
should be used on both sides. Let it not, my dear Marquis, be
considered as a derogation from the good opinion that I entertain of your prudence, when I caution you, as an individual desirous, of signalising yourself in the cause of your country and
freedom, against running into extremes and prejudicing your
cause. The King, though I think from every thing I have been

able to learn, he is really a good-hearted, tho' a warm-spirited man, if thwarted injudiciously in the execution of prerogatives that belonged to the Crown, and in plans which he conceives calculated to promote the national good, may disclose qualities he has been little thought to possess. On the other hand, such a spirit seems to be awakened in the Kingdom, as, if managed with extreem prudence, may produce a gradual and tacit Revolution much in favour of the subjects, by abolishing Lettres d[e] Cachet and defining more accurately the powers of government. It is a wonder to me, there should be found a single monarch, who does not realize that his own glory and felicity must depend on the prosperity and happiness of his People. How easy is it for a sovereign to do that which shall not only immortalize his, name, but attract the blessings of Millions.

In a letter I wrote you a few days ago by Mr Barlow (but which might not possibly have reached New York untill after his departure)[3] I mentioned the accession of Maryland to the proposed government and give you the state of politics, to that period. Since which the Convention of South Carolina has ratified the Constitution by a great majority: that of this State has been setting almost three weeks and so nicely does it appear to be ballanced, that each side asserts that it has a prepondenacy of votes in its favour. It is probable, therefore, the majority will be small, let it fall on which ever part it may; I am inclined to believe it will be in favour of the adoption. The Convention of New York and New Hampshire assemble both this week—a large proportion of members, with the Governor at their head, in the former are said to be opposed to the government in contemplation: New Hampshire it is thought will adopt it without much hesitation or delay. It is a little strange that the men of large property in [the] South, should be more afraid that the Constitution will produce an Aristocracy or a Monarchy, then the genuine democratical people of the East. Such are our actual prospects. The accession of one State more will complete the number, which by the Constitutional provision, will be sufficient in the first instance to carry the Government into effect.

And then, I expect, that many blessings will be attributed to our new government, which are now taking their rise from that industry and frugality into the practice of which the people have been forced from necessity. I really believe that there never was so much labour and economy to be found before in the country as at the present moment. If they persist in the habits they are acquiring, the good effects will soon be distinguishable. When the people shall find themselves secure under an energetic government, when foreign Nations shall be disposed to give us equal advantages in commerce from dread of retaliation, when the burdens of the war shall be in a manner done away by the sale of western lands, when the seeds of happiness which are sown here shall begen to expand themselves, and when every one (under his own vine and fig-tree) shall begin to taste the fruits of freedom—then all these blessings (for all these blessings will come) will be referred to the fostering influence of the new government. Whereas many causes will have conspired to produce them. you see I am not less enthusiastic than ever I have been, if a belief that peculiar scenes of felicity are reserved for this country, is to be denominated enthusiasm. Indeed, I do not believe that Providence has done so much for nothing. It has always been my creed that we should not be left as an awful monument to prove, "that Mankind, under the most favourable circumstances for civil liberty and happiness, are unequal to the task of Governing themselves, and therefore made for a Master."[4]

We have had a backward spring and summer, with more rainy and cloudy weather than almost ever has been known: still the appearance of crops in some parts of the country is favorable—as we may generally expect will be the case, from the difference of soil and variety of climate in so extensive a region—insomuch that, I hope, some day or another we shall become a storehouse and granary For the world. In addition to our former channels of trade, salted provisions, butter, cheese &c. are exported, with propht from the eastern States to the East Indies.[5] In consequence of a Contract, large quantities of f[l]our are lately sent from Baltimore for supplying the garrison of Gibralter. With sentiments of the tenderest affection—I am &c. &c.

Go. Washington

LB, DLC:GW.

1. For the Indian vocabularies, see Richard Butler to GW, 30 Nov. 1787, and enclosures.

2. GW probably wrote "exploits."

3. GW's letter of 28 May was to have been delivered by Joel Barlow.

4. The source of the quotation has not been determined.

5. See Robert Morris to GW, 29 April, and note 2 of that document.

## From James Madison

Dear Sir                      Richmond June 18. 88.

No question direct or indirect has yet been taken, by which the state of parties could be determined. of course each is left to enjoy the hopes resulting from its own partial calculations. It is probable the majority on either side will not exceed more than 3, 4, 5 or 6. I indulge a belief that at this time the friends of the Constitution have the advantage in point of number. Great moderation as yet marks our proceedings. Whether it be the effect of temper, or of the equality of forces & the uncertainty of victory, will be seen by the event. We are at present on the Executive Department. Mr H——y has not made a very[1] opposition to it though it was looked for. He may however still mean to make one; or he may lay by for an exertion agst the Judiciary. I find myself not yet restored & extremely feeble. With very affet. regards I remain Yrs

Js Madison Jr

ALS, DLC:GW; copy, in Madison's hand, DLC: Madison Papers.

1. Madison inadvertently omitted an adjective here.

*Letter not found*: from Mathew Carey, 19 June 1788. On 25 June GW wrote Carey about his "favor of the 19th."

## To Richard Henderson

Sir,                      Mount Vernon June 19th 1788

Your favour of the 5th instant was lodged at my house, while I was absent on a visit to my Mother. I am now taking the earliest opportunity of noticing its contents and those of its Enclosure. Willing as I am to give satisfaction so far as I am able, to every reasonable enquire (and this is certainly not only so, but may be highly important and interesting) I must however, rather deal in general than particular observations: as I think you will be able, from the length of your residence in the country and the extensiveness of your acquaintance with its affairs, to make the necessary applications and add the proper details.[1] Nor would I choos[e] that my interference in the business should be transmitted, lest, in a malicious world, it might be represented that I was officiously using the arts of seduction to depopulate other countries, for the sake of peopling our own.

In the first place it is a point conceded, that America, under an efficient government, will be the most favorable Country of any in the world for persons of industry and frugality, possessed of a moderate capital, to inhabit. It is also believed that it will not be less advantageous to the happiness of the lowest class of people because of the equal distribution of property the great plenty of unoccupied lands, and the facility of procuring the means of subsistance. The scheme of purchasing a good tract of freehold estate and bringing out a number of ablebodied men, indented for a certain time appears to be indisputably a rationale one. All the interior arrangements of transferring the property and commencing the establishment you are as well acquainted with, as I can possibly be. It might be considered as a point of more difficulty, to decide upon the place which should be most proper for a settlement. Although, I believe, that Emigrants from other countries to this, who shall be well-disposed and conduct themselves properly, would be treated with equal friendship and kindness in all parts of it; yet in the old settled States, land is so much occupied and the value so much enhanced by the contiguous cultivation, that the price would in general be an objection. The land in western country, or that on the Ohio, like all others, has its *advantages and disadvantages*. The neighbourhood of the Savages and the difficulty of transportation were the great objections. The danger of the first will soon cease by the strong establishments now taking place—the inconveniencies of the second will be, in a great degree, remidied by opening the internal Navigation. No Colony in America was ever settled under such favorable auspicies as that which has just commenced at the Muskingum Information, property and strength will be its characteristics. I know many of the settlers personally & that there never were men better calculated to promote the wellfare of such a community.[2]

If I was a young man, just preparing to begin the world or if advanced in life, and had a family to make a provision for, I know of no country, where I should rather fix my habitation than in some part of that region; for which the writer of the quæries seems to have a predilection. he might be informed that his name-sake and distant relation, Genl St Clair, is not only in high repute, but that he is Governor of all the Territory westward of the Ohio and that there is a Gentleman (to wit Mr Joel Barlow) come from New York by The last French Packet, who will be in London in the course of this year and who is authorised to dispose of a very large body of land in that Country.[3] The author of the quæries may then be referred "to the Information for those who would wish to remove to America": published in Europe in the year 1784, by the great Philosopher Dr Franklin. Short as it is, it contains almost every thing that need to be known on the subject of migrating to this Country. you may find that excellent little Treatise, in "Carey's American Museum for September 1787." It is worthy of being republished in Scotland and every other part of Europe.[4]

As to the European Publications respecting the United States, they are commonly very defective. The Abbe Raynale is quite erroneous. Guthrie, though somewhat better informed, is not absolutely correct. There is now "an American Geography preparing for the press by a Mr Morse of New Haven in Connecticut" which, from the pains the Author has taken in travelling through the States and acquiring information from the principal characters in each, will probably be much more exact and useful.[5] of books at present existing, Mr Jefferson's "Notes on Virginia," will give the best idea of this part of the Continent to a Foreigner: and the "American Farmer's Letters"—written by Mr Crevecœur (commonly called Mr St John) the French Consul in New York (who actually resided 20 years as a farmer in that State) will afford a great deal of profitable and amusive Information, respecting *the private Life* of the Americans; as well as the progress of agriculture, manufactures and arts in their Country.[6] Perhaps the picture he gives, though founded in fact, is in some instances embellished with rather too flattering circumstances—I am &ca

Go. Washington

LB, DLC:GW.

1. GW seems to have been tempted to provide "proper details" himself for potential settlers, for on the back of Henderson's letter of 5 June GW wrote a memorandum of the "Terms wch Servants may be Indented." He noted that

a carpenter or a mason could expect £12 per annum, and a carpenter "who is capable to work all Ho[use] Carprs Joine & Cabinet work," £36. Passage for these, GW fixed at 8 guineas and specified that their Employers would not "find Victuals or Cloaths" for them. An able-bodied male servant's pay he set at £3.3 and a female servant's at £2.2, "cloaths & victuals to be found" in both cases. Cost of passage for each servant he estimated would be £5.

2. In the spring of 1788 Rufus Putnam led the party that first settled Marietta in the Ohio Country. See Rufus Putnam to GW, 5 April 1784, and William Hull to GW, 25 Oct. 1786 and notes to these documents.

3. For the "writer of the quæries," see Henderson to GW, 5 June, n.1. For Barlow's journey to Europe, see GW to Lafayette, 28 May, n.2.

4. GW would have liked particularly Franklin's declaration: "people [in America] do not inquire concerning a Stranger, *What is he?* but *What can he do?* If he has any useful Art, he is welcome; and if he exercises it, and behaves well, he will be respected by all that know him" ("Information to Those Who Would Remove to America," [1782], printed in Smyth, *Writings of Franklin*, 8:603–14).

5. The tenth edition of William Guthrie's *A Geographical, Historical, and Commercial Grammar* was published in London in 1787. GW later secured a copy of the first American edition, published in two volumes in 1794 and 1795. The English translation of l'abbé Raynal (Guillaume-Thomas-François Raynal; 1713–1796), *A Philosophical and Political History of the British Settlements and Trade in North America*, was published in Edinburgh in two volumes in 1776 and 1779. Jedediah Morse published in 1789 his second book on geography, *The American Geography* (see also David Humphreys to GW, 1 Nov. 1786, n.2).

6. In July 1787 Crèvecoeur sent GW a copy of his three-volume French edition of *Letters from an American Farmer*. GW had read the English edition of 1782. GW had in his library at his death a copy of the second edition (1794) of Thomas Jefferson's *Notes on the State of Virginia* (1785).

# From John Hopkins

Sir.                                          Richmond June 20th 1788

Agreeably to your desire exprest, in your favor of the 27th April last, I have settled with, and paid the Sherif of Green Briar, the amount of your Taxes, and have given to Dr Stewart his receipts. The D[octo]r will pay the balance which is due me as appears, by an account delivered to him, which I presume he will forward to you, for your Satisfaction, before he leaves this City.[1]

The Sherif of Green Briar, and one of the Commissioners of the Land Tax, in that County, who was present—stated to me, that both the Tracts of Land of 10,990 Acres, and 2,000 Acres, on which Taxes were Charged, lies in the County of Montgomery, and the reason, these Lands were Taxed in Green Briar, was owing to the register of the Land Office having made his returns of the Lands in question, to that County. These Gentlemen inform me that the Great Kanawa does (as you suppose) seperate the County of Green Briar from any other, and that all the Lands, lying between the mouths of the great and little Kanawa, are within the Bounds of the County of Green Briar, Consequently the three tracts you mention of 2,314[,] 2,448 and 4,395 Acres making in the whole 9,157 Acres are in the said County of Green Briar, but no returns having been made of them, nor of the one patented in your Name, and that of M. George Muse of 7,276 acres, from the registers Office, they have never been Taxed. The tract of 587 Acres Called the round Bottom, is they think in the same predicament, but lies in the County of Harrison.[2] I have the honor to be with great respect & Esteem Sir Your most obt humble servant

Jno: Hopkins

ALS, DLC:GW.

   1. See GW to David Stuart, 24 July.

   2. For GW's inquiry about the counties in which his Ohio lands lay, see his letter to Hopkins of 27 April.

## To Eliza Harriot O'Connor

Madam,                    Mount Vernon June 20th 1788

   I have received the letter which you did me the favor to write to me on the 17th instant, and am happy that the acknowledgment of it affords me an occasion of expressing my real satisfaction at the present flourishing state of your Academy and ardent wishes for its future prosperity. Should my avocations (whh have been multiplied by two Journeys I have lately been obliged to make) and my attentions at home (which this busy season of the year will peculiarly demand) permit it to be in any manner convenient, I shall cheerfully attend either at the first or some subsequent exhibition of the Pupils in your Institution: and doubt not of my being highly gratified with their proficiency in useful and elegant accomplishments.

   These Madam, are the ideas I must have intended to intimate to Mr O'Connor on his first mentioning the subject to me. If he understood my having no objection to an occasional or casuale visititation, as a willingness to become one of the official and stated visitors at the examinations, he must have misconceived my meaning. The reasons are well known, why, at my time of life, under my actual circumstances, and assailed (as I may say) with a multiplicity of applications of different kinds sence the termination of the war, I have studiously declined entering into any new engagements which may tend to draw me, in the least degree, from my agricultural and private pursuits.[1]

I though[t] it necessary to be thus explicit in order to have obviate any misapprehensions that might have taken place, and to assure you with how great truth I have the honour to be Madam Your sincere Well-wisher & Most humble Servant

Go. Washington

LB, DLC:GW.

1. Mrs. O'Connor acknowledged GW's letter the next day, 21 June, in these terms: "I this moment received your letter of the 20th Instant, and take the liberty of detaining your servant while I express my gratitude for those good wishes you have for the Institution now under my particular direction, which can never be repaid by any other means than an endeavour on my part to deserve them which I hope you will be assured shall be my earnest endeavour" (DLC:GW).

# From Jonathan Trumbull, Jr.

My Dear General                    Lebanon [Conn.] 20th June 1788
I have this Day been made very happy in the receipt of your favor of the 8th instant. The information you have been so good as to communicate, and the pleasing prospects whih that information has excited in my Mind, have formed such an accession to my common stock of Joys as rarely falls in my Way—The Support which the new Constitution will receive from the State of Virginia must fill every Well Wisher to its Adoption, with heart felt pleasure & satisfaction. Under the Influence of these feelings, I anticipate the Joy of soon hearing the compleat ratification of your State.

The Triumph of Fœderalism has been great in Connecticut since last Winter. The Opposition which then existed, is now dwindled into meer unimportance. At our late Elections—which you know Sir! are formed by the people at large—a Genl Wadsworth, who was the Champion of Opposition in our Convention, lost his place as an Assistant, by great Odds—his Seat at the Council Board, was filled by Colo. Chester, late Speaker of our House of Assembly—a Gentleman of independant, liberal Sentiments, & a firm friend to general Government—Your Old Secretary being placed in the Speaker's Chair, on the removal of Colo. Chester, was an additional Blow to Opposition—and, he being considered as a warm supporter of the fœderal Interest—a fast friend to the Army, & to public Justice, this Event had its influence towards compleating the Triumph.[1]

Indeed much pleased have I been in the Course of our late Sessions of Assembly, to observe a Disposition towards public Measures much better than has prevailed for some Years past—Pray God this happy Change may continue!

A like Triumph I am told—and a similar good disposition has taken place in Massachusetts. And it is confidently said—so that it gains my belief—that N. Hampshire, at the Adjournment of her Convention, will asssuredly ratify the new Constitution, by a considerable Majority. A Dawn of better Times, my Dear Genl! appears—may the Day soon break upon us in full Lustre & brightness.

Under these circumstances, can the State of N. York have hardiness eno' to refuse their Assent? or will she consent to stand on the same Ground with our deluded Sister R. Island. I would fain hope, that shameless Prostitute will not be able to find an Associate in her Sins & Follies.

I have a late Letter from my Brother, who still continues in London—the Confidence with which he has been honored by Mr Adams, has led him near the Channels of the best information—and his Intimacy with Mr West, who, from a particular foible attendant on Majesty, has perhaps as much domestic intercourse with the King as almost any private Subject—has brot *him* more nearly acquainted with the Character of his Majesty, than is commonly obtained.

My Brother speaks warmly of the new Constitution—of the happy Effects he hopes from it—& of the urgent necessity of its speedy adoption. "No unforeseen Event (he says) will I hope occur to dash our hopes of Union—it was never more necessary than at this Hour—there are those who neither forget nor forgive our past successes; & who would rejoice in a fresh Opportunity of dispute, if they saw but a hope of success—& a late Event (he adds) has taken place which may perhaps inspire that hope—A Bill has just passed in Parliament for the better regulation of affairs in India—which vests the supreme Goverment & Defence of that Country in a Board of Controul, to be appointed by the King—this Board is supreme, & being charged with the defence of the Country, are consequently made directors of the territorial Revenues, which are said to amount to Seven Millions a year—This Sum is an addition to the Royal purse—independt of Parliament—and has for its natural attendant the Army at present under the Orders of the India Compa.—a no inconsiderable Body of Men—likewise independt of Parliament.[2] Those who know the British Constitution, may judge what will be the Effect of such an addition to the Power of One Branch. and those who know the Character of him who now constitutes that Branch, may judge what will be his future conduct. Ours obviously ought to be guarded, united & preparatory. We may perhaps be secured for a little time by the Quarrels of Europe— there is some reason to *hope*, that the Ambition & resentment which frowns on us may find other Occupations for some time: yet we shall not be forgotten—there is One who never forgets nor forgives—& be assured we shall be the Objects of his earliest Vengeance, as we are of his continual remembrance & Detestation."[3]

These circumstances are committed to me in Confidence— on the same ground I mention them to you, my Dear Sir!— with this one Observation only—that the Writer having been once frowned upon in England, would not willingly be brot into trouble again from the freedom of his pen.[4]

I beg pardon for troubling you with the above detail—at the present period however, such information, rightly improved, may not be useless. With the warmest cordiality of friendship—& the highest Sentiments of respect & regard I have the honor to be Dear Sir Your most Obedient & Obliged humble Servant

Jona. Trumbull

ALS, DLC:GW; ADf, CSmH.

1. John Chester of Wethersfield, Conn., was a member of the state's ratifying convention. "Your Old Secretary" was Trumbull himself.

2. "An Act for removing any Doubt respecting the Power of the Commissioners for the affairs of India . . ." was passed (*Statutes at Large*, 407–8).

3. John Trumbull (1756–1843) went to London in 1780 to study with Benjamin West with whom he continued to work.

4. After his arrival in London in 1780, John Trumbull was briefly imprisoned on charges of treason.

# From George Washington

Dr Sir                North Carolina Tarborough June 20th [1788]

From a most distresd Situation, have taken up my Pen to request your Attention, though I have not the least reason to Expect it, owing to my entering myself into a Matrymonial State too soon, & allowing myself to be led astray by the deceitfull Tongue of a Woman, one beyond expression & occasioned through my haveing so great an Attachment to her, that she rul'd me as she thought proper, & made me enter into all kind of Extravagancy; which has brought me to ruin, & depriv'd me of seeing my friends for some time past, I have, since her death Marryed another, who I can with propriety call a Wife, but as her Parrents weare so much averse to the match, I am kep oute of her Fortune untill she comes of Age, which will be in a twelve month from this, I have wrote to my Father for his Assistance he den'ys bitterly, which reduce's me to apply for your Astance, & am in hopes that you will take it under mature consideration—& grant it me, I should not have wrote at this time but I have lately Rented a House in greensVill Town, in this State, & am reduc'd to the necessaty of Keeping a Tavern; though I am not able to carry it on for the want of Moneys to set up a good one, therefore begg your assistance most seriously should you incline to assist me you may by Post, which will deliver me any service's that your undoubted goodness may send me, if you could assist me in leting me have a place on the Dismall Swamp to live on I had much rather be a Planter, or I will take care of your Business there, let me know by the first post after this, as I shall wait with expectations of heareing from you. I am Sir with every sentiment of reguard

                                        Geo. Washington

N.B. pray do not let my Father know of what I wrote to you for.[1]

ALS, ViMtV. The letter was sent "℔ post."

1. This George Washington may be the son of Lawrence Washington of Chotank, GW's boyhood friend. Lawrence of Chotank had a son George (b. 1758) who is thought to have died young. However on 15 Feb. 1777 GW wrote George Baylor about commissions for "Two young gentn namesakes of mine, the one Son to Mr Lawrence Washington, the other to Mr Robt Washington, both of Stafford County . . ." (ALS, DLC:GW). It is uncertain whether GW meant that the two young men both were named George. It is certain from this letter to GW, however, that this young George Washington and his father were well known to GW. The writer of the letter seems to have been still living in Tarboro in 1792 when Henry Irwin of Edgecombe County, N.C., wrote a will leaving £100 to "George Washington of Tarboro" (Ruth Smith Williams and Margarette Glen Griffin, *Abstract of the Wills of Edgecombe County, North Carolina, 1733–1856* [Rocky Mount, N.C., 1956], 178).

## From John Langdon

Sr        State of New Hampshire Concord June 21, 1788

I have the great pleasure of informing your Excellency that this State has this day Adopted the Federal Constitution, 57 yeas 46 Nays—thereby placing the Key Stone in the great Arch, this I hope will Apologize in some measure, for our heretofore Miss-doings—please to Excuse haste, and Beleive me with the highest Sense of Esteem and Respect your Excellencys most Obt Servt

John Langdon

ALS, DLC:GW.

## To John Lathrop

Reverend & respected Sir,      Mount Vernon June 22d 1788.

Your acceptable favour of the 16th of May, covering a recent publication of the proceedings of the Humane Society, has, within a few days past, been put into my hands.

I observe, with singular satisfaction, the cases in which your benevolent Institution has been instrumental in recalling some of our fellow creatures (as it were) from beyond the gates of Eternity, and has given occasion for the hearts of parents & friends to leap for joy. The provision made for Ship-wrecked Marriners is also highly estimable in the view of every philanthropic mind & greatly consolatory to that suffering part of the Community. These things will draw upon you the blessings of those who were nigh to perish. These works of charity & good-will towards men reflect, in my estimation, great lustre upon the Authors, and presage an æra of still farther improvements. How pitiful, in the eye of reason & religion, is that false ambition which desolates the world with fire & sword for the purposes of conquest & fame; when compared to the milder virtues of making our neighbours and our fellow men as happy as their frail conditions & perishable natures will permit them to be!

I am happy to find that the proposed general government meets with your approbation—as indeed it does with *that* of most disinterested and discerning men. The Convention of this State is now in Session, and I cannot but hope that the Constitution will be adopted by it—though not without considerable opposition. I trust, however, that the commendable example exhibited by the minority in your State will not be without its salutary influence in this. In truth it appears to me that (should the proposed government be generally & harmoniously adopted) it will be a new phœnomenon in the political & moral world; and an astonishing victory gained by enlightened reason over brutal force. I have the honor to be with very great consideration Reverd & respected Sir Yr Most Obedt & Hble Sert

Go: Washington

ALS, PWacD; LB, DLC:GW.

## From Tobias Lear

My dear Sir,                        Portsmouth [N.H.] 22 June 1788.

I have the pleasure to inform you that the Constitution was yesterday adopted by the Convention of this State after a Session of four days; the number in favor of the adoption was 57—against it 46. The majority, tho' small, is very respectable, as it is pretty well ascertained that at least ¾ of the property, & a larger proportion of the abilities in the State are friendly to the proposed system. The opposition here (as has generally been the case) was composed of men who were involved in debt; and of consequence would be averse to any government which was likely to abolish their tender Laws and cut off every hope of accomplishing their favorite plan of introducing a paper currency. The behaviour of the minority (except a few) was however candid & conciliatory; and the event was peculiarly pleasing to every inhabitant of this town & its vicinity.

The Independent Companies of Horse & the Militia will assemble tomorrow to conduct his Excellency President Langdon into town, but whether there will be any procession, as has been exhibited in other places on the occasion, I do not know, but think there will not.

I take the liberty to enclose a copy of the amendments recommended by this Convention; they were drawn up more with a view of softening & conciliating the adoption to some who were moderate in their opposition than from an expectation that they would ever be engrafted in the Constitution.[1]

I hope to be at Mount Vernon some time in the latter part of July or first of Augt—my inclination would lead me there sooner was that alone to be consulted, but there are several matters to be settled relative to my father's Estate which require my attention, and which will detain me in this part of the Continent a few weeks longer than I expected.[2]

You will be so obliging as to give my best respects to Mrs Washington—and be assured that I am, My dear Sir, With the warmest affection & highest respect, Yr most Obedt & Hble Servant
                                                    Tobias Lear

P.S. The Constitution was ratified on Saturday at 1 P.M. I am thus particular as Virginia might have adopted it on the same day, & in that Case the hour must be known to determine which was the ninth State.

ALS, DLC:GW.

1. The enclosure is in DLC:GW. After formally ratifying the Constitution on 21 June, the members of the New Hampshire convention voted to recommend certain "alterations and provisions be introduced into the said Constitution." The proposed amendments, twelve in number, included several parts of the bill of rights later incorporated in the first ten amendments to the Constitution (Walker, *New Hampshire Convention*, 44–52).

2. Lear "returned home" to Mount Vernon on 11 Sept. (*Diaries*, 5:393).

## To James Madison

My dear Sir, Mount Vernon June 23d 1788.

Since my last, acknowledging the first letter you did me the favor to write to me after your arrival in Richmond, I have received your subsequent ones of the 13th & 18th instant; which, tho' less favourable than the former, are more pleasing than suspence.

I will yet hope that the good sense of this Country, maugre all the arts of opposition, will ultimately decide right on the important question now depending before the Convention.

I hear with real concern of your indisposition. At Fredericksburgh (on a visit to my aged and infirm mother) I understood that you intended to proceed immediately from Richmond to New York, when the Convention shall have arisen. Relaxation must have become indispensably necessary for your health, and for that reason I presume to advise you to take a little respite from business and to express a wish that part of the time might be spent under this roof on your journey thither.[1] Moderate exercise, and books occasionally, with the mind unbent, will be your best restoratives. With much truth I can assure you that no one will be happier in your company than your sincere & affecte Servt

Go: Washington

ALS, NjP: Washington Miscellaneous Manuscripts; LB, DLC:GW.

1. Madison accepted GW's invitation, arriving at Mount Vernon on the afternoon of 4 July and staying until 7 July (*Diaries*, 5:357).

## From James Madison

Dear Sir Richmond—June Tuesday [23, 1788].[1]

We got through the constitution by paragraphs today. Tomorrow some proposition for closing the business will be made. On our side a ratification involving a few declaratory truths not affecting its validity will be tendered. The opposition will urge previous amendments. Their conversation to day seemed to betray despair. Col. Mason in particular talked in a style which no other sentiment could have produced. He held out the idea of civil convulsions as the effects of obtruding the Government on the people. He was answered by several and concluded with declaring his determination for himself to acquiesce in the event whatever it might be. Mr H——y endeavoured to gloss what had fallen from his friend, declared his aversion to the Constitution to be such that he could not take the oath; but that he would remain in peaceable submission to the result. We calculate on a majority, but a bare one. It is possible nevertheless that some adverse circumstance may happen. I am Dr Sr in haste Yrs entirely

Js Madison Jr

ALS, DLC:GW; copy, DLC: Madison Papers.

1. Madison dated the letter "Richmond—June Tuesday 25," but the contents of the letter indicate that Madison wrote it on Monday, 23 June. The final vote on ratification was taken on Wednesday, 25 June. Madison wrote again on 25 June.

## To David Stuart

Dear Sir,                                    Mount Vernon June 23d 1788.

Upon the receipt of your favor of the 13th instt[1] I caused enquiry to be made into the foundation for the report which you said was industriously circulated in Richmond, respecting the notice taken of the proposed Constitution by the Assembly of Maryland; and am told that it is a time serving falsehood; as you will be particularly informed by an enclosure from Colo. Fitzgerald.[2]

The hopes & fears of each party are, by this, I presume, realised. Important will be the decision. I wish it may be auspicious of the happiness of this Country.

The mode in which you propose to settle with Mr Hopkins, for my taxes in the County of Green Brier, is perfectly agreeable to me.[3] I have heard nothing yet from Mr Custis (of the Eastern Shore)[4]—nor has Colo. Thos Lewis ever acknowledged the receipt of my Letter to him; tho' he was particularly requested to do so (that I might know what I had to trust to) and a certain channel pointed out to him by which it could be done.[5]

Mrs Stuart went from this yesterday for Mount Airy;[6] and talked of being back again tomorrow. She & the Children are all well. The Rains have been so frequent and abundant on *my*

Plantations, that I am, in a manner drowned; this is not the case I am told at Abingdon.[7] and higher up, they rather *wanted* than were *overdone* with it when I was in Berkley—In the Neighbourhood of Fredericksburgh (from whence I came this day Se'night) nothing could be more seasonable. The Wheat with me, (& I believe it is the case generally, in a greater or lesser degree) has got the speck (Defective grains) but I have not, as yet, discovered rust among it. Rye is more injured than Wheat by the non-impregnation; and where it is thin, is still more hurt by entanglement and falling. Oats & Flax would have been very fine had not the best of *both* lodged[8]—What will become of *my* Corn is not easy, at this moment, to decide; I am working it ancle deep in Water & mud, & can destroy no other plant than the one I am aiming to preserve. I am—Dear Sir Yr Affecte & Obedt Servt

Go: Washington

ALS, owned (1976) by Mr. Fred Casoni, Washington, D.C.

1. Letter not found.
2. The enclosure has not been found.
3. See John Hopkins to GW, 20 June.
4. GW is probably referring to the Mr. Custis, identified as Edmund Custis, about whom GW wrote to Stuart on 15 January.
5. See GW to Thomas Lewis, 25 Dec. 1787.
6. Mount Airy in Prince Georges County, Md., was the childhood home of Mrs. Stuart, née Eleanor Calvert.
7. David Stuart lived at Abingdon on the Potomac, just above Alexandria.
8. I.e., beaten down to the ground by wind or rain.

*Letter not found*: from David Stuart, 23 June 1788. On 27 June GW wrote that his "letter of the 23d . . . came duly to hand."

## From Ebenezer Hazard

General Post Office,
Sir,                                     New York June 24th 1788.

By sending the enclosed under Cover to me, our good Friend Dr Gordon has given me another Opportunity of testifying my Respect for your Excellency, without unnecessarily diverting your Attention from more important Objects. It came to hand yesterday from Boston, where Mr John Adams has at length arrived after a Passage of ten Weeks.[1]

The Attention of Politicians here is wholly engrossed by the new Constitution. The Information received of late from New Hampshire leaves little or no Reason to doubt of its Adoption by that State, and the Gentlemen in Congress from thence consider it as a certain Event. The Convention of this State is now sitting at Poughkeepsie, and the Antifederalists have a decided Majority in that Body: we are told that their Conduct is more temperate than was at first expected, and some are sanguine enough to believe that the Necessity of the Case will induce them to adopt the new Constitution: others, perhaps better informed, seem confident that they will make certain Amendments the Condition of their adopting it: in my Opinion much depends upon the Conduct of Virginia, for whose Decision we wait with anxious Impatience: should that be favorable, New York will have no Supporter, in Case of a Rejection, but Rhode Island, and the Union will have but little to apprehend from either the Politics or Power of both. With every Sentiment of Esteem and Respect, I have the Honor to be, Your Excellency's most obedient and very humble Servant

Ebenr Hazard

ALS, DLC:GW.

1. GW received a letter from William Gordon dated 3 April 1788, in which he put in a good word for Hazard. For GW's acknowledgment on 22 July of Hazard's letter and its enclosures, see Hazard to GW, 14 July, n.1.

## To Mathew Carey

Sir,　　　　　　　　　　　　　Mount Vernon June 25th 1788

Although I believe "the American Museum" published by you, has met with extensive, I may say, with universal approbation from competent Judges; yet, I am sorry to find by your favor of the 19th that in a pecuniary view it has not equalled your expectations.[1]

A discontinuance of the Publication for want of proper support would, in my judgment, be an impeachment on the Understanding of this Country. For I am of opinion that the Work is not only eminently calculated to disseminate political, agricultural, philosophical & other valuable information; but that it has been uniformly conducted with taste, attention, & propriety. If to these important objects be superadded the more immediate design, of rescuing public Documts from oblivion: I will venture to pronounce, as my sentiment, that a more useful literary plan has never been undertaken in America, or one more deserving public encouragement. By continuing to prosecute that plan with similar assiduity and discernment, the merit of your Museum must ultimately become as well known in some Countries of Europe as on this Continent; and can scarcely fail of procuring an ample compensation for your trouble & expence.[2]

For my self, I entertain an high idea of the utility of periodical Publications: insomuch that I could heartily desire, copies of the Museum and Magazines, as well as common Gazettes, might be spread through every city, town & village in America—I consider such easy vehicles of knowledge, more happily calculated than any other, to preserve the liberty, stimulate the industry and meliorate the morals of an enlightened and free People. With sincere wishes for the success of your undertaking in particular, and for the prosperity of the Typegraphical art in general[3] I am—Sir Yr Most Obedt & Most Hble ⟨Serv⟩t

⟨Go: Washington⟩

ALS, PHi: Lea and Febiger Collection; LB, DLC:GW.

1. Letter not found. For reference to an earlier missing letter in which Carey sought help from GW, see GW to Carey, 29 Oct. 1787.

2. In September 1787 when in Philadelphia attending the Constitutional Convention, GW paid Carey for the second volume of the *American Museum*, which Carey published in Philadelphia between 1787 and 1792. GW at that time also paid 10 shillings for a six-month subscription to the *Columbian Magazine*, from July through December 1788 (receipt signed by William Spotswood, n.d., CSmH).

3. GW sent this under the cover of the following letter to Carey, also dated 25 June: "Sir, I enclose herewith a letter, expressing very fully my sentiments of the merit & utility of your Publication—with liberty for you to make whatsoever use you shall think proper of it. If my opinion would be of any avail with the public, I believed this might be a more eligable mode of communication, than by confining it to a simple & formal Certificate and one which is preferd by Sir Yr Most Obedt &ca Go: Washington" (ALS, NN: Miscellaneous and Personal, M. Carey; LB, DLC:GW).

## From James Madison

Dear Sir                                        Rich[mon]d June 25. [1788]
On the question today for *previous* amendments, the votes
stood 80 ays—88 noes—on the final question the ratification
passed 89 ays—79 noes. Subsequent amendments will attend
the act; but are yet to be settled. The temper of the minority will
be better known tomorrow. The proceedings have been without
flaw or pretext for it; and there is no doubt that acquiescence if
not cordiality will be manifested by the unsuccessful party. *Two*
of the leaders however betray the effect of the disappointment,
so far as it is marked in their countenances. In haste Yours
                                                        Js Madison Jr

ALS, in private hands; copy, DLC: Madison Papers.

## From James Madison

Dear Sir                                        Richmd June 27. 1788
The Convention came to a final adjournment to day. The inclosed is a copy of their act of ratification with the yeas & nays.[1]
A variety of amendments have been since recommended; several of them highly objectionable; but which could not be parried.[2] The Minority are to sign an address this evening which is
announced to be of a peace-making complexion. Having not
seen it I can give no opinion of my own. I wish it may not have
a further object.[3] Mr H——y declared previous to the final
question that altho' he should submit as a quiet citizen, he
should seize the first moment that offered for shaking off the
yoke in a *Constitutional way.* I suspect the plan will be to engage
⅔ of the Legislatures in the task of undoing the work; or to get
a Congress appointed in the first instance that will commit sui-
cide on their own Authority. Yrs most affetly & respectfy
                                                        Js Madison Jr

ALS, DLC:GW; copy, DLC: Madison Papers.
    1. The enclosure has not been found. The text of the act of the Virginia
convention ratifying the new Constitution is printed in Kaminski and Saladino, *Documentary History of the Ratification of the Constitution*, 10:1546.
    2. The minutes of 27 June of the Virginia Ratifying Convention includes
the amendments to the Constitution being recommended by the convention

(ibid., 10:1550–59). The proposed amendment to which Madison most strongly objected was one "prohibiting direct taxes where effectual laws shall be passed by the States for that purpose" (Madison to Alexander Hamilton, 27 June, in Rutland and Hobson, *Madison Papers*, 11:181–82).

3. On 27 July some of the Antifederalists met and decided to prepare an address to their constituents, but after George Mason had drafted one they decided not to adopt it. See Madison to Hamilton, 30 June, ibid., 184, and Kaminski and Saladino, op. cit., 1560–61.

## From Richard Peters

Dr Sir                                          Belmont [Pa.] June 27. 1788

On my Arrival from an annual Tour my Affairs compel me to take over the Susquahanna I have the Honour of your Letter of the 8th inst.[1] The Crops in the western Country as fine as ever I saw them but those within 40 or 50 Miles of Philadelphia execrably bad, owing to the Snows not having covered them in the Winter added to a bad Stile of farming which too commonly prevails. My Grain is among the best I have seen on this Side Susquahanna tho' inferior to what I have had & indeed it is but a middling Crop. The Winter has injured it exceedingly. Among the best of it are those Parts which grow on the green manured Ground. I mention this as you say you are about making an Experiment in this Way. I am entirely satisfied of its Efficacy having tried it many Years. Be sure to give your Fallow Time enough for the Buckwheat &c. not only to rot but complete its Fermentation which it will do according to Weather in a Period of from 2 to 3 Weeks.

The Mode of cultivating the Disette,[2] I had the Pleasure to communicate to you, does not direct the cutting off the Leaves & I have never followed it tho' I have seen such a Direction somewhere which may also possibly have fallen into your Hands. The Leaves of the Plant taken from the Seed Bed generally perish on transplanting which at first alarmed me; but a new Vegetation commences from the Heart of the Root & after this I have never found these Plants delicate or troublesome. They are the surest Crop I know. I am yet in Hopes your polled Roots will recover as I know their Hardiness. I am inclined to think the Roots may be raized to a larger Size in the Ground the Seed is dropped in. I believe too this is mentioned by Dr Lettsom as having been proved by the Experience of a Norfolk Farmer in England who raized them by this Mode to 20 or 25 Pounds. But I never can get my Ground in Order Time enough as our Frosts continue so late. I think your Climate would admit of your practising this Method. I know there are great Disadvantages attendant on transplanting these as well as all tap roots. If the Root gets broken in taking up or if it be doubled in planting it never equals the perfect Roots. You must be careful on this Score in transplanting your Carrots which I believe will do very well, as I have often filled up Vacancies in my Drills by Transplantation from those Parts wherein they stood too thick. You can certainly bring your Ground into better Tilth before the Carrots are transplanted in your Corn Ground than you could by drilling them originally. They must not be disturbed when very young & on this Account I am so frequently pestered with Weeds that I am sick of the Crop. I can raize 3 Rows of Scarcity roots at the same Expence of one of Carrots. Next Year I will either transplant or sow them in Drills in Ridges as I do the Disette. You say you lay yourself out to raize Seed for another Year—Permit me to remind you that the Plants of this Year will not afford you Seed till next Year & unless you have Seed from Plants raized last Year you will have none for next Season. I hope to be able to spare you some.

Notwithstanding my bad Luck with Cabbages I continue to cultivate from one to three Acres annually which at least obliges me to keep my Ground clean & of Consequence meliorated—If you follow the Course you have prescribed for yourself you need not be afraid of sowing Wheat in Clover Lays. It will be so clean that neither mixed Grasses or Weeds will injure your Crop. As to Wheat with us it is pretty near at an End. The Hessian Fly is now within 10 Miles of us & next Year we shall have it lay us all Waste. This seems as great a Curse as the British Army was, if not greater. We could combat their other Hessian Auxiliaries; but this is unconquerable.[3]

The Drill you describe must be better than any I can fix to the Brake. The new one does not please me as well as my first Harrow. I must make the Hoes broader to make it run steadier. I sent the two for you a Month ago to Town & Col. Biddle told me he was waiting for a Conveyance to send them to you.[4] For refreshing Land in good Tilth I know of no Instrument better than the trowel tined one & yours is much better than mine as I have remedied some Defects in the one I had made from speculation. I will have the Potatoe Cleaner made for you by the Time you will have Occasion to use it.[5]

Altho' nine States have agreed to our new & most excellent Government I wait with Anxiety to hear of Virginia's agreeing to adopt it. The Execution of it will be unpleasant if so great a State should withdraw itself from the Confederacy. It will be in vain for us to cultivate our Fields unless better Fences are put round them than our former System of Government afforded. I am with the most sincere & respectful Esteem your obedt Servt

Richard Peters

I have on a small Scale tried your method of planting Corn & potatoes. The Crop is surprizingly promising.

ALS, DLC:GW.

1. Letter not found.

2. Peters wrote GW at length about the root of scarcity, or scarcity plant, in his letter of 27 April. "Disette" is French for "scarcity."

3. The Hessian fly (*Phytophaga destructor*) had been moving southward in the 1780s, but not until late in 1794 is there any reference to its attacking the wheat at Mount Vernon. See also GW to George Morgan, 25 Aug. 1788.

4. For references to the harrow that Peters had made for GW, see Clement Biddle to GW, 21 April, 7 July, 13 Aug., Peters to GW, 27 April, and GW to Peters, 7 September. GW's cash accounts show that on 10 July he paid 10 shillings for "Freight of two Harrows from Philadelphia" (Ledger B, 270).

5. Peters wrote about his potato cleaner on 27 April.

## To David Stuart

Dear Sir,                                    Mount Vernon 27th June 1788.

Your letter of the 23d,[1] which came duly to hand; still leaves us in a state of suspence with respect to the final decision on the pendent question—and nothing new having happened in this quarter since my last, the principal design of this letter is to afford a cover for Mrs Stuarts; who, no doubt, will have informed you of her own health and that of the little ones, &ca—I shall only add therefore that with sincere regard I am—Dr Sir Yr Most Obedt & Affe. Servt

Go: Washington

ALS, PWacD.
    1. Letter not found.

## To Charles Carter

Dear Sir,                                    Mount Vernon June 28th 1788
    When Mrs Washington was at the Church in Fredericksburg
she perceived the Tomb of her Father the late John Dandridge
Esqr. to be much out of sorts and being desirous to have it done
up again, will you permit me to request the favour of you to
engage a workman to do this, the cost of which I will remit as
soon as you shall signify to me that the work is accomplished,
and inform me of its amount. I would thank you, My dear Sir—
for the ascertainment of this before hand. I have (not inclining
to dispute Accounts) felt, in too many instances, the expansion
of Tradesmens consciences when no previous agreement has
been made ever to put it in their power to charge what they
please in future.[1] My best wishes, in which Mrs Washington Joins
me, is tendered to Mrs Carter—with much truth I am Dear Sir,
Yr most Ob. & Affe. Hbl. Set

                                                    Go. Washington

LB, DLC:GW.
    1. During their recent trip to Fredericksburg, GW and Mrs. Washington on
Wednesday, 11 June, dined with Charles Carter of Ludlow and his wife, Elizabeth Chiswell Carter, among others. Carter's response has not been found, but
GW wrote him again on 1 Aug: "Dear Sir, This letter, at the same time that it
acknowledges the receipt of your favor of the 13th ult., and thanks you for the
trouble you have taken with respect to the Tomb of Mr Dandridge, serves to
cover 30 p. which you agreed to pay for the repairs of it. Mrs Washington joins
me in every good wish for yourself and Mrs Carter—and with sentiments of
very great esteem & regard—I am—Dear Sir Your most Obednt Affect. Hble
serv. G. Washington" (typescript, ViMtV). See also Ledger B, 270. John Dandridge's tomb is in St. George's Parish graveyard in Fredericksburg.

## To Charles Cotesworth Pinckney

Dear Sir,                                    Mount Vernon June 28th 1788
    I had the pleasure to receive, a day or two ago, your obliging
letter of the 24th of last month, in which you advise me of the
ratification of the fœderal Constitution by South Carolina. By

a more rapid water conveyance, that good news had some few days before arrived at Baltimore, so as to have been very opportunely communicated to the Convention of this State, in session at Richmond. It is with great satisfaction, I have it now in my power to inform you that, on the 25th instant, the Delegates of Virginia adopted the Constitution, in toto, by a division of 89 in favour of it to 79 against it: and that, notwithstanding the majority is so small, yet, in consequence of some conciliatory conduct and recommendatory amendments, a happy acquiescence it is said is likely to terminate the business here—in as favorable a manner as could possibly have been expected.

No sooner had the Citizens of Alexandria (who are fœderal to a man) received the intelligence by the Mail last night, than they determined to devote this day to festivity. But their exhiliration was greatly encreased and a much keener zest given to their enjoyment; by the arrival of an Express (two hours before day) with the News that the Convention of New Hampshire had, on the 21st instant, acceded to the new Confœderacy by a majority of 11 voices, that is to say, 57 to 46.

Thus the Citizens of Alexandria, When convened, constituted the first public company in America, which had the pleasure of pouring libation to the prosperity of the ten States that had actually adopted the general government. The day itself is memorable for more reasons than one. It was recollected that this day is the Anneversary of the battles of Sullivan's Island and monmouth—I have Just returned from assisting at the entertainment; and mention these details, unimportant as they are in themselves, the rather because I think we may rationally indulge the pleasing hope that the Union will now be established upon a durable basis, and that Providence seems still disposed to favour the members of it, with unequalled opportunities for political happiness.[1]

From the local situation as well as the other circumstances of North Carolina, I should be truly astonished if that State should withdraw itself from the Union—On the contrary, I flatter myself with *a confident expectation* that more salutary counsels will certainly prevail. At present there is more doubt how the question will be immediately disposed of in New York. For it seems to be understood that there is a majority in the Convention opposed to the adoption of the New fœderal System. Yet it is hardly to be supposed, (or rather in my Judgment it is irrational to suppose) they will reject a government, which, from an unorganised embrio ready to be stiffled with a breath, has now in the maturity of Its birth assumed a confirmed bodily existence. Or, to drop the metaphor, the point in debate has, at least, shifted its ground from policy to expediency. The decision of ten States cannot be without its operation. Perhaps the wisest way, in this crisis, will be, not to attempt to accept or reject—but to adjourn, untill the people in some parts of the State can consider the magnitude of the question and of the consequences involved in it, more coolly and deliberately. After New York shall have acted, then only one little State will remain—suffice it to say, *it is universally believed, that the scales are ready to drop from the eyes and the infatuation to be removed from the heart of Rhode Island.* May this be the case, before that inconsiderate People shall have filled up the measure of inequity before it shall be too late! Mrs Washington and all with us desire their best Compliments may be presented to Mrs Pinckney and yourself: wishing that mine may also be made acceptable to you both, I am &c.

Go. Washington

LB, DLC:GW.

1. The celebration at Alexandria was described in the newspaper: "On Wednesday the 25th ult. the Convention of this State ratified the Constitution proposed to the United States of America by the late General Convention. The news of this important event arrived here on Friday evening—As a testimony of the joy which the inhabitants felt, the town was immediately illuminated in an elegant manner; and the agreeable intelligence was communicated to our neighbours, up and down the river, by a well-timed discharge of cannon.—On Saturday many of the gentlemen of the town and some from the country, who had heard the *glad tidings*, dined together at Mr. Wise's tavern on a sumptuous dinner prepared for the occasion, to which General Washington, Col. Humphreys, and many genteel strangers were invited.—The General was met some miles out of town by a party of gentlemen on horseback, and escorted to the tavern, having been saluted on his way by the light infantry company in a respectful manner.—His arrival was announced by a discharge of ten cannon under the direction of Captain Greenway. After dinner the following toasts, each followed by a discharge of cannon, were drank, expressive of the high satisfaction of the assembly, the happiness of which was rendered complete by that admirable harmony of sentiment which universally prevailed" (Kaminski and Saladino, *Documentary History of the Ratification of the Constitution*, 10:1716, transcribed from Baltimore *Maryland Gazette*, 8 July, a reprint of *Virginia Journal*, 3 July [see pp. 1717–18]).

# To William West

Revd Sir,                         Mount Vernon June 28th 1788
I was favoured with your letter of the 17th Ult.[1] by your Son, in consequence of which I send the enclosed for Mr Welch, the Surviving Partner of the House of Cary and Co. who used to transact, principally, my business in London, and who is the only Mercantile character in England with whom I have had any intercourse for the last 15 years.[2] Formerly I corrisponded with Messrs Hanbury & Co. who also sold Tobaco for me—but Mr Hanbury I think, is dead.[3] and I have not been at all Sollicitous to renew the old or to form new Connexions in that Kingdom. When you spoke to me formerly, on this subject, I had besides Mr Welch, My old Neighbour and friend Colo. Fairfax in vew to have written to, but he is no more.[4]
If the introductory letter to Mr Welch can be, in the smallest degree servicable to the young Gentleman, I shall feel much pleasure from having afforded it, because I think your determination to give him an opportunity of cultivating and improving his genius for painting is wise and because he will carry with him my best wishes for the accomplishment thereof as well as for a safe and pleasant voyage and a happy return to you. With very great esteem and regard I am &c.

                                        Go. Washington

LB, DLC:GW.
    The Rev. William West (c.1739–1791), brother of the late Capt. John West, Jr., of Fairfax County, was at this time rector of St. Paul's Parish in Baltimore.
    1. Letter not found.
    2. GW's letter of 28 June from Mount Vernon to Wakelin Welch on behalf of young George William West (1770–1795) reads: "Sir, This letter is equally introductory, and recommendatory of Mr West, Son to the Revd Mr West of Maryland; a very worthy Episcopal Clergaman of my Acquaintance—The young Gentleman having, in early life, displayed a prompt and masterly genius for Painting, is sent to England by his father to improve himself in this Art—and having at the same time discovered a goodness of disposition and an amiableness of manners worthy of notice. I have taken the liberty of bearing this testimoney of him and shall feel myself obliged by any civilities you may shew him, whilst he resides in London. with sentiments of esteem and regard I am Sir—Yr Most Obedt and Most Hbe Sert Go. Washington" (LB, DLC:GW). Young West studied under Benjamin West in London and returned to Baltimore before his death in 1795.
    3. For GW's dealings with the Hanburys, see particularly GW to Capel &

Osgood Hanbury, 12 June 1759, and GW to Hanburys & Lloyd, 4 Aug. 1774, and notes.

4. George William Fairfax died in April 1787.

## To Tobias Lear

Dear Sir,                              Mount Vernon June 29th 1788.
Your letter of the 2d instant came duly to hand, and obliged me by its communications.

On friday last, (by the Stage), advice of the decision of the *long* and *warmly* (with temper) contested question, in the Convention of this State, was received. 89 ayes—79 Noes, without previous amendments; and in the course of that night, Colo. Henley, Express from New York on his way to Richmond, arrived in Alexandria with the news of the ratification by the State of New Hampshire.[1] This flood of good news, almost at the same moment, gave, as you will readily conceive, abundant cause for rejoicing in a place, the Inhabitants of which are *all* fœderal. The Cannon roared, and the Town was illuminated Yesterday, as *magnificent* a dinner as Mr Wise could provide (to which this family were invited and went), was displayed before the principal *Male* Inhabitants of the Town; whose Ears were saluted at every quaff with the melody of fœderal Guns. And on Monday, the business it seems is to recommense and finish, with fiddling & Dancing, for the amusement, & benefit of the Ladies.[2]

The final question was taken on the 25th; and some recommendatory, or declaratory rights, it was supposed (by my correspondents in Richmond), would follow the ratification of the Constitution the next, or following day. As these two adoptions make ten affirmatives without a negative, and little or no question is made of North Carolinas treading in the steps of Virginia, it is hardly to be conceived that New York will reject it. Rhode Island, hitherto, has so far baffled all calculation, that he must be a hardy man, indeed, who will undertake to declare what *will be* the choice of the majority of *that* State, lest he should be suspected of having participated of *their phrensy*.

The Accts from Richmond are, that the Minority will acquiesce with a good grace—Mr Henry it seems having declared that, though he cannot be *reconciled* to the Government in its *present* form, and will give it every *constitutional* opposition in his power; yet, that he will submit to it peaceably; as every good citizen he thinks ought; and by precept and example will endeavour, within the sphere of his action, to inculcate the like principles into others.

You have the best wishes of every one in this family, but of none in a higher degree than those of, Your Affecte friend and Obedient Servt

Go: Washington.

Pray offer my Complimts to Mr Langdon.

ALS, owned (1989) by Mrs. Helen Marie Taylor, Orange, Virginia.

1. The express rider Col. David Henley left New York City in early afternoon on 25 June to carry the news of New Hampshire's ratification of the Constitution to James Madison in Richmond. He arrived in Alexandria before dawn on 28 June, when he forwarded the letters for Madison to Richmond. See Kaminski and Saladino, *Documentary History of the Ratification of the Constitution*, 10:1672–74.

2. See GW to Charles Cotesworth Pinckney, 28 June, and note 1 of that document. John Wise's tavern was at this time on the northeast corner of Fairfax and Cameron streets. In 1792 Wise erected a new building at Royal and Cameron streets which John Gadsby later rented.

## To Benjamin Lincoln

My dear Sir,                    Mount Vernon June 29th 1788.

I beg you will accept my thanks for the communications handed to me in your letter of the 3d instant. And my congratulations on the encreasing good dispositions of the Citizens of your State—of which the late Elections are strongly indicative.

No one can rejoice more than I do at every step taken by the People of this great Country to preserve the Union—establish good order & government—and to render the Nation happy at home & respected abroad. No Country upon Earth ever had it more in its power to attain these blessings than United America. Wonderously strange then, & much to be regretted indeed would it be, were we to neglect the means, and to stray from the road to which the finger of Providence has so manifestly pointed. I cannot believe it will ever come to pass! The great Author of all good has not conducted us so far on the Road to happiness and glory to withdraw from us, in the hour of need, his beneficent support. By folly & misconduct (proceeding from a variety of causes) we may now & then get bewildered; but I hope, and trust, that their is good sense and virtue enough left to bring us back into the right way before we shall be entirely lost.

Before this letter can have reached you, you will have heard of the Ratification of the proposed Constitution by this State, without previous amendments. The final question was taken the 25th—Ayes 89—Noes 79; but something recommendatory, or declaratory of the rights of the People, it is said, will follow; so as not to affect the preceeding decision. This account, and the news of the adoption by New-Hampshire, arrived in Alexandria nearly about the sametime on Friday evening; and, as you may easily conceive, gave cause for great rejoicing among the Inhabitants, who have not, I believe, an antifederalist among them.

Our Accts from Richmond are, that the debates (through all the different stages of the business, though long and animated) were conducted with great dignity & temper—that the final decision exhibited an awful and solemn scene—and that, there is reason to expect a perfect acquiescence thereto by the minority. not only from the good sense & conduct of that body during the Session, but from the declaration of Mr Henry the great leader of the opposition to the effect, that though he cannot be reconciled to the Constitution in its present form, and shall give it every *constitutional* opposition in his power, yet that he will submit to it peaceably, as he thinks every good Citizen ought to do when it is in exercise; and that he will, both by precept & example, endeavor to inculcate this doctrine.

But little doubt is *now* entertained, *here*, of the ratification of the proposed Constitution by the State of North Carolina—and however great the opposition to it may be in that of New York, the leaders thereof will, I should conceive, consider the consequences of rejection well, before it is given. With respect to Rhode Island, the power that governs there, has so far baffled all calculation on this subject that no man will hazard an opinion on their proceedings lest he should be suspected of participating in its phrensy. You have every good wish of this family—and the sincere regard of your Affecte friend & Servt

Go: Washington

ALS, MH; LB, DLC:GW.

## From Vioménil

Sir,                                   Nantz [France] 30h June 1788.
  The Count de Brienne has been so good as to send me the
Diploma of the Society of the Cincinnati which your Excely had
the goodness to address to him. This title will be very dear to
me & I shall always regard it as a distinguished honor—I beg
your Excellency to be convinced of this; and to receive my best
thanks for this mark of your kindness.[1] I likewise desire permission, upon this occasion, to felicitate you upon the new Glory
which you have acquired in contributing by precept & example
to strengthen the bonds which unite the individual Compatriots—and at the same time give dignity & respectability to the
United States of No. America. I have the honor to be, with as
much admiration as attachment & respect Yr Excellency's Most
Hble & most Obedt Servt
                                                    Vioménil

Translation, in the hand of Tobias Lear, DLC:GW; ALS, in French, NN: Em-
met Collection. The ALS is in CD-ROM:GW.
  1. Antoine-Charles du Houx, baron de Vioménil (1728–1792), was Rochambeau's second-in-command and succeeded him when Rochambeau returned to France after the victory at Yorktown. Vioménil was one of the original members of the French Society of the Cincinnati. See Rochambeau to GW,
19 Jan. 1784, n.5. Athanase-Louis-Marie de Loménie, comte de Brienne
(1730–1794), at this time was Louis XVI's minister of war; no letter from GW
to Brienne has been found.


## From John Jay

Dear Sir                                          [June, 1788]
  Your obliging Letter of the 8 Inst. found me at this Place—I
thank you for the interesting Circumstances mentioned in it.
The Complection of our Convention is such as was expected.
They have hitherto proceeded with Temper & moderation, but
there is no Reason to think that either Party has made much
Impression on the other. The Leaders in opposition seem to
have more extensive views than their Adherents, and untill the
latter percieve that circumstance, they will probably continue
combined. The greater Number are I believe averse to a vote
of Rejection—some would be content with recommendatory

amendments—others wish for explanatory ones to settle Con-
structions which they think doubtful—others would not be satisfied with less than absolute and previous amendments; and I am
mistaken if there be not a few who prefer a Separation from the
union to any national Government whatever. They suggest
Hints of the Importance of this State, of its capacity to command
Terms, of the policy of its taking its own Time, and fixing its
own Price & they intimate that an adjournment may be expedient, and that it might be best to see the operation of the new
Governmt before they recieve it—the people however are gradually coming right notwithstanding the singular Pains taken
to prevent it. The accession of new Hampshire does good—
and that of Virginia would do more. With the greatest Respect &
Esteem I am Dear Sir your affte & obt Servt

John Jay

ALS, DLC:GW; ADf, NNC. The contents of the letter indicate it was written
after the news of New Hampshire's ratification of the Constitution reached
New York on 24 June and before the news of Virginia's ratification came on
2 July.

## From Arthur Young

Sir                          Bradfield Hall [England] July 1. 1788
   I recd the honour of Your Excellency's Letter of Nov. 1 some
weeks past but I have been so engaged in opposing the progress
of our Wool Bill through both Houses of Parliament, that it was
utterly impossible for me to make the necessary enquiries for
answering it.[1]
   I am very glad to hear the things I sent arrived tolerably safe
but I am not surprized at the sainfoine coming up but thinly;
for it is a very delicate seed with us, & will bear no careless treatment, nor age, & every thing runs no small hazard on ship
board. I beg that you will not let any idea in your labourers of
the weight of those ploughs frighten them; it is mere ignorance;
in all probability the addition of an hundred wt in the body of
one of their own light ploughs would make it go lighter to the
horses. There are at least 200 of those ploughs constantly working here, & never drawn with more than two moderate horses.
   I have taken every means of ascertaining the merit of Winlaws

threshing machine, but the accounts I have recd are too vague to be satisfactory; I have too many doubts about it to put you to the expence of purchase and freight; & the more especially as there is another invented in Scotland more simple, less liable to be out of order, & more effective; the price is £40 timber included; of this the accounts I have received are much more clear, & decisive so that I have little doubt of its merit, & would if my farm was large enough have one myself wch I would not of Winlaw's, unless better convinced of its merit. Should you be inclined to have this new one, & you give me an order I will take care and procure it for you.

I know not how sufficiently to express my gratitude for the condescending manner in wch you have so satisfactorily replied to the enquiries I presumed to trouble you with. The course you mention of 1. maiz 2 Wheat. 3 Weeds for 18 Mo.—wth a very little alteration might be converted into a very good one. Wheat in the South of France succeeds extremely well after maiz kept clean the only alteration wanted is to sow grass seeds with the wheat, leave them 1, 2, or 3 yrs according to the sorts, & then the land would be prepared very richly for maiz again, or any thing else: I have seen no country in wch the improvement of it might not be made to flow from an alteration only in the rotation of cropping.

The prices of all your products are flattering prospects your country may speedily improve with them; but there is no proportion between 12/ the common price of a sheep & £3 for a cow; I suppose sheep are kept with more difficulty not pasturing equally well in woods, yet great flocks in France are fed on the leaves of trees. In case I have the honour of a further communication fro. you, I should take it as a particular favour if you would send me a small lock of the Wool which sells in common at 1s/ ℔ lb. We are making in England some very important and successful experiments on propagating the Spanish breed of sheep that yield the finest wool. The King, Lord Sheffield, Sir Joseph Banks & myself have of them, & there is every reason to beleive the race will be secured; the wool does not degenerate.[2]

I trouble you with three more Volumes of the Annals[3] and beg leave to repeat that your Excellency's Commands will at all times be a pleasure to Sir Your much obliged & faithful Servt

Arth: Young

Might I take the liberty to insert some extracts fro. yr correspondence with yr name in the Annals? I would not presume to think
of any such thing without yr express permission.[4]

ALS, DLC:GW.

1. Early in 1788 the wool growers of Suffolk asked Young to support their
petition to Parliament against the Wool Bill. Young testified before both houses
of Parliament and printed two pamphlets opposing the bill, called *The Question
of Wool Truly Stated*. After the passage of the bill, its supporters in Norwich
burned Young in effigy. Young included reports of his testimony in Parliament
in his *Annals of Agriculture*, 10:1–18, 139–86.

2. John Baker Holroyd (1735–1821) was raised to the Irish peerage in 1781
as Baron Sheffield of Dunamore. He was a leading authority on British commerce and agriculture and wrote extensively, especially on the wool trade. His
estate, Sheffield Place in Surry, was regarded as a model in farming. Holroyd
was later made first earl of Sheffield. Sir Joseph Banks (1743–1820) was a
great patron of science and was made president of the Royal Society in 1778.
Banks, who accompanied Captain Cook on one of his voyages to the South
Seas, was created a baronet in 1781. His extensive library went to the British
Museum after his death.

3. Young sent GW the first four volumes of his *Annals of Agriculture, and
Other Useful Arts* in January 1786. See Young to GW, 7 Jan. 1786, n.2.

4. See GW's response to this request in the last paragraph of his letter to
Young, 4 Dec. 1788.

# From Robert Morris

Sir                                    Richmond July 3d 1788
    Capt. Stephen Gregory the bearer of these lines being called
by business to Dumfries, cannot think of returning from thence
without gratifying his earnest desire of paying his respects to
Genl Washington, a gratification which he is very ambitious to
obtain on proper terms, but which his modesty forbad him
to seek without an introduction.[1] Excuse me therefore my Good
Sir for presenting to you, a Gentleman that has Served with
Reputation as a Lieutenant in our late Infant Navy under Capt.
Barry & others and who since the Peace has Commanded a Ship
of mine & so Conducted himself as to induce me to give favourable testimony to his merit. With great respect I have the honor
to be Dear Sir Your most obliged & obedient humble servt
                                 Robt Morris

ALS, DLC:GW.

1. When Gregory visited Mount Vernon on 9 July, GW identified him as "a french Gentlemn. who served in the American Navy last War" (*Diaries*, 5:359). Gregory dined at Mount Vernon again on 31 Aug. and on 2 Sept. (ibid., 386, 387). Gregory was master of the *Comte d'Artois*, trading between Bordeaux and Virginia. Thomas Jefferson, who sometimes used Gregory's vessel to ship wine to friends, called Gregory "a good humoured agreeable man" (Boyd, *Jefferson Papers*, 11:378–79). Gregory wrote GW on 6 July 1789, sending him a miniature ship as a gift, and again on 12 Aug. requesting an appointment in the new government.

## From John Jay

Poughkeepsie [N.Y.] 4[–8] July 1788

I congratulate you my dear Sir! on the adoption of the constitution by virginia. That Event has disappointed the Expectations of opposition here, which nevertheless continues pertinacious. The unanimity of the southern District, and their apparent Determination to continue under the wings of the union, operates powerfully on the minds of the opposite Party. The constitution constantly gains advocates among the People, and its Enemies in the Convention seem to be much embarrassed.

8 July 1788

We have gone thro' the Constitution in a Committee of the whole—we finished yesterday Morning—The amendments proposed are numerous—how we are to consider them, is yet a Question, wh. a Day or two more must answer. a Bill of Rights has been offered with a view as they say of having it incorporated in the *Ratification*—The Ground of *Rejection* therefore seems to be entirely deserted—we understand that a committee will this Day be appointed to arrange the amendments—we learn from albany that an affray happened there on the 4 Inst: between the two parties, in which near thirty were wounded, some few very dangerously.[1]

From what I have just heard the Party begins to divide in their opinions—some insist on *previous* conditional amendments— a greater number will be satisfied with *subsequent* conditional amendments, or in other words they are for ratifying the Constitution on Condition that certain amendments take place within a given Time—these circumstances afford Room for Hope. with

the greatest Respect & Esteem I am Dr Sir your affte & hble
Servt

John Jay

ALS, DLC:GW.
    1. Twelve supporters of the Constitution and six opponents were hurt in a
riot in Albany on 4 July.

*Letter not found*: from Mathew Carey, 5 July 1788. On 21 July GW wrote
Carey: "I have been favoured with your letter of the 5th instt."

## From Nathaniel Gorham

Sir                                    Boston July 5th 1788
    It is with the most sincere pleasure that I congratulate you on
the adoption of the Constitution by Virginia—This great event
affords the most sincere and heart-felt pleasure to all ranks of
People here—The importance of that State is fully understood
and our anxiety was in proportion—the business I now look
upon to be compleat & that every thing will go on harmoniously & with good will—The temper of the People in this State
is truly Federal—the late elections have fully evinced this—The
Legislature and Executive being fill'd with federalists—I have a
very general knowledge of characters throughout this State and
can confidently assert that there has never been since the revolution so peaceable and quiet a temper pervading the State as at
the present moment—Industry & frugallity is allso very prevalent & increasing—I please myself Sir with the idea of soon seing
you at the head of the American Government[1]—and in the
mean time remain very respectfully your most Obedient &
Hume Servt

Nathaniel Gorham

ALS, DLC:GW.
    1. GW responded from Mount Vernon on 21 July: "Sir, I received your
congratulatory letter of the 5th instt by the last Mail. It gives me reciprocal
satisfaction to find that the adoption of the Constitution by Virginia has diffused so general a joy through the other States. The good disposition manifested by the Citizens of your Commonwealth, excites also a flattering & consolatory reflection in all who wish well to the fœderal interest & the glory of
the American Nation. Much happiness may rationally be anticipated from the

encreasing prevalence of industry & frugality, invigorated and encouraged by the operation of a free, yet efficient general government.

"Although I am passing rapidly into the *vale of Years*, where the genial warmth of youth that fires its votary with a generous enthusiasm becomes extinct, & where the cheerfulness of the prospect often infects the animal spirits with a similar contageon; yet I trust there are few who rejoice more fervently in the expectation that the beams of prosperity will break in upon a Country, which has ever engaged my most disinterested wishes & fondest hopes. And although I shall not live to see but a small portion of the happy effects, which I am confident this system will produce for my Country; yet the precious idea of its prosperity will not only be a consolation amidst the encreasing infirmities of Nature, and the growing love of retirement, but it will tend to sooth the mind in the inevitable hour of seperation from terrestrial objects. With earnest prayers that you and all the worthy patriots of America may long enjoy uninterrupted felicity under the New Government—I have the honor to subscribe myself with due regard & esteem Sir, Yr Most Obedt and Most Hble Servt Go: Washington" (ALS, CLjJC; LB, DLC:GW).

## From Clement Biddle

July 7. 1788.

By Capt. Ellwood I shipped the Hoe plows or Harrows from Mr Peters for which the Bill of Loading is enclosed the Certificate to save Duties was given to Capt. Ellwood—I have waited some Days in hopes of geting the Bill from Mr Peters which I several times requested him to send & that it should be immediately paid but I imagine he has not been lately in Town except when much engaged.[1]

The Herrings appear to be very good but several Barrels which were opened appeared to want about ⅙ of being full & they must when sold be unpacked to answer our inspection Law but near or upwards of 1000 Barrels having Come to Market from the head of Elk they have sold as low as 15/ & I have put yours into a Store in hopes of a Better price a few weeks hence.[2] I am &c.

Clement Biddle

ADfS, ViMtV: Clement Biddle Letter Book.

1. For the correspondence regarding the harrows that Thomas Peters arranged to have made for GW, see Peters to GW, 27 June, n.4.

2. The ten barrels of shad and forty barrels of herring that GW sent Biddle in late May remained unsold at summer's end. See GW to Biddle, 29 May, 16 Sept., Biddle to GW, 7, 30 July, 13, 24 August.

# To Thomas Newton, Jr.

Sir,                                   Mount Vernon July 7th 1788
I am in want of a quantity of *good* eighteen Inch shingles and
am informed that they will come better & *cheaper* from Norfolk
than from the Eastern shore. Be so good, therefore, as to advise
me by the first Post after you shall have received this letter if
I can be supplied with 100,000 from the former. In what time
—and at what price; delivered at *my landing* distinguishing between what is called bald, and green Cyprus. As my work will
soon call for these Shingles I repeat my wish for early advice
on this subject—That there may be a clear understanding—the
length, breadth, and thickness under which the Shingles shall
not be should be specified—among them I shall want about
3000 of Twenty one Inches long.[1] I am Sir, Yr Most Obedt
Hble Sert

                                                  Go. Washington

P.S. It runs through my mind, that I have heard of Shingles
being had from No. Carolina on good terms.

LB, DLC:GW.
    1. Thomas Newton, Jr., the merchant in Norfolk with whom GW had fre-
quent dealings, wrote GW on 14 and 19 July, sending him samples of shingles.
Neither of Newton's letters has been found, but GW wrote Newton on 1 Aug.
explaining that he needed the shingles for the roof of the barn that he was
building and asking him to send 25,000 36-inch shingles or 100,000 18-inch
shingles. On 10 Oct. GW acknowledged the receipt of Newton's letters of 8
Aug. and 23 Sept., which also have not been found, and the arrival of nearly
36,000 shingles. On 17 Dec. he wrote Newton indicating that he had received
from him more than 64,000 additional shingles. See also GW to John Brent,
17 Dec. 1788.

# From John Sullivan

Sir,                                 Durham [N.H.] July 7th 1788
I am directed by the society of the Cincinnati in New Hampshire to convey their congratulations to your Excellency, and to
the society in general, on the ratification of the new Constitution, by a sufficient number of States, not only to establish
it as a national form of Government, but thereby to fix upon
a permanent basis, those liberties, for which, under the direc-

tion and order of your Excellency, they have so cheerfully contended.

They now view with inexpressible pleasure the arrival of that happy period, when by the establishment of a truly republican, energetic and efficient National Government, they and their posterity may enjoy those blessings, which as freemen, they esteem an ample reward for all the toils and dangers, which they experienced in the course of a long and perilous war.[1] I have the honor to be with the most exalted sentiments of esteem and respect, your Excellency's most obedient Servant

Jno. Sullivan<br>By order of the society

ALS, MHi: James Sullivan Papers. "Jere[miah] Fogg Sec'y" is written at the bottom of the document.

1. GW replied on 1 Sept.: "Sir, It is with great personal Satisfaction, I receive the Congratulations of the Society of the Cincinnati in New Hampshire, on the present State of our public Affairs.

"I shall take care to convey the Instrument expressive of their sentiments to the Secretary of the General Meeting, that, being deposited in the Archives, the purport may be made known accordingly.

"The prevalence of so good dispositions from one extremity of the Continent to the other (with few exceptions) seems indeed to afford a subject of mutual felicitations, to all who delight in their Country's prosperity. But the idea, that my former gallant associates in the field are now about to receive, in a good National government, some compensation for the toils and dangers which they have experienced in the course of a long & perilous war, is particularly consolatory to me.

"I entreat that the members of your State Society will believe that I interest myself much in their prosperity; and that you will accept the professions of sincere regard & esteem, with which I have the honor to be Sir Yr Most Obedt & Most Humble Servt Go: Washington" (ALS, MBSC; LB, DLC:GW). GW forwarded Sullivan's letter of 7 July to Henry Knox on 10 September. See GW's letter to Knox, 10 Sept., printed in note 1, de Grasse to GW, 18 August.

## From Richard Henry Lee

Dear Sir,                                    Chantilly July the 8th 1788

I have the honor to enclose for your consideration and signature papers relative to our execution of the trust reposed on us for selling Mr Booths land and purchasing the lands in lieu. The partys are very desirous to have this business finished, and I have no doubt but that the saving clause, and the provision at the end of the deed, renders this conveyance perfectly safe for us. You will please to observe that young Mr Booths letter requests us to convey to R. Lee; but circumstances in that family, unknown to him, renders this improper. It is this however that causes Mr Charles Lee in his letter enclosed to say "I expect Mr W.A. Booth will give his direction for conveying to Miss E.A. Lee instead of R. Lee &c. Till such direction be given by Mr W.A. Booth I presume the Trustees will forbear to execute the deed[.]" This circumstance, together with Mr Bealls letter herein also enclosed, render two things necessary to be observed, before the deed shall be parted with by you—the one is, that Mr W.A. Booth signify his assent to the alteration of the conveyance and also that Mr Brooke Beall certify his receipt of the ballance due on this purchase, as requested in his brother Mr S. Bealls letter.[1]

I wish that the late excessive rains may not have injured your Crops nearly as much this year, as did the drought of last summer.

This family join me in presenting respectful compliments to your Lady. I have the honor to be, with every sentiment of esteem and regard, dear Sir your affectionate and obedient servant

Richard Henry Lee

ALS, DLC:GW.

1. For a description of the transactions with regard to the Booth property for which both GW and Lee were trustees, see Lee to GW, 16 April 1787, n.1. The quoted letter from Charles Lee is to Richard Henry Lee, 6 April 1788 (DLC:GW). Booth's letter to Richard Henry Lee has not been found.

*Letter not found*: from Charles Carter, 13 July 1788. GW wrote Carter on 1 Aug. acknowledging "the receipt of your favr of the 13th ult."

## From Ebenezer Hazard

Sir,                                    New York July 14th 1788

Some short Time since Col. Morgan, of Princeton, left with me a Parcel for your Excellency, with a Request that I would forward it at any Time when we happened to have a small Mail; I have now the Honor to transmit it,[1] with Assurances of the warmest Attachment of Your Excellency's most obedient humble Servant

Ebenr Hazard

ALS, DLC:GW.

1. GW wrote Hazard from Mount Vernon on 22 July: "Sir, The letters with which you favored me—dated the 24th of June and 14th instant—together with the packet and parcel which respectively accompanied them, came safe in due course of Post. For your attention & trouble in forwarding of them I beg you will accept the thanks of Sir Your most Obedt Hble Ser⟨vt⟩ Go: Washington" (ALS, PHi: Hazard Family Papers). The parcel from George Morgan was a packet of wheat for GW to plant. See Morgan to GW, 31 July, and GW to Morgan, 25 August.

## From Jedidiah Morse

Sir                                      New York July 14th 1788

Colo. Humphreys intimated to me, when he was in Connecticut, that I might use the freedom to forward Letters to him, under cover to your Excellency. This, Sir, is my apology, for giving you the trouble of delivering the enclosed to the Colo. whh I beg you to excuse. I am with the highest respect & esteem Your Excellency's most Obdt & most humble Servt

Jedidiah Morse

ALS, DLC:GW.

*Letter not found*: from Thomas Newton, Jr., 14 July 1788. On 1 Aug. GW wrote Newton: "Your letters of the 14th & 19 Ulto came duly to hand."

## From Peterson & Taylor

Sir                                 Alexandria July the 14th 1788

We Sent your Account by Major Washington Some time past, agreable to the Measurement you furnished, and have never herd from you Since, wheather it was in any wise not to your Satisfaction—and necessaty compells us to call on you for the ballance—which is agreable to contract,[1] we are exceedingly distressed for Money, which renderes it intirely out of our power

to avoid calling on you at this Time—We are Sir Your Most Obediant humb. Sevts

Peterson & Taylor

LS, DLC:GW.

1. For GW's purchase of scantling and planks from the Alexandria firm of Peterson & Taylor for his new barn, see GW to Peterson & Taylor, 5 Jan., and notes. See also Peterson & Taylor to GW, 18 April, and George Augustine Washington's letter printed in note 2 of that document. GW wrote from Mount Vernon on 19 July: "Gentn Your letter of the 14th came duly to hand as did the other to which there is an allusion. The first time my Nephew comes to Town I will send you what money I have towards discharging your bill for the Scantling furnished me—I wish it may be recollected, however that you have not been kept longer from the former than I have been from the latter— and that you may be moreover convinced, and sure I am, That my disadvantages arising from the one is at least equal to what yours can be from the other, and with more injurious consequences. Fish two (in Barrls) which was the fund I allotted for payment. and which if my memory has not failed me it was so intimated at the time, has not yet brought me in Cash but notwithstanding what I have you shall receive as above. I am Gentn Yr Most Obedt Servant Go. Washington" (LB, DLC:GW). GW notes in his cash accounts on 13 Sept.: "By Messrs Peterson & Taylor pd to Hans Orman by th[e]ir Order the Balance due to them amounting to [£]38.11.11½" (Ledger B, 270).

## From Noah Webster

Sir.                                        New York July 14th 1788

Having engaged to write, for Mr Morse's Geography, a sketch of the History of the late war, I take the liberty of making an enquiry respecting a fact which I am told is commonly misrepresented, & which perhaps no person but the commander in chief of the late armies in America can set right. An opinion, Sir, is very general, that the junction of the French fleet & the American armies at York Town was the result of a preconcerted plan between Yourself & the Count de Grasse; & that the preparations made at the time for attacking New York were merely a feint. But the late Quater Master General has assured me that a Combined attack was intended to be made upon New York, & that the arrival of the French fleet in the Bay of Chesapeake was unexpected, & changed the plan of operations. A true state of the facts is all I have to request of your Excellency—& I fear that this request may be improper & indelicate. But in writing history, it is of infinite consequence to know the *springs* of action as well as the *events*; and a wish to discover & communicate truth, is my sole motive for writing.[1]

Be pleased, Sir, to accept this as an apology for giving trouble to a Gentleman, who must be oppressed by a multitude of attentions of more Consequence & be assured that with perfect respect for yourself & family, I am Sir, your Excellency's most obliged & most humble Servant

Noah Webster

ALS, DLC:GW.

1. See GW's response on 31 July in which he gives his recollection of the decision making with regard to the Yorktown campaign in 1781, but see also the rebuttal of Timothy Pickering, the quartermaster general of the Continental army at the time of the siege, printed in note 1 of GW's letter.

## To Samuel Holden Parsons

Dear Sir, Mount Vernon July 15th 1788

By some unusual delay in the Post office, I did not receive your kind[1] letter of the 21st of April untill the 30th of June; or I should have sooner done myself the pleasure of acknowledging the receipt and of returning my best thanks for your friendly sentiments and wishes. I beg you will be persuaded of the satisfaction I take in hearing from my old military friends and of the interest I feel in their future prosperity. you will then do me the Justice to believe that my ardent desires attend the success & happiness of an establishment, in which the fortunes of so many of that worthy description of Citizens are comprehended.

You will doubtless have heard, before you can receive this letter, that the proposed general Government has been accepted by the Conventions of ten States. The prospect br[i]ghtens apace, and I flatter myself, the interior Settlements will find their interest concur with their inclination in maintaining an intimate connection with the Atlantic States.

It is with sincer pleasure I can infor[m] you, that the navigation of the Potowmac, so interesting in its consequence to the welfare of your Establishment as well as to the emolument of this Country, is in a fair way of being opened in as short a time and in as beneficial a manner as could have been expected. In order to meet the Directors of the Potowmac Company on business, I have lately been obliged to make a visit to the Great falls, the Seneca and the Shenandoah; and, therefore, give you this information from my own knowledge. Indeed, I may venture to conjecture, from the enormous quantity of labour already established by the Legislatures of Virginia and Maryland to obtain the Subscription Money, that, instead of ten years which the Company is allowed for opening the navigation, it will be made passable in little more than half the time. I do not mean, however, but that it will take a considerably longer period (perhaps the ten years) to meliorate and improve the works in the best manner.

As I thought this intelligence might be agreeable to you[r] brother Settlers, I have been the more confident and precise in expressing it according to my observation and Judgment. With sentiments of esteem I am &c.

Go. Washington

LB, DLC:GW.
    1. The copyist wrote "kink."

## To Gustavus Scott

Sir,                              Mount Vernon July 15th 1788
I am much obliged to you for the two curiousities you were pleased to transmit, as well as for your distinct and ingenious account of them. The facts have been so clearly stated by you, as I believe, to render a farther elucidation or confirmation unnec[e]ssary.[1]

It is greatly to be regretted, that we have not in America some general Museum or Cabinet for receiving all the rare Phenomena and unusual productions of nature, which might be collected in this Country: especially as natural History affords, perhaps, a more ample field for investigation here, than in any other part of the world. It is, however, laudible under all disadvantages for men of leisure and abilities to devote some part of their attention to so rational and curious a study.

In the mean time, as I shall take a particular pleasure in letting the Marquis de la Fayette know to whose care he may consider himself indebted for those articles, so I shall ever be happy in demonstrating.[2] With great esteem and regard I am, Sir, Yrs &c.

Go. Washington

LB, DLC:GW.

Gustavus Scott (1753–1800), originally from Prince William County in Virginia, lived in Cambridge, Maryland. He attended King's College in Aberdeen, Scotland, and studied law at the Inns of Court, London. GW was later, in 1794, to appoint him a commissioner for the new capital city of Washington.

1. The "two curiousities" have not been identified.

2. GW may have referred to Scott in his letter to Lafayette of 15 Sept., which has not been found.

# From James Gibbon

Sir                    Petersburgh Virginia July 16th 1788

Having once wrote you on the subject of my claim, I am unwilling to repeat it, as applications similar to mine, from their frequency must become troublesome.[1]

Altho Sir, my case has, by Congress, been referr'd to Mr Pierce he yet in a late letter to me signifies the necessity of referring to yr records with respect to my brevett, the resignation of wh. appears to be consider'd of course with a regimentall comsn I held under wh. I had not acted for two years previous to the revolt of our line[2]—my motive for it was no other, than by holding it I depriv'd the Junior officers of a Grade without the least consequence to myself, added to a rappid decline of my health which compell'd me going to the West Indies, which I did by the advice of D. Rush whose certificate to that purpose Mr Pierce is possess'd of.[3]

The Head Quarters of the army being at the time I was to sail at Newburgh and the Oppy flattering, did not admitt an application for the sanction nor did I know Sir, that of Congress was proper or necessary for in either instance my situation wou'd have justified it. Yr taking the trouble to say how my brevett stands or is consider'd on yr records is all I wish, as it will be the ultimatum by wh. Mr Pierce will be govern'd, the matter being totally referr'd to him.

From a wish only to do myself justice have I again troubled

you, which I trust will plead my Excuse.[4] With respect I am Sir yr Mo. Obt

J. Gibbon

My regimentall Comsn is indors'd at New Burgh—My brevett is not.

ALS, DLC:GW.

1. See Gibbon to GW, 26 Mar. 1787.

2. James Gibbon (Gibbons) was brevetted captain in the 6th Pennsylvania regiment on 20 July 1779. The Pennsylvania line's "revolt" over back pay was in 1783.

3. William Leigh Pierce (c.1740–1789) attended Congress from Georgia from January to May 1787. For reference to Gibbon's petition, which has not been found, see DNA:PCC, item 190.

4. GW replied from Mount Vernon on 1 Aug.: "⟨Si⟩r, I received your letter of the 16th Ulto, and can only advise you (respecting the subject to which it refers) that, upon a recurrence to the General Orders, I find y⟨our⟩ Brevet promotion announced to the Army in ⟨t⟩he words of the resolve of Congress; and, that, by farther researches among the memorandums of resignations, I can discover nothing more on the Subject. What was the understanding at the time when you resigned your Regimental Commission, I cannot, at this distant period, undertake to say: but I do not think it was absolutely necessary that the resignation of a Commission in the line should have involved the resignation of one held by the same person, by Brevet. Congress or their Commissioner for settling the accounts of the Army must be the discretionary Judges of right & propriety, in these intricate ⟨ca⟩ses.

"Your conjecture is but too well founded, that the applications to me on similar questions are extremely numerous & perplexing: Whensoever I am possessed of data which can be of any avail in settling disputes, I submit to the t⟨r⟩ouble with the less reluctance, as I am ever desirous justice should be done. With due regard I am Sir Yr Obedt Hble Servt Go: Washington" (ALS, NcD: George Washington Papers; LB, DLC:GW).

# From Francis Adrian Van der Kemp

Sir!                                                                    New-york 16. Jul. 88.

The answer from your Exellency to my Letters of the 15th May, with the flattering invitation to Mount-Vernon have induce me to visit Virginy, before I Settled my in the country.[1] My ardent wishes will be Satisfied. I desired to know that man, to whom America so much was in detted for her Liberty, and, if the expences of the voyage, joined to the troubles of it, had it not forbidden, I Should have chosen my eldest Son, to be the partner of my pleasures and feelings—although a child, he merited the favour. May I be So happy to know, if General Washington will be at home—a Letter—a Single line adressed to John Ross Esq. in Front Street between Walnut Street & the Drawbridge at Philadelphia wil be forwarded to me—Friday next I intend to go to New-wark—or Elisabeth-town—to visit Gov. Livingston—Saturday or Sunday I hope to be at Philadelphia, and wished to depart from this city the 23 or 24 of this instant to Baltimore, and So farther to Mount Vernon.[2] I am, with Sentiments of the highest respect Sir! Your Excellency's Most obedient Servant

Fr. Ad. vdKemp

ALS, DLC:GW.

1. GW's letter is dated 28 May.

2. The Dutch refugee Francis Adrian Van der Kemp (1752–1829), a Mennonite minister, visited Mount Vernon on 29 July; he found in GW "somewhat of a repulsive coldness" (Fairchild, *Van der Kemp*, 115–16; *Diaries*, 5:369–70). Van der Kemp, whose son was named John Jacob, settled in upstate New York and lived there until his death in 1829. He became a close friend of John Adams.

# From John Jay

Dear Sir　　　　　　　　Poughkeepsie [N.Y.] 17 July 1788

Since my arrival here I have written you two or three hasty letters—being constantly involved in Business or Company from wh. it would not be here very practicable or perhaps prudent to retreat, I have been able to write but very little—The Convention this moment adjourned and I am writing in their Chamber—a Question being about to be put on the mode of adoption which you have seen, we moved that the House adjourn for a month or two—It was yesterday carried against us—the former Question was again pressed with Earnestness—at that Period Mr M. Smith seconded by Mr Platt (both of whom dislike the Constitution, and are classed with its opposers) proposed the mode of adoption, of which the above is a Copy[1]—their own party were not pleased and the House adjourned.[2] this morning it was expected that the Question to postpone the former plan, and proceed to the Consideration of the latter, would be put. The House went into a Committee of the whole according to the order of the Day—A long Silence ensued—the Party seemed embarrassed—fearful to divide among themselves, and yet many of them very averse to the new Plan. the Committee rose, and the House adjourned, with very little opposition—It is difficult to conjecture what may be done out of Doors to Day.[3] I am inclined to think that the new plan will expel the other, and I wish it may, not because I approve of it, but because I prefer it as being less exceptionable than the other. with the greatest Respect & Esteem I am Dr Sir your affte & hble Servt

John Jay

ALS, DLC:GW; ADf, NNC. In the draft, someone, Jay perhaps, attempted to convert the 7 in 17 July into an 8; see note 3.

1. Jay in fact wrote his letter to GW at the end of his copy of the statement presented by Melancton Smith and Zephaniah Platt as the proposed mode of conditional ratification of the Constitution. See note 2.

2. On 11 July Jay introduced a motion in the New York Ratifying Convention that the Constitution be ratified. On 15 July Melancton Smith, a leading Antifederalist in the convention, proposed an amendment to Jay's motion. Smith's amendment set forth a number of conditions under which the Constitution would be ratified. On the next day the convention voted down the federalist motion to have the convention adjourn until September. It was at this point, on 17 July, that Smith and Platt, his fellow delegate from Dutchess County, proposed the new "mode of adoption." This called for unconditional ratification but accompanied by the retention of the right of New York to secede if the new government did not promptly consider amendments to the Constitution (Elliot, *Debates*, 2:410–11; De Pauw, *Eleventh Pillar*, 221–27). In the end, on 25 July, the New York convention voted 30 to 27 to ratify the Constitution "in full confidence" that the necessary amendments would be adopted.

3. Jay is describing here what transpired in the convention on 18 July.

# To John Jay

My dear Sir,                    Mount Vernon July 18th 1788.

A few days ago, I had the pleasure to receive a letter of yours from Poughkeepsie—since which I have not obtained any authentic advices of the proceedings of your Convention. The clue you gave me, to penetrate into the principles & wishes of the four classes of men among you who are opposed to the Constitution, has opened a wide field for reflection & conjecture.[1] The

accession of ten States must operate forcibly with all the opposition, except that class which is comprehended in your last description. Before this time you will probably have come to some
decision. While we are awaiting the result with the greatest anxiety our Printers are not so fortunate as to obtain any Papers
from the Eastward. Mine, which have generally been more
regular, have, however, frequently been interrupted for sometime past.

It is extremely to be lamented that a new arrangement in the
Post Office, unfavorable to the circulation of intelligence, should
have taken place at the instant when the momentous question
of a general government was to come before the People. I have
seen no good apology, not even in Mr Hazards publication, for
deviating from the old custom of permitting Printers to exchange their Papers by the Mail. That practice was a great public
convenience & gratification. If the priviledge was not from convention an original right, it had from prescription strong pretensions for continuance; especially at so interesting a period.
The interruption in that mode of conveyance, has not only given
great concern to the friends of the Constitution, who wished the
public to be possessed of every thing that might be printed on
both sides of the question: but it has afforded its enemies very
plausible pretext for dealing out their scandals, & exciting jealousies by inducing a belief that the suppression of intelligence
at that critical juncture, was a wicked trick of policy, contrived
by an Aristocratic Junto. Now, if the Postmaster General (with
whose character I am unacquainted & therefore would not be
understood to form an unfavorable opinion of his motives) has
any candid advisers who conceive that he merits the public employment they ought to counsel him to wipe away the aspersion
he has incautiously brought upon a good cause—if he is unworthy of the Office he holds, it would be well that the ground of a
complaint, apparently so general, should be enquired into, and,
if founded, redressed through the medium of a better appointment. It is a matter, in my judgment, of primary importance
that the public mind should be relieved from inquietude on this
subject. I know it is said that the irregularity or defect has happened accidentally, in consequence of the contract for trans-
porting the Mail on horseback, instead of having it carried in
the *Stages*—but I must confess, I could never account, upon any

satisfactory principles, for the inveterate enmity with which the Post Master General is asserted to be actuated against that valuable institution. It has often been understood by wise politicians and enlightened patriots that giving a facility to the means of travelling for Strangers and of intercourse for Citizens, was an object of Legislative concern & a circumstance highly beneficial to any Country. In England, I am told, they consider the Mail Coaches as a great modern improvement in their Postoffice regulations. I trust we are not too old, or too proud to profit by the experience of others. In this article the materials are amply within our reach. I am taught to imagine that the horses, the vehicles, and the accomodations in America (with very little encouragement) might in a short period become as good as the same articles are to be found in any Country of Europe—and, at the sametime, I am sorry to learn that the line of Stages is at present interrupted in some parts of New England and totally discontinued at the Southward.[2]

I mention these suggestions only as my particular thoughts on an Establishment, which I had conceived to be of great importance—Your proximity to the person in question & connection with the characters in power, will enable you to decide better than I can on the validity of the allegations; and, in that case, to weigh the expediency of dropping such hints as may serve to give satisfaction to the Public—With sentiments of the highest consideration & regard—I am Dear Sir, Your Most Obedt & Affecte Hble Servt

Go: Washington

P.S. Since writing this letter, I have been favoured with the one which you begun on the 4th and finished on the 8th instant from Poughkeepsie and thank you for the information contained therein. A little time will, I hope, bring the agreeable account of the ratification by your State unfettered with *previous* amendments. Yrs &c.

Go: W——n

ALS, NNC; LB, DLC:GW.

1. GW was referring to the letter from Jay printed above at the end of June; he had not yet received Jay's letter of 4–8 July. See postscript.

2. On 15 Oct. 1787 Congress authorized Ebenezer Hazard as postmaster general to contract with postriders to carry the mail, and Hazard soon thereafter contracted with postriders, instead of stagecoaches, to carry the mail

north of Philadelphia, beginning in 1788. He also discontinued the practice of allowing printers to exchange their newspapers with one another without postal charges. The resulting disruption in the flow of news and newspapers provoked widespread protest. See the editors' summary of these developments in Kaminski and Saladino, *Documentary History of the Ratification of the Constitution*, 16:540–41.

*Letter not found*: from Thomas Nelson, Jr., 19 July 1788. On 3 Aug. GW wrote Nelson: "Your letter of the 19th Ulto came duly to hand."

*Letter not found*: from Thomas Newton, 19 July 1788. On 1 Aug. GW wrote Newton: "Your letters of the 14th & 19 Ulto came duly to hand."

## To Clement Biddle

Dear Sir,                             Mount Vernon July 20th 1788

Your favors of the 26th of May, 13th of June and 7th instt are before me;[1] and I believe unacknowledged—The several Articles sent by the Packet came safe, except one of the Wheels belonging to the harrows which was not landed by Captn Ellwood who dropped them at my landing as he passed by in the Night returning. Whether the omission was in *him* or in putting them on board in Philadelphia I know not.

I am sorry my Herrings are likely to meet so unfavourable a market. If the price should not rise, I could have got what you say those from the head of Elk are selling at, in Alexandria; and am not a little surprized to hear of the deficiency having repacked them (at least ordered them to be so) When they were shipped for Philadelphia.[2]

I beg you will send me 200 wt of single and 100 wt of dble refined Sugar of good quality and a groce of Mr Hairs best bottled Porter if the price of it is not much enhanced by the copius droughts you took of it at the late Procession.[3]

As you have not yet furnished with my account I know not to what amount I stand indebted to you; and it not being my wish to put you to the smallest inconvenience by advancing money for the purchase of articles for my use I pray you to forward the account that I may draw on the Bank of Philadelphia in you favor.

I beg you would be so obliging as to forward the enclosed

letter for General Parsons by the first *safe* conveyance.[4] I am Dear Sir, Yr Most Obedt Sert

Go. Washington

P.S. Pray send me by the *Post* 12 yards of Velvet ribbon of the width and equality of the enclosed sample.

LB, DLC:GW.

1. Biddle's letters of 26 May and 13 June have not been found.
2. See Biddle to GW, 7 July.
3. GW was referring to the great Philadelphia procession on 4 July. See Biddle to GW, 30 July. Mr. Hair is Robert Hare (1752–1812), a Philadelphia merchant whose brewery was on the corner of Fifth and Market streets in Philadelphia (see Biddle to GW, 13, 17 August).
4. GW's letter to Samuel Holden Parsons is dated 15 July.


## To John Langdon

Dear Sir,                         Mount Vernon July 20th 1788.

I had the satisfaction to receive regularly your favor of the 21st Ulto announcing the adoption of the Fœderal government by the Convention of New Hampshire. You will already have been informed, through the ordinary channels of communication, that the same event took effect in this State a few days afterwards. And I am happy to say, that, so far as I have been able to learn, a spirit of harmony and acquiescence obtained among the large & respectable minority in as great a degree as could possibly have been expected.

If we may calculate upon rectitude in the views & prudence in the conduct of the leading characters throughout the States, accompanied by industry & honesty in the mass of the people, we may assuredly anticipate a new æra; and, perhaps, we shall not deceive ourselves by expecting a more happy one than hath before appeared on this checquered scene of existence. But we ought not to be too sanguine or to expect that we shall be entirely exempted from the ills which fall to the lot of humanity.

With congratulations to your Excellency on your elevation to the Chief Magistracy of your State,[1] and with sentiments of consideration & respect, I remain Sir—Your Excellency's Most Obedt Hble Ser⟨vt⟩

Go: Washington

ALS, NhSB: John Langdon Collection; LB, DLC:GW.
    1. John Langdon took office for a new term as president of New Hampshire on 6 June. The New Hampshire Ratifying Convention reconvened on 18 June.

## To Jonathan Trumbull, Jr.

Dear Sir,                                 Mount Vernon July 20th 1788.
    I have received your favor of the 20th of June and thank you heartily for the confidential information contained in it. The character given of a certain great Personage, who is remarkable for neither forgetting or forgiving, I believe to be just. What effect the addition of such an extraordinary weight of power & influence as the arrangement of the East India affairs gives to one branch of the British governmt cannot be certainly foretold: but one thing is certain, that is to say, it will always be wise for America to be prepared for events. Nor can I refrain from indulging the expectation that the time is not very distant, when it shall be more in the power of the United States than it hath hitherto been, to be forearmed as well as forewarned against the evil contingencies of European politics.
    You will have perceived from the Public papers, that I was not erroneous in my calculation that the Constitution would be accepted by the Convention of this State. The majority, it is true, was small; & the minority respectable in many points of view. But the greater part of the minority here, as in most other States, have conducted themselves with great prudence & political moderation; insomuch that we may anticipate a pretty general and harmonious acquiescence. We shall impatiently wait the result from New York & North Carolina. The other State which has not yet acted is nearly out of the question. As the infamy of the conduct of Rhode Island outgoes all precedent, so the influence of her Counsels can be of no prejudice. There is no State or description of Men but would blush to be involved in a connection with the Paper-money Junto of that Anarchy. God grant that the honest men may acquire an ascendency before irrevocable ruin shall confound the innocent with the guilty.
    I am happy to hear from General Lincoln & others that affairs are taking a good turn in Massachusetts. But the triumph of

salutary & liberal measures over those of an opposite tendency seems to be as complete in Connecticut as in any State & affords a particular subject for congratulation. Your friend Colo. Humphreys informs me, from the wonderful revolution of sentiment in favor of fœderal measures, and the marvellous change for the better in the elections of your State, that he Shall begin to suspect that miracles have not ceased. Indeed, for myself, since so much liberality has been displayed in the construction & adoption of the proposed general Government, I am almost disposed to be of the same opinion. Or at least we may, with a kind of grateful & pious exultation, trace the finger of Providence through those dark & misterious events, which first induced the States to appoint a general Convention & then led them one after another (by such steps as were best calculated to effect the object) into an adoption of the system recommended by that general Convention—thereby, in all human probability, laying a lasting foundation for tranquility & happiness; when we had but too much reason to fear that confusion and misery were coming rapidly upon us.

That the same good Providence may still continue to protect us & prevent us from dashing the cup of National felicity just as it has been lifted to our lips, is the earnest prayer of My dear Sir Your faithful friend & Affectionate Servt

Go: Washington

ALS, DNDAR; LB, DLC:GW.

## To Mathew Carey

Sir,                                    Mount Vernon July 21st 1788.

I have been favoured with your letter of the 5th instt, and shall be happy if mine, to which you allude, may have any operation in favour of your literary undertaking.[1]

If I had more leizure, I should most willingly give you any such communications (that might be within my reach) as would serve to keep up the reputation of your Museum. At present, occupied as I am with my Agriculture & corrispondencies, I can promise little. Perhaps some Gentlemen connected with me may make some selections from my repositories: and I beg you will be persuaded that I can have no reluctance to permit any thing to be communicated that might tend to establish truth, extend knowledge, excite virtue & promote happiness among mankind. With best wishes for your success I am—Sir Yr Most Obedt Hble Servt

Go: Washington

ALS, owned (1994) by Mr. Joseph Maddalena, Profiles in History, Beverly Hills, Calif.; LB, DLC:GW.

1. Carey's letter of 5 July has not been found; GW's letters to Carey are dated 25 June.

## From Samuel Hanson

Sir                                              Alexandria July 21st 1788
I take the liberty of addressing a few lines to you as to a Trustee of the Alexandria Academy.

In consequence of an Advertisement by Mr McWhir, I have applied to him for the place of Assistant-Teacher. at the time of my application, I conceived that the Young Gentleman who has hitherto acted in that Capacity, had given in his resignation. He has, however, lately expressed an inclination to be continued. By the rule of the Academy, Mr McWhir has the appointment, provided 3 of the Visitors concur in, or rather, ratify it. But, being under some difficulty with respect to superseding this young Man, who has acquitted himself very well, he requests a meeting of the Trustees, that the Board may recommend the Candidate they may think preferable. I do not claim any Superiority over my Competitor with regard to any of the qualifications required for this employment, except the Knowledge of Arithmetic, of which he is professedly ignorant. It is true that the teaching of that useful branch is not, at present, connected with the Latin-School. In consequence of this defect, it has been hitherto entirely omitted in that School. Perhaps the Trustees may think proper to pass a rule annexing this branch to the others. The price of tuition is sufficient, it would seem, to justify Such an addition of duty. If the Board should be of Opinion that such an Alteration of the original plan will encrease the general utility of the Institution, I conclude that they will not reject it, merely because it would have the effect of excluding one Candidate, and of securing the appointment of the other. The meeting is fixed for Wednesday, 10 O'Clock. If it would not be too inconvenient, I would beg the favour of your attendance. A full meeting would remove all grounds of Complaint against Mr McWhir, in case Mr Parsons should be rejected, and, at the same time, give me, as I conceive, the best chance of obtaining an Employment, the profits of which, however trifling, are an object to one in my Situation.[1] With due respect, I rema⟨in⟩ Sir Your most obedt & most humble Sert

S. Hanson of Saml

ALS, DLC:GW.

1. William McWhir's advertisement has not been found. Parsons has not been identified, but he may be John Parsons, the only son of James Parsons (d. 1787) who was the builder of Christ Church in Alexandria before the Revolution. Hanson did not become a teacher in Alexandria Academy. GW replied to this letter on 26 July, expressing his regrets that he would not be able to attend the meeting.

# From James Madison

Dear Sir                                  N. York July 21. 1788.

I have deferred writing since my arrival here in the hourly hope of being enabled to communicate the final news from Poughkepsie. By a letter from Hamilton dated the day before yesterday I find that it is equally uncertain when the business will be closed, and what will be its definitive form. The inclosed gazettes state the form which the depending proposition bears. It is not a little strange that the Antifederal party should be reduced to such an expedient, and yet be able to keep their members together in the opposition. Nor is it less strange that the other party, as appears to be the case, should hesitate in deciding that the expedient as effectually keeps the State for the present out of the New Union as the most unqualified rejection could do.[1] The intelligent Citizens here see clearly that this would be its operation and are agitated by the double motives of fœderalism, and a zeal to give this City a fair chance for the first meeting of the new Government.

Congress have deliberated in part on the arrangements for putting the new Machine into operation, but have concluded on nothing but the times for chusing electors &c.[2] Those who wish to make N. York the place of meeting studiously promote delay. Others who are not swayed by this consideration do not urge despatch. They think it would be well to let as many States as possible have an opportunity of deciding on the Constitution: and what is of more consequence, they wish to give opportunities where they can take place for as many elections of State Legislatures as can precede a reasonable time for making the appointments and arrangements referred to them. If there be too great an interval between the acts of Congress on this Subject and the next election or next meeting of a State Legislature, it may afford a pretext for an intermediate summoning of the existing members, who are every where less federal than their successors hereafter to be elected will probably be. This is particularly the case in Maryland, where the antifederal temper of the Executive would render an intermediate and extraordinary meeting of the Assembly of that State the more likely to be called. On my way thro' Maryland I found such an event to be much feared by the friends and wished by the adversaries of the Constitution. We have no late news from Europe. Nor any thing from N. Carolina. With every sentiment of esteem & attachment I remain Dr Sir Your Obedt & Affete servt

Js Madison Jr

ALS, DLC:GW; copy, DLC: Madison Papers.

1. In his letter to Madison of 19 July, Alexander Hamilton asked about New York's being admitted to the Union if "the only qualification [in ratifying] will be *the reservation* of a right to recede in case our amendments have not been decided upon . . . within a certain number of years." Madison responded on 20 July: "My opinion is that a reservation of a right to withdraw if amendments be not decided on . . . within a certain time, is a *conditional* ratification, that it does not make N. York a member of the New Union, and consequently that she could not be received on that plan" (Rutland and Hobson, *Madison Papers*, 11:188–89).

2. At this time, for one of the few times in its history, the Congress of the Confederation had representation from all thirteen states. On 8 July, before Madison's return, Congress received the report of its committee on the new Constitution recommending that presidential electors be chosen on the first Wednesday in December and vote for a president on the first Wednesday in January, and that the new government begin its operations on the first Wednesday in February 1788 at a place to be chosen. For the next two months Madison kept GW informed about the developments in the prolonged fight over the naming of a temporary capital for the new government and his own views of it (see Madison to GW, 11, 24 Aug. and 14 September). In the end,

on 13 Sept., New York was chosen over Philadelphia, and it was decreed that the electors would be chosen in January and would vote in February and that the new government would get underway in March (*JCC*, 34:522–23).

## From John Jay

Dr Sir                                    Poughkeepsie [N.Y.] 23 July 1788
     I wrote to you a few Days ago and inclosed a copy of certain Propositions, or mode of adoption—great objections to it being urged it was withdrawn for the *present*[1]—The Convention proceeded to Day in debating on the Plan of *conditional* amendment. some of the anti Party moved for striking out the words on *Condition* and substituting the words *in full confidence*—it was carried 31 to 29 in the Committee—so that if nothing new should occur this State will adopt unconditionally—the Party however mean to rally their forces and endeavour to regain that Ground—It was but this Instant that I heard of a Person going to town—He waits—I can only that I am Dr Sir with the greatest Respect & Esteem your affec. & hble Servt

                                                        John Jay

ALS, DLC:GW.
     1. Jay wrote on 17 July. See also James Madison to GW, 21 July, n.1.

## From Henry Lee, Jr.

My dear Genl                          Norfolk [Conn.] July 24th [17]88.
     The misery of my situation in consequence of the continued ill health of Mrs Lee, has prevented me the gratification of congratulatin you on the auspicious prospect which the adoption of the new constitution presents to our country.[1]
     Indeed I am now so inadequate from my temper of mind to execute a task so agreable, & on which I wish to say much, that I should have posponed the satisfaction, till I was more equal to a full expression of my feelings & opinions, had not my desire to introduce to your acquaintance Mr Livingston an officer in our late navy, my countryman & friend prevailed over other considerations.
     It is needless for me to explain public characters to you, as your discerning eye has viewed them in the day of trial, with

certainty and with justice—I will say nothing therefore on this score relative to Mr L., & content myself with recomending him to you as a gentleman of honor & worth—He is about to engage in a commercial scheme & is desirous of being made known to Mr Gardoqui, conceiving it probable such an acquaintance might eventually be advantageous to his designs.

With this view he takes the liberty of asking a letter from you, which solicitation I beg leave to advocate as far as your opinion of my judgement may warrant you to consider me.[2]

You will beleive me sir; when I assure you that no man feels more sensibly than I do, the delicacy of requesting civilitys of this nature, & that no motives of personal esteem could influence me to risk the introduction of any gentleman, of whose honor & merit, I was not thoroughly convicted—I am now on my way to N. York & Rhode island,[3] in either of which places, should you have any commands, you will render me very happy by putting it in my power to manifest the unceasing respect & attachment which I unalterably possess for you. I have the honor to be dear Genl your most obt h. ser.

Henry Lee

ALS, DLC:GW.

1. Matilda Lee became very ill in the summer of 1788 and continued in ill health until her death in childbirth in August 1790.

2. Musco Livingston (d. 1798) of Essex County, the eldest son of Frances Musco and John Livingston, was a ship captain who went to France at the beginning of the Revolution and was commissioned a lieutenant in the navy of the United States on 27 July 1778. At this time, ten years later, he was using Norfolk as the base for his overseas trading ventures. No letter from GW in support of Livingston has been found, and no response to this particular letter from Lee has been found. On 27 July 1789 Lee recommended to GW that Livingston be appointed to "the office of Surveyor for the district of Norfolk & Portsmouth."

3. Lee was back in New York by 29 July when he attended Congress, a member of which he had been since 1785.

## To David Stuart

Dear Sir,                         Mount Vernon July 24th 1788.

From Mr Lund Washington's I received your letter of the 20th instant, enclosing Mr Hopkins's Accts, receipts &ca[1]—Enclosed you have a receipt for the amount of your statement; specify-

ing the several articles which constitute the aggregate sum of
£567.10.5. I am Yr Affecte & Obedt Servt

Go: Washington

ALS, owned (1975) by Dr. Ralph F. Brandon, Short Hills, New Jersey.

1. Letter not found, but see John Hopkins to GW, 20 June 1788. See also
GW to Hopkins, 27 April, and notes.

## From Thomas Pleasants, Jr.

Sir                                   Raleigh 25th July 1788

I duly received your obliging answer to the enquiry respecting Mr Dydsburys Claim under Van braam of Land on the Kanhawa—and the obligation will be increased, if you will enable
me to extend my enquiry into that part of the County, by Mentioning some person of Character, to whom I may apply for a
particular description of its situation and Value.[1]

When Mr Madison left this State he put into my hands some
queries to answer, and desired me to send the answers open,
under Cover to you, which I now have the honour of doing.[2]
I am, With sentiments of great respect & Esteem Yr Mo. ob.
Hbble st

Thomas Pleasants jr

ALS, DLC:GW.

1. Pleasants wrote to GW on 2 June and GW responded on 8 June.

2. Pleasants's answers to the queries that Moustier posed to James Madison
on 2 Mar. were enclosed in his letter to Madison of 25 July, both printed in
Rutland and Hobson, *Madison Papers*, 11:201–7.

## From John Polson, Jr.

Sir                                   London 25 July 1788

I did myself the honor of writing you the 2d September 1783
and took the liberty of puting under your Cover a letter for
my old friend and Attorney the late Mr Alexr Craig of Williamsburg: a freedom I would not have taken if I knew how to
direct to him if living, and was then uncertain whether he was
dead or alive. I am sorry if you were offended at it, which I have
reason to fear was the Case as I never received any Answer from

you, tho' I earnestly requested it, particularly as Mr Craig was dead, and I had no one to inform me, what was done with the 6000 acres of Land granted me as heir to my Brother Willm Polson who was killed with Genl Braddock.[1] The want of information on this point may have been very prejudical to my Interest: for if my land is still at my disposal and not Confiscated by any Law of the State of Virginia, It may have been encroached upon and destroyed; if it was Confiscated by any Law of the State, I fear I have lost the chance I might have had of applying to the Commissioners appointed by Act of Parliament for a Compensation. I remain yet in this State of uncertainty, for tho' Mr Jefferson the Minister from the united States to the Court of France, wrote to General Stephen (who is one of my Partners in the Kanhawa Tract) in the Summer 1785, and to some other Gentleman in Virginia to know what was done with my land, he had not received any answer to his letters in April 1786 when I had the pleasure of seeing him here.[2] The Commissioners appointed by Act of Parliament to examine into the losses and Services of American Loyalist are to finish their duty, it is said, about the latter end of this year. And if I am unfortunate enough to have had my lands Confiscated because I was in the Service of Great Britain, where I had been for twenty years before, but had not been within any of the States since novr 1772, I cannot claim a Compensation unless I can prove that my Property was Confiscated and Sold, and the time is now so short that I can hardly expect to have these Vouchers transmitted to me from the State of Virginia before the Commissioners ⟨*mutilated*⟩ close their accounts: besides that I do not know who to apply to to obtain the Necessary information. I therefore once more take the liberty to address you as a Gentleman to whom I have been under great obligations, and to request the favor, that you will inform me whether my lands were Confiscated and Sold, and if they were so, to put me in the way to have the Account Sales properly certified, & sent home to me to this place under Cover to Messrs John & George Whitehead, Bankers in Basinghall street, and any Expence that will attend the geting the proper Vouchers from the different offices will be chearfully paid by Mr Samuel Milford Master of the Ship Friendship now bound for York River in your State.[3] And if my Land has not been forfeited, I will esteem it a very great favour that you will recommend some fit person to be my Attorney to whom I will sent a Power.[4] It is with the utmost regret that I trouble you on this Subject, but I hope you will excuse it from the necessity I am under, of produceing proofs incase my lands were forfeited, otherwise I lose my land, and the money I advanced for them, which is something considerable including Interest to this time. But I have such a high Opinion of the Justice of your State, that I hope the lands are left at my own disposal.

Though its the General Opinion that our Commissioners will finish their business before next Jany, If the Vouchers can be sent home as early as that, I shall be glad to have them, in case my lands were Confiscated, any time before the Month of June but my best Chance is to have them soon. I write to General Steph⟨en⟩ on this subject, but I have been told that he lives so far back in the Cou⟨ntry⟩ that it will be long before I can hear from him.

I must again beg your pardon for the Liberty I ha⟨ve⟩ taken with you, and I am with great regard & Esteem Your most obedt and most humble Servt

Jno. Pols⟨on⟩

ALS, DLC:GW.

A man named Samuel Milford brought this letter from London and forwarded it from Richmond with his own letter to GW of 24 September.

1. Lt. William Polson served under GW at Fort Necessity in 1754. He was killed at the Battle of the Monongahela in 1755 when Gen. Edward Braddock's army was routed by French and Indian forces. When Polson's father, John Polson, Sr. (d. 1778), wrote to GW in 1771 from Georgia about the land due his son under the terms of Dinwiddie's Proclamation of 1754, GW replied on 24 June 1771 suggesting that he engage Alexander Craig to act for him in this matter.

GW responded to John Polson on 28 Sept. 1788 and to Samuel Milford on 29 Sept. 1788. The Milford letter is printed in *Papers, Presidential Series*, vol. 1, but a partial facsimile of the letter to Polson turned up after that volume was in print. This letter reads: "Sir, Your letter of the 25th of July by Captn Milford, came duly to hand; but I do not recollect to have received one dated septr 2d 1783, spoken of therein. At that period I was with the Army in the State of New York and did not return to Virginia until the beginning of the succeeding year. all foreign letters to me, therefore, must either have passed the British Lines or taken their chance in Merchantmen—Both, were hazardous conveyances.

"Every information (and small indeed it is) that I can give respecting your Land on the Great Kanhawa, is communicated to Captn Milford; with a request that he would transmit a copy of it, with this letter, to you. His ship lays near Williamsburgh where your late attorney Mr Craig, lived, at the time of his decease—and where I presume his Executors (from whom the best information I conceive is to be had) must now live. Besides, in this situation Captn Milford is not far distant from Richmond, the Seat of the government and information, on account of the general resort to it for the purposes of attending the Courts—the Assemblies—Public offices—&ca—&ca. From *me*, this place is far removed; and one to which I seldom or never go. Indeed I rarely stir from home, and having made no enquiry into the matter, am entirely ignoran⟨t⟩ as to the disposition of any of the Lands which were granted to the Virginia Regiment raised in 1754, after Patents were obtained for them except [those of my own—and those were within an ace of being sold for the payment of Taxes due on them, before I received information thereof . . .]" (ALS [facsimile], Sotheby's catalog no. 6250, item 44, 12 Dec. 1991). The lines in square brackets are taken from a quotation in the descriptive entry for the item. Polson's letter of 2 Sept. 1783 and its enclosure to Alexander Craig are in DLC:GW.

2. Polson wrote Thomas Jefferson on 13 May and 1 July 1785, and Jefferson wrote Adam Stephen about Polson's claims on 19 June 1785 (Boyd, *Jefferson Papers*, 8:152, 258, 237–38). Polson wrote Jefferson again c.20 July 1788, and Jefferson replied on 29 July 1788, saying that he had written to Joseph Jones of King George County as well as to Stephen and had heard from neither (ibid., 13:388–89, 433–34).

3. GW consulted a lawyer who told him: "it is not likely that his [Polson's] property is comprehended in any Confiscation Law of this Commonwealth" but acknowledged that the land may have been sold for taxes (GW to Samuel Milford, 29 Sept. 1788).

4. GW told Milford that Polson should get someone in Richmond to act as his attorney but declined to name anyone.

## To Samuel Hanson

Sir,                                            Mount Vernon July 26th 1788
The letter which you was pleased to write to me on the 21st instant did not get to my hands in time to attend the meeting of the Trustees of Alexandria Academy. It is not *always* that I send to the Post Office on Post days. But on Monday last I directed a white man who lives with me, and who *said* he had a business at Court to call for my letters in the evening. That, however which was infinitely more agreeable, and equally injurious to himself allowed him no time to think of Post office or letters and accordingly he came home, without the latter.[1]
The want of Arethmetical and Mathematical instruction at this Academy is in my Judgment, a very great defect in the Institu-

tion. To find boys who have been Six or seven years at the Classics *entirely* unacquainted with those parts of literature which are to fit them for the *ordenary* purposes of life—incapable of writing legibly; and *altogether* ignorant in accts does not in the smallest degree, comport with my ideas of useful and assential education. Of this, I have already informed Mr McWher; and shall feel myself under the necessity of withdrawing my Nephews from the Academy unless some change in this respect takes place, and that in a short time. With esteem and regard I am, Sir Yr most Obedt Hble Sert

Go. Washington

LB, DLC:GW.

1. For a clue to the possible identity and activities of the man who went into town, see Thomas Green to GW, 15 May 1788.

## From William Tudor

Sir　　　　　　　　　　　　　　　　　　Boston 26 July 1788

The strong Attachment which I know you have always felt, & in a Variety of Instances demonstrated, for the State of Massachusetts, induces me to send you, what is here considered, an interesting Pamphlet; which, with great Impartiality, states the rise, causes, & happy Termination of the late most alarming Insurrections in the Commonwealth. The Author is a young Lawyer, & Clerk to our lower House of Assembly. He had the best Sources of Information, & his little History carries the Marks of Intelligence & Candour in every Page of it.[1]

A suppressed Rebellion always adds Energy to the Government. And perhaps the late one in our State was a fortunate Event. It is true, that it cost some Lives, & added Eighty thousand pounds to our public Debt. But it's intire Extinction has confirmed the Constitution, given Security & Stability to Property, & most thoroughly tamed many turbulent Spirits in all Parts of the State. To universal Discontent, the most violent party Animosity, & a very alarming Decline of Industry & Manufactures, have succeeded Content, Quiet & productive Labour.

The Exports of our State exceeded the Imports, last Year, by two hundred & thirty thousand Pounds and upwards. And we have now rose to be the third exporting State in the Confederacy. The Town of Boston alone, that Year, exported twelve hundred & thirteen thousand Pounds. And it has been considered, in another Point of View, as being still more beneficial, from aiding the Erection of the great federal Fabric, which was so boldly conceived in the general Convention at Philadelphia, & which now, it is beyond a Doubt, will be ratified by the People.

But it is not, I confess, so much with a Design of furnishing you, my dear Sir, with the complete Information contained in the Pamphlet, that I have taken the Liberty of transmitting it, as it is from a Desire of evidencing that Respect & Gratitude which I must ever personally feel for you. The early and particular Favours I experienced from you at a critical Period of my Life, & which continued during the Time I was in the Army, will never be forgot untill I shall cease to consider You as the Saviour of our Country.[2] That you may very long live to enjoy the honest Fame, which was so arduously & nobly acquired, & which you so fully possess by the Consent of all Mankind is the fervent Wish of, Dear Sir, Your most affectionate hble Servant

Wm Tudor

Pray present my most respectfull Compliments to Mrs Washington.

ALS, DLC:GW.

   William Tudor (1750–1819) of Boston before the Revolution was John Adams's law clerk, and in 1775 he became continental judge advocate general with the rank of lieutenant colonel. He was a prominent Boston merchant with strong scholarly interests.

   1. George Richards Minot's *The History of the Insurrections, in Massachusetts, in the Year MDCCLXXXVI, and the Rebellion Consequent Thereon*, which remains an important source of information about Shays' Rebellion, was printed in Worcester in 1788. Minot himself sent GW a copy of his book on 7 August. GW thanked Tudor for the book on 18 Aug. and Minot on 28 August.

   2. For GW's early "Favours" to Tudor, see GW to John Hancock, 21 July 1775 (first letter), and Tudor to GW, 23 Aug. 1775.

## From Chartier de Lotbinière

My General                                   New York 27 July 1788.

   At length the State of New York, of which I had always the greatest doubt, as being the seat of British Corruption, has adopted the new Constitution like the others; whereupon I have the honour to make my most particular compliments—And from the extreme attention I have paid in pursuing the persons employed even through their most intricate windings & from the different movements I have made for almost three months to make their sinister designs prove abortive & evaporate in smoke, Your Excellency may judge whether it is not sincere & whether my individual joy at such an event does not approach almost to that which you experience yourself.[1]

It is happy for your States that they have pushed things with so much eagerness & inflexibility, seeing that from hence no person can doubt of the imminent danger of a certain communication, which, before, might have been regarded by many as indifferent: & of which they will all at present be decided to demand of you the total suppression, when as I hope most firmly, they shall have placed you at the head of their new government; then nothing will be more easy for your Excellency, with that entire confidence you possess from every part without the least exception, with that wisdom & consummate experience for which I have known you, than to fix for ever the constant happiness of those who live now & who shall live hereafter in these States.[2] I have the honor to be, with all the attachment which you have recognised in me & with infinite respect, My Genl Your very humble & most Obedt Servant

Le Marq. de Chartier De Lotbiniere

Translation, in the hand of Tobias Lear, DLC:GW; ALS, in French, DLC:GW.

1. Michel, marquis de Chartier de Lotbinière had been in New York since late June 1786. See Chartier de Lotbinière to GW, 8 July 1787.

2. GW responded from Mount Vernon on 18 Aug.: "Sir, Your congratulatory letter, on the adoption of the Constitution by the Convention of New York, has been placed in my hands: and I have, in return, to request that you will be assured it would be incompatible with the feelings of the good Citizens of America to be insensible to the friendly sentiments, expressed by patriotic foreigners for their public felicity. For myself, it might be superfluous to add more than that I remain, with due impressions for your partiality in my favour, Sir, Yr Most Obedient & Most Hble Servant Go: Washington" (ALS [photocopy], Kenneth W. Rendell catalog no. 183, item 135, June 1987).

# From James McHenry

My dear General                                    Baltimore 27 July 1788.

It is whispered here that some leading characters among you have by no means dropped their resentment to the new constitution, but have determined on some secret plan to suspend the proper organization of the government or to defeat it altogether. This is so serious and alarming a circumstance that it is necessary to be apprised of its truth, and extent that we may be on our guard against attempts of the antifederals to get into our assembly, as in all probability the next legislature will meet before the time for commencing proceedings by the new Congress. Here every means is made use of to do away all distincting between federal and antifederal and I suspect with no very friendly design to the federal cause. If such a plan has been hatched I think you must have heard of it. I shall therefore be much obliged to you to give me a hint of it as soon as possible.[1] With great respect and sincere attatchment I am Dr General Yours

James McHenry

ALS, DLC:GW.

1. GW on 31 July responded to McHenry's rumors with a careful statement of his view of the political situation existing in the United States now that the new Constitution had been adopted. The Virginia Antifederalists led by Patrick Henry continued into 1789 their efforts to secure the calling of a second constitutional convention.

*Letter not found*: from James Madison, 27 July 1788. On 3 Aug. GW wrote Madison: "Your favors of the 21st & 27th of last month came duly to hand."

# To Robert Hanson Harrison

Mount Vernon [28 July 1788]

The bearer hereof—the Honble Judge Harrison of Maryland—is hereby authorized to take possession of Houses and lotts in the Town of Bath in the County of Berkeley, and to have the Free and uninterupted use of them during his stay at that place who ever may have them in care or occupation is requested to surrender them accordingly.[1] Given under my hand this 28th day of July 1788

Go. Washington

LB, DLC:GW.

GW's friend and former military secretary Col. Robert Hanson Harrison (1745–1791), chief justice of the Maryland General Court, spent the night of 27 July at Mount Vernon.

1. GW had made little or no use of the house and dependencies that James Rumsey built for him in 1785 in Bath (or Berkeley Springs), Berkeley County.

## From Robert Townsend Hooe

Dr Sir,                    Alexandria July 28th 1788.

I have been for some time past endeavoring to state the claims and Collect the Debts due to Mr Bennetts Estate & as I find among others they claim a Sum due from the Estate of Mr Thomas Colville late of this County, I have applied to Mr Thomas West for an Acct of the disposition of the Monies arising from the Sale of the Maryland Tract, also the Legacy left by Mr Colville to Mr Bennett, and had hopes he could satisfie me upon looking into his Fathers Papers but he refers me to Your Excellency saying that such Papers as he had of his Fathers relating thereto are in your Possession, & that he thinks Bonds of the Purchasers of the Maryland Tract were lodged with you. If this be the case I shall be extremely obliged if Your Excellency will let me know whether they are to be Assign'd or if you intend to order the Money to be Collected & paid.[1] I have the Honor to be, Sir, Your Excellency's most Obt Servt

R. Td Hooe

ALS, DLC:GW.

1. For the claims, under the terms of Thomas Colvill's will of Charles Bennett, fourth earl of Tankerville, and of his brother Henry Astley Bennett, see GW to Tankerville, 20 Jan. 1784, and notes. GW replied to Hooe from Mount Vernon later in the day: "Dear Sir, Having had but very little agency in the management of Colo. Thomas Colvills Affairs, but (after my return from public life and the death of Mr John West) being very desirous of getting them settled; I applied to Mr Thomas West for such Papers as were in his possession which (unfortunately are very difficient and unsatisfactory) & more than a year ago placed them with such as, I had myself in the hands of Mr Kieth to make a final Statement for the Court—The incompetency of the Papers had from Mr West is I presume the cause why it has not been done ere this—From

him you may, possibly, get some information—from me till the Papers are returned it is impracticable for want of documents to refer to. I am Dear Sir Yrs &ca Go. Washington" (LB, DLC:GW). See GW to James Keith, 24 Jan. 1788, Keith to GW, 25 Jan. 1788, Thomas West to GW, 27 June 1786, and GW to West, 6 Nov. 1786. Hooe received from the Colvill estate £600 sterling in April 1789, £100 sterling in July 1789, and £1,697.0.1½ and £541.8.7½ sterling in May 1793 for the earl of Tankerville's brother "Henry Astley Bennett to whom the residue of the money arising from the sale of the Maryland Tract of Land, is due after paying John Colvills Debt" (Ledger C, 16–17).

## From Henry Knox

My dear Sir                                   New York 28 July 1788

It is with the most sincere satisfaction that I congratulate you on the unconditiona⟨l⟩ adoption of the constitution by the Convention of this state. The particulars of this important event are contained in this days paper herein enclosed.

Messrs Jay Hamilton and the rest of the federalists have derived great honor from their temperate and wise conduct during the tedious debates on this subject—nor ought those Gentlemen who were opposed to the constitution in the first instance, but afterwards voted for its adoption be deprived of their due share of praise for their candor and wisdom in assuming different conduct when it became apparent that a perseverance in opposition would most probably terminate in Civil War, for such and nothing short of it were the prospects.[1]

We have now thank Heaven eleven states which have adopted the system—Conduct and wisdom almost superior to the lot of humanity will be required in the first outset of the New Constitution.

Congress will soon publish an ordinance for the necessary elections and organization—The times of election and period of organization will not be difficult to be determind But the *place* where they shall assemble will be warmly contested[.] The two places generally thought on are Philadelphia and New York— at present it is difficult to say in favor of which it will be determined—a few days will more explain the matter.[2]

I shall set out in a few days for the Province of main to be absent six weeks or two months On my return I shall do myself the pleasure of addressing you—I have hitherto refrained from acknowledg the receipt of yr Kind favor of the 17th of June, as the affairs in this Convention were so gloomily circumstanced but it is now dissipated—Governor Clinton has most perseveringly opposed the constitution, and from being in the majority during Almost the whole time he has found himself so much deserted as to be in the minority A precise history of his conduct is difficult to be written and must be left to time to explain.

Mrs Knox and her little family are well. She unites with me in presenting our affectionate respect to you and Mr⟨s⟩ Washington. I am my dear Sir Your sincere friend & humble Servant

H. Knox

ALS, DLC:GW.

1. For reference to the debates in the New York Ratifying Convention, see John Jay to GW, 17 July, n.2.

2. See James Madison to GW, 21 July, n.2.

## From Clement Biddle

Dear General                    Philad[elphia] July 30. 1788

I was favour'd with yours of 20th and by the same post sent a ps. of velvet Ribbon to pattern 15 yards for 9/6—which I sent because it cost less in a store than 12 yds would do in a retale Shop.

Capt. Ellwood is arrived but I have not seen him yet (as I shall do) about the wheel of the Plough and by him I shall ship the Articles orderd & then forward the Account Current—Altho' we had plentiful libations of Porter at the procession it has not raised the price and the quality is such that it is in high repute and has superceded the use of English porter.

The herrings & shad are yet on hand but I hope will sell soon—I shall send the Letter to Genl Parsons by first Conveyance.

I was a little indisposed or should have answerd your Letter sooner.

I beg leave to refer you to the papers now put up for an account of the adoption of the Constitution unconditionaly by New York. I am with great respect Your Excellencys Obed. & very hume Serv.

Clement Biddle

ALS, DLC:GW.

*Letter not found*: from John Beale Bordley, 31 July 1788. On 17 Aug. GW wrote Bordley: "The letter with which you honord me, dated the 31st ult. . . . came safe to hand."

## From Tobias Lear

My dear Sir,                    Portsmouth N.H. July 31st 1788.

I received your very obliging favor of the 29th Ulto and feel grateful for the pleasure it gave me by communicating the joy which was felt in your vicinity upon receiving the doubly pleasing intelligence of the accession of New Hampshire & Virginia to the proposed Constitution. Its adoption by the latter State gave peculiar & inexpressible satisfaction to the good people in these parts; for notwithstanding the ratification by New Hampshire was the Key-stone of the fabrick, they still trembled for the consequences if Virginia should reject it—they knew the importance of the Dominion as an acquisition to the Union—they knew its ability, beyond any other State, to support independence—they had the best grounds to beleive that a rejection there would produce similar effects in New York & No. Carolina, and their fears were kept up by concurrent accts from that quarter of the strong & able opposition which it met with in the Convention. These fears were however happily done away by the joyous tidings of its adoption. No. Carolina is now looked upon as certain; and what will be the determination of New York at present they do not seem to regard, for it is not doubted but that they *must* ultimately accede to the general Government.

Is it not necessary, my dear Sir, that I should mention the cause of my being detained here so much beyond the time which I had fixed upon for my return to Mt Vernon? I feel that it is; and shall do it in full confidence of obtaining your indulgence if I have protracted the time beyond what you expected.

Previous to the late war with G. Britain my father had dealings with the House of Lane Son & Fraser of London to some considerable amount; and at the time of his death (in Novr 1785) there appeared by his Books to be a Bal[an]ce of £1500 Sterling due to him from that house; at the close of the war when a demand was made of the above Balance they asserted that instead of £1500 being due from them there was more than £1700 due to them by my father. This difference appeared strange till we had fully discussed the matter, when we found that their demand was originally small but had accumulated by interest, which we had not an idea of adding to our's, and the Balce in our favor arose from a Ship belonging to my father and insured by them, which Ship, at the commencement of hostilities was taken, on her passage from the West Indies to London, by an American Privateer & the insurance of course became due: this they refuse to pay & still hold up the validity of their demand. We have frequently endeavoured to bring them to a settlement without going into the tedious & expensive process of Courts, but without effect, and we now think it necessary to have the matter closed by some means or other and have therefore entered suit against them; and at the earnest request of my mother I have promised to attend to the business on her behalf and wait the issue of it which will be on the 3d week in Augt. As the determination of this matter, for or against my father's estate will immediately affect my mother more than any one else and as her welfare, care & happiness are exceeding dear to me I am induced to pay that attention to it in person which if it concerned me alone, I would willingly give up to another.[1]

You will pardon, my dear Sir, the expression of this particular (and to you uninteresting) detail—it should not have been offered had I not thought it necessary to show you that it is not inclination nor a common occurrence that prevents my being at Mount Vernon on or before the time which I intended. Nothing will detain me here a day after the decision of this matter.

I must beg you to present my best respects to Mrs Washington and believe me to be, with sentiments of the highest respect & warm affection Dear Sir Yr most Obedt & Hble Servt

Tobias Lear

P.S. Mr Langdon requests me to present his best respects to you.

ALS, DLC:GW.

1. On 2 July 1776 the ship *Polly*, Tobias Lear, Sr., owner and master, was captured by the Massachusetts privateer *Revenge* on a voyage from Antigua to London with a cargo of 350 hogsheads of rum and 12 hogsheads of sugar. Although Lear and his mate were "Americans, and high Liberty men, and the Ship Sailed from London, before the Ninth of September 1775 . . . yet the Jury . . . contrary to the most upright charge given by the Judge, condemn'd her, not even allowing the adventure, or any thing else, this I and many others

look upon as absolute Piracy, and hope a redress, Lear demanded an Appeal to Congress, but the Act of Massachusetts, would not allow it . . ." (John Langdon to Josiah Bartlett, 28 Sept. 1776, in Morgan, *Naval Documents*, 6:1031; see ibid., 27, 56, 347, and 506–8).

## To James McHenry

Dear Sir,                                 Mount Vernon July 31st 1788

In reply to your recent favour, which has been duly received,[1] I can only observe; that, as I never go from home except when I am obliged by necessary avocations, and as I meddle as little as possible with politics that my interference may not give occasion for impertinent imputations, so I am less likely than almost any person to have been informed of the circumstance to which you allude. That some of the leading characters among the Opponents [of] the proposed government have not laid aside their ideas of obtaining great and essential changes, through a constitutional opposition, (as they term it) may be collected from their public speeches. That others will use more secret and, perhaps, insidious means to prevent its organization may be presumed from their previous conduct on the subject. In addition to this probability, the casual information received from Visitants at my house, would lead me to expect that a considerable effort will be made to procure the election of Antifederalists to the first Congress; in order to bring the subject immediately before the State legislators, to open an extensive correspondence between the minorities for obtaining alterations, and in short to undo all that has been done. It is reported that a respectable Neighbour of mine has said, the Constitution cannot be carried in execution, without great amendments. But I will freely do the opposition with us the Justice to declare, that I have heard of no cabals or canvassings respecting the elections. It is said to be otherwise on your side of the river. By letters from the eastern States I am induced to believe the Minorities have acquiesced not only with a good grace, but also with a serious design to give the government a fair chance to discover its operation by being carryed into effect. I hope and trust that the same liberal disposition prevails with a large proportion of the same description of men in this State. Still, I think there will be great reason, for those who are well-affected to the government, to use their utmost exertions that the worthiest Citizens may be appointed to the two houses of the first Congress and where State Elections take place previous to this choice that the same principle govern in these also. For much will doubtless depend on their prudence in conducting business at the beginning; and reconciling discordant dispositions to a reasonable acquiescence with candid and honest measures. At the same time it will be a point of no common delicacy to make provision for effecting such explanations and amendments as might be really proper and generally satisfactory; without producing or at least fostering such a spirit of innovaton as will overturn the whole system.

I earnestly pray that the Omnipotent Being who hath not deserted the cause of America in the hour of its extremest hazard; will never yeild so fair a heritage of freedom a prey to *Anarchy* or *Despotism*. With sentiments of real regard I am Dr Sir &ca

                                                    Go. Washington

LB, DLC:GW.
    1. McHenry's letter is dated 27 July.

## From George Morgan

Dear Sir          Prospect New Jersey July 31st[–5 August] 1788
    Your Excellency is no doubt informed of the Ravages made in Connecticut, New York & New Jersey by the Hessian Fly, whose History is given in various Publications: As this Insect is now advanced to the Neighbourhood of Philadelphia, & its Progress southward is alarming to the Farmer, I have taken some Pains to inform myself of its Manners & Life, & to make several Experiments to oppose its destructive Depredations: From these it appears that good Culture of strong Soil, or well manured Lands, may sometimes produce a Crop of Wheat or Barley, when that sowed in poor or middling Soil, without the other Advantages, will be totally destroy'd: but as the Insect lives in its aurelia[1] State, in Straw & Litter, through the Winter, I find that unmixed Barn Yard Manure spread on Land in the Spring, multiplies the Fly to an astonishing Degree. Hence the Farmer will see the necessity of mixing his Yard Manure with Earth or Marle, in Heaps, adding (where he can do it) a Quantity of Lime, & changing the Heaps after they have undergone the necessary

Fermentation, that their Parts may be well incorporated, & a new Digestion brought on, which will effectually destroy the Insect.

Rolling of Wheat just before the first Frosts in Autumn, & after the last in the Spring, or before the Wheat begins to pipe or spindle, has good Effect. In the first Place it is a part of good Culture; & secondly, the Roller crushes & destroys a great Proportion of the Insect.

Top Dressings of Lime, or of live Ashes, are useful as Manures, & may (when applied about the Times I have mentioned as proper for Rolling) be offensive to the Insect; but if used in a sufficient Quantity to destroy them, would, I believe, destroy the Wheat also.

I have confined my Observations to Wheat & Barley, because this Insect seldom injures Rye materially, & has never attacked Oats, Buckwheat or Indian Corn.

In the Year 1782 a particular Species of Wheat was accidentally introduced on Long Island which is found to resist the Fly & to yield a Crop when all other Wheats in the same Neighbourhood are destroyed by it: but as this Wheat has been incautiously sowed in Fields with other kinds, it has generally become so mixed by the Farina as to suffer in its Character in Proportion to this Mixture; insomuch that some Farmers, from Inattention to this Circumstance, have condemned it altogether: Fortunately however some Crops have been preserved from this Degeneration, & I was so lucky as to procure the whole of my last Years Seed of the purest kind; the consequence of which has been a good Crop, whilst my neighbours Fields, sowed with other kinds of wheat, have been either totally destroyed or materially injured: I have nevertheless deemed it of Importance to the Public, to find from whence, & how this Species of Wheat was first introduced on Long Island, that we may be enabled to renew our Seed from the same Quarter, pure & unmixed: I hoped to have ascertained, not only the State it came from, but the Farm it grew on. My Success has not hitherto equalled my Industry, owing, possibly, to the contraband Trade carried on during the War, between Chesapeek, Delaware & New York, by Means of Passports from the British Admirals, which has caused a Reluctance in giving Information: I have satisfied myself however, that this Species of Wheat was thus brought to New York in April 1782—that a Cargo of it was then sent to Messrs Underhills Mill near Flushing, to be manufactured into Flour; & that from Seed saved out of this Parcel, the yellow bearded Wheat has been propagated.

I have sent Samples of this Wheat to Gentlemen in Maryland, Delaware, & Pennsylvania, & to your Excellency, that by sowing them it may be ascertained whether the exact Species is to be found in either of those States, or in Virginia, from whence our Country may procure unmixed Seed, & the Farmers of the more southern States be effectually guarded against the Fly, by a timely Knowledge of the Qualities of the *Yellow bearded Wheat*, by which name it is properly distinguished from the *red* & the *white bearded*; neither of which resist the Fly. It is a general received Opinion that the Capacity of the Yellow bearded Wheat in withstanding the Attack of the Hessian Fly, is oweing to the hardness or Solidity of its Straw—but when we reflect that other Wheats are sometimes wholly cut off in the Fall of the Year, & sometimes early in the Spring, before the Season of its running to Straw, we shall be induced to assign another Cause.

I am sorry that I cannot point out more than two Distinctions of this from other Wheats—The first is in the Ear, at, or after Harvest—The obvious Difference *then*, is the Coulour of the Chaff. The second can only be observed by the Miller, who says, "this Grain requires to be more aired & dried than any other Wheat, before Grinding, or it will not yield its Flour so kindly, as it is of a more oily Nature; but when thus aired & dried, the Quality & Quantity of its Flour, is equal to that of the best white Wheat.

As Mr Hazard, the Post Master General undertook to forward the Sample of Wheat for your Excellency some Weeks ago, I hope it has come safe to Hand.[2] I should have done myself the Honour of writing to your Excellency at the same time, but I wished to accompany it with the above Information: When it is ascertained that you have the yellow bearded Wheat in your State or in any particular District of it, your causing Information thereof to be given to the Philadelphia Agricultural Society will render a most important Service to the Farmers of Pennsylvania, New Jersey &c., & may possibly prevent the farther Progress southward of this destructive Insect. I have the Honour to be, with the greatest Respect Your Excellencys most Obedient, humble Servt

Geo: Morgan

New York August 5th 1788. The Organization of the New Government has been long retarded by a Difficulty in uniting seven States to vote for One Place—The Contest lay between New York & Philadelphia. As both Parties could not be indulged, a Vote was carried yesterday for Baltimore; so that the Ordinance will be completed this Morning, unless New York succeeds in their Intention to move for a Reconsideration of it, as the Place is not agreeable to several of the most southern States, tho' they voted for it.[3]

ALS, DLC:GW.

Col. George Morgan (1743–1810), a partner in the firm of Baynton & Wharton and one of the "Suffering Traders," was granted land in 1768 by the Six Nations. During the Revolution Morgan was an Indian agent for the United States and a deputy commissary general of purchases. In 1779 he retired to his farm near Princeton and became a gentleman farmer, dabbling in science and writing articles, most notably on the Hessian fly. See particularly *American Museum*, 1:456–57, 2:298, 4:48.

1. The chrysalis, especially of lepidopterous insects.

2. See Ebenezer Hazard to GW, 14 July, and note 1 of that document.

3. See Henry Knox to GW, 28 July, and the references in note 2 of that document.

## To Noah Webster

Sir,                                        Mount Vernon July 31st 1788.

I duly received your letter of the 14th instant, and can only answer you *briefly*, and generally from *memory*: that a combined operation of the land and naval forces of France in America for the year 1781, was preconcerted the year before: that the point of attack was not absolutely agreed upon, because it would be easy for the Count de Grasse, in good time before his departure from the West Indies, to give notice by Express, at what place he could most conveniently first touch to receive advice, because it could not be foreknown where the enemy would be most susceptible of impression; and because we (having the command of the water with sufficient means of conveyance) could transport

ourselves to any spot with the greatest celerity: that it was determined by me (nearly twelve months before hand) at all hazards
to give out & cause it to be believed by the highest military as
well as civil Officers that New York was the destined place of
attack, for the important purpose of inducing the Eastern &
Middle States to make greater exertions in furnishing specific
supplies than they otherwise would have done, as well as for
the interesting purpose of rendering the enemy less prepared
elsewhere: that, by these means and these alone, artillery, Boats,
Stores & Provisions were in seasonable preparation to move with
the utmost rapidity to any part of the Continent—for the difficulty consisted more in providing, than knowing how to apply
the military apparatus: that before the arrival of the Count de
Grasse it was the fixed determination *to strike the enemy in the most
vulnerable quarter* so as to ensure success with moral certainty, as
our affairs were then in the most ruinous train imaginable: that
New York was thought to be beyond our effort & consequently
that the only hesitation that remained was between an attack
upon the British Army in Virginia or that in Charleston—and
finally that (by the intervention of several communications &
some incidents which cannot be Detailed in a letter; and wch
were *altogether unknown* to the late Quarter Master General of
the Army, who was informed of nothing but what related to the
immediate duties of his own department) the hostile Post in Virginia, from being *a provisional & strongly expected* became *the definitive and certain object* of the Campaign.

I only add, that it never was in contemplation to attack New
York, unless the Garrison should first have been so far degar-
nished to carry on the Southern operations, as to render our
success in the siege of that place as infallible as any future military event can ever be made. For I repeat it, and dwell upon it
again & again—some splended advantage (whether upon a
larger or smaller scale was almost immaterial) was so essentially
necessary to revive the expiring hopes & languid exertions of
the Country, at the crisis in question, that I never would have
consented to embark in any enterprize, wherein, from the most
rational plan & accurate calculations, the favourable issue
should not have appeared as clear to my view, as a ray of light.
The failure of an attempt agst the Posts of the enemy, could, in

no other possible situation during the war, have been so fatal to our cause.

That much trouble was taken and finesse used to misguide & bewilder Sir Henry Clinton in regard to the real object, by fictitious communications, as well as by making a deceptive provision of Ovens, Forage & Boats in his Neighbourhood, is certain. Nor were less pains taken to deceive our own Army; for I had always conceived, when the imposition did not completely take place at home, it could never sufficienty succeed abroad.[1]

Your desire of obtaining truth is very laudable, I wish I had more leizure to gratify it as I am equally solicitous the undisguised verity should be known. Many circumstances will unavoidably be misconceived & misrepresented. Notwithstanding most of the Papers which may properly be deemed official are preserved yet the knowledge of innumerable things, of a more delicate & secret nature, is confined to the perishable remembrance of some few of the present generation. With esteem I am—Sir Your Most Obedt Hble Servt

Go: Washington

ALS, NNPM; LB, DLC:GW. Webster wrote on the cover, twice, "Genl Washington Mount Vernon July 31 1788. published in my Essay, page 180."

On 22 April 1812 Benjamin Rush reported to John Adams a conversation that he had had with Timothy Pickering regarding this letter of 31 July 1788 from GW to Noah Webster: "Colonel Pickering made me a visit [in 1791] and, finding me alone, spent a long evening with me. We had a multitude of conversation. I had then lately purchased Mathew Carey's *American Museum*, the ninth volume of which then lay upon my table. Colonel Pickering, observing the book, said he was acquainted with the work and particularly with that volume of it; and there was a letter in it that he was extremely sorry to see there. I asked what letter is that? Col. Pickering answered, 'It is a letter from General Washington.'. . . You, my Friend Rush, by looking into the 282nd page of that 9th volume, will find a letter from George Washington dated Mount Vernon, July 31st, 1788.

"Col. Pickering said he was extremely sorry to see that letter in print. I asked him why? What do you see amiss in it? What harm will it do? Col. Pickering said, 'It will injure General Washington's character.' How will it injure him? Stratagems are lawful in war. Colonel Pickering answered me, 'It will hurt his moral character. He has been generally thought to be honest and I own I thought his morals were good, but that letter is false, and I know it to be so. I knew him to be vain and weak and ignorant, but I thought he was well meaning; but that letter is a lie, and I know it to be so.' I objected and queried.

"Pickering explained and descended to particulars. He said it was false in

Washington to pretend that he had meditated beforehand to deceive the enemy and to that end to deceive the officers and soldiers of his own army; that he had seriously meditated an attack upon New York for near a twelvemonth and had made preparations at an immense expense for that purpose. Washington never had a thought of marching to the southward, till the Count de Grasse's fleet appeared upon the coast. He knew it, and Washington knew it; consequently that letter was a great disgrace" (*The Spur of Fame: Dialogues of John Adams and Benjamin Rush, 1805–1813*, ed. John A. Schutz and Douglass Adair [San Marino, Calif., 1966], 212–13). Pickering continued to insist until as late as 1825 that GW had misrepresented the facts in this letter (see Pickering to Richard Peters, 12 Feb. 1825, MHi: Pickering Papers).

A close reading of GW's Yorktown journal, through August 1781, casts some doubt about the accuracy of GW's memory regarding the timing of the decision "that New York was thought to be beyond our effort & consequently that the only hesitation that remained was between an attack upon the British Army in Virginia or that in Charleston [S.C.]," which GW appears to say, here, was made "nearly twelve months before hand." For instance, in his journal, or diary, under the date of 1 Aug. 1781, three weeks before marching from New York with his army to Virginia, GW wrote: "Thus circumstanced . . . I could scarce see a ground upon wch. to continue my preparations against New York—especially as there was much reason to believe that part (at least) of the Troops in Virginia were recalled to reinforce New York and therefore I turned my views more seriously (than I had before done) to an operation to the Southward . . ." (*Diaries*, 3:404–5).

# To Thomas Newton, Jr.

Sir,                                    Mount Vernon August 1st 1788

Your letters of the 14th & 19 Ulto came duly to hand, as did the sample of Shingles by Captn Slacum.[1] I did not conceive that under the present dearth of Cash that the price of this article would have been so high as you mentioned.

Capt. Slacum, with whom I have conversed on this subject, thinks as you do, that Juniper Shingles would answer my purpose as well as any other would—and suggested farther, the propriety (their[2] covering being intended for a Barn) of making it of 3 feet shingles instead of 18 Inches which (according to his account) are of sufficient thickness and run from 7 to 10 Inches broad—suppose 8 Inches on an average the price he says is 7 or 8 Dollars pr M[3]—but whether he meant delivered here, or that it was the price at the place of Exportation it did not *at the time* occur to me to ask him. If the former, & he is right as to the weadth &c. tho' the original cost of them would amount to about the same as 18 Inch shingles, yet as I should save in the Articles of Nails, laths &c. they would be preferable.

Under this statement, if you could send me 25,000, the money (except for the freight which I would pay on delivery) to be paid in 3 or 4 Months (which is as soon as I could Raise it from my Wheat or Barley) I should be very glad to have them forwarded to me without delay; & shall depend on your doing the whole on the best terms, for me—pray let me hear from you immediately as the Walls of my building will soon require a roof.[4] If these cannot be had or do not come up to Captn Slacums discription, I must in that case request you to send me 100,000 18 Inch Shingles (if to be had on the above credit) of Juniper, agreeably to your own account of them. I am &ca

Go. Washington

LB, DLC:GW.

1. Neither of Newton's letters has been found, but see GW to Newton, 7 July, n.1. George Slacum (Slackum) was captain of the packet boat that ran between Norfolk and Alexandria.

2. The copyist wrote "they."

3. The copyist wrote "M."

4. Brissot de Warville describes the nearly finished barn which he saw when he visited Mount Vernon in November as "a huge one" (Warville, *New Travels*, 343). See also *Diaries*, 5:272.

## From William Pierce

Sir                        Savannah August 1st 1788.

I enclose you a small pamphlet which contains an Oration that I delivered in Savannah on the 4th ultimo. Independant of the common ceremony practised on these occasions I present it to you with the highest sentiments of respect and esteem. With honor I subscribe myself Your obedient servant

Wm Pierce

ALS, DLC:GW.

1. William Pierce's pamphlet *An Oration, Delivered at Christ Church, Savannah, on the 4th July, 1788* was delivered before the Georgia Society of the Cincinnati and was printed in Savannah.

2. GW acknowledged on 1 Sept. the receipt of Pierce's letter and enclosure: "Sir, I am happy to find that the same patriotic sentiments have been displayed, throught the Union, by the Citizens of America and particularly by

those who were formerly members of the Army, on the ⟨XII⟩ Anniversary of Independence. That you might not apprehend your letter of the 1st of August, had miscarried throh, the great distance of the way, or that I had received your agreeable Present without feeling a due sense of the favour; I have concluded to take an early opportunity of rendering my best acknowledgments for your Oration and of assuring you that I am, with great regard, Sir, Your most obedt &c. Hble Servant Go. Washington" (LB, DLC:GW).

*Letter not found*: from William Stephens Smith, 1 Aug. 1788. GW wrote Smith on 30 Aug.: "I was favoured, a few days ago, with your letter, dated the first day of this Month."

## To George Gilpin and John Fitzgerald

Gentn                                           Mount Vernon Augt 2d 1788
    As Monday next is the day on which the Directors, by the Constitution of the Company, are to make their report—and it has generally fallen to the lott of those on the Virginia side of the river to do this; I beg that you would from the minutes to which you are accessable—or from memory, bring forward the occurrences which may be proper to report at the General Meeting, about to be held. If this be delayed untill the day, there may be omissions which *might* involve censure, at least incur the charge of inattention. I will be in Town by 10 'Oclock on Monday. The Treasurer should have his accts ready for exhibition[1]—I am with much esteem & regard—Gentn Yr Most Obt Servt
                                                        Go: Washington

ALS, CSmH.
    1. GW went "up to alexandria" on Monday, 4 Aug. "to a meeting of the Potomack Company; the business of which was finished about Sun down." He remained in town for the night for the meeting of the directors the next day (*Diaries*, 5:373). GW made his annual report to the Potomac River Company on 4 Aug.: "The President & Directors of the Potomack Company beg leave to report that, since the general Meeting of last year by which they were instructed to Petition the Legislatures of the two States to pass an Act Obliging the delinquent Subscribers to pay their respective Quotas in a more summary way than by the common course of Law they now have the pleasure to inform the Company that such Laws have been obtained which they expect will be competent to the intention although the good Effects of them have not been as yet very productive.
    "Since the call of Six ℔Cent laid before the last meeting We have been under the Necessity, from the Delinquency of the Subscribers, to call for Six & one

half ₱Cent more which in the whole makes ⟨40⟩ ₱Cent on each share subscribed.

"For the several orders in conducting the Business intrusted to our care We beg leave to refer you to the Secretary's Books The unusual hieght of the Waters this Spring & Summer have greatly retarded our Operations on the river but should the Weather become more favorable we have reason to believe that a partial though not a perfect Navigation may be effected this fall & winter from Fort Cumberland down to the great falls—at which latter place the Canal is nearly completed[.] Our principal force has been applied to the Shenandoah & Seneca Falls, which, considering the Number of hands & unfavorable Season are in as great forwardness as we could expect.

"It appears to us by the Books of the Treasurer which you have had before you that the Sum paid unto his hands since our last report amount to £2990.2.2 Sterling which added to the former sum received makes Thirteen Thousand Seven Hundred & Nineteen Pounds Eighteen Shillings & Six pence Sterling in which are to be consider'd the Servants Utensils &ca on hand belonging to the Company agreeably to the Lists herewith submitted to you. G: Washington P." (DS, NIC).

# To John Jay

Dear Sir,                                   Mount Vernon Augt 3d 1788.

The letters which you did me the favor of writing to me on the 17th & 23d of last Month from Poughkeepsie, came duly to hand, & claim my particular acknowledgments.

With peculiar pleasure I now congratulate you on the success of your labours to obtain an unconditional ratification of the proposed Constitution in the Covention of your State; the acct of which, was brought to us by the mail of yesterday.

Although I could hardly conceive it possible, after ten states had adopted the Constitution, that New York, seperated as it is from the remaining three—and so peculiarly devided in sentiments as it is—would withdraw herself from the Union; yet, considering the great majority which appeared to cling together in the Convention, and the decided temper of the leaders in the opposition I did not, I confess, see the means by which it was to be avoided.

The exertion of those who were able to effect this great work, must have been equally arduous and meritorious. It is to be hoped that the State of North Carolina will not spend much time in deciding upon this question and as to Rhode Island, its conduct hitherto has so far baffled all calcuation that few are disposed to hazard a conjecture thereon. With sentiments of the sincerest esteem & regard I am Dear Sir Yr Most Obedt & Affecte Servt

Go: Washington

ALS, NNC; LB, DLC:GW.

## To James Madison

My dear Sir,                              Mount Vernon Augt 3d 1788.

Your favors of the 21st & 27th of last month came duly to hand.[1] The last, contained the pleasing—and I may add (tho' I could not reconcile it with any ideas I entertained of common policy) unexpected account of the unconditional ratification of the Consitution by the State of New York—That No. Carolina will hesitate long in its choice I can scarcely believe; but what Rhode Island will do is more difficult to say, though not worth a conjecture; as the conduct of the Majority there, has, hitherto, baffled all calculation.

The place proper for the New Congress to meet at, will, unquestionably, undergo (if it has not already done it) much investigation; but there are certain things which are so self evident in their nature as to speak for themselves—this, possibly, may be one—where the true point lays I will not undertake to decide, but there can be no hesitation I conceive in pronouncing one thing, that in all Societies, if the bond or cement is strong and interesting enough to hold the body together, the several parts should submit to the inconveniencies for the benefits which they derive from the conveniencies of the compact.

We have nothing in these parts worth communicating. Towards New York we look for whatever is interesting, until the States begin to act under the New form, which will be an important epocha in the annals of this Country. With sentiments of sincere friendship and affection I am—Yours

Go: Washington

ALS, MA; LB, DLC:GW.

1. Madison's letter of 27 July has not been found.

# To Thomas Nelson, Jr.

My dear Sir, Mount Vernon August 3d 1788

Your letter of the 19th Ulto came duly to hand and could I have been of any service in the affair to which it refers no apology would have been necessary for requesting it.[1] I have no white Ditcher with me at present but a Dutch Redemptioner[2]—Nor has there *ever* lived with me one—to the best of my recollection—of the name of Clarke. *Last year* I employed a man who called himself James Lawson—He worked for me about nine Months as a Ditcher and left my employment in very bad health in the month of September since which I have not hea[r]d from him.[3] Two or three years before that one William Skilling died in my Service as a Ditcher—these are all the white persons I have employed in that way since my return to private life.

Far, very far indeed was it from my intention to embarrass you by the letter which enclosed the proceedings of the Genl Convention—and still farther was it from my wish that the communication should be received in any other light than as an instance of my attention and Friendship. I was well aware that the adoption or rejection of the Constitution would, as it ought to be, decided upon according to its merits & agreeably to the circumstances to which our public affairs had arriven. That all questions of this kind are, ever will—and perhaps ought to be (to accomplish the designs of infinite wisdom) viewed through different mediums by different men is as certain as that they have existance—all that can be expected in such cases therefore is charrity mutual-forbearance and acquiescence in the Genl voice; which, though it may be wrong is presumably right.[4]

Mrs Washington unites with me in every good wish for Mrs Nelson, yourself and family—and with sentiments of the highest esteem and friendship I am—my Dear Sir—Yrs &c.

Go. Washington

LB, DLC:GW.

1. Letter not found.

2. GW is referring to Daniel Overdonck whom he "bought the time of" in November 1786. See the exchange of letters between GW and Philip Marsteller, 27 Nov. 1786.

3. The last entry under James Lawson's account indicates that Lawson quit GW's service on 18 Aug. 1787 "without any previous notice" (Ledger B, 237).

4. In his missing letter of 19 July Nelson evidently took issue with GW's

letter enclosing a copy of the Constitution that GW sent to Nelson on 24 Sept. 1787, as he also did to Benjamin Harrison and Patrick Henry. At the time that GW sent the letters, Nelson was speaker of the house of delegates, Harrison was president of the Virginia senate, and Henry was the state's governor.

*Letter not found*: from Annis Boudinot Stockton, 3 Aug. 1788. On 31 Aug. GW thanked Mrs. Stockton for her "kind letter of the 3d instant."

## To Clement Biddle

Dear Sir,                                    Mount Vernon August 4th 1788
   Your letter of the 30th Ulto came to my hands by the last mail.

   Let me request that those articles which you propose to send me by Captn Ellwood may be accompained by 200 lbs. of *Sheet* Iron from the Trenton Works (proper for plating the Mould boards of Plows)—and a Jarr of best Spirma ceti Oil for House Lamps—That is a clear fine Oil which does not foul them—The Velvet Ribbon came safe and was Just the kind I wanted, and for your care in forwarding it so expeditiously I beg you to accept my thanks.

   As the price of Porter according to your Account has not been enhanced and is good in quality, I beg, if this letter gets to hand in time, that you would add another groce to the one ordered in my former letter.

   I want a pump for a well on a farm yard which is 13½ feet deep—how much it will require to be above the ground *I* certainly, know not—but say six feet. no cap is necessary because it will be under cover. What would such an on[e], made fit for use cost in Philadelphia?—and what the freight of it round? Your answer will determin whether I shall import one from that place or get one made in Alexandria where the price asked is, I think, unreasonable.[1] I am Dear Sir Yrs &c.

Go. Washington

LB, DLC:GW. The ALS was offered for sale by Sotheby and Co. in 1931.

   1. No answer regarding the pump has been found in any of Biddle's extant letters to GW.

## To James Craik

Dear Sir,                                    Mount Vernon August 4th 1788
With this letter you will receive the Horse I promised you; And which I now beg your acceptance of. He is not in such good order as I could wish, but as good as my means would place him.

I also send you Thirty pounds Cash for one years allowance for the Schooling of your Son G.W. I wish it was in my power to send the like sum for the other year, which is now about, or near due; and that could discharge your account for attendance and ministrens to the Sick of my family—but it really is not; for with much truth I can say, I never felt the want of money so sensibly since I was a boy of 15 years old as I have done for the last 12 Months and probably shall do for 12 Months more to come.[1] Sincerely and affectly I am Yrs &c.

Go. Washington

LB, DLC:GW.
1. GW entered in his diary on 31 Aug. 1785: "This day I told Doctr. Craik that I would contribute One hundred Dollars pr. Ann., as long as it was necessary, towards the Education of His Son Geo. Washington either in this Country or in Scotland" (*Diaries*, 4:188). After completing his education, GW's old friend's son George Washington Craik (1774–1808) practiced law in Alexandria briefly before becoming GW's private secretary in 1796.

## From Charles Pettit

Sir                                    Philadelphia 5th August 1788
On a Subject so pleasing as the Prospect of an established Government on Principles which bid fair to secure the Benefits of Society to the Citizens of the United States, Your Excellency will excuse me in approaching you with my hearty Congratulations.

The excellent Sentiments conveyed to the World in your circular Letter of the 18th of June 1783, confirmed and methodized in my Mind Ideas which before had been but indigested Conceptions, and reduced to some Degree of Systematic Order on a republican Plan, those Principles and Maxims which, tho' well known to be essential to the public Prosperity under any Form of Government, I was much at a Loss how to apply with proper Effect in our novel Situation, till the plan of Government lately framed made its Appearance.[1] The Confederation of 1777

could operate with proper Force no longer than the Glow of
Zeal for the public Good was kept far above the natural Pitch,
by the combined Influence of common Danger, and the Resentment which that Danger excited against the Authors of it. As this
Zeal subsided, the Weakness of the fœderal Government was
discovered; and long before the Peace the Want of energetic
Power in Congress became alarming to the discerning Friends
of this Revolution; but not sufficiently so to the People at large
to induce them to add the necessary Powers. The Construction
of Congress was, however, a great, if not the principal Cause
of Reluctance to vest them with Powers adequate to a proper
fœderal Government. To combine the Legislative, Executive
& Judicial Powers of Government in one Body of Men, was
thought incompatible with the fundamental Principles of Liberty and Safety; and that inequality of Representation, which
gave to the smallest States an equal Voice in the disposal of Property with those which were to contribute in a tenfold Proportion,
was thought to be unjust.

The new Plan, now so happily approaching to Maturity, removes these Objections in a great Degree. It comes nearer to my
Ideas of Perfection than I could have expected in a first Essay of
any representative Body, having so many Difficulties to encounter as must have presented themselves to the general Convention. And tho' I am one of those that suppose some Amendments
ought to be early made in it, yet I am clearly of Opinion that the
Road to political Safety and Happiness is through the Adoption
of it as it is, and that the Amendments be made in a Mode compatible with the concurrent exercise of it as a Constitution. That
a considerable Proportion of the People of this State have been
of a different Opinion, has arisen more from the indiscreet Measures and Modes of the Advocates for an early Adoption than
from a refractory Disposition of the People. The Men who have
been most stigmatized on this Occasion, as factious antifederalists, have generally distinguished themselves as the Friends of
good Order and just Government; and have on all Occasions
manifested a good Disposition towards supporting the fœderal
Government, and cloathing it with the necessary Powers for its
due Operation. But on this Occasion the Change proposed was
great and Sudden: the Plan laid before them was entirely new,
and involved in it so many important Considerations which in

their Apprehension required deliberate Examination & Discussion, that they wanted Time and Opportunity allowed them for this Purpose. The Prejudices of the Minority in the general Convention were, moreover, communicated to divers of the leading Members of the Assembly from the Country, at least as early as the Plan itself came to their Knowledge; they therefore viewed it, on its first Appearance, through the Medium of these Prejudices. Under such Circumstances, unfavourable Impressions were naturally to be expected, but I believe an Idea never entered their Minds of preventing its being laid before the People, and fairly taking their Sense upon it in the Manner recommended by the general Convention. A reasonable Time for its Circulation amongst the People previous to their Election of Delegates to decide upon it in State Convention, was all they demanded. This was denied them in a Manner that became too notorious to escape general Notice. These Measures, instead of conciliating, inflamed their Minds; gave deeper Root to their Prejudices, and excited fresh Jealousies and Suspicions which otherwise would not probably have had Existence. In this Situation of Affairs the Elections for a State Convention were hurried on. Scarcely a fifth Part of the Voters gave their Suffrages: the rest, especially those remote from the City, either from Indolence, or not having had Time and Opportunity to form Satisfactory Judgment of the Subject to be decided upon, remained inactive. Hence the Minority in the Convention conceived that a Majority of the People in the State were of their Opinion, and would oppose the operation of the Plan, notwithstanding the Majority of the Convention had agreed to adopt it; and for a Time there was much Reason to apprehend that the government would have been improved, and the Peace of the State, if not of the Union, endangered by the Frenzy of a Zeal thus inflamed and misapplied. The little Influence I have with these People, of whose Principles, Integrity, and good Intentions I have a very favourable Opinion, has been exercised to moderate their Jealousies and remove their Prejudices so as to give their reasoning Faculties fair Operation. What Effect my Endeavours have had, I will not pretend to say; but whatever may have been the Causes of their change of Temper, it is with great Pleasure that I now find Reason to believe that they will not only acquiesce peaceably, but cooperate in the Organization of the new

Plan of Government, and content themselves with asking in a constitutional Mode the Amendments they desire.

This being the present Temper & Disposition of the People of Pennsylvania, who have been thus peculiarly irritated, and, as it were, driven into a Degree of Intemperance incompatible with their usual Conduct and Character, we may reasonably hope for a general Acquiescence in the People of the other States, who have taken as much Time as they chose for Deliberation and Discussion before they came to a Decision or committed the Power of deciding to others. Hence I conclude that the Object is in a great Measure gained, and the Foundation of political Happiness securely laid: And I trust that the Wisdom and Fortitude, which under the Guidance of a superintending Providence has established our Independance, and thus far united us in a Plan for the peaceable Enjoyment of it, will procure in Fruition what we have hardly yet ta[s]ted but in Prospect.[2]

Having thus far intruded on your Excellency concerning the Public, permit me to solicit your Patience while I say a few Words concerning myself. To have served the Public with Fidelity has ever been a Recommendation to your favourable Notice: to have performed such Service with splendid Abilities, could not fail to strengthen the Recommendation. To the latter, however, I make no Claim, tho' I feel a Consciousness that I have some Title to the former. If I had attended to my own Interest with as much Care and Assiduity as I bestowed on that of the Public, the fair Emoluments of my Station would have been so improved as to place me in a Situation of Ease & Independance: if I had availed myself of the Opportunities my Situation afforded, to acquire all that I *legally* might have acquired, I might have abounded in Wealth. But the latter I could not perfectly reconcile to my Ideas of Fidelity; and the former I was restrained from, as well in some Measure to save Appearances lest the Public should suffer by an Opinion that its Servants were enriching themselves in a Time of Calamity, as because my Time was too much engaged in public Cares to admit of due Attention to private Concerns. At the same Time an undue Confidence (as the Event has proved it) in the Abilities & Justice of the Public, led me to deposit in their Hands not only the greater Part of my Earnings in the Service, but the Property I had before acquired. Hence I remain a public Creditor for nearly all that I am worth; not by speculative Purchases at a low Value, but by original Loans, and by Certificates taken in Exchange for Property at their nominal Value. I am not unaware that by this Declaration I arraign my own Prudence, and perhaps depreciate my Judgment. The Spirit of Party has imputed to me much more Wealth than I possess, together with considerable Acquisitions by speculating in the public Funds. The part I took in my Endeavours to obtain Justice to be done to the Public Creditors, will explain the Motives for raising such Reports, especially when it is known that they originated with, or at least obtained a Currency from a person of great Wealth, and at that Time in high Station, who took especial Care that the Public should never become his Debtor, and who wished to avoid contributing anything towards the Payment of others. It is my Misfortune, however, that these Reports are void of Truth; and that on the Contrary I am, in the present Situation of public Credit, almost entirely dependant on the Produce of Industry for the Means of supporting a Family, at a Time of Life when I expected to enjoy Ease in domestic Affairs, if not Ability to advance my Progeny in the World. My fellow Citizens have frequently honored me with their Suffrages, and are still desirous of placing me in a representative Capacity. It is not a little mortifying, after twenty years Employment chiefly in the public Service, to be obliged to decline Honors of this kind, and at the same Time to seek for Employment of more Emolument, tho' less honorable; and yet while my little Capital is thus withheld from me, Necessity imposes on me this Choice. The Organization of the new Government will necessarily call for confidential Servants of the Public. If I should be deemed worthy of your Excellency's Patronage, I may be thought of in the arrangement; at the same Time I beg Leave to assure you that I wish not to stand in the Way of more deserving Objects, nor to occasion you a Moment's Embarrassment on my Account.[3]

I have now to request your Pardon for this Intrusion. I hope my Congratulations will be as acceptable as they are sincere; and that what I have said concerning the People of Pennsylvania may have a tendency to place them in a more just point of View than they may have been exhibited in by some other Reports. As to what I have said concerning myself, if it should be found to have any tincture of unpleasantness mingled with its Effects, I have only to request that it may be forgiven and forgotten. As a Citizen I feel too much Gratitude for your eminent Services, and as a public Servant too much a Respect for your Person to suffer me willingly to occasion the least Interruption to your Happiness. With fervent wishes for your continued Prosperity, I have the Honor to be Your Excellency's most obedient & most humble Servant

Chas Pettit

ALS, DLC:GW.

1. Pettit is referring to GW's long circular to the states which was dated variously from 8 to 21 June 1783. This document is often referred to as "Washington's Legacy."

2. For the career of Charles Pettit, and for GW's correspondence with him in 1787 and 1788 regarding the making of firebacks for the fireplaces at Mount Vernon, see the notes in GW to Pettit, 7 Sept. 1787.

3. In a cordial response on 16 Aug., GW ignores Pettit's hints about employment in the new federal system. On 24 May 1789, and again on 19 Mar. 1791, 22 Oct. 1793, and 24 Feb. 1794, Pettit made direct applications to GW for an office in his administration, but he did not receive an appointment.

## To Hector St. John Crèvecoeur

Sir,                                        Mount Vernon Augt 6th 1788.

The enclosed packet came under cover to me, yesterday; The Box which ought to have accompanied it is yet on Ship-board, in the lower part of this River. I have requested that it may be forwarded to me without delay. When it arrives I will send it to the Stage Office and desire that particular attention may be paid to it.[1]

Conceiving it to be best not to detain the letters for the arrival of the Box is the cause of your receivg this trouble, at this time; accompanied with assurances of the esteem and respect with which I have the honor to be Sir Your Most Obedt and Most Hble Servant

Go: Washington

ALS (photocopy), DLC: Crèvecoeur Papers.

1. GW wrote Crèvecoeur again on 14 Aug., saying: "Herewith is forwarded, the parcel referred to in my last. It came to my hands yesterday, and I hope will get safe to yours as it is particularly recommended to the care of the Post master in Alexandria" (ALS, DLC: Crèvecoeur Papers). The packet of letters and the parcel from Lafayette, directed to Crèvecoeur and intended for Brissot

de Warville, apparently came to GW via James Swan through Christopher Gadsden. See GW to Christopher Gadsden and to James Swan, both 18 August.

# To Samuel Hanson

Sir,                                        Mount Vernon August 6th 1788

On my return home last night I found my Nephew Lawrence here—who said he was affraid to remain at your House and offered to shew me some bruises he had received. Being prepared for it, I was going this morning to correct him, but he begged so earnestly, and promised so faithfully that there should be no cause of complaint against him for the future that I have suspended the Punishment.[1]

The letter which I have written to his Brother on the subject, is under this cover and open for your perusal[2]—He is arrived at that *age* and *size* now as to be a fitter subject to be reasoned with than to receive corporal punishment. and my primary object in placing these boys with you, *last*, was that they (at least George) Should be treated more on the footing of Friendship, and as companians, tha[n] as *mere* School-boy's—This, I hoped, would draw Georges attention to objects, and conversations, that would improve, and might contribute in a *degree* to wean him from boyish amusements—the influence of which would extend to Lawrence.

Necessary and decent Clothes they shall have no cause to complain for the want of; and if you, Sir, once a month, or oftener, would be so obliging as to inspect them, & let me know what they need I will take care that they shall be provided. A line from one of them, lodged at the Post, signifying their desire of sending things to my Taylor to repair will induce the occasunal call of a servant which may be sent to Town on other business[3]—with esteem I am Sir Yrs &c.

                                                    Go. Washington

LB, DLC:GW.

1. Hanson told GW on Monday, 4 Aug., when GW was in Alexandria, of his intention to punish Lawrence Washington with a whipping. See Hanson to GW, 7 August.

2. See GW to George Steptoe Washington, this date.

3. See George Steptoe Washington to GW, 8 Aug., n.1.

*Letter not found*: from Thomas Smith, 6 Aug. 1788. On 15 Sept. GW wrote Smith: "Your favour of the 6th Ult. came duly to hand."

## To George Steptoe Washington

Dear George,                          Mount Vernon August 6th 1788

It was with equal pain and surprize I was informed by Colo. Hanson on Monday last, of your unjustifiable behaviour in rescuing your brother from that chastisement which was due to his improper conduct; and which you know, because you have been told it in explicit language, he was authorized to administer whensoever he should deserve it.[1]

Such refractory behaviour on your part, I consider as an insult equally offered to myself after the above communications and I shall continue to view it in that light, till you have made satisfactory acknowledgments to Colo. Hanson for the offence given him.[2]

It is as much my wish and intention to see Justice done to you and your Brother as it is to punish either when it is merited—but there are proper modes by whch this is to be obtained, and it is to be sought by a fair and candid representation of facts whch can be supported—and not by vague complaints disobedience, perverseness, or disobliging conduct, which make enemies without producing the smallest good.

So often, and strenuously have I endeavoured to inculcate this advice, and to Shew you the advantages which are to be expected from close application to your studies, that it is unnecessary to repeat it. If the admonitions of friendship are lost other methods must be tried which cannot be more disagreeable to you than it would be to one who wishes to avoid it who is solicitous to see you and your Brother (the only remaining Sons of your father) turn out well,[3] and who is very desirous of continuing your Affecte Uncle

                                        Go. Washington

LB, DLC:GW.

1. See GW to Samuel Hanson, 6 Aug., n.1.

2. For George Steptoe Washington's apology and defense, see his letter to GW of 8 August.

3. Samuel Washington's two eldest sons were Thornton Washington (c.1760–1787) and Ferdinand Washington (1767–1788). Ferdinand died of

consumption in Lancaster County in early February before his brother George Steptoe could reach his bedside (*Diaries*, 5:272, 278).

## From Samuel Hanson

Sir                                        Alexandria, 7th Augt 1788
   Your favour, per Mastr Lawrence, was handed to me last Night.[1]
   Any "bruises" he may be able to shew, were not, as he well knows, given by me *with design*, but may be the consequences of the struggle which ensued upon my attempt to take him into a room for chastisement. I am certain he did not receive more than 3 strokes, and these with a Whip. Whether they could occasion any *bruises*, you, Sir, will determine. After the declaration of my intention to flog him, made to you on Monday, and your approbation of my Conduct, I can have no inducement to misstate this matter. The fact is, more than 24 hours had elapsed between the offence, & my *attempt* to punish it; so that I cannot be supposed to have acted from the sudden impulse of passion. Indeed; I had become so cool, that I hesitated considerably upon the subject: and nothing but the necessity of asserting my authority (which *expressly* depended upon the issue of this affair) could have impelled me to such a disagreeable measure. This is the true state of the matter. When compared with the one given by Lawrence, it confirms the propriety of those deductions which you made from his former Accounts. I beg leave to remark that the reputation of those who undertake the accommodation of Boys, is much in their power, & that this circumstance is not the least irksome of those which attend the employment It is natural for Parents or Guardians to be partial to the representations of their children, or their Connections: and it is not every one who would have listened to them with the same allowances in my favour which you, Sir, have been pleased to make.
   It has been my wish to consider, & treat, your Nephews as friends rather than School-Boys. George will do me the justice to own that I always inform him when we expect Company to Tea, (which is the only kind we have had for a long time) that he may join in it. Lawrence has not had the same invitation from his being a great Sloven. It is with pleasure I repeat that George

is of an obliging, amiable disposition. But he is a little subject to the natural warmth of his temper. This, added to the puerile ambition of giving him self consequence with the smaller boys, may, in some measure, account for the occasional impropriety of his behaviour. An *adequate* Acct would, perhaps, go farther. To treat with *voluntary* respect a Person under the humiliating necessity of accommodating Boys for pay, requires, I fear, the exercise of more consideration, and liberality of sentiment, than usually fall to the lot of the young.

Your directions respecting their cloathes shall be strictly observed. The care & inspection of their Dress I have always considered as a part of the duty I owe them: and I have frequently urged them to address you upon this point, when there was occasion; & recommended the Post-office as a proper place for their Letters. with the utmost respect & Esteem, I am Sir your most obedt & most humble Servant

S. Hanson of Saml

ALS, DLC:GW.
1. GW's letter is dated 6 August.

## From George Richards Minot

Sir                                   Boston 7th August 1788

Permit me to offer for your perusal, a copy of the History of the late Insurrections &c. in Massachusetts. The share which you had, in the great and glorious events of America, must interest your feelings in all subsequent transactions; and, I hope, this little narrative will not be unacceptable to you, as a continuance of information, upon the important subject of domestick History.[1]

The difficulty of stating facts on the spot where they happen, and under the view of the actors, will readily occur; and must be my apology with you in reading the book. If this circumstance however, has had influence in checking the remarks of the writer, I hope it has had none, in the relating of the events, which is the part wherein the publick are most concerned.

General Lincoln has kindly offered to introduce my production to your notice; and, my confidence in the goodness of your character, has led me to anticipate a favourable reception to an effort, which was dictated by a love of truth, and a wish to pre-serve the reputation of the country.[2] With the highest respect, I am, Sir, Your most obedient, & most humble Servant,

George Richards Minot

ALS, DLC:GW.

George Richards Minot (1758–1802) studied law under William Tudor and was appointed clerk of the Massachusetts house of representatives in 1781. From January to February 1788, he served as secretary of the Massachusetts Ratifying Convention.

1. William Tudor had sent GW a copy of Minot's history of Shays' Rebellion on 26 July. See also GW to Minot, 28 August.

2. Minot's letter was sent from Boston under cover of the following letter to GW of 9 Aug. from Benjamin Lincoln: "I congratulate your Excellency on the adoption of the new constitution by your State and thank your Excellency for the information It is important to all that New York has at last come in. Things remain much as they were in this State—I have no doubt but that the people here will embrace the new constitution. Your Excellency will receive herewith Mr Minots history of the late rebellion in this State—He is a Gentle-man of the Law and has I think done as much justice to the subject as could be expected whilst the different parties are all on the stage" (DLC:GW).

*Letter not found*: from Thomas Newton, Jr., 8 Aug. 1788. On 10 Oct. GW wrote Newton about "Your letter of the 8th of August."

## From George Steptoe Washington

Dear Uncle                                        Alexandria Augt 8th 1788

I received your letter from Col. Hanson, and after consider-ing the contents, think it necessary to transmit to you an account of the late occurrence, in which you have been informed I acted an improper part; my object in writing this letter is not to ex-culpate m[y]self, it is only to state matters as they really were; whither my conduct was justifiable in doing what I have, I am not a judge, but with pleasure leave it to be determin'd by you when made acquainted with the circumstances of the case. You have been informed that Laurence has attended divine servise but once or twice, if the information was received from Col. Hanson I wish not to contradict him, but of late he has attended pretty constant, and the reason of his absence from Church that day, was on account of his coat, but of this also I am not to judge, if Col. Hanson thinks proper to correct him I acknolidge it is not my business to interfere, neither would I have had the least idea of doing it if it had been done in an orderly manner, especially since I know it to be your desire; but it was the manner in which it was done and the instrument with which it was to be performed that caused my interference; when it happened, I was in my way to school, but was recalled by the cries of Laurence (which drew the attention of the neighbours) calling me to his assistance; upon my spedy return I found him on the floor with Col. Hanson on the top of him and a cowhide laying on the table, alarmed at this unexpected sight, I enterposed, without thinking on what I was about to do, and even then I offered no insult to Col. Hanson, but hindered my brother from being beat with an instrument which I deemed improper to inflict a punishment for so slall a crime. This was what I did but no more, it was not to deny Col. Hansons authority, it was not to call in question the justise of his punishment. but I was driven to it by brotherly affection; If it has meet with your disapprobation, I am sorry for it, and if you continue to be of that opinion, I will make any concessions to Col. Hanson, and as what is done cannot be undone, I shall persue that only method of atonement for folly, to be sorry for it, and do so no more.

It ony remains that I should express my thanks for your kind advise and assuring you that I will never deviate from any instructions which I shall be favoured with from you; these are the unaltered intentions. Of Dear Uncle Your most Obedient Nephew

George S. Washington.

Both of us are in want of coats and a pair of breeche's.[1]

ALS, DLC:GW.

1. Ledger B contains the following entries for 22 Aug.: "By Messrs Geo. & Lawce Washington pd to Messr Porter & Ingraham on their Acct . . . 27.0.0[,] By ditto pd Rd Weightman for making their Cloaths . . . 5.2.7[,] By ditto pd for trimgs for making Cloaths for them . . . 0.4.5" (270).

# From Samuel Powel

Dear Sir                                   Philadelphia August 9. 1788

On board Capt. Ellwood, who sails for Alexandria Tomorrow, I have shipped an Arm-Chair for you, which he has promised to deliver at Mount-Vernon, if practicable, or to a Gentleman at Alexandria to whom, he says, he commonly delivers any Articles he carries from hence for you. It is a neat chair, & will, I hope, please you.

Mrs Powel desires me to apologize for it's having been so long delayed. The Fact is, that the Maker living near Trenton, she employed a Friend of her's to communicate her Ideas of the Form of it to him. But, from some Cause or other, nothing appeared to have been done in the Business, 'till I, accidentally met the Man & spoke to him. This I mention to account for the Delay. At present I fear it will not fully accord with your Ideas, as he said that a Circle in the Back to have received a Cushion, would weaken the chair; & it did not appear practicable to prevail on him to deviate from his accustomed Mode of working with any Prospect of Success. The chair, such as it is, is the neatest I have seen of his making; &, should you be desirous of having a Sett of them, may be made for less than Two dollars each. The tedious Time that you have waited for this Trifle, will not, I hope, deter you from honoring us with any little Commission that you may wish to have executed here, as it will ever give us real pleasure to be, in any way, serviceable to you.[1]

I hope that you have been more fortunate in your Saintfoin than myself. Some few of the Seeds that you were so obliging as to send me, vegetated—but the Plants are since dead. I imagine that the Heat of the Ship's Hold had destroyed their vegetative Powers.

Have you heard of the Machine for rubbing out Grain invented by Mr Winlaw? I have not seen it, but have had a Description of it from Mr Bordley of Wye River in Maryland, who is in possession of a very compleat one sent him by Governor Sharpe. I am told that it will rub, or thresh, between Fifty and an Hundred Bushells in a Day.[2]

The Accounts from New York are that Congress after appointing Baltimore as the Seat of the new Government, in a Committee of the whole House, rejected the Report of the Committee, & named New York as the Place, after agreeing upon this, it was found that Rhode Island could not, with propriety sign the Mandate for the Elections in the different States, so that the place of meeting is yet to be fixed upon.[3] Is not this manner of Proceeding destitute of all Dignity. I confess that as an American

I feel mortified at this trifling with the Sensibilites of the Union, which I believe were never more alive than on the present Occasion—But I trust all will yet end well.

Mrs Powel request to join in the best Wishes for you & Mrs Washington. I am, with real Regard dear Sir your most obedt humble Servt

Samuel Powel

Capt. Ellwood sends me Word that he shall not sail before Wednesday. I have seen a Letter from a Member of Congress which says the Rhode Island Delegates are gone home—that new caballing is taking Place, & that Lancaster in Pennsylvania is now much talked of as the future Seat of Government—Some of the southern States who are averse to meeting at Philadelphia, are it is said willing to concur in this Measure[4]—Rhode Island, is said to have formally rejected the new Constitution—I do not know from whence the writer derives his Information, as I have not heard of any Convention in that State. This Intelligence I have collected since closing the foregoing Page.

ALS, DLC:GW.

1. GW wrote Powel on 15 Sept. that the chair had just arrived and that he was pleased with it.

2. GW had not yet received Arthur Young's unfavourable report on the Winlaw thresher, written on 1 July. See also GW to Young, 1 Nov. 1787, and note 4 of that document.

3. See James Madison to GW, 21 July, n.2.

4. See note 3.

# To Clement Biddle

Dr Sir,                                     Mount Vernon August 10th 1788

Should this letter get to your hands in time for the Sailing of Captn Ellwood—and you can readily procure 25 bushls of the *best* kind of *Winter* Barley I beg you to send it by him that I may try the success of it—The continual rains destroyed my Crop of spring Barley this year—but, if it had been otherwise, the Barley which you sent me the year before was so mixed with Oats (a circumstance I did not know till this Summer, as it was harvested while I was in Philadelphia) that it would no longer do to sow it. Could I be supplied with a quantity of that (spring Barley) whi[c]h is really good from your City? Could I get it upon better terms from Rhode Island? and at what price (delivered here) might it be received from either place?[1]

If you send the 25 bushels of Winter Barley, let it be put in good 4 bushel Sacks marked G.W. and they will be useful thereafter. With esteem & regard I am Dr Sir Yrs &c.

Go. Washington

LB, DLC:GW.

    1. See Biddle's response, 17 August.

## From Brissot de Warville

Sir                          New York 10th Augst 1788

Not knowing precisely at what time I shall be able to go to Virginia to pay my respects, I take the resolution to address by the Post to you the annexed Letter, which the Marq. de la Fayette hath sent to me & in which he makes mention of me[1]—as it may contain news that may be interresting to you, I hasten to forward it.[2] I have the honor to be &c.

de Warville

Translation, by David Humphreys, DLC:GW; ALS, in French, DLC:GW. The ALS is in CD-ROM:GW.

    1. Lafayette's letter to GW is dated 25 May 1788.

    2. GW replied from Mount Vernon on 28 Aug.: "Sir, The letter which you did me the honor to address to me on the 10th of August accompanied by one from the Marquis de la Fayette, arrived by the last post. Whensoever you can make your Journey to Virginia convenient for yourself, I shall hope to have the pleasure of seeing you at Mount Vernon, and of testifying my regard for a gentleman who interests himself so much in the Wellfare and reputation of America. With sentiments of consideration and regard I have the honor to be &c. Go. Washington" (LB, DLC:GW).

## From James Madison

Dear Sir                      New York Augst 11. 1788

I have been duly favored with yours of the 3d instant. The length of the interval since my last has proceeded from a daily expectation of being able to communicate the final arrangements for introducing the new Government. The place of meeting has undergone much discussion as you conjectured and still remains to be fixed. Philada was first named, & negatived by a voice from Delaware. N. York came forward next. Lancaster was opposed to it & failed. Baltimore was next tried and to the surprise of every one had seven votes. It was easy to see that that ground had it been free from objections was not maintainable. Accordingly the next day N. York was inserted in the place of it with the aid of the vote of Rhode Island. Rhode Island however has refused to give a final vote in the business and has actually retired from Congress.[1] The question will now be resumed between N. York & Philada. It was much to be wished that a fit place for a respectable outset to the Govt could be found more central than either. The former is inadmissible if any regard is to be had to the Southern or Western Country. It is so with me for another reason, that it tends to stop the final & permanent seat short of the potowmac certainly, and probably in the State of N. Jersey. I *know* this to be one of the views of the Advocates for N. York. The only chance the potowmac has is to get things in such a train that a coalition may take place between the Southern & Eastern States on the subject, and still more that the final seat may be undecided for two or three years, within which period the Western & S. Western population will enter more into the estimate. Wherever Congress may be, the choice if speedily made will not be sufficiently influenced by that consideration. In this point of view I am of opinion Baltimore would have been unfriendly to the true object. It would have retained Congress but a moment, so many States being North of it, and dissatisfied with it, and would have produced a coalition among those States—a precipitate election of the permanent seat & an intermediate removal to a more northern position.

You will have seen the circular letter from the Convention of this State.[2] It has a most pestilent tendency. If an Early General Convention cannot be parried, it is seriously to be feared that the System which has resisted so many direct attacks may be at last successfully undermined by its enemies. It is now perhaps to be wished that Rho. Island may not accede till this new crisis of danger be over. Some think it would have been better if even N. York had held out till the operation of the Government could have dissipated the fears which artifice had created and the attempts resulting from those fears & artifices. We hear nothing yet from N. Carolina more than comes by the way of Petersburg. With the highest respect & attachment I remain Dr Sir, your affecte servt

Js Madison Jr

ALS, DLC:GW; copy, DLC: Madison Papers. Madison's copy is incorrectly dated 15 August.

1. See Madison to GW, 21 July, n.2.
2. Governor George Clinton as president of the New York Ratifying Convention signed a circular letter addressed to the executives of the other states calling for the state legislatures to push for another general convention to consider amendments to the Constitution. GW found this quite alarming; see, for instance, the third paragraph of his long letter to Henry Lee, 22 September.

## From Charles Love, Jr.

Sir                                          Boyds hole 12th August 1788

The Bearer has my instructions to deliver you 50-Barrels of Corn on a/c of Wm Hunter Junr Esqr. which I hope will get to hand in time to answer your purpose although much later than I wished or expected when I last had the pleasure of seeing you—However Sir should you be supplyed be pleased [to] order the Skipper to proceed on to Alexandria, as it will be no Inconvenience to Mr Hunter or myself, should you decline receiving the Corn.[1] I am Sir very Respectfully Your Most Obdt Servt

Charles Love Junr

ALS, DLC:GW.
1. Charles Love, Jr., son of Samuel Love (d. 1787) of Prince William County, again wrote GW on 2 April 1789 from Boyd's Hole, a small trading center on the Potomac River in Stafford (later King George) County. William Hunter, Jr., was a merchant in Alexandria.

## From Neil McCoull

Sir                                  Fred[ericksbur]g 12th Augt 1788

I have your Bond ℀ £450 dated 12th Decemr 1774 & payable 10th Novemr 1775 to Mr Alexr Blair & myself—Mr Blair being since deceased I am to request you will write me how soon it will be convenient to you to take up this Bond[1] and am very respectfully—Sir Your mo: Obt hu: Servt

Neil McCoull

ALS, DLC:GW.

1. GW wrote to James Mercer from Mount Vernon on 17 Aug.: "Dear Sir, By the last Post I received the enclosed letter from Mr McCoull—to whh I have given the answer that accompanies it. I pray your direction for my conduct, as there can be little doubt, of Mr McCoulls intention to prosecute the Bond—since he has made application for payment of it after what has passed between you and him on the subject. I am Dr Sir, Yrs &c. Go. Washington" (LB, DLC:GW). On the same day GW wrote McCoull: "Sir, In answer to your letter of the 12th inst. The Honble Judge Mercer (with whom I have settled for the Bond therein mentioned and to whom I beg leave to refer) can better than I, inform you, and I hope he will do it satisfactorily, of the circumstances which attends this case. I am &c. G. Washington" (LB, DLC:GW). James Mercer had agreed to relieve GW of the payment of £450 for George Mercer's half of Four Mile Run tract which GW purchased in 1774, in return for GW's crediting the John Mercer estate with the payment of that amount on its debt to GW. For a fuller explanation of this, see GW to James Mercer, 19 Nov. 1786, n.1.

Neil McCoull and Alexander Blair were the Virginia attorneys for English creditors of the late George Mercer.

# From Thomas Thomson

Sir                    Nomony Westmoreland 12 Augst 1788

The distress'd Situation of a Family in who's welfare & happiness I am much interested, must plead my apology for thus addressing a person to whom I am unknown But the people of America both collectively and as individuals have long been taught to look up to your excellency for Assistance & protection against the worst of all evils, that of Slavery.

The circumstance that has induced me to Address your excellency on this Occasion, is the very unhappy fate, of a very deserving Gentleman, a Dr William Spence, who left Great Britain with a Wife & Child in Septr 81, to return to his native Country, having been Sent to Britain for his Education when a Boy, they took their passage with many others, both Americans & British on board the Buckskin Hero, Capt. Gordon for New york, they had a prosperous voyage for 30 days, & Suppos'd themselves within 2 or 3 days Sail of Sandy hook, as Appears by a Letter wrote by the D[octo]r to his friends in Glasgow, dated the 24th of Octr & Sent by a vessel they spoke at Sea—Since that time 'till the 3d of April last no Acct was ever heard of them, and it was confidently believ'd the Ship had foundred at Sea. But by the Information of a certain James Joshua Rynolds of Philadelphia Just return'd from Slavery at Algiers, & who's narrative I have inclos'd for your excellencys perusal, it appears that the Buckskin Hero was captured by the Algerins, and condemn'd as American property having first destroy'd her mediterranian pass; She had a very rich cargo on Board, which was too great a temptation for an Algerin to with stand, by which means the Ships Company & about 30 passengers have been carried into Slavery In Such a case, & under Such circumstances, might I hope your excellency would be so good as to interest yourself with the Court of France in behalf of this unhappy Family. I am perfectly perswaded, that Court would get the matter laid before the Regency of Algiers, by their Consul there in consiquence of your recommendation, with very probable hopes of redress.[1]

I am so well Satisfied Sir with your inclination to assist the unfortunate, that I need say nothing more on this Occasion to engage your feelings & humanity in the Interest of this distress'd family I can only add that it will greatly aleviate the Grief of the unhappy Mother of Dr Spence if you Should Espouse his cause, & lay under obligations a person who is with due Respect your Excellencys most obdt Humble Servt

Thos Thomson

P.S. This will be deliverd by George Thomson half Brother to the unhappy Sufferer Dr Spence who will receive any Answer you may pleas to give, & get it forewarded to its place of destination. T.T.

ALS, DLC:GW.

1. An entry in GW's diary for 23 Aug. reads: "A Mr. George Thompson, from the Academy in Alexandria with a letter to me from his father Doctr. Thompson respecting his Son in law Doctr. Spence . . . came here to dinner" (*Diaries*, 5:382). Dr. Thomas Thomson of Westmoreland County was the stepfather of William Spence, the son of his second wife. Spence took his medical degree at Glasgow in 1780 before sailing the next year for New York. For GW's efforts to ascertain whether the *Buckskin Hero* was among the ships taken

by the Algerine pirates and for the confirmation that it was not, see GW to Thomson, 24 Aug., 18 Sept., and GW to Thomas Barclay, 31 Aug., 18 Sept. See also James Madison to Thomas Jefferson, 8 Oct. 1788, and Jefferson to Madison, 12 Jan. 1789 (Rutland and Hobson, *Madison Papers*, 11:276–77, 412–14). James Reynold's narrative was printed in the *Pennsylvania Packet, and Daily Advertiser* (Philadelphia) on 23 July 1788: "The following Narrative of James Joshua Reynolds, late master of the Rising States of Philadelphia, was taken from his own mouth at Greenock, 3d April 1788 before witnesses.

"Mr. Reynolds says, he was born at Philadelphia, his parents quakers: That he was bred to the sea, served some time in the British navy, and commanded the Schooner Hammond, belonging to Mr Robert Sheddan, then of New York, now of London: That in the year 1784, he sailed from Philadelphia as master of the Rising States, bound for Lisbon: And on the 3d of April, that he was taken off the rock of Lisbon, by two Algerine cruisers; viz. the Polacre Selucia, Amet Homet Commander; and the Galley Ochlanchia, and carried into slavery, at Algiers, where he contined until January last." He was ransomed for 6,000 dollars by "John Jacobs, a Jew, he accidentally fell in with," whose brother Israel Jacobs lived in Philadelphia.

In his narrative, Reynolds reported that "during his stay at Algeirs he saw Captain Gordon," of the ship *Buckskin Hero*, of Glasgow, and he gave the names of five or six people from the *Buckskin Hero* who were on the same chain with him for two years. It was at this time that "he was told that a Doctor Spence and his lady were captured in the Buckskin Hero," but he "never saw either of them." Reynolds also reported that the *Buckskin Hero* "was taken before he arrived at Algiers, and carried into Sallee, where the pirates destroyed her pass, and got her condemned as an American. . . ."

Reynolds left Algiers on 2 Jan. 1788 and arrived in Philadelphia on 1 Aug., according to the paper. For the refutation of Reynolds's story printed in the *Packet* on 25 July, and probably written by Thomas Barclay, see GW to Thomson, 24 August.

# From Clement Biddle

Dear General                    Philadelphia August 13. 1788

By Capt. Ellwood who sails this day I have shipped the single & double refined Sugar, a Jug with two gallons of Spermaceti Lamp oil, two barrels containing six dozen of Porter, as Mr Hare advised leaving the remaining 18 dozen to be shipped next trip as it is now rather too brisk to ship and I shall send 1 Cwt of the plate Iron only for plow moulds as I have asked Mr Morris if he knew the kind & he did not and the smiths here not using it (I mean the City smiths) I have taken the best choice I could get but was too uncertain to send the whole.[1]

I shall forward the Invoices and account Current by next post.

I am sorry the herrings are yet on hand tho' I have offerd them to every probable purchaser, but I hope they will be wanted before long.

Having seen Mr Peters (and paid him for the harrow) I enquired for the wheel supposed to be missing—he tells me there was but one wheel which would serve for both or serve for a model to make others by.

A pump 13½ feet made of Pine & fitted with two boxes and a nozzle will cost 45/ for the wood work—the Ironwork about 6½d. a pound, the freight about 5/.

I expect to send the Letter for Genl Parsons by a Colonl St: Bayard who goes for Pittsburg in a few days.

Congress after a months debate & trying different Questions, on the future Seat of Government, have divided equally (Rhode Island not voting) and that Question, which we so ardently wished to be in favour of our City, seems now to be suspended for a time.

Mrs Biddle begs her Compliments may be made to Mrs Washington. With great respect I am Your Excellencys Most obedt & very humle servt

Clement Biddle

ALS, DLC:GW; ADfS, ViMtV: Clement Biddle Letter Book.

   1. Biddle's letter is in response to GW's of 4 August.

## From Alexander Hamilton

Sir                                  New York Aug. 13. 1788

Capt. Cochran of the British navy has requested my aid in recovering a family watch worn by his brother, who fell at York Town, (and now in the possession of —— ——). In compliance with this request I have written the letter herewith to —— —— which I take the liberty to convey through you, in hope that if you see no impropriety in it, you would add your influence to the endeavour to gratify Capt. Cochran. It is one of those things in which the affections are apt to be interested, beyond the value of the object; and in which one naturally feels an inclination to oblige.[1]

I have delivered to Mr Madison to be forwarded to you a sett of the papers under the signature of Publius, neatly enough bound, to be honored with a place in your library. I presume you have understood that the writers of these Papers are chiefly Mr Madison & myself with some aid from Mr Jay.[2]

I take it for granted, Sir, you have concluded to comply with what will no doubt be the general call of your country in relation to the new government. You will permit me to say that it is indispensable you should lend yourself to its first operations—It is to little purpose to have *introduced* a system, if the weightiest influence is not given to its firm *establishment*, in the outset. I remain with the greatest esteem Dr Sir Yr Obed. & hum. servant

A. Hamilton

ALS, DLC:GW.

1. Alexander Forester Ingles Cochrane served during the American Revolution in the West Indies as a British naval officer. His brother Maj. Charles Cochrane, an aide to Lord Cornwallis, was killed at Yorktown in 1781 (Syrett, *Hamilton Papers*, 5:202, n.1). The editors of the *Hamilton Papers* identify the possessor of the watch as well as the addressee of Hamilton's letter as Daniel Morgan (ibid., nn.2 and 3). See GW to Hamilton, 28 August.

2. GW received copies of the *Federalist Papers* from James Madison and John Jay as well as from Hamilton.

# To Joseph Caverly

Sir,                                    Mount Vernon August 14th 1788

I have not yet been able to examine the drifted wood on my shores—but as I am informed you have been a considerable sufferer by the Storm[1]—you shall be welcome to all that *now* lays from the Gut which formerly divided Simpsons plantation and Johnsons, to the point of Pocoson opposite to the mouth of Piscataway Creek—excepting Walnut logs.[2] or such pieces as will do for the framing of a wharf—These I reserve for my own use, in that district. and above it, my Nephew, Major Washington, has occasion for the wood for purposes of his own. It will be necessary for you to acquaint his Overseer and mine that this priviledge is allowed you, as orders have been given them to stop all encroachments of this kind and your own interest will prevent them from doing it till you shall have taken of[f] the Drift Wood which at *present* (for I do not mean this as a general

priviledge) lies on that shore which is here described. I am Dr
Sir &c.

Go. Washington

LB, DLC:GW.

Joseph Caverly, a ship carpenter who was living in Alexandria as early as
1783, owned a wharf in the city which evidently had been heavily damaged by
the hurricane of 24 July 1788.

1. For GW's own description of the hurricane and for other reports of the
damage the storm did in the Alexandria area, see *Diaries*, 5:366–67.

2. In 1760 GW bought from William Clifton an 1,806-acre tract lying across
Little Hunting Creek from Mount Vernon. Samuel Johnston (Johnson) and
Gilbert Simpson, Sr. (d. 1773), at that time were renting land on Clifton's Neck
on either side of Carneys Gut which was just above where Little Hunting
Creek flows into the Potomac. GW confirmed Simpson's lease but exchanged
two Johnston two leases for one farther upstream on Clifton's Neck. (See Lease
to Samuel Johnson, 25 Dec. 1761, and notes, printed above.) On 25 Oct. 1786
GW offered to turn over to his nephew and estate manager, George Augustine
Washington, for his own use the upper part of the Clifton tract on which Clif-
ton and later Johnston had once lived, with the understanding that George
Augustine would receive at GW's death the whole of Clifton's Neck. In effect,
GW was giving Caverly permission to collect driftwood along the shore of Clif-
ton's Neck from Carneys Gut along the riverbank of River farm to the end of
Pocoson Swamp at the lower end of George Augustine Washington's place.

# To John Marshall

Sir,             Mount Vernon August 15th 1788

Your letter of the 10th Ulto to Doctr Stuart enclosing a Summons for L. Washington &c. did not come to my hand till lass
Night.[1]

I am at a loss what step to take in this matter, and should
be glad of your advice. Luther Martin is the Attorney Genl of
Maryland and lives in Baltimore. Elizabeth and Sarah Cresap I
have always understood live with one Jacobs who Married there
Mother, and is said to be a resident of Hampshire County; but
two or three summons having been already Sent to the Sheriff
thereof and no return of them made, the presumption I think
is that there must have been either a Miscarriage—or that *these*
Daughters of Michl Cresap are not residents of that County—
Possibly they are Married, and living in Maryland where their
Father did.[2]

I should be glad to know whether, the issuing of the Patent, if the summons now sent is not executed and returned, or good reason assigned for the non execution is *merely* an *Officis* actor—will be in consequence of application from the heirs of Michael Cresap or any person in their behalf and who? My reason for it is, I have been informed and I believe from good authy that Jacobs *was* so well convinced of the legality and *equity* of my Title as to declare he should cease all further prosecution of the claim in behalf of the Childrin to whom I have heard he was guardian—This however may not be true—nor may it be the case with Mr Martin. The dismission of the Caveat will not invalidate my title to the land but may involve me in a more letigeous and expensive prosecution, or defence of it—and on this principle it was that Mr Randolph advised the Caveat. Under this relation of the Matter I shall be very glad to hear from you[3]—with very great esteem and regard I am—Sir, Yrs &ca

Go. Washington

LB, DLC:GW.

   1. Letter not found.

   2. A copy of the most recent summons, dated 26 April 1788, is in DLC:GW. Michael Cresap's two younger daughters, Elizabeth and Sarah, were married to Luther Martin's brother Lenox Martin and to Osborn Sprigg (c.1741–1815), respectively. For GW's earlier response to the claims of the heirs of Michael Cresap to GW's Round Bottom tract on the Ohio River, see John Harvie to GW, 20 May, 5 Aug. 1785, and GW to Harvie, 31 May 1785, to Edmund Randolph, 12 July 1786.

   3. No response from Marshall has been found, but see GW to Marshall, 17 Mar. 1789, and note 2 of that document. It may be that the copyist garbled a portion of this paragraph.

# From Thomas Ridout

Sir—                                         Montreal 15 August 1788

   I presume that your Excellency has heard that I had the misfortune to be taken by a party of Indians on my way to the Falls of the Ohio—although I lost every thing I was possessed of, I may reckon myself fortunate in having my life preserved—after remaining rather more than three months amongst the shawanese, I was brought into Detroit and there given up to a Trader for a debt of 340 dollars which I have obliged myself to pay at this place, and where I must remain at least for some months, perhaps the winter.

I have presumed to trouble your Excellency with this letter, to sollicit your recommendation to any vacant office under the Federal Government of the U. States which I may be thought adequate to, and if there be any that would suit me, that you would be so obliging as to advice me thereof by way of New York directed to the Care of Messrs Todd & McGill Merchts at this place.[1] I have the Honor to be very respectfully Your Excellency's most obedient servant

Thos Ridout

Present if you please my best respects to your Lady.

ALS, DLC:GW.

On 23 Dec. 1784 GW wrote a letter to Charles-Louis de Secondat de Montesquieu introducing Ridout, a Marylander engaged in the French trade, and Ridout had written to GW from Bordeaux as recently as 10 Sept. 1786.

1. No answer to Ridout's letter has been found.

## To Charles Pettit

Sir,                   Mount Vernon August 16th 1788

I have to acknowledge with much sensibility the receipt of your letter, dated the 5th instant, in which you offer your congratulations on the prospect of an established government, whose principles seem calculated to secure the benefits of society to the Citizens of the United States; and in which you also give a more accurate state of fœderal Politics in Pennsylvania than I had before received. It affords me unfeigned satisfaction to find that the acrimony of parties is much abated.

Doubtless there are defects in the proposed system which may be remedied in a constitutional mode. I am truly pleased to learn that those who have been considered as its most voilent opposers will not only acquiese peacably, but co-operate in its organization and content themselves with asking amendments in the manner prescribed by the Constitution. The great danger, in my view, was that every thing might have been thrown into the last stage of Confusion before any government whatsoever could have been established; and that we should have suffered a political shipwreck, without the aid of one friendly star to guide us into Port. Every real patriot must have lamented that private feuds and local politics should have unhappily insinuated themselves into, and in some measure obstructed the discussion of a great national question. A just opinion, that the People when rightly informed will decide in a proper manner, ought certainly to have prevented all intemperate or precipitate proceedings on a subject of so much magnitude, Nor should a regard to common decency have suffered the Zealots in the minority to have stigmatized the authors of the Constitution as Conspirators and Traitors. However unfavorably individuals, blinded by passion and prejudice, might have thought of the characters which composed the Convention; the election of those characters by the Legislatures of the several States and the refferrence of their Proceedings to the free determination of their Constituents, did not carry the appearance of *a private combination to destroy the liberties of their Country.*

Nor did the outrageous disposition which some indulged in traducing and vilifying the members seem much calculated to produce concord or accomodation.

For myself, I expected not to be exempted from obloquy any more than others. It is the lot of humanity.

But if the shafts of[1] malice had been aimed at me in ever so pointed a manner, on this occasion, involved as I was in a consciousness of having acted in conformity to what I believed my duty, they would have fallen blunted from their mark. It is known to some of my countrymen and can be demonstrated to the conviction of all, that I was in a manner constrained to attend the general Convention in compliance with the earnest and pressing desires of many of the most respectable characters in different parts of the Continent.

At my age, and in my circumstances, what sinister object, or personal emolument had I to seek after, in this life? The growing infirmities of age and the encreasing love of retirement, daily confirm my decided predilection for domestic life: and the great searcher of human hearts is my witness, that I have no wish which aspires beyond the humble and happy lot of living and dying a private citizen on my own farm.

Your candour and patriotism in endeavoring to moderate the jealousies and remove the prejudices which a particular class of Citizens had conceived against the new government, are certainly very commendable;[2] and must be viewed as such by all true friends to their Country. In this discription, I shall fondly hope I have a right to comprehend myself; and shall conclude by professing the grateful sense of your favorable opinion for me, with which I am, Sir, Your Most Obedient Servant

George Washington

LB, DLC:GW; Df, DNA:PCC, Miscellaneous Papers. The draft, in David Humphreys' hand and docketed by GW, reads exactly as the letter-book copy through "But if the shafts of" (see note 1). Part of the last paragraph of the draft has been scratched through and GW substituted the words as they appear in the last part of the paragraph in the letter-book copy.

1. Here the draft ends except for a short paragraph which has been scratched through by GW. See note 2.

2. GW's writing begins at the last syllable of the word "commendable."

## From Clement Biddle

Dr General                              Philadelphia Aug. 17 1788

By last post, I forwarded a Letter from Mrs Morris which Came with a pair of Stays. The stays I put in charge of Capt. Ellwood who promised great Care of them, inclosed is the Bill of loading of sundry Articles by said Captain of which a Certificate was delivered him to save the Duties. the Invoice & of Course the Account Current lays open for want of Mr Hare's bill for the Porter which have not yet got, the rest paid & the Accounts shall be made up by next Post.[1] I also forwarded a Letter from Thomas Smith Esqr. of Carlisle which Came to my hands with Fifty Pounds Cash which is to your Credit.[2]

Your favour of the 10th came to hand just as Capt. Ellwood was fully loaden & geting under sail therefore could not ship the Barly. The last sent I had from Mr Reuben Haines for the purpose of seed & relied on him that it was good. the next I will try from another Brewer.

If a direct Conveyance from Newport offered you could get the best spring Barley from thence. the best Winter Barley here. I am not able to inform the prices as I have been some days confined by indispotion but am better. Barley has yielded good Crops & must be cheap I am told, but the new Barley is not yet threshed or price fixed—it will by Capt. Ellwoods next Trip. I am with great respect Your Excellency's Mo. obedt & very hum. Servt

Clement Biddle

ALS, DLC:GW.

1. The letter from Mary White Morris has not been found.

2. Thomas Smith's letter of 6 Aug. has not been found, but see GW to Smith, 15 September.

## To John Beale Bordley

Sir,                                    Mount Vernon Augt 17th 1788.

The letter with which you honord me, dated the 31st Ult.; together with the Wheat, Barley and Madder came safe to hand.[1] For your kindness in presenting them, I pray you to accept my best acknowlegments and thanks.

Agriculture being my favourite amusement I am always pleased with communications that relate to it. To these the great improvemts in Husbandry, of late years, in England, may be attributed; and to a liberal communication of experiments must this Country be indebted for those profitable courses of crops which are best adapted to our climate—our soil—and our circumstances. Experiments must be made—and the practice (of such of them as are useful) must be introduced by Gentlemen who have leisure and abilities to devise and wherewithal to hazard something. The common farmer will not depart from the *old* road 'till the *new* one is made so plain and easy that he is sure it cannot be mistaken, and that it will lead him directly to his object. It is right perhaps it shd be so—for new ways are thorny and require time for amelioration.

No Wheat that has ever yet fallen under my observation exceeds the *White* which some years ago I cultivated extensively; but which, from inattention during my absence from home of almost nine years has got so mixed or degenerated as scarcely to retain any of its original characteristic properties. But if the march of the Hessian Fly, southerly, cannot be arrested; and Colo. Morgans experiments are corroborated by others of equal skill and attention, this *White Wheat* must yield the palm to the

*yellow bearded*, which alone, it seems, is able to resist the depredations of that destructive insect.[2] This makes your present of it to
me more valuable. It shall be cultivated with care.

The Cape Wheat I have cultivated three years successively.
The frost of the last, almost destroyed it. In neither, did it produce a full grain, though a large one. I have just harvested a
little of two sorts of wheat sent me by Arthur Young Esquire of
England; one of which he says is called the Harrison Wheat and
is in high estimation in that Country—the other is a large white
wheat to which I do not recollect his having given a name.[3] The
seed being injured in its passage came up badly, & with difficulty
was preserved from Weeds &ca—No conclusive opinion therefore can be formed of either from the trial of this year; but
should any thing indicate a superior quality in them next, I will
reserve some of the Seed for you.

That the system (if it deserves the appellation of one) of Corn,
Wheat, Lay;[4] has been injurious, and if continued would prove
ruinous to our lands, I believe no one who has attended to the
ravages which has been produced by it in our fields, is at a loss
to decide. But with deference let me ask if the substitute you
propose is the best that can be devised? Wheat follows Corn:
here are not only two corn crops, but those of the most exhausting nature following each other without the intervention
of a restorative; when, by the approved courses now practiced
in England, *Grain* and (what are called) *fallow* Crops, succeed
each other alternately. Though I am not *strongly* attached to a
particular course (being open to conviction) yet, that which has
obtained most in my mind, & which I have been endeavouring
(for it is not easy to go fully into any system that produces a
*material* change, at once) to carry into execution, is the following;
which for the better understanding of it, shall have dates to the
growth of the respective Crops.

By the usual mode (it is scarcely necessary to observe) we have
*three* fields—viz.—one in Corn—one in Wheat—and one in Lay.
By my plan these three fields are divided into Six. In 1788 for
instance, one of them (say no. 1) is planted with Corn 8 feet by
2, single stalks; with Irish Potatoes or Carrots, or partly both
between. That Corn planted in this manner will yield as much
to the Acre as in any other—That the quantity of Potatoes will

at least quadruple the quantity of Corn—and that the Potatoes do not exhaust the soil—are facts well established in my mind. In April 1789 it is sown with Buck Wheat for manure, which is plowed in before Harvest when the Seed *begins* to ripen and there is a sufficiency of it to seed the ground a second time. In July it is again plowed in; which gives two dressings to the land at the expence of a bushl of B[uck] Wheat and the plowings which would otherwise be essential for a summer fallow. In August, after the putrifaction & fermentation is over, Wheat is sown, & in 1790 harvested. In 1791 the best, and earliest kind of Indian Pease are sown broadcast, to be mowed when generally ripe Since the adoptn of this course & progress that has been made to carry it into effect, I have had too much cause to be convinced, that Pease harvested in this manr is a considerable exhauster of the Soil. I have some thoughts therefore of substituting a medley—of Pease—Buck Wheat for seed, Turnips, Pompions &ca in such parts of the field as best suit them—they will be useful—and serve as preparations. In 1792 Spring Barley or Oats, or equal quantities of each, will be sown with red clover; the latter to be fed with light Stock the first year after harvest. In 1793, the field remains in Clover for Hay, or grazing according to circumstances—And in 1794 comes into Corn again, and goes on as before. It may be remarked here—as an objection to this system—that Wheat, in the best farming Counties in England follows the Clover Lay—Is sown on a single ploughing—and has been found profitable from practice: My reasons for departing from that mode are—1. our ploughing is not equal to theirs, of course the clover is not so well buried, nor the ensuing crop (of Wheat) so free from grass as theirs. and 2. If we sow Wheat at an early and proper period, we loose a valuable part of the Clover crop. Whereas the ground for Corn need not be broken till the season for grazing is over, and the Beasts in their stalls. By the tillage too which the Corn Crop *ought* to receiv⟨e⟩; followed by Buck Wheat twice ploughed in, Weeds and grass, one would think, must be entirely subdued.

To contrast the probable yield of this system with the old course of Corn, Wheat & Lay, suppose a farm of 300 acres of arable Land.

### Old System

| | | | | |
|---|---|---|---|---|
| 100 Ac[re]s of Corn—12½ bushels is | 1250 | @ 3/ | £187.10. |
| 100 do | Wheat—6 | 600 | 5/ | 150 |
| 100 do | Pasture | | | |

|  |  |
|---|---|
| | 337.10 |
| In favr of the New | 116. 5 |
| | 453.15.0 |

### New System

| | | | | |
|---|---|---|---|---|
| 50 acs | Corn @ 12½ is | 625 | @ 3/ | £ 93.15 |
| Potatoes betwn the Corn Rows, will quadruple the quanty of Corn; but allowing for Seed, accidts &ca only dble, that gives 1250 bushl @ 1/ | | | | 62.10 |
| 50 acs. | Wheat @ 9 bl is | 450 | 5/ | 112.10 |
| 50 do | Barley 10 | 500 | 3/6 | 87.10 |
| 50 do | Pease 4 | 200 | 3/6 | 35. |
| 50 do | Clover Hay 25 Tons | | 50/ | 62.10.0 |
| 50 do | Pasture | | | |

|  |  |
|---|---|
| | £453.15.0 |

In the above statement, as much I conceive is allowed to the old, and taken from the New System, as can be done with justice. The Pastures of the latter will be fine, and improving—Those of the former, bad—declining—and running into gullies.

The Land-machine spoken of by you for sowing clover seed, I have wished to see, but never yet have seen one; but I cannot conceive that by *this*, or *any other* contrivance, a bushel of Clover seed can be made to subserve 20 acrs of Land without a considerable mixture of other grass Seeds; which would, in a manner, be wasted in so short a Lay as is proposed by either of our systems.

I have been informed that you have in possession one of Winlaws machines for threshing Wheat: Pray how do you approve of it on trial? Many of these newly invented things meet the approbation of the moment, but will not stand the test of constant use, or the usage of common labourers. I have requested Mr Young, if this machine has supported its reputation either in his opinion (if he has attended to the use of it) or in the judgment of those on whom he can confide, to send me one. I wish, notwithstanding, to receive your acct of it.⁵ With sentiments of esteem & regd I have the honor—to be—Sir Yr Most Obedt and Most Hble Servt

Go: Washington

ALS, MHi: Waterston Papers; LB, DLC:GW.

1. Letter not found. On Saturday, 6 Sept. GW sowed at the Mount Vernon farm recently secured from Penelope French a bushel of "the plain white wheat" that Bordley had sent him. Two days later he sowed "One bushel of the White bearded Wheat sent me by Beale Boardly Esqr. adjoining to the plain Wht. sowed on Saturday—and adjoining this again (likewise in drills) 9 Gallons of the Cape Wheat from that Gentleman also" (*Diaries*, 5:390, 391).

2. See George Morgan to GW, 31 July–5 August.

3. Young sent the grain on 1 Feb. 1787; GW received it in May 1787; and he wrote Young about it on 1 Nov. 1787.

4. The term "lay by" is also used to denote leaving a field unplanted for a growing season.

5. See GW's query to Arthur Young about Winlaw's threshing machine, 1 Nov. 1787, and Young's evaluation of the machine for GW, 1 July 1788.

# To James Madison

My dear Sir,                     Mount Vernon Augt 17[–18]th 1788.

Although the letter of Mr Pleasants and its enclosure will appear under date of the 25th of July, it never got to my hand till friday last. Tomorrow is the first Post by which I could forward it. It is now sent with thanks for the perusal. I shall write to the Count de Moustier, but in pretty general terms—giving the substance rather than the detail of this business.¹

That the circular letter from the Convention of New York should be handed to the public as the unanimous sense of that body is, to me, surprizing. It will, I fear, be attended with pernicious consequences. The decision of North Carolina—unaccountable as it is—is not, in my opinion, more to be regretted.² With sentiments of the highest esteem & regard—I am—My dear Sir Yr Most Obedient and Affectionate Hble Servt

Go: Washington.

Augt 18th
I had written this letter, but had not sent it to the Post-Office, when your favor of the 11th was brought to me.

I am clearly in sentiment with you that the longer the question respecting the permanent Seat of Congress remains unagitated, the greater certainty there will be of its fixture in a central spot. But not having the same means of information and judging that you have; it would have been a moot point with me, whether a *temporary* Residence of that body at New York would not have been a less likely mean of keeping it *ultimately* from the center (being farther removed from it) than if it was to be at Philada, because, in proportion as you draw it to the center, you lessen the inconveniences and of course the solicitude of the Southern & Western extremities; and when to these are super-added the acquaintances and connections which naturally will be formed—the expences which more than probably will be incurred for the accomodation of the public Offices—with a long train of etceteras, it might be found an arduous task to approach nearer to the Axis there after. These, however, are first thoughts; and may not go to the true principles of policy which governs in this case. I am as before Yrs very sincerely

Go. Washington

ALS, NN: Berg Collection; LB, DLC:GW.

1. For the French minister's query about American trade and other matters and the responses of GW and Madison, see Thomas Pleasants, Jr., to GW, 25 July, n.2, and GW to Moustier, 26 Mar., n.3., and 17 August.

2. For the New York circular letter, see Madison to GW, 11 Aug., n.2. In the North Carolina convention no vote on ratification was taken; instead, the Antifederalists passed by a vote of 184–84 a proposal for a declaration of rights of twenty articles as well as twenty-six proposed amendments to the Constitution. The proposed amendments were to be submitted to Congress and to a new convention of states to be called for the purpose of amending the Constitution (Delbert Harold Gilpatrick, *Jeffersonian Democracy in North Carolina, 1789–1816* [New York, 1967], 33).

## To Moustier

Sir, Mount Vernon Augt 17th 1788.

In the letter which I did myself the honor to address to your Excellency on the 26th of last March, I intimated that as soon as I should have obtained more particular information concerning the commercial intercourse between France and the United States, I would most willingly communicate the result. Ill pre-

pared as I still am to treat of a subject, so complicated in its
nature and so extensive in its consequences, I will now hazard
a few facts and general observations; without confining myself
strictly to your questions, to which, however, you may find there
will be a constant allusion.

Respecting the utility or hurtfulness of the Tobacco-Contract
between Mr Morris and the Farmers General, I have heard[1] so
many specious arguments on the one side and the other, that I
find myself embarrassed in making a fair Judgment. In ordinary
cases I know that all exclusive previleges and even partial mo-
nopolies are pernicious. How far in this instance, the contract
has been only a transferrence of the business from the foreign
Agents (English or Scottish) who used to conduct it, into other
hands; and whether the same exportations, in quantity, would
have been made directly to France through more advantageous
channels, I cannot pretend to determine. A free competition in
the purchase of that article here, as well as in the sale at the place
of market, it seems reasonable to conclude, would be mutually
beneficial to both Nations, however, it might be inconvenient to
Individuals. Though the present Contract will soon expire of
course and leave an equal field of speculation on this side the
Atlantic; I have been taught to believe that the Farmers General
will not so readily give up their share in the Monopoly, on the
other. So the business must, in all probability, revert to its original channel.

In reply to your second, third & fourth questions, I would
only briefly observe, that we are yet scarcely sufficiently acquainted with the coarse French woolens and their lowest price,
to determine how far they can come in rivalship with those of
Britain. The prevaling opinion is in the latter: but I see no reason why the former, when calculated for the particular purpose
may not be made equally cheap and good. As to other articles
of importation, directly from France, they might consist in, su-
perfine Broad Cloth's (particularly blue, which can be afforded
cheaper and better than from England) Glass, Gloves, Ribbons,
Silks, Cambricks, plain Lawns, Linens, Printed Goods, Wine,
Brandy, Oyl, Frute, and in general every thing necessary for carrying on the Indian Trade: from the Islands, Sugar and Coffee,
in addition to the Molasses and Rum which alone are permitted
to be exported to the United States at present. Our produce in

Return to Europe might comprehend, Tobacco (as the staple from this State) and from the States aggregately, wheat, Rice, other Grain, Bread, Flour, Fish, Fish Oyl, Pot-ashes, Pearl-ashes, Skins, Furs, Peltry, Indigo, Madder, different dying Woods, Lumber, Naval Stores, Iron, Coals, and Ships ready-built: to the Islands, Lumber, Bar-iron, Coals, Live stock, and Provisions of all kinds.

It may be mentioned here as a first principle of extending the intercourse, and as a theory which will be found incontestably true in experiment: *That in proportion as France shall encrease the facility of our making remittance, in the same ratio shall we encrease the consumption of her produce and manufactures.* Common Sense and sound Policy speak thus on our part: "We can furnish new materials of great value and our ability to do it will augment with our population every day: we want no money for them and we desire no credit may be given to us: we cannot manufacture fine articles so cheaply as we can import them and must while we continue an agricultural People be supplied from some quarter: we offer you the preferrence and will take in different Goods, to the amount to receive from us in our staple Commodities."

This Doctrine has been already verified so far as an opportunity has been affor'ded to observe the effect. The use of French Brandy, in common Taverns as well as private Houses, has been substituted, for two or three years past, very much in the room of Jamaica Rum; Probably not less than 24,000 gallons have been imported into this State, in one year. The consumption of French wines is also much greater than it has formerly been; and may by a moderate calculation amount to between one half and one third of all that is imported. The demand for both these articles might still be extended with the means of making remittance.

Not much French salt is made use of for curing provisions in Virginia The opinion is; that it is not so clean as that imported from other parts of Europe. If it was properly purified it might and certainly would be brought out as ballast in great quantities, and find a ready market.

About half the exports from Virginia are carried in American bottoms, the remainder principally in British bottoms. There are, however, a number of other foreign vessels employed in the trade.

I know not of any other equivalents, than those to be derived by France from the extension of her commerce, which we can give for any new favours in your Islands. Under the present rigorous restrictions it is thought that trade is unprofitable for us and will decay or be disused as soon as other avenues for receiving our produce shall be gradually opened. The Maritime Genius of this Country is now steering our Vessels in every ocean; to the East Indias, the North-west Coasts of America and the extremities of the Globe. I have the best evidence that the scale of commerce, so long against us, is beginning to turn in our favour, and that (as a new thing in our new world) the amount of exports from one State, last year, exceeded that of the imports, more than 230,000 Pounds.

What chance in systems and amelioration in the general complexion of our affairs, are likely to be produced in consequence of the national government, which is on the eve of being estabblished, I will not undertake to predict, I hope & trust the ties which connect this Nation with France will be strengthened and made durable by it. In the mean time, there are three things, which I flatter myself will counterbalance on the side of the French commerce the three advantages, of which I conceived the British Merchants to be possessed. The circumstances to which I allude are, 1st, The encreasing prejudices of this country against a commercial intercourse with England, occasioned by provocations and augmented by impositions on her part; 2ndly The facility given in many instances by the French government for our making remittances in the staple commodities of this Country: and 3dly the change of taste in favor of articles, pro-duced or manufactured in France, which may indeed in a great degree be attributed to the affection and gratitude still felt for her generous interposition in our favor.

I should be truly happy to learn that this Country and Inhabitants have become agreeable to your Excellency by acquaintance. For you may be assured, Sir, no one can be more zealous than myself in promoting a friendly connection between our Nations, or in rendering your situation perfectly satisfactory, while the United States shall enjoy the benefit of your residence in them. With the highest sentiments of consideration and respect I have the honor to be &ca

Go. Washington

ALS (incomplete facsimile), listed in Sotheby's sale catalog for 20 May 1993, item 158; LB, DLC:GW.

1. The remainder of the letter is taken from the letter-book copy.

## From Thomas Ruston

Sir                                        Philad[elphi]a Augt 17th 1788.

Will your Excellency permit me to congratulate you on the acceptance of the new constitution by eleven of the States? An event that I think must be highly pleasing to your Excellency, for as there is no one who has contributed so much towards the establishment of the liberty and independence of this Country, so I am convinced that there are none who have her happiness and prosperity more at heart. With regard to the two delinquent States (North Carolina and Rhode Island) when we consider the diversity of opinion that takes place amongst mankind upon almost every subject, it is perhaps more to be wondered at that eleven out of the thirteen should so immediately come into the measure, than that there should be two defaulters. the measure of Independence, so indispensible and necessary, if I remember right, was not immediately come into by all the States. Whatever ostensible reasons may be offered by those two States for the rejection of this constitution, from what I can learn the true one is the inhibition of paper money, a system which, as it has been practised, is founded in fraud, and the advocates of it seem loth to part with this darling privelege of cheating their neighbours according to law, but it is to be presumed that a little time and reflection will bring them to a right use of their reason.

Amidst the variety of important concerns that must necessarily engross your Excellencies attention at this crisis, it may perhaps be scarcely excusible in a private individual to attempt to call off your thoughts but for a moment to his particular concerns. as the subject however is of considerable importance to him, relying on your Vonted goodness, and the notice with which you have already indulged him, he is encouraged to mention the circumstance, leaving it entirely to your Excellency to take such notice of it as you shall think proper.

Your Excellency may possibly recollect that I mentioned to you, transiently, that I had some claims on the Principio Company. These claims were set forth in a petition which I presented to the Legislature of Maryland, at their last session, of which the inclosed is a copy.[1] This petition was read in both houses, but it being a short session, and the members in a great hurry to get home, it was, with a great deal of other business refered over to next session. Upon a perusal of it I presume there is nothing that appears unreasonable, and I flatter myself I shall be able to make good all the allegations contained in it. You may perceive that I ask nothing but what I shall prove that I have a clear right to, nor do I expect any part of that which has been given to other claims—but only my proportional part out of that which still remains in the hands of the State. To this Claim permit me to observe, that, as far as I have gone, I have hitherto met with no obstruction, but it was observed by some of my friends that as I was necessarily almost an entire stranger, it would be well if I could procure some leters of introduction to some of the Members of the Senate, or house of Delegates, or both, against the next session.[2] Pray make my best respect to Mrs Washington the Major & his Lady not forgeting Master Custis from Dr Sr Yr obliged and obedt humble Servt

Thos Ruston

N.B. Mr Morris's Ship, the Alliance, from India is arrived ⟨*mutilated*⟩ the capes.

ALS, DLC:GW.

1. GW, who owed his acquaintance with Dr. Ruston to George William Fairfax, may have learned of Ruston's interest in the Principio Iron Company in November 1787 or January 1788, when Ruston visited Mount Vernon. See George William and Sarah Cary Fairfax to GW, 2 July 1785, and *Diaries*, 5:217, 268. For references to the involvement of the Washington family in the Principio Iron Company, see GW to George Plater, Charles Carroll, John Cadwalader, and Samuel Chase, 11 Dec. 1784, and the source note of that document. In the enclosed petition directed to the Maryland legislature, Ruston asked that the shares in the Principio Company which his grandfather had acquired as one of the initial investors be restored to him.

2. GW wrote to Ruston from Mount Vernon on 31 Aug.: "Sir, I have been regularly favored with your letter of the 17th instant, and am much obliged by your polite congratulations on the ratification of the Constitution by eleven States. Your remark seems to be well-founded, that it is much more wonderful so many States should have adopted, than that two only should not as yet have accepted the government. It remains for us to hope the best; and I would fain persuade myself that the same power, which hath hitherto kept us from Disunion and Anarchy, will not suffer us to be disappointed.

"Although I am not personally acquainted with many of the Gentlemen who compose the Senate of Maryland, I have, according to your desire, given you introductory letters to some of them. As a New House of Delegates is to be Elected before the next Session of Assembly, it might not be so easy for me to know & address any of them, in time. Ever disposed to testify my regard and esteem for you, I remain Sir Your Most Obedt and very Humble Servt Go: Washington" (ALS, PWacD; LB, DLC:GW). There are three letters dated 25 Aug. in GW's letter book recommending Ruston in almost identical terms, one to Charles Carroll of Carrollton, one to George Plater, and one to William Smallwood. The letter to Carroll reads: "Dear Sir, This letter will be presented to you by Doctr Ruston who came warmly recommended to me by my deceased Friend Colo. Fairfax of England as a Gentleman of merit and a firm friend to the American cause during its contest with Great Britian. The Doctor has business with your assembly whch will call him to Annopolis and take the liberty of introducing him to your acquaintance. I am &ca Go. Washington" (LB, DLC:GW). The main differences in the three letters is that while GW introduces Ruston only to Carroll's acquaintance, he introduces him to Plater's "acquaintance and civilities," (LB, DLC:GW; copy, PHi: Tench Coxe Papers) and Smallwood only to his "civilities" (LB, DLC:GW; copy, PHi: Tench Coxe Papers). The full text of each of the three letters is in CD-ROM:GW.

## To Hector St. John Crèvecoeur

Sir,                                        Mount Vernon Augt 18th 1788.
Will you permit me to take the liberty of addressing the enclosed Letters to your care, to be forwarded when a conveyance shall offer for France?[1]
I will make no apology for the freedom, because you have encouraged me to use it. With sentiments of esteem & consideration I have the honor to be Sir Yr Most Obedt and Most Hble Servt

Go: Washington

ALS, DLC: Crèvecoeur Papers; LB, DLC:GW.
1. GW also wrote to Chartier de Lotbinière and Auguste deGrasse on this date.

## To Christopher Gadsden

Sir,                                        Mount Vernon August 18th 1788
I take the earliest opportunity of acknowledging the receipt of the letter, which you did me the favor to write to me on the

5th of June last;[1] and of informing you that I have received and forwarded the letters of Mr Warville, in conformity to your desires.

You have done perfectly right in appreciating the full value of the esteem and attachment by which I am connected with that amiable young nobleman, the Marqs de la Fayette; and in transmitting to my care the Packets, which he had addressed to you.[2]

The extremely polite manner in which you are pleased to offer your services, in case I might have occasion for them; at the same time that it tends to confirm the charactiristic generosity of your nation, entitles you to the most grateful acknowledgments of him, who has the honor to be With the greatest consideration, Sir yrs &c.

Go. Washington.

LB, DLC:GW. The copyist wrote "Cadran" rather than Gadsden.
  1. Letter not found.
  2. See GW to Hector St. John Crèvecoeur, 6 Aug., n.1.

## To Auguste, Comte de Grasse

Sir,                                    Mount Vernon August 18th 1788
  The letter which you did me the honor to write on the 11th of March last is before me, and affords an occasion of testifying the sincerity of my regrets for the distressing event announced in it. Be persuaded, Sir, I should do injustice to my feelings, if my disinterested friendship did not sympaithize with your filial duty, in expressions of the most genuine grief, for the death of your father. Indeed the merits of the Count de Grasse and the services which he had the happiness of rendering to this country, have given a singular poignancy to the melancholly, which United America feels for his loss. You need not doubt but those merits and those services will be as long had in remembrance here, as the honorable testimony of this Nations gratitude for them shall be preserved in your family.

After these pointed assurances and expressions of real esteem for your father; the son of my gallant friend and successful associate in arms will not find it difficult to comprehend the interest I take in whatever concer[n]s his reputation and Glory. But it rests not with me to grant permission for any one to bear the

Insignia of the Cincinnati. All I can do will be to refer your request and pretentions to the Genl meeting of that Society, who alone are competent to gratify your wishes. The General Meeting are Triennial. The next will not be untill a year from next May: Although I am the President, I do not expect to attend, because it is stipulated and understood that I shall be exempted from the trouble of the Office. For this reason, I will forward a transcript of your Letter to Genl Knox, who is the Secretary, with a request that it may be laid before the General meeting and that the result may be made known to you.[1] With sentiments of the highest regard and consideration, I am Sir Your most obedt & Very huble Servant

Go. Washington

LB, DLC:GW.

1. GW wrote Henry Knox from Mount Vernon on 10 Sept.: "Sir, In order that they may be laid before the next General Meeting of the Society of the Cincinnati, I enclose you the Congratulatory address of the State Society of New Hampshire on the Ratification of the new Constitution by a ⟨suffi⟩cient number of States to give efficacy thereto &c.—and an Extract of a letter from Count Aug: de Grasse, Son of the Admiral of that name—our compatriot in Arms. with sentiments of the highest esteem and regard, I have the honor to be Sir Yrs &c. Go. Washington" (LB, DLC:GW). The New Hampshire Society of Cincinnati's letter, dated 7 July and signed by John Sullivan, is printed above.

# From John Mary

Sir                                    New york August 18. 1788.

your Excellency will hardly remember of me, but when i will mention to you that i was secretary to the Consulate general of France under Mr Gerard's orders during the late war, & that i had the honour of dining there with you & your lady several times, then likely you will recollect me.[1]

however give me leave to wish you a very good health, your lady & all that belongs to you.

I have lately delivered a speech which relates very much with the present circumstances. It has met with the approbation of the most respectable & learned gentlemen of this place. i take the liberty of inserting a copy of the same in this letter.[2]

I have met honourable Sir, with great misfortunes since i had the happiness of seeing you in Philadelphia & in New port, so that i am obliged to teach both languages to live with as much decency as possible as there is an university that goes by your name, i would be much obliged to your Excellency if you would speak in my favor or to some Gentlemen who would have some body to instruct in their family. I would teach french, English writing & arithmetick.

I have compiled an english & french grammar, which has been approved of.

My loss during the late war is at least 4000. dollars for which i have authentical certificates.[3]

If it is not too much trouble i will beg of your Excellency to honor me with an answer.[4] I am with great respect sir your most obedient & humble servant

John Mary
late Secretary to the consulate general of France,
& now teaching both languages in this City, at M.
de Montaudevert merchant.

ALS, DLC:GW.

1. Conrad-Alexandre Gérard (1729–1790) arrived in America in 1778 with d'Estaing's flotilla, as the French minister to the United States. In ill health, he was replaced by La Luzerne in August 1779.

2. *A Speech on the Government of Good Morals* was enclosed.

3. In 1785 he advertised "A NEW French and English Grammer. By JOHN MARY" which was "Just Published, at Boston." Mary identified himself as "French Instructer a[t] the University at Cambridge" (*United States Chronicle* [Providence], 29 Sept. 1785).

4. GW's reply from Mount Vernon on 29 Aug. was unusually brusque: "Sir, Agreeably to your desire I am sitting down to acknowledge the receipt of the letter, which you was pleased to address to me on the 18th of this Month. In the multitude of persons, public and private, of whom I may have had some knowledge, it will not be thought strange, that I should retain no recollection of you. I am only sorry for the losses which you say you have sustained, without being able to remedy them.

"You are doubtless informed, Sir, that I lead altogether a private life. It would hardly be expected then that I should go abroad in search of employment for a gentleman, with whose talents and character, I have not the honor of being acquainted. Not having any agency with the College that bears my name, or knowledge of any family that, at present, wants an Instructor in the French language: you will excuse me for giving this laconic reply, with my wishes for your success. I am &ca Go. Washington" (LB, DLC:GW).

## To James Swan

Sir,                                    Mount Vernon August 18th 1788

I have received your favor of the 5th of June from Havre de Grace.[1] The measure you took, in recommending to Mr Cadson[2] the transmission of the Marqs de la Fayette's letters for Mr Crevecœur through my hands, was very acceptable to me and did not stand in need of an apology.[3]

About the time I was occupied in forwarding the Packet to New York, I had the satisfaction to hear of Mr Warville's safe arrival in Boston. From the favorable character given of that Gentleman, and the important object which has occasioned his advent. I hope his visit to America may become equally interesting and satisfactory in a personal and national point of view.[4] With sentiments of esteem I am &c.

                                                    Go. Washington

LB, DLC:GW.
   1. Letter not found.
   2. The copyist should have written "Gadsden."
   3. See GW to Crèvecoeur, 6 Aug., n.1.
   4. See Lafayette to GW, 25 May 1788, n.3.

## To William Tudor

Sir,                                    Mount Vernon Augt 18th 1788.

I have just received your friendly letter of the 26th of July, together with the History of the Insurrections in Massachusetts; and cannot delay to return you my thanks for these tokens of your regard.[1]

Though I have not yet had time to look through the book, from the interesting nature of the subject, and the judicious manner in which it seems to be handled, I anticipate considerable amusement and information. The apology for the publication at the present time is well conceived, and forms a just discrimination between the circumstances of our own and some other Countries.

The troubles in your State, may, as you justly observe, have operated in proving to the comprehension of many minds the necessity of a more efficient government. A Multiplicity of circumstances, scarcely yet investigated, appears to have *co-operated* in bringing about the great, and I trust, the happy revolution, that is on the eve of being accomplished. It will not be uncommon that these things, which were considered at the moment as real ills, should have been no inconsiderable causes in producing positive and permanent national felicity. For it is thus that Providence works in the mysterious course of events "from seeming evil still educing good."

I was happy to hear from several respectable quarters that liberal policy & fœderal sentiments had been rapidly encreasing in Massachusetts for sometime past: it gives me an additional pleasure to find that labour is becoming more productive & commerce more flourishing among the Citizens.

If I have formerly approved myself inclined to subserve the public interest by fostering youthful merit—I shall now claim to be credited, when I assert that my cordial desires for the happiness of the Republic & the prosperity of its friends are by no means diminished: and particularly when I add that with great esteem—I am—Sir Yr Most Obedt and Most Hble Servant

Go: Washington

ALS, MHi: Tudor Papers; LB, DLC:GW.
    1. See also George Richards Minot to GW, 7 August.

## From Thomas Hanson Marshall

Sir                    Maryland Marshall Hall 21st Augt 1788
    Your Farmer applyed to me on Sunday last, to know if I had any Wheat for sale, which you wanted for seed, I have not any out, nor will it now be in my power, conveniantly, to have aney ready, for that purpose, until about the first of next month weather &c. permiting: I will let you have, as fast as can get it out &c. from the above mention'd time, Two hundred Bushels at Five shillings Virginia Cury per Bushel.[1]
    You will pleas let me have your answar respecting the above, as may Act accordingly, And in case you encline to take the wheat, can give notice to the Farmr when it may, from time, be sent for with sertinty, that no disappointment may take place.[2] I am sir Yr Very Hble Servt

T.H: Marshall

N.B. there is more Cockle amongst my Wheats, then could wish.

ALS, DLC:GW.
1. James Bloxham was GW's farmer.
2. See GW to Marshall, 24 August.

## To John Fitzgerald and George Gilpin

Gentlemen,                                  Mount Vernon August 22d 1788

It is of so much consequence to the Company, that *necessary* and *legal* measures should be pursued to obtain Judgments againts its delenquent members at the ensuing General Court—now little more than five weeks distant—that I beg a moment may not be lost in complying with the requisition of Mr Lee for this purpose.[1]

In the mean time, if one of two things must take place which seem very likely—a stagnation in this business or an other call upon the subscribers for 2½ or 5 pr Ct I am decidedly in favor of the latter. To advance more money for this purpose when there are such sums unpaid, cannot be more irksome, or less convenient to any one than it is to myself—but when the interest of the company, or the reputation of the undertaking is at stake, I will chearfully submit to it: When the subscribers see and are satisfied, that we are pursuing rigorous measures to recover the unsatisfied calls, they ought to submit to it—but if there is the least remissness in the latter, or blunders on our side, they will, indeed, have great and Just cause to complain. For this reason let Mr Lee direct the essentials—Let us cause them to be executed without delay, precisely agreeable to his orders. I am &c.

                                                           Go. Washington

LB, DLC:GW.
1. For the new legislation that the Potomac River Company secured from the Virginia and Maryland legislatures to enable it to sue delinquent stockholders in the state courts, see GW to George Mason and David Stuart, 4 Nov. 1787, and notes.

## From Clement Biddle

Dear General                            Philad[elphi]a Aug. 24th 1788

Inclosed is your Account Currt (including the Goods ⅌ Cap. Ellwood) balance in my favour £5.3.8[1]—If you choose to have the barley please to inform me & I will procure it by Capt. Ell-woods return—the price is not yet ascertained[2]—I have not yet disposed of the herrings but have the preference from two vessels intended for Hispaniola if they load any—they have been very low in that Island which is our Chief market.

The Oil which I sent you for Lamps was of the best quality, but I have found it less offensive in a chamber to burn hogs Lard. fill a Tea or Coffee cup with Lard, sink a paper such as is inclosed in the Lard lightly & cover it about the Thickness of a dollar, or less, with Lard & cover the piece in the middle with Lard & then light it and it will burn a whole night—after a little use in fixing, it will seldom or ever go out in the night & there is no smell from it—I am with great respect Yr Exc[e]llencys Mo. obedient & very humle serv.

Clement Biddle

ALS, DLC:GW; ADfS, ViMtV: Clement Biddle Letter Book.
    1. The account current has not been found.
    2. See GW to Biddle, 10 August.

## From James Madison

Dear Sir                              New York Augst 24. 1788.

I was yesterday favored with yours of the 17th 18th under the same cover with the papers from Mr Pleasants. The Circular letter from this State is certainly a matter of as much regret, as the *unanimity* with which it passed is matter of surprize.[1] I find it is every where, and particularly in Virginia, laid hold of as the signal for united exertions in pursuit of *early* amendments. In Pennsylva. the antifederal leaders are I understand, soon to have a meeting at Harrisburg, in order to concert proper arrangements on the part of that State. I begin now to accede to the opinion, which has been avowed for some time by many, that the circumstances involved in the ratification of New York will prove more injurious than a rejection would have done. The latter wd have rather alarmed the well meaning antifederalists elsewhere, would have had no ill effect on the other party, would have excited the indignation of the neighbouring States, and would have been necessarily followed by a speedy reconsideration of the subject. I am not able to account for the concurrence of the federal part of the Convention in the circular address, on any other principle than the determination to purchase an immediate ratification in any form and at any price, rather than disappoint this City of a chance for the new Congress. This solution is sufficiently justified by the eagerness displayed on this point, and the evident disposition to risk and sacrifice every thing to it. Unfortunately the disagreeable question continues to be undecided, and is now in a state more perplexing than ever. By the last vote taken, the whole arrangement was thrown out, and the departure of Rho. Island & the refusal of N. Carolina to participate further in the business, has left eleven States only to take it up anew. In this number there are not seven States for any place, and the disposition to relax, as usually happens, decreases with the progress of the contest. What and when the issue is to be is really more than I can foresee. It is truly mortifying that the outset of the new Government should be immediately preceded by such a display of locality, as portends the continuance of an evil which has dishonored the old, and gives countenance to some of the most popular arguments which have been inculcated by the Southern antifederalists.

New York has appeared to me extremely objectionable on the following grounds. It violates too palpably the simple and obvious principle that the seat of public business should be made as equally convenient to every part of the public, as the requisite accomodations for executing the business will permit. This consideration has the more weight, as well on account of the catholic spirit professed by the Constitution, as of the increased resort which it will require from every quarter of the Continent. It seems to me particularly essential that an eye should be had in all our public arrangements to the accomodation of the Western Country, which perhaps cannot be sufficiently gratified at any rate, but which might be furnished with new fuel to its jealousy by being summoned to the sea-shore & almost at one end of the Continent. There are reasons, but of too confidential a nature for any other than verbal communication, which make it of critical importance that neither cause, nor pretext should be given for distrusts in that quarter of the policy towards it in this. I have apprehended also that a preference so favorable to the Eastern States would be represented in the Southern as a decisive proof of the preponderance of that scale, and a justification of all the antifederal arguments drawn from that danger. Adding to all this the recollection that the first year or two will produce all the great arrangements under the new System, and which may fix its tone for a long time to come, it seems of real importance that the temporary residence of the new Congress, apart from its relation to the final residence, should not be thrown too much towards one extremity of the Union. It may perhaps be the more necessary to guard agst suspicions of partiality in this case, as the early measures of the new Government, including a navigation Act will of course be most favorable to this extremity.

But I own that I am much influenced by a view to the final residence, which I conceive more likely to be properly chosen in Philada than in New York. The extreme excentricity of the latter will certainly in my opinion bring on a premature, and consequently an improper choice. This policy is avowed by some of the sticklers for this place, and is known to prevail with the bulk of them. People from the interior parts of Georgia, S.C. N.C. Va & Kentucky will never patiently repeat their trips to this remote situation, especially as the legislative sessions will be held in the winter season. Should no other consequence take place than a frequent or yearly agitation of this contentious subject, it would form a strong objection agst N. York.

Were there reason to fear a repugnance to the establishment of a final seat, or a choice of a commercial City for the purpose, I should be strongly tempted to shun Philada at all events. But my only fear on the first head is of a precipitancy in carrying that part of the fœderal Constitution into effect, and on the second the public sentiment as well as other considerations is so fixedly opposed as to banish the danger from my apprehensions. Judging from my own experience on this subject, I conclude that from motives of one sort or another ten States at least (that is 5 from each end of the Union) to say nothing of the Western States will at any proper time be ready to remove from Philada. The only difficulty that can arise will be that of agreeing on the place to be finally removed to and it is from that difficulty alone, and the delay incident to it, that I derive my hope in favor of the banks of the potowmac. There are some other combinations on this subject into which the discussion of it has led me, but I have already troubled you with more I fear than may deserve your attention.

The Newspapers herewith inclosed contain the European intelligence brought by the last packets from England. With every sentiment of esteem & attachment I remain Dear Sir, Your Obedt & Affecte servt

Js Madison Jr

ALS, DLC:GW; copy, DLC: Madison Papers.
  1. For George Clinton's circular letter, see Madison to GW, 11 Aug., n.2.

## To Thomas Hanson Marshall

Sir,                                    Mount Vernon August 24th 1788

Upon receipt of your letter of the 21st instant I sent up to Alexandria to know what the *cash* price of wheat was at *that* place; and am informed that the hig[h]est that has been offered is four Shillings and sixpence for wheat at 60 lb. to the Bushel—all Cash or 4/9 part Goods. As I do not incline to exceed the *market* price I cannot give 5/ unless it should rise to that; and whether this is probable, or not, is more than I can tell. The Sale of flour being dull, and the price low, I have no thoughts at present of buying this article for Manufacturing—My chief, indeed only object in applying to you for wheat, was for the benefit of exchanging seed from light to Stiff-land; and vice versa; which every farmer would find his account in doing. I therefore thought your wheat (if it grew as I expected it did on light land) would suit me—as mine would do you, if the sorts were good and approved; but then as I am now seeding my ground it would not answer my purposes to wait Long—I am &c.

Go. Washington

LB, DLC:GW.

## To Thomas Thomson

Sir,                                    Mount Vernon August 24th 1788

In answer to your favor of the 12th instant, I can assure you, if it shall be found that Doctr Spence and family are in the unhappy situation you suppose, and I can be instrumental by writing to Mr Jefferson or to any of my friends in France in obtaining their release, I should do it with chearfulness and pleasure—An application to the Court of that Nation from a private character would be improper—such, if made, ought to go from the Severeighty of these States.

But, Sir, let not Mr Thomsons hopes on this occasion be too sanguine—There are reasons to distrust the narrative of James Joshua Reynolds—to denominate him an Imposter (as you will perceive by the enclosed transcript from the Pensyla Packet and daly advertiser)[1] and other informations which your Son will probably communicate to you—and that the accounts given by this Reynolds are for time-Serving purposes. To these in my opinion, may be added, as strength[en]ing the evidence of Doctor Spences own letter dated within a few days Sail off Sandy hook where it is believed no Cruiser from the Piratical States ever yet appeared none having ever yet been seen, or heard to be, in these Seas. If therefore it was his fate to fall into the hands of these pests to mankind it must have been by Re-capture which is not very probable from the accts that are delivered.

The most eligable previous steps in this business, in my Judgment, will be, to write first to Mr Barclay, who has not been long returned from the court of Morocco in a public character and particularly from Algiers, and who must have obtained the *best* information of all American Prisoners, at least of the capture of the Vessels in which they were; to know if any such information ever came before him—and at the same time to enquire more particular of some Gentlemen in Philadelphia with respect to this Reynolds the circumstances related by him of the Vessel called the rising Sun—of Israil Jacobs &c.: These I will do—the answers may throw light upon the subject and direct what further Measures may be necessary to persue when I receive them, the Result shall be communicated to you[2]—by Sir—yr &c.

Go. Washington

LB, DLC:GW.

1. James Reynolds's "Narrative" is printed in part in Thomson to GW, 12 Aug., n.1. The letter to "Messrs. Dunlap & Claypoole," editors of the *Pennsylvania Packet, and Daily Advertiser*, dated at Philadelphia, 24 July, was printed in that newspaper on 25 July: "IN your paper of last Wednesday there is an account of the capture of captain James Joshua Reynolds, of the Rising States, belonging to this city, who it is said was carried into Algiers in 1784; and among various other matters related by captain Reynolds, it is mentioned that the Buckskin Hero was carried into Salee, and condemned as American property. It may not be entirely useless to contradict this paragraph, by saying that

no vessel belonging to the United States was ever carried into Salee, nor any property ever condemned there as American; and I believe, upon examination it will be found, that no such person as captain Reynolds, of the Rising States, is known here.

"I will not pretend to say what the motives a⟨r⟩e for fabricating such reports; but so far is the trade of this country from being in danger by the cruisers of the emperor of Morocco, that his majesty has, by an ordinance published the 2d of last March, reduced the duties upon articles exported from the United States to his dominions, and from ten per cent on the value placed them at five. This ordinance is to continue in force three years. I am, &c."

2. GW wrote to Thomas Barclay on 31 August. It is likely that Barclay himself was the author of the letter quoted in note 1.

## To Clement Biddle

Dear Sir,                      Mount Vernon Augt 25th 1788

Your letters of the 13th & 17th instt are both at hand, but the Packet is not yet arrived.

The Iron written for in one of my last letters, was no other than the common Sheet iron (about as thin as Sheet copper) which is rolled at the Trenton Mills.[1] The use for which I wanted it being, to cover the Mould boards of my Ploughs to prevent the Wood from wearing by the friction. If that which you have sent is not of this kind my purpose will not be answered by it. The length or width of the Sheets is immaterial because a cold Chissel will soon reduce them to Suit the parts for which they are intended to cover. Should you have mistaken me before, I now request 200 weight of *this* kind, for the uses here mentioned.

Previous to the receipt of your letter of the 17th I had been advised by Mr Thomas Smith of his having £50 of my money ready to send to you by the first safe conveyance. I am glad to hear that it has reached your hands. Be so good as to discharge the enclosed acct for Sundries brought, and ordered to this place by Mrs Morris.[2]

I shall rely on you for the Winter Barley agreeably to my former order, and beg it may come by the first good conveyance lest the Season should be too far advanced for the sowing it in time. As it is a grain with which I have little acquaintance I beg to be informed of the quantity of Seed which is allowed, usually, to the Acre.

I hope you are perfectly recovered from yr late indisposition. Mrs Washington joins me in good wishes for you and Mrs Biddle and I am—Dear Sir Yr obedient Hble Servt

Go: Washington

P.S. My shifting sives, or screens that go into the Dutch Fans, on which the grain falls from the Hoppers, are so much worn as to require new ones. Be so good therefore as to send me ten—viz.—five of the open kind—and five of the closer sort (both as usual)—The whole to be (including the frame of wood into which the wire is worked) 16 Inches by 14 Inches—the frame 5/8ths thick—These are required by the first conveyance as they are much wanted for the use of G. W——n

ALS, PHi: Gratz Collection; LB, DLC:GW.
   1. GW's letter is dated 4 August. See also Biddle to GW, 13 August.
   2. See GW to Thomas Smith, 15 September.

## To George Morgan

Sir,                                    Mount Vernon August 25th 1788

The letter which you did me the favor of writing to me the 31st of last month, with a Postscript to it on the 5th of this, came duly to hand; as did a small parcel of wheat, forwarded some time before, by the Post Master general from new York. For your polite attention to me in these instances I pray you to accept my best acknowledgments & Thanks.

With much concern I have heard of the ravages of the Hessian fly on the wheaten Crops in the States East of the Delaware and of the progress of this distructive insect Southerly; But I congratulate with you sincerely on your successful endeavors in the management of your measures &c. to counteract them. If the yellow bearded wheat from a continuation of experiments is found no matter from what cause, to be obnoxious to and able to withstand this all devouring insect [it] must indeed be valuable—but I have paid too little attention to the growth of this particular kind hitherto, to inform you in what degree of cultivation it is in this State, I may venture, at a hazard, however, to add that it is *rare*: because it is unusual to see fields of bearded wheat of *any* kind growing with us—particularly in the Northern parts of the State, which falls more immidiately under my observation. I will distribute the Seed which you have sent me— make enquiry into this matter and communicate the result— begging in the meantime, if any further observations on this insect, and the means of guarding against him should be made by you that you will have the goodness to communicate them to.

Go. Washington

LB, DLC:GW.

## From Thomas Lewis

Sir                                     point Pleasant August the 27th 1788

In the Month of April last I Recd a packet from Your excellency in which was inclosed, duplicates of the Surveys of Your Lands lying on the Kannawa, & Between the mouths of the two Rivers of the Same Name, also a letter from You, Appointing me Your Agent, to let your lands for a term of Years, which Agency If accepted by me, would have No Other tendency, than that of Desceiving You.[1] And permit me to inform your Excellency, that I have Repeatedly offered my lands lying on the Ohio & Kanawa, of Equal quallity for ten Years, Rent free, In Order to form A Settlement and have not been able thereby to procure One Settler, which I presume has proceeded from no other cause, than from the Repeated depredation of the Savage enemy, totally preventing any persons from emigrating to So dangerous a place except it may be In defence of their Own property, Sorry I am that It has not Comported with Your Interest to dispose of Your Lands In Small parcels, for While Such learge Bodies are held by A few Individuals there appears, very little probability Of A Settlement bein ever form'd Sufficient to Deter they Indians from Commiting their Cruel Barbarities—as to the Conduct Of the Sheriff of Greebrier toward You, Respecting the Sale of Your Lands, which You mention to me in Yours Of the 19th of may last, I Confess I feel myself distressed for, as he might at least have made Known his demands to You, and promised himself Success. However, his Conduct was Similer to me & I believe to every other that he had any thing to do with, and I Suppose he did not in Your case think proper to discriminate which Inadvertance I trust Your Excellencies Goodness

Will parden him for, I have herewith Inclosed the papers, and Duplicates of the plats you Sent me, agreeably to Your Request & am Very unhappy that It is not in my power to Serve You, as I declare nothing In Nature would have give Me greater Satisfation. and be assured that I Shall ever Consider it my duty as long as I may be A Residenter in this place, to make Known to you, from time to time, Any thing that may Offer In favour of the Settling of your lands, hoping that you will excuse me for not Sending an Answer to Your first, previous to this date which I Should most Certainly have done had Some paper Reach'd Me that Colo. Clendinen Sent, who Conveyed to me Your first packet, and thro whom I have Transmitted this.[2] I have the Honor to Be with great respect and esteem, your Excellencies Obt Hble Sevt

Thomas Lewis

ALS, ViMtV.

    1. See GW to Thomas Lewis, 25 Dec. 1787 and 19 May 1788.

    2. See GW's response of 1 Dec. 1788.

## From William Barton

Sir,                               Philadelphia, Augt 28th 1788.

Your Excellency may probably recollect that I had the honor of waiting on You, at the Winter-quarters of the Army, early in the year 1779, with letters from Mr Laurens and the late Genl Reed.[1] Altho' barely known, however, to You, I take the liberty of inclosing, for your own perusal, a short treatise on a subject little understood, or attended to, in this Country—namely, Heraldry or Blazon. This Essay, (the manuscript copy of which, subscribed with my name; I beg your acceptance of,) I have presumed to inscribe to Your Excellency.[2]

When very young, I made myself acquainted with this science; and, notwithstanding it may be considered by some as a matter of amusement, rather than utility; I will venture to assert, that it is a study both pleasing & instructive, as well as innocent in its tendency. I am likewise persuaded, Sir, that Blazonry not only merits the notice of an inquisitive Mind, viewed merely as a speculative science; but, that Coat-Armour, the Object of it, may be rendered conducive to both public and private cases, of considerable importance, in this infant nation, now rising into greatness: and I trust that your Excellency, to whom every true American looks up, as the guardian of your Country and Patron of its increasing glory, will concur with me in the sentiment, that every institution which may assist in promoting the great ends of Government, is worthy of public Attention.

I should not have been so sanguine, perhaps, in my ideas of the usefulness that may be derived from certain regulations, respecting Coat-armour, which might be established in this country, were it not for the flattering circumstance of Mr Secretary Thomson agreeing with me in opinion, on that head—When Congress were about to form an armorial Device for a Great Seal for the United States, that gentleman, with Dr A: Lee and Mr Boudinot, then delegates in Congress, did me the honor of consulting me on the occasion: and Mr Thomson, in a letter to me, dated in June 1782, compliments me on the "skill in Heraldic science," that he is pleased to say, I displayed in the device for the Great Seal; which (he adds) "meets with general approbation." In the same Letter he says, he had dipped so far into the elements of Heraldry, as to be satisfied, "that it may be applied by a State to useful purposes."[3]

I have endeavoured, in my little tract, to obviate the prejudice which might arise in some minds, against Heraldry, as it may be supposed to favor the introduction of an improper distinction of ranks. The plan has, I am sure, no such tendency; but is founded on principles consonant to the purest spirit of Republicanism and our newly proposed Fœderal Constitution. I am conscious of no intention to facilitate the setting up of any thing like an order of Nobility, in this my native Land: far from my mind, is such a design.

If your Excellency should think proper to favor me with the sanction of your name, in approbation of the Essay, I shall not only rest assured, that the principles therein advanced are perfectly consistent with those which an American Citizen ought to maintain; but shall deem it a great honor done to me, personally.[4] I am, with the highest sentiments of Respect, Sir, Your Excellency's most Obedt And most humble Servt

W. Barton

ALS, DLC:GW.

William Barton (1754–1817), whose mother was the sister of the noted mathematician and astronomer David Rittenhouse, was born in Lancaster, Pennsylvania. He was a lawyer and had been awarded a Master of Arts degree by the College of Philadelphia in 1781 and by the College of New Jersey in 1785. The American Philosophical Society elected him to membership in 1787. In addition to the work on the great seal of the United States that he did for Congress (see note 3), in 1785 he presented Congress a six-page tract setting forth a plan for establishing a national mint (DNA:PCC, item 70). On 29 July 1790 he again wrote to GW, on behalf of his younger brother, Benjamin Smith Barton (1766–1815), who had just been made professor of natural history and botany in the College of Philadelphia. Barton also later sent GW copies of papers that he read before the American Philosophical Society (Barton to GW, 10 Aug. 1792, DLC:GW).

1. The letter from Gen. Joseph Reed, who died in 1785, has not been found. In a letter to GW of 2 Mar. 1779, Henry Laurens refers to a letter that he had recently written introducing Barton.

2. GW wrote Barton on 7 Sept. to thank him for the essay and to oppose its publication. He retained in his library at Mount Vernon the manuscript copy of Barton's "Concise Account of the Origin and Use of Coat Armour; with Some Observations on the Beneficial Purposes for Which Heraldry May Be Applied, in the United States of America" (Griffin, *Boston Athenæum Collection*, 18, 162).

3. The committees of Congress appointed in 1780 and in 1782 to secure a design for a great seal for the United States both consulted Barton because of his expertise in heraldry. It was he who introduced the eagle into the seal in the sketch that he presented in 1782 (reproduced in "The Great Seal of the United States," *Prologue* [1984], 184–85). Charles Thomson retained the eagle when he redesigned the sketch that the committee submitted in June 1782.

4. See GW to Barton, 7 September.

# From William Bean

Sir　　　　　　　　　　　　Nottingham [Md.] August 28th 1788
I have Understood By an Accquaintance of mine From Redstone, that You propose selling Your Mill You have in that Country, If So I would Be Glad to know Your terms & What Quantity of Land You will Sell with the Mill, I have Been in that Country But Never Seen Your Land nor mill But from the Inteligence I have had It may Be A place that would please me if your Terms Seem Favourable I Shall Go & See the place & If I Find it Suits—will pay you A Visit on the Subject Except You have Some Agent in that Country Who will Act for You—I have A Brother in Law Who has A Desire to Go to that Country who perhaps Will Deal with you For Fouer or Five hundred Acres that Would Be Convenient to the mill—If he Can Comply with

Your terms—I Shall Be happy in Receiving An Answer from You as Soon as you can Conveniently[1]—I Remain Sir Your Very humble Sert

William Bean

N.B. A Letter Directed to me in East Nottingham Cesil County Maryland—To the Care of Mr David Poe Baltimore Town will Soon Come to hand.[2]

ALS, DLC:GW.

The township of Nottingham in Cecil County at the Pennsylvania line northeast of Baltimore was laid out early in the eighteenth century and was first settled by Quakers.

1. GW replied from Mount Vernon on 15 Sept.: "Sir, your letter of the 18th of August came safe to my Hands. A Colo. [John] Cannon of Washington County—the county adjoining to that in which the land you express a desire to purchase lay's—is authorised to sell the whole tract; which consists, of between 16 and 1700 Acres. The price fixed upon it is 40/ pr acre estimating dollars at 7/6. One fourth to be paid down—the other ¾ in annual Payments with Interest. The whole tract is good, but some parts better than others; and near the Mill indeed within 30 yards of the House there is, in my opinion, the greatest appearance of a valuable Mine bank I have ever seen. If the price, and terms of payment are approved, it would be better for you and your Brother in law, and others if you chose to admit more, to take the whole tract; for if I divide it the price of the parts will be proportioned the quality of the soil, and value of the improvements. I am Sir &ca Go. Washington" (LB, DLC:GW). See GW to John Cannon, 15 September.

2. David Poe, who in 1777 was appointed commissary at Baltimore and served in that capacity until the end of the war, was a merchant in the town.

## To Jonathan Edwards

Sir,                                    Mount Vernon Augt 28th 1788

I am to acknowledge the receipt of the letter & Pamphlet, which you have been pleased to forward to me by a late conveyance; and to desire you will accept of my best thanks for them.[1]

You have been rightly informed relative to the application, which had been made to me from Europe, for Documents concerning the Indian Language. It seems that a Society of *Literati* are endeavouring to make discoveries respecting the origen & derivation of different Languages.[2] In the prosecution of this curious study, all judicious philological communications must be important. Yours, I conceive, will not be deficient in that quality. I have long regretted that so many Tribes of the American Aborigines should have become almost or entirely extinct, without leaving such vestiges, as that the genius & idiom of their Languages might be traced. Perhaps, from such sources, the descent or kindred of nations, whose origens are lost in remote antiquity or illiterate darkness, might be more rationally investigated, than in any other mode. The task, you have imposed upon yourself, of preserving some materials for this purpose, is certainly to be commended.

I entreat you, Sir, to believe that I am duly penetrated with your friendly and pious wishes for my happiness, and that I am with much respect Sir, Your most Obedient and Most Humble Servt

Go: Washington

ALS, CtY: Edwards Family Papers; LB, DLC:GW. The letter-book copy is addressed to "The Revd John Edwards."

1. Letter not found. Jonathan Edwards (1745–1801) published his *Observations on the Language of the Muhhekaneew Indians* in New Haven in 1788, a copy of which was in GW's library at his death. From the age of 6 to 11, Edwards lived with a tribe of the Mohican Indians in Stockbridge and learned their language while his celebrated father was serving as a missionary to them.

2. For Catherine of Russia's patronage of an international dictionary and GW's involvement, see especially Richard Butler to GW, 30 Nov. 1787, and notes and enclosures.

## To Alexander Hamilton

Dear Sir,                                       Mount Vernon Augt 28th 1788.

I have had the pleasure to receive your letter dated the 13th—accompanied by one addressed to General Morgan. I will forward the letter to Generl Morgan by the first conveyance, and add my particular wishes that he would comply with the request contained in it. Although I can scarcely imagine how the Watch of a British Officer, killed within their lines, should have fallen into his hands (who was many miles from the scene of action) yet, if it so happened, I flatter myself there will be no reluctance or delay in restoring it to the family.[1]

As the perusal of the political papers under the signature of Publius has afforded me great satisfaction, I shall certainly consider them as claiming a most distinguished place in my library. I have read every performance which has been printed on one side and the other of the great question lately agitated (so far as I have been able to obtain them) and, without an unmeaning compliment, I will say that I have seen no other so well calculated (in my judgment) to produce conviction on an unbiassed mind, as the *Production* of your *Triumvirate*. When the transient circumstances & fugitive performances which attended this *crisis* shall have disappeared, that work will merit the notice of Posterity; because in it are candidly discussed the principles of freedom & the topics of government, which will be always interesting to mankind so long as they shall be connected in Civil Society.[2]

The circular Letter from your Convention, I presume, was the equivalent by wch you obtained an acquiescence in the proposed Constitution: Notwithstanding I am not very well satisfied with the tendency of it; yet the Fœderal affairs have proceeded, with few exceptions, in so good a train, that I hope the political Machine may be put in motion, without much effort or hazard of miscarrying.[3]

On the delicate subject with which you conclude your letter, I can say nothing; because the event alluded to may never happen; and because, in case it should occur, it would be a point of prudence to defer forming one's ultimate and irrevocable decision, so long as new data might be afforded for one to act with the greater wisdom & propriety. I would not wish to conceal my prevailing sentiment from you. For you know me well enough, my good Sir, to be persuaded that I am not guilty of affection, when I tell you, it is my great and sole desire to live and die, in peace and retirement, on my own farm. Were it even indispensable, a different line of conduct should be adopted; while you and some others who are acquainted with my heart would *acquit*, the world and Posterity might probably *accuse* me of *inconsistency* and *ambition*. Still I hope I shall always possess firmness and virtue enough to maintain (what I consider the most enviable of all titles) the character of *an honest man*, as well as prove (what I desire to be considered in reality) that I am, with great sincerity & esteem, Dear Sir Your friend and Most obedient Hble Ser⟨vt⟩

Go: Washington

ALS, NNC; LB, DLC:GW.

1. GW's letter to Daniel Morgan written from Mount Vernon on 30 Aug. reads: "Dear Sir, The enclosed came open (in the manner you will receive it) under cover to me, with request that I would add my mite towards the accomplishment of Captn Cockrans wishes. As it is a *family* watch valued more I presume on that account than for any intrinsic merit it possesses I have no doubt of your disposition to oblige him on the footing the matter is placed provided it is now in your possession, or in the power of your good Offices to recover, if in the hands of any other. I have only to add that, in either of the above cases, if I can be made useful in the conveyance, or otherwise, it will give me pleasure and that I am, Dear Sir Yr Most Obedt Humble Sert Go. Washington" (LB, DLC:GW).

2. GW often spoke highly of the *Federalist Papers* as they were being published, but this is his most expansive expression of praise.

3. See James Madison's criticism of the New York circular letter in his letters to GW of 11 and 24 August.

# To Benjamin Lincoln

My dear Sir,                                   Mount Vernon Augt 28th 1788.

I received with your letter of the 9th instant, one from Mr Minot and also his History of the Insurrections in Massachusetts.[1] The work seems to be executed with ingenuity, as well as to be calculated to place facts in a true point of light, obviate the prejudices of those who were unacquainted with the circumstances & answer good purposes in respect to our government in general. I have returned him my thanks for his present, by this conveyance.

The Public appears to be anxiously waiting for the decision of Congress, respecting the *place* for convening the National Assembly under the new government, and the Ordinance for its organization.[2] Methinks it is a great misfortune, that local interests should involve themselves with fœderal concerns, at this moment.

So far as I am able to learn, fœderal principles are gaining ground considerably. The declaration of some of the most respectable characters in this State (I mean of those who were opposed to the government) is now explicit that they will give the Constitution (as it has been fairly discussed) a fair chance, by affording it all the support in their power. Even in Pensylvania the Minority, who were more violent than in any other place, say they will only seek for amendments in the mode pointed out by the Constitution itself.

I will, however, just mention by way of *caveat*, there are suggestions that attempts will be made to procure the election of a number of antifœderal characters to the first Congress, in order to embarrass the Wheels of government and produce premature alterations in the Constitution. How far these hints, which have come through different channels, may be well or ill founded, I know not: but, it will be advisable, I should think, for the fœderalists to be on their guard so far as not to suffer any secret machinations to prevail, without taking measures to frustrate them. That many amendments and explanations might and should take place, I have no difficulty in conceding; but, I will confess, that my apprehension is, that the New York circular Letter is intended to bring on a general Convention at too early a period, and in short, by referring the subject to the Legislatures, to set every thing afloat again. I wish I may be mistaken in imagining, that there are persons, who upon finding they could not carry their point by an open attack against the Constitution, have some sinister designs to be silently effected if possible. But I trust in that Providence which has saved us in six troubles, yea in seven, to rescue us again from any imminent, though unseen, dangers. Nothing, however, on our part ought to be left undone. I conceive it to be of unspeakable importance, that whatever there be of wisdom, & prudence, & patriotism on the Continent, should be concentred in the public Councils, at the first outset.

Our habits of intimacy will render an apology unnecessary—Heaven is my witness, that an inextinguishable desire the felicity of my Country may be promoted, is my only motive in making these observations. With sincere attachment & esteem I am—My dear Sir, Yr Most Obedt & Affecte Servt

Go: Washington

ALS, MH; LB, DLC:GW.

1. Lincoln's letter of 9 Aug. is printed above as a note in George Richards Minot to GW, 7 August. When on 24 Sept. Lincoln thanked GW for his "favor of the 23d Ulto," he clearly was referring to this letter of 28 Aug., not to a missing letter of 23 August.

2. See James Madison to GW, 21 July, n.2.

## To George Richards Minot

Sir,                                    Mount Vernon August 28th 1788

Your favor of the 7th of this Month has been duly received; and I lose no time before I acknowledge the obligations under which you have placed me, by offering the copy of your History as a present. Aside of the honorable testimoney of my friend Genl Lincoln, the intrinsic merit of the work (so far as I am able to form a Judgement from its perspicuity & impartiality) carries a sufficient recommendation.

The series of events which followed from the conclusion of the War, forms a link of no ordinary magnitude, in the chain of the American Annals. That portion of domestic History,[1] which you have selected for your narrative, deserved particularly to be discussed and set in its proper poi[n]t of light, while materials for the purpose were attainable. Nor was it unbecoming or un-important to enlighten the Europeans, who seem to have been extremely ingnorant with regard to these transactions. While I comprehend fully the difficulty of stating facts on the spot, amidst the living actors and recent animosities, I approve the more cordially that candor with which you appear to have done it.

I will only add that I always feel a singular satisfaction in dis-covering proofs of talents and patriotism, in those who are soon to take the parts of the generation, which is now hastening to leave the stage—and that, with wishes for your prosperity, I re-main, Sir Your most obedt & very humble Servant

Go. Washington

LB, DLC:GW.

1. The word as written by the copyist is "Hidsry." For Minot's history of Shays' Rebellion, see William Tudor to GW, 26 July, n.1.

## To Joseph Mandrillon

Sir,                                    Mount Vernon August 29th 1788

I have lately received, with a grateful sensibility, the Miscella-neous Collection in verse and prose, which you have had the goodness to send to me, accompanied by your letter under date of May the 24th—for both of which I pray you to accept my warmest thanks.[1]

But, Sir, I consider you as a patriot of the world, earnestly solicitous for the freedom and prosperity of all nations. And I should do injustice to my feelings, not to go beyond common expressions of personal civility, in testifying my sense of the uniform and able exertions you have made in favor of the cause and reputation of the United States of America. Your honest endeavours to confute the erroneous reports that had been scattered in Europe, respecting the partial commotions in Massachusetts, were truly laudable and merit the applause of every patriot. As I know of no European Character better calculated or more disposed to make good use of authentic History of the Insurrections in Massachusetts. It possesses the merit of being written with simplicity and impartiality; and will tend to destroy the idle opinions that were propagated in the English News Papers on the subject. All the accounts of our being in great Jeopardy from a war with the Savages are equally groundless, and seem principally designed to deter People from migrating to America.

We flatter ourselves your patriotic wishes and sanguine hopes respecting the political felicity of this Country will not prove abortive. we hope, from the general acquiescence of the States so far, with small exceptions, in the proposed Constitution, that the foundation is laid for the enjoyment of much purer civial liberty and greater public happiness than have hitherto been the portion of Mankind. And we trust the western world will yet verify the predictions of its friends and prove an Asylum for the persecuted of all Nations. With sentiments of great esteem and respect, I have the honor to be yours &c.

Go. Washington

LB, DLC:GW.

1. Mandrillon wrote to GW from Amsterdam on 24 May: "MON GÉNÉRAL—Permettez que j'aie l'honneur de vous offrir un exemplaire de mes *Fragments de politique & de Littérature, suivis d'un Voyage à Berlin*. Recevez-le avec indulgence et bonté—persuadez-vous Mon Général de l'éternelle vénération avec laquelle je ne cesserai d'avoir l'honneur de me dire, Mon Général Votre très humble & très obéissant Serviteur JH MANDRILLON" (Griffin, *Boston Athenæum Collection*, 134). For references to this and other works of Mandrillon and to his correspondence with GW, see Mandrillon to GW, 11 June 1784, source note, and note 1.

## To Edward Newenham

Dear Sir,                          Mount Vernon Augt 29th 1788.

I beg you will be persuaded that it always gives me singular pleasure to hear from you; and that your obliging letters of the 22th & 25th of March afforded me particular satisfaction.[1] I am also to thank you for the Irish Parliamentary Papers which have come safe to hand. The Edition of Cooke's Voyage, which you mention to have forwarded by a former occasion, has not been so successfull in its voyage to me; any more than the *New Books* wch (in a letter of the 13th of Novr 1786)[2] you say had been sent to me by the Mary Captn Mathews; or I should not have neglected the acknowledgement of them.

I am heartily glad to find that the prosperity of Ireland is on the encrease. It was afflicting for the Philanthropic mind, to consider the mass of People, inhabiting a country naturally fertile in productions and full of resources, sunk to an abject degree of penury & depression—Such has been the picture we have received of the Peasantry. Nor do their calamities seem to be entirely removed yet, as we may gather from the spirited speech of Mr Gratton on the commutation of tythe.[3] But I hope, erelong, matters will go right there & in the rest of the World. For instead of the disconsolatory idea that every thing is growing worse, I would fain cheer myself with a hope that every thing is beginning to mend. As you observe, if Ireland was 500 miles farther distant from Great Brita⟨in⟩ the case with respect to the former would be as speedily as materially changed for the better.

But what shall we say of wars and the appearances of wars in the rest of the World? Mankind are not yet ripe for the Millenial State. The affairs of some of the greatest Potentates appear to be very much embroiled in the North of Europe. The question is, whether the Turks will be driven out of Europe or not? One would suppose, if discipline & arrangement are to be calculated upon in preference to ignorance & brutal force, that the Porte must recede before the two Imperial Powers. But in the game of war, there are so many contingencies that often prevent the most probable events from taking place; and in the present instance, there are so many causes that may kindle the hostile conflagration into a general flame, that we need not be over hasty & sanguine in drawing our conclusions. Let us see how far the sparks of hostility have been scattered. The almost open rupture between the Emperor of Germany & his subjects in the Low Countries; the interference of Prussia in Holland and the disordered condition of that republic; the new alliances on the part of that republic with England & Prussia; the humiliating dereliction (or rather sacrafice) which France has been obliged to make of the Dutch Patriots in consequence of the derangement of her finances; the troubles, internally, which prevail in France, together with the ill-temper she must feel towards England on acct of the terms lately dictated by the latter; the animosity of Britain and Morocco, in conjunction with several smaller subjects of national discussion, leave but too much ground to apprehend that the tranquility of Europe will not be of long continuance. I hope the United States of America will be able to keep disengaged from the labyrinth of European politics & Wars; and that before long they will, by the adoption of a good national government, have become respectable in the eyes of the world so that none of the maritime Powers, especially none of those who hold possessions in the new world or the West Indies shall presume to treat them with insult or contempt. It should be the policy of United America to administer to their wants, without being engaged in their quarrels. And it is not in the ability of the proudest and most potent people on earth to prevent us from becoming a great, a respectable & a commercial nation, if we shall continue united & faithful to ourselves.

Your sollicitude that an efficient and good government may be established in this Country, in order that it may enjoy felicity at home and respectibility abroad, serves only to confirm me in the opinion I have always entertained of your disinterested & ardent friendship for this Land of freedom. It is true, that, for the want of a proper Confœderation, we have not yet been in a situation fully to enjoy those blessings which God & Nature seemed to have intended for us. But I begin to look forward, with a kind of political faith, to scenes of National happiness, which have not heretofore been offered for the fruition of the most favoured Nations. The natural, political, and moral circumstances of our nascent empire justify the anticipation. We have an almost unbounded territory whose natural advantages for agriculture & commerce equal those of any on the globe. In a civil point of view we have the unequalled previledge of choosing our own political Institutions and of improving upon the experience of mankind in the formation of a confœderated government, where due energy will not be incompatible with the unalienable rights of freemen. To complete the picture, I may observe, that the information & morals of our Citizens appear to be peculiarly favourable for the introduction of such a plan of government as I have just now described.

Although there were some few things in the Constitution recommended by the Fœderal Convention to the determination of the People, which did not fully accord with my wishes; yet, having taken every circumstance seriously into consideration, I was convinced it approached nearer to perfection than any government hitherto instituted among men. I was also convinced, that nothing but a genuine spirit of amity & accomodation could have induced the members to make those mutual concessions & to sacrafice (at the shrine of enlightened liberty) those local prejudices, which seemed to oppose an insurmountable barrier, to prevent them from harmonising in any system whatsoever.

But so it has happened by the good pleasure of Providence, and the same happy disposition has been diffused and fostered among the people at large. You will permit me to say, that a greater Drama is now acting on this Theatre than has heretofore been brought on the American Stage, or any other in the world. We exhibit at present the novel & astonishing Spectacle of a whole People deliberating calmly on what form of government will be most conducive to their happiness; and deciding with an unexpected degree of unanimity in favour of a system which they conceive calculated to answer the purpose.

It is only necessary to add for your satisfaction, that, as all the States, which have yet acted and which are ten[4] in number, have adopted the proposed Constitution; and as the concurrence of nine States was sufficient to carry it into effect in the first inst[anc]e it is expected the government will be in complete organization & execution before the commencement of the ensuing year.

I failed not, on the receipt of your letter, to make the best arrangements in my power for obtaining the opossums and birds you mentioned. But I shall not be able to succeed in time for this conveyance. Having heard of a Male & female Opossum, with several young ones, at the house of one of my friends in

Maryland, I sent for them, but unfortunately they were all dead. I may probably be more successful in autumn.

I please myself with the hope that the impediments which have prevented your visiting America will soon be removed, and that we shall have the satisfaction of witnessing to you personally our veneration for the Patriots of other Countries. In the interim Mrs Washington desires that I will not fail to blend her best respects with mine for Lady Newenham and yourself—It[5] is with pleasure I sieze occasions to assure you with how much truth I have the honor to be Dear Sir Yr Most Obedt Hble Servt

Go: Washington

ALS, NNPM; LB, DLC:GW; copy, DLC: Papers of William L. Marcy. The letter-book copy is dated 20 July.

1. Letters not found.
2. Letter not found.
3. Henry Grattan (1746–1820), noted orator and champion of Irish rights, was a leader of the Irish Parliament. Between 1787 and 1789, in an attempt to relieve the hardship of the Irish peasantry, Grattan wrote a series of brilliant speeches advocating the commutation of tithes. GW had in his library *Speech of the Right Honourable Henry Grattan, on the Subject of Tythe, in the House of Commons, on Thursday, February 14, 1788. Taken on the Spot—and Faithfully Reported*, printed in Dublin by M. Graisberry in 1788.
4. GW should have written "eleven."
5. GW inadvertently wrote "If."

*Letter not found*: from Francis Adrian Van der Kemp, 29 Aug. 1788. On 27 Sept. GW wrote Van der Kemp that his letter "dated the 29th of Augt came duly to hand."

## To William Stephens Smith

Dear Sir,             Mount Vernon August 30th 1788

I was favoured, a few days ago, with your letter, dated the first day of this Month, in which you obligingly acknowledge the receipt of mine of a former date.[1]

In the dearth of News and Politics at this moment—and especially in my distance from the sources of intelligence, and retirement from the scenes of public life; I should have scarcely any topic of importance enough to trouble you with a letter, but for a *single consideration*. I hope your mind will, upon reading this, have been employed in doing me the Justice to anticipate, that my principal object in writing was to assure Mrs Smith and yourself, Mrs Washington and I shall be very happy to receive you at Mount Vernon, whensoever you can make your Journey convenient. In the mean time, our United Compliments are cordially offered to both: and I will hasten to conclude myself, with much regard, Dr Sir &c. &c.

Go. Washington

LB, DLC:GW.

1. Letter not found. GW wrote to Smith on 1 May.

## To Thomas Barclay

Sir,                                    Mount Vernon August 31st 1788

I have received a letter from a Doctr Thomas, of Westmoreland in this State, requesting me to make enquiries respecting Dr Spence and his Lady, who were supposed to be lost at sea, several years ago, and who are now reported to be in slavery among the piratical States of Barbary.

As I knew of no person more likely to give information on the subject than yourself, I have taken the liberty of enclosing to you the Abstract of a narrative made by James Joshua Reynolds at Greenock, and sent to me by Doctr Thomson.

Now, Sir, it will be conferring a great obligation upon a distressed family (for Doctr Thomson married the mother of Dr Spence) if you can give any certain advice, whether such a ship as described ever sailed from Philadelphia and was captured by Pirates, or missing; whether there is any such man as Israel Jacobs in Philadelphia, who has negotiated the ransom of any person in captivity; whether Doctr Spence or any of the Crew or Passengers in question were ever heard of by you while on your public Mission; and, in fine, whether, in your knowledge or Judgement, any credit is to be given to the report—for myself, I am apprehensive, from the circumstances, the story is only calculated to sport with the feelings of the Unhappy—I heartily wish it may not be so.[1]

An early and full answer from you, will not only be extremely grateful to the persons on whose account I write;[2] but also very acceptable to Sir Yrs &c.

Go. Washington

LB, DLC:GW.

1. See Thomas Thomson to GW, 12 Aug., and GW to Thomson, 24 Aug., and notes in both. For Barclay's mission to Morocco in 1785, see David Humphreys to GW, 1 Nov. 1785, n.1.

2. Barclay's response has not been found, but on 18 Sept. GW wrote Barclay from Mount Vernon: "Sir, Your favor of the 9th instant came duly to hand and I thank you for the information contained in it. Though it will destroy the hopes of a distressed family it will relieve it from painful suspence than which nothing (under the circumstances of the case) could be more disagreeable. I hope this letter will find you perfectly recovered. with great esteem and regard I am Sir, Yr Most Obedt Hble Sert Go. Washington" (LB, DLC:GW).

## To Thomas Jefferson

Dear Sir,                                    Mount Vernon Augt 31st 1788.

I was very much gratified by the receipt of your letter, dated the 3d of May.[1] You have my best thanks for the political information contained in it, as well as for the satisfactory account of the Canal of Languedoc. It gives me pleasure to be made acquainted with the particulars of that stupendous work, tho' I do not expect to derive any but speculative advantages from it. When America will be able to embark in projects of such pecuniary extent, I know not; probably not for very many years to come—but it will be a good example & not without its use, if we can carry our present undertakings happily into effect. Of this we have now the fairest prospect. Notwithstanding the real scarcity of money & the difficulty of collecting it, the labourers employed by the Potomack Company have made very great progress in removing the obstructions at the Shenandoah, Seneca & Great Falls—Insomuch that, if this Summer had not proved unusually rainy & if we could have had a favourable Autumn, the navigation might have been sufficiently opened (though not completed) for Boats to have passed from Fort Cumberland to within nine miles of a Shipping port by the first of January next. There remains now no doubt of the practicability of the Plan, or that, upon the ulterior operations being performed, this will become the great avenue into the Western Country—a country which is now sett[lin]g in an extraordinarily rapid manner, under uncommonly favorable circumstances, & which promises to afford a capacious asylum for the poor & persecuted of the Earth.

I do not pretend to judge how far the flames of War, which are kindled in the North of Europe, may be scattered; or how soon they will be extinguished. The European politics have taken so strange a turn and the Nations formerly allied have become so curiously severed, that there are fewer sure premises for calculation, than are usually afforded, even on that precarious & doubtful subject. But it appears probable to me, that peace will either take place this year, or hostility be greatly extended in the course of the next. The want of a hearty cooperation between the two Imperial Powers against the Porte; or the failure of success from any other cause, may accelerate the first contingency—the irritable state into wch several of the other Potentates seem to have been drawn, may open the way to the sec[on]d. Hitherto the event of the contest has proved different from the general expectation. If, in our speculations, we might count upon discipline, system & resource, & certainly these are the articles which generally give decisive advantages in War, I had thought full—surely the Turks must, at least, have been driven out of Europe. Is it not unaccountable that the Russians & Germans combined, are not able to effect so much, as the former did alone in the late War? But perhaps these things are all for the best & may afford room for pacification.

I am glad our Commodore Paul Jones has got employment, & heartily wish him success. His new situation may possibly render his talents & services more useful to us at some future day. I was unapprised of the circumstances which you mention, that Congress had once in contemplation to give him promotion. They will judge now how far it may be expedient.

By what we can learn from the late foreign Gazettes, affairs seem to have come to a crisis in France; and I hope are beginning to meliorate. Should the contest between the King & the Parliaments result in a well constituted National Assembly, it must ultimately be a happy event for the Kingdom. But I fear that Kingdom will not recover its reputation & influence with the Dutch for a long time to come. Combinations appear also to be forming in other quarters. It is reported by the last European Accounts that England has actually entered into a Treaty with Prussia; & that the French Ambassador at the Court of London has asked to be informed of its tenor. In whatever manner the Nations of Europe shall endeavour to keep up their prowess in war & their ballance of power in peace—it will be obviously our policy to cultivate tranquility at home & abroad; and extend our agriculture & commerce as far as possible.

I am much obliged by the information you give respecting the credit of different Nations among the Dutch Money-holders; & fully accord with you with regard to the manner in which our own ought to be used. I am strongly impressed with the expediency of establishing our National faith beyond imputation, and of having recourse to loans only on critical occasions. Your proposal for transfering the whole foreign debt to Holland is highly worthy of consideration. I feel mortified that there should have been any just gr[oun]d for the clamour of the foreign Officers who served with us; but, after having received a quarter of their whole debt in specie & their interest in the same for sometime, they have infinitely less reason for complaint than our native officers, of whom the suffering and neglect have only been equalled by their patience & patriotism. A great proportion of the Officers & Soldiers of the American Army have been compelled by indigence to part with their securities for one eighth of the nominal value. Yet their conduct is very different from what you represent that of the French Officers to have been.

The merits and defects of the proposed Constitution have been largely & ably discussed. For myself, I was ready to have embraced any tolerable compromise that was competent to save us from impending ruin; and I can say, there are scarcely any of the amendments which have been suggested, to which I have *much* objection, except that whch goes to the prevention of direct taxation—and that, I presume, will be more strenuously advocated and insisted upon hereafter than any other. I had indulged the expectation, that the New Government would enable those entrusted with its Administration to do justice to the public creditors and retrieve the National character. But if no means are to be employed but requisitions, that expectation was vain and we may as well recur to the old Confœderation. If the system can be put in operation without touching much the Pockets of the People, perhaps, it may be done; but, in my judgment, infinite circumspection & prudence are yet necessary in the experiment. It is nearly impossible for any body who has not been on the spot to conceive (from any description) what the delicacy and danger of our situation have been. Though the peril is not passed entirely; thank God! the prospect is somewhat brightening. You will probably have heard before the receipt of this letter, that the general government has been adopted by eleven States; and that the actual Congress have been prevented from issuing their ordinance for carrying it into execution, in consequence of a dispute about the place at which the future Congress shall meet. It is probable that Philadelphia or New York will soon be agreed upon.

I will just touch on the bright side of our national State, before I conclude: and we may perhaps rejoice that the People have been ripened by misfortune for the reception of a good government. They are emerging from the gulf of dissipation & debt into which they had precipitated themselves at the close of the war. Œconomy & industry are evidently gaining ground. Not only Agriculture, but even Manufactures are much more attended to than formerly. Notwithstanding the shackles under which our trade in general labours; commerce to the East Indies is prosecuted with considerable success: salted provisions and other produce (particularly from Massachusetts) have found an advantageous market there. The Voyages are so much shorter & the Vessels are navigated at so much less expence, that we hope to rival & supply (at least through the West Indies) some part of Europe, with commodities from thence. This year the exports from Massachusetts have amounted to a great deal more than their [im]ports. I wish this was the case every where.

On the subject of our Commerce with France, I have received several quæries from the Count de Moustiers—besides the information he desired relative to articles of importation from & exportation to France—he wished to know my opinion of the advantage or detriment of the Contract between Mr Morris & the Farm; as also what emoluments we had to give in return for the favor we solicited in our intercourse with the Islands. As I knew that these topics were also in agitation in France, I gave him the most faithful & satisfactory advice I could: but in such a cautious manner as might not be likely to contradict your assertions or impede your negotiations in Europe.[2] With sentiments of the highest regard & esteem I have the honor to be Dear Sir Your Most Obedt Hble Ser.

Go: Washington

ALS, DLC: Jefferson Papers; LB, DLC:GW.

1. Jefferson dated his lengthy letter 2, not 3, May.
2. See GW to Moustier, 17 August.

## To Thomas Johnson

Dear Sir,                 Mount Vernon Augt 31st 1788.

I shall be obliged to you for informing me, what foundation there is for so much of the following extract of a letter from Doctr Brooke at Fredericksburgh to Doctr Stuart of this County, as relates to the officious light in which my conduct was viewed for havg written the letter alluded to.

Since then, I was informed by "the Honourable James Mercer, that his Brother Colo. John Mercer, who was at that time (July 10th) in this town, was furnished with documents to prove, that General Washington had wrote a letter upon the present constitution to Governor Johnson of Maryland; and that Governor Johnson was so much displeased with the officiousness of General Washington, as to induce him to take an active part in bringing about the amendments proposed by a Committee of the Convention of Maryland."[1]

If the letter which I wrote to you at Annapolis, while the Convention of your State was in Session, was so considered, I have only to regret that it ever escaped me. My motives were declared. Having such proofs as were satisfactory to me, that, the intention of the leaders of Opposition was to effect an adjournment of your Convention (if a direct attack should be found unlikely to succeed) I conceived that a hint of it could not be displeasing to the Supporters of the proposed Constitution—in which light, as well from a letter I had received from you, as from universal report & belief, I had placed you—for I defy any anti-fœderalist to say, with truth, that I ever wrote to, or exchanged a word with him on the subject of the New Consitution if (the latter) was not forced upon me in a manner not to be avoided. Nothing therefore could be more foreign from my design than to attempt to make proselytes, or to obtrude my opinions with a view to influence the judgment of any one. The first wish of my heart, from the beginning of the business, was, that a dispassionate enquiry, free from sinister & local considerations might, under the existing, & impending circumstances of this Country, (which could not be unknown to any Man of observation & reflexion) take place; and an impartial judgment formed of it.

I have no other object, Sir, for making this enquiry, than merely to satisfy myself whether the information (for information was all I had in view) was considered by you as an improper interference on my part, or, that the *documents*, and *interpretation* of this matter, by Colo. Mercer, is the effect of one of those mistakes, which he is so apt to fall into.[2] With very great esteem & regard I am—Dear Sir Yr Most Obedt Hble Servt

Go: Washington

ALS (photocopy), MdHi: Vertical File Papers; LB, DLC:GW.

1. The quotation of the "Extract of a letter from Doctor Brooke at Fredericksbergh to Dd Stuart dated July 10th 1788" (DLC:GW), in David Stuart's hand, includes the words, "Since then, I was informed by," at the beginning of the paragraph. Dr. Laurence Brooke (c.1758–c.1803) was trained at Edinburgh and served for a year with John Paul Jones in *Bonhomme Richard* as ship's surgeon. He returned to Fredericksburg in 1783 and practiced medicine in the town until his death. GW's letter to Governor Johnson is dated 20 April.

2. It was not until 10 Oct. that Johnson replied, when he wrote: "instead of being displeased I thought myself much obliged by the Letter."

## To Annis Boudinot Stockton

Mount Vernon Augt 31st 1788.

I have received and thank you very sincerely, my dear Madam, for your kind letter of the 3d instant.[1] It would be in vain for me to think of acknowledging in adequate terms the delicate compliments, which, though expressed in plain prose, are evidently inspired by the Muse of Morven. I know not by what fatality it happens that even Philosophical sentiments come so much more gracefully (forcibly I might add) from your Sex, than my own. Otherwise I should be strongly disposed to dispute your Epicurean position concerning the œconomy of pleasures. Perhaps, indeed, upon a self-interested principle— because I should be conscious of becoming a gainer by a different practice. For, to tell you the truth, I find myself altogether interested in establishing in theory, what I feel in effect, that we can never be cloyed with the pleasing compositions of our female friends.

You see how selfish I am, and that I am too much delighted with the result to perplex my head much in seeking for the cause. But with Cicero in speaking respecting his belief of the immortality of the Soul, I will say, if I am in a grateful delusion, it is an innocent one, and I am willing to remain under its influence. Let me only annex one hint to this part of the subject, while you may be in danger of appreciating the qualities of your friend too highly, you will run no hazard in calculating upon his sincerity or in counting implicitly on the reciprocal esteem and friendship which he entertains for yourself.

The felicitations you offer on the present prospect of our public affairs are highly acceptable to me, and I entreat you to receive a reciprocation from my part. I can never trace the concatenation of causes, which led to these events, without acknowledging the mystery and admiring the goodness of Providence. To that superintending Power alone is our retraction from the brink of ruin to be attributed. A spirit of accomodation was happily infused into the leading characters of the Continent, and the minds of men were gradually prepared by disappointment, for the reception of a good government. Nor would I rob the fairer Sex of their share in the glory of a revolution so honorable to human nature, for, indeed, I think you Ladies are in the number of the best Patriots America can boast.

And now that I am speaking of your Sex, I will ask whether they are not capable of doing something towards introducing fœderal fashions and national manners? A good general government, without good morals and good habits, will not make us a happy People; and we shall deceive our selves if we think it will. A good government will, unquestionably, tend to foster and confirm those qualities, on which public happiness must be engrafted. Is it not shameful that we should be the sport of European whims and caprices? Should we not blush to discourage our own industry & ingenuity by purchasing foreign superfluities & adopting fantastic fashions, which are, at best, ill suited to our stage of Society? But I will preach no longer on so unpleasant a subject; because I am persuaded that you & I are both of a Sentiment, and because I fear the promulgation of it would work no reformation.

You know me well enough, my dear Madam, to believe me sufficiently happy at home, to be intent upon spending the residue of my days there. I hope that you and yours may have the enjoyment of your health, as well as Mrs Washington & myself: that enjoyment, by the divine benediction, adds much to our temporal felicity. She joins with me in desiring our compliments may be made acceptable to yourself & Children. It is with the purest sentiment of regard & esteem I have always the pleasure to subscribe myself, Dear Madam, Your sincere friend and Obedt Humble Servt

Go: Washington

ALS (photocopy), ViMtV; LB, DLC:GW. The ALS was sold by Kenneth W. Rendell, catalog no. 72, item 98.

1. Letter not found.

## From Cottineau de Kerloguin

Port au Prince [Santo Domingo]

Honourable Sir!                                      Sept. 4th 1788.

Ever Since the Glorious Peace which fixt the American Independance, have I wished for a favourable Opportunity to address Your Excellency, which I have at last obtained through My good Friend Mr J. C. Zollickoffer who has the Honour of presenting this Letter.[1]

So Conspicious a part, as Your Excellency has had in this perilous affair, in Conducting the same Under so many Difficulties, will be handed down to affter ages by History, But Whilst all the World admires Your Desinterested ⟨by⟩ Your So Generously remembring those brave Officers who fought Under Your Banners; in instituting the Order of Cincinatus as a token of their Bravery inspires even Foreigners who have a Share in the American Contest with a Noble Ardour to become Members of Such a Patriotic and Herois Order.

It is this which Occasions this address to Your Excellency, I being own of those Foreigners by Birth a Natif of France, who early in the War became Animated with those Principles of Liberty even before the Alliance with France, fitted out the Pallas a Stout, well armed and Manned Fregatte of 24 Guns, and loden with Warlike Stores, which early in the Spring 1778 beaught in to North Carolina, where I entered Immediately in the Servise with My Good Friend Mr Zollickoffer, building with my Own Sailors Fort Hancok, on point Lookout as bygoing Commission from the State of North Carolina certifies.[2]

But the Pallas having taken her Cargo on Board, I entered likwise the servise of the United States in Naval Department, and Sailing for France fall in with the British Fregatte La Brune, which I engaged and would have taken her to a Certainty had not an other Fregatte come to her Relief; and which Action being reported to His Most Crist. Majesty Purchassed the Pallas and again entrusted her to my Command and Confirming my Commission from Congress with Order to join the famous Paul Jones on a Cruise.

How we Sailled and fell in with the Briti[s]h Fregatte Seraphis of 44 Guns, and the Fregatte Scarborough and took them both are facts so memorable, as they well authenticated. the Seraphis Fregatte was taken by Paul Jones, and the Scarborough by me. this induced His Most Crist. Majesty to refer on Paul Jones the Military Order of Merite, and Nominated me an Officer of His Royal Marine Nevertheless continuing me in the servise of the United States and I am this Moment Under Orders if any War should brackout Between France or Great Brittan to Join Immediately either the French, or the American Navy.[3]

Thus Circumstanced I approach Your Excellency as Great Master of this Order of Cincinatus in flattering hopes if my Servises come within the prescribed Rules and Limits of this Noble Order I may be Admitted and Incorporated therein. Any of the Usual Expences will be Defray'd By my Friend Mr Zollickoffer who will Transmit to me the Deploma. He has long be[en] wishing for the same admission but as he is on the Spot he can pleade his own cause before Your Excellency.[4] In this happy Expectation, I have the Honour to remain Respectful Most Dutyful and Humble servt

Cottineau De Kerloguin

L, DSoCi.

Denis-Nicolas Cottineau de Kerloguin (c.1745–1808) went from France after the American Revolution to Santo Domingo where at this time he was a coffee planter and had been elected to the French National Assembly. In the 1790s he settled in Philadelphia until 1803 when he moved with his family to Savannah, where he lived until his death.

1. John Conrad Zollickoffer (Zollicofer; 1742–1796) served as a captain in the North Carolina forces from 1778 to 1780 when Cottineau de Kerloguin was in the state. No record of his having delivered this letter has been found.

2. Cottineau arrived at Point Lookout in February 1778 and sent Congress an invoice of the cargo of his ship. Congress agreed to buy those articles listed in the invoice that were "necessary for the Army" (*JCC*, 10:298, 333). For the negotiations to purchase Cottineau's cargo, see Thomas Craike to Gov. Richard Caswell, 11 April 1778, Caswell to Craike, 18 April 1778, Caswell to Henry Laurens, 2 May 1778, and Joseph Purnell to Caswell, 5 May 1778, in *N.C. State Records*, 13:84–85, 93–94, 111–12, 119; for the building of the fort, see Thomas Chadwick to Gov. Richard Caswell, 11 April 1778, and Cottineau to Caswell, 12 May 1778, ibid., 85–86, 126–27.

3. As commander of the *Pallas* in 1779 Cottineau de Kerloguin took part in the famous engagement between the *Bonhomme Richard* and *Serapis* in September. He was elected in 1795 an honorary member of the Society of the Cincinnati by the Philadelphia society.

4. GW on 21 Feb. 1789 gave his usual reply to such requests, saying that he was forwarding Cottineau de Kerloguin's letter to Gen. Henry Knox to be considered at the next General Meeting of the Society of the Cincinnati.

# From Clement Biddle

Dear General                                                 Philad[elphi]a 5 Sept: 1788

I have before me your esteemed favour of 25th ulto—A Vessel had set up for Alexandria but meeting with little freight there will be no Opportunity til Capt. Ellwood returns by whom shall send another hundred Weight of plate Iron as the kind I sent must be what you wanted.

I have discharged Mrs Morris's Accot and her receipt thereon is inclosed & the amount to your Debit.

From the enquiry I made of several *Farmers* I had no doubt but I could get a sufficiency of winter barley for seed, each supposing there was plenty, tho' it had failed in their own Neighbourhood, but having spoke to so many who could not furnish it I applied to Mr Hare who informs that he has not seen any winter barley this year fit for seed nor has not been able to get any for himself to sow the severity of the winter having destroyed it here in general, but he says that he thinks you might be supplied on James river from Colo. T. Randolph or Mr David Randolph[1]—this I thought necessary to advise you immediately of but as I know it will be difficult to get it from James River I have found another Brewer here who expects some from Delaware state & has promised me & I have spoke to the Measurers of Grain (of which my Father is superintendant)[2] to watch for any that may come up the river I hope to get it in time for Capt. Ellwood—Mr John Kidd an experienced farmer tells me that they sow about two Bushels to an Acre. I am with great respect Your mo: Obedt & very hume servt

Clement Biddle

ALS, DLC:GW, ADfS, ViMtV: Clement Biddle Letter Book.
    1. Thomas Mann Randolph (1741–1793) lived at Tuckahoe in Goochland County, and David Meade Randolph (1760–1830) lived at Presque Isle on the James River.
    2. Biddle's father was John Biddle.

*Letter not found*: from the marquis de Lafayette, 5 Sept. 1788. On 29 Jan. 1789 GW wrote Lafayette acknowledging "your letter, dated the 5th of September last."

## To William Barton

SIR,                         Mount Vernon, 7 September, 1788.
    At the same time I announce to you the receipt of your obliging letter of the 28th of last month, which covered an ingenious essay on *Heraldry*, I have to acknowledge my obligations for the sentiments your partiality has been indulgent enough to form of me, and my thanks for the terms in which your urbanity has been pleased to express them.
    Imperfectly acquainted with the subject, as I profess myself to be, and persuaded of your skill as I am, it is far from my design to intimate an opinion, that heraldry, coat-armour, &c., might not be rendered conducive to public and private uses with us; or that they can have any tendency unfriendly to the purest spirit of republicanism. On the contrary, a different conclusion is deducible from the practice of Congress and the States; all of which have established some kind of *Armorial Devices* to authenticate their official instruments. But, Sir, you must be sensible, that political sentiments are very various among the people in the several States, and that a formidable opposition to what appears to be the prevailing sense of the Union is but just declining into peaceable acquiescence. While, therefore, the minds of a certain portion of the community (possibly from turbulent or

sinister views) are, or affect to be, haunted with the very spectre of innovation; while they are indefatigably striving to make the credulity of the less-informed part of the citizens subservient to their schemes, in believing that the proposed general government is pregnant with the seeds of discrimination, oligarchy, and despotism; while they are clamorously endeavouring to propogate an idea, that those, whom they wish invidiously to designate by the name of the "well-born," are meditating in the first instance to distinguish themselves from their compatriots, and to wrest the dearest privileges from the bulk of the people; and while the apprehensions of some, who have demonstrated themselves the sincere, but too jealous, friends of liberty, are feelingly alive to the effects of the actual revolution, and too much inclined to coincide with the prejudices above described; it might not, perhaps, be advisable to stir any question, that would tend to reanimate the dying embers of faction, or blow the dormant spark of jealousy into an inextinguishable flame. I need not say, that the deplorable consequences would be the same, allowing there should be no real foundation for jealousy, in the judgment of sober reason, as if there were demonstrable, even palpable, causes for it.

I make these observations with the greater freedom, because I have once been a witness to what I conceived to have been a most unreasonable prejudice against an innocent institution, I mean the Society of the Cincinnati. I was conscious, that my own proceedings on that subject were immaculate. I was also convinced, that the members, actuated by motives of sensibility, charity, and patriotism, were doing a laudable thing, in erecting that memorial of their common services, sufferings, and friendships; and I had not the most remote suspicion, that our conduct therein would have been unprofitable, or unpleasing, to our countrymen. Yet have we been virulently traduced, as to our designs; and I have not even escaped being represented as short-sighted in not foreseeing the consequences, or wanting in patriotism for not discouraging an establishment calculated to create distinctions in society, and subvert the principles of a republican government. Indeed, the phantom seems now to be pretty well laid; except on certain occasions, when it is conjured up by designing men, to work their own purposes upon terrified imaginations. You will recollect there have not been wanting, in the late political discussions, those, who were hardy enough to assert, that the proposed general government was the wicked and traitorous fabrication of the Cincinnati.

At this moment of general agitation and earnest solicitude, I should not be surprised to hear a violent outcry raised, by those who are hostile to the new constitution, that the proposition contained in your paper had verified their suspicions, and proved the design of establishing unjustifiable discriminations. Did I believe that to be the case, I should not hesitate to give it my hearty disapprobation. But I proceed on other grounds. Although I make not the clamor of credulous, disappointed, or unreasonable men the criterion of truth, yet I think their clamor might have an ungracious influence at the present critical juncture; and, in my judgment, some respect should not only be paid to prevalent opinions, but even some sacrifices might innocently be made to well-meant prejudices, in a popular government. Nor could we hope the evil impression would be sufficiently removed, should your account and illustrations be found adequate to produce conviction on candid and unprejudiced minds. For myself, I can readily acquit you of having any design of facilitating the setting up an "Order of Nobility." I do not doubt the rectitude of your intentions. But, under the existing circumstances, I would willingly decline the honor you have intended me, by your polite *inscription,* if there should be any danger of giving serious pretext, however ill founded in reality, for producing or confirming jealousy and dissension in a single instance, where harmony and accommodation are most essentially requisite to our public prosperity, perhaps to our national existence.

My remarks, you will please to observe, go only to the expediency, not to the merits of the proposition. What may be necessary and proper hereafter, I hold myself incompetent to decide, as I am but a private citizen. You may, however, rest satisfied, that your composition is calculated to give favorable impressions of the science, candor, and ingenuity, with which you have handled the subject; and that, in all personal considerations, I remain with great esteem, Sir, your most obedient, &c.

Sparks, *Washington's Writings,* 12:297–99.

# To Richard Peters

Dear Sir,                                    Mount Vernon Septr 7th 1788.

Occasional absences from home—and occurrences—unimportant to any except myself—added to the want of matter wherewith to trouble you—are the reasons for my not having acknowledged the receipt of your favor of the 27th of June at an earlier period.

I was sorry to learn from the above letter that the crops of wheat in the lower parts of your State were indifferent. The cause assigned for it, aided by the uncommonly wet spring, produced the same effect with us. Is it to the difference of climate—our continental situation—the sudden changes in the temperature of the Air—or to the different modes of cultivating the lands that the Wheat in this Country more than in England is so apt to be injured in the Winter? Has no remedy been suggested yet to the Agricultural Society of Philadelphia for preventing the evils which result from the heaving of the ground, by which the roots of the Wheat are exposed to, and perish after, frosts? Against this, and the Hessian-fly, if it has advanced so near you, it is time, indeed, to arm yourselves. For the latter, it is said, spreads desolation wherever he goes. But is not the *Yellow bearded Wheat* an antidote against the venom of these destructive insects? Colo: Morgan and others have informed us that it is.[1] The fact ought in my opinion, to be ascertained by *repeated* experiments; because, if true, the remedy is at hand—is easy—and can be applied with little additional expence; and, perhaps, no diminution in the Crop.

The Buck Wheat which I sowed in the Spring (or rather in the early part of Summer) for manure, was, I apprehend, put in too late, and stood too long before it was plowed in; for I have been amazingly plagued with it. Perhaps the extreme wetness of the Season may have contributed as much or more than either to my difficulties. The Buck Wheat, in many places yeilded to a super-abundance of Weeds (distinguished with us by the name of Carrot & Hog Weeds) and in low places to a course grass which subdued every thing else—None of these, more than the Buck Wheat, could I plow in till after Harvest; before which, all of them had passed the meridian of their bloom, and that succulent state which must have fitted them best for speedy putrifaction & fermentation. They were not buried so well at the first plowing as they ought and now that I am crossing the former plowing, I find it next to impossible to make tolerable work; or to go ten steps together before the Plough is choked. How this might have been in a Season not more than usually wet I will not undertake to decide; but the inference I am inclined to draw from the whole, is, that the Buckwheat should be sown in April—ploughed in before it begins to seed, in June—the ground when this takes place being again sown, The expence of which, in my opinion, will be amply compensated by the succulency of the plant—seasonable plowings in—and superior preparation—The plants having time to rot, and ameliorate the Soil.

The Harrows which you were so obliging as to provide for me, came safe;[2] but my fields being, in a manner, always underwater, I could make no use of them. I am not less pleased with them, however, on that account. for I think them well calculated for the cultivation of Corn in my mode; with Potatoes and Carrots intermixed. Of the advantages of wch husbandry, I am more and more convinced as I advance in my experiments; having tried this mixture with success in very dry—very wet—and in ordinary seasons. The greatest difficulty lyes, in judiciously working the Corn; as the Plows can never cross their last furrows and the Hoe harrows after a good plowing before the ground gets foul—or hard—will, I conceive, effectively do this.

I do not know to what cause to attribute it, but my plants of Scarcity have not answered (fully) my expectations—probably from improper management; for the leaves never having grown to the size I have been taught to expect, have not, I presume, been often enough pulled. I shall thank you, however for a little seed for next year. And beg leave to remind you of the Potatoe cleaner. The sooner it comes to me *now* the better.[3] My Cabbages between the Corn rows have failed entirely. They will not do in this mode of cultivation—and for that reason I am disposed to discard them altogether. Potatoes & Carrots will, I am certain succeed in it, and are a very good substitute for this vegitable. Pease also I am affraid will not be a beneficial crop in my rotation system. One of two things I have had demonstrative proof of, *this season*, namely, that Pease exhaust, or Irish Potatoes enrich the Soil, considerably—I mean when the first are sown broad-mowed—and carried off the ground. A field which was in these articles last year, was sown with oats & clover this year. The difference in the quality of them, though there was no perceivable in the quality of the soil previous to the preceeding crops was so apparent as to be discovered almost as far as the field could be seen—Those on the Potatoe ground being so much[4] the most luxurient.

It would seem from the public Gazettes that the minority in your State are preparing for another attack of the—*now*-adopted Government; how formidable it may be, I know not. But that Providence which has hitherto smiled on the honest endeavours of the well meaning part of the People of this Country will not, I trust, with-draw its support from them at this crisis.[5] With best respects to Mrs Peters & yourself, in which Mrs Washington joins me, I am—Dear Sir Your Most Obedt Humble Servant

Go: Washington

ALS, anonymous donor. Addressed on cover to Peters at "Belmont—near Philadelphia."

1. See George Morgan to GW, 31 July–5 August.

2. See Peters to GW, 27 June, and note 4 of that document.

3. Peters wrote GW about roots of scarcity and the potato cleaner on 27 April and 27 June.

4. GW wrote "must."

5. Peters was at this time speaker of the lower house of the Pennsylvania legislature.

*Letter not found*: from Thomas Barclay, 9 Sept. 1788. On 18 Sept. GW wrote to Barclay: "Your favor of the 9th instant came duly to hand."

# From Samuel Powel

Dear Sir                              Philadelphia September 9. 1788

About three Weeks, or a Month, since I did myself the Honor of writing to you and informing you that I had shipped a chair for you by Capt. Ellwood, who promised to deliver it at Mount Vernon or Alexandria. The chair is, I hope, in your Possession before this Time.[1]

In one of your Letters you have requested me to remind you of the Spanish chestnuts. I now take the Liberty to request the

Favor of you to oblige me with a few of them, in hopes that they may succeed better than those of the last Year.[2]

From the present Appearances there seems to be little Doubt that the new Government will be put in Motion at New York. The Delegates from Rhode Island, who had withdrawn, are returned there, & have determined to vote upon that Question. Thus after so long trifling with the Dignity of the Union, this long & unworthy Point of altercation, will be settled in the same Manner that it might & I think ought to have been done at first—My meaning is that the necessary Steps for organizing the Government should have been instantly taken on the Accession of a Ninth State to the Union, without Regard to local Interests, leaving it to the future Government to chuse its own Place of Residence.

The late Proclamation of the King and Council of Great Britain to prevent the Importation of american wheat, on account of the Hessian Fly, has created an Alarm here, in Consequence of which our Supreme Executive Council, have made a long Publication in the Pennsylvania Packett, of this Day, with a Design to show that the Plant alone & not the Grain of the wheat is injured by this destructive Insect—of Course that the Propagation of this Scourge cannot happen from sowing wheat that has grown on Land infested by this animal.[3] Mrs Powel begs Leave to add her affectionate Comps. to Mrs Washington & all the good Family to those of dear Sir your most obedt humble Servt

Samuel Powel

ALS, DLC:GW.

1. Powel wrote GW about the chair on 9 August. See GW's response, 15 September.

2. See GW to Powel, 30 Nov. 1787.

3. The *Pennsylvania Packet, and Daily Advertiser* (Philadelphia) for 10, not 9, Sept., devoted more than a page to the Pennsylvania Council's action regarding the Hessian fly. A resolve of the council on 4 Sept. reads: "That the letter from Council to the Agricultural Society, dated the 1st inst. together with the answer of the said Society thereto, touching the nature of the Hessian Fly, be published in the Pennsylvania Packet—and that the Printers of the said newspaper be requested to republish the several letters from Mr. George Morgan of New-Jersey, dated May 20th and July 25th, 1787, and June 24th, 1788; and the letters from James Vaux, John Jacobs, and Henry Wynkoop, dated

the 16th of August, 1788, upon the same subject—immediately following the publication of the first mentioned letter's."

The letter of 1 Sept., signed by Peter Muhlenberg, vice-president of Pennsylvania, and addressed to Samuel Powel, president of the agricultural society, reads: "SIR, A PROCLAMATION was issued on the twenty-fifth of June last by His Britannic Majesty, prohibiting the entry of Wheat, the growth of any of the territories of the United States into any of the ports of Great Britain: And as there is reason to believe that the said proclamation has been occasioned by some misinformation respecting insect called the Hessian Fly;—

"Council therefore request your useful Society to investigate and report to them, as soon as convenient, the nature of the Hessian Fly, particularly as to the manner of its being propagated, and the effects of it on the crops of wheat; and to ascertain with all possible precision, whether the loss of the crops is not occasioned by the destruction of the plant; and whether the small quantity of wheat produced from a field infected with the Fly is good grain, or otherwise. Likewise, the most successful method that has hitherto been discovered for preventing the effects of this insect." Powel answered the Muhlenberg letter on 3 Sept. and enclosed copies of all the letters mentioned in the 4 Sept. resolve.

# From Samuel Thurber, Jr.

Dear Sir,                                    Providence R. I., 10th Sept. 1788

Being Informed that the State of Virginia is Endeaviouring to entroduce diferant species of Manufactrey & I cannot learn that the Article of Paper is Manufactried there, I as being acquainted with that buisnis am induced (as I would wish to be in a place whire there is some encouragement) to lay a Request before your Excellency (knowing of no other Man who is so great a friend to all that is Good) It is that I may be informed wheather a Conveniant seat for a Paper Mill may be had, in that, highley favoured State, & wheather a Substantial Friend may be found who will assist, in Errecting such a Mill, I am unable to do it & indeed unable to seek after my desires, therefore I am Constraned to trouble the Man, who nothing but the fullest assurance of his being one of the greatest & best of Friends to his Countrey & to all Mankind, would have emboldened me to have done it, pardon Oh pardon such a peace of presumtion, in One who with all Sincerety wishes nothing more, then, that Heaven will ever continue to power down upon that Eloustrious Head every desired Blessing. I am, Dear Sir, with all Submission your Excellency's Devote, Most Obt & Very Humbe Sarvt

Saml Thurber Junr

ALS, DLC:GW.
Samuel Thurber, Jr.'s paper mill was in the "North-End of Providence" (*United States Chronicle* [Providence], 29 Sept. 1785). Thurber (1724–1807) erected the mill in 1780 and in 1812 it was converted to a cotton manufactory.

# From Nicholas DuBey

Sir                               Philad[elphi]a 11th Sepber 1788.

At the latter End of 1786, I bought of Messrs Savary & Gallatin of Richmond[1] a tract of 20 thausend acres of Land, Scituated 2 miles from the ohio, between Little & Great Canaway, joigning your Excellency's possessions on the Same River, near Sandy Creek Harrisson's County. This Parcel is undivided between Mr Ostervald, a rich Swiss, for the greatest part, Mr J. P. Jeanneres of the Same Country & me Self.[2] The first of those Gentlemen Desires to Know which would be the best mode for the improuvement of these Lands. before I answer him, I take the liberty to inquire if Your Excellency has had no thoughts as yet to form Settlements On your tracts, Also what would be the most adviseable Method to be pursued in opposing the Savages & Erect at once Settlements of Some Consequence, in Case that Mr Osterwald Should bring over from Swiss a Certain nombre of families, which would be very easy, in this Supposition, what Certain advantage, would he reap from it?[3]

I have the honor to beg your Excellency to be willing to impart your intentions, that I might Acquaint Mr Ostervald with them & who would be more disposed, Should Your Excellency join with him to undertake it on a Large Scale.

I beg your Excellency would let me Know what Kind of Lands they are, and if there are Some Settlemen⟨ts⟩ near, or adjoining them. I have the honor to be Your Excellency's Very humble & obedient Servant.

N: DuBey

ALS, DLC:GW. The letter was sent under cover of Clement Biddle's letter to GW of 17 September.

1. Albert Gallatin (1761–1849) arrived in America from Switzerland in July 1780, and Jean Savary de Valcoulon came from Lyon in France in 1783 to collect from the state of Virginia debts claimed by Réné Rapicault. The two men became partners in claiming 120,000 acres on the Ohio adjacent to one of GW's tracts in that area. Gallatin went out to the land on the Ohio in the

summer of 1784 and again in 1785. At this time, in 1788, Gallatin was living in
Pennsylvania and Savary de Valcoulon in Richmond (Henry M. Dater, "Albert
Gallatin—Land Speculator," *Mississippi Valley Historical Review,* 26 [1939–40],
21–38).

2. These were Jean-Pierre Jeanneret and De Luze Osterwald.

3. See GW's response of 27 September.


# From Henry Lee, Jr.

My dear General.                          New York 13th Septr 88.

at length the new govt has received the last act necessary to
its existence. This day Congress passed the requisite previous
arrangements. The first Wednesday in January the ratifying
states are to appoint electors, on the first wednesday in february
the president is to be chosen, & the first wednesday in March is
the time, & this city the place for commencing proceedings.[1]

Some delay has attended this business from a difference in
opinion respecting the place of meeting, but this delay has not
in the least affected the sooner or later operation of the constitution. The southern gentlemen did not accord in the place of
temporary residence, from a discordance in sentiment, of its effect on the establishment of the permanent seat of govt. Some
considered this city, others a more southern position, as the most
favorable theatre to negotiate the determination of the ten miles
square. Many plausible & some cogent reasons are adducible
in support of either opinion & time only can shew which is
founded in propriety.

The solemnity of the moment, & its application to yourself,
has fixed my mind in contemplations of a public & a personal
nature and I feel an involuntary impulse which I cannot resist
of communicating without reserve to you, some of the reflexions
which the hour has produced. Solicitous for our common happiness as a people, & convicted as I continue to be, that our
peace & prosperity depends on the proper improvement of the
present period, my anxiety is extreme, that the new govt may
have an auspicious beginning—To effect this & to perpetuate a
nation formed under your auspices, it is certain that again you
will be called forth.

The same principles of devotion to the good of mankind

which has invariably governed your conduct, will no doubt, continue to rule your mind however opposite their consequences may be, to your repose & happiness. It may be wrong, but I cannot suppress in my wishes for national felicity, a due regard to your personal fame & content[ment].

If the same success should attend your efforts on this important occasion, which has distinguished you hitherto, then to be sure you will have spent a life, which providence rarely if ever before gave to the lot of one man. It is my beleif it is my anxious hope that this will be the case, but all things are uncertain, & perhaps nothing more than political events. The new govt tho about to commence its proceedings & r[e]ceived by a large majority of the people with unprecedented unanimity & attachment, must encounter from the nature of human affairs many difficultys—these obstacles to its harmonious progress will receive additional weight & influence from the active & enterprizing characters who continue to inflame the passions & to systemize the measures of opposition—the circular letr from this state, seems to be the standard, to which the various minoritys will repair, & if they should succeed in bringing quickly into action the objects of that letr, new & serious difficu[l]tys must arise, which will cross & may destroy the govt in its infancy —Much will depend on the part which the assembly of Virginia may adopt in this business, & from the complexion of that body, little is to be hoped. They appeared to be generally opposed, & Mr Henry with many other conventional coadjutors, are members of the legislature—Madison will not be there, nor is there a friend to govt in the assembly of comparative ability—It would be fortunate if this gentleman could be introduced into that body, & I think it is practicable— Mr Gordon one of the orange members would readily vacate, to let him in & the county would certainly elect him. In my letr of this date to Doctor Stuart, I have mentioned this suggestion.[2]

It would certainly be unpleasant to you & obnoxious to all who feel for your just fame, to see you at the head of a tumbling system—It is a sacrifice on your part, unjustifiable in any point of view—But on the other hand no alternative seems to be presented.

Without you the govt can have but little chance of success, & the people of that happiness which its prosperity must yield— In this dilemma, it seems wise that such previous measures be in time adopted, which most promise to allay the fury of opposition, to defer amendments, till experience has shewn defects & to ensure the appointments of able & honest men in the first Congress.

One of the best means to accomplish this seems to me to bring into the assembly of Virga the aid before mentioned.

Indeed I know of nothing so effective, for on the conduct of Virga every thing will depend—Her example will be followed, & if she supports with promptitude the system recommended by this state, confusion & anarchy may be the substitutes of order & good govt.

With much freedom have I disclosed to you & to you only, my sentiments on the present epocha as it involves in it, yourself. I am persuaded you will attribute my conduct to the motives which gave birth to it—zeal for the public prosperity, solicitude for your fame & happiness.

In a few weeks I shall return to Virga, if by land, I shall pay my respects to Mount Vernon, when it will be more in my power to explain fully my opinion.[3]

If any thing in this city would be agreable to you, it will give me pleasure to obey your commands & I can send articles procured, by water to Alexa. It is most probable we shall return by sea, in which case they can be taken with me. Mrs Lee begs to be presented to your lady. I have the honor to be with unalterable attachment yours truely

Henry Lee.

ALS, DLC:GW.

1. See James Madison to GW, 21 July, n.2., and Madison to GW, 14 September.

2. GW wrote to Madison on 23 Sept. referring to the dangers of leaving Patrick Henry unchallenged in the Virginia legislature. Madison chose to remain in New York until December, however, when he returned to Orange and was in Virginia until his election to the U.S. House of Representatives in February 1789. James Gordon, Jr. (1755–1799), who in 1787 was elected with Madison to represent Orange County in the state ratifying convention, at this time was one of the delegates from the county in the lower house of the Virginia legislature.

3. Before Lee came to spend the night of 30 Nov. at Mount Vernon, GW had responded to him on 22 Sept. in a letter which constitutes GW's fullest statement of his reservations and misgivings about assuming the office of president under the new Constitution.

## From James Madison

Dear Sir                                                   N. York Sepr 14. 1788

The delay in providing for the commencement of the Government was terminated yesterday, by an acquiescence of the minor number, in the persevering demands of the major. The time for chusing the electors is the first wednesday in Jany, and for chusing the President the first wednesday in Feby. The meeting of the Govt is to be the first wednesday in March, and in the City of New York. The times were adjusted to the meetings of the State Legislatures. The place was the result of the dilemma to which the opponents of N. York were reduced of yielding to its advocates or strangling the Government in its birth. The necessity of yielding, and the impropriety of further delay, has for some time been obvious to me, but others did not view the matter in the same light. Maryland & Delaware were absolutely inflexible. It has indeed been too apparent that local & State Considerations have very improperly predominated in this question, and that something more is aimed at than merely the first Session of the Govt at this place. Every circumstance has Shewn that the policy is to keep Congress here till a permanent seat be chosen, and to obtain a permanent seat at farthest not beyond the Susquehannah. N. Jersey, by its Legislature as well as its Delegation in Congress, has clearly discovered her view to be a temporary appointment of N. York as affording the best chance of a permanent establishment at Trenton. I have been made so fully sensible of these views in the course of the business as well as of the impropriety of so excentric a position as N. York that I woud have finally concurred in any place more Southward to which the Eastern States wd have acceded, and previous to the definitive vote, a motion was made tendering a blank for that purpose. At any place South of the Delaware, the Susquehannah at least would have been secured, and a hope given to the potowmac. As the case is I conceive the Susquehannah to be the utmost to be hoped for, with no small danger of being stopped at the

Delaware. Besides this consequence, the decision will I fear be regarded as at once a proof of the preponderancy of the Eastern strength, and of a disposition to make an unfair use of it. And it cannot but happen that the question will be entailed on the New Governmt which will have enough of other causes of agitation in its Councils.

The meeting at Harrisburg is represented by its friends as having been conducted with much harmony & moderation.[1] Its proceedings are said to be in the press, and will of course soon be before the public. I find that all the mischeif apprehended from Clinton's circular letter in Virginia will be verified. The Antifederalsts lay hold of it with eagerness as the harbinger of a second Convention; and as the Governor espouses the project it will certainly have the co-operation of our Assembly.

I inclose a sensible little pamphlet which falls within the plan of investigating and comparing the languages of the Aboriginal Americans.[2] With the sincerest attachment I am Dear Sir; your Obedt & very hb. ⟨*mutilated*⟩

Js Madison ⟨*mutilated*⟩

ALS, DLC:GW; copy, DLC: Madison Papers.

1. The Harrisburg Convention met on 3 September. Blair McClenachan was elected chairman; George Bryan and Albert Gallatin were among the thirty-three men attending. The convention agreed that the new Constitution should be accepted as an improvement over the Articles of Confederation but called for a new general convention to amend it (Elliot, *Debates*, 2:542–46).

2. This was Jonathan Edwards's pamphlet on the "Muhhekaneew Indians," which Edwards had sent to GW. GW acknowledged its receipt on 28 August.

## To John Cannon

Sir,                           Mount Vernon September 15th 1788

As I have not received a line from you for more than fifteen months, and am altogether in the dark respecting the business which was committed to your care[1]—I would thank you for information respecting the tenements—the Rents &ca of my Lands in Fayette and Washington Counties. And, as the latter— that is the Rents—may have been received in specific articles I should be glad to know they are disposed off. Letters Lodged at the Post office (and I believe one is now established from Philadelphia to Pittsburgh) will come safe—by private hands they rarely do—and any money which may have arisen from the Rents, or the produce of them, Mr Smith,[2] I am certain, will undertake if committed to his care, to forward to me.

If any proposals have been made to you for purchasing either, or part of the above tracts, I should be glad to know on what terms. As also to whom they are now tenanted, and what the Rents are. I am Sir Yrs &c.

Go. Washington

LB, DLC:GW.

1. Cannon wrote GW on 22 Jan. 1787. See GW to Cannon, 13 April 1787. For GW's arrangements with Cannon, see GW to Tobias Lear, 30 Nov. 1786, n.6.

2. This is GW's Pennsylvania lawyer Thomas Smith. See GW to Smith, this date.

*Letter not found*: GW to Lafayette, 15 Sept. 1788. On 27 Nov. 1788 GW wrote Lafayette: "I wrote to you my dear Marquis, on the 15th day of September last."

## To Samuel Powel

Dear Sir,                                   Mount Vernon Septr 15th 1788.

It was many days after the receipt of your obliging favour of the 9th ult.; by the Post, that Captn Ellwood arrived in the Packet. He brought the chair in very good order, and you and Mrs Powell have the best thanks of Mrs Washington and myself for the trouble you have been at to procure it. I think it handsome & neat; and with some additions which I will take the liberty sometime hence of proposing (such as can readily be inserted) they may be made to suit the colour and furniture of the room for which they are intended as well as a chair of quadruple their cost. In the meantime I have requested Colo. Biddle who does business for me in Philadelphia to pay the cost of the one which you have sent me.

I have not been more fortunate in my Sainfoin seed than you were. Though from the appearance one would not judge so, yet it is a tender Seed. Of my first sowing last autumn, a few vegetated & came up, but were destroyed by the Frost. Of those reserved till Spring seeding not one ever appeared above ground—and *now* I have not a single plant of this grass growing.

I have never seen Winlaws threshing Machine, but as the account of its utility is contained in Youngs Annals of Agriculture, I have requested that Gentleman if from his *own* experience, or that of others in whose judgment he can *entirely* rely, it is not (as most of these things are) too complicated for unskilful labourers—or, a vision of the day, and pass away like it—to send me one.

The present Congress, by its *great* indecision in fixing on the place at which the new one is to meet, have hung the expectations & patience of the Union on Tenter hooks—and thereby (if further evidence had been wanting) given a fresh instance of the unfitness of a government so constituted to regulate with precision and energy the Affairs of such an extensive Empire. In every good wish for Mrs Powell and yourself I am joined by Mrs Washington and this family—and with great esteem and regard I am—Dear Sir Yr Most Obedt Hble Servant

Go: Washington

ALS, ViMtV; LB, DLC:GW.

## To Thomas Smith

Sir,                                    Mount Vernon September 15th 1788

Your favour of the 6th Ult. came duly to hand[1] and I beg you to accept my thanks for the trouble you have had in collecting my money and for the punctuality and dispach with which you have transacted my business. The Sum of £50.0.2 sent to Colo. Biddle got safe; and the receipt of it is acknowledged by him in a letter to me. It is far, very far indeed, Sir, from my wish that you should make good the Counterfiet money which you received on my account—the Act of receiving it in [the] manner you do is confering a favour on me—to be made liable for the accidents which may attend the doing it would, if I could do it, be worse than ungenerous—it would be unjust. I therefore request that you would deduct the Sum of £7.6.8 from your next Account—Colo. Biddle could do no less than refuse it—but in doing so he has done more than I wished.[2]

I would thank you for giving the enclosed a safe conveyance. Colo. Cannon is vested with the care of my Landed property in the Counties of Fayette & Washington but owing to miscarriages of letters, or other causes, I have heard nothing from him for more than 15 months—and am agnorant of the Situation in which my tenements are.[3] Letters sent by Post by way of Philadelphia will always come safe, it is somewhat strange therefore to be so long with out one from him. with very great esteem—I am—Sir Yr most Obedt Hble Servant

Go. Washington

LB, DLC:GW.

1. Letter not found, but see Clement Biddle to GW, 17 August.

2. For the "Counterfiet money," see Clement Biddle to GW, 5 Mar., and GW to Smith, 3 April 1788.

3. See GW's letter to John Cannon, this date, and note 1 of that document.

## To Clement Biddle

Dear Sir,                                       Mount Vernon 16th Septr 1788

I have your letters of the 24th Ulto[1] & the 5th inst. now before me. The articles sent by Captn Ellwood arrived safe and agreeable to the invoice.

If you have not already purchased the Winter Barley I would not wish you to do it, for I think it is very probable that I may be able to get the quantity which I shall want of the Brewer in Alexandria in exchange for Spring Barley, or if I should be disappointed there, that I can obtain it upon better terms & perhaps of a better quality upon James River than at Philadelphia, as you observe that the crops of it have generally failed, and none has yet been seen that is fit for seed.

I should be glad to have the Herrings & Shad which are in your hands disposed of if it can be done without making an unreasonable sacrifice of them, that you may receive the Balance which is due upon your acct and have money of mine in your hands to procure any articles that I may have occasion for from Philadelphia—should you not be able to dispose of them immediately I will remit you a Bank Note.

I will thank you to pay Samuel Powell Esqr. for a chair which he was so good as to procure for me as a pattern.[2] With great esteem, I am, Dear Sir, Yr Most Obedt Hble Servt

Go: Washington

P.S. You will oblige me by forwarding the inclosed letter to Mr Smith.[3]

LS, in the hand of Tobias Lear, PHi: Washington-Biddle Correspondence; LB, DLC:GW. The letter is addressed by GW.

  1. Biddle's letter is dated 25 August.
  2. See Powel to GW, 9 Sept., and GW to Powel, 15 September.
  3. This is the letter to Thomas Smith of 15 September.

# To John Lewis

Dear Sir,                                    Mount Vernon September 16th 1788

I have to acknowledge the reception of your letter of the 15th of December 1787 together with the copy of my account inclosed therein—since which time I have received the two inclosed letters from Mr John Couper expressing a desire to purchase the tract of Land in No. Carolina which was the Joint property of your father Colo. Fielding Lewis and myself—These two letters, together with my answer to the first (a copy of which is also inclosed) will shew you upon what footing the matter now stands with respect to me—I will thank you to let me know, as soon as is convenient, your determination respecting the sale of this land that I may give Mr Cowper a decided answer.[1]

I will be much oblige[d] to you if you will look among your fathers papers for a protested Bill of Exchange drawn by the Executrs of Willm Armisted Esqr.—I am almost certain it was among other matters committed to his care to transact for me at the General Court of May 1775, when I was called of to the northward.[2]

I will likewise thank you for the amount of those charges in my Acct which are not extended that I may see how the Balance stands. Mrs Washington Joins her best wishes for you and those of your Family. I am Sir Yr Most Obedt Hble Sert

                                                               G. Washington

LB, DLC:GW.

  1. Neither of the letters from John Cowper has been found, but see GW to Cowper, 25 May 1788, and the references in note 2 of the document. See also Lewis to GW, 7 Dec. 1788, n.1.

  2. For GW's attempt to collect the debt from the estate of William Armistead which was owed to the Daniel Parke Custis estate and had been assigned to Martha Washington, see GW to John Armistead, 17 April 1786, n.1. See also GW to John Marshall, 17 Mar. 1789, n.1.

## To Peters and Company

Mount Vernon 16th Septr 1788

I have some Spring Barley for sale, and if you incline to buy it, would be glad to know what you will give delivered at my landing; or if this is not convenient for you what your price at Baltimore is.

It is raised from seed which Colo. Biddle of Philadelphia procured for me from a Mr Haynes a Brewer of that City; who had it (I am informed) from Rhode Island. It is, which I did not discover till growing, mixed, in a small degree, with oats. I mention it for the sake of plain dealing—and not because I am told it is a common case—and because it is generally so this year in the Eastern States.

Your answer by the first post will much oblige,[1] Sir, Yr most Obedt Hble Servt

Go: Washington

LS, in the hand of Tobias Lear, ViMtV; LB, DLC:GW.

1. See the noncommittal response from the commercial firm of Peters & Company of Baltimore, dated 21 October.

## From Clement Biddle

Dear General            Philad[elphia] Sept: 17. 1788.

Since I wrote you respecting the Winter barley for seed I find Mr Morris has some at his farm where I can be supplied if Capt. Ellwood arrives in time[1]—One Vessel put up for Alexandria but finding little freight altered her Voyage to James river therefore no Conveyance has Offered since your Order came to hand— The Wire work for the Wheat fans is ready for the first Vessel.[2]

The inclosed Letter from Mr Dubey is from a Swiss Gentleman of respect—Your answer under Cover to me will safely reach him.[3] I am with great respect Your Excellencys Mo: Obed. serv.

Clement Biddle

The Ordinance for organizing the new Government & fixing the meeting at New York Came from Congress to the Speaker of our Assembly last Evening.

ALS, DLC:GW.
    1. See Biddle to GW, 5 September.
    2. See GW to Biddle, 25 August.
    3. The letter from Nicholas DuBey is dated 11 September.

# From Richard Peters

Dear Sir                                        Philad[elphi]a Septr 17. 1788
    Yesterday I had the Honour of yours of the '7th I was in
Hopes the Crops with you would make up the Deficiency of ours
which are wretched indeed. I have the best Crop in my Neighbourhood tho' compared with that of a good Year it is but moderate. Our Situation removed from saline Particles in the Air &
the Moisture & Warmth they occasion added to our bad Culture—hard Winter &, too frequently, improper Choice of Soil
are among the Causes of Failure of our Wheat Crops. The Agricultural Society offered a Premium for a remedy against the
spewing out of our Grain, but I do not know that they have
recieved any satisfactory Scheme on that Subject. Deep & frequent ploughing & (what the Fly will now preclude us from for
even the Yellow Wheat must be sowed late) early sowing, are the
only remedies I know & these will not do in wet Ground without
a favourable Winter. Hard Frosts & sudden Thaws heave out
the Grain in this variable Climate. I have heard that drilled
Grain stands the best against this Evil. The Yellow bearded
Wheat is certainly in a great Degree an Antidote against the Ravages of the Fly but this will be destroyed if sown early. I think
therefore that our Wheat Crops will never be so heavy as formerly tho' this Discovery is a happy Instance of providen-
tial Care.
    You failed in your Green Manure from a Desire to do too
much—One Crop of good succulent Buckwheat ploughed in
some Time in July is enough & I know it from Experience to be
an admirable Manure. I have never suffered the Seeds to set but
have rolled down the Plant when in full Bloom & have ploughed
it in easily. At the common Time of crossing in August I have
ploughed my Fields again without Difficulty Since scattering
Seeds would vegetate but not so as to be inconvenient. Your Idea
of sowing early is right. I would not sow it doubly for there is

not Time for both Crops to putrify nor have Farmers on any large Scale Leisure to attend to such a Complication of the Bussiness. I have cut a Crop for the Grain, which I intended to have ploughed in, because it got too forward before I could set my Ploughs at Work. This has too been an uncommon Season for Weeds. I am happy the Harrows please you. I have improved on the one with three Hoes; but your multiplied one is better than mine. I have made free Use of mine & my Crops are clean even in this very weedy Season. I hope Mr Biddle has sent you all the Iron Work. Remember that these Harrows *are Preventatives more than Remedies*. If you let your Ground get too foul they will choak. Therefore it must always be taken in Time.

The Scarcity Plant is worse this Year with me than I ever had it, yet I am content with it. The Leaves are generally smaller than I ever knew them. My Seed has degenerated, tho' a Change will recover it. I will spare you some but do not fail to procure some elsewhere. If I get any I will share it with you. I believe too wet a Season is not advantageous to them. The Man I employed to make the Riddle has been dilatory but I have now set him to work & he promises to have it done speedily. I have so often failed in Cabbages that I will not plant many of them hereafter tho' I now have a tolerable Crop. Pease are at least doubtful the Horse Bean is worse. Our Suns are too hot & Vermin too plenty—Potatoes & Carrotts are sure & excellent. I hesitate about transplanting Carrots. They are apt to grow hairy & forked when transplanted.

Our Antifederalists have changed their Battery. They are now very federal. They want Amendments & they must get into the Seats of Government to bring them about—or what is better—to share the Loaves & Fishes—Their Harrisburg Convention have agreed to submit to & support the Government, & some of them, like the moderate Men & converted Tories formerly, now make up in Sound what they want in Patriotism. In short their Convention was a mere Election Jobb & no Harm is to be expected from it except they get into the Government which in the whole cannot be prevented. When they have got warm in their Seats they will, as it always happens in such Cases, find it their Interest to support a Government in which they are Sharers tho' they may make a little Bustle ad captandum—Mrs Peters returns her affectionate & respectful Compliments to you & Mrs Washington & I beg you to accept the Addition of mine. I am very truly & respectfully your obedt Servt

Richard Peters

I am hurried with the Bussiness of our House therefore excuse my Haste. We shall take up the federal Subject having received the Ordnance of Congress & on our Parts organize the Government. I believe Mr Morris will certainly be a Senator. Who the other will be is not so certain.

ALS, DLC:GW.

# From William Barton

Sir,                                    Philadelphia, Septr 18th 1788.
    I cannot forbear intruding upon your Excelly again, to return You my most sincere and thankful acknowledgments for the Candor and Politeness, with which You have been pleased to communicate to me Your sentiments on the subject of my Essay: And I should be wanting in that respect which is due to Your Character, as well as committing a Violation of my own feelings, were I *now* to publish it, had I before designed to do so; but my intention was to reserve it, for some future day.[1] The force and justness of your Observations must, of themselves, have impressed Conviction on my mind: But, Sir, the truth is, that I am myself sensible of the political prejudices, which obtain among many People in this Country; and I well know how extremely jealous they are, at this time, of every thing that bears the most distant *appearance* of favoring a distinction of ranks. I am entirely of your Excellency's Opinion, that, at the present truly important crisis, it is highly expedient to make some sacrifices to that Jealousy wch is entertained by many honest, well-meaning men. Every person in the least degree acquainted with human Nature must have observed, that the most unreasonable prejudices may be overcome, by prudence and moderation: and, in *some* stages of political ferment, a temporary suspension of public measures founded even in the most virtuous principles, may undoubtedly become advisable; lest, in their investigation, the views of the promoters of them may be purposely misrepre-

sented, by ill-disposed intriguing Characters, to answer their own ends; by means whereof, upright tho' weak men might be influenced to a wrong bias. Prejudices being, however, the result either of defective or erroneous information, it is evident that the most effective means of eradicating them, are Discussion and free Enquiry; provided that the public mind be not assailed, in matters of general and political concern, at an improper season: If this caution be observed, truth must, eventually, ever prevail over Error.

It has been under the impression of prejudices without doubt, that so much has been said and written, both against the Institution of the Cincinnati and our Fœderal Constitution; yet, Sir, I am persuaded that this very circumstance, instead of producing the effects intended by the violent and persevering opposers of both, has been a great mean of quieting the fears of many good Citizens, by giving others an opportunity of shewing how little foundation for jealousy really existed. With regard to the Cincinnati, though I have not the honor of being a member of that Society, I have always viewed it as an innocent, well-meant institution, formed on principles of humanity and benevolence: And, as to the new plan of our National Government, I frankly acknowlege that it is not, in my humble Opinion, *wholly* unexceptionable; but, notwithstanding this confession, my uniform sentiment has been, that it was the duty of every good citizen not only chearfully to acquiesce in, but to promote, its being carried into operation. Had I ever lent even *my* feeble support to such as opposed the attainment of this great and desirable Object, by writing or otherwise, the reflection would give me pain—For, I have long been convinced that a more efficient Government than the old Confederation, was necessary to our existence, as an independent people, a position which I have endeavoured to establish in two publications, in Carey's Museum (for Jany 1787, page 13—and May 1788, page 442):[2] And I had no doubt that the goodness of the American people would, in *due time*, introduce such alterations in the new Constitution, as experience and sound reason might suggest the propriety of, and in *such mode* as is directed by the Constitution itself. These, Sir, are my undisguised sentiments on this subject, and I have always avowed them. I anticipate, with pleasure, the happiness this Country will enjoy, under a virtuous administration of a good Government; and, tho' an humble Citizen, I am as anxious as any man to see it carried into effect. It is, therefore, with the most heart-felt satisfaction that I congratulate you, Sir, who have been so eminently instrumental in raising up this great Empire; on the peaceable declension of that spirit of jealousy, which threatened to mar our national prosperity—We have been witnesses, in this Country, to an almost total extinction of the violent prejudices, which were formerly entertained against an American Episcopate; and it is highly probable, that a similar moderation and liberality to that, which has since taken place on *that* subject, supported by patriotism, will soon supersede the unreasonable discontents which have been harboured in the minds of many, against the Fœderal Constitution.

You will, I hope, Sir, pardon my presumption, in thus trespassing on your patience—I am gratified by the honor You have done me, by your excellent letter; and I have, undesignedly, been drawn into this lengthy acknowledgment of it, by the train of reflexions which have crouded upon my Mind, on the Occasion. I have the honor to be; With the most respectful Attachmt Sir, Your Excellency's most obedt And most humble Servt

W. Barton

ALS, DLC:GW.

1. GW replied to Barton's letter of 28 Aug. on 7 September.

2. Barton's two pieces in Mathew Carey's *American Museum* are entitled: "On the propriety of investing congress with powers to regulate the trade of the united states" (3:13–16) and "Extract from 'the true interests of the united states'" (3:442–46) which also deals with trade.

## From Moustier

Sir,                                        New York 18th Septr 1788

I have but this moment recd, upon my return from Fort Stanwix, the letter which your Excellency did me the honor to write to me on the 17th of last month. I am much obliged to you for the detail which you gave me respecting the commerce between France & the United States, but shoud have wished it had been more particular. The expected departure of the squadron of M. de Saineville from Boston, which I am desireous of visiting, will not permit me to remain in New York more than 15 hours, to prepare myself for my new Journey.[1] I hope to return in a few weeks and to answer more particularly to the different interesting Objects which you have touched upon in your letter.

I flattered myself, Sir, that I should have had the honor of paying my personal respects to you in the course of this summer, but my tour to Fort Stanwix having detained me longer than I expected, I begin to fear that I shall be obliged to postpone my intended journey to the Southward 'till next year—I am very glad to have it in my power to congratulate you upon the adoption of a plan of Government, which you have strongly recommended to your Citizens, and the success of which cannot but be infinitely interesting to every friend of the United States. I have the honor to be, with the most respectful & inviolable attachment Sir, Yr Excellency's Most Obedt & very Hble Sevt

Le Cte de Moustier

Translation, in the hand of Tobias Lear, DLC:GW; ALS, in French, DLC:GW.

1. The following story appeared in the *Boston Gazette, and the Country Journal* on Monday, 22 Sept.: "On Monday last a very elegant Entertainment was given on board the SUPERB, by the Marquis de SAINNEVILLE, commandant of the French Squadron in this Harbour.—The Governor, the Lieutenant-Governor, His Excellency John Adams, Esq. the Hon James Bowdoin, Esq. the Consul of France, the Dutch Consul, the Gentlemen of the Senate, and of the House of Representatives who were in town, the Treasurer, Secretary, &c. formed the party on this occasion.

"On Wednesday His Excellency the Governor, gave an elegant Entertainment to the Marquis de Sainneville and the other French officers, &c. and in the evening a superb ball.

"A series of mutual and polite attentions from the officers of the French squadron to our citizens, and from our citizens to them, has been received ever since their arrival. Foremost in these attentions has been his Excellency the Governour, who has omitted no opportunity to render the stay of the officers here as agreeable and as happy as possible.

"The fleet will probably depart hence during the course of the present week."

# To Thomas Thomson

Sir,                                Mount Vernon September 18th 1788
    The enclosed, which I have Just received, is so full on the subject of your enquiry that I shall add nothing thereto[1]—although I am sorry, and feel for the disappointed hopes of your

Lady to recover her lost Son, yet I am glad that it is in my power to remove, as soon as possible the painful suspence which the Impositions of Reynalds must have thrown her and the family into. I am &c.

Go. Washington

LB, DLC:GW.

1. This was Thomas Barclay's letter to GW of 9 Sept., which has not been found. See GW to Barclay, 31 Aug., n.2.

## From William Drayton

Dear Sir,                    Charleston, So. Carolina. Septr 20. 1788.

I have the Honour to transmit to you a late Publication by our agricultural Society in this State. It is a Beginning only; but I hope the Subject will increase in it's Progress.[1] The Prospect, which the new Confederation opens to America, of an energetic Government, must doubtless stimulate the Genius of every Citizen to exert those means, by which not only his own Interests will be increas'd, but at the same time will be secur'd with the general welfare & Strength of his Country. Permit me to offer my best Compliments to the Ladies of your Family, & to assure your Excellency of my being, with the greatest Respect & Regard, your most obedient humble Servant

Wm Drayton.

ALS, DLC:GW.

1. Drayton wrote GW on 23 Nov. 1785 informing him that he had been elected the first honorary member of the South Carolina Agriculture Society. The enclosed pamphlet, *Letters and Observations on Agriculture, &c. Addressed to, or Made by the South-Carolina Society for Promoting and Improving Agriculture, and Other Rural Concerns*, printed in Charleston in 1788, was in GW's library at his death.

*Letter not found*: from Benjamin Fishbourn, 20 Sept. 1788. On 23 Dec. 1788 GW wrote to Fishbourn: "Your letter of the 20th of September, has been put into my hands, only a few days ago."

# From John Jay

Dear Sir                                         New York 21 Sepr 1788

Your Ideas relative to the Diffusion of Intelligence and useful Information by means of news Papers and the Press, appear to me exceedingly just; nor do I percieve any good Objection to preferring the Stages to Post Riders for the Transportation of the Mail, on the contrary I think the Ballance of Advantages is clearly in favor of the former.

How far it was the Duty of the Post office to recieve and forward News papers is a Question respecting which I confess I have Doubts. If I am rightly informed the Post Riders were formerly *permitted* to carry news Papers, on such Terms as might be settled between them and the Printers. The Number of Printers & of news Papers are now so great, that if the latter were admitted into the Mail the Expence to the public would be considerably enhanced; and it seems but reasonable that as the Printers (as well as the public) would derive much advantage from such a Regulation, they should contribute somewhat to it.

The Direction of the Post Office, instead of being as hitherto, consigned chiefly to a committee, and managed without much System; should I think be regulated by Law, and put under the Superintendence, and in some Degree under the controul of the Executive. The Public are not well satisfied on this Head, as Mattrs now stand, and there is but little Reason to expect any important change during the Existence of the present Government. The succeeding one will have an opportunity of doing a very *acceptable* Service to their Constituents by regulating the Post office in a proper Manner; and the more of *such* things they may have to do, the better. as to what ought to have been the conduct of Government on the occasion, there can be no Doubt—But my dear Sir we cannot expect it from such a Body as Congress: nay unless personal Qualities should supply the Deficiency, I am not sure that the new Government will be found to rest on Principles sufficiently stable to produce a uniform adherence to what Justice, Dignity and liberal Policy may require: for however proper such Conduct may be, none but great minds will always deem it expedient. Men in general are guided more by conveniences than by Principles. This Idea accompanies all my Reflections on the new Constitution, and induced me to remark to our late Convention at Poughkeepsie, that some of the most unpopular and strong Parts of it appeared to me to be the most unexceptionable. Government without Liberty is a curse but on the other Hand Liberty without Government is far from being a Blessing.

The opponents in this State to the Constitution decrease and grow temperate. many of them seem to look forward to another Convention rather as a Measure that will justify their opposition, than produce *all* the Effects they pretended to expect from it. I wish that Measure may be adopted with a good Grace, and without Delay or Hesitation. So many good Reasons can be assigned for postponing the *Session* of such a Convention for three or four Years, that I really believe the great Majority of its advocates would be satisfied with that Delay. After which I think we should not have much Danger to apprehend from it; especially if the new Governmt should in the mean Time recommend itself to the People by the wisdom of its Proceedings, which I flatter myself will be the Case. The Division of the Powers of Govt into three Departments is a great and valuable point gained; and will give the People the best opportunity of bringing the Question whether they can govern themselves, to a Decision in their Favor. with the greatest Esteem and Regard I am Dr Sir your affte Fd & obt Servt

John Jay

ALS, DLC:GW; ADfS, NNC.

1. For GW's criticism of the policy adopted by the postmaster general, Ebenezer Hazard, to bar newspapers from the mail, see his letter to Jay of 18 July.

# To Henry Lee, Jr.

(Private)

Dear Sir, Mount Vernon Septr 22d 1788

Your letter of the 13th instant was of so friendly & confidential a complexion, as to merit my early attention and cordial acknowledgments.

I am glad Congress have at last decided upon an Ordinance for carrying the New government into execution. In My Mind, the place for the meeting of the new Congress was not an object of such very important consequence: but I greatly fear that the question entailed upon that body, respecting their permanent residence, will be pregnant with difficulty & danger. God grant that true patriotism & a spirit of moderation may exclude a narrow locality and all ideas unfriendly to the Union from every quarter.

Your observations on the solemnity of the crisis & its application to myself, bring before me subjects of the most momentous & interesting nature. In our endeavours to establish a new general government, the contest, nationally considered, seems not to have been so much for glory, as existence. It was for a long time doubtful whether we were to survive as an independent Republic, or decline from our fœderal dignity into insignificant & wretched fragments of Empire. The adoption of the Constitution so extensively, & with so liberal an acquiescence on the part of the Minorities in general, promised the former: until, lately, the Circular letter of New York carried, in my apprehension, an unfavorable, if not an insidious tendency to a contrary policy. I will hope for the best, but before you mentioned it, I could not help fearing it would serve as a Standard to which the disaffected might resort. It is now evidently the part of all honest men, who are friends to the New Constitution, to endeavor to give it a chance to disclose its merits and defects, by carrying it fairly into effect, in the first instance. For it is to be apprehended, that by an attempt, to obtain amendments before the experiment has been candidly made "more is meant than meets the ear"—that an intention is concealed to accomplish slily, what could not have been done openly—to undo all that has been done. If the fact so exists, that a kind of combination is forming to stifle the government in embrio; it is a happy circumstance that the design has become suspected. Preparation should be the sure attendant upon forewarning. Probably, prudence, wisdom, & patriotism were never more essentially necessary than at the present moment: and so far as it can be done in an irreproachable direct manner, no effort ought to be left unessayed to procure the election of the best possible characters to the new Congress. On their harmony, deliberation & decision every thing will depend. I heartily wish Mr Madison was in our Assembly: as I think, with you, it is of unspeakable importance Virginia should set out in her fœderal measures under right auspices.

The principal topic of your letter is, to me, a point of great delicacy indeed: insomuch that I can scarcely, without some impropriety, touch upon it. In the first place, the event to which you allude may never happen—amongst other reasons—because, if the partiality of my fellow Citizens conceive it to be a mean by which the sinews of the new government would be strengthened, it will of consequence be obnoxious to those who are in opposition to it; many of whom, unquestionably, will be placed among the Electors. This consideration alone would supercede the expediency of announcing any definitive, and irrevocable resolution. You are among the small number of those, who know my invincible attachment to domestic life, and that my sincerest wish is to continue in the enjoyment of it, solely, until my final hour. But the world would be neither so well instructed, or so candidly disposed as to believe me to be uninfluenced by sinester motives; in case any circumstance should render a deviation from the line of conduct I had prescribed myself indispensable. Should the contingency you suggest take place, and (for argument sake alone let me say) should my unfeigned reluctance to accept the Office be overcome by a deference for the reasons and opinions of my friends; might I not, after the Declarations I have made (and Heaven knows they were made in the sincerity of my heart) in the judgment of the impartial World and of Posterity, be chargable with levity and inconsistency; if not with rashness & ambition? Nay farther, would there not even be some apparent foundation for the two former charges? Now justice to myself and tranquility of conscience require that I should act a part, if not above imputation, at least, capable of vindication. Nor will you conceive me to be too solicitous for reputation. Though I prize, as I ought, the good opinion of my fellow Citizens; yet, if I know myself I would not seek or retain popularity at the expence of one social duty or moral virtue. While doing what my conscience informed me was right, as it respected My God, my Country & myself, I could despice all the party clamour and unjust censure, which must be expected from some, whose personal enmity might be occasioned by their hostility to the governmt. I am conscious, that I fear alone to give any real occasion for obloquy—and that I do not dread to meet with unmerited reproach—And certain I am, whensoever I shall be convinced the good of my Country requires my reputation to be put in risque, regard for my own fame will not come in competition with an object of so much magnitude. If I declined the task it would be upon quite another principle. Notwithstanding my advanced season of life, my encreasing fondness for Agricultural amusements, and my growing love of retirement augment and confirm my decided predeliction for the character of a private Citizen: Yet it would be no one of these motives, nor the hazard to which my former reputation might be exposed, or the terror of encountering new fatigues & troubles that would deter me from an acceptance—but a belief that some other person, who had less pretence & less inclination to be excused, could execute all the duties full as satisfactorily as myself. To say more would be indiscreet; as a disclosure of a refusal beforehand, might incur the application of the Fable, in which the Fox is represented as undervaluing the Grapes he could not reach. You will perceive, my dear Sir, by what is here observed (and which you will be pleased to consider in the light of a confidential communication) that my inclinations will dispose & decide me to remain as I am; unless a clear & insurmountable conviction should be impressed on my mind, that some very disagreeable consequences must in all human probability result from the indulgence of my wishes.[1]

If you return by land, I shall expect without failure the pleasure of your Company. I am much indebted to you for your obliging offer of forwarding such articles as I might want from New York; though I shall not have occasion at this moment to avail myself of your goodness. Mrs Washington offers her best Compliments to Mrs Lee, with ardent wishes for the reestablishment of her health; which joined with my own, will conclude me, with great regard and esteem Dear Sir Yr most Obedt & Affecte Sert

Go: Washington

ALS, Vi; LB, DLC:GW.

1. In his correspondence with friends, GW continued to argue with himself in much these same terms until he was elected president in the spring of 1789.

# From Richard OBryen

Esteemed Sir,                    City of Algiers Septembr the 22d 1788.

We the unfortunate Americans in Slavery, takes the Liberty of writeing you a Narrative of our Captivity, by the Algerines and petioning you as the advocate for Liberty Hopeing you will be pleased to Lay before the Congress of the united States of America our Truly Lamentable Situation of Slavery.

the Ship Dauphin Richard OBryen Master belonging to Mr Mathew and Ths Irwins Merchants of the City of Philadelphia was Captured the 30th July 1785 by & algerine Cruiser 50 Leauges to the Westward of Lisbon and on the 16th of August was brought into Algiers where we were made Slaves of to this Regencey.

the Schooner Maria Isaac Stephens Master belonging to Mr Wm Foster of Boston in Massachusets was Captured the 25th July 1785 and brought to Algiers and Condemned to Slavery.

Humbly Sheweth that your Petioners Situation is truly miserable and unhappy much beyond our Expression or your Conception For Since the unhappy period our Captivity Commenced we have Experienced nothing but an uninterrupted Scene of Griefe and misery and for the major part of our Slavery, Surrounded with the pest and other Contagious Distempers which has numbered Six of our Countrymen in the Bills of mortality, & we are left but fifteen unfortunate Americans in Slavery.

that your petioners being Sensible of the multiplicity of Business that has occupied the attention of Congress Since our lot of Slavery Commenced and that the United States was Employed on affairs of more Importance to the Justice Happiness and welfare of the Riseing Empire, So that your petioners being fully Sensible that untill Such time as affairs So important was adjusted at home nothing Could be Done abroad But now Sir that it hath pleased God that the new Constitution of a futre Government is formed and Ratafied by the United States your Humble Petioners hopes that there Situation will be taken into Consideration So that ways and means will be adopted for our Restoration from Slavery without which we must be Ever wretched and miserable and with which we will be Ever Content and thankful to our Country. The Same time we Return our thanks to our Country for the Comfortable provision that has been allowed us and we are much indebted to the American Ambassadors in Europe for their attention towards us which has helped to alleviate some what our Sufferings without which allowance and attention our lives would be Rendered much more Burthensome and Unhappy.

Your Most Humble petioners further prays you will Consider what our Sufferings must have been for more then three years in this Country where we have Experienced Turkish Severity our Crews Being Employed on the most Laborious work Consumeing and Declineing under the Scorching heats of this Climate ⟨Far⟩ distant from our Families Friends and Connections, without any prospect of Ever Seeing them More.[1]

But now Sir that the new Constitution is Ratafied we hope that Congress will give Such powers to thier ministers in Eu⟨rope⟩ So as finally to Extricate your Unfortunate Countrymen and petitioners from thier wretched State of Slavery. Sir your most Obt most Humble and unfortunate Countrymen the Americans in Slavery, in Algiers In behalf of myself & brother Sufferers.

Richard OBryen

LS, DLC:GW. The random dots in the manuscript have been omitted. The letter is docketed in an unknown hand: "Office for foreign Affairs Feby 10th 1789—Recd & forwarded."

1. For a full description of the capture in 1785 of Richard OBryen (O'Bryen; c.1758–1824) by the Algerian corsairs and the measures OBryen took during the ensuing decade to secure his own release and that of an increasing number of American seamen being held in Algiers, see the note in Mathew Irwin to GW, 9 July 1789. .

# To James Madison

My dear Sir,          Mount Vernon Septr 23d 1788.

I duly received your letter of the 24th of last Month, but as we had no intelligence or circumstance in this quarter worthy of your acceptance, I postponed even the acknowledgment untill I was gratifyed by the receipt of your subsequent favor of the 14th instant. Indeed I have now little more to give you in return, than this information to prevent your apprehension of miscarriage; and my thanks for your illustration of the subject which has lately engaged the attention of Congress.

Upon mature reflection, I think the reasons you offer in favor of Philadelphia as the place for the first meeting of Congress are conclusive: especially when the farther agitation of the question respecting its permanent residence is taken into consideration. But I cannot, however, avoid being satisfied that the minority should have acquiesced in any place, rather than to have prevented the system from being carried into effect. The delay had already become the source of clamours and might have given advantages to the Antifœderalists. Their expedient will now probably be an attempt to procure the Election of so many of their own Junto under the New government, as, by the introduction of local and embarrassing disputes, to impede or frustrate its operation.

In the meantime it behoves all the advocates of the Constitution, forgetting partial & smaller considerations, to combine their exertions for collecting the wisdom & virtue of the Continent to one centre; in order that the Republic may avail itself of the opportunity for escaping from Anarchy, Division, and the other great national calamities that impended. To be shipwrecked in sight of the Port would be the severest of all possible aggravations to our misery; and I assure you I am under painful apprehensions from the single circumstance of Mr H——'s having the whole game to play in the Assembly of this State, and the effect it may have on others—It should be counteracted if possible. With sentiments of the highest esteem & regard I am— My dear Sir Your Affectionate Hble Servt

Go: Washington

P.S. Permit me to request the favor of you to forward the Letters under cover with this by a favourable conveyance.

ALS, NN: Lee Kohns Memorial Collection; LB, DLC:GW.

*Letter not found*: from Thomas Newton, Jr., 23 Sept. 1788. On 10 Oct. GW wrote Newton: "Your letter of the 23d Ulto was handed to me."

## To Samuel Powel

Dear Sir,                                  Mount Vernon Septr 23d 1788.
    Although I had not forgot the promise I made you, respecting the Spanish Chestnuts, yet I am glad you have reminded me of

it as we have the pleasure of knowing, from your letter, that Mrs Powell & yourself were well.[1] I am sorry to add, however, that though the prospect of an abundant crop of these Nuts was once great—appearances are now against it. Whether to the uncommonly wet Summer or to what other cause to attribute it I know not; but the fact is that as fast as the Burs get to a certain size they drop immaturely from the trees—whether this will continue to be the case now the weather has grown drier I am unable to decide—but this you may be assured of—Participation[2]

The Proclamation of His Britanic Majesty & the publication of the Executive Council of your State, I have seen. The former seem unwilling to receive any part of their own bounty, whilst the latter are encouraging them not to be affraid of it.

I am glad Congress have at *last,* decided upon an Ordinance for carrying the New government into execution. The patience of the Union was too long tried on a question of so temporary a nature. Mrs Washington and all under this roof unite with me in every good wish for Mrs Powell & yourself; and with sentiments of great esteem I am Dear Sir Your Most Obedt Hble Servt

Go: Washington

ALS, PHi: Gratz Collection; LB, DLC:GW.

1. Powel wrote on 9 September.
2. Instead of finishing the sentence, GW began a new paragraph here.

# Addenda

# From Hugh Williamson

Dear Sir                    Annapolis [Md.] 24th March 1784
    You are proba[b]ly informed that there is a Company in
North Carolina called the Lebanon Company, who own 40 or
50 thousand a[cre]s of Land on the South side of Drummonds
Lake or the great Dismal, I presume thier Lands are bounded
to the Northward by the Lands of the Virginia Company of
which you are a member, by the last Post I recived letters from
some gentlemen who are of the Lebanon Company, proposing
a Plan which they apprehend will not only tend to the improvement of all the Lands on albemarle sound and greatly promote
the Commerce of Virginia, they propose to dig a canal from the
head of Pasquetank into the Lake in the dismal & thence into
some navigable water which leads into Chesapeak Bay. The part
of the Canal on the [C]arolina Side I Presume may be 4 or 5
miles long on the Virginia side you know best what length it may
be. Your are doubtless informed that the Lands in some of the
Counties on albemarle sound are the most fertile in North Carolina and that no Vessel can go to Sea from albemarle sound, after
passing though ⟨*illegible*⟩ sound with more then ⟨nine⟩ feet water,
which is a prodigious tax on our Navigation Could we get a safe
navigation to Norfolk every article of our produce must rise at
least 5 prCt in its value. I need not say how much norfolk would
gain by our trade. an act passed at the Last session of the Virginia assembly for cuting a canal from Kemps Landing to the
North Landing. a river leads from the place last mentioned into
Currituck sound in our state, but such a canal can be of very
little use to ⟨us⟩. The navigation from albemarle sound into Virginia through Currituck is equal to an east India voyage, not
quite so long but rather more troublesome, our people in general disclaim it. The proposed Canal would be partly in Virginia & partly in carolina for which reason Some Gentlemen
wish that the Company, i.e. the Canal company could be incorporated by Congress. They are not aware how incompetent our
Purses are to such objects. I presume however that neither of
the states would refuse a Charter of Incorporation, & if such an
act should be passed by the two States in the form of a convention the proprietors would have all the security they could desire. Inclosed is one of the plans that was sent me from our state

for executing the proposed Canal; it is not very explicit. Wishing as far as possible to ⟨*illegible*⟩ perpetual Servitudes in a free count[r]y, I have taken the Liberty of Submiting the following Plan.

1st That the Canal Company to be incorporated by the Legislatures of Virginia & N. Carolina by an act which shall be stated and considered as a Convention, not revocable unless by mutual Consent.

2 That they be impower'd to receive from all vessels pasing through the Canal such a Toll as they may think proper to impose provided the annual amount does not excede an interest of 8 PrCt on the money that shall be expended in finishing the Canal together with the contingent expences of repairs & collecting the Toll. provided that the toll shall be uniformly imposed according to thier Tonage & that Vessels shall only pay toll in proportion to the distance which they pass in the Canal.

3d If it shall happen on any certain year that the Toll imposed does not amount to the annual Expences together with the proposed Interest of 8 PrCt It shall be permitted for the Company to charge the ballance remaining on some future years.

If the Legislatures of Virginia & N. Carolina or either of them for the general advancement of Commerce shall repay into the hands of the Company the whole sum they have expended in diging and opening the Canal together with any arrearages that may be due of Interest or incidental expences and shall declare the Canal to be open & free forever, on these considerations, the Charter shall be desolved. Perhaps those conditions as they respect the company may not appear very liberal, but it is to be considered that the primary objects with every man who may engage in the Company will be the improvement of his private estate and serving the public by extending Navigation, with those views a man may be fully satisfyed with the Interest of 8 PCt on all the money that he advances while it is Vested in the Canal. If the interest is moderate the public will the sooner be enable'd to redeem the Canal & the sooner it is made free the more perfectly does every man obtain the chief objects of his enterprise.

If you should agree with the gentlemen in our state to whom I have refered, in your Ideas concerning the Importence of such a Canal to the Commerce of both states, I am perswaded you will not fail to recommend it in such terms that the company shall not fail in obtaining the necessary act of incorporation in the state of Virginia. In the mean while I should be extremly happy in receiving your observations on this subject, that a Bill may be brought in with the advantages of such improvement. It has been said that in rainy Seasons the Waters of Drummonds Lake flow into some of the Rivers that are in our state; from this it appears that there is no elevated ground in the way, but there may be a de[s]cent of some value. If it was certain that the surface of the water in Drummonds Lake is not much above the Level of the waters in the adjacent rivers, when the Tides are up, i.e. if the difference is not above 3 or 4 feet the expence of the Canal must be inconsiderable, for Locks would not be required, unless perhaps one on the Virginia side, to prevent the water runing out on the ebing of the Tides, on the Carolina side where there are no tides the troubles would be less. I have the Honour to be with the utmost Conside[ratio]n your Most obedient Hble Servant

H: Williamson

very bad paper
Copy T. Walker

Copy, in hand of Thomas Walker, NcD: Dismal Swamp Land Company Papers. This may have been the copy of Williamson's letter made by Walker and sent to David Jameson, "who had the cheif mannagement" of the Dismal Swamp Company at this time. See Walker to GW, 29 Aug. 1784. Williamson's letter was answered by GW on 31 Mar. 1784.

# From Richard Henry Lee

DEAR SIR                    NEW YORK, April 18, 1785

I should before this have thanked you for your favour of March 15th, if I had not been in daily expectation that the arrival of the packets would bring us some intelligence from Europe worth communicating to you; the February packet has but just come in after a passage of eight weeks, and neither she or other vessels in short passages, bring us any thing interesting. War or peace in Europe, hangs yet in doubtful balance; both parties arming with assiduity, and nothing determined upon. Mr. John Adams, is sent plenipotentiary to the court of London, and Mr. Jefferson is the minister at Versailles, Dr. Franklin having leave, at his own request, to retire. Returning appearances of good humour, and a proposition first made by the British court, to treat of our differences in London, has induced hopes of an amicable adjustment of disputes. Mr. Gardoque is not arrived, but expected about the last of this month from the Havana, to which place he went from Spain previous to his coming here.[1] If the commenced bickering between Madrid and London on the Musquito shore should go on, we may probably have easier work with both courts in our business with them.[2] I have the honour to enclose you the report of a respectable committee on the subject of selling the western lands, which has not yet been acted upon, though it speedily will. What changes may be made in this plan before it finally passes, cannot yet be told, but probably there will be some. Your idea of settling a state at a time, would most certainly be the wisest and the best, if the excessive rage for taking lands there could be possibly restrained. But really it seems that either Congress must sell quickly, or possession will be so taken as to render doubtful this fine fund for extinguishing the public debt. It has been impossible to get a vote for more than seven hundred men to garrison all the posts to be fixed in the trans-Alleghanian country, from north to south; a number very inadequate, I fear, to the purpose of even suppressing illegal trespasses upon the western lands. Our friend the Marquis La Fayette, arrived after a short passage, but I believe it was a very boisterous one.[3] Your letter for Mr. Lee I sent after him to Virginia, whither he was returning before I received it.[4] My best respects attend your lady.

I have the honour to be, with the truest esteem and regard, dear Sir, your most obedient and very humble servt.

RICHARD HENRY LEE.

Richard Henry Lee, *Memoir of the Life of Richard Henry Lee*, 2 vols. (Philadelphia, 1825), 2:63–64.

1. Diego Maria de Gardoqui, the new Spanish chargé d'affaires arrived in Philadelphia from Havana on 20 May 1785.

2. The Mosquito Coast, along the eastern coast of Central America, had been a British protectorate since 1655.

3. Lafayette arrived at New York on 4 Aug. 1784 for a triumphal tour of the United States. He left New York again for France on 21 Dec. 1784, arriving at Brest on 20 January.

4. GW's letter to Arthur Lee is dated 15 Mar. 1785.

# To William Heth

Dear Sir,                                    Mount Vernon Aprl 6th 178⟨6⟩

An honest confession of the truth, is the best apology I can make for my not acknowledging the receipt of your favor of the 24th of Decr before this.[1] The fact is, the letter was mislaid, and entirely forgot, till chance recovered it. I now send you Colo. De Corny's third Bill of Exchange on Colo. Wadsworth. his second I have never (I believe) seen. the first you have.[2] With esteem I am—Dear Sir Yr Most Obedt Sert

Go: Washington

ALS, owned (1994) by Mr. Joseph Rubinfine, West Palm Beach, Florida. This letter was found after the publication of vol. 4 of *Papers, Confederation Series.*

1. Heth's letter is printed in note 2 of GW to Dominique-Louis Ethis de Corny, 5 Dec. 1785.

2. For Ethis de Corny's membership in the Society of the Cincinnati, see also Barbé-Marbois to GW, 12 June 1785, GW to George Weedon, 23 July 1785, and Weedon to GW, 10 Aug. 1785.

# From Leven Powell

Dear Sir,                                    Loudoun Decr 18h 1786.

Supposing the Buck Wheat was intended only for Sowing & having pretty full employment for our Waggons Occassion'd me not to send Any down to you sooner than I did; When that Waggon was loaded I was so engaged in business that I had not time to write. The residue of the Buck Wheat I have now by me, but again our Waggons are much engaged in getting down a Quantity of Tobacco for a vessel that is now waiting for it & it will be very convenient to me if you can wait for the Buck Wheat 'till a more Leisure time. If you cannot conveniently do so be pleased to inform my son At Alexandria & it shall be immediately sent to you.[1] When this load is sent down I shall do myself the pleasure of writing you with respect to the usefulness of this Grain & how it is to be managed.[2] With much respect I am Dr Sir Yr Obt Hble Servt

Leven Powell

ALS, DLC:GW.

1. Powell's son William Henry Powell had a general merchandise store in Alexandria.

2. GW answered this letter on 21 Dec. 1786. Leven Powell wrote to GW on 8 April 1787 giving him instructions about the planting and cultivation of the buckwheat that he had purchased for GW.

# From Unknown Frenchman

Sir                                                                  [1786]

Mr Houdon Delivered me the Letter that Your Excellency Honoured me with, of the 5th Novr And I have learnt with very Great Satisfaction that you have Enjoyed very Good Health, & that you[r] Promise, to your Acquaintances a long life, that has been Glorious, & Usefull to your Country.[1] I return Your Excelly my most Sincere Thanks for the Distinct Account you have given me Of the Affairs of the United States, & the Same Opinion prevails at Versailles that you have, Of the Powers, that the Different States, Ought to Grant to Congress, for to enable them, to Regulate the Commerce in General, & that Wise & Prudent measure could not assuredly, Do any Dretriment, to their Liberty, & the Americans have Sense, & to[o] Good a Knowledge, for not to be Sensible (or know) that the foreign powers, who are Interested in Commerce with them, could not Possibly Treat with the Thirteen Different States, who also having all Different Interests, Could not but Ruin them, ⟨Than⟩ for the Congress to Adopt the General Measures, which alone could enable them, to Conduct it, for the Good of the Republick; I hope that the First News that we Receive from America, will Inform us that the Different Assembly's have put the finishing Stroke to this Grand Affair. We are likewise very desirous, that Something Decisively could be done upon the article of Finances, for the Payment of the Publick Debt, or at least for the Interest of that Debt, in the Advent of Ground Ceded by Treaty, Some of whc. was not Inhabited, before the War, they Should find it insufficient to Satisfy the Creditors, I hope that the legislators will be of the Same mind, & that they will Seriously think of means, to Clear themselves of it. We agree here to give to the American Trade all the Assistance that could be Capable of admitting, agreeing with the Interests of Both nathions.

All the Publick News Assure us, that the Forts Situated upon the lakes & the River St Lawrence, will not be given up to the Americans, & that the English, have mad[e] it a kind of Compensation for the Pretended Infractions of the Treaty of Peace I have too good an opinion of Mr Pitt, for to Believe, that if he had it in his power to decide this dispute, that it not be in favor of America, but the Minister, has found a Party very Powerfull in the opposition, that he is so much affraid of, that he Cannot follow the Measures, that he Believes reasonable to Propose— Some People Believe that there will be Soon a Change of the British Ministry, The Cabinett of London is full of Dissentions, All Europe is very Tranquill, & the Change of the Barrier, which has made Such a noise, makes War appear more Distant than ever, It is Probable that the line of Germany (whc. has been he Fruits of Jealousies, that this Bartering was the Cause of it) will Produce the Repose of Europe for a long time, The Interior Dissensions of Holland whc. was the Cause of a great noise in Europe has not been of very troublesome Consequences, that State has been at its ease Since the Treaty with the Emperor, & its alliance Deffensive with France, the Republican Party, & the Stadtholder appeared very much incense, it is nevertheless probable that they will reconcile him for the Good of the Re-publick.

I hope that Your Excy will in these moments, remember that you have in France a Servt, very much attached & who Desires very Sincerely to Give Some dissinterested Proofs of the Perfect consideration & of the respect with whc. he is Your ⟨E⟩.

Will Madame Washtn do him the Honour to accept of his Respects.

Translation, DLC:GW.
   1. Houdoun arrived back in France in mid-December 1785.

# Index

(A cumulative index for the *Confederation, Presidential,* and *Retirement Series* will be compiled upon the completion of the *Presidential Series.*)

NOTE: Identifications of persons, places, and things in previous volumes of the *Confederation Series* are noted within parentheses.

Abingdon (house), 353
Adam, John: id., 249
Adam, Robert: id., 60
Adams, Abigail, 251
Adams, John, 251, 525; at Mount
    Vernon, 250; in Holland, 254;
    and Van der Kemp, 279; ap-
    proves Constitution, 291; and
    John Trumbull, 347; returns to
    U.S., 353; and William Tudor,
    401; and Benjamin Rush, 415;
    as U.S. minister to Britain,
    541
Adams, Samuel: opposes Constitu-
    tion, 22, 40, 119; supports rati-
    fication of Constitution, 106,
    108; defeated in Mass. election,
    310
Agriculture: GW's views on, 48–49;
    plowing, 239–40; GW's discus-
    sion of, 450–54; and soil enrich-
    ment, 520–21
  crops: corn, 111–13, 142–43, 154,
    236, 238, 353, 359, 369, 411,
    451, 452, 453, 505; carrots, 112,
    113, 236, 237, 358, 451, 452,
    505; potatoes, 112, 113, 142,
    236, 237, 239, 359, 451–52,
    453, 505, 521; turnips, 112,
    113, 236, 452; failure of, 130;
    gooseberries, 130; roots of scar-
    city (mangel-wurzel), 154, 236,
    357–58, 505, 506, 521; cab-
    bages, 236, 358, 505, 521;
    beans, 237, 521; peas, 237, 452,
    453, 505–6, 521; wheat, 237,
    238, 239, 353, 358, 369, 410–
    12, 450–51, 474–75, 504–5, 520;
    oats, 237–38, 353, 452; rotation
    of, 237–38, 451–53; clover, 238,

452, 453; and excessive rain,
    352–53, 436; flax, 353; rye, 353,
    411; in Pennsylvania, 357; grass,
    368, 369; barley, 410–11; pump-
    kins, 452
  equipment: plows, 20, 238, 239,
    368; harrows, 142, 144, 154,
    238, 239, 358, 443, 505, 521;
    Winlaw's thresher, 190, 191,
    368–69, 435, 436, 453–54, 516;
    Chateauvieux cultivator, 238;
    potato cleaner, 239–40, 358,
    505, 506; wheat fans, 519
  fertilizer: plaster of paris, 155–56,
    239; lime, 236, 410; manure,
    236–37, 410
  livestock: jackasses, 9–10, 138,
    217; sheep, 369
  seed: from England, 13, 79–80,
    110–11, 451, 454; rhubarb, 79–
    80, 138; clover, 109, 125, 138;
    grass, 110, 111, 130, 145, 156,
    157, 515; turnip, 110; vetch,
    110; wheat, 110, 111, 377, 450,
    451, 452, 453, 454, 466, 471,
    543, 544; timothy, 125; white
    pine, 154; roots of scarcity
    (mangel-wurzel), 155, 220, 230–
    31, 267–68; peas, 266, 282, 296;
    barley, 284, 436–37, 449–50,
    450, 452, 453, 468, 474, 500–
    501, 517, 519; oats, 436; mad-
    der, 450. *See also* Hessian fly
Agriculture Society of Philadelphia,
    412, 504, 508; and raising
    grain, 520
Alexander, Robert: debt of, 77–78
Algerine pirates: and the *Buckskin
    Hero,* 440–42; captives of,
    532–33